Fundamentals of Java Programming

Mitsunori Ogihara

Fundamentals of Java Programming

 Springer

Mitsunori Ogihara
Department of Computer Science
University of Miami
Miami, FL, USA

ISBN 978-3-030-07785-3   ISBN 978-3-319-89491-1   (eBook)
https://doi.org/10.1007/978-3-319-89491-1

This Springer imprint is published by the registered company Springer Nature Switzerland AG
The registered company address is: Gewerbestrasse 11, 6330 Cham, Switzerland

To my family

Preface

This book was born from the desire of having an introductory Java programming textbook whose contents can be covered in one semester. The book was written with two types of audience in mind: those who intend to major in computer science and those who want to get a glimpse of computer programming. The book does not cover graphical user interfaces or the materials that are taught in a data structure course. The book very quickly surveys the Java Collection Framework and the generics in the penultimate chapter. The book also covers the concepts of online and recursive algorithms in the last chapter. The instructors who choose to use this textbook are free to skip these chapters if there is no sufficient time. Except for the code examples that receive parameters from the command line, the code examples can be compiled and run in a command-line environment as well as in IDEs. To execute those code examples in an IDE, the user must follow the step of provide args before execution. The code examples appearing in the book have very few comments, since the actions of the code are explained in the prose. The code examples with extensive comments are available for the publisher. There are PDF lecture slides accompanying the book. They are prepared using the Beamer environment of LaTeX. The source codes of the lecture slides may be available through the publisher.

Acknowledgements I would like to take this opportunity to thank those who helped me in writing this book: Paul Drougas (Springer), Victor Milenkovic (University of Miami), Ted Pawlicki (University of Rochester), Ken Regan (University at Buffalo), Geoff Sutcliffe (University of Miami), and Osamu Watanabe (Tokyo Institute of Technology). Huge thanks go to my daughter Ellen, who painstakingly read through the draft and provided constructive criticisms.

Miami, FL, USA   Mitsunori Ogihara

Contents

List of Figures

List of Tables

Part I

Programming Basics

"Hello, World!"

1

1.1 The Programming Environment for Java

1.1.1 The Java Virtual Machine (JVM)

Java is one of the most popular programming languages. It is a descendant of the programming language C and is much related to C++. Java, like C++, embodies the concept of *object-oriented programming*, which allows a programmer to define a type of data with its permissible set of operations.

To execute a Java program on a machine, the machine needs an installation of the Java Running Environment (JRE). A major part of JRE is the Java Virtual Machine (JVM). JVM creates an environment where Java programs interact with the hardware.

A programmer creates a Java program by writing its source code. A source code is a text file that describes the program according to the syntax of Java and has the file name extension .java. An executable Java program generated from a source code is called Java bytecode, and has the file name extension .class. To generate a Java program from a source code, the machine needs an extension of JRE called the Java Development Kit (JDK) (see Fig. 1.1).

The Java language that comes with JDK consists of two parts. The first part, called java.lang, is an essential component of Java. The second part is a collection of source codes that can be selected and added to the Java program being written.

To write and edit a Java source code, a text editor is needed. Some editors understand the syntax of Java and offer a variety of assistance. Popular text editors, which can be used for editing general text, include: vim, emacs, and sublime.

The process of generating Java bytecode from a Java source code is called compilation. A primitive way to compile a Java source code is to execute a compilation command in a command line interface. Modern computers usually come with command line interfaces. For example, Mac OSX has **Terminal** and Windows has **cmd**. There are other downloadable command line interfaces. A command line interface is a program that interacts with the user on a text screen (see Fig. 1.2). The user types, according to the syntax of the command line interface, a character sequence representing an action he/she wishes to take. This sequence is called a command or a command line. On the interface screen, the characters that the user types appear (or "echo") as they are being typed. After completing the command, the user hits the return key. The command line interface then attempts to parse the entered

© Springer Nature Switzerland AG 2018
M. Ogihara, *Fundamentals of Java Programming*,
https://doi.org/10.1007/978-3-319-89491-1_1

Fig. 1.1 The program layers, JVM, JRE, and JDK

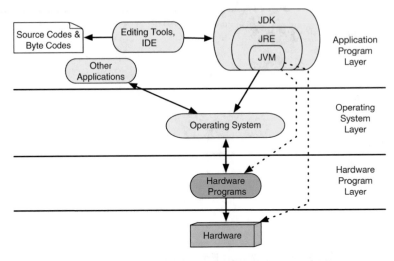

Fig. 1.2 A screen shot of Terminal on a Mac OS X machine. The prompt is the percent sign followed by one white space

command according to its syntax. If the command is syntactically correct, the interface executes the action represented by the command. When the action occurs, some characters may appear on the screen after the command line. If there are many such characters, the text screen scrolls down to show however many characters will fit on the screen, starting with the most recent. If the command is not syntactically correct, the command line interface prints an error message. To inform the user that it is ready to accept a new command, the command line interface prints a special sequence of characters, called prompt, e.g., the "percent" symbol % followed by one white space, or the "greater than" symbol >. Table 1.1 is a select list of commands.

An interactive development environment (IDE) is a program that combines a program editor and a command line interface with many additional features that make it easy to write (in particular, large) computer programs (see Fig. 1.3). The most famous IDEs for Java are Eclipse and Netbeans.

1.1.2 Changing Folders in a Command Line Interface

A command line interface (such as the program Finder for Mac and the program Folder for Windows) works in one specific file folder. The specific folder is called the **working folder** (or the **working directory**). In Finder and Folder, switching to a different folder is done by clicking icons. In a

Table 1.1 A short list of commands available in the Terminal programs for Mac OSX and Linux, as well as their counterparts in the Windows cmd

Terminal (Mac OSX/Linux)	cmd (Windows)	Function
cd FOLDER	cd FOLDER	Change folder to FOLDER
cd	cd	Change to the home folder
cd ..	cd ..	Change to the parent folder
pwd	chdir	Print the working folder
ls	dir	Listing of all files in the folder
ls FILE	ls FILE	Listing of FILE in the folder
rm FILE	del FILE	Remove the file FILE
rmdir FOLDER	del FOLDER	Remove the folder FOLDER (must be empty)
mv FILE1 FILE2	move FILE1 FILE2	Rename FILE1 to FILE2
cp FILE1 FILE2	copy FILE1 FILE2	Copy FILE1 to FILE2
mkdir FOLDER	mkdir FOLDER	Create the folder FOLDER
cat FILE	type FILE	Show the contents of FILE
more FILE	more FILE	Show the contents of FILE in chunks

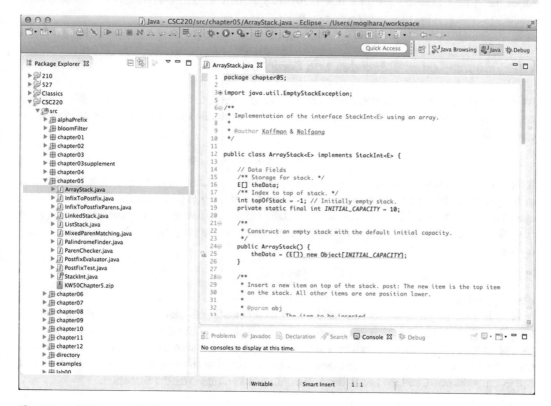

Fig. 1.3 An IDE screen of Eclipse

command line interface, this switch is made by typing a special command. The name of the command is cd (which stands for "change directory"). The syntax of cd is:

```
cd FOLDER_PATH
```

Here, FOLDER_PATH specifies how to get to the target folder from the working folder. In Chap. 15, we study the general concept of file paths.

The folder moves are composed of two basic moves: moving to one of the folders that belong to the present folder or moving to the parent (that is, the folder that the working folder belongs to as a subfolder). To move to a child folder, the path that is specified is this child folder's name. To move to the parent, the path that is specified is . . (i.e., two periods).

It is possible to combine successive folder moves into one path. For a non-Windows system like Mac OSX and Linux, this is done by inserting / between the individual moves. For Windows, \ is the folder separator. For example, in Mac OSX,

$$\texttt{cd ../foo/bar}$$

changes the working folder to the parent, to a child of the parent named foo, and then to a child of the child named bar. bar is thus a grandchild folder of the parent of the present working folder.

To check what the working folder directly is, the command pwd can be used for a non-Windows system, and chdir for Windows. These commands print the path to the working folder, starting from the "home" folder on the screen. It is also possible to take the inventory of the files in the working folder using the command ls for a non-Windows system, and dir for Windows. This command produces a list of all the files in the working folder.

1.1.3   Source Codes, Bytecodes, and Compilation

As mentioned earlier, all Java source files must have the file name extension .java. We call them Java files. To compile the source code Foo.java in a command line interface, one must type the command:

$$\texttt{javac Foo.java}$$

If the source code compiles without error, a file named Foo.class is created. This is the bytecode of the program. We call it a **class file**. If the class file already exists, then the file is overwritten upon successful compilation. In the case of IDE, .class files are generated only during the execution process. If Foo.java has compiled successfully, the program can be executed by using the command:

$$\texttt{java Foo}$$

after the prompt.

Here is an example of a user interaction with a command line interface, where the user tries to compile and then execute a program whose source code is HelloWorld.java (Fig. 1.4). The prompt of the command line interface is the percent symbol followed by one white space. The first line is the compilation command, the second line is the execution command, the third line is the result of executing the code, and the fourth line is the command prompt after the execution.

Fig. 1.4 The compilation and execution of HelloWorld.java

```
% javac HelloWorld.java
% java HelloWorld
Hello, World!
%
```

1.2   The First Program, "Hello, World!"

Let us start writing Java programs. Our first program is the popular `Hello, World!` program.

```
1  public class HelloWorld
2  {
3    public static void main( String[] args )
4    {
5      System.out.println( "Hello, World!" );
6    }
7  }
```

Listing 1.1 `HelloWorld.java`

Executing this program produces a single line of output:

```
Hello, World!
```

Using this code, we shall learn some important ingredients of Java programs.
The three words in the first line:

$$\texttt{public class HelloWorld}$$

state that:

(a) this is a program unit of type `class`,
(b) the unit is named `HelloWorld`, and
(c) the unit is accessible from all other Java program units.

There are four kinds of program units: `class`, `interface abstract class`, and `enum`. This book covers `class` and `interface` only.

The keyword `public` specifies that the unit is accessible from other program units. A keyword that specifies the accessibility of program units and their components is called a **visibility attribute**. There are three explicit visibility types: `public`, `private`, and `protected`. The default visibility type, when there is no explicit visibility attribute, is the `package visibility`.

The order of appearance of the three components,

$$\texttt{VISIBILITY\_TYPE UNIT\_TYPE NAME}$$

applies to all Java source code files.

Every source file in Java has the file extension `.java`. In a single `.java` file, multiple classes can be defined, simply by concatenating their source codes. In such a case, at most one class may be `public`. In addition, if a source file contains a unit with the public visibility, the name of the unit must match the file name. For example,

```
1  class Foo
2  {
3    ...
4  }
5  class Bar
6  {
7    ...
8  }
```

is okay, but

```
1  public class Foo
2  {
3  ...
4  }
5  public class Bar
6  {
7  ...
8  }
```

is not.

```
1  public class Foo
2  {
3  ...
4  }
5  class Bar
6  {
7  ...
8  }
```

is acceptable as well, but the source file must be Foo.java.

Let us do an experiment. If the class name is changed from HelloWorld to Hello while preserving the file name HelloWorld.java:

```
1  public class Hello
2  {
3     public static void main( String[] args )
4     {
5        System.out.println( "Hello, World!" );
6     }
7  }
```

attempting to compile the source code (that is, the command javac HelloWorld.java) produces the following error message:

```
1  HelloWorld.java:1: error: class Hello is public, should be
2  declared in a file named Hello.java
3  public class Hello
4  {
5            ^
6  1 error
```

The first two lines of the error message state the nature of the error, which is that, to define a class by the name of Hello, the file name must be Hello.java. The next three lines of the error message specify the location of the error using the "caret" symbol ^. According to the marking, the error is at the class declaration. The last line of the error message is the total number of errors found in the source code.

If the source file name HelloWorld.java is retained but the public attribute is removed, like this one:

```
1   class Hello
2   {
3     public static void main( String[] args )
4     {
5       System.out.println( "Hello, World!" );
6     }
7   }
```

the code compiles, but the .class generated is Hello.class, not HelloWorld.class.

1.2.1 Methods and Their Declarations

In Java, curly brackets { } are used to enclose units, components, and code blocks. For example, the declaration of each program unit (such as class and interface) should be followed by a matching pair of curly bracket. Two matching pairs appear either one after the other or one inside the other; that is,

$$\text{either } \{ \ \dots \ \{ \ \dots \ \} \ \dots \ \} \ \text{ or } \ \{ \ \dots \ \} \ \dots \ \{ \ \dots \ \}$$

For a source file to compile successfully, all of its curly brackets must have unique matching partners. Thus, the **depth** of a text in a source code can be defined as the number of matching pairs enclosing it. Multiple methods may appear in one source code.

In the source code of HelloWorld.java, the opening line public class HelloWorld is at depth 0, public static void main(String[] args) is at depth 1, and System.out.println(...) is at depth 2. The component appearing between lines 3 and 6 is called a **method**.

A **method** has a name and defines a set of actions needs to be performed. Some methods process information given to the in the form of **parameters**. Some methods report the results through the use of **return values**. We cover this topic in Chap. 5.

A special kind of method is the **method main**. Each method main takes the form of:

$$\text{public static void main(String[] args)}$$

as its declaration. The term args appearing in the parentheses represents the sequence of characters that the user types in the command line after the name of the program. We study args in Sect. 13.4. Only Java classes with a method main can be executed.

The general method declaration consists of the following, where the parts in boxes are optional.

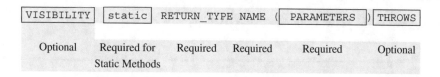

VISIBILITY	static	RETURN_TYPE	NAME	(PARAMETERS)	THROWS
Optional	Required for Static Methods	Required	Required	Required	Optional

In the case of the method main, the attribute public states that the method is accessible from outside, the attribute static states that the method is part of some executable program, the return type void states that the method has no return value, and String[] args specifies that the parameter is args and its data type is String[]. We study the meaning of square brackets in Chap. 12. The last component is about handling errors that occur during the execution of the program. We study this in Chap. 15.

1.2.2 `System.out.println` and `System.out.print`

The method `main` has only one action:

$$\texttt{System.out.println("Hello, World!");}$$

This produces the output of `Hello, World!`. A sequence of characters that defines one unit of action is called a **statement**.

Generally, a statement ends with a semicolon. The role of a statement is to perform a certain task. A method can contain any number of statements, including none. The statements are executed in the order they appear.

The period plays a special role in Java; it implies possession. `System.out.println` refers to a method (by the name of `println`) associated with `System.out`, which is part of a group of virtual hardware components named `System`. The siblings of `System.out` include: `System.err`, for printing error messages, and `System.in`, for keyboard input.

The method `println` converts the data appearing inside its parentheses to a series of characters, and then prints the series on the screen with the newline character (the equivalent of the return key) at the end. The sequence `"Hello, World!"` is the thirteen character sequence:

$$\texttt{'H' 'e' 'l' 'l' 'o' ',' ' ' 'W' 'o' 'r' 'l' 'd' '!'}$$

The double quotation mark `"` that surrounds the thirteen-character sequence is for marking the start and the end of the sequence. A character sequence encased in a pair of double quotation marks is called a **String literal**.

The method `System.out.println` automatically prints the newline character at the end. Sometimes the attachment of the newline is not desirable, e.g., when a single line of output is built by combining multiple outputs. The method `System.out.print`, a sibling of `System.out.println`, is helpful in such an occasion. The method `System.out.print` does the same as `System.out.println`, except that it does not append the newline character at the end. Furthermore, `System.out.println()` has the effect of typing the return key (that is, going to the next line without printing any other character), while `System.out.print()` is syntactically incorrect because `System.out.print()` means "print nothing".

If the method call is changed from `System.out.println` to `System.out.print`, how will the output change? Here is the new code. The program has a new name `HelloWorld01`.

```
1  public class HelloWorld01
2  {
3    public static void main( String[] args )
4    {
5       System.out.print( "Hello, World!" );
6    }
7  }
```

Listing 1.2 A version of `HelloWorld` that uses `System.out.print` in place of `System.out.println`

The execution produces the following:

```
1  Hello, World!%
```

Listing 1.3 The result of executing `HelloWorld.java`

Note that the prompt `%` appears at the end line because of the use of `System.out.print`.

1.2.3 Spacing in the Source Code

In Java source code, the white space, the tab-stop, and the newline all serve as spacing characters. The following spacing rules must be followed in Java:

- There should be some spacing between two consecutive occurrences of any of the following: type, attribute, and name.
- Some mathematical and logical symbols run together to mean special operations. In this situation, there should not be spacing between symbols.
- There should not be any newlines appearing inside a `String` literal (a character sequence within a pair of double quotation marks).

Proper spacing makes Java source codes easy to read. For example, it is possible to write:

```
1  System   .   out   .   println   (   "Hello, World!"
2       )
3       ;
```

instead of the plain

```
System.out.println("Hello, World!");
```

Although the Java compiler finds no problem in understanding this line of code, a human may find it to be a bit difficult to parse.

It is advisable to limit the number of characters per line and work within that limit, breaking up long lines into multiple smaller ones. The spacing, indentation, and the line width are up to the programmer.

Furthermore, indenting from the left end proportionally to the depth of code is good practice (recall the discussion in Sect. 1.2.1). In other words, using some fixed quantity M, the code at depth D receives an indentation of $M \cdot D$ white spaces. The code in this book utilizes this scheme with $M = 2$.[1] Most code examples that appear in this book present each curly bracket as a stand-alone in one line.

1.2.4 Commenting

It is possible to insert texts that have no relevance to how the code runs. Such texts are called **comments**. Comments are free-form texts. Java compilers ignore comments when producing class files and so they exist only in the source file. A programmer can use comments to make notes to him or herself. For example, comments can be about the expected behavior of the program and about the underlying algorithms. To save space, the code examples presented in this book use comments sparingly.

Java has three kinds of comment formats.

The first kind starts with two forward slashes `//` appearing outside `String` literals. If two side-by-side forward slashes appear outside multiple-line comments (see below) and outside `String` literals, the two characters and all the characters appearing after them are treated as comments.

---

[1] Some people use $M = 4$ or $M = 8$. The latter is equivalent to the tab-stop; i.e., a tab-stop with a depth of 1.

Because a programmer tends to limit the number of characters per line in the source code, the comments that start with two forward slashes are naturally suitable for short comments. For example, in

```
1    System.out.println( "Hello!" ); // first line
2    System.out.println( "How are you!" ); // second line
```

`// first line` and `// second line` are comments.

To place longer comments, multiple consecutive lines starting with two forward slashes after some indentation can be used, e.g.,

```
1    /////////////////////////////////////////
2    // This program receives two numbers from
3    // the user and prints the result of performing
4    // addition, subtraction, multiplication, and
5    // subtraction on the two.
6    /////////////////////////////////////////
```

are long comment lines.

There is a special way of specifying multiple-line comments. If a line starts with /* after an indentation, then all the characters starting from the /* and ending with the next */ are comments. Using this option, a comment can be stated as:

```
1    /*
2     * This program receives two numbers from
3     * the user and prints the result of performing
4     * addition, subtraction, multiplication, and
5     * subtraction on the two.
6     */
```

The * appearing in the middle four lines are extraneous, but programmers tend to put that character to make the vertical array of * look like the left border of the comments.

Be mindful of the following:

- /* appearing inside a matching pair of double quotation marks behaves as part of the String literal. The same holds for */ and //.
- All characters appearing between /* and the matching */ are comments. Therefore, /* appearing in a matching pair of /* and */ is part of the comment represented by the pair.

This means that the code

```
1   public class Foo
2   {
3     public static void main( String[] args )
4     {
5       /* here is a comment
6       /* one more comment? */
7       */
8       System.out.println( "/*//" );
9     }
10  }
```

has no matching /* for the */ in Line 7.

The last kind of comment is the **Javadoc**. The Javadoc is a variant of the aforementioned multiple-line comment and uses a pair of /** and */ in place of /* and */. Javadocs are for publicizing information about methods and classes and are written using a special syntax. IDEs such as Eclipse are capable of presenting information available through Javadocs.

The following code shows some examples of commenting.

```
1   /*
2    * Class for showing comment examples
3    * Written by Mitsunori Ogihara
4    */
5   public class Comments
6   {
7     /**
8      * main method
9      * @param args the arguments
10     */
11    public static void main( String[] args )
12    {
13      // There are two lines in the program
14      System.out.println( "A code needs comments!" );
15    }
16  }
```

Listing 1.4 Examples of comments. Lines 1–4 form a multiple-line comment. Lines 7–10 form a Javadoc comment. Line 13 is a single-line comment

1.2.5 Errors

A **syntax error** is a part of source code that fails to conform to the Java syntax. If a source code contains syntax errors, the Java compiler, instead of producing the bytecode, produces an error message stating that there are syntax errors. If there is a bytecode generated from the prior successful compilation, that code remains the same without being updated.

The syntax error that a compiler produces is a bit cryptic and takes some experience to comprehend. Mainly because the compiler is not aware of the true intension of the programmer who wrote the erroneous code, the stated number of syntax errors does not necessarily agree with the actual number of syntax errors.

Consider the following code, which is intended to execute three println statements successively.

```
1   //---- This is the class name
2   public class BuggyHelloWorld
3     /----
4     //---- Main method of the code
5     //----
6     public static void main( String[] args )
7     {
8       System.out.pritnln( "Hello, World! );
9       System.out.printin( Hello, Class!" );
10      System.out.printin( "Hello, its' me!" ):
11    }
12  }
13  }
```

Listing 1.5 A buggy version of the HelloWorld program. The intended class name is BuggyHelloWorld

There are four syntax errors in the code:

1. the forward slash in line 3 should be a double forward slash,
2. the `String` literal in line 7 does not have a closing double quotation mark,
3. the colon at the end of line 7 should be a semicolon, and
4. There should be one more "}" at the end.

At the compilation step, we encounter the following error messages:

```
1    BuggyHelloWorld.java:2: error: '{' expected
2    public class BuggyHelloWorld
3                                 ^
4    BuggyHelloWorld.java:8: error: unclosed string literal
5        System.out.pritnln( "Hello, World! );
6                            ^
7    BuggyHelloWorld.java:8: error: ';' expected
8        System.out.pritnln( "Hello, World! );
9                                             ^
10   BuggyHelloWorld.java:9: error: illegal start of expression
11       System.out.printin( Hello, Class!" );
12                           ^
13   BuggyHelloWorld.java:9: error: ';' expected
14       System.out.printin( Hello, Class!" );
15                                 ^
16   BuggyHelloWorld.java:9: error: ')' expected
17       System.out.printin( Hello, Class!" );
18                                          ^
19   BuggyHelloWorld.java:9: error: unclosed string literal
20       System.out.printin( Hello, Class!" );
21                                          ^
22   BuggyHelloWorld.java:10: error: ';' expected
23       System.out.printin( "Hello, its' me!" ):
24                           ^
25   BuggyHelloWorld.java:10: error: ';' expected
26       System.out.printin( "Hello, its' me!" ):
27                                              ^
28   BuggyHelloWorld.java:13: error: class, interface, or enum expected
29   }
30   ^
31   10 errors
```

Each error message consists of the source file name, the line number of the error, the nature of the error, and the actual location of the error (indicated by the caret symbol). In the case of an IDE, instead of presenting the errors in its command line interface screen, these errors are highlighted in the source code editor screen.

As can be seen, the number of error messages is greater than the actual number of errors. Although the number of error messages may exceed the number of true errors, it is always the case that the very first error message corresponds to the very first syntax error. In the above example, "illegal start of type" pointing to / - - - is a true syntax error. Fixing the very first syntax error in the source code first is a good strategy.

There are two other types of errors: **run-time errors** and **logic errors**. Runtime errors are those that occur during the execution of code, interrupting the execution. They often result in a premature termination of the program. Logic errors do not necessarily result in run-time errors, but occur due to misconception or flaws in the logic of the programmer.

1.3   Using Multiple Statements

1.3.1   `System.out.println` and `System.out.print` (Reprise)

As mentioned earlier, a method can contain multiple statements. If multiple statements appear in a method, they act in the order of appearance. Multiple statements can be used to write a program that executes a complex task.

Consider the following program that prints the "ABC Song":

```
1  public class MultiLines
2  {
3    public static void main( String[] args )
4    {
5      System.out.println( "A B C D E F G" );
6      System.out.println( "H I J K L M N O P" );
7      System.out.println( "Q R S and T U V" );
8      System.out.println( "W X Y and Z" );
9      System.out.println( "Now I know my A B C" );
10     System.out.println( "Won't you sing along with me" );
11   }
12 }
```

Listing 1.6 A source code with multiple `println` statements

The program executes the six `System.out.println` statements from top to bottom, and produces the following six-line output.

```
1  A B C D E F G
2  H I J K L M N O P
3  Q R S and T U V
4  W X Y and Z
5  Now I know my A B C
6  Won't you sing along with me
```

Recall that `System.out.print` is the version of `System.out.println` without the newline at the end.

The next code is a variant of the previous code. We have changed the first, third, and fifth `System.out.println` statements to `System.out.print` statements.

```
1  public class MultiLines01
2  {
3    public static void main( String[] args )
4    {
5      System.out.print( "A B C D E F G" );
6      System.out.println( "H I J K L M N O P" );
7      System.out.print( "Q R S and T U V" );
8      System.out.println( "W X Y and Z" );
9      System.out.print( "Now I know my A B C" );
10     System.out.println( "Won't you sing along with me" );
11   }
12 }
```

Listing 1.7 A source code with multiple `print` and `println` statements

The result of executing the code is as follows:

```
1   A B  C D E F  GH  I J K L  M N O  P
2   Q R  S and T U  VW  X Y and Z
3   Now I know my A B  CWon't you sing along with me
```

The use of `System.out.print` at three places has reduced the number of output lines from six to three. In each of the three lines, two outputs appear side-by-side with no gaps in between. Thus, to make the connections appear correct, some characters are needed in between. The next code example fixes this spacing issue by appending the command and the space (i.e., `", "`) to the first, third, and fifth sequences.

```
1    public class MultiLines02
2    {
3      public static void main( String[] args )
4      {
5        System.out.print( "A B  C D E F  G, " );
6        System.out.println( "H I J K L M N O  P" );
7        System.out.print( "Q R S and T U V, " );
8        System.out.println( "W X Y and Z" );
9        System.out.print( "Now I know my A B  C, " );
10       System.out.println( "Won't you sing along with me" );
11     }
12   }
```

Listing 1.8 A source code with multiple `print` and `println` statements with some punctuation

The result of executing the code is as follows:

```
1   A B  C D E F  G, H I J K L M N O  P
2   Q R S and T U V, W X Y and Z
3   Now I know my A B  C, Won't you sing along with me
```

1.3.2 Printing Multiple-Line Texts on the Screen

In a manner similar to the code for the ABC song, we can write a program that produces some selected texts on the screen, for example, the poem "Autumn" by an American poet Henry Wadsworth Longfellow (February 27, 1807 to March 24, 1882).

Thou comest, Autumn, heralded by the rain
With banners, by great gales incessant fanne
Brighter than brightest silks of Samarcand,
And stately oxen harnessed to thy wain!
Thou standest, like imperial Charlemagne,
Upon thy bridge of gold; thy royal hand
Outstretched with benedictions o'er the land,
Blessing the farms through all thy vast domain!
Thy shield is the red harvest moon, suspended
So 'long' beneath the heaven's o'er-hanging eaves;
Thy steps are by the farmer's prayers attended;
Like flames upon an altar shine the sheaves;
And, following thee, in thy ovation splendid,
Thine almoner, the wind, scatters the golden leaves!

The code `Autumn.java` that appears next produces this poem on the screen by combining `System.out.print` and `System.out.println` statements, where each line of the poem is split into two statements.

```
1   public class Autumn
2   {
3     public static void main( String[] args )
4     {
5       System.out.println( "Autumn, by Longfellow" );
6       System.out.println();
7       System.out.print( "Thou comest, Autumn, " );
8       System.out.println( "heralded by the rain" );
9       System.out.print( "With banners, " );
10      System.out.println( "by great gales incessant fanne" );
11      System.out.print( "Brighter than brightest " );
12      System.out.println( "silks of Samarcand," );
13      System.out.print( "And stately oxen " );
14      System.out.println( "harnessed to thy wain!" );
15      System.out.print( "Thou standest, " );
16      System.out.println( "like imperial Charlemagne," );
17      System.out.print( "Upon thy bridge of gold; " );
18      System.out.println( "thy royal hand" );
19      System.out.print( "Outstretched with benedictions " );
20      System.out.println( "o'er the land," );
21      System.out.print( "Blessing the farms through " );
22      System.out.println( "all thy vast domain!" );
23      System.out.print( "Thy shield is the red harvest moon, " );
24      System.out.println( "suspended" );
25      System.out.print( "So long beneath the heaven's " );
26      System.out.println( "o'er-hanging eaves;" );
27      System.out.print( "Thy steps are by the farmer's " );
28      System.out.println( "prayers attended;" );
29      System.out.print( "Like flames upon an altar " );
30      System.out.println( "shine the sheaves;" );
31      System.out.print( "And, following thee, " );
32      System.out.println( "in thy ovation splendid," );
33      System.out.print( "Thine almoner, the wind, " );
34      System.out.println( "scatters the golden leaves!" );
35    }
36  }
```

Listing 1.9 A source code for Autumn.java

The program produces the following output:

```
1
2   Thou comest, Autumn, heralded by the rain
3   With banners, by great gales incessant fanne
4   Brighter than brightest silks of Samarcand,
5   And stately oxen harnessed to thy wain!
6   Thou standest, like imperial Charlemagne,
7   Upon thy bridge of gold; thy royal hand
8   Outstretched with benedictions o'er the land,
9   Blessing the farms through all thy vast domain!
10  Thy shield is the red harvest moon, suspended
11  So long beneath the heaven's o'er-hanging eaves;
12  Thy steps are by the farmer's prayers attended;
13  Like flames upon an altar shine the sheaves;
14  And, following thee, in thy ovation splendid,
15  Thine almoner, the wind, scatters the golden leaves!
```

1.3.3   Escaping Characters

Suppose we wish to print the following character sequence:

abc"def

To print a character sequence directly with System.out.print and System.out.println, we attach the double quotation mark before and after the sequence. What if the sequence were abc"def and we wrote out the statement as follows?

System.out.println("abc"def");

This would produce a compilation error.

The next code is one that has triple double quotation marks.

```
1   public class TripleQuote
2   {
3     public static void main( String[] args )
4     {
5        System.out.println( "abc"def" );
6     }
7   }
```

Listing 1.10   A code that attempts to use a quotation mark inside a character sequence

The compiler produces the following error messages:

```
1   TripleQuote.java:3: error: ')' expected
2       System.out.println( "abc"def" );
3                                ^
4   TripleQuote.java:3: error: unclosed string literal
5       System.out.println( "abc"def" );
6                                    ^
7   TripleQuote.java:3: error: ';' expected
8       System.out.println( "abc"def" );
9                                       ^
10  TripleQuote.java:5: error: reached end of file while parsing
11  }
12   ^
13  4 errors
```

What happened during the compilation attempt? The Java compiler tried to pair the first double quotation mark with another. It chose, however, to pair the second quotation mark with the first. The compiler then tried to make sense of the remainder def", but it could not.

To correct this problem, we need to tell the compiler that the middle double quotation mark is not the end marker. Attaching a backslash \ before the quotation mark accomplishes this.

"abc\"def"

With this modification, the code looks like:

```
1   public class TripleQuoteCorrect
2   {
3     public static void main( String[] args )
4     {
5        System.out.println( "abc\"def" );
6     }
7   }
```

Listing 1.11   A code that prints a quotation mark inside a character sequence and the code generates the output as intended:

```
abc"def
```

We call the action of attaching the backslash to relieve a symbol of its regular duties **escaping**.

With escaping, we can insert a newline character using the combination \n. To include a tab-stop character, we can use \t instead of using of the actual tab-stop. The benefit of using the \t is that the character is visible; if we use the tab-stop character as it is, it is difficult to tell later whether a gap we see is indeed a tab-stop or just a series of the white space.

Finally, to escape the backslash character, we use the double backslash \\.

Assuming that the tab-stop positions of a terminal program are at every eighth position starting from the left end, the statement:

```
System.out.println( "abcdefgh\n\"\\i\tj\nk" );
```

produces the following output:

```
1  abcdefgh
2  "\i        j
3  k
```

We can use escaping to print texts with quotation marks and backward slashes. Listing 1.12 is a program that prints a quotation from Mark Twain's *Adventures of Huckleberry Finn*. In one line of the quote, the addition of System.out.println and the indentation makes the line too long to fit in the width of 72 characters. To solve this issue, we split the line into two: the first half with System.out.print and the second half with System.out.println (Lines 17 and 18).

```
1  public class HuckleberryFinn
2  {
3    public static void main(String[] args)
4    {
5      System.out.println("\\Quoted from Huckleberry Finn\\");
6      System.out.println("I broke in and says:");
7      System.out.println("\"They're in an awful peck of trouble, and\"");
8      System.out.println("\"Who is?\"");
9      System.out.println("\"Why, pap and mam and sis and Miss Hooker;");
10     System.out.println("\tand if you'd take your ferryboat and go up
           there\"");
11     System.out.println("\"Up where?  Where are they?\"");
12     System.out.println("\"On the wreck.\"");
13     System.out.println("\"What wreck?\"");
14     System.out.println("\"Why, there ain't but one.\"");
15     System.out.println("\"What, you don't mean the Walter Scott?\"");
16     System.out.println("\"Yes.\"");
17     System.out.print("\"Good land! what are they doin' there, ");
18     System.out.println("for gracious sakes?\"");
19     System.out.println("\"Well, they didn't go there a-purpose.\"");
20   }
21 }
```

Listing 1.12 A program that prints a quotation from Mark Twain's *Adventures of Huckleberry Finn*

Executing the code produces the following output.

```
1   \Quoted from Huckleberry Finn\
2   I broke in and says:
3   "They're in an awful peck of trouble, and"
4   "Who is?"
5   "Why, pap and mam and sis and Miss Hooker;
6           and if you'd take your ferryboat and go up there"
7   "Up where? Where are they?"
8   "On the wreck."
9   "What wreck?"
10  "Why, there ain't but one."
11  "What, you don't mean the Walter Scott?"
12  "Yes."
13  "Good land! what are they doin' there, for gracious sakes?"
14  "Well, they didn't go there a-purpose."
```

Using \n as the newline, we can print multiple short lines into single statements, as shown in List 1.13. Note that most of the lines contain \n in the character sequence that needs to be printed.

```
1   public class HuckleberryFinn01
2   {
3     public static void main(String[] args)
4     {
5       System.out.print( "\\Quoted from Huckleberry Finn\\\n" );
6       System.out.print( "I broke in and says:\n\"They're in" );
7       System.out.print( " an awful peck of trouble, and\"\n" );
8       System.out.print( "\"Who is?\"\n\"Why, pap and mam and " );
9       System.out.print( "sis and Miss Hooker;\n\tand if you'd " );
10      System.out.print( "take your ferryboat and go up there\"" );
11      System.out.print( "\n\"Up where?  Where are they?\"\n" );
12      System.out.print( "\"On the wreck.\"\n\"What wreck?\"\n" );
13      System.out.print( "\"Why, there ain't but one.\"\n" );
14      System.out.print( "\"What, you don't mean the Walter " );
15      System.out.print( "Scott?\"\n\"Yes.\"\n\"Good land! " );
16      System.out.print( "what are they doin' there, for " );
17      System.out.print( "gracious sakes?\"\n\"Well, they " );
18      System.out.print( "didn't go there a-purpose.\"\n" );
19    }
20  }
```

Listing 1.13 A program that uses squeezed print statements to produce the same quotation from Mark Twain's *Adventures of Huckleberry Finn* as before

The execution produces exactly the same result as before.

Java uses many symbol sequences, including escaping. Table 1.2 summarizes all such symbol sequences.

1.3.4 Printing Shapes

Previously, we used multiple System.out.println statements to produce multiple-line texts on the terminal screen. Expanding on the idea, now we write Java programs that print shapes on the terminal screen.

Table 1.2 The list of meaningful symbols in Java

`[]`	Arrays	`()`	Parameters
`{}`	Code block	`<>`	Type parameter
`.`	Class membership	`=`	Assignment
`;`	Statement separator	`,`	Parameter separator
`?`	If-then-else value selection	`:`	Case presentation
`+`	Addition/concatenation	`-`	Subtraction, negative sign
`*`	Multiplication	`/`	Quotient
`%`	Remainder, format type parameter		
`++`	Increment	`-`	Decrement
`+=`	Direct addition	`-=`	Direct subtraction
`*=`	Direct multiplication	`/=`	Direct quotient
`%=`	Direct remainder		
`==`	Equality	`!=`	Inequality
`>`	Greater than	`<`	Smaller than
`>=`	Greater than or equal to	`>=`	Smaller than or equal to
`&&`	Logical AND	`||`	Logical OR
`!`	Negation		
`«`	Signed left shift	`»`	Signed right shift
`«<`	Unsigned left shift	`»>`	Unsigned right shift
`&`	Bit-wise AND	`	`	Bit-wise OR
`^`	Bit-wise XOR		
`&=`	Direct bit-wise AND	`	=`	Direct bit-wise OR
`^=`	Direct bit-wise XOR		
`@`	Javadoc keyword	`//`	Line comment
`/*`	Multiple-line comment start	`/**`	Javadoc start
`*/`	Multiple-line comment/Java end		
`\`	Escape	`\\`	Backslash character
`\n`	The newline character	`\t`	The tab-stop character
`\'`	Single quote in a char literal	`%%`	the % Character in format strings
`%n`	The newline character in format strings		

Suppose we want to print the figure of a right-angled triangle like the one appears next:

In the drawing, we use the forward slash / for the left side of the triangle, the vertical | for the right side of the triangle, and the underscore _ for the bottom side.

The following code will do the job:

```
 1  //-- print a triangle
 2  public class Triangle
 3  {
 4    public static void main( String[] args )
 5    {
 6      System.out.println( "        /|" );
 7      System.out.println( "       / |" );
 8      System.out.println( "      /  |" );
 9      System.out.println( "     /   |" );
10      System.out.println( "    /    |" );
11      System.out.println( "   /     |" );
12      System.out.println( "  /_____|" );
13    }
14  }
```

Listing 1.14 The code for producing a right-angled triangle

How about an isosceles triangle, like this one?

```
1         /\
2        /  \
3       /    \
4      /      \
5     /        \
6    /          \
7   /_____\
```

Using the \ for the right edge, we come up with the following code:

```
 1  //-- print an isosceles
 2  public class Isosceles
 3  {
 4    //-- main method
 5    public static void main( String[] args )
 6    {
 7      System.out.println( "      /\\" );   // line 1
 8      System.out.println( "     /  \\" );  // line 2
 9      System.out.println( "    /    \\" );   // line 3
10      System.out.println( "   /      \\" );  // line 4
11      System.out.println( "  /        \\" );   // line 5
12      System.out.println( " /          \\" );  // line 6
13      System.out.println( "/_____\\" );   // line 7
14    }
15  }
```

Listing 1.15 A code for printing on the screen an isosceles triangle

Let's try printing an isosceles upside down, as shown next:

```
1  \------------/
2   \          /
3    \        /
4     \      /
5      \    /
6       \  /
7        \/
```

The shape looks a bit unwieldy, since we are using the dash to draw the top line. The triangle will look better if we draw the top line using an over-line bar character, but unfortunately, such a character does not exist in our standard character set, so the dash is our only option.

```
1   //-- print an isosceles upside down
2   public class UpsideDownIsoscelesCorrect
3   {
4     //-- main method
5     public static void main( String[] args )
6     {
7       System.out.println( "\\-------------/" );   // line 7
8       System.out.println( "  \\           /" ); // line 6
9       System.out.println( "   \\         /" );  // line 5
10      System.out.println( "    \\       /" );  // line 4
11      System.out.println( "     \\     /" );   // line 3
12      System.out.println( "      \\ /" );      // line 2
13      System.out.println( "       \\/" );       // line 1
14    }
15  }
```

Listing 1.16 The code for producing an upside-down isosceles triangle on the screen

Try writing programs that draw other interesting shapes!

Summary

■ A command line interface is an environment in which the user, through typing commands after a prompt, interacts with the system.

■ In command line interfaces and programming environments, there exists a "working folder".

■ The standard header of a Java class is public class CLASS_NAME. Its file name should be CLASS_NAME.java.

■ An executable Java class has public static void main(String[] arg).

■ To compile a Java program, use the command javac CLASS_NAME.java.

■ The Java compiler may produce compilation errors due to syntax errors.

■ The command to use when executing a Java bytecode by the name of CLASS_NAME is java CLASS_NAME.

■ A code that compiles may produce terminating errors. Such terminating errors are called run-time errors.

■ A code that compiles and is free of run-time errors may still not run correctly. Logical errors are the culprits.

■ Java programs use pairs of curly braces to define code blocks.

■ Unless they are appearing in the source code for an object class, methods need to have the static attribute.

■ Methods and classes may have a visibility attribute.

■ Method declarations must have both a return value specification and a parameter specification.

■ In a method, multiple statements may appear. Each statement ends with a semicolon.

■ System.out.println is a method that produces the value of its parameter on the screen and then prints a newline.

■ System.out.print is a method that produces the value of its parameter on the screen.

■ To print the double quotation mark, the escape sequence of \ " is used.
■ To print the backslash as a character, the escape sequence of \ \ is used.
■ There are three types of comments: single line comments, multiple-line comments, and Javadocs.

Exercises

1. **Terminology** Answer the following questions:
   (a) What is the formal name of the process for creating an executable Java code from a .java file? What about the command used in the Unix environment for creating such an executable code?
   (b) What is the file extension of a Java byte code?
   (c) What is the command used for executing a Java byte code?
   (d) In a .java file two words usually appear before its class name. What are they?
   (e) What are the three words that precede the main method in a .java file?
   (f) State the differences between System .out.print and System.out.println.
   (g) What are the three categories of errors in programming?
   (h) In String literals, what sequences of characters must you use to print the double quote, the backslash, and the newline?

2. **Main Declaration** Of the following possible declarations for the method main, which ones will compile?
   (a) public static void main(String[] args)
   (b) static void main(String[] args)
   (c) public static main(String[] args)
   (d) public static void(String[] args)
   (e) public static void main( )
   (f) public static void main(String[])
   (g) public static void main(args)

3. **Fixing errors** The following code contains some errors and will not compile. State what we must fix so that it will compile.

```
1  public class MyBuggyProgram {
2    public static main( []String args )
3    [
4      System.out.prink( 'Hello!' ):
5    ]
6  }
```

4. **Escaping** Which of the following require a backslash when being included in a String literal (i.e., a series of characters flanked by a pair of double quotation marks)?
   • A
   • /
     (i.e., the forward slash)
   • \
     (i.e, the backslash)
   • "
   • %
     (i.e., the percentage symbol)
   • @
     (i.e., the at sign)

Programming Projects

5. **Alma Mater**   Write a program named `AlmaMater` that upon execution prints the Alma Mater of your school. For the University of Miami, the output of the program should look like:

```
1   UM ALMA MATER
2
3   Southern suns and sky blue water,
4   Smile upon you Alma mater;
5   Mistress of this fruitful land,
6   With all knowledge at your hand,
7   Always just to honor true,
8   All our love we pledge to you.
9   Alma Mater, stand forever
10  On Biscayne's wondrous shore.
```

6. **Printing a Diamond**   Write a program named `Diamond.java` that prints the shape of a diamond of height 10 and width 10 as shown:

```
1          /\
2         /  \
3        /    \
4       /      \
5      /        \
6      \        /
7       \      /
8        \    /
9         \  /
10         \/
```

7. **Printing a Filled Diamond**   Write a program named `DiamondFilled.java` that prints the shape of a diamond of height 10 and width 10 with the white space filled with forward slashes on the left-hand side and backward slashes on the right-hand side, as shown:

```
1         /\
2        //\\
3       ///\\\
4      ////\\\\
5     /////\\\\\
6     \\\\\/////
7      \\\\////
8       \\\///
9        \\//
10        \/
```

8. **Printing an X with 'X'**

   Write a program, `XwithXs`, that produces the following shape on the screen:

```
1   X           X
2    X         X
3     X       X
4      X X
5       X
6      X X
7     X       X
8    X         X
9   X           X
```

9. **Cascaded printing**   Write a program, `CascadedChildren`, that prints the first two verses of "Children" by Henry Wadsworth Longfellow with increasing indentations:

```
1   Come to me, O ye children!
2    For I hear you at your play,
3     And the questions that perplexed me
4      Have vanished quite away.
5
6       Ye open the eastern windows,
7        That look towards the sun,
8         Where thoughts are singing swallows
9          And the brooks of morning run.
```

10. **Slashes**   Write a program, `Slashes`, that produces the following shape on the screen:

```
1   / / / / / / / / / / / /
2    / / / / / / / / / / / /
3   / / / / / / / / / / / /
4    / / / / / / / / / / /
5   / / / / / / / / / / / /
6    / / / / / / / / / / /
7   / / / / / / / / / / / /
8    / / / / / / / / / /
9   / / / / / / / / / / / /
10   / / / / / / / / / /
```

11. **Backlashes**   Write a program, `BackSlashes`, that produces the following shape on the screen:

```
1   \ \ \ \ \ \ \ \ \ \ \ \
2    \ \ \ \ \ \ \ \ \ \ \
3   \ \ \ \ \ \ \ \ \ \ \ \
4    \ \ \ \ \ \ \ \ \ \ \
5   \ \ \ \ \ \ \ \ \ \ \ \
6    \ \ \ \ \ \ \ \ \ \ \
7   \ \ \ \ \ \ \ \ \ \ \ \
8    \ \ \ \ \ \ \ \ \ \ \
9   \ \ \ \ \ \ \ \ \ \ \ \
10    \ \ \ \ \ \ \ \ \ \
```

12. **Tabstop**   You can use the tab-stop character `\t` to line things up (to improve the readability of the text output). Consider the following code:

```
1   public class TestTabStop
2   {
3     public static void main( String[] args )
4     {
5       System.out.println( "Abbie Zuckerman 23yrs Soccer" );
6       System.out.println( "Brittany Ying 21yrs Swimming" );
7       System.out.println( "Caty Xenakis 22yrs Softball" );
8       System.out.println( "Dee Wick 20yrs Basketball" );
9       System.out.println( "Eva Venera 19yrs Polo" );
10    }
11  }
```

The code produces the following output:

```
1   Abbie Zuckerman 23yrs Soccer
2   Brittany Ying 21yrs Swimming
3   Caty Xenakis 22yrs Softball
4   Dee Wick 20yrs Basketball
5   Eva Venera 19yrs Polo
```

Revise the program so that it uses the same code, but replaces the whitespace (inside each pair of double quotation marks) with the tab-stop. Run the program to see how it changes the way the information appears on the screen.

13. **Self introduction**   Write a program named `SelfIntro` that introduces yourself as follows:

```
1   My name is NAME.
2    I was born in PLACE.
3     My favorite television program is PROGRAM.
4      I woke up at HOUR:MINUTE today.
5       I own NUMBER books.
6        My target grade point average is GPA.
```

The uppercase words NAME, PLACE, PROGRAM, HOUR, MINUTE, NUMBER, and GPA, are placeholders, so you must substitute them with appropriate text. PROGRAM must appear with double quotation marks. For example,

```
1   My name is Mitsu Ogihara.
2    I was born in Japan.
3     My favorite television program is "Parks and Recreation".
4      I woke up at 6:30 today.
5       I own 1000 books.
6        My target grade point average is 4.0.
```

Using Data for Computation

2

2.1 Data

2.1.1 Data and Their Taxonomy

The previous chapter presented how to write programs using only `System.out.println` and `System.out.print` statements. This chapter introduces how to store, modify, and retrieve information. The medium in which information is stored is called **data**.[1]

In Java, every data has its **type**, which specifies how the data encodes its information, as well as what operations can be performed on the data. There are two broad classifications of data types in Java: **primitive data types** and **object data types**.

A primitive data type is one that uses only a predetermined number of **bits** in representation, where a bit is the fundamental unit of information and has two possible values (0 and 1). There are eight primitive data types: `boolean` for the logical values, `char` for the characters, `byte`, `short`, `int`, and `long` for whole numbers of various capacities, and `float` and `double` for real numbers of various capacities.

On the other hand, an object data type is a custom-designed data type. A programmer designs a new object data type by putting together existing data types and defining the permissible operations for acting on the information stored. Some object data types require an indefinite number of bits for representation.

In addition to the major difference between primitive and object data types, the following distinctions can be made among data.

1. There are data with names referencing and data without these names.
   (a) The former kind is a **variable**. A special variable is one whose value cannot be changed during the course of program. Such a variable is called a **constant**
   (b) The latter kind consists of **literals** and **return values**. A literal is a data whose value is exactly specified. A return value is a value that a method returns.

---

[1]The term data is used for both singular and plural forms. The original singular form of "data" is "datum", but this is rarely used nowadays.

© Springer Nature Switzerland AG 2018
M. Ogihara, *Fundamentals of Java Programming*,
https://doi.org/10.1007/978-3-319-89491-1_2

2. Some variables and constants are accessible only inside the method in which they appear; others are accessible from everywhere in the class. The former ones are **local**, and the latter ones are **global**.

    (a) Some global variables in an object class play the role of storing information for individual objects of the class. Those variables are **instance variables** (or **field variables**).

    (b) Each global constant, as well as each instance variable, has a specific visibility type (public, private, protected, and package).

2.1.2 Number Literals

The sequence `"Hello, World!"` is a literal of the data type `String`. Literals are available not only for `String` but also for all the primitive data types.

The following is an example of a code using literals:

```
1  public class Literals
2  {
3    public static void main( String[] args )
4    {
5      System.out.print( "Rank number " );
6      System.out.print( 1 );
7      System.out.print( " in my all-time favorite NFL QB list is " );
8      System.out.print( "Steve Young" );
9      System.out.println( "." );
10     System.out.print( "His overall quarterback rating is " );
11     System.out.print( 96.8 );
12     System.out.println( "." );
13   }
14 }
```

Listing 2.1 A program that produces a comment about an NFL quarterback

In Lines 5, 7–9, and 12, `String` literals appear inside the parentheses. In Lines 6 and 11, literals 1 and 96.8 appear inside the parentheses. These are number literals (an `int` literal and a `double` literal, to be precise).

When this program runs, `System.out.print` converts these two numbers to character sequences, then prints those sequences on the screen.

```
1  Rank number 1 in my all-time favorite NFL quarterbacks is Steve Young.
2  His overall quarterback rating is 96.8.
```

By adding the same sequence of statements for two more quarterbacks, the following program is obtained.

```
1   public class Literals01
2   {
3     public static void main( String[] args )
4     {
5       System.out.print( "Rank number " );
6       System.out.print( 1 );
7       System.out.print( " in my all-time favorite NFL QB list is " );
8       System.out.print( "Steve Young" );
9       System.out.println( "." );
10      System.out.print( "His overall QB rating is " );
11      System.out.print( 96.8 );
12      System.out.println( "." );
13
```

Listing 2.2 A program that produces comments about three NFL quarterbacks (part 1). The program header and the part that produces comments about the first player

For these additional two players, number literals appear in Lines 15, 20, 24 and 29.

```
14      System.out.print( "Rank number " );
15      System.out.print( 2 );
16      System.out.print( " in my all-time favorite NFL QB list is " );
17      System.out.print( "Peyton Manning" );
18      System.out.println( "." );
19      System.out.print( "His overall QB rating is " );
20      System.out.print( 96.5 );
21      System.out.println( "." );
22
23      System.out.print( "Rank number " );
24      System.out.print( 3 );
25      System.out.print( " in my all-time favorite NFL QB list is " );
26      System.out.print( "Tom Brady" );
27      System.out.println( "." );
28      System.out.print( "His overall QB rating is " );
29      System.out.print( 97.0 );
30      System.out.println( "." );
31    }
32  }
```

Listing 2.3 A program that produces comments about three NFL quarterbacks (part 2). The part that produces comments about the second and the third players

The program produces the following output[2]:

```
1   Rank number 1 in my all-time favorite NFL quarterbacks is Steve Young.
2   His overall quarterback rating is 96.8.
3   Rank number 2 in my all-time favorite NFL quarterbacks is Peyton Manning.
4   His overall quarterback rating is 96.5.
5   Rank number 3 in my all-time favorite NFL quarterbacks is Tom Brady.
6   His overall quarterback rating is 97.0.
```

---

[2]Jon Steven "Steve" Young (born October 11, 1961) is a former NFL quarterback and a sportscaster. He played 13 seasons with the San Francisco 49ers, and led the team to three Super Bowl wins. Peyton Williams Manning (born March 24, 1976) is a former NFL quarterback who played with the Indianapolis Colts and later with the Denver Broncos. He led each team to one Super Bowl win. Thomas Edward Patrick Brady Jr. (born August 3, 1977) is an NFL quarterback for the New England Patriots. He led the team to five Super Bowl wins.

2.1.3   Variable Declarations

A variable is a type of data with a reference name. Simply by putting its name in the code, the value of the data in that specific moment can be looked up.

Since each data has a unique type, a variable is specified with its name and its type. This is called a **declaration**. A declaration takes the following form:

$$DATA\_TYPE\ VARIABLE\_NAME;$$

Remember that the tab-stop can be used in place of the white space, and adding more tab-stops or white space after that is possible as well.

One example is the following:

```
1   public static ...
2   {
3     ...
4     int myInteger;
5     ...
6   }
```

Here, `int` is the data type and `myInteger` is the name of the data. Notice the semicolon `;` appearing at the end. Each line of local/global variable/constant declarations requires a semicolon at the end. The above is an instance in which the variable is a local variable. A local variable belongs to a method and its declaration appears inside the method that it belongs to. The "locality" of variables becomes important when multiple methods are written in a source code.

To declare a global variable, its declaration is placed outside the methods, at depth 1. For example, the following declares a global variable named `myInteger` of data type `int`.

```
1     static int myInteger;
2
3     public static ...
4     {
5       ...
6     }
```

The attachment of `static` is required for the declaration of a global variable.

It is possible to join declarations of multiple variables of the same type in one line via separating the names with commas, as shown next:

```
int oneInteger , anotherInteger , yetAnotherInteger ;
```

Here, `oneInteger`, `anotherInteger`, and `yetAnotherInteger` are all of the `int` data type. This single-line declaration is equivalent to:

```
1   int oneInteger;
2   int anotherInteger;
3   int yetAnotherInteger;
```

To name a variable, a sequence of contiguous characters chosen from the alphabet, numerals, the **underscore** _, and the **dollar sign** $ must be used. In addition, the first character of the sequence must be a letter of the alphabet.[3] Thus, according to this rule, 55 cannot be a variable name. The

---

[3]Technically, a variable name can start with the underscore or the dollar sign, but the convention is to start a variable name with a lowercase letter.

variable names, method names, and class names are all case-sensitive. The following conventions are generally used:

- The name of a variable must start with a lowercase letter.
- The name of a constant must contain no lowercase letter.
- The name of a class must start with an uppercase letter.

2.1.4 Assigning Values to Variables

As mentioned earlier, variables (or constants) are places where information is stored. The action of giving a value to a variable/constant is called an **assignment**.

The syntax for an assignment is:

```
VARIABLE = VALUE;
```

Here, the equal sign = appearing in the middle symbolizes the assignment. The left-hand side of the assignment, VARIABLE, is the name of the variable in which a value is to be stored. The right-hand side of an assignment, VALUE, is the value being stored. JVM can interpret this as a data having the same type as the variable. The value in an assignment can be:

- a literal of the same type;
- a variable of the same type;
- a call to a method that returns with data of the same type; or
- a formula of the same type.

Next is an example of assigning a value to a variable:

```
1  int myInteger;
2  myInteger = 55;
```

The first line here is a variable declaration. The type of the data is int and the name of the data is myInteger. The second line is an assignment. The right-hand side of the assignment is an int literal with the value of 55. This action stores the value of 55 into the variable myInteger.

It is possible to combine a declaration of a variable and an initial value assignment to the variable all in a single statement, like this one:

```
int myInteger = 55;
```

It is also possible to combine multiple declarations and assignments of multiple variables in one line, so long as they all have the same type. The following is an example of such combinations:

```
int oneInteger = 17, anotherInteger, yetAnotherInteger = 23;
```

This single line of code declares int variables, oneInteger, anotherInteger, and yetAnotherInteger, and assigns the value of 17 to oneInteger and the value of 23 to yetAnotherInteger (note that 17 and 23 are literals).

Here, anotherInteger does not have an assignment. Does it have a value? Yes, the default value of a variable of a primitive number type immediately after declaration is 0.

This one-line code is equivalent to:

```
1   int oneInteger, anotherInteger, yetAnotherInteger;
2   oneInteger = 17;
3   yetAnotherInteger = 23;
```

as well as to:

```
1   int oneInteger, anotherInteger, yetAnotherInteger;
2   oneInteger = 17, yetAnotherInteger = 23;
```

For the code to compile, the value assigned to a variable must match the data type of the variable. In the above code fragment, an attempt to assign numbers with a decimal point,

```
1   int oneInteger, anotherInteger, yetAnotherInteger;
2   oneInteger = 17.5;
3   yetAnotherInteger = 23.0;
```

results in a syntax error, because neither 17.5 nor 23.0 are integers.

The Attribute final

By attaching final in front of the data type specification in a variable declaration, any future value assignments to the variable are prohibited. Thus, by the attachment of final, a variable becomes a constant.

```
1       static final int YOUR_INTEGER = 20;
2
3       public static void main( String[] args )
4       {
5          final int MY_NUMBER = 17;
6          ...
7       }
```

The first variable, YOUR_INTEGER, is a global constant and the second variable, MY_NUMBER, is a local constant. Java requires that a value must be assigned to a constant using a combined declaration and assignment. Therefore, in the above code example, splitting the declaration and assignment of either constant into a standalone declaration and a standalone assignment is rejected as a syntax error.

A global constant may have an explicit visibility specification. As mentioned in Chap. 1, there are three explicit visibility specifications: public, private, and protected. In the source code:

```
1    public class PubConstEx
2    {
3       public static final int COMMONINTEGER = 20;
4
5       public static void main( String[] args )
6       {
7          final int MY_NUMBER = 17;
8          ...
9       }
10   }
```

COMMONINTEGER is a global constant accessible from outside and MY_NUMBER is declared to be a local constant. By combining the class name and the global variable name, as in PubConstEx.COMMONINTEGER, the value 20 can be accessed from other source codes.

Reassignment

If a variable is not a constant, the value of the variable can be updated any number of times. Consider the next code:

```
1  int myInteger;
2  myInteger = 63;
3  ...
4  myInteger = 97;
5  ...
6  myInteger = 20;
```

The dotted parts represent some arbitrary code. Assuming that no assignments to myInteger appear in the dotted part, the value of myInteger changes from 63 to 97 in Line 4 and from 97 to 20 in Line 6.

2.2 The Primitive Data Types

Java has eight primitive data types. They are **boolean, byte, short, int, long, float, double**, and **char**. Table 2.1 shows the range of possible values for each type.

boolean

The boolean is a data type for storing a logical value. There are only two possible values for a boolean data type: true and false. Here is an example of declaring boolean variables and assigning values to them.

```
1  boolean logicA, logicB, logicC;
2  logicA = true;
3  logicB = false;
```

Table 2.1 The primitive data type

Type	No. bits	Data representation
boolean	1	Logical value, true or false
byte	8	Integer, $[-128, 127]$
short	16	Integer, $[-32,768, 32,767]$
int	32	Integer, $[-2,147,483,648, 2,147,483,647]$
long	64	Integer, $[-9,223,372,036,854,775,808, 9,223,372,036,854,775,807]$
float	32	Floating point number, approximately from $1.4013 \cdot 10^{-45}$ to $3.4028 \cdot 10^{+38}$ (positive or negative)
double	64	Floating point number, approximately from $4.9407 \cdot 10^{-324}$ to $1.7977 \cdot 10^{+308}$ (positive or negative)
char	16 (unsigned)	UNICODE character, $[0, 65,535]$

There are three operators available for `boolean`: the **negation** `!`, the **conjunction** `&&`, and the **disjunction** `||`. The `boolean` data type will be discussed in Chap. 6.

byte

The data type `byte` consists of eight bits, so there are $2^8 = 256$ possible values. The value range of `byte` is between $-2^7 = -128$ and $2^7 - 1 = 127$. The **hexadecimal encoding** is an encoding that is often used for specifying a `byte` literal. This is the encoding that divides the bits into groups of four and uses a unique character to represent each of the 16 possible values for each group. The value range of four bits is between 0 and 15, so naturally the numerals 0 through 9 are used for representing numbers 0 through 9. For the numbers 10 through 15, the letters a through f (or their upper case letters A through F) are used. In hexadecimal encoding, a byte must be represented with two characters. The combination YZ represents

The number Y represents multiplied by 16, plus the number Z represents.

Thus, "5f" in hexadecimal is not 65 ($= 5 * 10 + 15$) but 95 ($= 16 * 5 + 5$) and "dc" in hexadecimal is 220 in decimal ($= 13 * 16 + 12$). Hexadecimal encoding makes it possible to represent bit sequences compactly: four characters for sixteen bits, eight characters for 32 bits, and sixteen characters for 64 bits. In hexadecimal encoding, to indicate that a literal is presented, the prefix `0x` must be attached. For example, `0x33` is 33 in hexadecimal, which is equal to 51 in decimal.

```
byte myByteValue = 0x3f;
```

short

The data type `short` consists of sixteen bits. It has 65,536 possible values. The value range is between $-2^{15} = -32,768$ and $2^{15} - 1 = 32,767$.

int

`int` is a data type that consists of 32 bits. It has 4,294,967,296 possible values. The value range is between $-2^{31} = -2,147,483,648$ and $2^{31} - 1 = 2,147,483,647$. The default data type of a whole number literal is `int`.

long

The data type `long` consists of 64 bits. It has 18,446,744,073,709,551,616 possible values. The value range is between $-2^{63} = -9,223,372,036,854,775,808$ and $2^{63} - 1 = 9,223,372,036,854,775,807$. When presenting a literal in `long`, if the value that the literal represents goes beyond the range of `int`, the letter L must be attached as a suffix at the end of the number sequence, like this one:

```
long myLongNumber = 1234567890987654321L;
```

float **and** double

`float` and `double` are data types for real numbers. They use floating point representations. Basically, a floating point representation divides the available bits into three parts: the **sign**, the **significand**, and the **exponent**. Let S be the sign ($+1$ or -1). The number of bits for the sign is one, and the bit is at the highest position of the bits allocated for the data type. The bits of the significand represent a number between 0 and 1. If that part has m bits and the bit sequence is $b_1 \cdots b_m$, that part represents the sum of all 2^{-i} such that $b_i = 1$. Let C be this fractional number. Each floating point encoding system uses a fixed "base" for exponentiation, which is either 2 or 10. Let B be this base. If there are n bits in the exponent, that part encodes a number between -2^{n-1} and $2^{n-1} - 1$ (for whole number types). Let E be this number. Now, the bits of the floating number altogether represent

$$S \cdot (1 + C) \cdot B^E.$$

To designate that a floating point number literal is a `float`, the letter F must be attached as a suffix.

Here is an example of declaring and assigning a literal value to one variable for each primitive number type:

```
1   byte myByte;
2   short myShort;
3   int myInt;
4   long myLong;
5   float myFloat;
6   double myDouble;
7   myByte = 0x3d;
8   myShort = 1345;
9   myInt = 90909;
10  myLong = 1234567890123456789L;
11  myFloat = -3.145F;
12  myDouble = 1.7320504;
```

The numbers appearing after '=' in lines 7–12 are all literals.

char

The last primitive data type is `char`. The representation of `char` requires sixteen bits. By attaching the apostrophe before and after of a character, a `char` literal is specified, as in `'A'` and `'x'`.

```
1   char myChar1 = 'A';
2   char myChar2 = 'x';
```

The default value of a `char` type variable is `\0`. This is the character corresponding to the number 0. This must not be confused this with the numeral 0. There is no direct arithmetic operation that can be applied to `char` data for producing another `char`, but if a `char` data appears in a mathematical formula, it acts as if it were an `int`. Since the single quotation mark is used for a `char` literal, to specify the single quotation mark itself as a `char` literal, attaching a backslash as is must be done to represent the double quotation mark in `String` literals; that is, `'\"` represents the single quotation mark. Because of this special use of backslash, two backslashes are used to mean the backslash itself as a literal, as in `'\\'`. The other escape sequences, `'\t'` and `'\n'`, are valid for `char` literals too.

2.3 Using Variables for Computation

2.3.1 Quarterbacks Program (Reprise)

Using the fact that reassignments of values can be made to non-final variables, the previous three-favorite-quarterback program can be rewritten using three variables:

- an `int` variable, `rank`, for specifying the rank in the list
- a `String` variable, `name`, for the name of the quarterback, and
- a `double` variable, `qbr`, for the quarterback rating.

```
1   public class Literals02
2   {
3     public static void main( String[] args )
4     {
5       int rank;
6       String name;
7       double qbr;
8
9       rank = 1;
10      name = "Steve Young";
11      qbr = 96.8;
12      System.out.print( "Rank number " );
13      System.out.print( rank );
14      System.out.print( " in my all-time favorite NFL QB list is " );
15      System.out.print( name );
16      System.out.println( "." );
17      System.out.print( "His overall QB rating is " );
18      System.out.print( qbr );
19      System.out.println( "." );
20
```

Listing 2.4 A program that produces comments about three NFL quarterbacks using variables (part 1). The variable declarations and the part that produced the comments about the first player

Note that the variable declarations appear in Lines 4, 5, and 7. The variable declarations are followed by three blocks of the same format, each consisting of eleven lines. The first lines of each block assign values to the variables. For example, the first lines of the first block are:

```
1       rank = 1;
2       name = "Steve Young";
3       qbr = 96.8;
```

The next eight lines of code make the presentation, with the three literals for rank, name, and rating substituted with their respective names.

```
1       ...
2       System.out.print( rank );
3       ...
4       System.out.print( name );
5       ...
6       ...
7       System.out.print( qbr );
8       ...
```

In these three lines, the values of these variables substitute their respective locations into the print statements. Note that the action order is:

$$\text{declaration} \rightarrow \text{assignment} \rightarrow \text{reference}$$

Since assignments can be made multiple times to non-final variables, a variable declaration is effective until the end of the innermost pair of curly brackets that contains it. This means that two declarations of the same variables cannot intersect. In the above program, the innermost matching pair containing a variable declaration appears at Lines 4 and 44. Thus, the declarations are valid until Line 44. Formally, the range of lines in which a variable declaration is valid is called the **scope of the variable**.

```
21      rank = 2;
22      name = "Peyton Manning";
23      qbr = 96.5;
24      System.out.print( "Rank number " );
25      System.out.print( rank );
26      System.out.print( " in my all-time favorite NFL QB list is " );
27      System.out.print( name );
28      System.out.println( "." );
29      System.out.print( "His overall QB rating is " );
30      System.out.print( qbr );
31      System.out.println( "." );
32
33      rank = 3;
34      name = "Tom Brady";
35      qbr = 97.0;
36      System.out.print( "Rank number " );
37      System.out.print( rank );
38      System.out.print( " in my all-time favorite NFL QB list is " );
39      System.out.print( name );
40      System.out.println( "." );
41      System.out.print( "His overall QB rating is " );
42      System.out.print( qbr );
43      System.out.println( "." );
44   }
45 }
```

Listing 2.5 A program that produces comments about three NFL quarterbacks using variables (part 1). The part that produces the comments about the second and the third players

Reserved Names

The names appearing in Table 2.2 cannot be used as the name of a variable, a method, or a class. These are called the **reserved names**.

2.3.2 Number Arithmetics

2.3.2.1 Number Operations

In Java, the four standard arithmetic operations in mathematics (addition, subtraction, multiplication, and division) are represented with the standard mathematical symbols (+, -, *, and /, respectively). The negative sign - can be used for flipping the sign. The regular parentheses ( ) can be used for flipping the sign. There is no symbol for representing exponentiation.

The symbols that represent binary operations are called **operators**. The values that are evaluated with an operator are called **operands**. Since - acts on a single value, it is a **unary operator**. Since +, -, *, /, and % take two values, they are **binary operators**.

There are other additional operator types, such as unary bit shift («, », and »>), unary bit complement (~), and unary bit-wise (^, |, and &). This textbook does not use these bit operators (see Table 1.2)

Table 2.2 The list of reserved words in Java

abstract	boolean	break	case	catch	char	class
const	continue	default	do	double	else	enum
extends	final	finally	float	for	goto	if
import	implements	import	instanceof	int	interface	long
native	new	package	private	protected	public	short
static	strictfp	super	return	switch	synchronized	this
throw	throws	transient	try	void	volatile	while

In addition to using actual values (as represented by literals), variables can be used in mathematical formulas. When evaluating a formula that contains a variable, the value of the variable at the moment of evaluation is used. Consider the following code fragment:

```
1  double x, y, z;
2  x = 3.5;
3  y = 4.5;
4  z = -x + y + 1.0;
5  System.out.println( z );
```

In the fourth line of the program,

```
4  z = -x + y + 1.0;
```

the values that x and y hold (that is, 3.5 and 4.5, respectively) substitute their respective locations into the right-hand side of the formula. The result of the evaluation is 2.0. Since there is =, this value is assigned to the variable z. So, when the program executes System.out.println(z), this new value of 2.0 emerges in output:

```
2.0
```

It is possible to write more complicated formulas. For example, in

```
1  double x, w;
2  x = 2.0;
3  w = ( x + 1.0 ) * ( -1.0 + x );
4  System.out.println( w );
```

the value of x becomes 2.0 in Line 2. The value of the formula (x + 1.0) * (-1.0 + x) then becomes 3.0. This value is assigned to w. So, the output of the program is:

```
3.0
```

Alternatively, the code could be written as either

```
1  double x, w;
2  x = 2.0;
3  w = x * x - 1.0 * x + 1.0 * x - 1.0;
4  System.out.println( w );
```

or

```
1  double x, w;
2  x = 2.0;
3  w = ( x * x ) - 1.0;
4  System.out.println( w );
```

Both produce the same output as the original.

The Remainder Operator

The remainder operator % works as follows. Let a and b be two numbers. If the value of b is 0, a % b is undefined, an attempt to execute the operation produces a run-time error. Otherwise, if a and b have the same signs, the value of a % b is a - d * b, where d is the integer part of a divided by b, and if a and b have opposite signs, the value of a % b is a + d * b, where d is the integer part of $|a|$ divided by $|b|$. For example, `10 % 3` is equal to `1` and `-17.0 % 5.0` is `-2.0` since the integer part of `-17.0 / 5.0` is equal to `-3`.

2.3.2.2 Evaluation of Formulas

To evaluate formulas with more than two operations, Java prioritizes these operators in the same way we would in arithmetics.

- `*`, `/`, and `%` have the same level of priority.
- `+` and `-` have the same level of priority.
- The `-` for switching the sign has the highest priority. Next in priority is the { `*`, `/`, `%` } group. Last is the { `+`, `-` } group.
- The evaluation of a formula is from left to right using the following principles:
  - If there are parentheses in the formula, evaluate the leftmost and innermost parenthetical clause to reduce it to a single value.
  - If the formula does not have parentheses and has one of `*`, `/`, and `%`, process the leftmost one of the three kinds.
  - If the formula does not have parentheses and has no `*`, `/`, and `%`, process the leftmost operation.

In the code

```
1  double myDouble = 10.5;
2  int myInt = 11;
3  myDouble = -3 % 2 + (3 * 8 + myDouble * myInt) % 6;
```

the evaluation proceeds as follows:

```
1  -3 % 2 + (3 * 8 + 10.5 * 11) % 6
2  -1 + (3 * 8 + 10.5 * 11) % 6
3  -1 + (24 + 10.5 * 11) % 6
4  -1 + (24 + 115.5) % 6
5  -1 + 139.5 % 6
6  -1 + 1.5
7  0.5
```

`0.5` becomes the value of `myDouble`.

Here is how to use data (and some arithmetics on the data) to perform computation. Consider a program that evaluates several formulas involving a set of unknowns (which may appear in more than one formula). The user enters the values for the unknowns. It is possible to ask the user to enter the value of a variable whenever the calculation needs to use the value. However, since some variables are used more than once and there is no guarantee that the user enters a consistent value to a variable, the program instead stores the values of the unknowns into variables.

This first example is for computing various geometric values with respect to a radius R. A `double` variable, `radius`, is used to represent the value of the radius. Suppose the following four quantities are to be computed from R:

1. the perimeter of a circle having radius R,
2. the area of a circle having radius R,
3. the surface area of a sphere having radius R, and
4. the volume of a sphere having radius R.

The following mathematical formulas can be used in calculating the four quantities:

$$2\pi R, \ \pi R^2, \ 4\pi R^2, \ \text{and} \ \tfrac{4}{3}\pi R^3.$$

The program uses four variables, circlePerimeter, circleArea, ballArea, and ballVolume, to record the quantities. Lines 5 and 6 of the code declare these variables.

In Line 8, the value of radius is set to 10.0. The program then successively computes the four quantities in Lines 10 through 13, and uses the literal 3.14159265 for π. Lines 15 through 18 print the four quantities.

```
1   public class RadiusPrimitive
2   {
3     public static void main( String[] args )
4     {
5       double radius;
6       double circlePerimeter, circleArea, ballArea, ballVolume;
7
8       radius = 10.0;
9
10      circlePerimeter = 2.0 * 3.14159265 * radius;
11      circleArea = 3.14159265 * radius * radius;
12      ballArea = 4.0 * 3.14159265 * radius * radius;
13      ballVolume = 4.0 * 3.14159265 * radius * radius * radius / 3.0;
14
15      System.out.println( circlePerimeter );
16      System.out.println( circleArea );
17      System.out.println( ballArea );
18      System.out.println( ballVolume );
19    }
20  }
```

Listing 2.6 A preliminary version of the program for computing values for a given radius

This code produces the following output:

```
1   62.831853
2   314.159265
3   1256.63706
4   4188.7902
```

Two changes will be made to the program to obtain the next code. First, noticing that the value 3.14159265 as π appears in multiple formulas, a variable can be used to store a value for π. Second, the four quantities that are calculated will be printed with their names.

Line 8 declares a new variable, pi, in which the value of π is stored (Line 10). In the ensuing calculation, the variable pi is used in places where the value of π is needed. Also, the attribute of final is attached to the variable so as to make it a local constant and prevent value changes.

```
1   // compute values given a radius
2   public class Radius
3   {
4     public static void main( String[] args )
5     {
6       double radius;
7       double circlePerimeter, circleArea, ballArea, ballVolume;
8       double pi;
9       //--- set the values of pi and radius
10      pi = 3.14159265;
11      radius = 10.0;
```

Listing 2.7 The code for computing values for a given radius (part 1). Quantity calculation

The second part of the code is for reporting the results of the calculation.

```
12        // calculcate the values
13        circlePerimeter = 2.0 * pi * radius;
14        circleArea = pi * radius * radius;
15        ballArea = 4.0 * pi * radius * radius;
16        ballVolume = 4.0 * pi * radius * radius * radius / 3.0;
17        //-- output the values
18        System.out.print ( "circlePerimeter = " );
19        System.out.println ( circlePerimeter );
20        System.out.print ( "circleArea = " );
21        System.out.println ( circleArea );
22        System.out.print ( "ballArea = " );
23        System.out.println ( ballArea );
24        System.out.print ( "ballVolume = " );
25        System.out.println ( ballVolume );
26    }
27 }
```

Listing 2.8 The code for printing the values of the four quantities. The part for calculating the quantities and printing the results

To make clear which value represents which quantity, the program uses a `print` statement. The program prints the name of the quantity preceding the presentation of the value. The statement

$$\texttt{System.out.println (circlePerimeter);}$$

prints the value of the variable `circlePerimeter` and proceeds to the next line.

This code produces the following output:

```
1  circlePerimeter = 62.831853
2  circleArea = 314.159265
3  ballArea = 1256.63706
4  ballVolume = 4188.7902
```

With this arrangement, the correspondence between the value and the meaning will be clear to the user when reading the output.

Here is another, more obscure, way of calculating the four quantities in a row. The program uses the facts that, for a fixed radius value,

(a) the area of the circle is the perimeter times the radius divided by 2,
(b) the surface area of the ball is four times the area of the circle, and
(c) the volume of the ball is the area of the ball times the radius divided by 3.

Based upon these facts, the program obtains the value for the variable `circleArea` with a formula that contains `circlePerimeter`, obtains the value for the variable `ballArea` with a formula that contains `circleArea`, and obtains the value for the variable `ballVolume` with a formula that contains `ballArea`. Note that the variable `pi` is now a constant named `PI` with the attribute of `final` (with its name in all uppercase according to the naming convention).

```
1    // compute values given a radius
2    public class RadiusAlternative
3    {
4      public static void main( String[] args )
5      {
6        double radius;
7        double circlePerimeter, circleArea, ballArea, ballVolume;
8        final double PI = 3.14159265;
9        //--- set the values of PI and radius
10       radius = 10.0;
11       // calculcate the values
12       circlePerimeter = 2.0 * PI * radius;
13       circleArea = radius * circlePerimeter / 2.0;
14       ballArea = 4.0 * circleArea;
15       ballVolume = ballArea * radius / 3.0;
16       //-- output the values
17       System.out.print( "circlePerimeter = " );
18       System.out.println( circlePerimeter );
19       System.out.print( "circleArea = " );
20       System.out.println( circleArea );
21       System.out.print( "ballArea = " );
22       System.out.println( ballArea );
23       System.out.print( "ballVolume = " );
24       System.out.println( ballVolume );
25     }
26   }
```

Listing 2.9 An alternative for the calculation of values associated with a circle and a ball

Yet another modification will be made by moving the constant PI outside the method, thereby changing it from a local constant to a global constant.

Note that the `static` attribute must be attached to the declaration.

```
1    // compute values given a radius
2    public class RadiusAlternative2
3    {
4      static final double PI = 3.14159265;
5      public static void main( String[] args )
6      {
7        double radius;
8        double circlePerimeter, circleArea, ballArea, ballVolume;
9        //--- set the values of PI and radius
10       radius = 10.0;
11       // calculcate the values
12       circlePerimeter = 2.0 * PI * radius;
13       circleArea = radius * circlePerimeter / 2.0;
14       ballArea = 4.0 * circleArea;
15       ballVolume = ballArea * radius / 3.0;
16       //-- output the values
17       System.out.print( "circlePerimeter = " );
18       System.out.println( circlePerimeter );
19       System.out.print( "circleArea = " );
20       System.out.println( circleArea );
21       System.out.print( "ballArea = " );
22       System.out.println( ballArea );
23       System.out.print( "ballVolume = " );
24       System.out.println( ballVolume );
25     }
26   }
```

Listing 2.10 The radius code with the value of π as the global constant

2.3.2.3 Mixing Different Number Types in a Formula

There are two rules that Java applies when two different number types appear as operands.

- Either one of them is a floating point number type (i.e., `float` or `double`) if and only if the result is a floating point number type.
- The number of bits of the resulting data type is the maximum of the numbers of bits for the two number types.

For example, if the operands are `byte` and `float`, the result will be a `float`. Table 2.3 shows the primitive data type that results by mixing data types.

The next code attempts to compute the product and division between two numbers, 11 and 3. Each number is either an `int` or a `double`. In each of the statements in Lines 14, 15, 18, 19, 22, 23, 26, and 27, there appears an unfamiliar use of `System.out.println`. For example, Line 14 goes:

```
14    System.out.println( aInt / bInt );
```

Appearing inside the parentheses is a formula. Conveniently, if a formula appears inside the parentheses, both `System.out.print` and `System.out.println` evaluate the formula, convert the result to a character sequence, and print the sequence on the screen.

The program first declares the variables it is going to use:

```
1   public class NumberTest
2   {
3       //--- try four possible cases of "11 divided by 3"
4       public static void main( String[] args )
5       {
6           int aInt, bInt;
7           double aDouble, bDouble;
8           aInt = 11;
9           bInt = 3;
10          aDouble = 11.0;
11          bDouble = 3.0;
```

Listing 2.11 A program that demonstrates the use of operators on `double` and/or `int` variables (part 1)

The program then executes a number of operations on the variables.

Table 2.3 The number types chosen when two primitive data types are processed in binary arithmetic operations

Type	byte	short	int	long	float	double
byte	byte	short	int	long	float	double
short	short	short	int	long	float	double
int	int	int	int	long	float	double
long	long	long	long	long	double	double
float	float	float	float	float	double	double
double	double	double	double	double	double	double

```
12        // case 1
13        System.out.println( "aInt vs bInt. / and %" );
14        System.out.println( aInt / bInt );
15        System.out.println( aInt % bInt );
16        // case 2
17        System.out.println( "aInt vs bDouble. / and %" );
18        System.out.println( aInt / bDouble );
19        System.out.println( aInt % bDouble );
20        // case 3
21        System.out.println( "aDouble vs bInt. / and %" );
22        System.out.println( aDouble / bInt );
23        System.out.println( aDouble % bInt );
24        // case 4
25        System.out.println( "aDouble vs bDouble. / and %" );
26        System.out.println( aDouble / bDouble );
27        System.out.println( aDouble % bDouble );
28     }
29  }
```

Listing 2.12 A program that demonstrates the use of operators on `double` and/or `int` variables (part 1)

The result of executing the code is as follows:

```
1   aInt vs bInt. / and %
2   3
3   2
4   aInt vs bDouble. / and %
5   3.6666666666666665
6   2.0
7   aDouble vs bInt. / and %
8   3.6666666666666665
9   2.0
10  aDouble vs bDouble. / and %
11  3.6666666666666665
12  2.0
```

When a literal of a primitive number type appears, its default type is `int` for a whole number and `double` for a floating point number. To treat a data as an alternate type, attach, in front of it, the alternate type enclosed in a matching pair of parentheses. For example, `(byte) 12` instructs to treat the `int` type value of `12` as a `byte` type. The action of attaching a data type to treat a data as a different type is called **casting**.

Using casting, a floating point number can be truncated to an integer; that is, for a floating point number `x`, `(int) x` is a 32-bit whole number that is equal to the integer part of `x`.

2.3.3 Computing the Body-Mass Index

The next example is a program for computing the **Body-Mass Index** for multiple combinations of weight and height. The Body-Mass Index measures the balance between the height and weight of a human body. The lower the index is, the lighter the person is. The following formula defines the Body-Mass Index:

$$\text{BMI} = 703 * \text{weight (in pounds)} / (\text{height} \times \text{height}) \text{ (in inches)}$$

In the program, the computation is carried out in the following steps:

- declare variables for storing weight, height, and the BMI value;
- assign a value to weight and a value to height;
- compute the BMI value;
- print the result;
- reassign a value to weight and a value to height;
- compute the BMI value with respect to the reassigned weight and height;
- print the result.

Next is the program BMI.java that does this.

```
1   public class BMI
2   {
3     public static void main( String[] args )
4     {
5       // first time
6       double weight = 140.0;    // weight
7       double height = 67.0;     // height
8       double bmi = 703.0 * weight / (height * height);
9       System.out.print( "BMI = " );
10      System.out.println( bmi );
11      // second time
12      weight = 150.0;           // weight
13      height = 70.0;            // height
14      bmi = 703.0 * weight / ( height * height );
15      System.out.print( "BMI = " );
16      System.out.println( bmi );
17    }
18  }
```

Listing 2.13 The code for computing the BMI for predetermined combinations of height and weight

Here is what happens in the code:

- What appears after the first comment is the declaration of a `double` variable `weight` (Line 6). Here, the program assigns the value of 140.0 immediately to the variable. The next line (Line 7) does the same for `height` with the value of 67.0. Both these lines use the idea of combining a variable declaration and a value assignment in one line.
- The next line (Line 8) declares a `double` variable `bmi` and assigns to it a value using the formula `703.0 * weight / (height * height)`. This line also uses the idea of combining a variable declaration and a value assignment in one line. Furthermore, the line takes advantage of the fact that by the time the code execution reaches this third declaration and assignment, both `weight` and `height` have acquired new values.
- The parentheses surrounding the second multiplication line designate that the multiplication must take place before the division (again, Java follows our common sense evaluation of mathematical formulas). If the parentheses are removed, the last multiplication symbol must be replaced with the division symbol; that is,

```
double bmi = 703.0 * weight / height / height;
```

Otherwise, the code

```
double bmi = 703.0 * weight / height * height;
```

will divide the product of `703.0` and the value of `weight` by the value of `height` and then multiply it by the value of `height`.

- The ensuing two lines are for producing the result on the screen. The first of the two is for printing the `String` literal `"BMI = "`, and the second is for printing the value and proceeding to the next line.
- Then the program assigns new values to `weight` and `height` and then recomputes the BMI value. Since these lines are in the scope of the three variables, the type declaration `double` must not appear again.

The execution of the code results in the following:

```
1   BMI = 21.92470483403876
2   BMI = 21.520408163265305
```

Note the difference, between the two lines, in the number of digits after the decimal point. The first one has fourteen digits and the second one has fifteen. In both cases the actual BMI value has infinitely many digits and thus the floating point expression cannot correctly represent the value. The value that appears on the screen is only an approximation. Chapter 8 describes how to control the number of digits appearing after the decimal point.

2.3.4   Sum of Integers from 1 to 100 à la Gauss

Johann Carl Friedrich Gauss (April 30, 1777 to February 23, 1855) is a German mathematician who made important contributions to many fields of mathematics. There is a famous story stating that he was a genius even as a school kid. The story goes like this.

> One day a teacher asked the class to calculate, on a sheet of paper, the sum of integers from 1 to 100. While all the other classmates were adding the numbers one after another, Gauss raised his hand to tell his teacher he had completed the task. Miraculously, the answer he gave was correct. Stunned, the teacher asked Gauss to explain how he had gotten to his answer. Gauss explained: If you add the first number, 1, and the last number, 100, the result is 101. If you add the second number, 2, and the second to last number, 99, the result is 101. If you keep going this way, the smaller number increases by 1 and the larger number decreases by 1, and so the sum is always 101. Since there are 100 numbers to add, there are 50 such pairs. Thus, the total is 101 * 50 = 5050.

Based upon his observation, the sum of all integers between 1 and $n \geq 1$ can be quickly computed. If n is an even number, the total is given as the following formula

$$(n + 1) * n/2$$

If n is an odd number, the middle number $(n + 1)/2$ does not pair with other numbers, and since there are $(n - 1)/2$ pairs, the total is

$$(n + 1) * (n - 1)/2 + (n + 1)/2 = (n + 1) * ((n - 1)/2 + 1/2) = (n + 1) * n/2$$

Thus, regardless of whether n is even or odd, the total is $(n + 1) * n/2$.

The following program demonstrates the use of integer variables, which computes the sum of integer sequences à la Gauss.

```
1  public class Gauss
2  {
3    public static void main( String[] args )
4    {
5      int n, sum;
6      n = 100;
7      sum = ( n + 1 ) * n / 2;
8      System.out.print( "The sum of integers from 1 to " );
9      System.out.print( n );
10     System.out.print( " = " );
11     System.out.println( sum );
12     n = 1000;
13     sum = ( n + 1 ) * n / 2;
14     System.out.print( "The sum of integers from 1 to " );
15     System.out.print( n );
16     System.out.print( " = " );
17     System.out.println( sum );
18   }
19 }
```

Listing 2.14 The code for computing $1 + \cdots + n$ for $n = 100$ and $n = 1000$

The code uses two int variables, n and sum. The program assigns the value of 100 and then the value of 1000 to the variable n. The five lines that appear after the first assignment are identical to the five lines that appear after the second assignment. With these identical five lines, the program does the following:

(a) it computes the sum using the formula,
(b) it prints a String literal "The sum of integers from 1 to ",
(c) it prints the value of n,
(d) it prints another String literal " = ", and
(e) it prints the value of sum.

The output of the program is as follows:

```
1  The sum of integers from 1 to 100 = 5050
2  The sum of integers from 1 to 1000 = 500500
```

2.3.4.1 Truncation of Real Numbers

Each of the floating point data types, float and double, has a finite number of bits for representation. This limitation sometimes results in odd output. The next program shows such an example. It works with two variables, v and a. The program assigns the initial value of 17.0 to v, fixes the value of a to 3.42567824 (many digits!) and then updates the value v four times by: dividing by a, subtracting 1.0, multiplying by a, and adding a. Before starting the series of modifications, as well as after each of the four modifications, the program prints the value of v with additional information regarding what value v represents. Since $(((v/a)-1)*a)+a = v$, the value is anticipated to return, at the end, to the original value, 17.0.

```
1   public class RepresentationTest
2   {
3     public static void main ( String [] args )
4     {
5       double v = 17.0;
6       double a = 3.42567824;
7
8       System . out . print ( "Start: " );
9       System . out . println ( v );
10
11      v = v / a;
12      System . out . print ( "/ a :   " );
13      System . out . println ( v );
14
15      v = v - 1.0;
16      System . out . print ( "- 1.0: " );
17      System . out . println ( v );
18
19      v = v * a;
20      System . out . print ( "* a :   " );
21      System . out . println ( v );
22
23      v = v + a;
24      System . out . print ( "+ a :   " );
25      System . out . println ( v );
26    }
27  }
```

Listing 2.15 A program that shows the limitation of using a finite number of bits for representating real numbers

The result is the following:

```
1   Start: 17.0
2   / a :   4.96252094008689
3   - 1.0: 3.9625209400868897
4   * a :   13.574321760000002
5   + a :   17.0
```

The first line of the output is the original value of 17.0. The second is the value immediately after v = v / a. The third is the value immediately after v = v - 1.0. The fourth is the value immediately after v = v * a. The last is the value immediately after v = v + a.

Notice that there is a difference between the length of the second output line (noted as / a) and the length of the third output line (noted as - 1.0). Again, the difference is due to the fact that the correct value of v / a requires an infinite number of digits. Also notice the 0000002 at the end of the fourth line. With a pencil calculation, the value is 13.57432176, but the representation does not capture this correctly, hence the extra seven digits appearing at the end. Even though there are some discrepancies, when the output moves to the last line, the tiny quantity of 0.000000000000002 at the end vanishes, and so the output is 17.0 instead of 17.000000000000002.

2.3.5 Simplified Expressions

There is a way to simplify a mathematical formula that updates a variable using its current value. For a formula of the type

$$a = a \circ b;$$

where $\circ$ is one of the five operations $\{+, -, /, *, \%\}$, the expression:

$$a \circ = b;$$

can be used instead. For example,

```
1  int a, b;
2  a = 20;
3  b = 13;
4  a = a + b;
5  b = b * 3;
```

can be simplified as

```
1  int a, b;
2  a = 20;
3  b = 13;
4  a += b;
5  b *= 3;
```

A special case of this short-hand is when the intended operation is either adding 1 to a or subtracting 1 from a. In this situation, the short-hand of either a++ or ++a can be used for adding 1 and the short-hand of either a- or -a can be used for subtracting 1. The difference between having the ++ or - before or after the variable name is based on whether the change (i.e., adding 1 or subtracting 1) takes place *before* or *after* the evaluation of the entire formula takes place. For example, in the next code, adding 1 to b occurs before setting the value of a to the product of the value of b and the value of c, and adding 1 to e occurs after setting the value of d to the product of the value of e and the value of f.

```
1  a = ++b * c
2  d = e++ * f
```

The following program demonstrates the use of the simplified operations. The program uses two int variables, myInt and other, and initializes the two variables with the values 10 and 13. The program updates myInt five times using

- += other,
- *= other,
- -= other,
- /= other, and
- %= other

in this order, and reports the action it has performed, as well as the outcome.

```
 1   public class ShortHandExperiment
 2   {
 3     public static void main( String[] args )
 4     {
 5       int myInt , other;
 6       myInt   = 10;
 7       other = 13;
 8       System.out.print( "myInt is " );
 9       System.out.print( myInt );
10       System.out.print( ", other is " );
11       System.out.println( other );
12
13       myInt += other;
14       System.out.print( "Executed myInt += other\tmyInt is " );
15       System.out.println( myInt );
16
17       myInt *= other;
18       System.out.print( "Executed myInt *= other\tmyInt is " );
19       System.out.println( myInt );
20
21       myInt -= other;
22       System.out.print( "Executed myInt -= other\tmyInt is " );
23       System.out.println( myInt );
24
25       myInt /= other;
26       System.out.print( "Executed myInt /= other\tmyInt is " );
27       System.out.println( myInt );
28
29       myInt %= other;
30       System.out.print( "Executed myInt %= other\tmyInt is " );
31       System.out.println( myInt );
32
```

Listing 2.16 A program that demonstrates the use of mathematical short-hand expressions (part 1)

In the second part, the program executes myInt += other four times while modifying the value of other with

- ++other,
- other++,
- -other, and
- other-

in this order, and reports the action it has performed and the outcome.

```
33      myInt += ++other;
34      System.out.print( "Executed myInt += ++other\tmyInt is " );
35      System.out.print( myInt );
36      System.out.print( ", other is now " );
37      System.out.println( other );
38
39      myInt += other++;
40      System.out.print( "Executed myInt += other++\tmyInt is " );
41      System.out.print( myInt );
42      System.out.print( ", other is now " );
43      System.out.println( other );
44
45      myInt += --other;
46      System.out.print( "Executed myInt += --other\tmyInt is " );
47      System.out.print( myInt );
48      System.out.print( ", other is now " );
49      System.out.println( other );
50
51      myInt += other--;
52      System.out.print( "Executed myInt += other--\tmyInt is " );
53      System.out.print( myInt );
54      System.out.print( ", other is now " );
55      System.out.println( other );
56   }
57 }
```

Listing 2.17 A program that demonstrates the use of mathematical short-hand expressions (part 2)

The program produces the following output:

```
1  myInt is 10, other is 13
2  Executed myInt += other myInt is 23
3  Executed myInt *= other myInt is 299
4  Executed myInt -= other myInt is 286
5  Executed myInt /= other myInt is 22
6  Executed myInt %= other myInt is 9
7  Executed myInt += ++other        myInt is 23, other is now 14
8  Executed myInt += other++        myInt is 37, other is now 15
9  Executed myInt += --other        myInt is 51, other is now 14
10 Executed myInt += other--        myInt is 65, other is now 13
```

The next code uses two variables, int myInt and double myReal, to store an integer and a floating point number, respectively. The program computes the product of the two variables and stores the value of the product in a double variable, result. In addition, in the assignment of the product, the program executes one of ++ or - either before or after the two variables:

```
1  result = myReal++ * myInt++;
2  result = ++myReal * ++myInt;
3  result = myReal-- * myInt--;
4  result = --myReal * --myInt;
```

These actions appear in Lines 19, 35, 51, and 66.

Before each operation, the program prints the values of myInt and myReal, using four statements:

```
1    System.out.print( "myReal = " );
2    System.out.print( myReal );
3    System.out.print( " and myInt = " );
4    System.out.println( myInt );
```

The first and third lines announce the variables whose values are to be printed and the second and the fourth lines print their values.

After the operation, the program reports the action it has performed and the values of the three variables, and then draws a bunch of dashes.

Here is the code, presented in multiple parts. ++ or - appears in Lines 19, 35, 51, and 67.

```
1    public class ShortHandNew
2    {
3      public static void main( String[] args )
4      {
5        ////////////////////////////////////////////////////////
6        // declaration and initialization
7        ////////////////////////////////////////////////////////
8        int myInt;
9        double myReal, result;
10       myReal = 89.5;
11       myInt = 17;
12       ////////////////////////////////////////////////////////
13       // first round
14       ////////////////////////////////////////////////////////
15       System.out.print( "myReal = " );
16       System.out.print( myReal );
17       System.out.print( " and myInt = " );
18       System.out.println( myInt );
19       result = myReal++ * myInt++;
20       System.out.println( "Execute myReal++ * myInt++" );
21       System.out.print( "The result is " );
22       System.out.println( result );
23       System.out.print( "Now myReal = " );
24       System.out.print( myReal );
25       System.out.print( " and myInt = " );
26       System.out.println( myInt );
27       System.out.println( "-------------------------------------");
```

Listing 2.18 A program that demonstrate the use of ++ and −− (part 1)

```
28    //////////////////////////////////////////////////////////
29    // second round
30    //////////////////////////////////////////////////////////
31    System.out.print( "myReal = " );
32    System.out.print( myReal );
33    System.out.print( " and myInt = " );
34    System.out.println( myInt );
35    result = ++myReal * ++myInt;
36    System.out.println( "Execute ++myReal * ++myInt" );
37    System.out.print( "The result is " );
38    System.out.println( result );
39    System.out.print( "Now myReal = " );
40    System.out.print( myReal );
41    System.out.print( " and myInt = " );
42    System.out.println( myInt );
43    System.out.println( "-------------------------------------" );
44    //////////////////////////////////////////////////////////
45    // third round
46    //////////////////////////////////////////////////////////
47    System.out.print( "myReal = " );
48    System.out.print( myReal );
49    System.out.print( " and myInt = " );
50    System.out.println( myInt );
51    result = myReal-- * myInt--;
52    System.out.println( "Execute myReal-- * myInt--" );
53    System.out.print( "The result is " );
54    System.out.println( result );
55    System.out.print( "Now myReal = " );
56    System.out.print( myReal );
57    System.out.print( " and myInt = " );
58    System.out.println( myInt );
59    System.out.println( "-------------------------------------" );
60    //////////////////////////////////////////////////////////
61    // fourth round
62    //////////////////////////////////////////////////////////
63    System.out.print( "myReal = " );
64    System.out.print( myReal );
65    System.out.print( "and myInt = " );
66    System.out.println( myInt );
67    result = --myReal * --myInt;
68    System.out.println( "Execute --myReal * --myInt" );
69    System.out.print( "The result is " );
70    System.out.println( result );
71    System.out.print( "Now myReal = " );
72    System.out.print( myReal );
73    System.out.print( " and myInt = " );
74    System.out.println( myInt );
75    System.out.println( "-------------------------------------" );
76    }
77 }
```

Listing 2.19 A program that demonstrate the use of ++ and −− (part 2)

Executing the program produces the following result:

```
1    myReal = 89.5 and myInt = 17
2    Execute myReal++ * myInt++
3    The result is 1521.5
4    Now myReal = 90.5 and myInt = 18
5    -------------------------------------
6    myReal = 90.5 and myInt = 18
7    Execute ++myReal * ++myInt
8    The result is 1738.5
9    Now myReal = 91.5 and myInt = 19
10   -------------------------------------
11   myReal = 91.5 and myInt = 19
12   Execute myReal-- * myInt--
13   The result is 1738.5
14   Now myReal = 90.5 and myInt = 18
15   -------------------------------------
16   myReal = 90.5and myInt = 18
17   Execute --myReal * --myInt
18   The result is 1521.5
19   Now myReal = 89.5 and myInt = 17
20   -------------------------------------
```

2.4   An Introduction to the `String` Data Type

2.4.1   The `String` Data Type

Recall that `"Hello, World!"` is a `String` literal. `String` is not a primitive data type. Rather, `String` is an object type that encompasses a series of `char` data along with an `int` value representing the length of the series. To create data of an object type, a special method called **constructor** must be used. The use of any constructor requires a special keyword `new`. However, since `String` is such an important data type, the Java language designers have made it possible to create a `String` literal by specifying the character sequence that it encapsulates (using the double quotation mark at the beginning and end of the sequence). The way to declare a `String` variable and assign a value to it is the same as the other data types. The following source code is a new version of the previous quarterback program, with the use of `String` variables.

The program decomposes the messages into the variable parts and the common parts. The first line of the message takes the format of:

| Rank No. | 1 | in my all-time favorite NFL QB list is | Steve Young | . |

where the texts in a box are the unchanged parts. Thus, the first line is split into five parts total: the three parts in a box, the rank number, and the name of the quarterback. The boxed parts are character sequences. So is the name of the quarterback. The rank number can be thought of as an integer. The variable names, `rankText`, `favText`, and `period`, are given to the three unchanged text parts respectively, and the variable names, `rank` and `name`, are assigned to the remaining two. The output of the line is:

```
rankText rank favText name period
```

The texts appearing in the boxes, including all the white space, are stored in the variables `rankText`, `favText`, and `period`. The integer literal 1 is stored in the `int` variable `rank` and the `String` literal `"Steve Young"` is assigned to the variable `name`. By printing the first four of the five components (`rankText`, `rank`, `favText`, and `name`) successively with `System.in.print` and then the last of the five components, `period`, with `System.out.println`, the same output can be generated.

To be more precise, the following code will be used:

```
1       String rankText , favText , period;
2       int rank;
3       String name;
4
5       rankText = "Rank number ";
6       favText = " in my all-time favorite NFL QB's is ";
7       period = ".";
8
9       rank = 1;
10      name = "Steve Young";
11      System.out.print( rankText );
12      System.out.print( rank );
13      System.out.print( favText );
14      System.out.print( name );
15      System.out.println( period );
```

This series of actions produces the desired output line:

```
Rank number 1 in my all-time favorite NFL QB's is Steve Young.
```

The second line can be decomposed in the same manner. The line is

$$\boxed{\text{His overall QB rating is}} \; 96.8 \boxed{.}$$

Again, the texts in a box are the unchanged parts. Since we already have declared the variable `period` and assigned a literal consisting of a period to the variable, we will introduce only one new variable, `overText`, which holds the other unchanged part `His overall QB rating is`.

The variable part in this line is a floating point number, so a `double` variable is used. The name of the variable is `qbr`. By assigning the value `96.8` to `qbr` and printing the three components successively, the second line of the output is reproduced.

The following is the code that represents this decomposition:

```
1       String overText;
2       double qbr;
3       overText = "His overall QB rating is ";
4
5       qbr = 96.8;
6       System.out.print( overText );
7       System.out.print( qbr );
8       System.out.println( period );
```

the code will produce the output:

```
His overall QB rating is 96.8.
```

By grouping the same type of variables together, rearranging the assignments and the declarations, and making an assignment to each unchanged part immediately after declaring it, the next code is obtained. In the next code, Lines 5–7 are the variable declarations, Lines 8–11 are the assignments to the unchanged parts, Lines 13–15 are the assignments to the variable parts, and Lines 16–23 are the print statements.

```
1   public class Literals03
2   {
3     public static void main( String[] args )
4     {
5       int rank;
6       String name, rankText, favText, overText, period;
7       double qbr;
8       rankText = "Rank number ";
9       favText = " in my all-time favorite NFL QB list is ";
10      overText = "His overall QB rating is ";
11      period = ".";
12
13      rank = 1;
14      name = "Steve Young";
15      qbr = 96.8;
16      System.out.print( rankText );
17      System.out.print( rank );
18      System.out.print( favText );
19      System.out.print( name );
20      System.out.println( period );
21      System.out.print( overText );
22      System.out.print( qbr );
23      System.out.println( period );
24
25      rank = 2;
26      name = "Peyton Manning";
27      qbr = 96.5;
28      System.out.print( rankText );
29      System.out.print( rank );
30      System.out.print( favText );
31      System.out.print( name );
32      System.out.println( period );
33      System.out.print( overText );
34      System.out.print( qbr );
35      System.out.println( period );
36
37      rank = 3;
38      name = "Tom Brady";
39      qbr = 97.0;
40      System.out.print( rankText );
41      System.out.print( rank );
42      System.out.print( favText );
43      System.out.print( name );
44      System.out.println( period );
45      System.out.print( overText );
46      System.out.print( qbr );
47      System.out.println( period );
48    }
49  }
```

Listing 2.20 A program that produces comments about some NFL quarterbacks using variables and literals

Here is the output of the code:

```
1  Rank number 1 in my all-time favorite NFL QB's is Steve Young.
2  His overall QB rating is 96.8.
3  Rank number 2 in my all-time favorite NFL QB's is Peyton Manning.
4  His overall QB rating is 96.5.
5  Rank number 3 in my all-time favorite NFL QB's is Tom Brady.
6  His overall QB rating is 97.0.
```

2.4.2 String Concatenation

2.4.2.1 Concatenating Two String Data

A String object can represent a very, very long sequence.[4] To specify a String, the beginning and ending double quotation marks must appear in the same line. Therefore, to define a long (say, 900 characters) String literal, the width of the terminal screen is too small; viewing it on a screen results in wraparound, i.e., the character sequence flows into the next line. For example, if a command line interface window has the width of 64 characters (this quantity may change as the window is resized) and a String has 900 characters in a single line, the line will be divided into much smaller segments on the screen.

Fortunately, in Java, it is possible to **concatenate** String literals and variables using the + sign to mean concatenation. It is also possible to concatenate between a String data and data of other data types. Using concatenation, the process of generating output can be simplified.

The following code is a new version of the "favorite quarterbacks" program that uses the concatenation operator:

```
1  public class Literals04
2  {
3    public static void main( String[] args )
4    {
5      int rank;
6      String name;
7      double qbr;
8      String rankText = "Rank number ";
9      String favText = " in my all-time favorite NFL QB list is ";
10     String overallText = "His overall QB rating is ";
11     String period = ".";
12
13     rank = 1;
14     name = "Steve Young";
15     qbr = 96.8;
16     System.out.println( rankText + rank + favText + name + period );
17     System.out.println( overallText + qbr + period );
18
```

Listing 2.21 A program that produces comments about three NFL quarterbacks using String concatenation (part 1)

---

[4]Since int is the data type for specifying the position of a character letter in a character sequence, the limit on the length is $2^{31} - 1$.

```
19        rank = 2;
20        name = "Peyton Manning";
21        qbr = 96.5;
22        System.out.println( rankText + rank + favText + name + period );
23        System.out.println( overallText + qbr + period );
24
25        rank = 3;
26        name = "Tom Brady";
27        qbr = 97.0;
28        System.out.println( rankText + rank + favText + name + period );
29        System.out.println( overallText + qbr + period );
30    }
31 }
```

Listing 2.22 A program that produces comments about three NFL quarterbacks using String concatenation (part 2)

Here is another example of using the concatenation operator. The program prints a quote from *Gettysburg Address* by Abraham Lincoln (February 12, 1809 to April 15, 1865):

> *"Four score and seven years ago our fathers brought forth on this continent, a new nation, conceived in Liberty, and dedicated to the proposition that all men are created equal."*

It is possible to declare a String variable and store this sentence in one line. If the width of the screen is 64, the declaration and assignment will appear as:

```
1 String address1 = "Four score and seven years ago our fathers b
2 rought forth on this continent, a new nation, conceived in Libe
3 equal.";
```

with two mid-word breaks. Using the connector +, the code can be made easier to recognize:

```
1    String address1 = "Four score and seven years ago our"
2                    + " fathers brought forth on this continent,"
3                    + " a new nation, conceived in Liberty, and"
4                    + " dedicated to the proposition that all men"
5                    + " are created equal.";
```

Because of the white space appearing at the start of the second, the third, the fourth, and the fifth literals, System.out.println(address1) has the same effect as before:

```
1 Four score and seven years ago our fathers brought forth
2  on this continent, a new nation, conceived in Liberty,
3 and dedicated to the proposition that all men are create
4 d equal.
```

To avoid wraparound, the newline character \n to force line breaks can be inserted, e.g.,

```
1 String address1 =
2    "Four score and seven years ago our fathers brought forth\n"
3 + "on this continent, a new nation, conceived in Liberty,\n"
4 + "and dedicated to the proposition that all men are\n"
5 + "created equal.\n";
```

The output of `System.out.println( address1 )` then changes to:

```
1  Four score and seven years ago our fathers brought forth
2  on this continent, a new nation, conceived in Liberty,
3  and dedicated to the proposition that all men are
4  created equal.
```

Here is another example. The example uses a `String` variable named `row`. The variable `row` has the four lines of the song "Row, row, row your boat". The literal has the newline at the end of each line, so printing it produces the four lines, as shown next:

```
1  Row, row, row your boat,
2  Gently down the stream.
3  Merrily, merrily, merrily, merrily,
4  Life is but a dream.
```

The code for defining the `String` is as follows:

```
1  String row = "Row, row, row your boat,\n"
2              + "Gently down the stream.\n"
3              + "Merrily, merrily, merrily, merrily,\n"
4              + "Life is but a dream.\n"
```

When printing many short lines, the lines can be connected into a single line with a "\n in between, thereby reducing the number of lines in the program. For example,

```
1  String count = "One\nTwo\nThree\nFour\nFive\n"
2              + "Six\nSeven\nEight\nNine\nTen\n";
3  System.out.print( count );
```

produces the output

```
1   One
2   Two
3   Three
4   Four
5   Five
6   Six
7   Seven
8   Eight
9   Nine
10  Ten
```

2.4.2.2 Concatenating String Data with Other Types of Data

When multiple number data are connected with a `String` object using the plus sign, the concatenation shows some peculiar behavior. This is because the plus sign has two roles as both the addition operator of numbers and the `String` connector. Suppose the concatenation has more than two terms and is free of parentheses. The java compiler interprets this from left to right, and in each concatenation, if both terms are numbers, then the compiler treats it as the number addition.

In the following code fragment:

```
1  String word1 = "csc120";
2  String word2 = 4 + 5 + 6 + "ab" + word1;
```

The value of `word2` becomes the literal `"15abcsc120"`, but not `"456abcsc120"`. This is because the first and the second concatenations are additions.

Consider the following example:

```
1  //-- examples of string manipulation
2  public class StringVariables {
3    public static void main( String[] args ) {
4      String myString = "abcde";
5      int myInteger = 10;
6      double myDouble = 9.5;
7      System.out.print( "myString = " + myString );
8      System.out.print( ", myInteger = " + myInteger );
9      System.out.println( ", myDouble = " + myDouble );
10
11     System.out.print( "myString + myInteger + myDouble = " );
12     System.out.println( myString + myInteger + myDouble );
13
14     System.out.print( "myString + (myInteger + myDouble) = " );
15     System.out.println( myString + ( myInteger + myDouble ) );
16
17     System.out.print( "myInteger + myString + myDouble = " );
18     System.out.println( myInteger + myString + myDouble );
19
20     System.out.print( "myInteger + myDouble + myString = " );
21     System.out.println( myInteger + myDouble + myString );
22   }
23 }
```

Listing 2.23 A program that contains `print` statements that print values of `String` data generated by concatenation

In this code, both `System.out.print` and `System.out.println` have one or two concatenations appearing in their parentheses. The execution of the code produces the following result:

```
1  myString = abcde, myInteger = 10, myDouble = 9.5
2  myString + myInteger + myDouble = abcde109.5
3  myString + (myInteger + myDouble) = abcde19.5
4  myInteger + myString + myDouble = 10abcde9.5
5  myInteger + myDouble + myString = 19.5abcde
```

For `String` concatenation, the short-hand expression of `+=` is available. In other words, `w += x` can be used in place of `w = w + x`.

Summary

■ Data carries information.
■ A data with a name is a variable. An example of data without a name is a literal.
■ A variable declaration requires the type and the name of the variable.
■ It is possible to declare multiple variables of the same type with just one type specification.
■ A variable declaration with `final` is a declaration of a constant.
■ Each variable declaration is valid until the end of the innermost pair of matching curly brackets that contain it. This is the scope of the variable.
■ Two declarations having the same variable name must not have overlapping scopes.
■ The declaration of a variable must appear before an assignment to the variable.
■ A variable name must consist of letters and numerals, and must start with a letter.
■ The reserved words of Java cannot be used for names.
■ All the methods in a class have access to global variables.
■ Global variable declarations appear at depth 1 with the attribute of `static` while local variable declarations appear at depth 2.
■ There are eight primitive data types. Other data types are object data types.
■ `+`, `-`, `*`, `/`, and `%` are five elementary mathematical operations.
■ Five shorthand expressions are available for self-updating. They are `+=`, `-=`, `*=`, `/=`, `%=`, `++`, and `-`.
■ It is possible to attach `++` or `-` to a variable, and the position of the attachment can be either before or after the variable.
■ When a binary operator operates on two numbers of different types, the program chooses to represent both with a floating number if and only if one of them is of a floating number. Furthermore, for two numbers of different types, the program will choose the type with the larger number of bits to represent both numbers.
■ It is possible to concatenate `String` literals and `String` variables with the `+` sign.
■ When a number concatenates with a `String`, the result is a `String`.

Exercises

1. **Memory size**   The following are the four primitive data types in Java that represent whole numbers. State how many bits are required to represent each of them.
    (a) `byte`
    (b) `short`
    (c) `int`
    (d) `long`
2. **Memory size**   The following are the two primitive data types in Java that represent floating point numbers. State how many bits are required to represent each of them.
    (a) `float`
    (b) `double`
3. **Casting**   State whether or not the following statements are correct.
    (a) To represent a whole number literal as a `short`, attach S at the end, e.g., as in `120S`.
    (b) To represent a whole number literal as a `byte`, attach B at the end, e.g., as in `120B`.
    (c) To represent a floating point number literal as a `float`, attach F at the end, e.g., as in `120.5F`.

4. **Data type** Suppose a is a `long` variable, b is an `int` variable, and c is a `double` variable. State the data types of the following formulas:

   (a) a / b

   (b) a / c

   (c) b / c

5. **Declaring variables** Write a program, `MyFavorites`, that declares two variables, `String word` and `int lucky`, assigns some literals to them, and then prints the values as follows:

```
1   My favorite word is "XXX".
2   My lucky number is YYY.
```

where XXX is for the value of `word` and YYY is for the value of `lucky`.

6. **Value assignments to variables** Consider the following series of statements:

```
1   int a = 11;
2   int b = 3;
3   int c = a / b + a % b;
4   a = a + b;
5   b = a - b;
```

What are the values of a, b and c after the very last statement?

7. **Cyclic value assignments**

   Consider the following series of statements:

```
1   int a, b, c, d;
2   a = 11;
3   b = 12;
4   c = 13;
5   d = 14;
6   a = b;
7   b = c;
8   c = d;
9   d = a;
```

What are the values of the variables a, b, c, and d after each of the eight assignments?

8. **What's wrong with the code?** Assume that the code below is part of the method `main` of a class. State what is wrong with the code:

```
1   int numberX = 0, numberY = 2;
2   int numberX += numberY, numberZ;
3   numberZ = 0.5;
4   realW = 71.5;
5   double realW *= realW;
```

9. **What's wrong with the code?** Assume that the code below is part of the method `main` of a class. State what is wrong with the code:

```
1  int a = 11, b = 10;
2  int b = a * b;
3  final int c = a;
4  c = a - 7;
```

10. **Variable evaluation, ++ and --**   After executing the code below, what are the values of x, y, z and w?

```
1  int x, y, z, w;
2  x = 10;
3  y = 3;
4  z = x * y--;
5  w = --x * --y;
```

11. **Variable evaluation, ++ and -- with division**   After executing the code below, what are the values of z and w?

```
1  int x, y, z, w;
2  x = -11;
3  y = 4;
4  z = x / ++y;
5  w = ++x % y--;
```

12. **Variable evaluation, String and number**   After executing the code below, what are the values of z and w?

```
1  String x, y, z, w;
2  x = "emerson";
3  y = "palmer";
4  z = x + "lake" + y;
5  w = 1 + 2 + z + 3 + 4;
```

13. **Value exchanging**   Let a and b be int variables. Write a code for exchanging the values of a and b. For example, when a has the value of 10 and b has the value of 7, the exchange will make the value of a equal to 7 and b equal to 10. Assume that a and b have been already declared in the code and have been assigned values, so the task at hand is to swap the values of the two.

14. **Value exchanging, again**   Let a, b, and c be int variables. Write a code for exchanging the values of the three (the original value of a goes to b, the original value of b goes to c, and the original value of c goes to a).

15. **Short-hand**   Suppose a and b are int variables. What are the values of a and b after executing the following?

```
1  a = 3;
2  b = 2;
3  a *= b;
4  b *= a;
5  a *= b;
6  b *= a;
```

Programming Projects

16. **Gravity again**   Recall that if an object is released so that it falls, the speed of the object at t seconds after its release is gt and the distance the object has travelled in the t seconds after release is $\frac{1}{2}gt^2$. Here, g is the gravity constant. Its value is approximately 9.8. Write a program, `Gravity`, in which the method `main` performs the following actions:
    (a) The program declares variables `t` for the travel time, `speed` for the speed, and `distance` for the distance traveled;
    (b) The program assigns some value to `t`;
    (c) The program calculates the speed and the distance;
    (d) The program prints the calculated values.
    (e) The program assigns a different value to `t` and repeats Steps 1–4.

17. **Computing the tax from a subtotal and then the total**   Write a program, `ComputeTaxAndTotal`, that computes the tax and the total in the following manner:
    * The program uses an `int` variable `subtotal` to store the subtotal in cents. Since we do not know (yet) how to receive an input from the user, assign some int literal to this variable in the code.
    * The program use a `double` variable `taxPercent` to store the tax rate in percent. Again, since we do not know (yet) how to receive an input from the user, assign some int literal to this variable in the code (for example, the tax rate is 5.5% in the state of Massachusetts).
    * The program then computes the tax amount as a whole number in cents, in an `int` variable `tax`. Using the casting of `(int)`, a floating point number can be converted to a whole number by rounding it down.
    * The program then computes the total, and stores it in an `int` variable `total`. (Again, this quantity is in cents.)
    * The program reports the result of the calculation in dollars and cents for the subtotal, the tax, and the total, and then reports the tax rate.

    The output the code may look like:

```
1    The subtotal = 110 dollars and 50 cents.
2    The tax rate = 5.5 percent.
3    The tax = 6 dollars and 7 cents.
4    The total = 116 dollars and 57 cents.
```

18. **Speeding fine**   In the town of Treehead, the speeding fines are $20 times the mileage beyond the speed limit. For example, if a driver was driving at 36 mph on a 30 mph road, his fine is $120. Write a program, `SpeedingFine`, that produces the speeding fines for the following combinations of speed and speed limit:
    * (50 mph, 35 mph)
    * (30 mph, 25 mph)
    * (60 mph, 45 mph)

    In the program, declare `int` variables, `speed`, `limit`, and `fine`. Compute the fine by assigning values to the first two variables and multiplying it by the rate of `20`. To report the results, write a series of `print`/`println` statements in which the speed, the limit, and the fine appear as variables. The code should execute this series three times and, before each series, the assignment to the three variables must appear.

    Here is an execution example of the program.

```
1    The fine for driving at 50 mph on a 35 mph road is 300 dollars.
2    The fine for driving at 30 mph on a 25 mph road is 100 dollars.
3    The fine for driving at 60 mph on a 45 mph road is 300 dollars.
```

19. **The area of a trapezoid**   Write a program, `Trapezoid`, that computes the area of a trapezoid when given the top and bottom lengths and the height. The program specifies the top, the bottom, and the height of the trapezoid in individual `System.out.println` statements. The program computes the area by directly putting the formula (bottom + top) * height / 2 inside a System.out.println statement. Freely choose the variables for the top, the bottom, and the height.

For example, the output of the program can be:

```
1   Top: 10.0
2   Bottom: 20.5
3   Height: 24.4
4   Area: 372.09999999999997
```

Split each line of the output into two parts: the first part prints the text, including the whitespace, using a `System.out.print` statement, and the second part prints the quantity using a `System.out.println` statement. For example, the first line should use the following two statements:

```
1   System.out.print( "Top: " );
2   System.out.println( 10.0 );
```

Reading Keyboard Input

3

3.1 Class `Scanner`

3.1.1 Importing Source Codes

The class `Scanner` enables reading data from the keyboard, a `String` object, or a text file using the characters (the white space character ' ', the tab-stop '\t', and the newline '\n') as separators (such characters are called **delimiters**). The character sequences separated by the delimiters can be read not only as `String` data but also as data of other types (when such interpretations are possible). The class will play an important role in the programs presented in this book. The source code for `Scanner` is available as part of JDK but not part of `java.lang`. Therefore, to write a source code for a program that uses `Scanner`, the source code of `Scanner` must be included. To include `Scanner`, an **import statement** must be used. If a class `FooBar` uses `Scanner`, the declaration must take the following form:

```
1  import java.util.Scanner;
2  public class FooBar
3  {
4  ...
5  }
```

Here, `java.util` is the group called **package** that contains the source code for `Scanner`.

The source code library of JDK is a hierarchical (tree-like) structure. We call the top-level of the hierarchy the **root**. Underneath the root exists a number of **projects**. A project is a collection of **packages**, where a package is a collection of classes and/or hierarchies of classes serving common purposes. Popular projects include `java` and `javax`. Popular packages in the project `java` are `lang`, `io`, and `util`. The standard Java package `lang` belongs to the project `java`. The period . appearing in the import statement refers to these hierarchical relations, so `java.util.Scanner` means:

"the class `Scanner` in the package `util` of the project `java`".

Some packages have sub-packages, and so the actual number of times that the separator . appears in an import statement is more than two for some packages.

© Springer Nature Switzerland AG 2018
M. Ogihara, *Fundamentals of Java Programming*,
https://doi.org/10.1007/978-3-319-89491-1_3

Multiple import statements may appear in the header. For example, the following code:

```
1   import java.util.Scanner;
2   import java.util.ArrayList;
3   import java.util.LinkedList;
4   import java.io.File;
5   import java.io.FileNotFoundException;
6   class FooBar
7   {
8   ...
9   }
```

imports five distinct classes. Multiple import statements for classes from the same package can be substituted with a universal import statement.

```
1   import java.util.*;
2   class FooBar
3   {
4   ...
5   }
```

The asterisk, meaning "everything", is called the **wildcard**.

3.1.2   The Instantiation of a `Scanner` Object

To use the functions of the class `Scanner`, one needs a `Scanner` object. A `Scanner` object is created through a process called **instantiation**. The instantiation of an object of a type `CLASS_NAME` takes the form of:

```
new CLASS_NAME( PARAMETERS )
```

where `CLASS_NAME` is a special method called **constructor**. Each object class has its own `constructors`. The name of a constructor matches the name of the class it belongs to. Here, `PARAMETERS` represents the information given to the instantiation procedure. Many classes, including `Scanner`, accept more than one kind of parameter specification. In this book, we study three `Scanner` constructors: one that takes a `String` object, one that takes `System.in`, which refers to the keyboard, and one that takes a `File` object, which refers to a file.[1] The next code fragment uses the three `Scanner` constructors and assign them to `Scanner` variables.

```
1   Scanner strScanner, fileScanner, keyboard;
2   strScanner = new Scanner( "My GPA is 4.00!" );
3   fileScanner = new Scanner( new File( "theFile.txt" ) );
4   keyboard = new Scanner( System.in );
```

---

[1]Although we do not use them in this book, `String` has many constructors (for various examples, see https://docs.oracle.com/javase/7/docs/api/java/lang/String.html).

The first Scanner object strScanner scans the String literal "My GPA is 4.00!", the second Scanner object fileScanner scans a file named "theFile.txt", and the last Scanner object keyboard scans input from the keyboard. We will study the last type extensively in this chapter.

3.2   Reading Data with a Scanner Object

Regardless of whether the input source may be a String, a File, or System.in, the chief function of a Scanner is to read from the input source using a delimiter sequence as a separator. Scanner does this by scanning the input character sequence from the beginning to the end and discovering the longest stretch of characters free of delimiters. The delimiters are our usual suspect of spacing characters: the white space character, the tab-stop, and the newline. We call such a delimiter-free stretch of characters a **token**. When reading from a String and when reading from a File, the contents of the input are fixed, so dividing the contents into tokens and delimiters is easy. When reading from System.in, dividing the contents into tokens is a dynamic process, since the user can use the delete key (or backspace key) to change the contents dynamically until the return key is pressed, upon which no more changes are permitted.

Imagine that a String object myStringSource has contents

> " Programming\t\tis fun, \nisn't it?\n"

where \t and \n are the tab-stop, and the newline and the other gaps consist of the white space characters. We can break this String data into an alternating series of delimiters and tokens, as follows:

1. a delimiter " ",
2. a token "Programming",
3. a delimiter "\t\t",
4. a token "is",
5. a delimiter " ",
6. a token "fun,",
7. a delimiter "\n",
8. a token "isn't",
9. a delimiter " ",
10. a token "it?"

If we have instantiated a Scanner object myInput from this String literal, then myInput produces the five tokens in order of appearance.

To read data from the input source of a Scanner object, we apply a method to the object. Formally, a method applied to an object data is called an **instance method**. To execute an instance method on an object of an object class, we attach a period and the name of the method to the object, and then attach a pair of parentheses after the method name. Each execution of the method is called a **method call**.

This period has the same role as the second periods in `System.out.println` and
`System.out.print`, since `System.out` is an object of type `PrintStream` (which we will
study in Chap. 15).

The instance method used for reading a token as a `String` data from the input source of a
`Scanner` object is called `next`. Here is a code that uses the method:

```
1   String myStringSource;
2   Scanner myInput;
3   myStringSource = "  Programming\t\tis    fun, \nisn't it?";
4   myInput = new Scanner( myStringSource );
5   myInput.next();
```

`myInput.next()` produces the first token of the `String` object, `"Programming"`. If there
is no action that utilizes this token, the token disappears. The token that `next` produces in a `String`
variable can be saved via assignment; that is, after

```
1   String myStringSource, myFirstToken;
2   Scanner myInput;
3   myStringSource = "  Programming\t\tis    fun, \nisn't it?";
4   myInput = new Scanner( myStringSource );
5   myFirstToken = myInput.next();
```

the variable `firstToken` has the value `"Programming"`.

Earlier we quickly went over the return type of a method. In the case of the method `next` of
`Scanner`, its return type is `String`. In the case of the method `next`, the method comes back with
a `String`. We can obtain that value by assigning it to a `String` value. In a similar manner, we can
place the method call in a `System.out.println`, as shown next:

```
1   myInput = new Scanner( myStringSource );
2   System.out.println( myInput.next() );
```

The `System.out.println` receives the return value of `myInput.next()` and prints it on
the screen. Since the first token retrieved is `"Programming"`, the code produces the output:

```
Programming
```

By executing the `next()` four more times, we are able to retrieve all the tokens appearing in
`mySourceText`. For example,

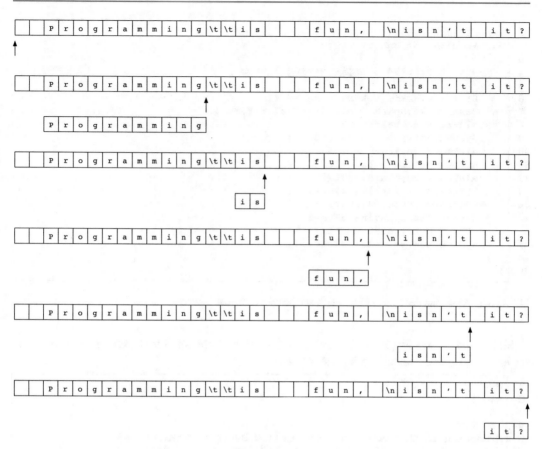

Fig. 3.1 The results of five consecutive calls of next. The arrows show the start positions of the Scanner object for the next read. The sequences immediately to the left of the arrows are the tokens that have been read

```
1   String myStringSource, token1, token2, token3, token4, token5
2   Scanner myInput;
3   myStringSource = "  Programming\t\tis   fun, \nisn't it?";
4   myInput = new Scanner( myStringSource );
5   token1 = myInput.next();
6   token2 = myInput.next();
7   token3 = myInput.next();
8   token4 = myInput.next();
9   token5 = myInput.next();
```

retrieves the five tokens as five variables in the order they appear.

The results of the five calls of next are shown in Fig. 3.1.

It is impossible to scan beyond the last token. If an attempt is made to read beyond the last token, a run-time error of NoSuchElementException occurs. The code appearing in the next source code demonstrates an attempt to read beyond the last token, as well as the resulting run-time error.

```
1   import java.util.Scanner;
2   public class BeyondLimit
3   {
4     public static void main( String[] args )
5     {
6       String aToken, tokens = new String( "My age is 20" );
7       Scanner keyboard = new Scanner( tokens );
8       aToken = keyboard.next();
9       System.out.println( aToken );
10      aToken = keyboard.next();
11      System.out.println( aToken );
12      aToken = keyboard.next();
13      System.out.println( aToken );
14      aToken = keyboard.next();
15      System.out.println( aToken );
16      aToken = keyboard.next();
17      System.out.println( aToken );
18    }
19  }
```

Listing 3.1 A program that attempts to read a token that does not exist

Since there are five `keyboard.next()` calls and there are only four tokens, an error occurs at the fifth `keyboard.next()` call, as shown next:

```
1   My
2   age
3   is
4   20
5   Exception in thread "main" java.util.NoSuchElementException
6           at java.util.Scanner.throwFor(Scanner.java:862)
7           at java.util.Scanner.next(Scanner.java:1371)
8           at BeyondLimit.main(BeyondLimit.java:16)
```

The fifth line of the output is the start of the error message. The type of the error appears, at the end, as `java.util.NoSuchElementException`.

It is vital to prevent attempts to read beyond the last token. When reading from the keyboard, because the texts are generated dynamically and the length of the text is indefinite, we usually do not encounter the error. (The error does not occur unless the user simultaneously presses the CTRL-key and the letter 'd' to indicate the end of the input. This combination is called CTRL-D. We will study the use of CTRL-D in Chap. 11.)

When reading tokens from a `String` data or from a file, however, some proactive measures are needed to prevent the error from happening. There are three possible approaches:

(a) know beforehand how many tokens are in the input source;
(b) check for the existence of a token before attempting to read;
(c) recover from `NoSuchElementException` using a special mechanism, called `try-catch`.

We will study the second approach in Chap. 11 and the third in Chap. 15.

Table 3.1 Selected
methods of Scanner

Name	Return type	Action
next	String	Obtains the next token
nextBoolean	boolean	Obtains the next boolean token
nextByte	byte	Obtains the next byte token
nextDouble	double	Obtains the next double token
nextFloat	float	Obtains the next float token
nextInt	int	Obtains the next int token
nextLong	long	Obtains the next long token
nextShort	short	Obtains the next short token
nextLine	String	Obtains the String before the next newline
hasNext	boolean	Checks whether or not the next token exists

All the methods in this table are usually called with an empty parameter, i.e., with () attached after the method names. We will study hasNext in Chap. 11

Using Scanner, we can fetch the next token not only as a String data but also as a token of a specific primitive data type, given that the token can be interpreted as a literal of that type. The type-specific fetch methods are: nextBoolean, nextByte, nextDouble, nextFloat, nextInt, nextLong, and nextShort. Note that there is no method corresponding to reading a char. If one of these methods is called and the next token cannot be interpreted as the type associated with the method, a run-time error of InputMismatchException occurs. For example, suppose the next token in the input sequence is -1.0. The token can be interpreted as a double data, a float data, and a String data, but not as a whole number data or as a boolean data. Thus, the use of nextBoolean, nextByte, nextDouble, nextFloat, nextInt, or nextLong will fail (and a run-time error will subsequently appear).

Table 3.1 presents a list of Scanner methods that appear in this textbook. We will study hasNext in Chap. 11.

There is one particularly interesting "next" method in Scanner and this is nextLine. If the remaining (or upcoming) character sequence has at least one occurrence of the newline character, the nextLine returns the entire character sequence appearing before the first newline character in the upcoming character sequence. After completing nextLine, the Scanner object scans the sequence starting from the character immediately after the identified newline character.

If a Scanner object is instantiated with either a String data or a File object, the remaining sequence may not contain any newline characters. If the nextLine method is called in such a situation, the method returns the String data corresponding to all the remaining characters. After that, no characters remain in the sequence.

Consider the following code:

```
1   import java.util.*;
2   public class NextLine
3   {
4     public static void main( String[] args )
5     {
6       String myStringSource =
7           "My lucky number is 17 , \n how about yours?   ";
8       Scanner myInput = new Scanner( myStringSource );
9       System.out.println( myInput.next() );
10      System.out.println( myInput.next() );
11      System.out.println( myInput.next() );
12      System.out.println( myInput.next() );
13      System.out.println( myInput.nextInt() );
14      System.out.println( myInput.nextLine() );
15      System.out.print( myInput.nextLine() );
16      System.out.println( ":::::" );
17    }
18  }
```

Listing 3.2 A program that combines `next` and `nextLine`

The source of the `Scanner` object is the `String` literal

```
"My lucky number is 17 , \n how about yours?   "
```

The fifth token of the input source is the `String` literal `"17"`. We can treat this as either a `String` type or an `int` (or any other number type since 17 can be represented as a `byte` data). The delimiter sequence that follows this number token consists of five characters, represented as `" , \n "`. (the double quotation marks are attached so as to clarify the beginning and the ending of the character sequence. If the method that is called at that point is `next`, then the `Scanner` will skip to the next token `","`. However, if the method that is called is `nextLine` instead, the `"\n"` appearing as the fourth character of the five-character sequence becomes the delimiter. When this happens, the `Scanner` object returns `" , "` as the result of executing `nextLine`, and then the `Scanner` object positions itself to the fifth character of the sequence, i.e., the `" "` after the newline. If `nextLine` and `next` are called successively, the method call to `next` returns `"how"`. If `nextLine` is called twice successively, the first call returns `" , "` as in the previous case, and the second call returns the remainder of the sequence, `" how about yours?  "`, because is no additional appearance of `\n`. Based upon this analysis, the output of the program is expected to be:

```
1   % java NextLine
2   My
3   lucky
4   number
5   is
6   17
7    ,
8    how about yours?   :::::
9   %
```

The `":::::"` appearing at the end is not part of the `String` literal, but is a marking that this program attaches to indicate the end of its output. Figure 3.2 shows the progress that the `Scanner` object makes during the execution of the program.

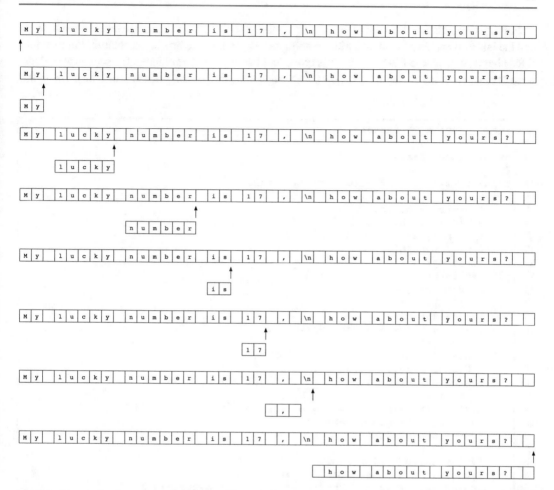

Fig. 3.2 The results of executing the program. The arrows show the positions of the Scanner object for the next read. The sequences immediately to the left of the arrows are the tokens that have been read. Note that the last two reads are done by nextLine so the delimiters other than the newline characters, if any, are included in the returned String data that are returned

3.3   Reading Input from the Keyboard

We will now explore how to read data from the keyboard. Note two things:

1. The Scanner objects instantiated with System.in cannot take action until the return key is pressed. This means that, depending on what actions are awaiting with the Scanner object, the single line of input may offer a return value to multiple next methods of the Scanner object.
2. When reading the output generated by a program that scans keyboard input, the coexistence of the output of the program and the echo of the keyboard input makes it difficult to distinguish between the two different types of screen output.

The next code demonstrates the use of the type-specific token reading methods. The program stores the result of each token it reads in a variable of an appropriate type, and then prints the value.

Notice that nextLine appears at the very beginning of the series of calls to next methods. This is because if nextLine comes after another call to the next method, then the result of nextLine will be an empty String.

Furthermore, when a `Scanner` object is instantiated with `System.in`, because the white space and the tab-stop are erasable after typing, nothing occurs until the return key is entered. For example, if the character sequence ABC 17 5.4 is typed and the return key is entered, the sequence includes three tokens, but none of the three tokens can be read until the pressing of the return key. Using this

```
 1  import java.util.Scanner;
 2
 3  public class Nexts
 4  {
 5    public static void main( String[] args )
 6    {
 7      Scanner keyboard;
 8      boolean myBoolean;
 9      byte myByte;
10      double myDouble;
11      float myFloat;
12      int myInt;
13      long myLong;
14      short myShort;
15      String myString;
16      keyboard = new Scanner( System.in );
17      // Nextline
18      System.out.print( "Enter any String: " );
19      myString = keyboard.nextLine();
20      System.out.println( "You've entered: " + myString );
21      // String
22      System.out.print( "Enter a String with no space: " );
23      myString = keyboard.next();
24      System.out.println( "You've entered: " + myString );
25      // boolean
26      System.out.print( "Enter a boolean: " );
27      myBoolean = keyboard.nextBoolean();
28      System.out.println( "You've entered: " + myBoolean );
29      // byte
30      System.out.print( "Enter a byte: " );
31      myByte = keyboard.nextByte();
32      System.out.println( "You've entered: " + myByte );
33      // double
34      System.out.print( "Enter a double: " );
35      myDouble = keyboard.nextDouble();
36      System.out.println( "You've entered: " + myDouble );
37      // float
38      System.out.print( "Enter a float: " );
39      myFloat = keyboard.nextFloat();
40      System.out.println( "You've entered: " + myFloat );
41      // int
42      System.out.print( "Enter an int: " );
43      myInt = keyboard.nextInt();
44      System.out.println( "You've entered: " + myInt );
45      // long
46      System.out.print( "Enter a long: " );
47      myLong = keyboard.nextLong();
48      System.out.println( "You've entered: " + myLong );
49    }
50  }
```

Listing 3.3 A program that demonstrates the use of various "next" methods of `Scanner`

information, if the user knows what types of tokens the program is expecting to receive, she can enter multiple tokens in succession.

In the next code, the program expects three input tokens from the keyboard, a `String`, an `int`, and a `double`. The program receives these input tokens and then prints them. Knowing what happens in the code, the user can type ABC 10 4.5 to enter all the tokens required by the program at once.

```java
import java.util.Scanner;
// an example of using Scanner
public class ScannerExample
{
  public static void main( String[] args )
  {
    Scanner console;
    String theWord;
    int theWholeNumber;
    double theRealNumber;
    console = new Scanner( System.in );
    System.out.print( "Enter a string: " );
    theWord = console.next();
    System.out.print( "Enter an int: " );
    theWholeNumber = console.nextInt();
    System.out.print( "Enter a double: " );
    theRealNumber = console.nextDouble();
    System.out.print( "You have entered " );
    System.out.print( theWord );
    System.out.print( ", " );
    System.out.print( theWholeNumber );
    System.out.print( ", and " );
    System.out.print( theRealNumber );
    System.out.println();
  }
}
```

Listing 3.4 A program that reads a `String` data, an `int` data, and a `double` data using methods of `Scanner`

The next program asks the user to enter two integers and then two real numbers. The program then multiplies the two integers and divides the first real number by the second. Finally, the program produces the output showing the results of the arithmetic operations.

```
1   import java.util.Scanner;
2   // an example of using Scanner
3   public class ScannerMath
4   {
5     public static void main( String[] args )
6     {
7       Scanner console;
8       int int1, int2, product;
9       double real1, real2, quotient;
10
11      console = new Scanner( System.in );
12
13      System.out.print( "Enter int no. 1: " );
14      int1 = console.nextInt();
15      System.out.print( "Enter int no. 2: " );
16      int2 = console.nextInt();
17      product = int1 * int2;
18
19      System.out.print( "Received " );
20      System.out.print( int1 );
21      System.out.print( " and " );
22      System.out.println( int2 );
23      System.out.print( "The product is " );
24      System.out.println( product );
25
26      System.out.print( "Enter double no. 1: " );
27      real1 = console.nextDouble();
28      System.out.print( "Enter double no. 2: " );
29      real2 = console.nextDouble();
30      quotient = real1 / real2;
31
32      System.out.print( "Received " );
33      System.out.print( real1 );
34      System.out.print( " and " );
35      System.out.println( real2 );
36      System.out.print( "The quotient is " );
37      System.out.println( quotient );
38    }
39  }
```

Listing 3.5 A program that performs arithmetic operations on the numbers received from the user

Again, when running this code, all the numbers can be typed at once. Such "ahead of the game" typing saves the wait time.

Summary

- We construct an object by calling a constructor new CLASS_NAME(PARAMETERS).
- A class may have more than one constructor, with each taking a unique set of parameters.
- To use a Scanner object in the source code, the class Scanner must be imported.
- To execute a method on an object, the method name along with parameters must be attached to the object, with a period before the method name.
- Scanner offers a variety of token reading methods: next, nextBoolean, nextByte, nextDouble, nextFloat, nextInt, nextLine, nextLong, and nextShort.

- An attempt to read beyond the last token results in a run-time error.
- The keyboard echo and the output of the program share the same screen.

Exercises

1. **Terminology test**
   (a) To be able to use a `Scanner`, which class must be imported?
   (b) To create a `Scanner` object that receives input from the keyboard, what statement is needed?
   (c) Write the names of the `Scanner` methods necessary for receiving a `String`, an `int`, and a `double`, respectively.
   (d) When a user types a floating point number into a location where the program has just called the `nextInt` method of a `Scanner` method, will an error occur? If so, what kind of error is it?
   (e) Does an `int` value of 15 pass for a `double`?
   (f) What is the formal term that refers to the process of creating an object of an object type?
   (g) What is the special keyword used in the source code when creating an object?
   (h) For one primitive data type, the class `Scanner` does not have the `next` method designated to read tokens of that type. Which type is this?

2. **Scanning errors**   Consider the following program:

```
1   import java.util.*;
2   public class SimpleInputOutput
3   {
4     public static void main( String[] args )
5     {
6       Scanner keyboard = new Scanner( System.in );
7       String word;
8       double real;
9       int value;
10      System.out.print( "Enter a real number (for a double): " );
11      real = keyboard.nextDouble();
12      System.out.print( "Enter a word: " );
13      word = keyboard.next();
14      System.out.print( "Enter an integer (for an int): " );
15      value = keyboard.nextInt();
16      System.out.print( "Your have entered: " );
17      System.out.println( real + ", " + word + ", " + value );
18    }
19  }
```

Suppose the user is considering the following key strokes when the code is compiled and run, where the strokes are presented as `String` literals, with `\t` and `\n` representing the tab-stop and newline respectively. Do they have enough tokens to finish the code? Which ones will run without causing an error? For those that lead to an error, where will its error occur, and what is the nature of the error?

(a) `"\t0.5\tprogramming\t10\n"`
(b) `"\t5\tprogramming\t10.5\n"`
(c) `"\n\n5\n\n5\n"`
(d) `" 0 0 0.5"`
(e) `" 0 0 0.5\n"`

3. **Scanning errors when `nextLine` is involved**   Consider the following program:

```
1  import java.util.*;
2  public class SimpleInputOutput
3  {
4    public static void main( String[] args )
5    {
6      Scanner keyboard = new Scanner( System.in );
7      String word1, word2;
8      double real;
9      int value;
10     System.out.print( "Enter a real number (for a double): " );
11     real = keyboard.nextDouble();
12     System.out.print( "Enter a word: " );
13     word1 = keyboard.nextLine();
14     System.out.print( "Enter an integer (for an int): " );
15     value = keyboard.nextInt();
16     System.out.print( "Enter another word: " );
17     word2 = keyboard.nextLine();
18     System.out.print( "Your have entered: " );
19     System.out.println(
20         real + ", " + word1+ ", " + value + ", " + word2 );
21   }
22 }
```

Suppose the user is considering the following key strokes when the code is compiled and run, where the strokes are presented as `String` literals with `\t` and `\n` representing the tab-stop and newline respectively. Do they have enough tokens to finish the code? Which ones will run without causing an error? For those that lead to an error, where will its error and what is the nature of the error?

(a) `"\t0.5\tprogramming\t10\tJava\n"`

(b) `"\t5\tprogramming\n10.5\tJava\n"`

(c) `"5\nprogramming\n10.5\nJava\n"`

(d) `"\n\n5\n\n5\n"`

(e) `" -3 -3\n-3.7 -3.5\n"`

(f) `" 0.5 0.5\n6 6\n"`

Programming Projects

4. **Inferences**   Write a program named `Inference` that receives three names, `name1`, `name2`, and `name3`, from the user and prints the following statements.

```
1  name1 is senior to name2
2  name2 is senior to name3
3  so
4  name1 is senior to name3
5
6  name3 is senior to name2
7  name2 is senior to name1
8  so
9  name3 is senior to name1
```

The output of the program is composed of the names entered, `" is senior to `, and `"so"`. Declare the last two as constants. Use three variables to store the entered names. Use these components to produce the output.

5. **Arithmetic short-hand**   Write a program named `ArithmeticShortHand` that receives two `double` numbers x and y from the user and then executes `x *= y`, `y = x/y`, and `x /= y`. The program should print the values of x and y after each of the three actions. Try running the program with various values for x and y. Also, see what happens when the value of y is set to 0.

6. **Receiving five numbers**   Write a program named `FiveNumbers` that prompts the user to enter five whole numbers, receives five numbers (u, v, x, y, and z) using `nextInt`, computes the product of the five numbers as a `long` data, and produces the values of the five values and the product on the screen. For example, the result could look like:

```
1   Enter five integers: 12 34 56 78 90
2   The five numbers are: 12, 34, 56, 78, 90
3   The product is: 160392960
```

7. **Adding six numbers with four variables**   Write a program named `Miser` that prompts the user to enter six whole numbers and produces the following output:

```
1   % java Miser
2   Enter six numbers: 1 10 3 4 -12 -6
3   You've entered: 1 10 3 4 12 -6 with the total sum of 0
```

Here, the numbers entered are 1, 10, 3, 4, -12, and -6. The program should be written so that it uses only four variables: one variable for the scanner, one variable for the number received, one variable for the total, and one variable for the message. The initial value of the variable storing the total is 0, and the initial value of the variable storing the message is `"You've entered:"`. After these initializations, the program should receive the input value from the user, add the value to the total, and update the value of the message variable by adding one white space followed by the input value.

8. **Favorite football player, an interactive program**   Write a program named `FavoriteFootballPlayer` that receives the name, the position, the team, and the jersey number from the user, and then produces the following message on the screen:

```
1   Enter name: Larry Fitzgerald
2   Enter position: Wide Receiver
3   Enter team: The Arizona Cardinals
4   Enter jersey number: 11
5   Your favorite football player is Larry Fitzgerald.
6   His position is Wide Receiver.
7   He is with The Arizona Cardinals and wears the jersey number 11.
```

Here, the first four lines show the interaction with the user. Since we do not need to perform math operations, treat all the four values as `String`. The name may have spaces, so read each input using `nextLine`.

9. **Gravity again**   Recall that if an object is released to fall, the speed of the object at t seconds after its release is gt and the distance the object has travelled in the t seconds after release is $\frac{1}{2}gt^2$. Here, g is the gravity constant, which is approximately 9.8 (the unit is m/s^2) on Earth. Write a program named `GravityInput` whose method `main` does the following:

(a) It declares variables t for the travel time, speed for the speed, and distance for the distance traveled;

(b) It receives a value for t from the user;

(c) It calculates the speed and the distance;

(d) It prints the calculated speed and distance.

(e) Repeat the last three steps two more times.

10. **Quadratic evaluation**   Write a program named `QuadraticEvaluation` that declares four variables (`a`, `b`, `c`, `x`), receives values for the four from the user, calculates $ax^2 + bx + c$ and $a/x^2 + b/x + c$, and prints the values.

11. **Adding time**   Write a program named `AddTime` that receives minutes and seconds from the user four times, and then computes the total in hours, minutes, and seconds. The user must specify the minutes and the seconds separately. Ideally, we want to be able to check if the values are valid (that is, the minutes and the seconds have to be between 0 and 59), but because we have not learned yet how to write code that does this, we will assume that the user always enters valid values. The interactions with the user can be as follows:

```
1   Enter time #1: 10 50
2   Enter time #2: 26 35
3   Enter time #3: 37 30
4   Enter time #4: 41 50
5   The total is 1 hours 56 minutes 45 seconds.
```

We may want to print `"hour"` instead of `"hours"` for this particular case, but again, we do not know yet how to identify that the number of hours is 1, so we will thus use `"hours"` throughout. The task can be accomplished as follows:

- Compute the total seconds and the total minutes from the input.
- Add the quotient of the seconds divided by 60 to the minutes and then replace the seconds with the remainder of the seconds divided by 60.
- Set the quotient of the minutes divided by 60 to the hour and then replace the minutes with the remainder of the minutes divided by 60.

Programming Projects

12. **Computing the tax, again**   Write a program named `ComputeTaxAndtotalInteractive` that computes the tax and the total in the following manner:

- The program uses an `int` variable `subtotal` to store the subtotal in cents. The program receives the value from the user.
- The program uses a `double` variable `taxPercent` to store the tax rate in percent. The program receives the value from the user.
- The program then computes the tax amount as a whole number in cents, in an `int` variable `tax`. Using the casting of `(int)`, a floating point number can be truncated to a whole number.
- The program then computes the total and stores it in an `int` variable `total`. (Again, this quantity is in cents.)
- The program reports the result of the calculation in dollars and cents for the subtotal, the tax, and the total, and then reports the tax rate.

The output of the code may look like:

```
1   Enter subtotal in cents: 11050
2   Enter tax percentage: 5.5
3   The subtotal = 110 dollars and 50 cents.
4   The tax rate = 5.5 percent.
5   The tax = 6 dollars and 7 cents.
6   The total = 116 dollars and 57 cents.
```

13. **Speeding fines, part 1**   In the town of Silver Hollow, the speeding fines are $20 times the mileage beyond the speed limit. For example, if a driver was driving at 36 mph on a 30 mph road, his fine is $120. Write a program named `SpeedingFineNew1` that receives the speed and the limit from the user, and then computes the fine in Silver Hollow. The result could look like:

```
1  Enter the speed and the limit: 50 35
2  The fine for driving at 50 mph on a 35 mph road is 300 dollars.
```

14. **Speeding fines, part 2**   In the town of Golden Valley, the speeding fines are $15 times the percentage of the speed exceeding the limit. The percentage is rounded down to a whole number. For example, if a driver was driving at 35 mph on a 30 mph road, the percentage of excess is the integer part of `(35 - 30) / 30`, which is 16. Thus, the fine is 16 times $5 = $80. Write a program named `SpeedingFineNew2` that receives the speed and the limit from the user and then computes the fine. The result could look like:

```
1  Enter the speed and the limit: 35 30
2  The fine for driving at 35 mph on a 30 mph road is 80 dollars.
```

15. **Fractional difference**   Write a program named `FractionalDifference` that receives four integers a, b, c, and d from the user, and then computes the difference `(a/b) - (c/d)`. Compute the difference by treating the four numbers as integers and then as floating point numbers. To convert an integer to `double`, use casting of `(double)`, e.g., `(double) a`. The result could look like:

```
1  Enter the four numbers: 10 3 20 7
2  The difference is 1 using int and 0.4761904761904763 using double.
```

16. **Volume of a rectilinear box**   Write a program named `RectilinearBox` that receives three quantities, `height`, `width`, and `length`, from the user, and then computes the volume of the rectilinear box whose dimensions are represented by these quantities. Assume that these quantities are `double` (so the volume should be `double`).

Decomposing Code into Components

4

4.1 Procedural Decomposition

4.1.1 Printing Rectangles

In this chapter, we learn how to decompose a source code into multiple methods.

We previously studied programs that draw shapes using multiple `System.out.println` statements. Consider, this time, drawing a rectangle. Suppose we draw a rectangle with 3×3 white space characters and surrounding borders, as shown next:

```
1  +---+
2  |   |
3  |   |
4  |   |
5  +---+
```

We can accomplish the task using five `System.out.println` statements corresponding to the five horizontal strips of the shape, as shown next.[1] For clarification, the five `System.out.println` statements are marked with line comments indicating their correspondence to the strips.

```
1   public class Rectangle
2   {
3     public static void main( String[] args )
4     {
5       System.out.println( "+---+" );      // top line
6       System.out.println( "|   |" );      // middle section 1
7       System.out.println( "|   |" );      // middle section 2
8       System.out.println( "|   |" );      // middle section 3
9       System.out.println( "+---+" );      // bottom line
10    }
11  }
```

Listing 4.1 The source code for a program that produces a 3×3 white space rectangle with encompassing borders

---

[1]The program name for this is Rectangle, not Square, although the size of the white-area is 3×3. This is because the shape does not look like a square, which is because the computer characters have longer height than width.

© Springer Nature Switzerland AG 2018
M. Ogihara, *Fundamentals of Java Programming*,
https://doi.org/10.1007/978-3-319-89491-1_4

Suppose, instead of just one rectangle, we want to print the same rectangle three times, on top of one another, as shown next.

```
1    +---+
2    |   |
3    |   |
4    |   |
5    +---+
6    +---+
7    |   |
8    |   |
9    |   |
10   +---+
11   +---+
12   |   |
13   |   |
14   |   |
15   +---+
```

We can accomplish the task by repeating the five statements two more times:

```
1   public class Rectangle00
2   {
3     public static void main( String[] args )
4     {
5       System.out.println( "+---+" );      // top line
6       System.out.println( "|   |" );      // middle section 1
7       System.out.println( "|   |" );      // middle section 2
8       System.out.println( "|   |" );      // middle section 3
9       System.out.println( "+---+" );      // bottom line
10      System.out.println( "+---+" );      // top line
11      System.out.println( "|   |" );      // middle section 1
12      System.out.println( "|   |" );      // middle section 2
13      System.out.println( "|   |" );      // middle section 3
14      System.out.println( "+---+" );      // bottom line
15      System.out.println( "+---+" );      // top line
16      System.out.println( "|   |" );      // middle section 1
17      System.out.println( "|   |" );      // middle section 2
18      System.out.println( "|   |" );      // middle section 3
19      System.out.println( "+---+" );      // bottom line
20    }
21  }
```

Listing 4.2 A program that produces three rectangles

Alternatively, the same output can be generated using a source code that uses, three times, a method that prints just one rectangle.

A method that prints a single rectangle can be defined as follows (where we use the name oneRectangle for the method):

```
1     public static void oneRectangle()
2     {
3       System.out.println( "+---+" );
4       System.out.println( "|   |" );
5       System.out.println( "|   |" );
6       System.out.println( "|   |" );
7       System.out.println( "+---+" );
8     }
```

The method declaration conforms to the format we saw in Chap. 1:

ATTRIBUTES RETURN_TYPE METHOD_NAME(PARAMETERS)

oneRectangle is a public executable method requiring no parameters, with the return type of void.

As mentioned earlier, one can define multiple methods in a source code. If oneRectangle is the name of a method defined in a source code, all the methods appearing in the same source code can execute the code oneRectangle. This is done by stating the name, and then attaching a pair of parentheses followed by a semicolon:

```
1    public static ... fooBar( ... )
2    {
3       ...
4      oneRectangle();
5       ...
6    }
```

We call the action of executing a code (written in a method) by stating its name a **method call**.

Unlike the concept of method calls that we saw in Chap. 3, the method call oneRectangle stands alone and does not require an instantiation of an object.

When a method call occurs, the present execution of the code is suspended temporarily, and the code of the method that has been called is executed. Once the execution of the method is completed, the suspended execution resumes.

Returning to the task of printing the three rectangles: now that we have written oneRectangle as he method for printing one rectangle, the task can be accomplished by three successive calls of oneRectangle, as shown next:

```
1    public static void main( String[] args )
2    {
3      oneRectangle();
4      oneRectangle();
5      oneRectangle();
6    }
```

Remember that the declaration of a method in a class appears at depth 1 of a source code. If a class has some k methods, the source code of the class will look like:

```
1  public class Foo
2  {
3    ATTRIBUTES_1 METHOD_1(...)
4    {
5       ...
6    }
7    ATTRIBUTES_2 METHOD_2(...)
8    {
9       ...
10   }
11   ...
12   ATTRIBUTES_k METHOD_k(...)
13   {
14      ...
15   }
16 }
```

Here, `ATTRIBUTES_i` is a series of attributes for `Method_i`. These methods may appear in any order.

Here is a complete source code for printing three rectangles using the method `oneRectangle`:

```
1   public class Rectangle01
2   {
3     public static void oneRectangle() {
4        System.out.println( "+---+" );
5        System.out.println( "|   |" );
6        System.out.println( "|   |" );
7        System.out.println( "|   |" );
8        System.out.println( "+---+" );
9     }
10    public static void main( String[] args )
11    {
12       oneRectangle();
13       oneRectangle();
14       oneRectangle();
15    }
16  }
```

Listing 4.3 A program that produces three rectangles. An alternate version

Since the order in which the two methods, `oneRectangle` and `main`, appear in the source does not affect the way the source code works, the following code, in which the order of their appearances is reversed, behaves exactly the same:

```
1   public class Rectangle01_Rev
2   {
3     public static void main( String[] args )
4     {
5        oneRectangle();
6        oneRectangle();
7        oneRectangle();
8     }
9     public static void oneRectangle()
10    {
11       System.out.println( "+---+" );
12       System.out.println( "|   |" );
13       System.out.println( "|   |" );
14       System.out.println( "|   |" );
15       System.out.println( "+---+" );
16    }
17  }
```

Listing 4.4 A program that produces three rectangles. The order of the two methods have been switched

Figure 4.1 shows how the two methods work together. Each method is visualized in a column, where the statements appearing in it are presented from top to bottom. When the first call of `oneRectangle` occurs, C is recorded as the return location after completion of `oneRectangle`, and then the execution of `oneRectangle` starts. When the execution of `oneRectangle` completes, the return location of C is retrieved, and from there the execution of `main` resumes (Fig. 4.2). We call the concept of using multiple methods with specific roles assigned to the methods a **procedural decomposition**. The procedural decomposition of the three-rectangle program has three benefits:

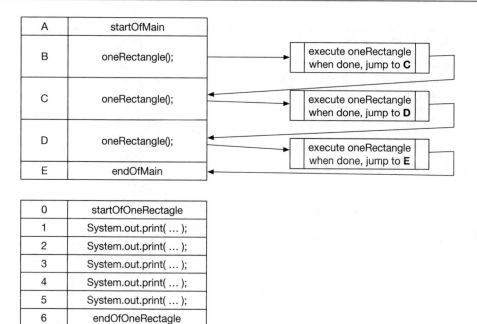

Fig. 4.1 The method calls in `Rectangle01`

1. In the source code of `main`, it is clear that some set of actions is repeated three times.
2. To change the shape, only one shape (i.e., the shape printed with `oneRectangle`) needs to be modified.
3. To change the number of times the shape is printed, only the number of calls of `oneRectangle()` needs to be modified.

Procedural decompositions improve the understanding of the code and make modifications easy. Procedural decompositions can be made in a bottom-up manner, building a new method out of already existing ones, as in case of the three identical rectangles. Procedural decompositions can be made in a top-down manner as well, dividing an existing method into smaller components, as we will see now.

We notice that there are only two distinct strips in the rectangle: `+---+` and `|---|`. We define methods, `line` and `section`, that present these strips, respectively:

```
1   public static void line ()
2   {
3       System.out.println( "+---+" );
4   }
```

and

```
1   public static void section ()
2   {
3       System.out.println( "|   |" );
4   }
```

We can then rewrite `oneRectangle` as:

```
1    public static void oneRectangle()
2    {
3      line();
4      section();
5      section();
6      section();
7      line();
8    }
```

The overall program looks like this:

```
1   public class Rectangle02
2   {
3     public static void line()
4     {
5       System.out.println( "+---+" );
6     }
7     public static void section()
8     {
9       System.out.println( "|   |" );
10    }
11    public static void oneRectangle()
12    {
13      line();
14      section();
15      section();
16      section();
17      line();
18    }
19    public static void main( String[] args )
20    {
21      oneRectangle();
22      oneRectangle();
23      oneRectangle();
24    }
25  }
```

Listing 4.5 A program that produces three rectangles. The final version

The way the method calls are handled is now two-tiered. Added benefits of using this structure are:

1. To change the width of the rectangle, the programmer only needs to edit the String literals appearing in line and section.
2. To modify the number height of the rectangle, the programmer only needs to change the number of times oneRectangle calls section.

4.1.2   Printing Quadrangles

Consider drawing four rectangles of same dimensions, two on top of the other two, where neighboring rectangles share their adjacent sides and corners, as shown next:

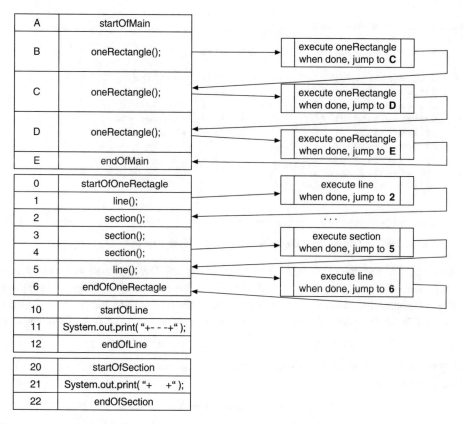

A	startOfMain
B	oneRectangle();
C	oneRectangle();
D	oneRectangle();
E	endOfMain
0	startOfOneRectagle
1	line();
2	section();
3	section();
4	section();
5	line();
6	endOfOneRectagle
10	startOfLine
11	System.out.print("+- - -+");
12	endOfLine
20	startOfSection
21	System.out.print("+ +");
22	endOfSection

execute oneRectangle
when done, jump to **C**

execute oneRectangle
when done, jump to **D**

execute oneRectangle
when done, jump to **E**

execute line
when done, jump to **2**

. . .

execute section
when done, jump to **5**

execute line
when done, jump to **6**

Fig. 4.2 The method calls in `Rectangle02`

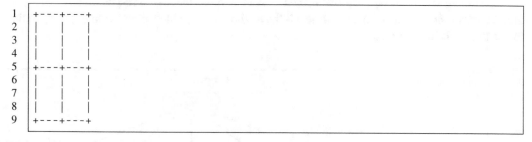

```
1  +---+---+
2  |   |   |
3  |   |   |
4  |   |   |
5  +---+---+
6  |   |   |
7  |   |   |
8  |   |   |
9  +---+---+
```

With all the actions placed in the `main` method, the code will look like:

```
1   public class Quadrant01
2   {
3     public static void main( String[] args )
4     {
5       System.out.println( "+---+---+" ); // top line
6       System.out.println( "|   |   |" ); // top section 1
7       System.out.println( "|   |   |" ); // top section 2
8       System.out.println( "|   |   |" ); // top section 3
9       System.out.println( "+---+---+" ); // middle line
10      System.out.println( "|   |   |" ); // bottom section 1
11      System.out.println( "|   |   |" ); // bottom section 2
12      System.out.println( "|   |   |" ); // bottom section 3
13      System.out.println( "+---+---+" ); // bottom line
14    }
15  }
```

Listing 4.6 A program that prints four rectangles with two on top of the other two

As in the case of the three rectangles, there are only two different printed strips that are printed: (a) the pattern appearing at the top, in the middle, and at the bottom of the shape and (b) the pattern appearing elsewhere. So, as before, we define two methods representing the patterns: `line` for the former and `side` for the latter. We can decompose the drawing of the shape as the following sequence:

line, side, side, side, line, side, side, side, line

We can group the series of `side` into one and assign the name `section` to this group. The whole sequence then becomes:

line, section, line, section, line

The above discussion is summarized in the diagram shown in Fig. 4.3. We then use this analysis to decompose the original source code to a new one that employs multiple methods, `Quadrant03`.

Appearing first in the program is the method `line` that prints the line corresponding to the top, the middle, and the bottom lines. Appearing next is the method `side`, which prints the line corresponding to one line of the middle section.

Fig. 4.3 The decomposition of actions in the generation of the quadrant

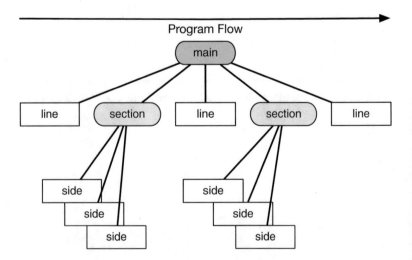

```
1    public class QuadrantDecomposed
2    {
3       // the horizontal line
4       public static void line()
5       {
6          System.out.println( "+---+---+" ); // border line
7       }
8       // the side line
9       public static void side()
10      {
11         System.out.println( "|   |   |" ); // one line of section
12      }
```

Listing 4.7 A program that produces four rectangles using method class (part 1). The methods that are responsible for producing single lines

Appearing next is the method section that calls side three times. At the end, the method main appears and calls line, section, line, section, and line in this order.

```
13      // the middle block between the horizontal lines
14      public static void section()
15      {
16         side(); // section 1
17         side(); // section 2
18         side(); // section 3
19      }
20      // the main
21      public static void main( String[] args )
22      {
23         line();
24         section(); // top section
25         line();
26         section(); // bottom section
27         line();
28      }
29   }
```

Listing 4.8 A new version of the quadrant generation program that uses method calls (part 2). The methods for printing the middle section and the method main

4.1.3 "Old MacDonald Had a Farm"

Suppose we are to write a code that produces on the screen the lyrics to a popular nursery rhyme "Old MacDonald Had A Farm". Each verse of the song introduces one new animal and then presents the sound that the animal makes as well as the sounds of all the other animals in the reverse order of introduction.

There are many variations of this rhyme, with regards to the number of animals and the order of appearance. Here is one version with four animals (a cow, a pig, a duck, and a horse) with no "repeats" from previous verses.

```
1    Old MacDonald had a farm
2    E-I-E-I-O
3    And on his farm he had a cow
4    E-I-E-I-O
5    With a moo moo here
6    And a moo moo there
7    Here a moo, there a moo
8    Everywhere a moo moo
```

```
 9  │ Old MacDonald had a farm
10  │ E-I-E-I-O
11  │
```

Listing 4.9 The lyrics to the rhyme "Old MacDonald Had A Farm" with four animals. Presented without repeats

```
12  │ Old MacDonald had a farm
13  │ E-I-E-I-O
14  │ And on his farm he had a pig
15  │ E-I-E-I-O
16  │ With a oink oink here
17  │ And a oink oink there
18  │ Here a oink, there a oink
19  │ Everywhere a oink oink
20  │ Old MacDonald had a farm
21  │ E-I-E-I-O
22  │
23  │ Old MacDonald had a farm
24  │ E-I-E-I-O
25  │ And on his farm he had a duck
26  │ E-I-E-I-O
27  │ With a quack quack here
28  │ And a quack quack there
29  │ Here a quack, there a quack
30  │ Everywhere a quack quack
31  │ Old MacDonald had a farm
32  │ E-I-E-I-O
33  │
34  │ Old MacDonald had a farm
35  │ E-I-E-I-O
36  │ And on his farm he had a horse
37  │ E-I-E-I-O
38  │ With a neigh neigh here
39  │ And a neigh neigh there
40  │ Here a neigh, there a neigh
41  │ Everywhere a neigh neigh
42  │ Old MacDonald had a farm
43  │ E-I-E-I-O
44  │
```

Listing 4.10 The lyrics to the rhyme "Old MacDonald Had A Farm" with four animals. Presented without repeats (cont'd)

With the repeats from previous verses, the rhyme looks like:

```
 1  │ Old MacDonald had a farm
 2  │ E-I-E-I-O
 3  │ And on his farm he had a cow
 4  │ E-I-E-I-O
 5  │ With a moo moo here
 6  │ And a moo moo there
 7  │ Here a moo, there a moo
 8  │ Everywhere a moo moo
 9  │ Old MacDonald had a farm
10  │ E-I-E-I-O
11  │
12  │ Old MacDonald had a farm
13  │ E-I-E-I-O
14  │ And on his farm he had a pig
15  │ E-I-E-I-O
```

Listing 4.11 The lyrics to the rhyme "Old MacDonald Had A Farm" with four animals (part 1)

```
16  With a oink oink here
17  And a oink oink there
18  Here a oink, there a oink
19  Everywhere a oink oink
20  With a moo moo here
21  And a moo moo there
22  Here a moo, there a moo
23  Everywhere a moo moo
24  Old MacDonald had a farm
25  E-I-E-I-O
26
27  Old MacDonald had a farm
28  E-I-E-I-O
29  And on his farm he had a duck
30  E-I-E-I-O
31  With a quack quack here
32  And a quack quack there
33  Here a quack, there a quack
34  Everywhere a quack quack
35  With a oink oink here
36  And a oink oink there
37  Here a oink, there a oink
38  Everywhere a oink oink
39  With a moo moo here
40  And a moo moo there
41  Here a moo, there a moo
42  Everywhere a moo moo
43  Old MacDonald had a farm
44  E-I-E-I-O
45
46  Old MacDonald had a farm
47  E-I-E-I-O
48  And on his farm he had a horse
49  E-I-E-I-O
50  With a neigh neigh here
51  And a neigh neigh there
52  Here a neigh, there a neigh
53  Everywhere a neigh neigh
54  With a quack quack here
55  And a quack quack there
56  Here a quack, there a quack
57  Everywhere a quack quack
58  With a oink oink here
59  And a oink oink there
60  Here a oink, there a oink
61  Everywhere a oink oink
62  With a moo moo here
63  And a moo moo there
64  Here a moo, there a moo
65  Everywhere a moo moo
66  Old MacDonald had a farm
67  E-I-E-I-O
68
```

Listing 4.12 The lyrics to the rhyme "Old MacDonald Had A Farm" with four animals (part 2)

The structure of these verses is simple. Each verse consists of four parts:

part number	the lines	characteristic
1	"Old MacDonald ... -O"	common among all the verses
2	"And ... had a XXX ... -O"	unique to each verse
3	"With a YYY ... Everywhere a YYY"	cumulative
4	"Old MacDonald ... -O"	the first block, then one empty line

Based upon this observation, we design the following code:

```
1   public class OldMacDonaldDecomposed
2   {
3     // start and end of each verse
4     public static void macDonald()
5     {
6       System.out.println( "Old MacDonald had a farm" );
7       System.out.println( "E-I-E-I-O" );
8     }
9     // possession of a cow
10    public static void cowPossession()
11    {
12      System.out.println( "And on his farm he had a cow" );
13      System.out.println( "E-I-E-I-O" );
14    }
15    // possession of a pig
16    public static void pigPossession()
17    {
18      System.out.println( "And on his farm he had a pig" );
19      System.out.println( "E-I-E-I-O" );
20    }
21    // possession of a duck
22    public static void duckPossession()
23    {
24      System.out.println( "And on his farm he had a duck" );
25      System.out.println( "E-I-E-I-O" );
26    }
27    // possession of a horse
28    public static void horsePossession()
29    {
30      System.out.println( "And on his farm he had a horse" );
31      System.out.println( "E-I-E-I-O" );
32    }
```

Listing 4.13 A program that print the lyrics to "Old MacDonald Had A Farm" using decomposition (part 1). The method that produces the opening and ending lines of the verses and the methods for producing the lines about the animals

```
33    // the sound of a cow
34    public static void cowSound()
35    {
36      System.out.println( "With a moo moo here" );
37      System.out.println( "And a moo moo there" );
38      System.out.println( "Here a moo, there a moo" );
39      System.out.println( "Everywhere a moo moo" );
40    }
41    // the sound of a pig
42    public static void pigSound()
43    {
44      System.out.println( "With an oink oink here" );
45      System.out.println( "And an oink oink there" );
46      System.out.println( "Here an oink, there an oink" );
47      System.out.println( "Everywhere an oink oink" );
48    }
49    // the sound of a duck
50    public static void duckSound()
51    {
52      System.out.println( "With a quack quack here" );
53      System.out.println( "And a quack quack there" );
54      System.out.println( "Here a quack, there a quack" );
55      System.out.println( "Everywhere a quack quack" );
56    }
57    // the sound of a horse
58    public static void horseSound()
59    {
60      System.out.println( "With a neigh neigh here" );
61      System.out.println( "And a neigh neigh there" );
62      System.out.println( "Here a neigh, there a neigh" );
63      System.out.println( "Everywhere a neigh neigh" );
64    }
```

Listing 4.14 A program that print the lyrics to "Old MacDonald Had A Farm" using decomposition (part 2). The methods for printing the lines that introduce the sounds that the animals make

```
65    // the cow verse
66    public static void cowVerse()
67    {
68      macDonald();
69      cowPossession();
70      cowSound();
71      macDonald();
72    }
73    // the pig verse
74    public static void pigVerse()
75    {
76      macDonald();
77      pigPossession();
78      pigSound();
79      cowSound();
80      macDonald();
81    }
82    // the duck verse
83    public static void duckVerse()
84    {
85      macDonald();
86      duckPossession();
87      duckSound();
88      pigSound();
89      cowSound();
90      macDonald();
91    }
92    // the horse verse
93    public static void horseVerse()
94    {
95      macDonald();
96      horsePossession();
97      horseSound();
98      duckSound();
99      pigSound();
100     cowSound();
101     macDonald();
102   }
103   // main
104   public static void main( String[] args )
105   {
106     cowVerse();
107     System.out.println();
108     pigVerse();
109     System.out.println();
110     duckVerse();
111     System.out.println();
112     horseVerse();
113   }
114 }
```

Listing 4.15 A program that produces the lyrics to the rhyme "Old MacDonald Had A Farm" (part 3). The methods that build individual verses and the method main

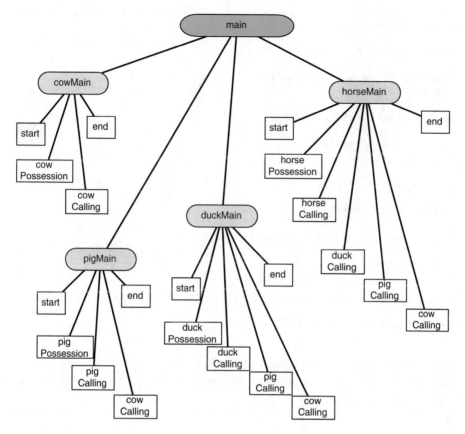

Fig. 4.4 The dependency among methods in OldMacDonaldDecomposed.java

Figure 4.4 presents the dependencies among the methods.

4.1.4 A General Strategy for Procedural Decomposition

While procedural decomposition helps better understand the code and makes future revisions easier, it does not necessarily reduce the length of the source code because each additional method has its own header and encompassing curly brackets.

In the next chapter, Chap. 5, we will study methods that take parameters and/or return a value. By combining procedural decomposition and the use of multiple source code files, we will be able to write a program divided into reasonably small units that are all easy to understand.

Since each method appearing in a source code can call each method appearing in the same source code, it is possible to create a circle of method calls.

Suppose we have the program:

```
1   public class Parts123
2   {
3     public static void partOne()
4     {
5       System.out.println( "One" );
6       partTwo();
7     }
8     public static void partTwo()
9     {
10      System.out.println( "Two" );
11      partThree();
12    }
13    public static void partThree()
14    {
15      System.out.println( "Three" );
16    }
17    public static void main( String[] args )
18    {
19      partOne();
20    }
21  }
```

Listing 4.16 A program with methods that print 1, 2, and 3

The action of the entire code is simple: main calls partOne, partOne calls partTwo, and partTwo calls partThree. This produces the output of "One", "Two", and "Three". The execution of the program produces the output:

```
1   One
2   Two
3   Three
```

By making a slight change to the code we can produce a bizarre effect.

```
1   public class InfiniteCalls
2   {
3     public static void partOne()
4     {
5       System.out.println( "One" );
6       partTwo();
7     }
8     public static void partTwo()
9     {
10      System.out.println( "Two" );
11      partThree();
12    }
```

Listing 4.17 A program that produces a bizarre effect (part 1)

```
13    public static void partThree()
14    {
15       System.out.println( "Three" );
16       partOne();
17    }
18    public static void main( String[] args )
19    {
20       partOne();
21    }
22 }
```

Listing 4.18 A program that produces a bizarre effect (part 2)

The code produces the following:

```
1  % javac InfiniteCalls.java
2  % java InfiniteCalls
3  One
4  Two
5  Three
6  ...
7  ...
8  Exception in thread "main" java.lang.StackOverflowError
9     at sun.nio.cs.UTF_8$Encoder.encodeLoop(UTF_8.java:691)
10    at java.nio.charset.CharsetEncoder.encode(CharsetEncoder.java:579)
11    at sun.nio.cs.StreamEncoder.implWrite(StreamEncoder.java:271)
12    at sun.nio.cs.StreamEncoder.write(StreamEncoder.java:125)
13    at java.io.OutputStreamWriter.write(OutputStreamWriter.java:207)
14    at java.io.BufferedWriter.flushBuffer(BufferedWriter.java:129)
15    at java.io.PrintStream.write(PrintStream.java:526)
16    at java.io.PrintStream.print(PrintStream.java:669)
17    at java.io.PrintStream.println(PrintStream.java:806)
18    at InfiniteCalls.partOne(InfiniteCalls.java:3)
19    at InfiniteCalls.partThree(InfiniteCalls.java:12)
20    at InfiniteCalls.partTwo(InfiniteCalls.java:8)
21    at InfiniteCalls.partOne(InfiniteCalls.java:4)
22 ...
23    at InfiniteCalls.partThree(InfiniteCalls.java:12)
24    at InfiniteCalls.partTwo(InfiniteCalls.java:8)
25    at InfiniteCalls.partOne(InfiniteCalls.java:4)
26 %
```

The actual output of the code is much longer. The ... signifies the visual cut made to the output. The import thing to notice is the line

```
Exception in thread "main" java.lang.StackOverflowError
```

The error message states that the method calls have used up all the memory space available for JVM to run, so JVM had to abort the execution of the code. The direct cause of this termination is due to the method call structure from Fig. 4.5. You can see that there is a loop going from one to three. This loop repeats over and over again, which results in the exhaustion of the memory space. In general, we call a loop structure that makes the program run forever an **infinite loop**. Thus, we say that the code InfiniteClass.java has an infinite loop.

The word "Exception" appearing in the error message is a word that refers to a **run-time error**.

Fig. 4.5 The dependency among methods in the two source code. Left panel: the original code. Right panel: the modified code

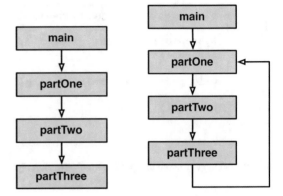

4.2   Using Multiple Program Files

We extend the idea of extracting components from a method to create another method, and write multiple classes and use methods from one in another Java class.

The benefits of reusing existing source codes are twofold. First, the use of recycling code from another class saves the coder from having to write the same code from scratch again. Second, sharing the code among applications may make it easier to revise the code.

Consider the following class `Signature`.

```
1   public class Signature
2   {
3     public static void sign()
4     {
5       System.out.println();
6       System.out.println(
7         "+-----------------------------------------+" );
8       System.out.println(
9         "| THIS PROGRAM IS CODED BY MITSU OGIHARA  |" );
10      System.out.println(
11        "+-----------------------------------------+" );
12    }
13  }
```

Listing 4.19 A program that produces a signature

`Signature.java` has one method, `sign`, which produces four lines of output as follows:

```
1
2   +-----------------------------------------+
3   | THIS PROGRAM IS CODED BY MITSU OGIHARA  |
4   +-----------------------------------------+
```

There is no `main` method in this class, so we cannot execute the code by itself. By attaching the class name `Signature` and a period before the method name, we can call this method from outside:

                                        `Signature.sign();`

Knowing this capability we can write a new version of `HelloWorld`, which produces the signature lines along with the `"Hello, World!"` message.

```
1  public class HelloWorldCall
2  {
3    public static void main( String[] args )
4    {
5      System.out.println( "Hello, World!" );
6      Signature.sign();
7    }
8  }
```

Listing 4.20 A HelloWorld program that print a signature at the end

To run the above code, you need both HelloWorldCall and Signature. Since the former used the latter, one can compile the latter first and then compile the former. Alternatively, we may simply compile both at the same time:

javac Signature.java HelloWorldCall.java

Summary

- A class can have any number of methods in it.
- Methods are defined at depth 1 of the class in which they appear.
- Methods can appear in any order in a class.
- The process of creating a method that is in charge of performing a certain part of the actions another method performs is called procedural decomposition.
- The benefits of procedural decomposition include better readability and easier code modification.
- It is possible to write multiple classes with methods making calls across classes. When using multiple program files, the files can be compiled either individually or all at once.

Exercises

1. **Number manipulation** Suppose we are writing a program PlayWithNumbersDecomposed, in which we have two tasks:
   (a) The program receive two integers, a and b, from the user and then prints a + b, a - b, a * b, a / b, and a % b (we anticipate that the user will not enter 0 for the second number).
   (b) The program receives three integers, a, b, and c, from the user and then prints the result of (a - b) / c for each of the six possible permutations among the three numbers.
   Write the code for this program so that it has two separate methods that handle the two tasks. The method main calls the two methods one after the other. Each non-main method instantiates its own Scanner object with System.in. Here is an example of how the program may interact with the user.

```
1    Enter two integers: 1000435 345
2    a + b is equal to 1000780
3    a - b is equal to 1000090
4    a * b is equal to 345150075
5    a / b is equal to 2899
6    a % b is equal to 280
7    Enter three integers: 34325 79 -40
8    (a - b)/c is equal to -856
9    (a - c)/b is equal to 435
10   (b - c)/a is equal to 0
11   (b - a)/c is equal to 856
12   (c - a)/b is equal to -435
13   (c - b)/a is equal to 0
```

2. **Shape Presentation**   Suppose we are writing a program `HouseShape` that produces the following output on the screen:

```
1             /\
2            /  \
3           /    \
4          /  +--+  \
5         /   |  |   \
6        /    +--+    \
7       -+---------+-
8        |         |
9        |   +--+   |
10       |   |  |   |
11       |   +--+   |
12       |         |
13      -+---------+-
14    This is my house!
```

The action of the program can be divided into three parts:
- printing the roof (including the bottom of the roof),
- printing the body of the house, and
- printing the message.

Write a program with three methods (in addition to `main`) which correspond to the above three tasks, where the method `main` simply calls the three methods in order.

3. **Forward slashes**   Previously we wrote a program that produced on the screen:

```
1     / / / / / / / / / /
2      / / / / / / / / / /
3     / / / / / / / / / /
4      / / / / / / / / / /
5     / / / / / / / / / /
6      / / / / / / / / / /
7     / / / / / / / / / /
8      / / / / / / / / / /
9     / / / / / / / / / /
10     / / / / / / / / / /
```

This output consists of five repetitions of the pattern of the first two lines. Write an alternate version, `SlashesWithMethodCalls`, that performs this task with five identical method calls (in the method `main`) to a method, `twoLines`. The method `twoLines` produces the consecutive pair of two lines.

Programming Projects

4. **This Old Man**   "This Old Man" is a popular children rhyme that consists of ten verses. All the verses are identical, except for the two words, which we present below as XXX and YYY, where XXX goes from one to ten

```
1   This old man, he played XXX,
2   He played knick-knack on his YYY;
3   With a knick-knack paddywhack,
4   Give the dog a bone,
5   This old man came rolling home
```

Here is the list of ten words for YYY:

drum, shoe, knee, door, hive, sticks, heaven, gate, spine, again

We can decompose the common parts of the verses into:

(a) The first line excluding XXX,. In other words, it is "This old man, he played "
(b) The second line excluding YYY;. In other words, it is "He played knick-knack on his "
(c) The third to fifth lines plus one empty line.

Let first, second, and rest be methods that print the three parts, where first and second use System.out.print and rest uses System.out.println. Using this decomposition, write a program that prints the first three verses of the rhyme.

5. **Die face printing**   Consider printing the six sides of a die using in a 5 × 5 grid as follows:

```
+---+
|   |
| o |
|   |
+---+

+---+
|   |
|o o|
|   |
+---+

+---+
|  o|
| o |
|o  |
+---+

+---+
|o o|
|   |
|o o|
+---+
```

```
+---+
|o  o|
|  o |
|o  o|
+---+

+---+
|o  o|
|o  o|
|o  o|
+---+
```

Write a program named `Dice` that prints the six faces using a method call to print each line of the faces.

6. **Digits in** 5×5 **rectangles**   Consider writing a program that prints digits $0, \ldots, 9$ in 5×5 rectangles using the following design: Here is the code:

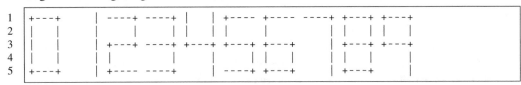

To save space, the digits are placed side by side, but in the actual code, the digits will be stuck on top of each other. There are only six patterns appearing in the digits:

```
1  +---+
2  +---
3     ---+
4  |    |
5  |
6       |
```

We can give these six patterns unique pattern names and write six methods that print the individual six patterns. With the addition of one more method that prints one empty line, the seven methods can be used as the building blocks for digit printing. Write a program named `Digits` that accomplishes this task. The program should have the seven building blocks as methods, ten methods that print the ten digits with one blank line as their sixth lines, and the method `main` that calls the ten methods one after another.

7. **A Pop song**   Select one of the No. 1 hits by *The Beatles* (e.g., "I Want To Hold Your Hand") and write a program that prints the lyrics to the song line by line. A popular song lyrics search engine can be used to find the lyrics. Consider the following points:

   - If a line is repeated more than once, define a method for printing that line alone.
   - If a series of lines are repeated more than once, find a maximally long stretch for that series and define a method for printing that series.
   - It is natural to define a method for each verse or bridge (a verse and a bridge are the units that are presented with no blank lines in them).

Passing Values to and from Methods

5

5.1 Passing Values to Methods

5.1.1 Methods That Work with Parameters

In this chapter, we will advance the concept of method decomposition and learn how to exchange information with methods.

Recall the rhyme "Old MacDonald Had a Farm" that we examined in Chap. 4. The verses of the song became longer and longer as each new verse introduced one new animal. The contents of the verses are repetitive because they have the same principal structures. We now consider a new program in which the song introduces only three animals: a cow, a pig, and a dog in this order. With slight changes in capitalization and punctuation, our goal is to generate this output:

```
 1  Old MacDonald had a farm, E-I-E-I-O
 2  And on his farm he had a cow, E-I-E-I-O
 3  With a Moo, Moo here
 4  And a Moo, Moo there
 5  Here a Moo, there a Moo
 6  Everywhere a Moo, Moo
 7  Old MacDonald had a farm, E-I-E-I-O
 8
 9  Old MacDonald had a farm, E-I-E-I-O
10  And on his farm he had a pig, E-I-E-I-O
11  With an Oink, Oink here
12  And an Oink, Oink there
13  Here an Oink, there an Oink
14  Everywhere an Oink, Oink
15  With a Moo, Moo here
16  And a Moo, Moo there
17  Here a Moo, there a Moo
18  Everywhere a Moo, Moo
19  Old MacDonald had a farm, E-I-E-I-O
20
```

Listing 5.1 The expected output our new "Old MacDonald Had A Farm" program (part 1)

© Springer Nature Switzerland AG 2018
M. Ogihara, *Fundamentals of Java Programming*,
https://doi.org/10.1007/978-3-319-89491-1_5

```
21  Old MacDonald had a farm, E-I-E-I-O
22  And on his farm he had a dog, E-I-E-I-O
23  With a Bow, Wow here
24  And a Bow, Wow there
25  Here a Bow, there a Bow
26  Everywhere a Bow, Wow
27  With an Oink, Oink here
28  And an Oink, Oink there
29  Here an Oink, there an Oink
30  Everywhere an Oink, Oink
31  With a Moo, Moo here
32  And a Moo, Moo there
33  Here a Moo, there a Moo
34  Everywhere a Moo, Moo
35  Old MacDonald had a farm, E-I-E-I-O
```

Listing 5.2 The expected output our new "Old MacDonald Had A Farm" program (part 2)

Look at the lines that introduce the animal names:

```
1  And on his farm he had a cow, E-I-E-I-O
2  ...
3  And on his farm he had a pig, E-I-E-I-O
4  ...
5  And on his farm he had a dog, E-I-E-I-O
```

The three lines appear in all the verses with their unique animal names, `"a cow"`, `"a pig"`, and `"a dog"`. By hiding the variable part with . . ., the lines are:

```
And on his farm he had ..., E-I-E-I-O
```

We thus construct a method that takes the . . . and replaces it with the input when printing the line. Suppose `name` is a `String` variable whose value is one of the three possible values and, for what it is worth, any `String`. We can be substitute the line with:

```
System.out.println( "And on his farm he had " + name
      + ", E-I-E-I-O" );
```

Based upon what we have learned so far, we know that this statement accomplishes the required task. We can turn this into a method by the name of "had," since it is about an animal.

```
1  public static void had()
2  {
3    System.out.println( "And on his farm he had " + name
4        + ", E-I-E-I-O" );
5  }
```

Note that the declaration of `name` is missing in the code for `had`. Thus, for this code to function correctly, the declaration must appear in the method or appear outside the method as the declaration of a global variable. To make the declaration appear in the method, one can think of defining it as:

```
1  public static void had()
2  {
3    String name;
4    System.out.println( "And on his farm he had " + name
5        + ", E-I-E-I-O" );
6  }
```

Unfortunately, this does not allow the code outside the method to assign a value to name. The correct way to do so, according to the Java syntax, is to place it inside the parentheses of the method header, as shown next:

```
1    public static void had( String name )
2    {
3       System.out.println( "And on his farm he had " + name
4           + ", E-I-E-I-O" );
5    }
```

We call the variables appearing in the parentheses of a method declaration **parameters**, or **formal parameters**, to be more precise.

The way we call this method is the same as the way we call the print methods of System.out, e.g.,

```
1    ...
2    public static void main( String[] args )
3    {
4       had( "a cow" );
5       ...
6       String name = "a pig";
7       had( name );
8       ...
9    }
10   public static void had( String name )
11   {
12      System.out.println( "And on his farm he had " + name
13          + ", E-I-E-I-O" );
14   }
```

The first method call is had("a cow"). Before executing this call, JVM stores the value of the String literal "a cow" to the method had. To pass the value, JVM stores the value in the formal parameter name of the method had.

The second method call is had(name). This time, JVM stores the value of the variable name appearing in the main method, which is "a pig", in the formal parameter name of the method had.

As opposed to the term formal parameter, we call the variables that the JVM transfers to the formal parameters of a method call **actual parameters**.

```
1    ...
2    public static void main( String[] args )
3    {
4       had( "a cow" );
5       ...
6       String name = "a pig";
7       had( name );
8       ...
9    }
10   public static void had( String name )
11   {
12      System.out.println( "And on his farm he had " + name
13          + ", E-I-E-I-O" );
14   }
```

Note that the `name` appearing in the second method call is different from the `name` appearing in the method itself due to their scopes. The range of the first `name` starts at the { immediately after the `main` declaration and ends at the } before the `had` declaration. The range of the second `name` starts at the { immediately after the `had` declaration and ends at the last }. Therefore, we can safely change the names stored in the variables without causing any problems.

We apply a similar decomposition to the section that prints the calling of the animals. In this section, the output for the pig is:

```
1   With an Oink, Oink here
2   And an Oink, Oink there
3   Here an Oink, there an Oink
4   Everywhere an Oink, Oink
```

and the output for the dog is:

```
1   With a Bow, Wow here
2   And a Bow, Wow there
3   Here a Bow, there a Bow
4   Everywhere a Bow, Wow
```

We can identify the following pattern:

```
1   With xxx, yyy here
2   And xxx, yyy there
3   Here xxx, there xxx
4   Everywhere xxx, yyy
```

where xxx and yyy are respectively `"an Oink"` and `"Oink"` for the pig and respectively `"a Bow"` and `"Wow"` for the dog. (Naturally, we wish we could dispose of the article appearing in each xxx, but unfortunately that appears impossible, since the article is `"an"` for the pig and `"a"` for the others.) The pattern is encode in a method named `with` as follows:

```
1   public static void with( String xxx, String yyy )
2   {
3      System.out.println( "With " + xxx + ", " + yyy + " here" );
4      System.out.println( "And " + xxx + ", " + yyy + " there" );
5      System.out.println( "Here " + xxx + ", there " + xxx );
6      System.out.println( "Everywhere " + xxx + ", " + yyy );
7   }
```

Unlike `had`, which takes just one formal parameter, the method `with` has two formal parameters. Both are `String` data. When there is more than one formula parameter, we use a comma to separate them. For variable declaration, we can combine multiple declarations of the same type by connecting the variable names with a comma inserted between two variable names. Such abbreviations are not permissible in formal parameter specifications; each parameter must have its own type specification.

In general, the parameter part of a method declaration is a list of parameter types and parameter names.

```
( TYPE_1 NAME_1, ..., TYPE_k NAME_k )
```

If there is no parameter that the method takes, this part is empty; if there is only one parameter, there will be no comma, since the number of commas is one fewer than the number of parameters. We call the sequence of the types

```
[ TYPE_1, ..., TYPE_k ]
```

the **parameter type signature** of the method. The entire code appears next, shown in two parts:

```
 1   public class OldMacDonaldPassing
 2   {
 3       //--  the cow verse
 4       public static void cowVerse()
 5       {
 6           macDonald();
 7           had( "a cow" );
 8           with( "a Moo", "Moo" );
 9           macDonald();
10       }
11       //--  the pig verse
12       public static void pigVerse()
13       {
14           macDonald();
15           had( "a pig" );
16           with( "an Oink", "Oink" );
17           with( "a Moo", "Moo" );
18           macDonald();
19       }
20       //--  the dog verse
21       public static void dogVerse()
22       {
23           macDonald();
24           had( "a dog" );
25           with( "a Bow", "Wow" );
26           with( "an Oink", "Oink" );
27           with( "a Moo", "Moo" );
28           macDonald();
29       }
30       //--  start and end of each verse
31       public static void macDonald()
32       {
33           System.out.println( "Old MacDonald had a farm, E-I-E-I-O" );
34       }
```

Listing 5.3 A source code for the parameterized version of the "Old MacDonald" program (part 1)

```
35        //--   the "Had" line
36     public static void had( String name )
37     {
38        System.out.println( "And on his farm he had " + name
39            + ", E-I-E-I-O" );
40     }
41        //--   the "With a" lines
42     public static void with( String xxx, String yyy )
43     {
44        System.out.println( "With " + xxx + ", " + yyy + " here" );
45        System.out.println( "And " + xxx + ", " + yyy + " there" );
46        System.out.println( "Here " + xxx + ", there " + xxx );
47        System.out.println( "Everywhere " + xxx + ", " + yyy );
48     }
49        //--   main
50     public static void main( String[] args )
51     {
52        cowVerse();
53        System.out.println();
54        pigVerse();
55        System.out.println();
56        dogVerse();
57     }
58  }
```

Listing 5.4 A source code for the parameterized version of the "Old MacDonald" program (part 2)

Note that, in this version, `main` appears as the very first method. As mentioned earlier, methods are free to call others regardless of their order of appearance in the source code.

The formal parameters of a method are local variables. The method can use them in the computation by making modifications to them. If they are primitive data, the values of the corresponding actual parameters are copied to the formal parameters. This means that the modifications that occur to the formal parameters in the method do not reflect on the value of the actual parameters. In contrast, if they are object data, the actual parameters inform the method the locations of the object data in the computer memories. We call the locational information the **reference**. If the method assigns a value to the formal parameter, the reference of the formal parameter changes, but the reference of the actual parameter does not and the method loses the reference to the original data. From that point on, any actions taken on the formal parameter will have no effect on the actual parameter. If the method executes an instance method on the formal parameter without assigning a new value, and that method modifies the status/contents of the object data, the actual parameter will be affected.

To see how this mechanism works, consider the following code. The two assignments in `test` have no effect on `word` or `radius` in `main`. The `t.next()`, on the other hand, because `t` and `textScanner` are referring to the same `Scanner` object, has the effect of advancing the scanning position. This means that, when `main` executes `textScanner.next()`, the method `next` returns the second token of `"Madman across the water!"`, across.

```
1    import java.util.*;
2    public class Levon
3    {
4      public static void main( String[] args )
5      {
6        String word = "Tiny Dancer";
7        double radius = 19.7;
8        Scanner textScanner = new Scanner( "Madman across the water!" );
9        test( word, textScanner, radius );
10       System.out.println( radius );
11       System.out.println( word );
12       System.out.println( textScanner.next() );
13     }
14     public static void test( String w, Scanner t, double r )
15     {
16       w = "Levon";
17       r = 4.5;
18       System.out.println( t.next() );
19     }
20   }
```

Listing 5.5 A code that demonstrates call-by-reference

Executing the code produces the following result:

```
Madman
19
Tiny Dancer
across
```

Figure 5.1 explains this effect. w, r, and t appearing in the lower part of the picture are the formal parameters of test. word, radius, and textScanner appearing in the higher part of the picture are the variables of main. The solid arrows originating from them represent the values they have at the end of test. The dashed arrows originating from these variables represent the values they used to have. The start positions for obtaining the next tokens are shown with big arrows. At the start of test, w and r have the same values as word and radius. When the assignments to w and r are made in test, the values of w and r change, but the values of word and radius are preserved. The effect of t.next is different. While t and textScanner still have the Scanner object as their values, the call t.next changes the position of the next available token.

We call the mechanism in which Java handles parameter passing **call by reference**.

5.1.2   Method Overloading

Java permits multiple methods having the same names appear in the same code unit as long as their parameter type signatures are different. We call this **method overloading**.

The following code example demonstrates method overloading. The program defines seven methods by the name of response. The first six of the seven methods take one parameter each: a String, a boolean, a int, a byte, a double, and a float. The last of the seven takes no parameter. These methods simply print on the screen what the parameter type is, as well as the value of its parameter.

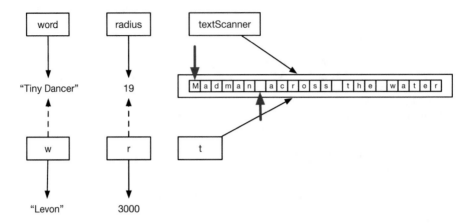

Fig. 5.1 The call-by-reference concept. On the top side, the boxes are actual parameters

```
1
2     /* ****************************************
3      * A toy example of method overloading
4      * **************************************** */
5
6    public class ResponseOverload
7    {
8      /* *****************
9       * the String version
10      * *************** */
11     public static void response( String data )
12     {
13        System.out.println( "The data is a String \"" + data + "\"." );
14     }
15
16      /* *****************
17       * the boolean version
18       * *************** */
19     public static void response( boolean data )
20     {
21        System.out.println( "The data is a boolean " + data + "." );
22     }
23
24      /* *****************
25       * the int version
26       * *************** */
27     public static void response( int data )
28     {
29        System.out.println( "The data is an int " + data + "." );
30     }
31
32      /* *****************
```

Listing 5.6 A program that demonstrates the use of method overloading (part 1)

```
33       * the byte version
34       * ************** */
35      public static void response( byte data )
36      {
37        System.out.println( "The data is a byte " + data + "." );
38      }
39
40      /* ******************
41       * the float version
42       * ************** */
43      public static void response( float data )
44      {
45        System.out.println( "The data is a float " + data + "." );
46      }
47
48      /* *******************
49       * the double version
50       * ************** */
51      public static void response( double data )
52      {
53        System.out.println( "The data is a double " + data + "." );
54      }
55
56      /* ******************
57       * the empty version
58       * ************** */
59      public static void response()
60      {
61        System.out.println( "There is no data." );
62      }
63
64      /* ******************
65       * the main method
66       * ************** */
67      public static void main( String[] args )
68      {
69        String myString = "hello";
70        boolean myBoolean = false;
71        int myInteger = 10;
72        byte myByte = 0x7f;
73        double myDouble = -98.5;
74        float myFloat = 99.9F;
75
76        response( myString );
77        response( myBoolean );
78        response( myInteger );
79        response( myByte );
80        response( myDouble );
81        response( myFloat );
82        response();
83      }
84  }
```

Listing 5.7 A program that demonstrates the use of method overloading (part 2)

The method `main` appearing at the end of the source code declares variables of six different types, assigns values to them, and then makes seven calls. Six out of the seven take one variable each. The one appearing at the end takes none.

The Java compiler assigns these calls to their respective types. Because each version announces itself, it is possible to tell which one of the seven is called by looking at the output generated. Note that if the letter F that appears at the end of the assignment to `myFloat`, this indicates that the literal is a `float`.

Here is the result of executing the code:

```
1   The data is a String "hello".
2   The data is a boolean false.
3   The data is an int 10.
4   The data is a byte 127.
5   The data is a double -98.5.
6   The data is a float 99.9.
7   There is no data.
```

Notice that the output for `myByte` is in decimals, although the value specified is hexadecimal.

If the type signature of a method call does not match the type signature of any method having the same name, a compiler checks if the data types of the actual parameter can be interpreted as different types so that the interpreted type signature has a match. The interpretation is applied to number types, by treating a whole number type as a floating point number type and/or by treating a number type as a larger number type. If no match can be found even with the parameter type interpretation, the compiler produces a syntax error.

The next code is a new version of `ResponseOverload`. The number of type signatures for `response` has been reduced from seven to just two. The types are `int` and `double`.

```
1
2     /* *****************************************
3      * A toy example of method overloading
4      * ***************************************** */
5
6   public class ResponseOverloadLimited
7   {
8     /* ******************
9      * the int version
10     * **************** */
11    public static void response( int data )
12    {
13       System.out.println( "The data is an int " + data + "." );
14    }
15
16    /* ******************
17     * the double version
18     * **************** */
19    public static void response( double data )
20    {
21       System.out.println( "The data is a double " + data + "." );
22    }
23
```

Listing 5.8 A program with method overloading in which available methods are fewer than the method call types (part 1)

```
24    /* ******************
25     * the main method
26     * *************** */
27    public static void main( String[] args )
28    {
29        int myInteger = 10;
30        byte myByte = 0x7f;
31        double myDouble = -98.5;
32        float myFloat = 99.9F;
33
34        response( myInteger );
35        response( myByte );
36        response( myDouble );
37        response( myFloat );
38    }
39 }
```

Listing 5.9 A program with method overloading in which available methods are fewer than the method call types (part 2)

For myByte, the compiler uses the int version as its surrogate, and for myFloat, the compiler uses the double version as its surrogate. These substitutions come naturally, since both int and byte are for whole numbers with more bits in int, and both double and float are for floating point numbers with more bits in double. Here is the result of executing the program.

```
1   The data is an int 10.
2   The data is an int 127.
3   The data is a double -98.5.
4   The data is a double 99.9.
```

If we take this further and eliminate the int version, then double will be used for all number types.

5.2   Receiving a Value from a Method

It is possible to receive a value from a method as the outcome of its calculation. A method returns a value of a specific data type (and that specific data type must appear in the method declaration). All the methods we have seen so far had void as the return type. By changing it to something else, we can write a declaration with a real return type.

```
ATTRIBUTES RETURN_TYPE METHOD_NAME( PARAMETERS )
```

For example, we can define a method named bmiCalculate that calculates the BMI value of a person (given the weight value and the height value, where the return type is double) as follows:

```
public static double bmiCalculate( double weight, double height )
```

Here is another example. Suppose we want to write a method calculateSum that computes the sum of integers from 1 to n for an integer n. We can declare the method as follows:

```
public static int calculateSum( int n )
```

When a method that returns a value finishes its computation, the program execution goes back to the location where the call took place, carrying the return value. Upon returning, JVM completes the statement in which the method call appears, using the value it is carrying back from the method. For example, in the case of calculateSum, if the method call appears in the form of:

```
int mySum = calculateSum( 10 );
```

and if the method returns some value (in this case 55 is the value we wish to receive), the end result is the same as:

```
int mySum = 55;
```

We can use the data that a method returns in an assignment. We can also use it as a formal parameter. If the data is an object type, we can directly apply a method for the type to the data that the method returns. Consider the following two hypothetical methods:

```
1    public static Scanner generateScanner( int inputData )
2    {
3      String phrase;
4      // some computation to determine the value of phrase
5      // from inputData
6      Scanner yourScanner = new Scanner( phrase );
7      return yourScanner;
8    }
9    public static String firstToken( int inputInt )
10   {
11     Scanner myScanner = generateScanner( inputInt );
12     String myToken = yourScanner.next();
13     return( myToken );
14   }
```

The statement return has the role of returning a value. The parentheses surrounding the data to be returned can be omitted.

The first method, generateScanner, determines the value of a String variable, phrase, based upon the value of the parameter inputData. The method then calls the constructor for a Scanner with the phrase as the parameter (i.e., new Scanner(phrase)). This call come back with a Scanner object. The method stores this Scanner object in yourScanner. The method concludes by returning yourScanner.

The second method, firstToken, calls the first method, generateScanner, with inputInt as the actual parameter (note that there is transfer of value from inputInt to inputData) and stores the Scanner that the first method returns in myScanner. Then, the method executes next on myScanner to obtain its first token and stores the token in the variable myToken. The method concludes by returning myToken.

We can simplify this code by disposing of the three variables, yourScanner, myScanner, and myToken, as follows:

```
1    public static Scanner generateScanner( int inputData )
2    {
3      String phrase;
4      // some computation
5      return new Scanner( phrase );
6    }
7    public static String firstToken( int inputData )
8    {
9      return generateScanner( inputData ).next();
10   }
```

In the first method, the `return` statement returns the `Scanner` object that the constructor generates. In the second method, the program executes the method `next` directly on the `Scanner` object that the first method returns.

Method calls can appear in another method call. If a method `methodA` takes some *k* parameters of types TYPE_1, ..., TYPE_k and methods METHOD_1, ..., METHOD_k return the same types of data respectively, and the value sequence to pass to these methods is SEQUENCE_1, ..., SEQUENCE_k, then:

```
1    TYPE_1 value_1 = method_1( SEQUENCE_1 );
2    ...
3    TYPE_k value_k = method_k( SEQUENCE_k );
4    methodA( value_1, ..., value_k );
```

can be substituted with:

```
methodA( method_1 ( SEQUENCE_1 ), ..., method_k( SEQUENCE_k ) );
```

Here is an illustration of how we may use this feature. In the previous code for computing BMI values, we used pounds for the weight unit and feet and inches for the height units.

```
1    import java.util.Scanner;
2    public class BMIInteractive
3    {
4      public static final double BMI_SCALE = 703.0;
5      public static final int FEET_TO_INCHES = 12;
6
7      public static double bmiFormula( double weight, double height )
8      {
9        return BMI_SCALE * weight / (height * height);
10     }
11
```

Listing 5.10 A program for computing the BMI values interactively. Reprise (part 1)

```
12    public static void oneInteraction ()
13    {
14      Scanner keyboard = new Scanner ( System.in );
15      System.out.print ( "Enter weight: " );
16      double weight = keyboard.nextDouble ();
17      System.out.print ( "Enter height in feet and inches: " );
18      double feet = keyboard.nextDouble ();
19      double inches = keyboard.nextDouble ();
20      double height = FEET_TO_INCHES * feet + inches;
21      double bmi = bmiFormula ( weight, height );
22      System.out.println ( "Your BMI is " + bmi + "." );
23    }
24    public static void main ( String[] args )
25    {
26      oneInteraction ();
27      oneInteraction ();
28    }
29  }
```

Listing 5.11 A program for computing the BMI values interactively. Reprise (part 2)

To compute the BMI value using these three values, we convert the feet and the inches to a single value named `height` using the formula (Line 20), and then use the method `bmiFormula` to obtain the BMI value (Line 21).

We can develop methods to conduct these calculations. One method, `combineFeetAndInches`, takes the feet and inches for `height` and returns its inch-only value as follows:

```
1    public static double combineFeetAndInches ( double feet, double inches )
2    {
3      return FEET_TO_INCHES * feet + inches;
4    }
```

The other method we introduce is a three-parameter version of `bmiFormula`. The method takes three values, the weight, the feet, and the inches. The method computes the inch-based representation of the height using `combineFeetAndInches` with `feet` and `inches` as the actual parameters. Then, the method calls the two-parameter version of `bmiFormula` to obtain the BMI, and returns the BMI. Since the inch-based representation of `height` is used nowhere else, we can dispose of the variable for storing the inch-based value, as follows:

```
1    public static double bmiFormula ( double weight, double feet,
2        double inches)
3    {
4      return bmiFormula ( weight, combineFeetAndInches ( feet, inches ) );
5    }
```

The return value of the method call to `combineFeetAndInches` is used as the second actual parameter of the call to `bmiFormula`.

The following is a version of the program with these new features. The output of the program is different from that of the previous, and the program states what the input values are. The first part of the code consists of the constants and the methods for computing the BMI values.

```
1   import java.util.Scanner;
2   public class BMIFeeding
3   {
4     public static final double BMI_SCALE = 703.0;
5     public static final int FEET_TO_INCHES = 12;
6
7     public static double bmiFormula( double weight, double height )
8     {
9       return BMI_SCALE * weight / (height * height);
10    }
11
12    public static double combineFeetAndInches( double feet, double inches )
13    {
14      return FEET_TO_INCHES * feet + inches;
15    }
16
17    public static double bmiFormula( double weight, double feet,
18        double inches)
19    {
20      return bmiFormula( weight, combineFeetAndInches( feet, inches ) );
21    }
22
```

Listing 5.12 A new version of the program for computing the BMI values for the input provided by the user (part 1)

The next part consists of the method for interacting with the user and the method `main`.

```
23    public static void oneInteraction()
24    {
25      Scanner keyboard = new Scanner( System.in );
26      System.out.print( "Enter weight: " );
27      double weight = keyboard.nextDouble();
28      System.out.print( "Enter height in feet and inches: " );
29      double feet = keyboard.nextDouble();
30      double inches = keyboard.nextDouble();
31      double bmi = bmiFormula( weight, feet, inches );
32      System.out.println( "Weight = " + weight + " pounds" );
33      System.out.println( "Height = " + feet + " feet and "
34          + inches + " inches" );
35      System.out.println( "BMI = " + bmi );
36    }
37    public static void main( String[] args )
38    {
39      oneInteraction();
40      oneInteraction();
41    }
42  }
```

Listing 5.13 A new version of the program for computing the BMI values for the input provided by the user (part 2)

Here is an execution example of the new program:

```
1   Enter weight: 170
2   Enter height in feet and inches: 5 7
3   Your BMI is 26.62285586990421.
4   Enter weight: 160
5   Enter height in feet and inches: 5 7
6   Your BMI is 25.056805524615726.
```

5.3   Class Math

5.3.1   Mathematical Functions in Java

In the very early days of computing, programmers had to write the code for mathematical functions from scratch (even fundamental ones, such as the square root and the logarithm). Fortunately, modern programming languages offer a plethora of pre-written mathematical functions allowing programmers to skip that tedious process.

In Java, the class Math provides mathematical functions. To use a mathematical function in Math, we attach a period and the name of the function to the class name, e.g., Math.sin. The class Math is available without writing import. Since all important mathematical functions are available under a single class and the web documentation of Java comes in classes, it is easy for a programmer who needs mathematical functions to explore the Java provision of the functions.[1]

There are two constants in Math.

- Math.PI is a double constant that provides the value of π.
- Math.E is a double constant that provides the value of the base of the natural logarithm.

Since these quantities are irrational, the values that the class Math provides are approximations.

Next, we present some of the methods in Math. The order of presentation is based on the number of formal parameters.

There is only one Math method that takes no parameters: Math.random(). The method Math.random() returns under a uniform distribution a random double value between 0 and 1. The value is strictly less than 1 and greater than or equal to 0. Since double has finite length, the number of values that Math.random may generate is finite.

---

[1]The link for the class Math is:
https://docs.oracle.com/javase/8/docs/api/java/lang/Math.html .

Table 5.1 One-parameter
functions in `Math`

Name	What it computes
`sin`	The sine of the parameter value (radian)
`cos`	The cosine of the parameter value (radian)
`tan`	The tangent of the parameter value (radian)
`asin`	The inverse of sine, return value in $[-\frac{\pi}{2}, \frac{\pi}{2}]$
`acos`	The inverse of sine, return value in $[0, \pi]$
`atan`	The inverse of sine, return value in $[-\frac{\pi}{2}, \frac{\pi}{2}]$
`sqrt`	The square root
`cbrt`	The cubic root
`log`	The natural logarithm
`log10`	The logarithm base 10
`signum`	The sign of the number, -1.0, 0.0, or $+1.0$
`exp`	The exponential function base the natural logarithm.
`ceil`	The smallest whole number that is $>=$ parameter
`floor`	The largest whole number $<=$ parameter
`round`	The rounded whole number, as an `int`
`abs`	The absolute value

Table 5.2 Two-parameter
functions in `Math`

`max`	The maximum of two numbers given as parameters
`min`	The minimum of two numbers given as parameters
`pow`	The first parameter raised to the power of the second

Table 5.1 presents selected methods in `Math` that take just one parameter. For all but two of the methods on the table, the return type is `double`. For `Math.round`, there are two versions. The return type of `Math.round` that takes a `double` parameter is `long`, and the return type of `Math.round` that takes a `float` parameter is `int`. For `Math.abs`, there are four versions. The types of their input parameters are `double`, `float`, `long`, and `int`. For each version of `Math.abs`, the return type is identical to the parameter type.

Table 5.2 presents some two-parameter methods of `Math`.

As in the case of `abs`, both `max` and `min` have four versions. The parameter types of the four versions are `double`, `float`, `long`, and `int`. They compute the maximum (respectively, minimum) of its two parameters.

Here is a code example that shows the use of the constants and the random number generator.

```
1   public class MathNoParameters
2   {
3     public static void main( String[] args )
4     {
5       System.out.println( "PI: " + Math.PI );
6       System.out.println( "E: " + Math.E );
7       System.out.println( "Random round 1: " + Math.random() );
8       System.out.println( "Random round 2: " + Math.random() );
9       System.out.println( "Random round 3: " + Math.random() );
10      System.out.println( "Random round 4: " + Math.random() );
11      System.out.println( "Random round 5: " + Math.random() );
12    }
13  }
```

Listing 5.14 A program that demonstrates the use of constants and the method `random` of the class `Math`

Running the code produces the following result:

```
1   Math.PI = 3.141592653589793
2   Math.E= 2.718281828459045
3   Round 1: Math.random() = 0.056618315818746656
4   Round 2: Math.random() = 0.30658632116385387
5   Round 3: Math.random() = 0.07808433189065977
6   Round 4: Math.random() = 0.27893273824439646
7   Round 5: Math.random() = 0.752651071169672
```

Another execution produces the following result:

```
1   Math.PI = 3.141592653589793
2   Math.E= 2.718281828459045
3   Round 1: Math.random() = 0.2509009548325596
4   Round 2: Math.random() = 0.2199297628318726
5   Round 3: Math.random() = 0.4874309775816027
6   Round 4: Math.random() = 0.830865085635181
7   Round 5: Math.random() = 0.8592438408895406
```

The value `Math.round` generates is random, so we can expect the results to be different each time.

Since the number that `Math.random` produces is between 0 and 1 (not including 1), by multiplying the result of `Math.random` with a positive integer b and then adding another integer a, a random real number between a and b can be generated. By applying the casting (`int`) to such a number, it is possible to generate a random integer between a and a + b.

```
(int)( a + b * Math.random() );
```

Since a is an `int` parameter, the effect is the same if we take a outside the parentheses:

```
a + (int)( b * Math.random() );
```

The following code uses this idea. The program receives two values and produces a random integer using the latter formula four times.

The program execution produces the following result:

```
1   import java.util.Scanner;
2
3   public class MathRandomInt
4   {
5     public static void main( String[] args )
6     {
7       Scanner keyboard = new Scanner( System.in );
8       int a, b;
9       System.out.print( "Enter the size of the interval: " );
10      b = keyboard.nextInt();
11      System.out.print( "Enter the smallest number: " );
12      a = keyboard.nextInt();
13      System.out.println( a + (int)( b * Math.random() ) );
14      System.out.println( a + (int)( b * Math.random() ) );
15      System.out.println( a + (int)( b * Math.random() ) );
16      System.out.println( a + (int)( b * Math.random() ) );
17    }
18  }
```

Listing 5.15 A program that generates random integers using Math.random

```
1   Enter the size of the interval: 5
2   Enter the smallest number: 4
3   5
4   8
5   7
6   5
```

Here is another run:

```
1   Enter the size of the interval: 10
2   Enter the smallest number: 20
3   28
4   26
5   22
6   27
```

The next code example shows the use of methods for algebraic and analytical functions that return a double value. The program receives a real number from the user and then executes the methods for the functions. For each function, the program produces an output line in the format of:

```
NAME(XXX)=ZZZ
```

where NAME is the name of the function, XXX is the value the user has entered, and ZZZ is the value the method has returned. The program also demonstrates the use of a two-parameter method pow. For that method, we want to produce the output in the format of:

```
NAME(XXX,YYY)=ZZZ
```

For this purpose, the program uses two methods named nameArgValue via method overloading. The first version takes three parameters. The three parameters are expected to be the name of the function, the value of the input given to the function, and the value of the function. The second version takes four parameters. The four parameters are expected to be the name of the function, the values of the two inputs to the function, and the value of the function. The parameter type signatures of the two methods are:

```
[String, double, double] and [String, double, double, double]
```

Next is the code for the method `main`. The program receives one floating point number from the user, and then makes a series of calls to `nameArgValue`. In each call, the program passes the name of the `Math` method it is using, the real number that the user has entered, and the return value of the call to the `Math` method. To print the return value, the program executes `System.out.println` with the method calls as the actual parameters.

```java
import java.util.Scanner;

public class MathPoly
{
  public static void nameArgValue( String name, double argument,
      double value )
  {
    System.out.print( name );
    System.out.print( "(" );
    System.out.print( argument );
    System.out.print( ")=" );
    System.out.println( value );
  }

  public static void nameArgValue( String name, double arg1,
      double arg2, double value )
  {
    System.out.print( name );
    System.out.print( "(" );
    System.out.print( arg1 );
    System.out.print( "," );
    System.out.print( arg2 );
    System.out.print( ")=" );
    System.out.println( value );
  }

  public static void main( String[] args )
  {
    Scanner keyboard = new Scanner( System.in );
    double real, real2;

    System.out.print( "Enter a positive real number: " );
    real = keyboard.nextDouble();

    nameArgValue( "sqrt", real, Math.sqrt( real ) );
    nameArgValue( "cbrt", real, Math.cbrt( real ) );
    nameArgValue( "log10", real, Math.log10( real ) );
    nameArgValue( "log", real, Math.log( real ) );
    nameArgValue( "exp", real, Math.exp( real ) );
    nameArgValue( "exp", -real, Math.exp( -real ) );
    nameArgValue( "abs", real, Math.abs( real ) );
    nameArgValue( "abs", -real, Math.abs( -real ) );
    nameArgValue( "signum", real, Math.signum( real ) );
    nameArgValue( "signum", -real, Math.signum( -real ) );

    System.out.print( "Enter another real number: " );
    real2 = keyboard.nextDouble();
    nameArgValue( "pow", real, real2, Math.pow( real, real2 ) );
  }
}
```

Listing 5.16 A program that demonstrates the use of algebraic and analytical functions of Math

The next code shows an example of rounding numbers. As before, the source code has two versions of `nameArgValue` via method overloading. In the first version, the third parameter is `double`, and in the second version, the third parameter is `long`.

The action of the method `main` is very similar to the action of the previous program. The program receives input from the user, and then calls the three functions twice each. The first call is with the value entered, and the second call is with the value having the opposite sign.

```
1   import java.util.Scanner;
2
3   public class MathRounding
4   {
5     public static void nameArgValue( String name, double argument,
6         double value )
7     {
8       System.out.print( name );
9       System.out.print( "(" );
10      System.out.print( argument );
11      System.out.print( ")=" );
12      System.out.println( value );
13    }
14
15    public static void nameArgValue( String name, double argument,
16        long value )
17    {
18      System.out.print( name );
19      System.out.print( "(" );
20      System.out.print( argument );
21      System.out.print( ")=" );
22      System.out.println( value );
23    }
24
25    public static void main( String[] args )
26    {
27      Scanner keyboard = new Scanner( System.in );
28      System.out.print( "Enter a real number: " );
29      double real = keyboard.nextDouble();
30      nameArgValue( "ceil", real, Math.ceil( real ) );
31      nameArgValue( "ceil", -real, Math.ceil( -real ) );
32      nameArgValue( "floor", real, Math.floor( real ) );
33      nameArgValue( "floor", -real, Math.floor( -real ) );
34      nameArgValue( "round", real, Math.round( real ) );
35      nameArgValue( "round", -real, Math.round( -real ) );
36    }
37  }
```

Listing 5.17 A program that demonstrates the use of rounding methods in `Math`

Here is an execution example of the code. Note that while the ceiling of 45.78 produces 46.0, the ceiling of −45.78 produces −45.0, not −46.0. The same difference exists for the flooring.

```
1  Enter a real number: 45.78
2  ceil(45.78)=46.0
3  ceil(-45.78)=-45.0
4  floor(45.78)=45.0
5  floor(-45.78)=-46.0
6  round(45.78)=46
7  round(-45.78)=-46
```

The next code demonstrates the use of the trigonometric functions. Again, the program uses methods named nameAndValue. The first method has four parameters, name, arg1, arg2, and value, and produces the output in a new format:

$$\text{xxx}(\text{Pi}*(\text{yyy}/\text{zzz}))=\text{vvv}$$

with xxx, yyy, zzz, and vvv replaced with the values of name, arg1, arg2, and value, respectively. Previously, we had a comma in place of the forward slash. Both nameArgValue methods in this program combine some components to be printed into a single line with the use of concatenation. As the result, the codes are shorter.

```
1   import java.util.Scanner;
2   public class MathTrigonometry
3   {
4     public static void nameArgValue( String name, int arg1, int arg2,
5         double value )
6     {
7       System.out.print( name );
8       System.out.print( "(Pi*(" + arg1  + "/" + arg2  + "))=" );
9       System.out.println( value );
10    }
11
12    public static void nameArgValue( String name, double arg,
13        double value )
14    {
15      System.out.print( name );
16      System.out.print( "(" + arg + ")=" );
17      System.out.println( value );
18    }
19
```

Listing 5.18 A program that demonstrates the use of trigonometric methods in Math (part 1)

In the remainder of the code, the program receives two integers, a and b, from the user. The two integers are expected to represent the fraction r defined by a/b. The program then computes the sine, cosine, and tangent of πr. These values are stored in sinVal, cosVal, and tanVal. The program then applies the inverse functions to the three quantities, and stores the values returned in asinVal, acosVal, and atanVal. After obtaining these values, the program uses nameArgValue methods to report the results.

```
20   public static void main( String[] args )
21   {
22     Scanner keyboard = new Scanner( System.in );
23     System.out.print( "Enter integers a and b for Pi*(a/b): " );
24     int a = keyboard.nextInt();
25     int b = keyboard.nextInt();
26     double sinVal = Math.sin( Math.PI * a / b );
27     double cosVal = Math.cos( Math.PI * a / b );
28     double tanVal = Math.tan( Math.PI * a / b );
29     double asinVal = Math.asin( sinVal );
30     double acosVal = Math.acos( cosVal);
31     double atanVal = Math.atan( tanVal );
32     nameArgValue( "sin", a, b, sinVal );
33     nameArgValue( "cos", a, b, cosVal );
34     nameArgValue( "tan", a, b, tanVal );
35     nameArgValue( "asin", sinVal, asinVal );
36     nameArgValue( "acos", cosVal, acosVal );
37     nameArgValue( "atan", tanVal, atanVal );
38   }
39 }
```

Listing 5.19 A program that demonstrates the use of trigonometric methods in `Math` (part 2)

Here is an execution example of the code:

```
1 Enter integers a and b for Pi*(a/b): 2 3
2 sin(Pi*(2/3))=0.8660254037844387
3 cos(Pi*(2/3))=-0.4999999999999998
4 tan(Pi*(2/3))=-1.7320508075688783
5 asin(0.8660254037844387)=0.33333333333333337
6 acos(-0.4999999999999998)=0.6666666666666666
7 atan(-1.7320508075688783)=-0.3333333333333334
```

Note that there are many digits appearing after the decimal point.

5.3.2 Mortgage Calculation

Suppose we are to take out a mortgage for some n months, with the principal of p dollars and the fixed annual rate of $a\%$. Our loan starts on the first day of a month, and each monthly payment will be on the last day of the month.

We want to use a computer program to calculate the monthly payment as well as the total payment for various loan scenarios. Since we can compute the total payment by simply multiplying the monthly payment by the total number of payments, the key thing to compute is the monthly payment.

One calculates the monthly payment as follows.

If the annual percentage interest rate is $a\%$, then the monthly interest rate r is the twelfth root of $b = (1 + a/100)$. This is because the annual interest rate is calculated as the compound rate of its monthly rate. In other words, the annual interest rate is the twelfth power of the monthly rate.

If the residual principal is x on the first day of a month, then on the last day of the same month, the residual principal balloons to rx. Since the payment of m occurs on the last day of the same month, on the first of the next month, the principal will be:

$$rx - m.$$

In the next month, the same calculation takes place and the new residual amount after the next payment will be:

$$r(rx - m) - m.$$

Then, again one month after, the principal becomes:

$$r(r(rx - m) - m) - m.$$

Let $\{p_i\}_{i=0}^{n}$ be a series representing the residual principals, such that for each i, $0 \leq i \leq n$, the residual after i months of payment is p_i. The value of p_0 is p since payments have not started yet and the value of p_n is 0 since the payment must be completed on the last day of the n-month period. By using the calculation from the previous step, we obtain:

$$p_1 = rp - m, \; p_2 = r(rp - m) - m, \; p_3 = r(r(rp - m) - m) - m, \ldots$$

We can see that for all $k \geq 0$,

$$p_k = r^k p - (r^{k-1} + r^{k-2} + \cdots + r + 1)m.$$

We need to obtain the sum on the right-hand side. Define Q by:

$$Q = r^{k-1} + r^{k-1} + \cdots + r + 1.$$

By multiplying Q by r then adding 1 to the product we have:

$$rQ + 1 = r^k + r^{k-1} + \cdots + r + 1.$$

Also, by adding r^k to Q, we have:

$$r^k + Q = r^k + r^{k-2} + \cdots + r + 1.$$

Since the right-hand sides are the same between the two equalities, we have:

$$rQ + 1 = r^k + Q.$$

Solving this for Q, we obtain:

$$Q = \frac{r^k - 1}{r - 1}.$$

Thus,

$$p_k = r^k p - \frac{r^k - 1}{r - 1} m.$$

Since the loan is paid off in exactly n months, we have $p_n = 0$. Substituting k with n in the above equation, we have:

$$p_n = r^n p - \frac{r^n - 1}{r - 1} m = 0.$$

Solving this for m, we have:

$$m = \frac{r^n (r - 1)}{r^n - 1} p.$$

Noting that r^n appears twice in the formula, we substitute r^n with s. Then we have:

$$m = \frac{s(r - 1)}{s - 1} p.$$

We now have the following process for computing the monthly payment m from p, a, b, and n.

1. Compute $b = (1 + a/100)$.
2. Compute $r = b^{1/12}$.
3. Compute $s = r^n$.
4. Compute $m = ps(r - 1)/(s - 1)$.
5. Compute the total amount $t = mn$.

Here is the code based upon the above analysis.

The code uses the following variables for receiving information about the loan from the user:

- `int nMonth`: number of months (n in the above discussion);
- `int principal`: the principal amount in dollars (p in the above discussion);
- `double aRate`: annual rate in percentage (a in the above discussion).

Then the code uses the following variables for calculating the parameters:

- `double bRate`: the rate of annual increase (b in the above discussion);
- `double rRate`: the rate of monthly increase (r in the above discussion);
- `double power`: the n-th power of r (s in the above discussion);
- `double mPay`: the monthly payment (m in the above discussion);
- `double totalPay`: the total payment (t in the above discussion).

The declarations of these variables appear in Lines 8 through 12. In Line 7 we also declare a `Scanner` variable.

```
1    import java.util.*;
2
3    public class Loan
4    {
5      public static void main( String[] args )
6      {
7        Scanner keyboard;
8        int nMonth, principal;
9        double aRate, bRate, rRate;
10       double power;
11       double mPay, totalPay;
12
13       keyboard = new Scanner( System.in );
14
15       System.out.print( "Enter nMonth, principal, annual rate: " );
16       nMonth = keyboard.nextInt();
17       principal = keyboard.nextInt();
18       aRate = keyboard.nextDouble();
19
20       bRate = ( 1 + aRate / 100 );
21       rRate = Math.pow( bRate, 1.0 / 12 );
22       power = Math.pow( rRate, nMonth );
23       mPay = principal * power * ( rRate - 1 ) / ( power - 1 );
24       totalPay = mPay * nMonth;
25       System.out.print( "monthly = " + mPay );
26       System.out.println( ", total = " + totalPay );
27     }
28   }
```

Listing 5.20 A program that calculates mortgage payments

Lines 13–18 are for receiving input from the user. Notice that the use of `nextInt` is for the `int` variables, and the use of `nextDouble` is for the `double` variable. Notice, also, the use of `1.0 / 12` for 1/12 in Line 21. The `.0` is essential here, since `1 / 12` would produce 0 as the integer quotient. Such treatment is not necessary for Line 20, because `aRate` is `double`.

Here is how the code runs[2]:

```
1    Enter nMonth, principal, annual rate: 360 100000 3.65
2    monthly = 454.10190144665336, total = 163476.6845207952
```

The code we have just seen does not use rounding. Since we cannot make payments carrying a fraction of a cent, it is natural for us to round each currency amount with a fraction of a cent to one without. In presenting currencies, we want to present exactly two digits after the decimal point. We

---

[2]So about 63.5% more over the period of 30 years. Not bad, I think.

can make the number of digits to be printed after the decimal point to exactly two in the following manner. We multiply mPay by 100 and then round it down to a whole number using the floor function. We then split the number into two parts, as the quotient divided by 100 and the remainder divided by 100. The result looks like this:

```
1  Enter nMonth, principal, annual rate: 360 100000 3.65
2  monthly = 454.1, total = 163476.0
```

The number of digits after the decimal point has been reduced, but in this case, there appears only one digit after the decimal point for both numbers.

Java has a convenient way of adjusting the numbers to appear on the screen: a special print command System.out.printf. The printf stands for "print with formatting" and it takes a format String and a series of data as parameters.

```
System.out.printf( FORMAT_STRING, DATA_1, ..., DATA_k );
```

Here FORMAT_STRING is a String that contains some k placeholders, where each placeholder starts with a symbol % and ends with a letter specifying the type of data required for the position, e.g., s, d, and f. Between the % and the type-specifying letter may appear characters that specify how the value of the data may appear when printed. Examples include the number of character spaces to use and whether the value appears flush left or flush right.

In our particular case, we need to print two real values with exactly two digits after the decimal point. A bonus would be to have a punctuation with every three digits, since the two values are currencies.

```
System.out.printf(
     "monthly = $%,.2f, total = $%,.2f%n", mPay, totalPay );
```

The format String contains two placeholders. Both place holders are %,.2f. The letter f means that the data is a floating point number. The character , means that the currency punctuation must appear. The character sequence .2 specifies that exactly two digits must after the decimal point. The remaining parts, monthly = $, , total = $, and %n, print as they appear in the format String. The %n specifies the newline and is essentially the same as \n. Using this formatting, the output becomes:

```
monthly = $454.10, total = $163,476.00
```

The complete code of the program that computes the loan payments and produces a fancy output is shown next. Just for comparison, the code includes the somewhat incomplete truncation print line that we previously used.

```
1   import java.util.*;
2
3   public class LoanFancy
4   {
5     public static void main( String[] args )
6     {
7       Scanner keyboard;
8       int nMonth, principal;
9       double aRate, bRate, rRate;
10      double power;
11      double mPay, totalPay, mPay2, totalPay2;
12
13      keyboard = new Scanner( System.in );
14
15      System.out.print( "Enter nMonth, principal, annual rate: " );
16      nMonth = keyboard.nextInt();
17      principal = keyboard.nextInt();
18      aRate = keyboard.nextDouble();
19
20      bRate = ( 1 + aRate / 100 );
21      rRate = Math.pow( bRate, 1.0 / 12 );
22      power = Math.pow( rRate, nMonth );
23      mPay = principal * power * ( rRate - 1 ) / ( power - 1 );
24      totalPay = mPay * nMonth;
25      System.out.print( "monthly = " + mPay );
26      System.out.println( ", total = " + totalPay );
27
28      mPay2 = Math.floor( mPay * 100 ) / 100.0;
29      totalPay2 = mPay2 * nMonth;
30      System.out.printf( "monthly = $%,.2f, total = $%,.2f%n",
31          mPay2, totalPay2 );
32    }
33  }
```

Listing 5.21 A new program that computes mortgage payments with fancy output

Summary

- The formal parameters are those parameters that appear in a method declaration. In the declaration, each formal parameter is specified with its type and name.
- When a method A calls a method B, the values appearing in the method call are transferred to the formal parameters of B. These values are called actual parameters.
- The mechanism used in Java for transferring parameter values to methods is call-by-reference. If an object data is given to a method as a formal parameter, executing an instance method on the parameter may affect the contents/status of the object.
- The parameter type signature of a method is the sequence of the parameter types appearing in its parameter specification.
- Method overloading refers to the concept in which a class may define multiple methods having the same name, so long as the type signatures are distinct.
- A method may return a value. The type of the return value of a method is specified in the method declaration immediately before the method name. If there is no return value, a special keyword void is used in the return type specification.

■ When a program makes a method call and no version of the method available through method overloading has a completely matching parameter type signature, a close match, if available, is used.

■ Class Math provides a number of methods for mathematical and analytical functions as well as mathematical constants.

■ The method Math.random returns a random double between 0 and 1. Using this method, it is possible to generate an integer within a finite range.

Exercises

1. **Concept check** What do you call the concept that states that, in one class, multiple methods with identical names can be declared, so long as the required parameters among them are different?

2. **Concept check** Can void methodX(int a, int b) and int methodX(int c, int d) coexist in the same Java class?

3. **Concept check** For each mathematical function, state the name of the method from class Math used for calculating the function.
   (a) the sine function
   (b) the cosine function
   (c) the inverse of the tangent function
   (d) the natural logarithm
   (e) the square root
   (f) the cubic root

4. **Ceil, floor, and round** Let x be a double variable with value 3.5 and let y be a double variable with value 4.0. Find the values of the following:
   (a) Math.ceil(x) and Math.ceil(y)
   (b) Math.floor(x) and Math.floor(y)
   (c) Math.max(x, y) and Math.min(x, y)
   (d) x % y

5. **Feeding the output of a method to a method** Consider the following three methods:

```
1   public static int method1( int a, int b )
2   {
3     return 2 * a * b;
4   }
5   public static int method2( int a )
6   {
7     return a / 2;
8   }
9   public static int method3( int a )
10  {
11    return a * 3;
12  }
```

What is the value of method1(method2(3), method3(3))?
What is the value of method3(method2(method1(3, 4)))?

6. Write a method named getInt that takes one Scanner parameter s and one String parameter prompt, prints the prompt on the screen, receives an int from the user using the Scanner type s, and then returns the int received from the user.

7. Write a void method named message that receives a String name and a double v as parameters and prints on the screen

```
The value of [name] is [v]
```

where [name] is the value of the variable name and [v] is the value of v

8. **Combining methods** Suppose a method cross is defined as follows:

```
1  public static int cross( int a,  int b )
2  {
3      return a - b;
4  }
```

State what value is returned by cross(10, cross(9, 4)).

9. **Combining method** Suppose a method cute is defined as follows:

```
1  public static int cute( int a,  int b )
2  {
3      return a * b + b;
4  }
```

State what value is returned by cute(cute(10, 4), 5). Also, state the value of cute(cute(10, 5), 4).

10. **The volume of a cylinder** Write a public static method named cylinderVolume (including its method declaration) that receives two double values dValue and hValue as parameters, and then returns the volume of the cylinder whose diameter is equal to dValue and whose height is equal to hValue.

11. **Solving a quadratic equation** Write a program named SimpleQuadraticEq that receives three double value coefficients a, b, and c from the user, and then solves the equation $ax^2 + bx + c = 0$ using Math.sqrt. If the equation has no real solution, the code may halt with a run-time error. If the two solutions are identical to each other, the program may print the unique solution twice.

For example, the program may execute as follows:

```
1  Enter the coefficients a,  b,  and c: 2 -5 2
2  The roots are 2.0 and 0.5
```

12. **Computing the radius of a ball given its volume** Write a program named RadiusFromCubeVolume that receives the volume of a ball in cubic meters from the user, and then computes the radius of the ball.

Programming Projects

13. **Summing numbers** Write a program named SimpleSumGauss that receives an integer top from the user and returns the sum from 1 to top, using the formula by Gauss. The program should contain a method computeSum that takes an int as its formal parameter and returns the sum. The program may not work correctly if the input the user provides is not positive.

14. **Coordinate system conversion** There are two coordinate systems for a point on the two-dimensional space with the origin. One system, the Cartesian system uses a pair of axes that are perpendicular to each other and specifies the point suing the x and y values of that point.

The other system, the polar system, has one axis and uses the distance from the origin and the counter-clockwise angle from the axis in the range of $-\pi$ to π degrees. Write a program named `CoordinateConversion` that demonstrates the conversions between the two. The program should have two methods, one for converting from the former type to the latter and the other for converting from the latter type to the former. The method `main` prompts the user to enter information and makes the calls to these methods, where the methods perform their respective conversions and print the results on the screen. Use the fact that the angle (in radian) of (x, y) is the sign of y times the arc-cosine of y/x and that the cosine is $x/\sqrt{x^2 + y^2}$. To compute the sign, `Math.signum` can be used and to compute the arc-tangent `Math.acos` can be used.

15. **Balancing a ship**   Determine how deep the bottom of a ship sinks when it is placed in water. Assume that the shape of the ship is an elongated triangle (in the shape of a Toblerone package for instance).

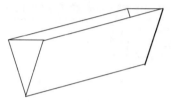

The front view of the ship is an isosceles with the base at the top. Use variables `height` and `base` for the height and the base of the triangle. Use a variable `length` for the length of the ship. All these quantities should be in meters. Use a variable `weight` for the weight of the ship in tons. To describe how much of the ship will be in water, use a `double` variable `ratio` that is between 0 and 1. The height of the ship under water is `ratio * height`. For the ship to balance, the weight of the water it displaces should be equal to the weight of the ship. The first quantity is:

$$0.5 * (\text{ratio} * \text{height}) * (\text{ratio} * \text{base}) * \text{length}$$
$$= 0.5 * \text{ratio}^2 * \text{height} * \text{base} * \text{length}$$

If the ship is balanced in water, then this quantity is equal to `weight`. By solving the equality, the value for `ratio` can be obtained.

Write a program named `BalancingShip` that takes `height`, `base`, `length`, and `weight` from the user, and computes the height of the ship above water.

16. **Euclidean distance**   Write a program named `Euclidean` that takes six double numbers `a1`, `b1`, `c1`, `a2`, `b2`, `c2` as parameters, and then prints the Euclidean distance between the points `(a1, b1, c1)` and `(a2, b2, c2)` as

$$\sqrt{(a1 - a2)^2 + (b1 - b2)^2 + (c1 - c2)^2}.$$

17. **String parameters**   Write a program named `NamePermute` that takes three `String` tokens from the user. These tokens are supposed should be proper nouns. Print a statement in which the three names appear in six possible orders.

```
1   % java NamePermute
2   Enter three names: Kris Luke Mike
3   Kris is friendly with Luke, but not with Mike
4   Kris is friendly with Mike, but not with Luke
5   Luke is friendly with Kris, but not with Mike
6   Luke is friendly with Mike, but not with Kris
7   Mike is friendly with Kris, but not with Luke
8   Mike is friendly with Luke, but not with Kris
9   %
```

To write the code, use a method that takes three `String` parameters and prints a single line with the three parameter values. To present the common parts, `String` variables can be used.

18. **This Old Man, again**   Previously we looked at decomposing "This Old Man". Now we know how to pass values. Write a method named `oldManVerse` that prints one verse of *This Old Man*, given two formal parameters XXX and YYY, which are both `String` objects, and prints

```
1   This old man, he played XXX,
2   He played knick-knack on his YYY;
3   With a knick-knack paddywhack,
4   Give the dog a bone,
5   This old man came rolling home
6
```

Then, using the method `oldManVerse`, write a program `ThisOldManPassing` that prints all ten verses of the rhyme, where the value of XXX goes from `one` to `ten`, while the value of YYY goes:

drum, shoe, knee, door, hive, sticks, heaven, gate, spine, again

19. **Area of a regular polygon having N vertices**   For an integer $N \geq 3$, a polygon having N vertices $v_1, \ldots, v_N$ is a shape formed by connecting v_i and v_{i+1} for all i, $1 \leq i \leq N-1$, and connecting v_1 and v_N, each with a straight line. A regular polygon is a polygon such that the vertices are on a circle, the line segments connect between the two neighbors on the circle, and the line segments are equal in length. Examples of a regular polygon are squares and equilaterals. Write a program named `PolygonArea` that receives the number of vertices `number` and the common length `length`, the latter of which is `double`, from the user and reports the area. In the program, include a method `computeArea` that takes the two quantities as its parameters and returns the area.

20. **How far does a baseball go?**   If a baseball is thrown at an angle, how far will it reach? Simplify the problem by assuming that the ball is released at height 0 above ground, there is no wind or air resistance, and the ball flies on a plane. Under these assumptions, the ground distance that the ball travels is determined by the speed and the angle when the ball is released. Let the ball be at the speed of s at the start and the angle is θ in radian. The vertical speed of the ball, v, is $s \sin(\theta)$ and the horizontal speed of the ball, u, is $s \cos(\theta)$. The time that it takes for the ball to reach the highest point, t, is v/g, where g is the gravity constant ($= 9.8$). The height that it reaches, h, is $vt - gt^2/2$. The time that it takes for the ball to hit the ground, t', is $\sqrt{2h/g}$. Thus, the travel distance is $(t + t')u$.

Write a program named `HowFar` that does this calculation. Design the code so that it contains a method that does the calculation from s and θ, while printing the intermediate quantities on the screen. Receive the values for the two variables from the user and call the method for calculation. The user gives the angle, in degrees, between 0 and 90, so the program must convert the angle to radian.

Here is a possibility of how the program may interact with the user:

```
1   Enter the speed: 100 45
2   Enter the angle in degrees: The horizontal speed is 70.71067811865476
3   The vertical speed is 70.71067811865474
4   The time required to reach the top is 7.215375318230075
5   The height is 255.10204081632642
6   The time required to hit the ground is 7.215375318230075
7   The distance traveled is 1020.4081632653059
```

Conditions and Their Use for Controlling the Flow of Programs

6

6.1 Condition and Its Evaluation

A **condition** is a literal, a variable, a formula, or a method call whose value is `boolean`.[1] **Conditional evaluation** is the action of obtaining the value of a condition. Recall, as we studied in Sect. 2.2, that `boolean` is a primitive data type with just two possible values, `true` and `false`, which are opposite to each other. `System.out.print` and its variants print these two values as the `String` literals `"true"` and `"false"`, respectively, as demonstrated in the next code:

```
1  public class BooleanPrint
2  {
3    public static void main( String[] args )
4    {
5      boolean t = true;
6      boolean f = false;
7      System.out.println( t );
8      System.out.println( f );
9    }
10 }
```

Listing 6.1 An program that prints `boolean` literals and variables

The code produces the following result:

```
1  true
2  false
```

To build a `boolean` formula, **conditional** or **logical operators** can be used. There are three conditional operators, the **negation**, **conjunction** (or **logical-and**), and **disjunction** (or **logical-or**).

Negation   The **negation** of a condition has the opposite value of the original; that is, if x has the value of `true`, `!x` has the value of `false`; and if x has the value of `false`, `!x` has the value of `true`. The negation operator must be attached immediately in front of the condition it acts upon.

---

[1]The name "boolean" comes from **George Boole** (November 2, 1815 to December 8, 1864), a nineteenth century English mathematician who did fundamental work in logic and algebra.

© Springer Nature Switzerland AG 2018
M. Ogihara, *Fundamentals of Java Programming*,
https://doi.org/10.1007/978-3-319-89491-1_6

The negation can be applied multiple times. When the negation is applied to something that is already negated, a pair of matching parentheses is needed before attaching the additional negation. In other words, for any condition x, the double negation !!x must be written as !(!x). The double negation of a condition has the same value as the original.

Disjunction   The disjunction asks whether or not at least one of the conditions given as the operands have the value of true. For operands x1, ..., xk such that k is greater than or equal to 2,

$$x1 \ || \ ... \ || \ xk$$

has the value of true if and only if for some i, xi has the value of true.

Conjunction   The conjunction asks whether or not all of the conditions given as the operands have the value of true. For operands x1, ..., xk such that k is greater than equal to 2,

$$x1 \ \&\& \ ... \ \&\& \ xk$$

has the value of true if and only if for all i, xi has the value of true.

De Morgan's laws state[2]:

$$!(x \ \&\& \ y) \ \text{is equivalent to} \ !x \ || \ !y \ \text{and}$$
$$!(x \ || \ y) \ \text{is equivalent to} \ !x \ \&\& \ !y$$

Since the double negation flips the value back to the original, we have:

$$x \ \&\& \ y \ \text{is equivalent to} \ !(!x \ || \ !y) \ \text{and}$$
$$x \ || \ y \ \text{is equivalent to} \ !(!x \ \&\& \ !y)$$

The evaluation of conditional formulas with more than two operands follows rules analogous to the rules used in evaluating mathematical formulas, with !, ||, and && acting as -, +, and *, respectively.

The next code demonstrates the effect of the three boolean operations. In this program, we make a number of conditional evaluations. To make the code look simpler, we use the method nameAndValue. The method receives a String data name and a boolean data value as formal parameters and prints them in a single line with a String literal " : " in between:

```
1  public class BooleanConnectivesNew
2  {
3     public static void nameAndValue( String name , boolean value )
4     {
5        System.out.println( name + ": " + value );
6     }
```

Listing 6.2 A program that demonstrates the use of boolean operators (part 1)

We use the method nameAndValue as follows. Line 9 of the program goes:

```
9        System.out.println( "---------- NOT --------------" );
```

Here, the first parameter "true && true" is a String literal that presents as a String literal a conditional formula to be made and the second parameter true && true is the actual formula to be evaluated. Note that the first actual parameter is a String literal and the second is a boolean formula.

The method nameAndValue simplifies the somewhat awkward single println statement of the form:

---

[2] Augustus De Morgan (27 June 1806 to 18 March 1871) was a British mathematician and logician, a contemporary of George Boole. He worked on logic and algebra.

```
System.out.println( "true && true: " + (true && true) );
```

To execute this statement, `println` evaluates the conditional formula `(true && true)`. The value of the formula is `true`. After the evaluation, `println` converts the boolean value to a `String` literal `"true"`, and appends it to `"true && true: "`. As the results, `println` produces the output:

```
true && true: true
```

The method `main` that is shown next demonstrates how the three logical operators work by applying them to `boolean` literals:

```
1    public static void main( String[] args )
2    {
3       System.out.println( "---------- NOT --------------" );
4       nameAndValue( "!true", !true );
5       nameAndValue( "!false", !false );
6       nameAndValue( "!!true", !!true );
7       nameAndValue( "!!false", !!false );
8       System.out.println( "--------- AND --------------" );
9       nameAndValue( "true && true", true && true );
10      nameAndValue( "true && false", true && false );
11      nameAndValue( "false && true", false && true );
12      nameAndValue( "false && false", false && false );
13      System.out.println( "--------- OR --------------" );
14      nameAndValue( "true || true", true || true );
15      nameAndValue( "true || false", true || false );
16      nameAndValue( "false || true", false || true );
17      nameAndValue( "false || false", false || false );
18   }
```

Listing 6.3 A program that demonstrates the use of `boolean` operators (part 2)

The execution of the code produces the following result:

```
1    ---------- NOT --------------
2    !true: false
3    !false: true
4    !!true: true
5    !!false: false
6    --------- AND --------------
7    true && true: true
8    true && false: false
9    false && true: false
10   false && false: false
11   --------- NO --------------
12   true || true: true
13   true || false: true
14   false || true: true
15   false || false: false
```

Two conditions can be compared for equality and inequality. Given two conditions x and y, x == y tests whether or not the value of x is equal to the value of y, and x != y tests whether or not the value of x is not equal to the value of y. If x (or y) is a formula, it may be necessary to surround it with a pair of parentheses.

Numbers and `char` data can be compared for equality and inequality. Let x and y be data of some non-`boolean` primitive data types, where the data type of x may be different from the data type of y. We can apply six different comparisons to them:

- `x > y` tests whether or not the value of x is strictly greater than the value of y.
- `x >= y` tests whether or not the value of x is greater than or equal to the value of y.
- `x < y` tests whether or not the value of x is strictly less than the value of y.
- `x <= y` tests whether or not the value of x is less than or equal to the value of y.
- `x == y` tests whether or not the value of x is equal to the value of y.
- `x != y` tests whether or not the value of x is not equal to the value of y.

In the case where either x or y is `char`, the `char` type is treated as an unsigned 16-bit number. For this treatment, we use the character table called **Unicode**.[3] An important subset of the character set is the set of characters whose values are between 0 and 127. We call the subset the **ASCII Table**.[4]

The equality and inequality tests can be applied to object data types, e.g., `String` data, but the tests do not compare the contents of the objects, but the data locations. A special value for object type data is `null`. `null` means that the value is undefined. The following program:

```
1    boolean flag;
2    String unknown;
3    flag = ( unknown == null );
4    System.out.print( flag );
5    unknown = "abc";
6    flag = ( unknown == null );
7    System.out.print( flag );
```

produces two lines of output:

```
1  true
2  false
```

Many object types in Java offer a method specifically for comparisons. They are usually called `equals` and `compareTo`. We shall see such methods for the `String` type in Chap. 9.

In the next code, the program prompts the user to enter two integers, receives two numbers, and then performs the six comparisons between the two values entered. The program then executes the same series of action by receiving two real numbers from the user. The results of the six comparisons are stored in six `boolean` variables using the statement of the form:

$$\text{BOOLEAN\_VARIABLE} = \text{OPERAND1 OPERATOR OPERAND2};$$

For variable naming, the code uses the form eqXXX, neXXX, gtXXX, geXXX, ltXXX, and leXXX for ==, !=, >, >=, <, and <=, with `Int` for XXX for integers and `Double` for floating point numbers.

Here is the header part of the program. It states what variables will be used:

---

[3]For example, `https://unicode-table.com/en/#control-character`.
[4]For example, `http://www.asciitable.com`.

```
1   import java.util.*;
2   // various comparisons
3   public class Comparisons0
4   {
5     public static void main( String[] args )
6     {
7       Scanner keyboard = new Scanner( System.in );
8       int int1, int2;
9       double double1, double2;
10      boolean eqInt, neInt, gtInt, geInt, ltInt, leInt;
11      boolean eqDouble, neDouble, gtDouble, geDouble, ltDouble, leDouble;
```

Listing 6.4 A program that shows comparisons between numbers (part 1)

In the next part, the program receives two `int` data from the user, compares them in six different ways, saves the outcomes in their respective variables, and prints the outcomes along with the numbers:

```
12        //------------- enter int values
13        System.out.print( "Enter two int: " );
14        int1 = keyboard.nextInt();
15        int2 = keyboard.nextInt();
16        //------------- compare the int values
17        eqInt = ( int1 == int2 );
18        neInt = ( int1 != int2 );
19        gtInt = ( int1 > int2 );
20        geInt = ( int1 >= int2 );
21        ltInt = ( int1 < int2 );
22        leInt = ( int1 <= int2 );
23        //------------- print the results
24        System.out.printf( "int1 = %d, int2 = %d%n", int1, int2 );
25        System.out.printf( "int1 == int2 returns %s%n", eqInt );
26        System.out.printf( "int1 != int2 returns %s%n", neInt );
27        System.out.printf( "int1 > int2 returns %s%n", gtInt );
28        System.out.printf( "int1 >= int2 returns %s%n", geInt );
29        System.out.printf( "int1 < int2 returns %s%n", ltInt );
30        System.out.printf( "int1 <= int2 returns %s%n", leInt );
```

Listing 6.5 A program that shows comparisons between numbers (part 2)

To print the outcome, we use `System.out.printf` that we saw earlier in Sect. 5.3.2. The method `printf` follows the syntax:

```
printf( FORMAT_STRING, PARAMETER1, ..., PARAMETERk );
```

where k represents the number of placeholders for data values appearing in `FORMAT_STRING`. `FORMAT_STRING` is a `String` data. We call the first parameter of `printf` the **formatting String**.

In `System.out.printf`, each data placeholder takes the form of `%XXXt`, where t is a letter that refers to the expected data type and XXX is a character sequence that specifies the way in which the data value is printed. In this book we will see five types for t: c for `char`, d for any whole number, f for any floating point number, s for `String` and `boolean`, and, much later, e for exponential representation. If the XXX part is empty, `System.out.printf` uses the default formatting for the type t (see Chap. 8).

The first `printf` statement in our code is:

```
System.out.printf( "int = %d, int2 = %d%n", int1, int2 );
```

The format `String` of the statement is `"int = %d, int2 = %d%n"`. Two placeholders appear in it. Both placeholders are `%d` and thus meant for printing integers. The `%n` is equivalent to `\n` and is for printing the newline character. Since two placeholders appear, the `printf` statement works if and only if exactly two whole numbers appear after the format `String`. In our case, those numbers are `int1` and `int2`. When printing the values, `printf` formats use the minimum number of characters required to print the values. Suppose the value of `int1` is 987 and the value of `int2` is −456. Then `printf` produces the output:

$$\text{int = 987, int2 = -456}$$

According to the rule, if the values are 10 and −98, respectively, the output is:

$$\text{int = 10, int2 = -98}$$

In the ensuing six lines, the placeholder is `%s` and `printf` substitutes each placeholder with the value of the `boolean` variable appearing in the statement.

The last part of the code uses `%f` for printing the `double` values:

```
31      //------------- enter double values
32      System.out.print( "Enter two floating point numbers: " );
33      double1 = keyboard.nextDouble();
34      double2 = keyboard.nextDouble();
35      //------------- compare the Double values
36      eqDouble = ( double1 == double2 );
37      neDouble = ( double1 != double2 );
38      gtDouble = ( double1 > double2 );
39      geDouble = ( double1 >= double2 );
40      ltDouble = ( double1 < double2 );
41      leDouble = ( double1 <= double2 );
42      //------------- print the results
43      System.out.printf( "double1 = %f, double2 = %f%n",
44          double1, double2 );
45      System.out.printf( "double1 == double2 returns %s%n", eqDouble );
46      System.out.printf( "double1 != double2 returns %s%n", neDouble );
47      System.out.printf( "double1 > double2 returns %s%n", gtDouble );
48      System.out.printf( "double1 >= double2 returns %s%n", geDouble );
49      System.out.printf( "double1 < double2 returns %s%n", ltDouble );
50      System.out.printf( "double1 <= double2 returns %s%n", leDouble );
51  }
52 }
```

Listing 6.6 A program that shows comparisons between numbers (part 3)

Here is one execution example of the program:

```
1  Enter two int: -9834 5343
2  int1 = -9834, int2 = 5343
3  int1 == int2 returns false
4  int1 != int2 returns true
5  int1 > int2 returns false
6  int1 >= int2 returns false
7  int1 < int2 returns true
8  int1 <= int2 returns true
9  Enter two floating point numbers: -194.5 -34.5
```

```
10   double1 = -194.500000, double2 = -34.500000
11   double1 == double2 returns false
12   double1 != double2 returns true
13   double1 > double2 returns false
14   double1 >= double2 returns false
15   double1 < double2 returns true
16   double1 <= double2 returns true
```

6.2   The If Statements

6.2.1   If

Using conditional evaluations, we can control the flow of programs. We can create a code that adjoins two sequences of statements, A and B, with the evaluation of a condition C, in the following format:

"if C then execute A; otherwise, execute B"

We call this **conditional execution**. All programming languages, including Java, have conditional executions. The standard expression of a conditional execution is the use of the keyword if, so we call it an **if-statement**. For the alternate action (which corresponds to "otherwise"), the accompanying keyword is else.

The primary structure for an if-statement in Java, with no action to perform in C, is:

```
1   if ( CONDITION )
2   {
3      STATEMENTS
4   }
5   AFTER_IF_PART
```

Here, the CONDITION is the condition to be evaluated and AFTER_IF_PART is the actions to be performed after completing the if-statement. If the evaluation of CONDITION produces the value false, the execution jumps to this part.

In other words, this code fragment is executed as follows:

- CONDITION produces true: STATEMENTS followed by AFTER_IF_PART.
- CONDITION produces false: AFTER_IF_PART.

We can draw a diagram that describes this action (see Fig. 6.1).

A special feature of if-statements is that the pair of curly brackets following the conditional evaluation can be omitted if there is *only one statement* in the block. While the ability to omit the curly brackets is convenient, the omission can lead to logical errors.

The next code is our first example of using if-statements. The program receives a temperature value from the user and makes a comment.

Fig. 6.1 The execution
diagram of an if-statement

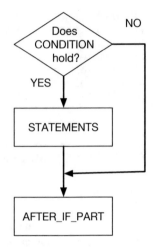

```
1   import java.util.Scanner;
2   // ask about temperature and respond
3   public class Temperature01
4   {
5     public static void main( String[] args )
6     {
7       Scanner keyboard = new Scanner( System.in );
8       //-- prompt answer
9       System.out.print( "What is the average high temperature in "
10        + "August in your area? : " );
11      double temp = keyboard.nextDouble();
12      //-- response
13      if ( temp > 90.0 )
14      {
15        System.out.println( "Wow! That must be very hot!" );
16      }
17    }
18  }
```

Listing 6.7 A program that receives a temperature value and makes a comment when appropriate

Here is the if-statement appearing the code:

```
1       if ( temp > 90.0 )
2       {
3         System.out.println( "Wow! That must be very hot!" );
4       }
```

The program prints the statement "`...  very hot!`" if the value the user has entered is strictly greater than 90.0 and prints nothing otherwise.

Here are three separate executions of the program.

In the first round of execution, the value is 85 and strictly greater than 90.0, so no message appears, as shown next:

```
What is the average high temperature in August in your area? : 85
```

In the second round, the value is 90 and not strictly less than 90.0, so no message appears, as shown next:

```
What is the average high temperature in August in your area? : 90
```

In the third round, the value is 91 and is strictly greater than 90.0, so the message appears, as shown next:

```
1  What is the average high temperature in August in your area? : 91
2  Wow! That must be very hot!
```

Figure 6.2 shows the diagram of the program.

Our next code example uses two if-statements. The first if-statement tests if the value entered is strictly greater than 90.0 as before. The second one tests if the temperature value is less than or equal to 70.0 (notice the equality sign placed on the second one). There are two messages from which the program chooses to print. The program prints the first message if and only if the temperature is strictly greater than 90.0, and the second message if and only if the temperature is less than or equal to 70.0. The program prints no statement if the temperature is strictly greater than 70.0 and less than or equal to 90.0:

```
1  import java.util.Scanner;
2  // ask about temperature and respond
3  public class Temperature02
4  {
5    public static void main( String[] args )
6    {
7      Scanner keyboard = new Scanner( System.in );
8      //-- prompt answer
9      System.out.print( "What is the average high temperature in "
10         + "August in your area? : " );
11     double temp = keyboard.nextDouble();
12     //-- response no.1
13     if ( temp > 90.0 )
14     {
15       System.out.println( "Wow! That must be very hot!" );
16     }
17     //-- response no.2
18     if ( temp <= 70.0 )
19     {
20       System.out.println( "Wow! That must be very cold!" );
21     }
22   }
23 }
```

Listing 6.8 Another program that receives a temperature value and makes a comment when appropriate

Fig. 6.2 The execution
diagram of
`Temperature01.java`

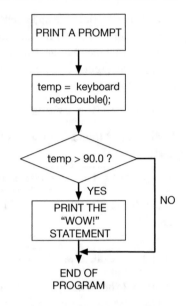

Here are three separate executions of the program:

```
1  What is the average high temperature in August in your area? : 60
2  Wow! That must be very cold!
```

```
   What is the average high temperature in August in your area? : 80
```

```
1  % java Temperature02
2  What is the average high temperature in August in your area? : 91
3  Wow! That must be very hot!
```

In the next code example, the program asks the user to enter a temperature value and then a humidity value. The if-statements of the program combine the tests on the temperature and humidity values using the conjunction operator `&&`:

```
1   import java.util.Scanner;
2   // ask about temperature and humidity and provide response
3   public class Temperature03
4   {
5     public static void main( String[] args )
6     {
7       Scanner keyboard = new Scanner( System.in );
8       //-- prompt answer
9       System.out.print( "What is the average high temperature in "
10        + "August in your area? : " );
11      double temp = keyboard.nextDouble();
12      System.out.print( "How about the average humidity? : " );
13      double humidity = keyboard.nextDouble();
14      //-- response no.1
15      if ( temp >= 90.0 && humidity >= 90.0 )
16      {
17        System.out.println( "Wow! That must be hot and humid!" );
18      }
19      //-- response no.2
20      if ( temp >= 90.0 && humidity <= 50.0 )
21      {
22        System.out.println( "Wow! That must be hot and dry!" );
23      }
24      //-- response no.3
25      if ( temp <= 70.0 )
26      {
27        System.out.println( "Wow! That must be cool!" );
28      }
29      //-- response no.4
30      if ( temp > 70.0 && humidity < 90.0 )
31      {
32        System.out.println( "Wow! That must be very comfortable!" );
33      }
34    }
35  }
```

Listing 6.9 A program that receives a temperature value and a humidity value, and then makes a comment when appropriate

Here are some execution examples:

```
1   What is the average high temperature in August in your area? : 80
2   How about the average humidity? : 100
```

```
1   What is the average high temperature in August in your area? : 70
2   How about the average humidity? : 50
3   Wow! That must be cool!
```

```
1   What is the average high temperature in August in your area? : 91
2   How about the average humidity? : 90
3   Wow! That must be hot and humid!
```

Fig. 6.3 The
combinations of
temperature and humidity
considered in
`Temperature03`

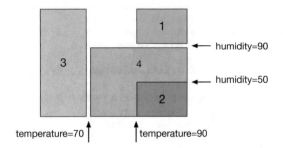

1	What is the average high temperature in August in your area? : 95
2	How about the average humidity? : 40
3	Wow! That must be hot and dry!
4	Wow! That must be very comfortable!

What are the cases in which the program produces no output? Also, what are the cases in which the program produces more than one statement?

The four cases the program tests are as follows:

Case 1   `temp >= 90.0 && humidity >= 90.0`
Case 2   `temp >= 90.0 && humidity <= 50.0`
Case 3   `temp <= 70.0`
Case 4   `temp > 70.0 && humidity < 90.0`

We can draw a diagram shown in Fig. 6.3 to discern these four cases with the temperature as the x-axis, the humidity as the y-axis, and the rectangles representing the cases.

We thus have:

• the program produces no comments if and only if the temperature is strictly greater than 70.0 and is strictly less than 90.0 and the humidity is greater than or equal to 90.0

and

• the program produces two comments if the temperature is strictly greater than 70.0 and the humidity is less than or equal to 50.0.

Here is one more example of the use of if-statements.

The program presents a list of four colors indexed 1, ..., 4 to the user. It then asks the user to select a number that represents her favorite color. Upon receiving the input, the program produces a message based upon the choice that the user has made. The program stores the response from the user in an `int` variable, `answer`, by assigning the value that the `nextInt` method returns.

There are four if-statements in the code. In the order of appearance, they have the following roles.

1. `if ( answer < 1 || answer > 4 )` checks whether or not the user's selection is invalid—the selection has to be one of 1, 2, 3, and 4. This one thus checks whether or not the number is either (strictly less than 1) or (strictly greater than 4). If either is the case, the program produces a message that says the choice is invalid.
2. `if ( answer >= 1 && answer <= 4 )` tests the validity of the choice. It uses the condition exactly opposite to the first one.

3. if (answer == 1 || answer == 2) is for producing a special message when the choice corresponds to one of the University of Miami (UM) colors (orange and green).
4. if (answer == 3 || answer == 4) is for producing a special message when the choice corresponds to one of the University of Michigan (UM) colors (maize and blue).

Note that the messages that the first two if-statements generate use printf for formatting:

```
1   import java.util.Scanner;
2   // ask about a color and respond
3   public class ColorSelection
4   {
5     public static void main( String[] args )
6     {
7       //-- scanner
8       Scanner keyboard = new Scanner( System.in );
9       System.out.println( "What is your favorite color?" );
10      System.out.println(
11          "1. Orange, 2. Green, 3. Maize, 4. Blue" );
12      System.out.print( "Select from 1 to 4 : " );
13      int answer = keyboard.nextInt();
```

Listing 6.10 An interactive program that responds to the user's color selection (part 1)

```
14        if ( answer < 1 || answer > 4 )
15        {
16          System.out.printf( "Your choice %d is invalid.%n", answer );
17        }
18        if ( answer >= 1 && answer <= 4 )
19        {
20          System.out.printf( "Your choice %d is excellent.%n", answer );
21        }
22        if ( answer == 1 || answer == 2 )
23        {
24          System.out.println( "It is a U. Miami color!" );
25        }
26        if ( answer == 3 || answer == 4 )
27        {
28          System.out.println( "It is a U. Michigan color!" );
29        }
30      }
31  }
```

Listing 6.11 An interactive program that responds to the user's color selection (part 2)

Following is an example of executing the program:

```
1   What is your favorite color?
2   1. Orange, 2. Green, 3. Maize, 4. Blue
3   Select from 1 to 4 : 6
4   Your choice 6 is invalid.
```

```
1   What is your favorite color?
2   1. Orange, 2. Green, 3. Maize, 4. Blue
3   Select from 1 to 4 : 3
4   Your choice 3 is excellent.
5   It is a U. Michigan color!
```

Fig. 6.4 The execution
diagram of an if-else
statement

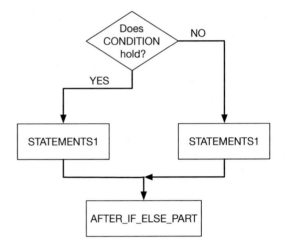

```
1   What is your favorite color?
2   1. Orange, 2. Green, 3. Maize, 4. Blue
3   Select from 1 to 4 : 1
4   Your choice 1 is excellent.
5   It is a U. Miami color!
```

6.2.2 Else

Now we look at the if-statements having the "otherwise" part, which we call if-else statements:

```
1   if ( CONDITION )
2   {
3      STATEMENTS1
4   }
5   else
6   {
7      STATEMENTS2
8   }
9   AFTER_IF_ELSE_PART
```

Figure 6.4 shows the execution diagram of an if-else statement as it appears in the above hypothetical code.

In an if-else statement, an `if` and an `else` work as a pair. For each `if-else` pair, the `if` part must appear before the `else` part. Furthermore, the `if` part and the `else` part must be at the same depth. Furthermore, there must be no other statements or code blocks between the paired `if` and `else` parts.

The following example shows syntactically incorrect if-else statements:

```
1   public static void SOME_METHOD()
2   {
3      else
4      {
5         ...
6      }
7      if ( CONDITION1 )
8      {
```

```
 9        ...
10      }
11      System.out.println( "Wow!" );
12      else
13      {
14        ...
15      }
16   }
```

Similar to the case of if-statements, the curly brackets for the else-part can be omitted if there is only one statement in it. In other words,

```
1   if ( CONDITION )
2      FIRST_STATEMENT;
3   else
4      SECOND_STATEMENT;
5   AFTER_IF_ELSE_PART
```

is the same as:

```
1   if ( CONDITION )
2   {
3      FIRST_STATEMENT;
4   }
5   else
6   {
7      SECOND_STATEMENT;
8   }
9   AFTER_IF_ELSE_PART
```

The code:

```
1   if ( CONDITION )
2      FIRST_STATEMENT;
3      ADDITIONAL_STATEMENT;
4   else
5      SECOND_STATEMENT;
```

is syntactically incorrect, because the code is basically saying:

```
1   if ( CONDITION )
2   {
3      FIRST_STATEMENT;
4   }
5      ADDITIONAL_STATEMENT;
6   else
7   {
8      SECOND_STATEMENT;
9   }
```

meaning ADDITIONAL_STATEMENT is wedged between the if-part and the else-part.

Using else we can rewrite ColorSelection as follows:

```
1   import java.util.Scanner;
2   // ask about a color and respond
3   public class ColorSelectionElse
4   {
5     public static void main( String[] args )
6     {
7       //-- scanner
8       Scanner keyboard = new Scanner( System.in );
9       System.out.println( "What is your favorite color?" );
10      System.out.println(
11          "1. Orange, 2. Green, 3. Maize, 4. Blue" );
12      System.out.print( "Select from 1 to 4 : " );
13      int answer = keyboard.nextInt();
14      if ( answer < 1 || answer > 4 )
15      {
16        System.out.printf( "Your choice %d is invalid.%n", answer );
17      }
18      else
19      {
20        System.out.printf( "Your choice %d is excellent.%n", answer );
21      }
22      if ( answer == 1 || answer == 2 )
23      {
24        System.out.println( "It is a U. Miami color!" );
25      }
26      if ( answer == 3 || answer == 4 )
27      {
28        System.out.println( "It is a U. Michigan color!" );
29      }
30    }
31  }
```

Listing 6.12 A program that responds to a color selection of the user. The program uses `else`

6.2.3 If-Else Inside If/Else

Any number of if-statements and/or if-else statements can be placed in an `if`-block and in an `else`-block to build complex flow control.

The next code utilizes two `if-else` blocks, with the second one appearing inside the `else` block of the first, to accomplish exactly the same task as before:

```
1   import java.util.Scanner;
2   // ask about a color and respond
3   public class ColorSelectionInside
4   {
5     public static void main( String[] args )
6     {
7       //-- scanner
8       Scanner keyboard = new Scanner( System.in );
```

Listing 6.13 A color-selection program that uses two `if-else` blocks (part 1)

In the second occurrence of if-else (Lines 21–28), if the code reaches Line 20, the value of answer is guaranteed to be one of 1, 2, 3, and 4. Therefore if the code reaches the second else (Line 25), the value of answer is guaranteed to be either 3 or 4. This implies that the code works as we intended.

```
9     System.out.println( "What is your favorite color?" );
10    System.out.println(
11        "1. Orange, 2. Green, 3. Maize, 4. Blue" );
12    System.out.print( "Select from 1 to 4 : " );
13    int answer = keyboard.nextInt();
14    if ( answer < 1 || answer > 4 )
15    {
16        System.out.printf( "Your choice %d is invalid.%n", answer );
17    }
18    else
19    {
20        System.out.printf( "Your choice %d is excellent.%n", answer );
21        if ( answer == 1 || answer == 2 )
22        {
23            System.out.println( "It is a U. Miami color!" );
24        }
25        else
26        {
27            System.out.println( "It is a U. Michigan color!" );
28        }
29    }
30  }
31 }
```

Listing 6.14 A color-selection program that uses two if-else blocks (part 2)

A special case of successive if-else statements is else if as follows:

```
1 if ( CONDITION1 ) { STATEMENTS1 }
2 else if ( CONDITION2 ) { STATEMENTS2 }
3 else if ( CONDITION3 ) { STATEMENTS3 }
4 else { STATEMENTS4 }
```

Because of the rule allowing the omission of the curly-brackets after else (if the section has only one statement), and because a single-pair of if-else is an inseparable block of code, this is syntactically equivalent to:

```
1 if ( CONDITION1 ) { STATEMENTS1 }
2 else {
3   if ( CONDITION2 ) { STATEMENTS2 }
4   else { if ( CONDITION3 ) { STATEMENTS3 }
5     else { STATEMENTS4 }
6   }
7 }
```

In the above if-else statement, the evaluation of CONDITION2 occurs only if the evaluation of CONDITION1 produces false and the evaluation of CONDITION3 occurs only if both the evaluation of CONDITION1 and the evaluation of CONDITION2 produces false. In general, if an if-statement is followed by a series of else-if statements, the condition evaluation terminates at the point where the result is true and evaluations beyond that point never take place. If there is no condition producing true, the statements corresponding to the final else will run.

Using this option, we can rewrite the previous code as follows:

```
1  import java.util.Scanner;
2  // ask about a color and respond
3  public class ColorSelectionWithElse
4  {
5    public static void main( String[] args )
6    {
7      //-- scanner
8      Scanner keyboard = new Scanner( System.in );
9      System.out.println( "What is your favorite color?" );
10     System.out.println( "1. Orange, 2. Green, 3. Yellow, 4. Blue" );
11     System.out.print( "Select from 1 to 4 : " );
12     int answer = keyboard.nextInt();
13     if ( answer < 1 || answer > 4 )
14     {
15       System.out.printf( "Your choice %d is invalid.%n", answer );
16     }
17     else if ( answer == 3 || answer == 4 )
18     {
19       System.out.printf( "Your choice %d is great, but%n", answer );
20       System.out.println( "it is not a UM color!" );
21     }
22     else
23     {
24       System.out.printf( "Your choice %d is great.%n", answer );
25     }
26   }
27 }
```

Listing 6.15 A color-selection program that uses else-if

The benefit of else is that when the flow control uses more than two mutually exclusive conditions, the expression can be simplified without having to spell out each condition succinctly.

To explain this a little, consider the hypothetical situation in Fig. 6.5. If we are to write the code without the use of else, it may look like:

Fig. 6.5 A hypothetical situation with interwoven conditions

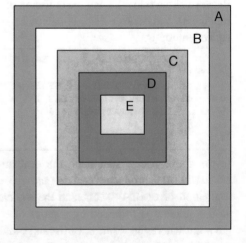

```
1   if ( cond_A ) { ... }
2   if ( !cond_A )
3   {
4     if ( cond_B ) { ... }
5     else ( !cond_B )
6     {
7       if ( cond_C ) { ... }
8       if ( !cond_C )
9       {
10        if ( cond_D ) { ... }
11        if ( !cond_D )
12        {
13          if ( cond_E ) { ... }
14          if ( !cond_E ) { ... }
15        }
16      }
17    }
18  }
```

or:

```
1   if ( cond_A ) { ... }
2   if ( !cond_A && cond_B ) { ... }
3   if ( !cond_A && !cond_B && cond_C ) { ... }
4   if ( !cond_A && !cond_B && !cond_C && cond_D ) { ... }
5   if ( !cond_A && !cond_B  && !cond_C && !cond_D && cond_E ) { ... }
```

On the other hand, if we use else, we can simplify it as:

```
1   if ( cond_A ) { ... }
2   else if ( cond_B ) { ... }
3   else if ( cond_C ) { ... }
4   else if ( cond_D ) { ... }
5   else if ( cond_E ) { ... }
```

Here is an example that demonstrates the benefit of else.

Suppose we are to write a program that receives an int value from the user and produces an output line depending on the value: message X for values 0, 4, 8, and 12, message Y for values less than 0 and values greater than 12, and message Z for the rest. Without using else the code may look like:

```
1   if ( value == 0 || value == 4 || value == 8 || value == 12 )
2   {
3     System.out.println( X );
4   }
5   if ( value < 0 || value > 12 )
6   {
7     System.out.println( Y );
8   }
9   if ( value > 0 && value < 4
10     || value > 4 && value < 8
11     || value > 8 && value < 12 )
12  {
13    System.out.println( Z );
14  }
```

Using `else`, we can avoid using one conditional evaluation:

```
1   if ( value == 0 || value == 4 || value == 8 || value == 12 )
2   {
3      System.out.println( X );
4   }
5   else if ( value < 0 || value > 12 )
6   {
7      System.out.println( Y );
8   }
9   else
10  {
11     System.out.println( Z );
12  }
```

By swapping the order between the first and the second conditions, we can further simplify the code, since 0, 4, 8, and 12 are all multiples of 4, as shown next:

```
1   if ( value < 0 || value > 12 )
2   {
3      System.out.println( Y );
4   }
5   else if ( value % 4 == 0 )
6   {
7      System.out.println( X );
8   }
9   else
10  {
11     System.out.println( Z );
12  }
```

6.2.4 Truncation of Conditional Evaluations

The evaluations of a conditional formula generally proceeds from left to right and stops immediately when the value of the formula has been determined. For example, in the evaluation of a formula (A || B || C), the evaluation order of the operands is A, B, and C. If the value of A is found to be `true`, regardless of the values of B and C, the value of the formula is `true`, so neither B nor C are evaluated. For a similar reason, if the value of A is found to be `false` and the value of B is found to be `true`, C is not evaluated. Similarly, in the condition (A && B && C), if the value of A is found to be `false`, neither B nor C are evaluated, and if the value of A is found to be `true` and the value of B is found to be `false`, C is not evaluated.

This feature can be taken advantage of in many ways. Here is a simple example.

Suppose we are to write an application in which we receive two integers, a and b, from the user and test whether or not a is divisible by b. We can test the divisibility using the condition a % b == 0.

```
1   Scanner keyboard = new Scanner( System.in );
2   int a, b;
3   System.out.print( "Enter two integers a and b: " );
4   a = keyboard.nextInt();
5   b = keyboard.nextInt();
6   if ( a % b == 0 )
7   {
8      System.out.println( a + " divides " + b );
9   }
```

With this code, if the user enters 0 for b, the execution results in a run-time error of `ArithmeticException`.

To prevent this error from happening, we can test b `!= 0` first to ensure that the division is performed only if b is not 0:

```
1   Scanner keyboard = new Scanner( System.in );
2   int a, b;
3   System.out.print( "Enter two integers a and b: " );
4   a = keyboard.nextInt();
5   b = keyboard.nextInt();
6   if ( b != 0 )
7   {
8     if ( a % b == 0 )
9     {
10      System.out.println( a + " divides " + b );
11    }
12  }
```

We can apply the "truncation rule" to this code:

```
1   Scanner keyboard = new Scanner( System.in );
2   int a, b;
3   System.out.print( "Enter two integers a and b: " );
4   a = keyboard.nextInt();
5   b = keyboard.nextInt();
6   if ( b != 0 && a % b == 0 )
7   {
8     System.out.println( a + " divides " + b );
9   }
```

If b `== 0`, the conditional evaluation halts immediately with the outcome of `false`, so the remainder operator a `%` b will not occur. Thus, the program works the same way.

Another nice feature of conditional evaluation is that each of the six comparisons can be combined with an assignment. For example, consider the following code fragment:

```
1   int a, b
2   ...
3   if ( ( a = 2 * b ) > 17 )
4   {
5     ...
6   }
```

Here, a acquires the value of 2 `*` b, and then the value is compared with 17.

In a little more complicated situation, an assignment of a value obtained by a `Scanner` object can be subjected to a test:

```
1   Scanner keyboard = new Scanner( System.in );
2   int a;
3   System.out.println( "Enter an integer: " );
4   if ( ( a = keyboard.nextInt() ) % 2 == 0 )
5   {
6     System.out.println( a + " is an even number." );
7   }
```

Summary

- A condition is a formula, a variable, a literal, or a method call that has a `boolean` value.
- Numbers, including `char`, can be compared using mathematical comparisons `x > y`, `x >= y`, `x < y`, `x <= y`, `x == y`, and `x != y`.
- `!`, `||`, and `&&` are `boolean` operators.
- `if` and `if-else` statements control the flow of the program.
- Multiple `else-if` blocks may appear after one `if`.
- The evaluation of a conditional formula involving multiple operands terminates as soon as the value of the formulas has been found.

Exercises

1. **Flattening multi-level if-then statements** Consider the following code:

```
1   if ( x > 10 )
2   {
3     if ( x > 20 )
4     {
5       methodA();
6     }
7     else
8     {
9       methodB();
10    }
11  }
12  else if ( x < -10 )
13  {
14    if ( x < -20 )
15    {
16      methodA();
17    }
18    else
19    {
20      methodB();
21    }
22  }
23  else
24  {
25    if ( x == 0 )
26    {
27      methodA();
28    }
29    else
30    {
31      methodB();
32    }
33  }
```

Rewrite the code in the form of:

```
1  if ( CONDITION_X )
2  {
3     methodA();
4  }
5  else
6  {
7     methodB();
8  }
```

2. Flattening multi-level if-then statement, alternate

```
1   if ( x > 10 )
2   {
3      if ( x < 20 )
4      {
5         methodA();
6      }
7      else
8      {
9         methodB();
10     }
11  }
12  else if ( x < -10 )
13  {
14     if ( x > -20 )
15     {
16        methodA();
17     }
18     else
19     {
20        methodB();
21     }
22  }
23  else
24  {
25     if ( x == 0 )
26     {
27        methodA();
28     }
29     else
30     {
31        methodB();
32     }
33  }
```

Rewrite the code in the form of:

```
1  if ( CONDITION_X )
2  {
3     methodA();
4  }
5  else
6  {
7     methodB();
8  }
```

3. **Tracing a nested if-statement**   Consider the following code:

```
1  public static String test( int primary , int secondary )
2  {
3    if ( primary > 0 )
4    {
5      if ( secondary > 0 )
6      {
7        return "1";
8      }
9    }
10   return "0";
11 }
```

State:
- for which input combinations the method returns `"1"`;
- for which input combinations the method returns `"0"`.

4. **Tracing a nested if-statement**   Consider the following code:

```
1  public static String test( int primary , int secondary )
2  {
3    if ( primary > 0 )
4    {
5      if ( secondary == primary )
6      {
7        return "1";
8      }
9      else if ( secondary == 2 * primary )
10     {
11       return "2";
12     }
13     return "X";
14   }
15   return "0";
16 }
```

The return value of the method is `"1"`, `"2"`, `"X"`, or `"0"`. For each of the four possible return values, state one combination of the values of `primary` and `secondary` for which the method returns the value.

5. **Divisibility testing**   Write a program, `Divisibility`, that receives two int values from the user and asserts whether the first number is a multiple of the second. The method asserts that the answer is in the negative if the second number happens to be 0.

6. **Boolean evaluation**   Suppose a, b, and c are `boolean` variables. Then (a == b) != c is a valid formula, since a == b evaluates to a `boolean`. There are eight possible combinations for the values of the three variables. For each of the combinations, state the value of the condition.

7. **Discriminant of a quadratic formula**   Write a program, `DiscriminantTest`, that receives three real values a, b, and c from the user, and returns the number of real solutions of the equation $ax^2 + bx + c = 0$ as an int.

8. **Following the code execution to determine the output**   State the value that the method `method123` below returns with each of the values below as the actual parameter:

```
1   public static double method123( double input )
2   {
3     if ( input < 11.0 )
4     {
5       return input + 1;
6     }
7     if ( input < 12.0 )
8     {
9       return input + 2;
10    }
11    return input - 5;
12  }
```

(a) 10.0

(b) 11.0

(c) 12.0

(d) 13.0

9. **Following the code execution to determine the output** State the value the method methodABC below returns with each of the values below as the actual parameter:

```
1   public static double methodABC( int input )
2   {
3     if ( input == 10 )
4     {
5       return input * 2;
6     }
7     if ( input < 11 )
8     {
9       return input * 3;
10    }
11    return input * 7;
12  }
```

(a) 9

(b) 10

(c) 11

10. **Return value determination 1** Let a method cute be defined as follows:

```
1   public static boolean cute( boolean x, boolean y, boolean z )
2   {
3     return x == (y == z);
4   }
```

For each of the eight possible input values, state the value the method returns.

11. **Return value determination 2** Let the method neat be defined as follows:

```
1   public static boolean neat( boolean x, boolean y, boolean z )
2   {
3     return x != y || y != z || z != x;
4   }
```

State, for each of the eight possible value combinations for the three parameters, the return value of the method.

Programming Projects

12. **Triangle validity** Write a method, `isValidTriangle`, that receives three `double` values `sideA`, `sideB`, and `sideC` as parameters and returns whether or not each value is strictly less than the sum of the other two. The return type must be `boolean`.

13. **Right angle** Write a method, `isRightAngleTriangle`, that receives three `double` values `sideA`, `sideB`, and `sideC` as parameters, and returns whether or not the three edges form a right-angled triangle. The return type must be `boolean`.

14. **Checking whether or not three values are all positive** Write a public static method named `allPositive` that receives three `double` values `valueA`, `valueB`, and `valueC` as parameters, and returns whether or not the three values are all strictly positive. The return type must be `boolean`.

15. **What does this function compute?** Analyze the following code, and state what this method computes.

```
1  public static int mystery ( int a,  int b,  int c )
2  {
3     if ( a == Math.max( a, Math.max( b, c ) ) )
4     {
5        return Math.max( b, c );
6     }
7     return Math.max( a, Math.min( b, c ) );
8  }
```

16. **Solving a system of linear equations with two unknowns** Consider solving the system of linear equations with two unknowns x and y:

$$ax + by = s$$

$$cx + dy = t$$

To solve the problem, we first check the value of the determinant of the system: $h = ad - bc$. If h is not 0, we have $x = (ds - bt)/h$ and $y = (-cs + at)/h$. If h is 0, the system is degenerate, and falls into one of the following four cases:

- the system is unsolvable;
- the system is equivalent to one linear equation;
- the value of x is arbitrary and the value of y is fixed;
- the value of y is arbitrary and the value of x is fixed

Write a program, `LinearEquation2`, that receives the six coefficients from the user and solves the problem if the determinant h is not 0. The program should state, in the case that $h = 0$, that it cannot solve the system.

17. **Fully solving a system of linear equations with two unknowns** Continuing on the previous problem, write a program `LinearEquation2Full` that completely solves the problem including the cases in which only x or only y is determined. Here are five examples that show the behavior of the program.

```
1  Enter a, b, s for number 1: 1 2 3
2  Enter c, d, t for number 2: 3 1 2
3  x = 0.2, y = 1.4.
```

```
1   Enter a, b, s for number 1: 0 0 0
2   Enter c, d, t for number 2: 0 0 0
3   Both x and y are arbitrary.
```

```
1   Enter a, b, s for number 1: 1 0 2
2   Enter c, d, t for number 2: 2 0 4
3   y is arbitrary and x = 2.0.
```

```
1   Enter a, b, s for number 1: 1 2 3
2   Enter c, d, t for number 2: 2 4 6
3   Any point on 1.0x+2.0y=3.0.
```

```
1   Enter a, b, s for number 1: 1 2 3
2   Enter c, d, t for number 2: 2 4 5
3   Unsolvable.
```

Implement a series of cases to consider, which can be expressed as a series of if-else-if:

- "if" $h \neq 0$: solve it as before;
- "else if" either $a = b = 0$ and $s \neq 0$ or $c = d = 0$ and $t \neq 0$: unsolvable;
- "else if" either $a = b = s = c = d = t = 0$: arbitrary x and y;
- "else if" $a = b = s = 0$: equivalent to $cx + dy = t$;
- "else if" $c = d = t = 0$: equivalent to $ax + by = s$;
- "else if" $a = c = 0$ and $s/b = t/c$: equivalent to $ax + by = s$.
- "else if" $b = d = 0$ and $s/b = t/c$: equivalent to $ax + by = s$.
- "else if" either $a = c = 0$ or $b = d = 0$: unsolvable;
- "else if" $s/a \neq t/b$: unsolvable;
- "else": equivalent to $ax + by = s$.

Write a method named justOne(double p, double q, double r) that handles the situation in which the system is equivalent to just one equation, where it is guaranteed that either $p \neq 0$ or $q \neq 0$. Using this method, the series of actions can be handled in a slightly simpler manner.

Part II

Loops

For-Loops

7

7.1 Using For-Loops for Repetition

A **loop** is a program structure for executing a block of code repeatedly. The code for a loop usually comes with a specification of when to stop the repetition. Java has four loop structures: the for-loop, the while-loop, the do-while loop, and the for-each loop. We study the for-loop in this chapter, the while-loop and do-while loop in Chap. 11, and the for-each loop in Chaps. 17 and 18.

In Sect. 5.2, we studied computing the BMI value on height and weight values that the user enters. In BMIInteractive.java (List 7.1) we used a method named oneInteraction that received one pair of height and weight from the user and reported the BMI value with respect to the combination. The action of the method main in the program was to call oneInteraction twice.

Suppose we want to increase the number of repetitions from two to a much larger number, for example, ten. We can accomplish this by adding eight more lines of oneInteraction():

```
 1   public static void main( String[] args )
 2   {
 3     oneInteraction();
 4     oneInteraction();
 5     oneInteraction();
 6     oneInteraction();
 7     oneInteraction();
 8     oneInteraction();
 9     oneInteraction();
10     oneInteraction();
11     oneInteraction();
12     oneInteraction();
13   }
```

Now what should we do if we wanted to increase the number of repetitions to 20? Should we add ten more lines of the same oneInteraction()? Using a loop, it is possible to state the 20-time repetitions in just a few lines.

© Springer Nature Switzerland AG 2018
M. Ogihara, *Fundamentals of Java Programming*,
https://doi.org/10.1007/978-3-319-89491-1_7

```
1    public static void main( String[] args )
2    {
3      int i;
4      for ( i = 1;  i <= 10;  i = i + 1 )
5      {
6        oneInteraction();
7      }
8    }
```

Line 4 of the code,

$$\texttt{for (i = 1; i <= 10; i = i + 1)}$$

is the for-loop. It means

"repeat the following as long as i <= 10 by first assigning the value of 1 to i and then adding 1 to i each time."

The "following" refers to the block of code between Lines 5–7. We call this block the **loop-body**.
The actions that take place in the above for-loop are as follows:

- The value of 1 is stored in i.
- As long as the value of i is less than or equal to 10,
  - execute oneInteraction and
  - increase the value of i by 1.

The use of a for-loop in stating the repetition makes it easy to change the number of repetitions. Furthermore, if the name of the method changes, we only have to replace just one call, which appears in the body of the loop.

The variable i that refers to the "round" in the repetition can be used in the body of the loop. For example, before calling oneInteraction we can announce the round:

```
1    public static void main( String[] args )
2    {
3      int i;
4      for ( i = 1; i <= 10; i = i + 1 )
5      {
6        System.out.println( "This is round " + i + "." );
7        oneInteraction();
8      }
9    }
```

The code with the round announcement appears next:

```
1   import java.util.Scanner;
2   public class BMIRepetitive
3   {
4     public static final double BMI_SCALE = 703.0;
5     public static final int FEET_TO_INCHES = 12;
6
7     public static double bmiFormula( double weight, double height )
8     {
9       return BMI_SCALE * weight / (height * height);
10    }
11
12    public static void oneInteraction()
13    {
14      Scanner keyboard = new Scanner( System.in );
15      System.out.print( "Enter weight: " );
16      double weight = keyboard.nextDouble();
17      System.out.print( "Enter height in feet and inches: " );
18      double feet = keyboard.nextDouble();
19      double inches = keyboard.nextDouble();
20      double height = FEET_TO_INCHES * feet + inches;
21      double bmi = bmiFormula( weight, height );
22      System.out.println( "Your BMI is " + bmi + "." );
23    }
24    public static void main( String[] args )
25    {
26      int i;
27      for ( i = 1; i <= 10; i = i + 1 )
28      {
29        System.out.println( "This is round " + i + "." );
30        oneInteraction();
31      }
32    }
33  }
```

Listing 7.1 A program that repeatedly computes BMI using a for-loop. The program announces each round

The execution of the code, with some input from the user, produces the following:

```
1   This is round 1.
2   Enter weight: 150
3   Enter height in feet and inches: 5 6
4   Your BMI is 24.207988980716255.
5   This is round 2.
6   Enter weight: 150 5 7
7   Enter height in feet and inches: Your BMI is 23.490755179327245.
8   This is round 3.
9   Enter weight: 160 5 7
10  Enter height in feet and inches: Your BMI is 25.056805524615726.
11  This is round 4.
12  ...
```

As we have seen in the above, the header part of a for-loop has three components with a semicolon in between:

- **initialization,**
- **continuation (termination) condition,**
- **update**

Fig. 7.1 A generic flow
chart of for-loops

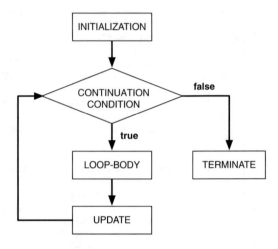

In other words, the header part of a for-loop takes the form of:

```
for ( INITIALIZATION; CONTINUATION CONDITION; UPDATE ) { ... }
```

The roles of these components are as follows:

- The initialization of a for-loop is a statement that is executed prior to entering the repetition.
- The continuation condition is one that must hold for the loop-body to execute. Before executing the loop-body, this condition is tested. If the condition does not hold, the loop is terminated immediately.
- The update is a statement that is executed after each execution of the loop-body.[1]

The roles of the three components are summarized in Fig. 7.1. Most typically, in a for-loop, the initialization is an assignment to a variable (usually an integer), the termination condition is a comparison involving the variable, and the update is a modification to the variable. We call such a variable an **iteration variable**.

The next program contains a for-loop with an interaction that changes its value from 0 to 7.

```
 1  public class ForExample
 2  {
 3    public static void main( String[] args )
 4    {
 5      int count;
 6      for ( count = 0; count < 8; count ++ )
 7      {
 8        System.out.println( "The value of count is " + count );
 9      }
10    }
11  }
```

Listing 7.2 An iteration over the sequence 0, ..., 7

---

[1]Both the initialization and the update can be composed of multiple statements. Those statements must be separated by a comma in between.

Fig. 7.2 The code
execution diagram of
`ForExample`

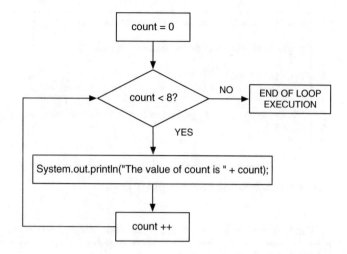

The iteration variable of the for-loop is count. Since the initial value of the iteration variable is 0, the termination condition is count < 8, and the update is count ++, the last value of count for which the loop-body is executed is 7. Figure 7.2 summarizes the above observation.

Running the code produces the following:

```
1   The value of count is 0
2   The value of count is 1
3   The value of count is 2
4   The value of count is 3
5   The value of count is 4
6   The value of count is 5
7   The value of count is 6
8   The value of count is 7
```

Consider changing the initialization to:

$$count = 8$$

while retaining the other two components of the loop header.

```
1   public class ForExampleNoOutput
2   {
3     public static void main( String[] args )
4     {
5       int count;
6       for ( count = 8; count < 8; count ++ )
7       {
8         System.out.println( "The value of count is " + count );
9       }
10    }
11  }
```

Listing 7.3 A for-loop that never executes its body

Since the new initial value already fails to satisfy the termination condition, the loop terminates without executing its body once.

Consider further changing the comparison in the termination condition to count <= 8, as shown next:

```
1  public class ForExampleJustOnce
2  {
3    public static void main( String[] args )
4    {
5      int count;
6      for ( count = 8; count <=8; count ++ )
7      {
8        System.out.println( "The value of count is " + count );
9      }
10   }
11 }
```

Listing 7.4 A for-loop that never executes its body

The loop-body will then execute just once, producing the output line:

```
The value of count is 8
```

Remember that the existence/absence of the equal sign often makes a significant difference in the behavior of a for-loop.

The variable type declaration of the iteration variable can be inserted in the initialization, like this:

```
1    public static void main( String[] args )
2    {
3      // int count;
4      for ( int count = 0; count < 8; count ++ )
5      {
6        System.out.println( "The value of count is " + count );
7      }
8    }
```

This requires the removal of the declaration of the variable count appearing in Line 3; otherwise, the scopes of the two declarations of the identical variable names overlap. Retaining the declaration (i.e., not adding the two forward slashes) will result in an error message during compilation, e.g.:

```
1  ForExample.java:6: error: variable count is already defined in method
     main(String[])
2      for ( int count = 0; count < 8; count ++ )
3                 ^
4  1 error
```

Here, the code uses // to make the line a comment.

If the iteration variable is declared in the initialization of a for-loop, then its scope is the entire for-loop, including the header-part. The scope of the variable count becomes the entire for-loop, not the entire main.

Let us go back to the use of a for-loop to repeat an action.

Suppose we want to generate a random number between 0 and 1 (using Math.random) N times and take the average of the random numbers. What can we expect? To compute the average, we only have to compute the total of the random numbers and then divide it by N. According to the statistical principal called the **law of large numbers**, if the random number generation is fair, the larger the value of N is, the closer the average is to 0.50.

Suppose we use a modest value, 20, for N and run an experiment to examine how close the average gets to the expected average of 0.50. Our program uses a double variable named random to record the random number Math.random produces at each round, an int variable named round to record the number of times a random number has been generated, and a double variable named sum to record the sum of the random numbers. At each round, the program announces the round number and the random number that has been generated. After the for-loop, the program divides the total by 20 and then prints the average.

Here is the code that follows this algorithm:

```
1  public class RandomAverage
2  {
3    public static void main( String[] args )
4    {
5      double random, sum;
6      sum = 0;
7      for ( int round = 1; round <= 20; round ++ )
8      {
9        random = Math.random();
10       sum += random;
11       System.out.print( "round=" + round );
12       System.out.println( ", number=" + random );
13     }
14     sum /= 20;
15     System.out.println( "average=" + sum );
16   }
17 }
```

Listing 7.5 A program that computes the average of 20 random numbers

Here is the result of one execution. Since the program uses a random number generator, it is unlikely that the same output result occurs twice:

```
1   round=1,  number=0.8157853753717103
2   round=2,  number=0.46775040606117546
3   round=3,  number=0.8441866465531849
4   round=4,  number=0.5829690931048322
5   round=5,  number=0.5599437446060029
6   round=6,  number=0.8672105406302983
7   round=7,  number=0.33033589637735683
8   round=8,  number=0.5881510375862207
9   round=9,  number=0.38566559572527037
10  round=10, number=0.31425625823536696
11  round=11, number=0.3286394398265723
12  round=12, number=0.9437308791253096
13  round=13, number=0.8607491030785093
14  round=14, number=0.008072130126899335
15  round=15, number=0.0477975147654055
16  round=16, number=0.2659779860979148
17  round=17, number=0.5987723989794204
18  round=18, number=0.8369910748406596
19  round=19, number=0.25924195790278215
20  round=20, number=0.005168580596320194
21  average=0.4955697829795607
```

Here is another run:

```
1    java RandomAverage
2    round=1, number=0.8920844233690451
3    round=2, number=0.3288527172059581
4    round=3, number=0.4933769583576755
5    round=4, number=0.8788336888081347
6    round=5, number=0.6212225634348153
7    round=6, number=0.7371533245256305
8    round=7, number=0.7485906839518522
9    round=8, number=0.5634098385103024
10   round=9, number=0.22549810357332067
11   round=10, number=0.8546489284189476
12   round=11, number=0.2905654125567769
13   round=12, number=0.24907615852772835
14   round=13, number=0.5800520831995266
15   round=14, number=0.2043575262026217
16   round=15, number=0.25741759539019937
17   round=16, number=0.4710648380419118
18   round=17, number=0.04850748397632787
19   round=18, number=0.6508157292281656
20   round=19, number=0.33074890481577923
21   round=20, number=0.7833542508320545
22   average=0.5104815606463388
```

In both cases, the average is quite close to 0.50.

7.2   Iteration

7.2.1   Simple Iteration

We formally call the process of generating a series of values using a loop an **iteration**. For-loops are useful for iteration. In many cases of iterations with a for-loop, the series is generated as the values of its iteration variable.

Using different initializations, termination conditions, and updating actions, it is possible to produce a wide variety of sequences. Here are some examples:

```
1        for ( int count = 10; count >= 1; count -- );
2        for ( int count = 10; count > 0; count -= 2 );
3        for ( int count = 89; count <= 100; count += 3 );
4        for ( int count = 1; count <= 100; count *= 2 );
5        for ( int count = 3; count <= 80; count = count * 2 - 1 );
```

These are all syntactically correct. Their iteration variables are named `count`. Each line ends with a semicolon, which indicates that there is no loop-body. The learners of Java often attach a semicolon after the closing parenthesis, which may produce a source code that compiles but does not run as anticipated.

The sequences generated by the for-loops are:

```
1    10, 9, 8, 7, 6, 5, 4, 3, 2, 1
2    10, 8, 6, 4, 2
3    89, 92, 95, 98
4    1, 2, 4, 8, 16, 32, 64
5    3, 7, 15, 31, 63
```

The next code executes the for-loop (now without the semicolon after the closing parenthesis) and prints the values generated in one single line for each loop, with a single white space character inserted before each value. To do this, the code uses `print` instead of `println`. Because `print` does not add the newline character at the end of its loop, the code must execute one `println` statement to go to the next line.

Furthermore, the two lines preceding each for-loop have the role of producing the three components of the loop on the screen:

```
1  public class IterationSamples
2  {
3    public static void main( String[] args )
4    {
5      int count;
6      System.out.println( "----- Loop Number 1 ----- " );
7      System.out.println( "count = 10; count >= 1; count --" );
8      for ( count = 10; count >= 1; count -- )
9      {
10       System.out.print( " " + count );
11     }
12     System.out.println( "\n----- Loop Number 2 ----- " );
13     System.out.println( "count = 10; count > 0; count -= 2" );
14     for ( count = 10; count > 0; count -= 2 )
15     {
16       System.out.print( " " + count );
17     }
```

Listing 7.6 Examples of iteration (part 1)

```
18       System.out.println( "\n----- Loop Number 3 ----- " );
19       System.out.println( "count = 89; count <= 100; count += 3" );
20       for ( count = 89; count <= 100; count += 3 )
21       {
22         System.out.print( " " + count );
23       }
24       System.out.println( "\n----- Loop Number 4 ----- " );
25       System.out.println( "count = 1; count <= 100; count *= 2" );
26       for ( count = 1; count <= 100; count *= 2 )
27       {
28         System.out.print( " " + count );
29       }
30       System.out.println( "\n----- Loop Number 5 ----- " );
31       System.out.println(
32           "count = 3; count <= 80; count = count * 2 - 1" );
33       for ( count = 3; count <= 80; count = count * 2 - 1 )
34       {
35         System.out.print( " " + count );
36       }
37       System.out.println();
38     }
39  }
```

Listing 7.7 Examples of iteration (part 2)

The code produces the following output:

```
1    ----- Loop Number 1 -----
2    count = 10; count >= 1; count --
3     10 9 8 7 6 5 4 3 2 1
4    ----- Loop Number 2 -----
5    count = 10; count > 0; count -= 2
6     10 8 6 4 2
7    ----- Loop Number 3 -----
8    count = 89; count <= 100; count += 3
9     89 92 95 95 98
10   ----- Loop Number 4 -----
11   count = 1; count <= 100; count *= 2
12    1 2 4 8 16 32 64
13   ----- Loop Number 5 -----
14   count = 3; count <= 80; count = count * 2 - 1
15    3 5 9 17 33 65
```

Using an iteration that decreases the value of its iteration variable from its start value, as well as a `Scanner` object that receives the start value, we can write the following simple program for executing a countdown from the start number to 0.

Note the following specifics of the code:

- The program uses a `Scanner` object. Line 1 is an `import` statement for using a `Scanner`. We use a generic `java.util.*` here.
- In Line 9, the program receives the start value and stores it in a variable named `start`. The variable `start` is declared in Line 6.
- The iterator has `value > 0` as the termination condition. Thus, the last value of `value` in which the loop-body executes is greater than 0. Since `value` is an integer, the smallest integer that satisfies `value > 0` is 1, so the condition is equivalent to `value >= 1`.

```java
1    import java.util.* ;
2
3    public class CountDown
4    {
5      public static void main( String[] args )
6      {
7        Scanner keyboard;
8        int start, value;
9        keyboard = new Scanner( System.in );
10       System.out.print( "Enter start: " );
11       start = keyboard.nextInt();
12       for ( value = start; value > 0; value -- )
13       {
14         System.out.println( ".." + value );
15       }
16       System.out.println( "BOOOOOOOOOOOOOOOOOOOOOOOM!" );
17     }
18   }
```

Listing 7.8 A program that counts down from an input number to 0

Executing the code produces the following result:

```
1  | Enter start: 10
2  | ..10
3  | ..9
4  | ..8
5  | ..7
6  | ..6
7  | ..5
8  | ..4
9  | ..3
10 | ..2
11 | ..1
12 | BOOOOOOOOOOOOOOOOOOOOOOOOOM!
```

Another run produces this result:

```
1  | Enter start: 13
2  | ..13
3  | ..12
4  | ..11
5  | ..10
6  | ..9
7  | ..8
8  | ..7
9  | ..6
10 | ..5
11 | ..4
12 | ..3
13 | ..2
14 | ..1
15 | BOOOOOOOOOOOOOOOOOOOOOOOOOOM!
```

We can accelerate the speed at which the number decreases by using "dividing by 2" instead of "decreasing by 1" in the iteration, a shown next:

```java
1  import java.util. * ;
2
3  public class CountDownFast
4  {
5    public static void main( String[] args )
6    {
7      Scanner keyboard;
8      int start, value;
9      keyboard = new Scanner( System.in );
10     System.out.print( "Enter start: " );
11     start = keyboard.nextInt();
12     for ( value = start; value > 0; value /= 2 )
13     {
14       System.out.println( ".." + value );
15     }
16     System.out.println( "BOOOOOOOOOOOOOOOOOOOOOOOOOOM!" );
17   }
18 }
```

Listing 7.9 A program that counts down from an input number to 0 by dividing the number by 2

Here is one execution:

```
1   Enter start: 1000
2   ..1000
3   ..500
4   ..250
5   ..125
6   ..62
7   ..31
8   ..15
9   ..7
10  ..3
11  ..1
12  BOOOOOOOOOOOOOOOOOOOOOOOOOOM!
```

Here is another:

```
1   Enter start: 10000
2   ..10000
3   ..5000
4   ..2500
5   ..1250
6   ..625
7   ..312
8   ..156
9   ..78
10  ..39
11  ..19
12  ..9
13  ..4
14  ..2
15  ..1
16  BOOOOOOOOOOOOOOOOOOOOOOOOOOOM!
```

The next program receives the value for an int variable, n, from the user, and then computes the sum of integers between 1 and n. In Chap. 2, we have seen the program performing this calculation, using Gauss's approach for a fixed value of n (as n * (n - 1) / 2). The version here computes the sum by adding the numbers one after another:

```
1   import java.util.*;
2   public class LimitedGauss
3   {
4     public static void main( String[] args )
5     {
6       int n, sum;
7       Scanner keyboard = new Scanner( System.in );
8       System.out.print( "Enter n: " );
9       n = keyboard.nextInt();
10      sum = 0;
11      for ( int i = 1; i <= n; i ++ )
12      {
13        sum += i;
14      }
15      System.out.println( "The sum = " + sum );
16    }
17  }
```

Listing 7.10 A program that calculates the sum of all integers between 1 and n by adding one number after another

The iteration variable i produces the sequence 1, ..., n for a positive integer n. The program adds the value of i to a variable, sum, whose initial value is 0. Thus, the value of sum becomes 1, 3, 6, 10, and so on, ending with n*(n-1)/2.

Here is one execution example:

```
1  Enter n: 10
2  The sum = 55
```

Note that if the value of n is less than or equal to 0, the loop-body is never executed, and so the value sum retains its initial value, 0:

```
1  Enter n: -10
2  The sum = 0
```

In a similar vein, we can write a program that computes the product of all integers between 1 and n, where n is a value that the user enters. The mathematical name for the product of consecutive numbers starting from 1 is the *factorial* of n, written n!. Since the factorial is a function that increases very quickly as the value of n increases, we use long instead of int. We compute the value of the factorial in a long variable named product. Then, we initialize product with the value of 1. During the loop, we update the value of product by multiplying it with the value of the iteration variable i.

```
1   import java.util.*;
2   public class Factorial
3   {
4     public static void main( String[] args )
5     {
6       int n;
7       long product;
8       Scanner keyboard = new Scanner( System.in );
9       System.out.print( "Enter n: " );
10      n = keyboard.nextInt();
11      product = 1;
12      for ( int i = 1; i <= n; i ++ )
13      {
14        product *= i;
15      }
16      System.out.println( "The product = " + product );
17    }
18  }
```

Listing 7.11 A program that computes the factorial function using a for-loop

Here is one execution example:

```
1  Enter n: 34
2  The product = 4926277576697053184
```

Note that if the value of n is less than or equal to 0, the loop-body is never executed, and so the value product retains its initial value, 1, as shown next:

```
1  Enter n: -10
2  The product = 1
```

The next program receives values for two variables, start and end, from the user. Using these two values, the program computes the sum of all numbers of the form start + 3 * i that fall in the range from start to end. At the end, the program prints the sum.

```
1   import java.util.Scanner;
2   public class SumEveryThird
3   {
4     public static void main( String[] args )
5     {
6       Scanner keyboard;
7       int sum, count, start, end;
8       keyboard = new Scanner( System.in );
9       System.out.print( "Enter start and end: " );
10      start = keyboard.nextInt();
11      end = keyboard.nextInt();
12      //-- initialize the sum
13      sum = 0;
14      //-- iterate the value of j from 1 to 100
15      for ( count = start; count <= end; count += 3 )
16      {
17        sum += count;
18      }
19      //-- output the result
20      System.out.println( "the sum = " + sum );
21    }
22  }
```

Listing 7.12 A program that computes the sum of every third number within a range

We use two successive calls to nextInt (Lines 8 and 9) to receive the input value of the user. The user may hit the return key after entering the first number, but at that point the program will still be waiting for the second number, meaning nothing will happen. After receiving the two numbers, the program executes an iteration with the initialization of count = start and the termination condition of count <= end (Line 15).

The execution of the code with three different pairs of input results is shown next.

```
1   Enter start and end: 100 10000
2   the sum = 16670050
```

```
1   Enter start and end: 599 599
2   the sum = 599
```

```
1   Enter start and end: 1000
2   100
3   the sum = 0
```

Note the following:

- In the second case, the loop-body executes exactly once, since start is equal to end.
- In the last case, the value of end is strictly smaller than the value of start, so the loop terminates before executing the loop-body.

7.2.2 Iteration with an Auxiliary Variable

The sequences that we produced through of iteration had no repetitions and were either monotonically increasing or monotonically decreasing. Is it possible to use a simple iteration to generate a sequence containing repetitions? Is it possible to use a simple iteration to generate a sequence that is not monotonic?

The answer to both questions is "yes". Such sequences can be generated using an auxiliary variable. For examples, consider the sequence

$$[0, 0, 0, 1, 1, 1, 2, 2, 2, 3, 3, 3, 4, 4, 4]$$

For all nonnegative integers k, 3k / 3, (3k + 1) / 3, and (3k + 2) / 3 are all equal to k. Therefore, the above sequence is identical to a / 3 for a = 0..14. We can then generate the sequence in an auxiliary variable, i, as follows:

```
1  int i, a;
2  for ( a = 0; a <= 14; a ++ )
3  {
4    i = a % 3;
5  }
```

By attaching an output statement to the body of the loop:

```
1  int i, a;
2  for ( a = 0; a <= 14; a ++ )
3  {
4    i = a / 3;
5    System.out.print ( " " + i );
6  }
7  System.out.println ();
```

we can verify the output:

```
0 0 0 1 1 1 2 2 2 3 3 3 4 4 4
```

In the above, if we use % instead of /, we generate the sequence:

```
0 1 2 0 1 2 0 1 2 0 1 2 0 1 2
```

Furthermore, by changing the operation to i = (a % 3) - 1, we have the following code:

```
1  int i, a;
2  for ( a = 0; a <= 14; a ++ )
3  {
4    i = ( a % 3 ) - 1;
5    System.out.print ( " " + i );
6  }
7  System.out.println ();
```

This code produces the sequence:

```
-1 0 1 -1 0 1 -1 0 1 -1 0 1 -1 0 1
```

7.3 Double For-Loops

The double for-loop is a special for-loop structure that comprises of two for-loops, with one loop appearing inside the other. Here is the general structure of the double for-loop:

```
1  for ( INITIALIZATION1; CONDITION1; UPDATE1 )
2  {
3    SOME_CODE;
4    for ( INITIALIZATION2; CONDITION2; UPDATE2 )
5    {
6      LOOP_BODY;
7    }
8    SOME_OTHER_CODE;
9  }
```

We call the first loop the **external loop** and the second loop the **internal loop**.

Suppose we have the following double for-loop:

```
1  int start1, start2, end1, end2, diff1, diff2, count1, count2;
2  ...
3  for ( count1 = start1; count1 <= end1; count1 += diff1 )
4  {
5    for ( count2 = start2; count2 <= end2; count2 += diff2 )
6    {
7      System.out.println( count1 + ":" + count2 );
8    }
9  }
```

The code uses two iteration variables, `count1` and `count2`. Iteration by `count1` follows values `start1`, `start1 + diff1`, `start1 + 2 * diff1`, etc., until it reaches a value greater than `end1`. For each value of `count1`, a similar iteration takes places for `count2`.

```
1  import java.util.Scanner;
2  //--- print a rectangular box with "#"
3  public class DarkBox
4  {
5    //-- main method
6    public static void main( String[] args )
7    {
8      int height, width, vertical, horizontal;
9      Scanner keyboard;
10     keyboard = new Scanner( System.in );
11     // set height and width
12     System.out.print( "Enter height: " );
13     height = keyboard.nextInt();
14     System.out.print( "Enter width: " );
15     width = keyboard.nextInt();
16     // exterior loop
17     for ( vertical = 1; vertical <= height; vertical ++ )
18     {
19       // interior loop
20       for ( horizontal = 1; horizontal <= width; horizontal ++ )
21       {
22         System.out.print( "#" );
23       }
24       //-- newline is needed
25       System.out.println();
26     }
27   }
28 }
```

Listing 7.13 A program that generates a rectangle drawn with hash marks

Double for-loops such as this one can be incorporated in the following example. The program receive two integers from the user and produces a rectangle made up of ' # ''s on the screen. The dimensions of the rectangle are equal to the numbers the user has entered.

The external loop is for counting the number of lines, and the internal loop is for counting the number of ' # ''s appearing in each line. Also, for both loops, if we change the start value to 1 and the termination condition to <, we still get the same result. This is because prior to the change, the vertical value iteration generates the sequence:

$$0, 1, 2, \ldots, \text{height} - 1$$

and the horizontal value iteration generates the sequence:

$$0, 1, 2, \ldots, \text{width} - 1$$

After the change, the vertical value iteration generates the sequence:

$$1, 2, \ldots, \text{height}$$

and the horizontal value iteration generates the sequence:

$$1, 2, \ldots, \text{width}$$

Here is an execution example of the code:

```
1   Enter height: 10
2   Enter width: 50
3   ##################################################
4   ##################################################
5   ##################################################
6   ##################################################
7   ##################################################
8   ##################################################
9   ##################################################
10  ##################################################
11  ##################################################
12  ##################################################
```

Here is another:

```
1   Enter height: 8
2   Enter width: 60
3   ############################################################
4   ############################################################
5   ############################################################
6   ############################################################
7   ############################################################
8   ############################################################
9   ############################################################
10  ############################################################
```

Here is one more execution example:

```
1   Enter height: 7
2   Enter width: 0
```

Since the width of the rectangle was 0, seven empty lines appeared.

The next code produces lines surrounding the rectangle, with - for the horizontal lines, | for the vertical lines, and ' + ' for the four corners.

The first part of the code consists of declarations and the user input. The values that the user enters are height and width (same as before).

```
1   import java.util.Scanner;
2   public class FramedBox
3   {
4   //--- print a rectangular box with "#" with a frame
5     //-- main method
6     public static void main( String[] args )
7     {
8       int height, width, horizontal, vertical;
9       Scanner keyboard;
10      keyboard = new Scanner( System.in );
11      // set height and width
12      System.out.print( "Enter height: " );
13      height = keyboard.nextInt();
14      System.out.print( "Enter width: " );
15      width = keyboard.nextInt();
```

Listing 7.14 A program that generates a rectangle of hash marks with surrounding lines (part 1)

The second part consists of three components. The first component is for printing the top line, which is a ' + ', a line of ' - ' having length width, and another ' + ' in the order of appearance. The second component is similar to the previous double for-loop, but has one ' | ' at the beginning and at the end. In addition, the program prints the second ' | ' with System.out.println instead of System.out.print. The third component is identical to the first one.

```
16        // * * * * the top line * * * * //
17        System.out.print( "+" );
18        for ( horizontal = 1; horizontal <= width; horizontal ++ )
19        {
20          System.out.print( "-" );
21        }
22        System.out.println( "+" );
23        // * * * * the middle lines * * * * //
24        for ( vertical = 1; vertical <= height; vertical ++ )
25        {
26          System.out.print( "|" );
27          for ( horizontal = 1; horizontal <= width; horizontal ++ )
28          {
29            System.out.print( "#" );
30          }
31          System.out.println( "|" );
32        }
33        // * * * * the bottom line * * * * //
34        System.out.print( "+" );
35        for ( horizontal = 1; horizontal <= width; horizontal ++ )
36        {
37          System.out.print( "-" );
38        }
39        System.out.println( "+" );
40      }
41  }
```

Listing 7.15 A program that generates a rectangle of hash marks with surrounding lines (part 2)

Here is one example of executing the code.

```
 1  java FramedBox
 2  Enter height: 10
 3  Enter width: 20
 4  +--------------------+
 5  |####################|
 6  |####################|
 7  |####################|
 8  |####################|
 9  |####################|
10  |####################|
11  |####################|
12  |####################|
13  |####################|
14  |####################|
15  +--------------------+
```

Specifying one of the two dimensions as 0 results in the following. This is when the height is 0:

```
 1  Enter height: 0
 2  Enter width: 10
 3  +----------+
 4  +----------+
```

and this is when the width is 0:

```
 1  Enter height: 7
 2  Enter width: 0
 3  ++
 4  ||
 5  ||
 6  ||
 7  ||
 8  ||
 9  ||
10  ||
11  ++
```

By using the value of the external iteration variable in the header of the internal iteration, it is possible to perform a complicated task. The next example shows this. The goal is to print an upside down triangle with the right angle at the upper-left corner, like this one:

```
 1  *********
 2  ********
 3  *******
 4  ******
 5  *****
 6  *****
 7  ****
 8  ***
 9  **
10  *
```

The number of '*' printed in one line starts from some number and decreases one by one, until it becomes 1. The start number is equal to the number of '*' printed in the first line. Suppose an int variable named down contains the number of '*'s that must be in a give line. Using an iteration variable, across, the task of printing that specific line can be accomplished as:

```
1        for ( across = 1; across <= down; across ++ )
2        {
3          System.out.print( "*" );
4        }
5        System.out.println();
```

By enclosing this for-loop in another for-loop that generates the sequence 10, 9, ..., 1 with the iteration variable down, the triangle can be generated:

```
1        for ( down = 10; down >= 1; down -- )
2        {
3          for ( across = 1; across <= down; across ++ )
4          {
5            System.out.print( "*" );
6          }
7          System.out.println();
8        }
```

We want this program to receive the length of the first line (or the number of lines) from the user. We will store the value in a variable named height. We modify the internal loop so that the last output of "*" is part of println. This reduces the number of times the inner loop-body is executed by 1.

These changes result in the following code:

```
 1  import java.util.Scanner;
 2  //-- print a triangle
 3  public class TriangleFlipped
 4  {
 5    //-- main method
 6    public static void main( String[] args )
 7    {
 8      int height, down, across;
 9      Scanner keyboard;
10      keyboard = new Scanner( System.in );
11      System.out.print( "Enter height: " );
12      height = keyboard.nextInt();
13      for ( down = height; down >= 1; down -- )
14      {
15        for ( across = 1; across <= down - 1; across ++ )
16        {
17          System.out.print( "*" );
18        }
19        System.out.println( "*" );
20      }
21    }
22  }
```

Listing 7.16 A program that prints an upside right-angled triangle of a given height

Here is an execution example of the code:

```
 1  Enter height: 17
 2  ****************
 3  ***************
 4  **************
 5  *************
 6  ************
 7  ***********
 8  **********
 9  *********
10  ********
11  *******
12  ******
13  *****
14  *****
15  ****
16  ***
17  **
18  *
```

7.4 Computing the Maximum and Minimum in a Series of Numbers

Here, we combine for-loops and conditional executions to write an application.

Our first application MaxAndMin receives a series of integer data from the user and computes the maximum and minimum of the series. Prior to receiving the series, the program asks the user to specify the series length: in other words, how many elements are in the series. The length, which is stored in a variable nData. The program then generates a sequence 1, ..., nData using a for-loop and receives the elements in the series.

We use if-statements in three places.

First, we use it to check if nData is greater than 0. If nData is less than or equal 0, the program terminates itself by announcing a run-time error. The type of the run-time error is IllegalArgumentException. We generate the error with a special statement of throw in the following manner:

```
throw new IllegalArgumentException(
       "\n    " + nData + " is not positive" );
```

The second line of the statement is interpreted as a String and printed as an error message before termination. Since it begins with "\n ", the error message will start in a fresh newline with four white space characters.

In general,

```
throw new ERROR_TYPE_NAME( MESSAGE );
```

is the syntax of terminating a program by generating a run-time error of type ERROR_TYPE_NAME with an error message of MESSAGE. The word new is a keyword indicating that this is a creation of an object data of type ERROR_TYPE_NAME, and MESSAGE is the actual parameter given to the constructor.

The second and third if-statements appear when the element that the user has entered is compared with the present maximum and minimum values for updates.

```
1   import java.util.*;
2   public class MaxAndMin
3   {
4     public static void main( String[] args )
5     {
6       int nData, max, min, input;
7       Scanner keyboard = new Scanner( System.in );
8       System.out.print( "Enter # of data: " );
9       nData = keyboard.nextInt();
10      if ( nData <= 0 )
11      {
12        throw new IllegalArgumentException(
13            "\n       " + nData + " is not positive" );
14
15      }
```

Listing 7.17 A program for computing the maximum and the minimum of an integer series (part 1). A part that is responsible for receiving the length and running a check

Next, the program receives the first element of the series and stores this in the variable `input`. Since this is the very first element, the program stores its value in both `maximum` and `minimum`. The declarations of all these variables appear in Line 6. If the value of `nData` is 1, then there will be no further input, and so the first number the user enters is both the maximum and the minimum.

```
16      System.out.print( "Enter Data No. 1: " );
17      input = keyboard.nextInt();
18      max = input;
19      min = input;
```

Listing 7.18 A program for computing the maximum and the minimum of an integer series (part 2). A part that is responsible for receiving the first number

Since the program has set the initial value to the variables for the maximum and the minimum, the for-loop iterates over `2, ..., nData` with the variable `round`. If we change the initialization to `round = 1`, the program will prompt the user to enter one extra element.

The prompt that the program uses in the for-loop is

$$\text{"Enter Data No. " + round + ": "}$$

This is consistent with the prompt

$$\text{"Enter Data No. 1: "}$$

that the program uses for the very first number. This way, the user sees no difference between the prompt for the first number and the prompt for the remaining numbers.

In the for-loop, the program compares the input that the user enters with the present maximum (Lines 25–28) and the minimum (Lines 29–32). If the input is greater than the maximum, the program stores the value of the input in the maximum. If the input is smaller than the minimum, the program stores the values of the input in the minimum. Note that we can substitute the `if` for the minimum with `else if`, because if the input is greater than the present maximum, then there is no way for the input to be smaller than the minimum.

Finally, the program uses `printf` to produce the result on the screen, using the placeholder `%d` for both the maximum and the minimum.

```
20      for ( int round = 2; round <= nData; round ++ )
21      {
22         System.out.print( "Enter Data No. " + round + ": " );
23         input = keyboard.nextInt();
24         if ( max < input )
25         {
26            max = input;
27         }
28         if ( min > input )
29         {
30            min = input;
31         }
32      }
33      System.out.printf( "max=%d, min=%d%n", max, min );
34   }
35 }
```

Listing 7.19 A program for computing the maximum and the minimum of an integer series (part 3). A part that is responsible for receiving the remaining numbers and printing the result

Here is an execution example where the run-time error `IllegalArgumentException` occurs:

```
1  Enter # of data: 0
2  Exception in thread "main" java.lang.IllegalArgumentException:
3     0 is not positive
4        at MaxAndMin.main(MaxAndMin.java:12)
```

The third line, " 0 is not positive" is the actual parameter of `throw new Illegal Argument Exception`.

Here is an execution example of the code in which the calculation is successful:

```
1   Enter # of data: 8
2   Enter Data No. 1: -1546
3   Enter Data No. 2: 345
4   Enter Data No. 3: 98035
5   Enter Data No. 4: -876
6   Enter Data No. 5: 5121
7   Enter Data No. 6: 100001
8   Enter Data No. 7: -4
9   Enter Data No. 8: -200000
10  max=100001, min=-200000
```

7.5   A Betting Game

7.5.1   For-Loops with Skipped Execution

The next application is a simple betting game, where the user is asked to throw a die and bet which side is facing up.

There are two bet types: specify the exact number of dots or specify odd/even of the number. Here are some rules:

- The player starts with 50 chips and plays 10 times. However, if the player has lost all his/her chips, the game ends, regardless of which round the player is on.
- The number of chips that can be bet is between 1 and the number of chips the player possesses at that moment.
- After throwing a die, the following occurs:

- If the player has bet on the exact number of dots and the side that has shown has the same number of dots, the player retains the bet chips and receives, as a reward, chips in the amount equal to five times the number of chips that have been bet.
- If the player has bet on even/odd parity and the number of dots on the side that has shown has the same parity as the player's bet, the player retains the bet chips and receives, as a reward, chips in the amount equal to the number of chips that have been bet.
- If neither is the case, the player loses the bet chips.

We design the code using the following algorithm:

- A for-loop is used to repeat a single round of action ten times.
- The loop-body takes its action only if the number of chips in possession at the start of the body is strictly positive. The body consists of the following sequence events.
  - The player is advised of the number of chips currently in possession and asked the number of chips to be bet.
  - The player enters the bet amount. If it is less than or equal to 0, the amount is adjusted to 1 (the body being executed guarantees that the number of chips in possession is at least 1). If the bet amount is greater than the number of chips in possession, the bet amount is reduced to the number of chips is possession.
  - The player is asked to enter the type of bet: -1 for the odd parity, 0 for the even parity, and one of 1, ... 6 for the exact number of dots.
  - The player enters the type. If the type is less than -1, then it is adjusted to -1, and if the type is greater than 6, then it is adjusted to 6.
  - Using `Math.random`, an `int` between 1 and 6 is generated to represent the number of dots on the face that is up.
  - The player is told if he/she has won the bet and is advised on the change has been made on the number of chips in possession.
- After completing the loop, the final number of chips in possession is reported.

Here is the program that implements this idea.

We use `int` variables `possession` to record the number of chips in possession, `betType` to record the bet type, `betAmount` to record the bet amount, and `number` to record the result after throwing the dice (Line 7).

```
1  import java.util.*;
2  public class BettingGame
3  {
4    public static void main( String[] args )
5    {
6      Scanner keyboard = new Scanner( System.in );
7      int betType, betAmount, number, possession = 50;
8
```

Listing 7.20 A betting game (part 1). The part that sets up the variables

Next is the for-loop and the beginning of its loop-body. The for-loop iterates the sequence 1, ..., 10 using an iteration variable, i (Line 9). For each round, an action is to be performed only if `possession` is positive (Line 11). The action is as follows:

- Inform the player of the round number and the current chip amount (Lines 13–15).
- Ask for the bet amount, receive it, and store it in `betAmount` (Lines 16 and 17).
- Make an adjustment to the amount if necessary as follows:

- If its value is not positive, raise it to 1 (Lines 18–21);
- if its value is greater than `possession`, reduce it to `possession`, since a player cannot bet more than what he/she has (Lines 22–25).
- After that, state the [possibly altered] bet amount (Line 26).

```
9    for ( int i = 1; i <= 10; i ++ )
10   {
11     if ( possession > 0 )
12     {
13        System.out.println( "===============================" );
14        System.out.println( "This is round " + i );
15        System.out.println( "You have " + possession + " chips" );
16        System.out.print( "How much do you want to bet? " );
17        betAmount = keyboard.nextInt();
18        if ( betAmount < 1 )
19        {
20           betAmount = 1;
21        }
22        else if ( betAmount > possession )
23        {
24           betAmount = possession;
25        }
26        System.out.println( "Your bet amount is " + betAmount );
27
```

Listing 7.21 A betting game (part 2). The part that processes the bet amount

The next part is for determining the betting type. The program does the following:

```
28        System.out.print( "Enter your bet type: " );
29        System.out.println( "-1 for odd, 0 for even," );
30        System.out.print( "1..6 for an exact bet: " );
31        betType = keyboard.nextInt();
32        if ( betType < -1 )
33        {
34           betType = -1;
35        }
36        else if ( betType > 6 )
37        {
38           betType = 6;
39        }
40
```

Listing 7.22 Betting game (part 3). The part that determines the bet type

- Ask the player to enter the bet type (Lines 28–30).
- Receive the bet type and store the value in `betType` (Line 31).
- Make an adjustment if necessary:
  - If the type is less than −1, raise it to −1 (Lines 32–35);
  - if the type is greater than 6, reduce it to 6 (Lines 36–39).

Next comes the part where a die is thrown. This is the end of the big if-statement as well as the for-loop.

- Generate the value for number using the formula 1 + (int)(6 * Math.random()) (Line 41) and report this number (Line 42).
- Check win/loss and make adjustments as follows (Lines 43–58):
  - If either (betType == -1 (odd) and number % 2 == 1) or (betType == 0 (even) and number % 2 == 0), then the player has won an odd/even bet, so add betAmount to possession (Lines 43–48).
  - Otherwise, if betType == number, then the player has won an exact-face bet, so add 5 * betAmount to possession (Lines 49–53).
  - Otherwise, subtract betAmount from possession (Lines 54–58).
- Line 59 is the end of the if-statement.
- Line 60 is the end of the for-loop.

```
41              number = 1 + (int)( 6 * Math.random() );
42              System.out.println( "The number is " + number );
43              if ( betType == -1 && number % 2 == 1 ||
44                  betType == 0 && number % 2 == 0 )
45              {
46                System.out.println( "You've won!" );
47                possession += betAmount;
48              }
49              else if ( betType == number )
50              {
51                possession += 5 * betAmount;
52                System.out.println( "You've won big time!!!!!!" );
53              }
54              else
55              {
56                possession -= betAmount;
57                System.out.println( "You've lost!" );
58              }
59          }
60      }
```

Listing 7.23 A betting game (part 4). The part that throws a dice and reports the result

At the end of the ten rounds, the program concludes by reporting the final amount of possession.

```
61
62      System.out.println( "===================================" );
63      System.out.println( "You ended with " + possession + " chips" );
64
```

Listing 7.24 A betting game (part 5). The part that produces the final reporting

The logical formula in Lines 43 and 44:

betType == -1 && number % 2 == 1 || betType == 0 && number % 2 == 0 is equivalent to:

$$betType + (\ number \ \% \ 2 \ ) \ == \ 0$$

as well as to:

$$Math.abs (\ betType \ ) \ == \ (\ number \ \% \ 2 \ )$$

7.5.2   The Statements `continue` and `break`

Two important statements that can be used in a for-loop body are `continue` and `break`. The statement `continue` instructs the program to skip the remainder of the loop-body and move on to the next round of the loop. The statement `break` instructs the program to terminate the execution of the loop immediately, ignoring the remainder of the present round and all the remaining rounds. If these statements appear inside an interior loop of multiple loops, their actions apply to the innermost loop that contains the statements.

Consider the following code block:

```
1    Scanner keyboard = new Scanner ( System.in );
2    int sum = 0;
3    for ( int i = 1; i <= 30; i ++ )
4    {
5       if ( i % 7 == 0 )
6       {
7          continue;
8       }
9       int input = keyboard.nextInt ();
10      if ( input == 0 )
11      {
12         break;
13      }
14      sum += i * input;
15   }
```

The program generates a sequence `1, ..., 30` with the iteration variable `i`, receives an input from the user if `i` is not a multiple of 7, and computes the sum of `i` multiplied by the input. However, if the user enters 0, the loop is terminated immediately.

Here is another example. In the following code, `a` is an `int` variable.

```
1    for ( int count = 1; count <= 100; count ++ )
2    {
3       a += 10;
4       System.out.println( count + ", " + a );
5       if ( a > 1000 )
6       {
7          break;
8       }
9    }
```

The program repeatedly increases `a` by 10 until the value of `a` exceeds 1000.

In the betting game program, we enclosed the entire action inside the for-loop in the if-statement whose condition was `possession > 0`, i.e.,

```
1   for ( int i = 1; i <= 10; i ++ )
2   {
3     if ( possession > 0 )
4     {
5       THE_ACTION
6     }
7   }
```

where THE_ACTION refers to the action to be performed. We can use continue to take THE_ACTION outside the if-block.

```
1   for ( int i = 1; i <= 10; i ++ )
2   {
3     if ( possession > 0 )
4     {
5       continue;
6     }
7     THE_ACTION;
8   }
```

Once possession becomes 0, there will be no action to be performed in the loop-body. Therefore, we can use break to terminate the loop as soon as possession becomes 0.

```
1   for ( int i = 1; i <= 10; i ++ )
2   {
3     THE_ACTION;
4     if ( possession == 0 )
5     {
6       break;
7     }
8   }
```

Because possession is decreased only at one location, we can move the if-statement containing the break statement inside after the statement for printing the message "You've lost!".

```
1    for ( int i = 1; i <= 10; i ++ )
2    {
3      ...
4      else
5      {
6        possession -= betAmount;
7        System.out.println( "You've lost!" );
8        if ( possession == 0 )
9        {
10         break;
11       }
12     }
13   }
```

7.6   Computing the Fibonacci Sequence

The Fibonacci sequence $F_0, F_1, F_2, \ldots$ is an infinite integer sequence defined by: $F_0 = F_1 = 1$ and for all $n \geq 2$, $F_n = F_{n-1} + F_{n-2}$. The sequence is as follows:

$$1, 1, 2, 3, 5, 8, 13, 21, 34, 55, 89, 144, \ldots$$

Consider receiving an integer n from the user and printing the value of F_i for $i = 2, \ldots, n$. To determine the value of F_i, we only need the values of F_{i-1} and F_{i-2}. Therefore, we can accomplish the task by using a for-loop and memorizing just the two previous values in the sequence.

Using a for-loop that iterates the sequence $2, \ldots, n$ with a variable named i, we compute the value of F_i. To record the values of F_i and its two predecessors, we use three `long` variables, instead of three `int` variables. This is because the values of the elements of the Fibonacci sequence increase very quickly. The three variables are `f`, `fp`, and `fpp`. They represent F_i, F_{i-1}, and F_{i-2} respectively. At the start of the loop body, it is ensured that the value of `fp` is equal to F_{i-1} and the value of `fpp` is equal to F_{i-2}. We obtain the value of F_i by `f = fp + fpp` and print its value. When the program returns to the start of the loop-body, the value of `i` has been increased by 1. Therefore, we must make sure that `fpp` and `fp` hold the values of F_{i-1} and F_{i-2} for the new value of `i`. This can be accomplished by first replacing the value of `fpp` with the value of `fp`, and then replacing the value of `fp` with the value of `f`. Also, before entering the loop, since the value of `i` starts with 2, we need to assign the value of F_1 to `fp` and F_0 to `fpp`.

The next code encapsulates the above ideas and prints the value of `f`, along with the values of `fp` and `fpp`.

```
1   import java.util.*;
2   public class FibonacciProgress
3   {
4     public static void main( String[] args )
5     {
6       long f, fp = 1, fpp = 1;
7       Scanner keyboard = new Scanner( System.in );
8       System.out.print( "Enter n: " );
9       int n = keyboard.nextInt();
10      for ( int i = 2; i <= n; i ++ )
11      {
12        f = fp + fpp;
13        System.out.println(
14            i + "\tf=" + f + "\tfp=" + fp + "\tfpp=" + fpp );
15        fpp = fp;
16        fp = f;
17      }
18    }
19  }
```

Listing 7.25 A program that computes the Fibonacci sequence

Note that the order of execution is (a) computing `f`; (b) printing the values of `i`, `f`, `fp`, and `fpp`; (c) updating `fpp`; (d) updating `fp`. Here is an execution example:

```
1   Enter n: 30
2   2: 2      fp=1, fpp=1
3   3: 3      fp=2, fpp=1
4   4: 5      fp=3, fpp=2
```

5	5: 8 fp=5, fpp=3
6	6: 13 fp=8, fpp=5
7	7: 21 fp=13, fpp=8
8	8: 34 fp=21, fpp=13
9	9: 55 fp=34, fpp=21
10	10: 89 fp=55, fpp=34
11	11: 144 fp=89, fpp=55
12	12: 233 fp=144, fpp=89
13	13: 377 fp=233, fpp=144
14	14: 610 fp=377, fpp=233
15	15: 987 fp=610, fpp=377
16	16: 1597 fp=987, fpp=610
17	17: 2584 fp=1597, fpp=987
18	18: 4181 fp=2584, fpp=1597
19	19: 6765 fp=4181, fpp=2584
20	20: 10946 fp=6765, fpp=4181
21	21: 17711 fp=10946, fpp=6765
22	22: 28657 fp=17711, fpp=10946
23	23: 46368 fp=28657, fpp=17711
24	24: 75025 fp=46368, fpp=28657
25	25: 121393 fp=75025, fpp=46368
26	26: 196418 fp=121393, fpp=75025
27	27: 317811 fp=196418, fpp=121393
28	28: 514229 fp=317811, fpp=196418
29	29: 832040 fp=514229, fpp=317811
30	30: 1346269 fp=832040, fpp=514229

After the first round, the value of fp is transferred to fpp and the value of f to fp.

Summary

- The format for a for-loop is:

  ```
  for ( INITIALIZATION; CONTINUATION CONDITION; UPDATE ) { ... }
  ```

  The initialization is the action to be performed before entering the loop. The update is the action to be performed after each execution of the loop-body.
- The declaration of the iteration variable may appear in the initialization part of a for-loop. The scope of an iteration variable whose declaration appears in the header of the loop is the entire loop.
- We formally call the process of generating a series of index values loop an "iteration". The variable we use in iteration is an iteration variable.
- A for-loop can be used for counting repetitions. The value of the iteration variable can be referred to in the loop-body to produce results that are dependent on the iteration variable.
- A double-loop is a loop inside a loop. Using a double-loop, one can manipulate a block of data that has two dimensions.
- The continue statement instructs the program to skip the present round of for-loop and move on the next round.
- The break statement instructs the program to terminate the execution of the for-loop immediately.

Exercises

1. **Evaluating a for-loop** How many lines of output will be generated by the code below?

```
1  for ( int i = 1; i < 1000; i *= 2 )
2  {
3      System.out.println(i);
4  }
```

2. **Evaluating double loops** State the output generated by each of the following for-loops:

```
1  for ( int i = 0; i < 4; i ++ )
2  {
3      for ( int j = i + 1; j <= 4; j ++ )
4      {
5          System.out.print( j );
6      }
7      System.out.println( "x" );
8  }
```

```
1  for ( int i = 0; i <= 4; i ++ )
2  {
3      System.out.print( "=" );
4      for ( int j = 0; j <= i; j ++ )
5      {
6          System.out.print( j );
7      }
8      System.out.println();
9  }
```

```
1  for ( int s = 5; s >= 1; s -- )
2  {
3      for ( int t = 5; t > s; t -- )
4      {
5          System.out.print( t );
6      }
7      System.out.println( "@" );
8  }
```

```
1  for ( int s = 33; s >= 0; s -= 6 )
2  {
3      for ( int t = 33 - s; t <= s; t += 5 )
4      {
5          System.out.print( t );
6      }
7      System.out.println( "#" );
8  }
```

3. **Double for-loop** Write a double for-loop that produces the following output:

```
1  123456789
2  3456789
3  56789
4  789
5  9
```

4. **Another double for-loop**   Write a double for-loop that produces the following output:

```
1   987654321
2   8765432
3   76543
4   654
5   5
```

5. **Number iterations**   For each of the number sequences below, write a for-loop with an iteration variable, n, that generates the sequence:

   (a) 1, 2, 3, 4, 5
   (b) 1, 10, 100, 1000, 10,000
   (c) 10, 8, 6, 4, 2, 0
   (d) 12, 9, 6, 3, 0, -3, -6, -9

6. **Generating a series of squares**   Write a program named `Squares` that receives an integer from the user, stores the value in an `int` variable n, and uses a for-loop to produce the following output lines:

```
1   1
2   4
3   9
4   . . .
5   n^2
```

   We can expect the value the user enters to be positive. Noting that $(m+1)^2 - m^2 = 2m + 1$, write an alternative version that keeps producing the squares by cumulatively adding odd integers to a variable that is initially 0.

7. **Printing a diamond of variable sizes**   Write a program named `Diamond2` that receives an integer value from the user (that is guaranteed to be positive and even) and prints a filled diamond with the input value as the height and width. (For the shape below the input value is 10.) The program may run by calculating one half of the input number and using it in iteration.

```
1          /\
2         //\\
3        ///\\\
4       ////\\\\
5      /////\\\\\
6      \\\\\/////
7       \\\\////
8        \\\///
9         \\//
10         \/
```

8. **Number sequence with decreasing repetitions**   Write a triple for-loop that produces the output below.

```
1    543210
2    554433221100
3    555444333222111000
4    5555444433332222111110000
5    555554444433333222221111100000
6    5555554444443333332222221111110000000
7    55555554444444333333322222221111111100000000
8    555555554444444433333333222222221111111100000000
9    5555555554444444443333333332222222221111111110000000000
10   55555555554444444444333333333322222222221111111111110000000000
```

9. **Number pyramid**   Write a program that produces the output in the shape of a pyramid as shown next using one double for-loop:

```
1    1
2    22
3    333
4    4444
5    55555
6    666666
7    7777777
8    88888888
9    999999999
```

10. **Output generated by for-loops 1**   State the output the following code generates:

```
1   int gap = 1, n = 1;
2   for ( int count = 1; count <= 10; count ++ )
3   {
4      System.out.println( n );
5      n += gap;
6      gap ++;
7   }
```

11. **Output generated by for-loops 2**   State the output the following code generates:

```
1   int gap = 1, n = 1;
2   for ( int count = 1; count <= 10; count ++ )
3   {
4      System.out.println( n );
5      n += gap;
6      gap += 2;
7   }
```

12. **Output generated by for-loops 3**   State the output the following code generates:

```
1   int gap = 1, n = 1;
2   for ( int count = 1; count <= 10; count ++ )
3   {
4      System.out.println( n );
5      n += gap;
6      gap *= 2;
7   }
```

13. **Output generated by for-loops 4**   State the output the following code generates:

```
1   int gap = 10, n = 100;
2   for ( int count = 1; count <= 10; count ++ )
3   {
4      System.out.println( n );
5      n -= gap;
6      gap --;
7   }
```

14. **Partial sums**   Write a program, `PartialSums`, that receives an integer `top` from the user and returns the sum of all the sums (m + ... + 2 * m) such that m is between 1 and `top`. The return value must be 0 if `top` is less than equal to 0. By appropriately designing the components of the loops, this requirement can be met without having to check whether or not `top` <= 0.

15. **Double iteration, A**   Write a program named `AllIJ1` that receives an integer `top` from the user and produces on the screen the output

    `(i,j)`

    for all values of i and j between 1 and `top`. Configure the loops so that in the output, the value of i does not decrease, and for each fixed i, the value of j is strictly decreasing.

    Here is an execution example:

```
 1  Enter one number: 4
 2  (1,1)
 3  (1,2)
 4  (1,3)
 5  (1,4)
 6  (2,1)
 7  (2,2)
 8  (2,3)
 9  (2,4)
10  (3,1)
11  (3,2)
12  (3,3)
13  (3,4)
14  (4,1)
15  (4,2)
16  (4,3)
17  (4,4)
```

16. **Double iteration, B**   Write a program named `AllIJ2` that receives an integer `top` from the user and produces on the screen the output

    `(i,j)`

    for all values of i and j between 1 and `top` such that i is no greater than j. Configure the loops so that in the output, the value of i does not decrease, and for each fixed i, the value of j is strictly increasing.

    Here is an execution example:

```
 1  Enter one number: 4
 2  (1,1)
 3  (1,2)
 4  (1,3)
 5  (1,4)
 6  (2,2)
 7  (2,3)
 8  (2,4)
 9  (3,3)
10  (3,4)
11  (4,4)
```

17. **Double iteration, C**   Write a program named `AllIJ3` that receives an integer `top` from the user and produces of the screen the output

    `(i,j)`

    for all values of i and j between 1 and `top` such that i is strictly less than j. Configure the loops so that in the output, the value of i does not decrease, and for each fixed i, the value of j is strictly increasing.

Here is an execution example:

```
 1  Enter one number: 4
 2  (1,1)
 3  (1,2)
 4  (1,3)
 5  (2,1)
 6  (2,2)
 7  (2,3)
 8  (3,1)
 9  (3,2)
10  (3,3)
11  (4,1)
12  (4,2)
13  (4,3)
```

18. **Coordinated iteration**   Suppose we want to print the coordinates of an N by N table, where N is greater than or equal to 2, and the rows and columns have indexes from 1 to N. The combination of a row number x and a column number y should be printed as (x,y). For each row, the coordinates should be printed in one line. Write CoordinatedIteration that accomplishes this task. The program receives the value for N from the user. The output for N = 3 is as follows:

```
 1  Series 1
 2  (1,1) (1,2) (1,3)
 3  Series 2
 4  (2,1) (2,2) (2,3)
 5  Series 3
 6  (3,1) (3,2) (3,3)
```

19. **Powers of a power**   Write a program named IntPowers that receives three integers, a, p, and k, from the user and prints the values of $a^p, a^{2p}, a^{3p}, \cdots, a^{kp}$, where these values are double and appear one value per line. Use Math.pow to compute the powers.

Programming Projects

20. **The size of a toilet paper**   Consider determining the length of toilet paper dispensed from a roll of toilet paper. To determine the length three parameters are needed: the radius of the core coreRadius, the maximum radius of the resulting roll of paper maxRadius, and the thickness of paper thickness. The way we will determine the length is as follows:
    • Each time the paper goes around the roll in one full circle, the radius increases by thickness. Therefore, for each round >= 1, if the paper goes around the roll round times, then the radius increases by round * thickness.
    • We want the resulting radius to be as large as possible, but not larger than maxRadius.
    • Based upon the above, we determine the exact number of times that the paper goes around the roll, represented by a variable numberOfRounds.
    • We assume that when the paper goes around the roll, which has radius radius, the length of the paper used for that particular round is 2π times radius.
    • The length of the roll generated is two times π times the sum of the radiuses of the roll from all rounds.
    Write a Java program named ToiletPaper.java that receives user coreRadius, maxRadius, and thickness from the user, and prints the length of the paper. Note that the integer part of any double y can be obtained by (int) (Math.floor(y)).

21. **BMI for ranges of weights and heights**   Write a program named RangeBMI that computes the BMI for a range of weights and heights. The user will specify the maximum and minimum

of the weights. He/she will also specify the maximum and minimum of heights. Furthermore, the user will specify the sizes of increments in weights and heights. The maximums, the minimums, and the increments are all integers. The program must use a double for-loop. In the external loop, the program generates an increasing sequence of weights to be considered. In the internal loop, the program generates an increasing sequence of heights to be considered. For each combination of weight and height, the program prints the weight, the height, and the BMI.

22. **Points on a circle**   Write a program named `PointsOnCircle` that receives two positive quantities, a `double` data `myRadius` and an `int` data `myFraction`, from the user and prints the coordinates of the points on a circle with radius `myRadius`, whose rotation angles from the x-axis is between $-180°$ and $180°$ (with the degree incremented by `360 / myFraction`). The following is an example of running the program:

```
 1   Enter the radius: 3
 2   Enter the fraction: 8
 3   (-3.6739403974420594E-16,-3.0)
 4   (-2.121320343559643,-2.1213203435596424)
 5   (-3.0,1.8369701987210297E-16)
 6   (-2.1213203435596424,2.121320343559643)
 7   (0.0,3.0)
 8   (2.1213203435596424,2.121320343559643)
 9   (3.0,1.8369701987210297E-16)
10   (2.121320343559643,-2.1213203435596424)
11   (3.6739403974420594E-16,-3.0)
```

23. **Computing the combinatorial numbers**   Write a program named `Combinatorial` that computes combinatorial numbers after receiving two integers, n and k, from the user.

   For integers $n \geq k \geq 0$, $C(n, k)$ is the number of possible ways to select k distinct elements from a group of n distinct elements. $C(n, k)$ is given as:

$$C(n, k) = \frac{n!}{k!(n - k)!}$$

Here, $n!$ denotes the factorial of n. The factorial of n is $n(n - 1) \cdots 1$ if $n \geq 1$ and 1 otherwise. Implement three ways to compute $C(n, k)$ on the values of n and k that the user enters.

(a) Write a method named `public static long factorial( int m )` that computes the factorial of m as a `long` data. Write a method named `combinatorial` that receives n and k as parameters and computes $C(n, k)$ using three calls to the method `factorial`.

(b) For all n and k, we know that $C(n, k) = C(n, n - k)$.

$$\frac{n!}{k!(n - k)!} = \frac{n(n - 1) \cdots 1}{(k(k - 1) \cdots 1)((n - k)(n - k - 1) \cdots 1)}$$

Let q be the smaller of k and $n - k$. Then we have

$$\frac{n!}{k!(n - k)!} = \frac{n(n - 1) \cdots 1}{(q(q - 1) \cdots 1)((n - q)(n - q - 1) \cdots 1)}$$

We can simplify the fraction to obtain

$$C(n, k) = \frac{n(n - 1) \cdots (n - q + 1)}{q(q - 1) \cdots 1}$$

Write a method, `public static long product( int start, int end )`, that returns the product of all the integers between `start` and `end`, where `end >= start`. Write a method named `combinatorial2` that computes the two products using the method `product`.

(c) By reversing the order of appearance of the terms in the denominator $n(n-1)\cdots(n-q+1)$, we have

$$C(n, k) = \frac{n(n-1)\cdots(n-q+1)}{1\cdot 2\cdots(q-1)q}$$

Write an additional method named `combinatorial3` that computes the factorial. For $i = 1, \ldots, q$, `combinatorial3` executes the multiplication by the i-th term in the numerator and the division by the i-th term in the denominator.

The combinations of n and k for which the program computes $C(n, k)$ correctly increases, as follows:

```
1   Enter n and k: 20 10
2   With method 1,  C(20,10)=184756
3   With method 2,  C(20,10)=184756
4   With method 3,  C(20,10)=184756
```

```
1   Enter n and k: 22 11
2   With method 1,  C(22,11)=-784
3   With method 2,  C(22,11)=705432
4   With method 3,  C(22,11)=705432
```

```
1   Enter n and k: 40 20
2   With method 1,  C(40,20)=0
3   With method 2,  C(40,20)=-1
4   With method 3,  C(40,20)=137846528820
```

24. **Treasure hunting**   Write a program named `TreasureHunting`, that plays a game defined as follows: The player's goal is to find a treasure hidden at a location between 1 and 100. The player can make at most ten guesses. If the guess is correct, the program announces `"You have found the treasure!"` and halts. In every round, if the player makes an incorrect guess, based upon the distance between the true location and the guess, the program announces the following:

(a) If the distance is between 1 and 3, the program announces
    `"The treasure is very close."`.
(b) If the distance is between 4 and 6, the program announces
    `"The treasure is somewhat close."`.
(c) If the distance is greater than 6, the program announces
    `"The treasure is not close."`.

Starting in the second round, if the player makes an incorrect guess, the program informs the player whether the guess is closer than the previous one. The message printed is: `"You are closer."`, `"You are farther."`, or `"The same distance."`. If the user fails to find the treasure, the program should reveal the true location.

Formatted Printing Using `printf`

8

8.1 General Rules for `printf`

This chapter discusses the syntax of `printf`, which we have already seen before. The general usage of `printf` is

```
System.out.printf( "u0w1u1w2 ...wkuk", d1, ..., dk );
```

where w1, ..., wk are placeholders that each specify the formatting of a single data, d1, ..., dk are the data to be formatted with the placeholders w1, ..., wk in this order, and u0, ..., uk are character sequences without formatting placeholders. For each i, the data di must be of the type specified in wi; if not, it must be converted to a data of that type. Any data can be interpretable as a `String` data, and any whole number data can be interpretable as a floating point data.

If a data supplied to a placeholder cannot be converted to the required type (for example, a `String` is supplied to a placeholder for a whole number), a run-time error occurs.

```
1  %d|Exception in thread "main" java.util.IllegalFormatConversionException:
      d != java.lang.String
2  at java.util.Formatter$FormatSpecifier.failConversion(Formatter.java:4302)
3  at java.util.Formatter$FormatSpecifier.printInteger(Formatter.java:2793)
4  at java.util.Formatter$FormatSpecifier.print(Formatter.java:2747)
5  at java.util.Formatter.format(Formatter.java:2520)
6  at java.io.PrintStream.format(PrintStream.java:970)
7  at java.io.PrintStream.printf(PrintStream.java:871)
8  at PrintFString.printStringWithFormat(PrintFString.java:28)
9  at PrintFString.main(PrintFString.java:22)
```

The same `IllegalFormatConversionException` error also occurs when the number of data supplied and the number of placeholders do not agree, as well as when a placeholder is incorrectly written.

Since each placeholder starts with a percent character, to include the percent character in a part that is not a placeholder, the `%%` is used via escaping. In `printf`, the newline character can be specified as `%n`.

© Springer Nature Switzerland AG 2018
M. Ogihara, *Fundamentals of Java Programming*,
https://doi.org/10.1007/978-3-319-89491-1_8

8.2   Formatted Printing of `String` Data

Next, we learn how to format `String` data using `printf`.

The general expression for `String` formatting is `%Xs`, where X consists of three options that can be selected independently of each other. Here are the three options, which must appear in this order:

1. The flush left positioning can be specified using a single minus sign `-`.

    If this option is not present, the data is automatically printed in flush right.
2. The minimum number of character spaces allocated for the data can be specified with a positive integer without leading 0's.

    If this option is not present, the default character space allocated is the exact number of character spaces required to print the data.

    If this option is present and the length of the data to be printed is smaller than the specified number of character spaces, the space character ' ' is added so as to make the length exactly the specified number. The adding of the space character occurs at the beginning of the data if the positioning is flush right (default), and at the end if flush left.

    However, if this option is present and the length of the `String` data to be printed is greater than the specified minimum character space, the entire data is printed with no padding.
3. It is possible to print only a prefix of the `String` data. The length of the prefix to be printed can be specified with a period immediately before the length.

    If this option is not present, the entire character sequence of the `String` data is printed.

    However, if the specified prefix length is greater than the length of the `String` data to be printed, the prefix length is automatically reduced to the exact length of the `String` data.

For example, `"%-10s"` specifies that the `String` data must be printed in flush left using at least ten character spaces, and `"%10.5s"` specifies that only the first five characters must be printed in flush right using at least ten character spaces. Thus, in

```
System.out.printf( "Message=%-10.5s-Mike",  "Table tennis is fun!" );
```

the 10-space formatting of the String `"Table tennis is fun!"` will appear after `"Message="`, and `"-Mike"` after that. This results in:

```
Message=Table     --Mike
```

The next program shows different effects in `printf` for `String`. The program presents the results in a two-column table, with the left column showing the format used and the right column showing the formatting generated. To print a row of the table, the program uses a method named `printStringWithFormat`. The method takes two `String` parameters, `fmt` and `message`, where the first formal parameter is used to format the second parameter. The formatting of the second parameter using the first parameter can be accomplished by

```
System.out.printf( fmt, message );
```

This will be the second column of the row.

For the first column, we want to print the first parameter fmt. Assuming that the length of fmt is no more than 10, we allocate exactly ten character spaces in flush right and print the vertical line character | after that as follows:

```
"System.out.printf( "%10s|", fmt );"
```

We also want to show if padding appears in the formatting of message using fmt as the formatting. Since the white space is invisible, we add a colon at the end to indicate the end of the line for this purpose.

Altogether, the method has the following code:

```
19   public static void printStringWithFormat (
20        String fmt, String message )
21   {
22       System.out.printf( "%10s|", fmt );
23       System.out.printf( fmt, message );
24       System.out.println( ":" );
25   }
```

The method main prints the String variable t using various formats. The method first stores the literal "Welcome to the Club!" to t (Line 5). The method then prints the header lines (Lines 7–9). The method then prints t in seven different formats by calling the printStringWithFormat method (Lines 10–16). At the end, in Line 17, the method prints a line identical to the one that it printed in Line 9.

```
1    public class PrintFString
2    {
3        public static void main( String[] args )
4        {
5            String t = "Welcome to the Club!";
6            System.out.println( "theString=\"Welcome to the Club!\"" );
7            System.out.println( "Format     |Position" );
8            System.out.println( "String     |012345678901234567890123 45" );
9            System.out.println( "----------+------------------------" );
10           printStringWithFormat( "%s:", t );
11           printStringWithFormat( "%25s:", t );
12           printStringWithFormat( "%-25s:", t );
13           printStringWithFormat( "%10s:", t );
14           printStringWithFormat( "%-10s:", t );
15           printStringWithFormat( "%-25.14s:", t );
16           printStringWithFormat( "%25.14s:", t );
17           System.out.println( "----------+------------------------" );
18       }
```

Listing 8.1 A code that shows various output formatting for String data. The main method

Executing the code produces the following:

```
1   theString="Welcome to the Club!"
2   Format      |Position
3   String      |012345678901234567890123 45
4   ----------+------------------------
5          %s:|Welcome to the Club!:
6        %25s:|       Welcome to the Club!:
7       %-25s:|Welcome to the Club!     :
8        %10s:|Welcome to the Club!:
9       %-10s:|Welcome to the Club!:
10   %-25.14s:|Welcome to the          :
11     %25.14s:|            Welcome to the:
12   ----------+------------------------
```

%c is used to format a char data. Only two options are available: the number of character spaces allocated and the flush left positioning.

8.3   Formatted Printing of Integers

To use printf for printing a whole number, we use a format String of the form %Xd, where the part X consists of four options that can be selected independently of each other. Here are the four options (the fourth option must appear the last):

1. The forced plus sign for a strictly positive value can be specified with a single plus sign +.
    If this option is not present, a strictly positive value appears without the plus sign.
2. A single comma , specified the forced currency punctuation. If the option is present, the punctuation appears with every three digits if the environment information the JVM has access to state that the country where the computer is running is the United States of America.
    If this option is not present, there will be no punctuation.
3. Either the flush left or leading 0s can be specified with a single minus sign - or a single 0 respectively.
    At most one of the two can be specified.
    If neither options are present, the data is printed in flush right.
4. The minimum number of character spaces allocated for the data can be specified with a positive integer without leading 0s.
    If this option is not present, the character space allocated is the exact number of character spaces required to print the data, meaning that the "leading-0" option will be ignored.

Note that the comma, the plus sign, and the minus sign are counted towards the number of characters used.

Here is a code that demonstrates the different formatting of a whole number. The method responsible for printing a row of the table is very much similar to the previous one, except that the second parameter is an int data named n.

```
 1  public class PrintFDecimal
 2  {
 3    public static void main( String[] args )
 4    {
 5      int num = 456789;
 6      System.out.println( "number=" + num );
 7      System.out.println( "Format     |Position" );
 8      System.out.println( "String     |01234567890123456789" );
 9      System.out.println( "----------+--------------------" );
10      printDecimalWithFormat( "%d:", num );
11      printDecimalWithFormat( "%+d:", num );
12      printDecimalWithFormat( "%,d:", num );
13      printDecimalWithFormat( "%+,d:", num );
14      printDecimalWithFormat( "%20d:", num );
15      printDecimalWithFormat( "%+20d:", num );
16      printDecimalWithFormat( "%,20d:", num );
17      printDecimalWithFormat( "%+,20d:", num );
18      printDecimalWithFormat( "%-20d:", num );
19      printDecimalWithFormat( "%+-20d:", num );
20      printDecimalWithFormat( "%,-20d:", num );
21      printDecimalWithFormat( "%+-,20d:", num );
22      printDecimalWithFormat( "%020d:", num );
23      printDecimalWithFormat( "%+020d:", num );
24      printDecimalWithFormat( "%,020d:", num );
25      printDecimalWithFormat( "%+,020d:", num );
26      System.out.println( "----------+--------------------" );
27    }
28    public static void printDecimalWithFormat( String fmt, int n )
29    {
30      System.out.printf( "%-10s|", fmt );
31      System.out.printf( fmt, n );
32      System.out.println();
33    }
34  }
```

Listing 8.2 A code that shows various output formatting for whole number data

The code produces the following output:

```
 1                01234567890123456789
 2  ----------+--------------------
 3  %d:       |456789:
 4  %+d:      |+456789:
 5  %,d:      |456,789:
 6  %+,d:     |+456,789:
 7  %20d:     |              456789:
 8  %+20d:    |             +456789:
 9  %,20d:    |             456,789:
10  %+,20d:   |            +456,789:
11  %-20d:    |456789              :
12  %+-20d:   |+456789             :
13  %,-20d:   |456,789             :
14  %+-,20d:  |+456,789            :
15  %020d:    |00000000000000456789:
16  %+020d:   |+0000000000000456789:
17  %,020d:   |0000000000000456,789:
18  %+,020d:  |+000000000000456,789:
19  ----------+--------------------
```

8.4   Formatted Printing of Floating Point Numbers

To use `printf` for printing a floating point number, we use a format `String` of the form `%Xf`, where the part X consists of five options that can be selected independently of each other. The first four options are the same as the options for `%d`. The last option specifies the exact number of digits printed after the decimal point. It is specified with a single period followed by a strictly positive integer, which is the number of digits.

Since there are so many options to apply to a floating number, we demonstrate the effect using two programs.

Here is the first program.

```
 1  public class PrintFFloat
 2  {
 3    public static void main( String[] args )
 4    {
 5      double num = 1974.9215;
 6      System.out.println( "number=1974.9215" );
 7      System.out.println( "Format      |Position" );
 8      System.out.println( "String      |01234567890123456789" );
 9      System.out.println( "----------+--------------------" );
10      printFloatWithFormat( "%f:", num );
11      printFloatWithFormat( "%+f:", num );
12      printFloatWithFormat( "%,f:", num );
13      printFloatWithFormat( "%+,f:", num );
14      printFloatWithFormat( "%20f:", num );
15      printFloatWithFormat( "%+20f:", num );
16      printFloatWithFormat( "%,20f:", num );
17      printFloatWithFormat( "%+,20f:", num );
18      printFloatWithFormat( "%-20f:", num );
19      printFloatWithFormat( "%+-20f:", num );
20      printFloatWithFormat( "%,-20f:", num );
21      printFloatWithFormat( "%+-,20f:", num );
22      printFloatWithFormat( "%020f:", num );
23      printFloatWithFormat( "%+020f:", num );
24      printFloatWithFormat( "%,020f:", num );
25      printFloatWithFormat( "%+,020f:", num );
26      System.out.println( "----------+--------------------" );
27    }
```

Listing 8.3 A code that shows various output formatting for floating point data (part 1). The `main` method

The auxiliary method is similar to the one from the previous programs.

```
28    public static void printFloatWithFormat( String fmt, double v )
29    {
30      System.out.printf( "%-10s|", fmt );
31      System.out.printf( fmt, v );
32      System.out.println();
33    }
34  }
```

Listing 8.4 A code that shows various output formatting for floating point data (part 2). A method used for printing the format `String` and the formatted data together

Here is the second program.

```
1   public class PrintFFloat2
2   {
3     public static void main( String[] args )
4     {
5       double num = 1974.9215;
6       System.out.println( "number=1974.9215" );
7       System.out.println( "Format     |Position" );
8       System.out.println( "String     |01234567890123456789" );
9       System.out.println( "----------+--------------------" );
10      printFloatWithFormat( "%.3f:", num );
11      printFloatWithFormat( "%+.3f:", num );
12      printFloatWithFormat( "%,.3f:", num );
13      printFloatWithFormat( "%+,.3f:", num );
14      printFloatWithFormat( "%20.3f:", num );
15      printFloatWithFormat( "%+20.3f:", num );
16      printFloatWithFormat( "%,20.3f:", num );
17      printFloatWithFormat( "%+,20.3f:", num );
18      printFloatWithFormat( "%-20.3f:", num );
19      printFloatWithFormat( "%+-20.3f:", num );
20      printFloatWithFormat( "%,-20.3f:", num );
21      printFloatWithFormat( "%+-,20.3f:", num );
22      printFloatWithFormat( "%020.3f:", num );
23      printFloatWithFormat( "%+020.3f:", num );
24      printFloatWithFormat( "%,020.3f:", num );
25      printFloatWithFormat( "%+,020.3f:", num );
26      System.out.println( "----------+--------------------" );
27    }
```

Listing 8.5 A code that shows various output formatting for floating point data (part 3). The `main` method of the second program

The auxiliary methods between the two programs are identical.

```
28      public static void printFloatWithFormat( String fmt, double v )
29      {
30        System.out.printf( "%-10s|", fmt );
31        System.out.printf( fmt, v );
32        System.out.println();
33      }
34  }
```

Listing 8.6 A code that shows various output formatting for floating point data (part 4). A method used for printing the format `String` and the formatted data together

Executing the two programs, `PrintFFloat` and `PrintFFloat2`, results in the following output.

The following is from `PrintFFloat`:

```
1                  01234567890123456789
2   ---------+--------------------
3   %f:        |1974.921500:
4   %+f:       |+1974.921500:
5   %,f:       |1,974.921500:
6   %+,f:      |+1,974.921500:
```

```
 7   %20f:       |            1974.921500:
 8   %+20f:      |           +1974.921500:
 9   %,20f:      |           1,974.921500:
10   %+,20f:     |          +1,974.921500:
11   %-20f:      |1974.921500           :
12   %+-20f:     |+1974.921500          :
13   %,-20f:     |1,974.921500          :
14   %+-,20f:    |+1,974.921500         :
15   %020f:      |0000000001974.921500:
16   %+020f:     |+000000001974.921500:
17   %,020f:     |000000001,974.921500:
18   %+,020f:    |+00000001,974.921500:
```

The following is from PrintFFloat2.

```
 1                      01234567890123456789
 2   ----------+--------------------
 3   %.3f:       |1974.922:
 4   %+.3f:      |+1974.922:
 5   %,.3f:      |1,974.922:
 6   %+,.3f:     |+1,974.922:
 7   %20.3f:     |           1974.922:
 8   %+20.3f:    |          +1974.922:
 9   %,20.3f:    |          1,974.922:
10   %+,20.3f:   |         +1,974.922:
11   %-20.3f:    |1974.922            :
12   %+-20.3f:   |+1974.922           :
13   %,-20.3f:   |1,974.922           :
14   %+-,20.3f:  |+1,974.922          :
15   %020.3f:    |0000000000001974.922:
16   %+020.3f:   |+000000000001974.922:
17   %,020.3f:   |000000000001,974.922:
18   %+,020.3f:  |+00000000001,974.922:
19   ----------+--------------------
```

8.5   Printing the Fibonacci Sequence (Reprise)

In Chap. 7, we learned how to compute the Fibonacci numbers using two variables to record two immediate predecessors in the sequence. Now, consider printing the square and cubic roots of the numbers obtained as a table, where we generate the sequence up to F_{80}:

```
 1   Enter n: 30
 2        i                    F_i                sqrt              cbrt
 3   ----------------------------------------------------------------------
 4        2                     2              1.41421           1.25992
 5        3                     3              1.73205           1.44225
 6        4                     5              2.23607           1.70998
 7        5                     8              2.82843           2.00000
 8        6                    13              3.60555           2.35133
 9        7                    21              4.58258           2.75892
10        8                    34              5.83095           3.23961
11        9                    55              7.41620           3.80295
12       10                    89              9.43398           4.46475
13       11                   144             12.00000           5.24148
14       12                   233             15.26434           6.15345
15       13                   377             19.41649           7.22405
16       14                   610             24.69818           8.48093
```

17	15	987	31.41656	9.95648
18	16	1597	39.96248	11.68876
19	17	2584	50.83306	13.72242
20	18	4181	64.66065	16.10992
21	19	6765	82.24962	18.91280
22	20	10946	104.62313	22.20335
23	21	17711	133.08268	26.06640
24	22	28657	169.28379	30.60156
25	23	46368	215.33230	35.92577
26	24	75025	273.90692	42.17632
27	25	121393	348.41498	49.51437
28	26	196418	443.19070	58.12912
29	27	317811	563.74728	68.24272
30	28	514229	717.09762	80.11593
31	29	832040	912.16227	94.05489
32	30	1346269	1160.28833	110.41904
33	31	2178309	1475.90955	129.63029
34	32	3524578	1877.38595	152.18402
35	33	5702887	2388.07182	178.66175
36	34	9227465	3037.67427	209.74622
37	35	14930352	3863.98137	246.23891
38	36	24157817	4915.06022	289.08079
39	37	39088169	6252.05318	339.37651
40	38	63245986	7952.73450	398.42293
41	39	102334155	10116.03455	467.74254
42	40	165580141	12867.79472	549.12272
43	41	267914296	16368.08773	644.66184
44	42	433494437	20820.52922	756.82333
45	43	701408733	26484.12228	888.49923
46	44	1134903170	33688.32394	1043.08477
47	45	1836311903	42852.21001	1224.56587
48	46	2971215073	54508.85316	1437.62195
49	47	4807526976	69336.33229	1687.74661
50	48	7778742049	88197.17710	1981.38919
51	49	12586269025	112188.54231	2326.12119
52	50	20365011074	142706.03027	2730.83137
53	51	32951280099	181524.87460	3205.95506
54	52	53316291173	230903.20737	3763.74314
55	53	86267571272	293713.41691	4418.57798
56	54	139583862445	373609.23763	5187.34425
57	55	225851433717	475238.29151	6089.86433
58	56	365435296162	604512.44500	7149.40935
59	57	591286729879	768951.70842	8393.29931
60	58	956722026041	978121.68264	9853.60747
61	59	1548008755920	1244189.99993	11567.98733
62	60	2504730781961	1582634.12764	13580.64357
63	61	4052739537881	2013141.70835	15943.47179
64	62	6557470319842	2560755.81027	18717.39668
65	63	10610209857723	3257331.70827	21973.94288
66	64	17167680177565	4143389.93791	25797.07926
67	65	27777890035288	5270473.41662	30285.38401
68	66	44945570212853	6704145.74818	35554.58645
69	67	72723460248141	8527805.12489	41740.55105
70	68	117669030460994	10847535.68609	49002.78069
71	69	190392490709135	13798278.54151	57528.52933
72	70	308061521170129	17551681.43427	67537.63032
73	71	498454011879264	22326083.66640	79288.16470
74	72	806515533049393	28399217.12036	93083.11578
75	73	1304969544928657	36124362.20792	109278.18137
76	74	2111485077978050	45950898.55463	128290.94539

77	75	3416454622906707	58450445.87432	150611.64511
78	76	5527939700884757	74350115.67499	176815.81168
79	77	8944394323791464	94574808.08223	207579.11010
80	78	14472334024676221	120301014.22962	243694.76088
81	79	23416728348467685	153025253.95655	286093.99305
82	80	37889062373143906	194651129.90462	335870.05549

We can generate this output using two coordinated formats, one for the first line of the header and the other for the data rows of the table. Both types have four entries, and the numbers of spaces allocated for them are 5, 20, 20, and 20 in this order. For the header line, all the entries are `String` data, so we use the place holders `"%5s"`, `"%20s"`, `"%20s"`, and `"%20s"`. For each data line, the first two entries are integers and the last entries are floating point numbers with five digits after the decimal point, so we use the placeholders `"%5d"`, `"%20d"`, `"%20.5f"`, and `"%20.5f"`. Each time a new element of the Fibonacci sequence is calculated, the element is stored in the variable `f`. The new element is calculated as the sum of the two variables, `fp` and `fpp`. `fp` and `fpp` hold the values of the previous Fibonacci number and the number right before the previous Fibonacci number. We calculate the two roots using the `Math` functions `sqrt` and `cbrt`.

Here is the code for this task, `FibonacciClean`.

```
1   import java.util.*;
2   public class FibonacciClean
3   {
4     public static void main( String[] args )
5     {
6       long f, fp = 1, fpp = 1;
7       double sqroot, cbroot;
8       Scanner keyboard = new Scanner( System.in );
9       System.out.print( "Enter n: " );
10      int n = keyboard.nextInt();
11      System.out.printf( "%5s%20s%20s%20s\n",
12           "i", "F_i", "sqrt", "cbrt" );
```

Listing 8.7 A program that prints the Fibonacci numbers and their square and cubic roots neatly (part 1)

```
13        for ( int i = 1; i <= 65; i ++ )
14        {
15          System.out.print( "-" );
16        }
17        System.out.println();
18        for ( int i = 2; i <= n; i ++ )
19        {
20          f = fp + fpp;
21          sqroot = Math.sqrt( f );
22          cbroot = Math.cbrt( f );
23          System.out.printf( "%5d%20d%20.5f%20.5f\n",
24               i, f, sqroot, cbroot );
25          fpp = fp;
26          fp = f;
27        }
28      }
29  }
```

Listing 8.8 A program that prints the Fibonacci numbers and their square and cubic roots neatly (part 2)

Summary

■ The formatting options that are available for printing a String data with a printf statement include the choice between the flush left and the flush right positioning, the number of character spaces allocated, and the length of the prefix to be printed.

■ The formatting options that are available for printing a whole number with a printf statement include the choice among flush left, flush right, and flush right with leading 0s, the forced plus sign, the forced punctuation, and the number of character spaces allocated.

■ The formatting options that are available for printing a floating point number with a printf statement include the choice among flush left, flush right, and flush right with leading 0s, the forced plus sign, the forced punctuation, the number of character spaces allocated, and the number of digits after the decimal point.

■ The formatting options that are available for printing a char data with a printf statement are the choice between flush left and flush right, and the number of character spaces allocated.

■ To include % in the format, use %%.

Exercises

1. **Printf output**   Let myVar be a double variable with the value of 10.345678. State what output the following printf statements generate.
   (a) System.out.printf("value=%4.1f", myVar);
   (b) System.out.printf("value=%5.2f", myVar);
   (c) System.out.printf("value=%.3f", myVar);

2. **(Approximately) simulating printf for a real number**   Write a method named dot2f that acts as if it were printf with "%.2f" as the format. The method does not return a value. The method has one formal parameter input, which is a double. The method must print the value of input.
   The strategy for achieving the goal is as follows:
   • Execute Math.round of input * 100.0 and convert it to an integer by casting (long), and then store its value into a long variable input100.
   • Divide input100 into two long values a and b, which are respectively the quotient of input100 by 100 and the remainder of input100 by 100.
   • Print a, the period, b / 10, and b % 10 in this order.

3. **(Approximately) simulating printf for a real number, continued**   Using the idea from the previous question, write a void method dot4f that takes a double variable input as its parameter and prints the value of input in "%.4f" format.

4. **A simple for-loop, leading 0s**   Using a for-loop whose body consists of just one printf statement, write a code that produces the following output:

```
1   001:
2   003:
3   005:
4   007:
5   009:
```

5. **Two values per line for-loop** Using a for-loop whose body consists of just one `printf` statement, write a code that produces the following output:

```
1  001,002
2  003,004
3  005,006
4  007,008
5  009,010
```

6. **A simple for-loop** Using a for-loop whose body consists of just one `printf` statement, write a code that produces the following output:

```
1  100!
2   88!
3   76!
4   64!
5   52!
6   40!
7   28!
8   16!
```

7. **Powering** Write a method named `powerList` that takes two parameters, a `double` d and an `int` k, and prints the i-th power of d for $i = 1, \ldots, k$. The output for each value of i appears in a single line along with the value of i, with r digits for i and four digits after the decimal point for the powers. The following is an example of the output produced by such a method:

```
1     1 3.1000
2     2 9.6100
3     3 29.7910
4     4 286.2915
```

Programming Projects

8. **Mimicking the simple formatting of a floating point number without rounding** Write a program named `PseudoPrintfF` that receives a `double` number x and a nonnegative `int` number d from the user, and then prints the absolute value of x with exactly d digits after the decimal point. If the user enters a negative integer for d, the program terminates with an error of `IllegalArgumentException`. If d `==` 0, the program prints only the integer part of the absolute value of x without a period. If d `>` 0, the program prints the integer part of the absolute value, prints a period, and prints d digits as follows: Let y be the absolute value of x minus the integer part of the absolute value. y is greater than or equal to 0 and strictly less than 1. The program repeats the following d times:
   - Multiply y by 10.
   - Print the integer part of y.
   - Subtract the integer part of y from y.

9. **Printing the calendar of a month** Write a program named `CalOfAMonth` that produces the calendar of a month. The program receives the number of days in the month and the position at which the first day of the month starts (0 for Sunday, 1 for Monday, etc.), and then prints the calendar in the example below, where the inputs are 31 and 2.

```
1   |   Sun     Mon     Tue     Wed     Thu     Fri     Sat
2   +------+------+------+------+------+------+------+
3   |      |      |   1  |   2  |   3  |   4  |   5  |
4   |   6  |   7  |   8  |   9  |  10  |  11  |  12  |
5   |  13  |  14  |  15  |  16  |  17  |  18  |  19  |
6   |  20  |  21  |  22  |  23  |  24  |  25  |  26  |
7   |  27  |  28  |  29  |  30  |  31  |      |      |
8   +------+------+------+------+------+------+------+
```

The number of days must be 28, 29, 30, or 31. Let `numberOfDays` and `startDay` be the number of days and the position of the first day of the month. A key calculation to make is (excluding the fixed lines) how many rows are in the table. The minimum number of cells required to produce the table is the sum of `numberOfDays` and `startDay`. If the sum is a multiple of 7, then the number of rows is the sum divided by 7; otherwise, it is the quotient plus 1. Based on this observation, we can write the code using a double for-loop. The exterior loop of the double for-loop produces the row values in a variable `row` starting from 0. The interior loop of the double for-loop produces the column values in a variable `col` between 1 and 7. The cell at (`row`, `col`) corresponds to the day index 7 * `row` + `col` - `startDay`. If the day index is greater than or equal to 0 and less than or equal to `numberOfDays`, we need to print the value of the index; otherwise, the index is invalid, so the cell should be six white spaces.

10. **Parsing `Prinrtf` parameter** Write a program named `ParsePrintfD` that receives a `String` data, w (which is a syntactically correct integer format placeholder for `printf`), and produces the answers to the following questions on the screen:

- Does it contain `'+'`?
- Does it contain `','`?
- Does it contain `'-'`?
- Does it contain a sequence of numerals?
- Does it contain a sequence of numerals and the sequence start with a `'0'`?

Here is an execution example:

```
1   Enter your format string: +-,45
2   Has a '+' = true
3   Has a '-' = true
4   Has a ',' = true
5   Has a number = true
6   Has a zero = false
```

Here is one more:

```
1   Enter your format string: 034,3
2   Has a '+' = false
3   Has a '-' = false
4   Has a ',' = true
5   Has a number = true
6   Has a zero = true
```

11. **Generating a BMI table**   Write a program named `BMITable` that generates a table of BMI values for a range of weights in pounds and for a range of heights in inches. The weight range is from 260 pounds down to 80 pounds with the value gap decreasing by 5 (the values are 260, 255, 250, . . . , 80). The height range is from 56 to 76 with the value increasing by 2 (the values are 56, 58, . . . , 76). The rows are the weights and the columns are the heights. Use the `printf` format of `"%5.1f"` to print the values. The output of the program should start with:

```
1    -------+----------------------------------------------------------
2    Weight | height (in.)
3    (lbs.) |   56   58   60   62   64   66   68   70   72   74   76
4    -------+----------------------------------------------------------
5    260    | 58.3 54.3 50.8 47.5 44.6 42.0 39.5 37.3 35.3 33.4 31.6
6    255    | 57.2 53.3 49.8 46.6 43.8 41.2 38.8 36.6 34.6 32.7 31.0
7    250    | 56.0 52.2 48.8 45.7 42.9 40.3 38.0 35.9 33.9 32.1 30.4
```

and end with:

```
1    95     | 21.3 19.9 18.6 17.4 16.3 15.3 14.4 13.6 12.9 12.2 11.6
2    90     | 20.2 18.8 17.6 16.5 15.4 14.5 13.7 12.9 12.2 11.6 11.0
3    85     | 19.1 17.8 16.6 15.5 14.6 13.7 12.9 12.2 11.5 10.9 10.3
4    80     | 17.9 16.7 15.6 14.6 13.7 12.9 12.2 11.5 10.8 10.3  9.7
5    -------+----------------------------------------------------------
```

Write and use a method for printing the separator line, a method for printing the two header lines, and a method for printing the rest of the table.

Classes `String` and `StringBuilder`

9

9.1 Methods for Obtaining Information from `String` Data

Java provides a variety of methods for extracting information from a `String` data. Since `String` is an object class, like `Scanner`, we execute a method on a `String` data by attaching a period, the name of the method, and the parameters:

STRING_DATA.METHOD_NAME(PARAMETERS)

A wide variety of methods are available for `String`. We can divide them roughly into four types:

1. the methods for obtaining information about the `String` data;
2. the methods for comparing the `String` data with another `String` data;
3. the methods for locating a pattern in the `String` data; and
4. the methods for producing a new `String` data from the `String` data.

Table 9.1 summarizes the `String` methods we will study. The table has two additional methods, `toCharArray` and `split`. We will study these methods later.

The first `String` method we lean is `length()`. This method belongs to the first category and returns the character length as `int`. The following code assigns the `String` literal `"the earth"` to a `String` variable named `message`. Next, the code obtains the character length of `message` and stores it in an `int` variable named `characterCount`. Finally, the code prints the values of `message` and `characterCount` using a `printf` statement.

```
1  String message = "the earth";
2  int characterCount = message.length();
3  System.out.printf( "\"\%s\" has length %d%n", message, characterCount );
```

The output generated by the code is:

```
"the earth" has length 9
```

Another method in the first category is `charAt`. `charAt` receives an `int` value as a parameter, and returns the character of the `String` data at the character position represented by the parameter. In Java, a position count starts from 0, instead of from 1. We see this in `String` and in arrays (see

© Springer Nature Switzerland AG 2018
M. Ogihara, *Fundamentals of Java Programming*,
https://doi.org/10.1007/978-3-319-89491-1_9

Table 9.1 A list of `String` methods

Name	Return type	Parameters	Action
`length`	`int`	None	Returns the character length of s
`charAt`	`char`	`int p`	Returns the character of s at position p
`toCharArray`	`char[]`	`void`	Returns the character array representation of s
`Split`	`String[]`	`String p`	Returns the `String` array generated by splitting with s as the delimiter
`equals`	`boolean`	`String o`	Returns whether or not s is equal to o
`compareTo`	`int`	`String o`	Returns the result of comparing s with o
`startsWith`	`boolean`	`String o`	Returns whether or not s starts with o
`endsWith`	`boolean`	`String o`	Returns whether or not s ends with o
`indexOf`	`int`	`String w`	Returns the lowest position where w occurs in s; if w does not occur in s, returns -1
`lastIndexOf`	`int`	`String w`	Returns the highest position where w occurs in s; if w does not occur in s, returns -1
`indexOf`	`int`	`String w,` `int p`	Returns the lowest position >= p where w occurs in s; if w does not occur in s at positions >= p, returns -1
`lastIndexOf`	`int`	`String w,` `int p`	Returns the highest position < p where w occurs in s; if w does not occur in s at positions < p, returns -1
`trim`	`String`	None	Returns a new `String` without the leading and trailing white space characters
`substring`	`String`	`int i`	Returns the suffix of s starting from position i
`substring`	`String`	`int i,` `int j`	Returns the substring of s between position i and position j - 1
`toUpperCase`	`String`	None	Returns a new `String` generated from s by converting all lowercase letters to uppercase
`toLowerCase`	`String`	None	Returns a new `String` generated from s by converting all uppercase letters to lowercase
`replace`	`String`	`String a,` `String b`	Returns a new `String` generated from s by substituting all occurrences of a by b
`replaceFirst`	`String`	`String a,` `String b`	Returns a new `String` generated from s by substituting the first occurrence of a by b

Here s represents the `String` data to which the methods appearing in the table are applied. For methods `indexOf` and `lastIndexOf`, a char value is also accepted as the first parameter

Chap. 12). For each `String` object having length N, its first character is at position 0, its second character is at position 1, and so on. The last character is at position N - 1. If s is a `String` data and p is an `int` value between 0 and `s.length()` - 1, then `s.charAt( p )` returns the char of s at position p.

Consider the following code fragment:

```
1   String message = "the sun";
2   System.out.println( "char at 1 is " + message.charAt( 1 ) );
3   System.out.println( "char at 5 is " + message.charAt( 5 ) );
4   System.out.println( "char at 6 is " + message.charAt( 6 ) );
```

This code produces the output:

```
1  char at 1 is h
2  char at 5 is u
3  char at 6 is n
```

If we call charAt with a position value outside the valid range, a run-time error, StringIndexOut OfBoundsException, occurs. The following program demonstrates the use of length and charAt, and generates StringIndexOutOfBoundsException. The program receives an input line from the user using the method nextLine of Scanner, and stores it in a String variable named line. The program then executes a for-loop that iterates over the sequence 0, ..., input.length() with an index variable named i. For each value of i, the program prints the value of i as well as the value of input.chatAt(i).

```
1  import java.util.Scanner;
2  public class StringIndices
3  {
4    public static void main( String[] args )
5    {
6      Scanner keyboard = new Scanner( System.in );
7      System.out.print( "Enter string: " );
8      String input = keyboard.nextLine();
9      for ( int i = 0; i <= input.length(); i ++ )
10     {
11       System.out.print( "position = " + i );
12       System.out.println( " .. char is " + input.charAt( i ) );
13     }
14   }
15 }
```

Listing 9.1 An example of StringIndexOutOfBoundsException

Since the valid range of the parameter for input.chatAt is from 0 to input.length() - 1, the program makes an invalid method call at the last round of the iteration. At that round, the value of i is equal to input.length(). Here is how the program runs and how the error is generated.

```
1  Enter string: Hello, World!
2  position = 0 .. char is H
3  position = 1 .. char is e
4  position = 2 .. char is l
5  position = 3 .. char is l
6  position = 4 .. char is o
7  position = 5 .. char is ,
8  position = 6 .. char is
9  position = 7 .. char is W
10 position = 8 .. char is o
11 position = 9 .. char is r
12 position = 10 .. char is l
13 position = 11 .. char is d
14 position = 12 .. char is !
15 position = 13Exception in thread "main"
       java.lang.StringIndexOutOfBoundsException: String index out of range:
       13
16   at java.lang.String.charAt(String.java:646)
17   at StringIndices.main(StringIndices.java:12)
```

The error message starts immediately after the output position = 13.

9.2   Methods for Comparing `String` Data with Another

9.2.1   The Equality Test and the Comparison in Dictionary Order

As mentioned earlier, the mathematical equality and inequality tests work correctly only for primitive data types. `String` has two methods for content equality and content comparison. They are methods `equals` and `compareTo`. Let s and t be two `String` objects. `s.equals( t )` returns a `boolean` that represents whether or not s and t have the same character sequences. The relation computed by `equals` is symmetric and reflexive. In other words, `s.equals( t )` and `t.equals( s )` have the same values, and for all s that is not `null`, `s.equals( s )` is `true`.

The method `s.compareTo( t )` returns an `int` value representing the result of performing character-by-character comparison from start to end between the two `String` objects. The is based upon the indexes of the characters in the Unicode table. The comparison is terminated when either all the characters of either s or t have been examined or the character of s at the present position has been found to be different from the character of t at the same position.

In the former situation, there are three possible outcomes.

1. If all the characters have been complete examined for both s and t, the method returns 0.
2. If s has at least character remaining, it means that t is a proper prefix of s and the method returns a strictly positive integer.
3. If t has at least character remaining, it means that s is a proper prefix of t and the method returns a strictly negative integer.

In the latter situation, there are two possible outcomes.

1. If the character of s has a higher position than the character of t in the Unicode character indexes, he method returns a strictly positive integer.
2. If the character of s has a lower position than the character of t in the Unicode character indexes, the method returns a strictly negative integer.

The relation defined by the method `compareTo` of `String` data is transitive, in the sense that if `s.compareTo( t )` and `t.compareTo( u )` are both positive, then `s.compareTo( u )` is positive, and if `s.compareTo( t )` and `t.compareTo( u )` are both negative, then `s.compareTo( u )` is negative. Because of the transitive property, the method `compareTo` induces a complete ordering of all `String` values. This property is used in the method `sort` of class `Arrays` that we will see later in Sect. 13.1. Furthermore, `s.compareTo( t ) + t.compareTo( s )` is equal to 0.

It is practically impossible to remember the position of each character in the Unicode table, but the following information may be helpful:

- the numerals appear consecutively in ten positions, starting with `'0'` and ending with `'9'`;
- the uppercase letters appear consecutively in 26 positions, starting with `'A'` and ending with `'Z'`;
- the lowercase letters appear consecutively in 26 positions, starting with `'a'` and ending with `'z'`;
- the numerals precede the uppercase letters and the uppercase letters precede the lowercase letters.

The next program, `StringCompExample`, receives three `String` data, `text1`, `text2`, and `text3`, from the user and compares them. The program has two methods, `performEquals` and

```
1   import java.util.*;
2   public class StringCompExample
3   {
4     public static void main( String[] args )
5     {
6       Scanner keyboard = new Scanner( System.in );
7       System.out.print( "Enter #1: " );
8       String text1 = keyboard.nextLine();
9       System.out.print( "Enter #2: " );
10      String text2 = keyboard.nextLine();
11      System.out.print( "Enter #3: " );
12      String text3 = keyboard.nextLine();
13
```

Listing 9.2 An example of String comparison (part 1). This section is for receiving the input data

performCompareTo. performEquals receives two String data, s and t, and reports the result of comparing s with t using equals. performCompareTo receives two String data, s and t, and reports the result of comparing s with t using compareTo. Both methods use printf for reporting the result. The method performEquals uses %s as the placeholder for printing the return value of the equals method, while the method performCompareTo uses %d as the placeholder for printing the return value of the compareTo. Using the two methods, the method main executes equals between text1 and text1 itself, between text1 and text2, and between text2 and text3. The method then executes comparesTo between text1 and text1 itself, and all distinct pairs (in this case, there are six of them).

```
14        performEquals( text1, text1 );
15        performEquals( text1, text2 );
16        performEquals( text2, text3 );
17
18        performCompareTo( text1, text1 );
19        performCompareTo( text1, text2 );
20        performCompareTo( text2, text1 );
21        performCompareTo( text2, text3 );
22        performCompareTo( text3, text2 );
23        performCompareTo( text3, text1 );
24        performCompareTo( text1, text3 );
25      }
26    public static void performEquals( String s, String t )
27    {
28      boolean result = s.equals( t );
29      System.out.printf( "\"%s\" equals \"%s\": %s%n", s, t, result );
30    }
31    public static void performCompareTo( String s, String t )
32    {
33      int result = s.compareTo( t );
34      System.out.printf( "\"%s\" compareTo \"%s\": %d%n", s, t, result );
35    }
36  }
```

Listing 9.3 An example of String comparison (part 2). This section is for executing comparisons

Here is an execution example of the program:

```
1   Enter #1: New Hampshire
2   Enter #2: New Mexico
3   Enter #3: New York
4   "New Hampshire" equals "New Hampshire": true
5   "New Hampshire" equals "New Mexico": false
6   "New Mexico" equals "New York": false
7   "New Hampshire" compareTo "New Hampshire": 0
8   "New Hampshire" compareTo "New Mexico": -5
9   "New Mexico" compareTo "New Hampshire": 5
10  "New Mexico" compareTo "New York": -12
11  "New York" compareTo "New Mexico": 12
12  "New York" compareTo "New Hampshire": 17
13  "New Hampshire" compareTo "New York": -17
```

The ordering among the three input data, from the smallest to the largest is:

`"New Hampshire"`, `"New Mexico""`, `"New York"`

Here is another example. This time, the input contains numerals:

```
1   Enter #1: ZeroOne
2   Enter #2: zeroone
3   Enter #3: 01
4   "ZeroOne" equals "ZeroOne": true
5   "ZeroOne" equals "zeroone": false
6   "zeroone" equals "01": false
7   "ZeroOne" compareTo "ZeroOne": 0
8   "ZeroOne" compareTo "zeroone": -32
9   "zeroone" compareTo "ZeroOne": 32
10  "zeroone" compareTo "01": 74
11  "01" compareTo "zeroone": -74
12  "01" compareTo "ZeroOne": -42
13  "ZeroOne" compareTo "01": 42
```

The ordering among the three inputs, from the smallest to the largest is:

`"01"`, `"ZeroOne"`, `"zeroone"`

9.2.2 The Prefix and Suffix Tests

The class `String` offers prefix and suffix tests, called `startsWith` and `startsWith`. Let `s` and `t` be `String` data.

- `s.startsWith( t )` returns a `boolean` value that represents whether or not `t` is a prefix of `s`.
- `s.endsWith( t )` returns a `boolean` value that represents whether or not `t` is a suffix of `s`.

The next code compares the `String` literal `"Computer Science"` with three other literals, `"Computer"`, `"Science"`, and `"Engineering"`, with respect to prefixes and suffices. The program uses methods, `prefixTest` and `suffixTest`, that receive two `String` parameters, performs either the prefix or the suffix tests, and reports the result.

```
1   public class PrefixSuffix {
2     public static void main( String[] args )
3     {
4       String cs = "Computer Science";
5       String comp = "Computer";
6       String sci = "Science";
7       String eng = "Engineering";
8
9       prefixTest( cs, comp );
10      prefixTest( cs, sci );
11      prefixTest( cs, eng );
12      suffixTest( cs, comp );
13      suffixTest( cs, sci );
14      suffixTest( cs, eng );
15    }
16    public static void prefixTest( String line, String pattern )
17    {
18      String neg = "";
19      if ( !line.startsWith( pattern ) )
20      {
21        neg = "not ";
22      }
23      System.out.printf( "\"%s\" is %sa prefix of \"%s\".%n",
24          pattern, neg, line );
25    }
26    public static void suffixTest( String line, String pattern )
27    {
28      String neg = "";
29      if ( !line.endsWith( pattern ) )
30      {
31        neg = "not ";
32      }
33      System.out.printf( "\"%s\" is %sa suffix of \"%s\".%n",
34          pattern, neg, line );
35    }
36  }
```

Listing 9.4 A program that demonstrates the use of beginsWith and endsWith

The execution of the code produces the following result:

```
1   Is "Computer" a prefix of "Computer Science"? true
2   Is "Science" a prefix of "Computer Science"? false
3   Is "Engineering" a prefix of "Computer Science"? false
4   Is "Computer" a suffix of "Computer Science"? false
5   Is "Science" a suffix of "Computer Science"? true
6   Is "Engineering" a suffix of "Computer Science"? false
```

9.3 Methods for Searching for a Pattern in a `String` Data

For two `String` data s and t, and an integer q, we say that t appears in s at position q, if the character sequence of s starting from position q has t as a prefix. More precisely, t appears in s at position q if q + t.length() <= s.length() and the character sequence s.charAt(q), ..., s.charAt(q + t.length() - 1) is equal to the characters of t. For instance, in "Panama", "a" appears at 1, 3, and 5.

indexOf and lastIndexOf are methods for pattern search. Both methods receive the pattern to search for as a parameter. The pattern is either a String data or a char data. Both methods may take a second parameter. The second parameter, if present, is an int data and represents the region of search. The return type is int for both. The return value represents the position at the pattern appears. If the pattern does not appear, the return value is -1. The method indexOf returns the lowest position at which the pattern appears. If the second parameter is present, the method indexOf returns the lowest position at which the pattern appears among the positions greater than or equal to the value of the second parameter. The method lastIndexOf returns the highest position at which the pattern appears. If the second parameter is present, the method lastIndexOf returns the highest position at which the pattern appears among the positions less than the value of the second parameter. If there is no match in the specified region, both two-parameter versions return -1. Let seq be a String data that contains opening lines from the hymn "Swing Low, Sweet Chariot" in all lower case, as follows:

```
"swing low, sweet chariot, comin' for to carry me home"
```

We can present the characters of seq with their positions in a table-like format as follows:

```
1   char: swing low, sweet chariot, comin' for to carry me home
2   ten:  0000000000011111111111122222222222233333333333444444444
3   one:  012345567890123455678901234556789012345567890123455567
```

In the table, the row starting with "char" shows the character sequence of seq, and the next two rows show their character positions. The row starting with "ten" represents the digit in the tens place, and the row starting with "one" represents the digit in the ones place. We can see that seq contains four occurrences of the letter 'e', at positions 12, 13, 43, and 47. The method call seq.indexOf('e') returns the smallest among the four, namely 12. The method call seq.indexOf('e', 20) returns the smallest among those that are greater than or equal to 20, namely 43. The method call seq.lastIndexOf('e') returns the largest among the four values, namely 47. The method call seq.lastIndexOf('e', 30) returns the largest among those that are strictly less than 30, namely 13. The method call seq.lastIndexOf('e', 12) returns -1 since none of the positions are smaller than 12. If the pattern to search for is "sw", the positions at which the pattern occurs are 0 and 11. Therefore, seq.indexOf("sw") returns 0, seq.indexOf("sw", 7) returns 11, seq.indexOf("sw", 12) returns −1, seq.lastIndexOf("sw", 7) returns 0, and seq.lastIndexOf("sw", 12) returns 11.

The next program, IndexOf, receives an input line, a pattern to search for in the input line, and a position that represents a search range, and then prints the result of executing the search methods. Here is the part for receiving the input from the user:

```
1   import java.util.*;
2   public class IndexOf
3   {
4     public static void main( String[] args )
5     {
6       Scanner keyboard = new Scanner( System.in );
7       System.out.print( "Enter the input: " );
8       String input = keyboard.nextLine();
9       System.out.print( "Enter the pattern: " );
10      String pat = keyboard.nextLine();
11      System.out.print( "Enter the position " );
12      int pos = keyboard.nextInt();
13
```

Listing 9.5 A program that demonstrates the use of pattern search methods of String (part 1). The part that receives the input

The program presents the input and the character positions using the table-like format shown above. If the input from the user has length between 0 and 100, the decimal representation of each character position requires at most two digits. If a value between 0 and 99 is represented by an int variable i, its digit in the tens place is i / 10 and its digit in the ones place is i % 10. Based upon this observation, the program uses the following code to produce the header.

```
14      System.out.println();
15      for ( int i = 0; i <= input.length() - 1; i ++ )
16      {
17         System.out.print( ( i / 10 ) % 10 );
18      }
19      System.out.println();
20      for ( int i = 0; i <= input.length() - 1; i ++ )
21      {
22         System.out.print( i % 10 );
23      }
24      System.out.println();
25      System.out.println( input );
26      for ( int i = 0; i <= input.length() - 1; i ++ )
27      {
28         System.out.print( '-' );
29      }
30      System.out.println();
31
```

Listing 9.6 A program that demonstrates the use of pattern search methods of String (part 2). The part that prints the header of the output

The program then executes pattern search. There are four different calls. The program announces the method it is about to call, and then prints the return value.

```
32      System.out.print( "indexOf(\"" + pat + "\"): " );
33      System.out.println( input.indexOf( pat ) );
34      System.out.print( "lastIndexOf(\"" + pat + "\"): " );
35      System.out.println( input.lastIndexOf( pat ) );
36      System.out.print( "indexOf(\"" + pat + "\"," + pos + "): " );
37      System.out.println( input.indexOf( pat, pos ) );
38      System.out.print( "lastIndexOf(\"" + pat + "\"," + pos + "): " );
39      System.out.println( input.lastIndexOf( pat, pos ) );
40      }
41  }
```

Listing 9.7 A program that demonstrates the use of pattern search methods of String (part 3). The part that calls the search methods and prints the results

Here is the result of executing the code with the two lines from "Swing Low, Sweet Chariot":

```
1  Enter the input: swing low, sweet chariot, comin' for to carry me home
2  Enter the pattern: e
3  Enter the position 20
4
5  00000000001111111111222222222233333333334444444444555
6  01234567890123456789012345678901234567890123456789012
7  swing low, sweet chariot, comin' for to carry me home
```

```
 8  | ---------------------------------------------------------
 9  | indexOf("e"):  13
10  | lastIndexOf("e"):  52
11  | indexOf("e",20):  47
12  | lastIndexOf("e",20):  14
```

Here is another example with the two lines from the second verse of the hymn "Jerusalem".

```
 1  | Enter the input: bring me my bow of burning gold! bring me my arrows of
    |     desire!
 2  | Enter the pattern: ow
 3  | Enter the position 10
 4  |
 5  | 00000000001111111111222222222233333333334444444444555555555566
 6  | 01234567890123456789012345678901234567890123456789012345678901
 7  | bring me my bow of burning gold! bring me my arrows of desire!
 8  | ---------------------------------------------------------
 9  | indexOf("ow"):  13
10  | lastIndexOf("ow"):  48
11  | indexOf("ow",10):  13
12  | lastIndexOf("ow",10):  -1
```

9.4   Methods for Creating New String Data from Another

The final group of String methods that we learn consists of those that generate a new String data.
Let s be a String object.

1. s.toUpperCase() returns a copy of s in which each lowercase letter is switched to its
   uppercase version; if no lowercase letter appears in s, the method returns the exact copy of s.
2. s.toLowerCase() returns a copy of s in which each uppercase letter is switched to its
   lowercase version; if no uppercase letter appears in s, the method returns the exact copy of s.
3. s.substring(int startIndex) returns a copy of s starting from position
   startIndex; if the index value is negative or greater than the length of s, the method produces
   a run-time error StringIndexOutOfBoundsException.
4. s.substring(int startIndex, int endIndex) returns a copy of s starting at position startIndex and ending at position endIndex - 1; if either index
   value is negative or greater than the length of s, the method produces a run-time error
   StringIndexOutOfBoundsException.
5. s.replace(String x, String y) returns a copy of s in which all the occurrences
   of x are replaced with y; if x does not occur in s, the method returns the exact copy of s. If
   there is only one occurrence of x in s, that occurrence is substituted with y. If there are multiple
   occurrences of x in s and if some consecutive occurrences overlap, the occurrences are chosen
   without overlap in a "greedy" fashion, as follows: The first occurrence chosen is the occurrence at
   the lowest position. From the second occurrence on, the occurrence chosen is the one at the lowest
   position that overlaps none of the previously chosen occurrences. For instance, "abababa" has
   three occurrences of "aba", at positions 0, 2, and 4. The second occurrence overlap the first and
   the last. Given "aba" as the first parameter, replace chooses the positions 0 and 4.
6. s.replaceFirst(String x, String y) is a variant of replace where the substitution applies only to the first occurrence of x.
7. s.trim() returns a copy of s without all of its leading and trailing white space characters.

The next program demonstrates the use of the String generation methods. The method main of the program calls three methods names changesOne, changesTwo, and changesThree (Lines 6–8).

```
1   import java.util.*;
2   public class ModifyString
3   {
4     public static void main( String[] args )
5     {
6       changesOne();
7       changesTwo();
8       changesThree();
9     }
```

Listing 9.8 A program that demonstrates the use of String methods for generating new String data (part 1). The method main

The first method of three, changesOne, demonstrates the use of toLowerCase(), toUpperCase(), and trim(). The method receives an input line from the user, stores it in a variable named input (Lines 13 and 14), and then executes input.toLowerCase() (Lines 15 and 16), input.toUpperCase() (Lines 17 and 18), and input.trim() (Lines 19 and 20). The program uses a String variable named result to receive the return values of these methods.

```
10    public static void changesOne()
11    {
12      Scanner keyboard = new Scanner( System.in );
13      System.out.print( "Enter the input String: " );
14      String input = keyboard.nextLine();
15      String result = input.toLowerCase();
16      System.out.println( "lower: " + result );
17      result = input.toUpperCase();
18      System.out.println( "upper: " + result );
19      result = input.trim();
20      System.out.println( "trim: " + input.trim() );
21    }
```

Listing 9.9 A program that demonstrates the use of String methods for generating new String data (part 2). The method changesOne

In changesTwo, the program receives an input line (Lines 25 and 26) and two position values (Lines 27–30) from the user, and then calls the method substring. To announce the action that has been performed and its result, the program uses printf, with the format:

$$\text{substring}(\%d) = \%s\%n$$

for the one-parameter version, and the format:

$$\text{substring}(\%d, \%d) = \%s\%n$$

for the two-parameter version. Each %d is the placeholder for the actual parameter, and each %s is the placeholder for the return value.

The nextLine appearing in Line 30 is necessary, for the following reason: After changesTwo, the method changesThree is called. The first action changesThree performs with a Scanner is to read an input line with nextLine. To receive the two position values, changesTwo uses `nextInt`. If there is no `nextLine` after the two calls of `nextInt` in `changesTwo`, the first `nextLine` in `changesThree` returns the sequence of characters entered between the last numeral of the second integer retrieved with `nextInt` in `changesTwo` and the return key that has been pressed to enter the numbers.

```
22    public static void changesTwo ()
23    {
24       Scanner keyboard = new Scanner ( System.in );
25       System.out.print ( "Enter the input String: " );
26       String input = keyboard.nextLine ();
27       System.out.print ( "Enter start and end positions " );
28       int pos1 = keyboard.nextInt ();
29       int pos2 = keyboard.nextInt ();
30       keyboard.nextLine ();
31       String result = input.substring ( pos1 );
32       System.out.printf ( "substring ( %d ): %s%n", pos1, result );
33       result = input.substring ( pos1, pos2 );
34       System.out.printf ( "substring ( %d, %d ): %s%n", pos1, pos2, result );
35    }
```

Listing 9.10 A program that demonstrates the use of `String` methods for generating new `String` data (part 3). The method `changesTwo`

In `changesThree`, the program receives an input line (Lines 39 and 40) and two additional lines representing the patterns (Lines 41–44) from the user, and then executes the pattern replacement (Lines 45–48).

```
36    public static void changesThree ()
37    {
38       Scanner keyboard = new Scanner ( System.in );
39       System.out.print ( "Enter the input String: " );
40       String input = keyboard.nextLine ();
41       System.out.print ( "Enter pattern 1: " );
42       String pat1 = keyboard.nextLine ();
43       System.out.print ( "Enter pattern 2: " );
44       String pat2 = keyboard.nextLine ();
45       String result = input.replaceFirst ( pat1, pat2 );
46       System.out.printf ( "replaceFirst ( %s,%s ): %s%n",
47           pat1, pat2, result );
48       result = input.replace ( pat1, pat2 ) ;
49       System.out.printf ( "replace ( %s,%s ): %s%n", pat1, pat2, result );
50    }
51 }
```

Listing 9.11 A program that demonstrates the use of `String` methods for generating new `String` data (part 4). The method `changesThree`

Here is one execution example of the code.

```
1  Enter the input String:     Sorry, Professor. My phone's alarm didn't
        work...
2  lower:    sorry, professor. my phone's alarm didn't work...
3  upper:    SORRY, PROFESSOR. MY PHONE'S ALARM DIDN'T WORK...
4  trim: Sorry, Professor. My phone's alarm didn't work...
5  Enter the input String: We have caught a possum resembling Fairway Frank.
6  Enter start and end positions 10 20
```

```
7   substring(10)=ught a possum resembling Fairway Frank.
8   substring(10,20)=ught a pos
9   Enter the input String: I've received an A in BIO101 and CHM101.
10  Enter pattern 1: A
11  Enter pattern 2: A+
12  replaceFirst(A,A+)=I've received an A+ in BIO101 and CHM101.
13  replaceF(A,A+)=I've received an A+ in BIO101 and CHM101.
```

9.4.1 String.format

There is one static `String` method that is used often. The method is `format`. We can use this method to mimic the action of `printf` and receive the result as a return value, instead of printing it on the screen. For example,

```
1   int x = 10;
2   double y = 1.7956;
3   String output = String.format( "x=%d,y=%.2f", x, y );
```

stores the character sequence x=10,y=1.80 in the `String` variable output (because the rounding for y occurs at the third position after the decimal point).

9.5   Class StringBuilder

Quite often, we need to produce a long `String` output spreading over multiple lines, either on the screen or to some file. We can build such an output using `String` concatenation, by adding components one after another. A `StringBuilder` object can be used to build a `String` data through insertion, deletion, and concatenation. To create a `StringBuilder` object, we use a constructor, either with a `String` as its initial contents or without, as shown next:

```
1   StringBuilder builder1 = new StringBuilder();
2   StringBuilder builder2 = new StringBuilder( "Hello, World!" );
```

A `String` data that a `StringBuilder` object represents can be obtained by calling the method `toString`. Some methods of `String` are available for `StringBuilder` too. They include `length`, `charAt`, `indexOf`, `lastIndexOf`, and `substring`. The `StringBuilder` versions of these methods are applied to the `String` data that the `StringBuilder` object represents.

There are methods that are available in `StringBuilder` but not in `String`. They include `append`, `insert`, and `delete`:

- The method `append` receives one formal parameter and appends its value to the contents. The type of the parameter can be `boolean`, `char`, `double`, `float`, `int`, `long`, or `String`.
- The method `insert` receives two formal parameters. The first parameter is an `int` and specifies where, in the contents of the `StringBuilder` object, an insertion must be made. The second parameter specifies the actual data to insert. The type of the second parameter can be `boolean`, `char`, `double`, `float`, `int`, `long`, or `String`.
- The method `delete` receives two `int` parameters, `start` and `end`, and removes the characters at positions between `start` and `end` - 1 from the contents. The use of an invalid index results in the run-time error of `StringIndexOutOfBoundsException` occurs. There is a one-parameter version of `delete`. This version removes all the characters starting from the position that the parameter specifies.

Here is a demonstration of how the methods of StringBuilder work. The program receives an input line from the user, and then collects all the lowercase letters appearing in the input line. The collected letters are simply connected without spacing in between and turned into a String data. The method main stores its input in a variable named input (Lines 7 and 8) and calls the method collect. The method stores the returned value in a variable named output (Line 9). The method then presents the two values (Line 11).

The method collect receives a String data as a formal parameter, and returns a String object (Line 13). The method instantiates a StringBuilder object (Line 15). It then goes through the characters of the input line one after another (Line 16). For each character encountered, if the character is a lowercase letter (Lines 18 and 19), the method appends the character to the builder (Line 21). After completing the examination, the method inserts the sequence -\n after every ten characters of the output. To accomplish this task, the method iterates the sequence builder.length(), ..., 1 with the variable i (Lines 24 and 25). At each round of the iteration, if the value of i is a multiple of 10 (Line 26), the method inserts the sequence at position i (Line 28). The values of i appear in decreasing order because an insertion changes the character positions of all the existing characters appearing after the position of insertion.

```
1   import java.util.*;
2   public class AlphabetCollection
3   {
4     public static void main( String[] args )
5     {
6       Scanner keyboard = new Scanner( System.in );
7       System.out.print( "Enter: " );
8       String input = keyboard.nextLine();
9       String output = collect( input );
10      System.out.println( "========" );
11      System.out.printf( "Input:%n%s%nhas become:%n%s%n", input, output );
12    }
13    public static String collect( String input )
14    {
15      StringBuilder builder = new StringBuilder();
16      for ( int i = 0; i < input.length(); i ++ )
17      {
18        char c = input.charAt( i );
19        if ( c >= 'a' && c <= 'z' )
20        {
21          builder.append( c );
22        }
23      }
24      int ell = builder.length();
25      for ( int i = ell; i >= 1; i -- ) {
26        if ( i % 10 == 0 )
27        {
28          builder.insert( i, "-\n" );
29        }
30      }
31      return builder.toString();
32    }
33  }
```

Listing 9.12 A program that demonstrates the use of StringBuilder objects

Here is an execution example of the code:

```
 1  Enter: The title of this album is "Sgt. Pepper's Lonely Hearts Club Band"
 2  ========
 3  Input:
 4  The title of this album is "Sgt. Pepper's Lonely Hearts Club Band"
 5  has become:
 6  hetitleoft-
 7  hisalbumis-
 8  gtepperson-
 9  elyeartslu-
10  band
```

Summary

- `String` has a wide variety of methods. None of them change the contents of the `String` to which the methods are applied.
- `StringBuilder` is a class for building a `String` object. Many methods of `String` can be applied to `StringBuilder` objects.
- `length` and `charAt` provide the character length of the `String` and the character at the specified position.
- The use of actual parameters outside the range for the `charAt` method produces `StringIndexOutOfBoundsException`.
- `indexOf` and `lastIndexOf` can be used to search for patterns in a `String` data and in a `StringBuilder` data. Both methods return `-1` if the pattern does not exist.
- `String` data and `StringBuilder` data can be compared using `compareTo`, `equals`, `startsWith`, and `endsWith`.
- `substring` generates a substring.
- `toUpperCase` and `toLowerCase` return a new `String` data after changing the cases.
- `trim` returns a new `String` data without leading and trailing white space characters.
- `replace` and `replaceFirst` return a new `String` data generated by substitution.
- `String.format` is a static method for generating the output of `System.out.printf` as a `String`.
- The methods available for `StringBuilder` but not for `String` include `append`, `delete`, and `insert`.

Exercises

1. **String arithmetic** Write a program named `ReceiveAndPrint` that receives a `String` value s, an `int` value m, and a `double` value d from the user, and then prints the following:
   - s
   - m
   - d
   - m + d + s
   - m + s + d
   - s + m + d

2. **Concept check**
   (a) Name the String method for comparing a String with another just for equality.
   (b) Name the String method for substituting all occurrences of one pattern with another.
   (c) State whether or not the following statement is true: For a String word having length 10, word.substring(1) and w.substring(1, 9) produce an identical result.
   (d) State whether or not the following statement is true: The compareTo method for String always produces +1, 0, or -1.
   (e) Name the String method that returns, when applied to a String data, a new String without leading and trailing whitespace characters.

3. **Connecting String values**   Write a public static method named connect. The method receives two String formal parameters: word1 and word2. The method must return a boolean. The return value must represent whether or not the last character of word1 is equal to the first character of word2, or the last character of word2 is equal to the first character of word1. If either word1 or word2 has length 0, the method must return false.

4. **String methods**   Let word be a String data whose value is "School.of.Progressive.Rock" (not including the quotation marks). State the return value of each of the following:
   (a) word.length()
   (b) word.substring(22)
   (c) word.substring(22, 24)
   (d) word.indexOf("oo")
   (e) word.toUpperCase()
   (f) word.lastIndexOf("o")
   (g) word.indexOf("ok")

5. **Understanding String methods**   Suppose String variables w and pat are given as follows:

```
1  w = "Singin'_in_the_rain";
2  pat = "in";
```

State the return value of each of the following:
   (a) w.indexOf(pat)
   (b) w.indexOf(pat, 3)
   (c) w.indexOf(pat, 6)
   (d) w.lastIndexOf(pat)
   (e) w.length()
   (f) w.toUpperCase()
   (g) w.charAt(0)

6. **Printing the letters of a String variable**   Suppose word is a String variable. Using a for-loop, write a code that prints the letters of word from the start to the end, one letter per line with no indentation. For example, if the value of word is equal to the literal "hurricanes", the output of the code is:

```
1   h
2   u
3   r
4   r
5   i
6   c
7   a
8   n
9   e
10  s
```

7. **Printing the suffixes of a `String` variable** Suppose word is a `String` variable. Using a for-loop, write a code that prints the suffixes of word starting from the longest to the shortest, one substring per line with no indentation. For example, if the value of word is equal to the literal `"hurricanes"`, the output of the code is:

```
1   hurricanes
2   urricanes
3   rricanes
4   ricanes
5   icanes
6   canes
7   anes
8   nes
9   es
10  s
```

8. **Concept check** Let s be a `String` variable whose value is the literal `"Mississippi"`. State the return value of each of the following:
   - (a) `s.length()`
   - (b) `s.indexOf( "si" )`
   - (c) `s.toUpperCase().indexOf( "si" )`
   - (d) `s.toLowerCase().indexOf( "si" )`
   - (e) `s.substring(0,s.indexOf( "i" ))`
   - (f) `s.substring( s.lastIndexOf( "i" ) )`

9. **Character order reversal** Write a program named `StringReverse` that receives a `String` data from the user, and then creates the reverse of the input. For example, the program may run as follows:

```
1   Enter an input String: Computer-Programming
2   The reverse of Computer-Programming is gnimmargorP-retupmoC.
```

The first line consists of the prompt (ending with `" : "`) and the input. The second line is the output of the program after receiving the input. Try to use `printf` in producing the output.

10. **Sum of all digits** Write a program named `NumeralSum` that receives a `String` data from the user, and then computes the sum of the values of all the numerals appearing in it. For example, if the input is `BIO542L`, the sum is $5 + 4 + 2 = 11$.

Programming Projects

11. **Cyclic shifts** Suppose w is a `String` variable such that `w.length()` is greater than or equal to 1. For a positive integer k whose value is between 0 and `w.length()`, the k-th left cyclic shift of w is the `String` constructed from w by moving the first k characters of w after the last character of w while preserving the order of the k characters. For instance, if w has the value `"abcdefgh"` and k is 3, then the k-th left cyclic shift of w is `"efghabc"`. If the value of k is either equal to 0 or equal to `w.length()`, the k-th left cyclic shift produces a `String` value equal to the value of w. Write a program named `CyclicShift` that does the following: The program receives an input line from the user, and stores the input line in a variable w. The program receives a nonnegative integer from the user, and stores it in an `int` variable k. The program then constructs the k-th cyclic shift of w and prints it. Design your code so that the program is able to receive a line that contains the whitespace as input. If the value of k is out of range, the program reports that the value is invalid and stop. Here are execution examples of such a program.

```
1   Enter your input line: How are you?
2   Enter the shift value k: 4
3   The 4-th cyclic shift of
4   "How are you?"
5   is
6   "are you?How "
```

```
1   Enter your input line: How are you?
2   Enter the shift value k: 34
3   Invalid value for k
```

12. **Factor of a String data**   The "minimum factor" of a character sequence w is the shortest prefix s of w such that w is a repetition of s. For example, the minimum factor of "ababababab" is "ab" and the minimum factor of "abcdef" is "abcdef". Put differently, the length of the minimum factor of w is the smallest positive k such that the k-th left cyclic shift of w is equal to w.

    Consider computing the minimum factor of a given String object w using a for-loop that iterates over the sequence 1, ..., w.length() with the variable k. At each round of the for-loop, the program checks if the k-th left cyclic shift of w is equal to w. The smallest value of k at which the shift produces the same String is the length of the factor.

    Write a program named StringFactor that receives an input line from the user, and then reports its minimum factor along with the length of the factor. Design the program so that it uses a method that returns the minimum factor.

13. **Enumerating all occurrences of a character pattern, part 1**   Consider finding all occurrences of a pattern pat in a String data input. We can solve the problem by checking at each position of input, whether or not pat appears at the position. Write a program named AllOccurrences that receives the values for pat and input from the user, finds all the matching positions, and prints the total number of occurrences.

    Here is an example of how such a code may work.

```
1    Input some text: I'm singin' in the rain, I'm singin' in the rain
2    Input pattern: in
3    Found at position 5.
4    Found at position 8.
5    Found at position 12.
6    Found at position 21.
7    Found at position 30.
8    Found at position 33.
9    Found at position 37.
10   Found at position 46.
11   The number of occurrences is 8.
```

    The smallest position possible for i is 0.

14. **Enumerating all occurrences of a character pattern, part 2**   Write another program named AllOccurrencesAlt that solves the previous problem with character-by-character comparisons between the input and the pattern. The task can be accomplished using a double for-loop.

15. **Switching between two neighbors**   Write a program named SwitchingBetweenNeighbors that executes the following: The program receives a String value from the user. From the input, the program creates a new String value by switching between every pair of the characters in the input. The switching occurs between positions 0 and 1, between positions 2 and 3, and so. If the input the user provides has an odd length, the last character will remain in the same position. For example, the method should produce "cseicne" from "science".

16. **Playing with StringBuilder**   Write a program named DoubleInsertion that receives a String value from the user using nextLine, and then builds a new String using StringBuilder as follows:
    - Initially the builder is empty.
    - The program scans the characters of the input, from the beginning to the end, and executes the following:
        - If the position of the character is 2m for some nonnegative integer m, the program inserts the character at position m.
        - If the position is 2m + 1 for some nonnegative integer m, the program appends the character at the very end.

    The program must print the input in one line, and then the output in the next line. For example, if abcdefghijkl is the input, the contents of the StringBuilder change as follows:

```
 1  a
 2  ab
 3  acb
 4  acbd
 5  acebd
 6  acebdf
 7  acegbdf
 8  acegbdfh
 9  acegibdfh
10  acegibdfhj
11  acegikbdfhj
12  acegikbdfhjl
```

17. **All substrings**   Write a program named AllSubstrings that receives a String from the user and produces all its nonempty substrings along with their ranges of character positions. Use a double for-loop to generate all pairs of index values (i,j) to provide the substring method as its actual parameters. Allocate three character spaces to each coordinate value. The output of the program may look like:

```
 1  Enter your input string: karma
 2  (  0,   1):k
 3  (  0,   2):ka
 4  (  0,   3):kar
 5  (  0,   4):karm
 6  (  1,   2):a
 7  (  1,   3):ar
 8  (  1,   4):arm
 9  (  2,   3):r
10  (  2,   4):rm
11  (  3,   4):m
```

18. **All anti-substrings**   Write a program named AllAntiSubstrings that receives a String from the user, and then produces all strings generated from the input by removing some substring. Use a double for-loop that iterates over all possible index pairs (i,j) such that i < j. For each pair, remove from the input the characters having indexes between i and j - 1. Allocate three character spaces to each coordinate value. Here is an example of how the code may work:

```
1   Enter your input string: walking
2   (  0,  1):alking
3   (  0,  2):lking
4   (  0,  3):king
5   (  0,  4):ing
6   (  0,  5):ng
7   (  0,  6):g
8   (  1,  2):wlking
9   (  1,  3):wking
10  (  1,  4):wing
11  (  1,  5):wng
12  (  1,  6):wg
13  (  2,  3):waking
14  (  2,  4):waing
15  (  2,  5):wang
16  (  2,  6):wag
17  (  3,  4):waling
18  (  3,  5):walng
19  (  3,  6):walg
20  (  4,  5):walkng
21  (  4,  6):walkg
22  (  5,  6):walkig
```

19. **All anti-substrings no.2**   Write a program named AllAntiSubstrings2 that receives a String from the user, and then produces all strings generated from the input by connecting two substrings. The substrings are generated using index triples (i,j,k) such that i < j < k and connecting substring(0, i) with substring(j, k). Allocate three character spaces to each coordinate value. Here is how the code may work.

```
1   Enter your input string: Davis
2   (  0,  1,  2):a
3   (  0,  1,  3):av
4   (  0,  1,  4):avi
5   (  0,  2,  3):v
6   (  0,  2,  4):vi
7   (  0,  3,  4):i
8   (  1,  2,  3):Dv
9   (  1,  2,  4):Dvi
10  (  1,  3,  4):Di
11  (  2,  3,  4):Dai
```

20. **Conversion to decimal**   Write a program named ToDecimal that receives a binary integer from the user, and then prints its decimal representation. For example, 1111000 in binary is 120 in decimal and 11111011111 in binary is 2015 in decimal. Assume that the binary input is given as a String value.

The Switch Statements

10

10.1 The Syntax of Switch Statements

The switch statement is a mechanism for controlling the flow of the program based on exact values of one data. Often a switch statement is used in a menu, where the action to be performed is selected based on a value.

A switch statement has three components, the header, the body, and the anchors. The header takes the form of:

```
switch ( x )
```

where x is a data and its type must be `int`, `char`, `short`, `long`, or `String`. The body is a series of statements encompassed in a pair of curly brackets. An anchor is either in the form of `default:` or `case A:` for some literal A whose type is the same as the type of x. Anchors appear between the statements in the body. Multiple `case`-type anchors may appear in the body, but no two of them can have the same associated literals. The anchor `default:` may or may not appear, but it cannot appear more than once. Furthermore, `break` can be used as a valid statement.

For instance, with an `int` variable x, the following switch statements can be written:

```
1  // Example No.1
2  switch ( x )
3  {
4     case 11: System.out.print( "Eleven" );
5     default: System.out.print( "Other" );
6     case 8: System.out.print( "Eight" );
7  }
```

```
1  // Example No.2
2  switch ( x )
3  {
4     case 11: System.out.print( "Eleven" ); break;
5     default: System.out.print( "Other" ); break;
6     case 8: System.out.print( "Eight" );
7  }
```

© Springer Nature Switzerland AG 2018
M. Ogihara, *Fundamentals of Java Programming*,
https://doi.org/10.1007/978-3-319-89491-1_10

Table 10.1 The output generated by the three examples of switch

Example no.	The value of x		
	11	8	Others
1	ElevenOtherEight	Eight	OtherEight
2	Eleven	Eight	Other
3	Eleven	Eight	

```
1   // Example No.3
2   switch ( x )
3   {
4      case 11: System.out.print( "Eleven" ); break;
5      case 8: System.out.print( "Eight" );
6   }
```

The anchors specify the entry points into the body. case A: means

"if the value of x is equal to A, start the execution of the body from here"

and default: means

"if none of the associated values of the case anchors match the value of x, start the execution of the body from here".

The execution of the body is terminated either when the execution reaches the end of the body or when the execution encounters break. For this reason, the break appearing at the end of the body is redundant and thus can be removed.

The above three examples produce the following results: In the first example, break does not appear in the body. Therefore, after entering the body, the execution continues until the very end. In the second example, each System.out.print statement is followed by break. Therefore, after entering the body, the program executes the System.out.print following the anchor, and then terminates the execution of the body. In the last example, if the value of x is either 11 or 8, the action to be performed is the same as that of the second example. However, if the value of x is neither, there is no action to perform, so nothing occurs.

Table 10.1 summaries this analysis.

To see how we can utilize a switch statement for a menu, consider printing various shapes on the screen upon the user's request. This program asks the user to choose, from a menu of possible shapes, one shape to print:

```
1   ********************************************
2   This program prints a shape of your choice
3   Select by entering number
4   0. Right-angle triangle
5   1. Isosceles
6   2. Square
7   3. Parallelogram
8   Enter your choice: 3
9   Enter height: 10
```

```
10   Here is your figure!
11   ##########
12    ##########
13     ##########
14      ##########
15       ##########
16        ##########
17         ##########
18          ##########
19           ##########
20            ##########
21
```

In Lines 8 and 9, the program prompts the user to choose the shape and its size, and receives 3 and 10 from the user. The output of the shape appears after receiving the size parameter.

As shown in the example, there are four possible shapes to choose in the menu. The user can choose the size of each shape. The generation of the four shapes are accomplished by four methods, `rightAngle`, `isosceles`, `square`, and `parallelogram`. Each of the four receives a size parameter. The task of directing the flow to the generation of the shape chosen by the user can be accomplished as follows using an if-else statement:

```
1        if ( choice == 0 )
2        {
3           rightAngle( height );
4        }
5        else if ( choice == 1 )
6        {
7           isosceles( height );
8        }
9        else if ( choice == 2 )
10       {
11          square( height );
12       }
13       else if ( choice == 3 )
14       {
15          parallelogram( height );
16       }
```

The switch statement replaces these `if` and `else if` conditional tests with case names:

```
1        switch ( choice )
2        {
3          case 0: rightAngle( height ); break;
4          case 1: isosceles( height ); break;
5          case 2: square( height ); break;
6          case 3: parallelogram( height ); break;
7        }
```

This probably makes it clearer that the choices are 0 through 3.

The entire program of the selective shape generation appears next. First comes the part in the method `main` that receives the input from the user: the value for the selection variable `choice` (Lines 18 and 19) and the value for the height variable `height` (Lines 20 and 21). The switch statement we discussed appears in Lines 25–31. This version lacks the final `break`, since a `break` statement at the end of the body of a switch statement is redundant.

```
1    import java.util.*;
2
3    public class ShapeSelection
4    {
5      public static void main( String[] args )
6      {
7        Scanner keyboard = new Scanner( System.in );
8        int choice, height;
9
10       System.out.println( "*******************************************" );
11       System.out.println( "This program prints a shape of your choice" );
12       System.out.println( "Select by entering number               " );
13       System.out.println( "0. Right-angle triangle                 " );
14       System.out.println( "1. Isosceles                            " );
15       System.out.println( "2. Square                               " );
16       System.out.println( "3. Parallelogram                        " );
17       System.out.println( "*******************************************" );
18       System.out.print( "Enter your choice: " );
19       choice = keyboard.nextInt();
20       System.out.print( "Enter height: " );
21       height = keyboard.nextInt();
22
23       System.out.println( "Here is your figure!" );
24
25       switch ( choice )
26       {
27         case 0: rightAngle( height ); break;
28         case 1: isosceles( height ); break;
29         case 2: square( height ); break;
30         case 3: parallelogram( height );
31       }
32     }
33
```

Listing 10.1 A program that uses a switch statement to generate a shape (part 1). The part for receiving an input from the user

The four shape-generation methods receive an int parameter height and print height lines using a for-loop that iterates over the sequence 1, ..., height with a variable named i. The action of the loop-body is to call a method named line with two parameters. Depending of the relations of the values of the two parameters to i, different shapes are printed.

The line receives two int parameters, whiteWidth and blackWidth (Line 34), and prints blackWidth hash marks after an indentation of length whiteWidth. The indentation is generated using a for-loop in Lines 36–39 and the hash marks are printed using a for-loop in Lines 40–43.

```
34    public static void line( int whiteWidth , int blackWidth )
35    {
36      for ( int i = 1; i <= whiteWidth; i ++ )
37      {
38        System.out.print ( " " );
39      }
40      for ( int i = 1; i <= blackWidth; i ++ )
41      {
42        System.out.print ( "#" );
43      }
44      System.out.println ();
45    }
```

Listing 10.2 A program that uses a switch statement to generate a shape (part 2). A method `line` that produces a line of `"#"` after some indentation

For `rightAngle` (Line 47), the actual call is `line ( 0, i )` (Line 51). This produces `i` hash marks with no indentation. Since the value of `i` is increasing, a right-angled triangle is produced. For `isosceles` (Line 55), the actual call is `line ( height - i, i * 2 - 1 )` (Line 59). As the value of `i` increases from 1 to `height`, the length of indentation decreases from `height - 1` to 0 while the number of hash marks increases from 1 to 2 `* height - 1` by 2 at a time. Therefore, an isosceles triangle is produced. For `square` (Line 63), the actual call is `line ( 0, height )` (Line 67). This produces `height` hash marks with no indentation. Therefore, a square is produced. For `parallelogram` (Line 71), the actual call is `line ( i - 1, height )` (Line 75). The length of indentation increases from 0 to `height - 1` while the number of hash marks is `height`. Therefore, a parallelogram is produced.

```
46
47    public static void rightAngle( int height )
48    {
49      for ( int i = 1; i <= height; i ++ )
50      {
51        line( 0, i );
52      }
53    }
54
55    public static void isosceles( int height )
56    {
57      for ( int i = 1; i <= height; i ++ )
58      {
59        line( height - i, i * 2 - 1 );
60      }
61    }
62
```

Listing 10.3 A program that uses a switch statement to generate a shape (part 3). Two shape-producing methods

```
63     public static void square( int height )
64     {
65       for ( int i = 1; i <= height; i ++ )
66       {
67         line( 0, height );
68       }
69     }
70
71     public static void parallelogram( int height )
72     {
73       for ( int i = 1; i <= height; i ++ )
74       {
75         line( i - 1, height );
76       }
77     }
78   }
```

Listing 10.4 A program that uses a switch statement to generate a shape (part 4). The two remaining shape-producing methods

Here are execution examples of the program.

```
1    ******************************************
2    This program prints a shape of your choice
3    Select by entering number
4    0. Right-angle triangle
5    1. Isosceles
6    2. Square
7    3. Parallelogram
8    Enter your choice: 0
9    Enter height: 10
10   #
11   ##
12   ###
13   ####
14   #####
15   ######
16   #######
17   ########
18   #########
19   ##########
20   ******************************************
21   This program prints a shape of your choice
22   Select by entering number
23   0. Right-angle triangle
24   1. Isosceles
25   2. Square
26   3. Parallelogram
27   Enter your choice: 1
28   Enter height: 5
29       #
30      ###
31     #####
32    #######
33   #########
```

```
34   ********************************************
35   This program prints a shape of your choice
36   Select by entering number
37   0. Right-angle triangle
38   1. Isosceles
39   2. Square
40   3. Parallelogram
41   Enter your choice: 2
42   Enter height: 7
43   #######
44   #######
45   #######
46   #######
47   #######
48   #######
49   #######
50   ********************************************
51   This program prints a shape of your choice
52   Select by entering number
53   0. Right-angle triangle
54   1. Isosceles
55   2. Square
56   3. Parallelogram
57   Enter your choice: 3
58   Enter height: 20
59   ####################
60    ####################
61     ####################
62      ####################
63       ####################
64        ####################
65         ####################
66          ####################
67           ####################
68            ####################
69             ####################
70              ####################
71               ####################
72                ####################
73                 ####################
74                  ####################
75                   ####################
76                    ####################
77                     ####################
78                      ####################
```

Multiple anchors can be assigned to the same entry points. Recall the program from Chap. 6 that shows four colors and produces statements based upon the choice made (List 6.10). In that code, 1 and 2 were the official University of Miami colors and 3 and 4 were the official University of Michigan colors. Using a switch statement with default as an anchor, we can write the following code that behaves exactly the same way:

```
1    import java.util.Scanner;
2    // ask about a color and respond
3    public class ColorSelectionSwitch
4    {
5      public static void main( String[] args )
6      {
7        Scanner keyboard = new Scanner( System.in );
8        System.out.println( "What is your favorite color?" );
9        System.out.println( "1. Orange, 2. Green, 3. Maize, 4. Blue" );
10       System.out.print( "Select from 1 to 4 : " );
11       int answer = keyboard.nextInt();
12
13       switch ( answer )
14       {
15         case 1:
16         case 2:
17           System.out.printf( "Your choice %d is excellent.%n", answer );
18           System.out.println( "It is a U. Miami Color!" );
19           break;
20         case 3:
21         case 4:
22           System.out.printf( "Your choice %d is excellent.%n", answer );
23           System.out.println( "It is a U. Michigan Color!" );
24           break;
25         default:
26           System.out.printf( "Your choice %d is invalid.%n", answer );
27       }
28     }
29   }
```

Listing 10.5 A program that responds to a color choice

The actions to be performed are identical between the choices 1 and 2, the actions to be performed are identical between the choices 3 and 4.

10.2   Using a `char` Data in a Switch-Statement

Consider computing the number of occurrences of six punctuation marks (the period, the comma, the question mark, the exclamation mark, the colon, and the semicolon) and everything else in an input character sequence. We can use seven `int` variables corresponding to the seven categories. After initializing the variables with the value of 0, we examine each character of the input sequence and increase the variable corresponding to the character. The following program executes this, using a switch-statement for handling the selection of the variable.

The program consists of three methods:

1. The method `receiveInput` receives a multiple-line input from the user.
2. The method `printInfo` prints the name of a punctuation mark and the number of its occurrences.
3. The method `main` handles the task of counting.

The program receives multiple lines of input from the user. The number of lines that the user enters is defined as a constant `LINENUMBER`. The value of the constant is 10 (Line 4).

The method `receiveInput` receives `LINENUMBER` lines from the user and returns a `String` that connects them with the newline at the end of each line. The method uses a `StringBuilder` object named `builder` to build the `String` to be returned (Line 11). The method announces the actions to be performed and instantiates a `Scanner` object for reading the keyboard (Lines 8–10). The method uses a for-loop to count the number of lines entered (Line 12). At each round of iteration, the method reads one line of input (Line 14), and then appends the line and the newline to `builder` (Line 15). At the end, the method converts the contents of `builder` to a `String` value and returns it.

```
1   import java.util.*;
2   public class CountPunctuations
3   {
4     public static final int LINENUMBER = 10;
5
6     public static String receiveInput ()
7     {
8       System.out.printf( "Enter text of %d lines.%n", LINENUMBER );
9       System.out.println( "The program will count each punctuation." );
10      Scanner keyboard = new Scanner( System.in );
11      StringBuilder builder = new StringBuilder();
12      for ( int count = 1; count <= LINENUMBER; count ++ )
13      {
14        String line = keyboard.nextLine();
15        builder.append( line + "\n" );
16      }
17      return builder.toString();
18    }
19
```

Listing 10.6 A program that counts punctuations (part 1). The program header and a program for receiving a multiple-line input

The method `printInfo` receives a `String` representing the name of a punctuation marks and an `int` representing the count, and prints the two values using `printf` (Line 22). The `String` appears in 20 character spaces and the count in three character spaces. The two are separated by a colon and one white space. The method `main` first calls the method `receiveInput` to obtain a

```
20    public static void printInfo( String name, int count )
21    {
22      System.out.printf( "%20s: %3d times%n", name, count );
23    }
24
```

Listing 10.7 A program that counts punctuations (part 2). The method `printInfo`

multiple-line input from the user. The method stores the input in a variable `input` (Line 27). The method then declares the variables for counting the occurrences of the six punctuation marks. The six variables are `nPeriod`, `nComma`, `nQuestion`, `nExclamation`, `nColon`, and `nSemicolon`. They correspond to the period, the comma, the question mark, the exclamation mark, the colon, and the semicolon. In addition, the method declares a variable, `nOthers`, for counting the occurrences of everything else. These seven variables are initialized with the value of 0 (Lines 28 and 29). The method then executes a for-loop that iterates over the sequence 0, ..., `input.length() - 1` with a variable named `i` (Line 30). The body of the loop is a switch statement. The switch statement examines `input.charAt( i )` (Line 32), and then depending on the value of the `char` data, it increases the value of one counter by 1. There are six `case` anchors corresponding to the six punctuation marks (Lines 34–39), and `default` that handles the remainder (Line 40).

```
25    public static void main ( String [] args )
26    {
27      String input = receiveInput();
28      int nPeriod = 0, nComma = 0, nQuestion = 0, nExclamation = 0;
29      int nColon = 0, nSemicolon = 0, nOthers = 0;
30      for ( int i = 0; i <= input.length() - 1; i ++ )
31      {
32        switch ( input.charAt( i ) )
33        {
34          case '.': nPeriod ++; break;
35          case ',': nComma ++; break;
36          case '?': nQuestion ++; break;
37          case '!': nExclamation ++; break;
38          case ':': nColon ++; break;
39          case ';': nSemicolon ++; break;
40          default: nOthers ++;
41        }
42      }
43
```

Listing 10.8 A program that counts punctuations (part 3). The part for counting the characters

The last part of the code handles the reporting of the result. First, the program prints a header (Lines 44 and 45). The header includes the input lines that the user enters. The `%s` appearing in the format `String`

```
Your input:%n%s%nThe counts:%n
```

serves as the placeholder for the input. Since `receiveInput` adds the newline after each input line received, each input line is printed in an individual line. After printing the input lines, the program prints the seven counts using the `print` method (Lines 46–52).

```
44      System.out.println( "\n===========================" );
45      System.out.printf( "Your input:%n%s%nThe counts:%n", input );
46      printInfo( "Period", nPeriod );
47      printInfo( "Comma", nComma );
48      printInfo( "Question Mark", nQuestion );
49      printInfo( "Exclamation Mark", nExclamation );
50      printInfo( "Colon", nColon );
51      printInfo( "Semicolon", nSemicolon );
52      printInfo( "Others", nOthers );
53    }
54  }
```

Listing 10.9 A program that counts punctuations (part 4). The part for generating a report

Here is an execution example of the program. The user enters ten lines from *Adventures of Huckleberry Finn* by Mark Twain.[1]

```
 1   Enter text of 10 lines.
 2   The program will count each punctuation.
 3   "Well, who said it was?"
 4   "Why, you did."
 5   "I DIDN'T nuther."
 6   "You did!"
 7   "I didn't."
 8   "You did."
 9   "I never said nothing of the kind."
10   "Well, what DID you say, then?"
11   "Said he come to take the sea BATHS--that's what I said."
12   "Well, then, how's he going to take the sea baths if it ain't on the sea?"
13   =========================
14   Your input:
15   "Well, who said it was?"
16   "Why, you did."
17   "I DIDN'T nuther."
18   "You did!"
19   "I didn't."
20   "You did."
21   "I never said nothing of the kind."
22   "Well, what DID you say, then?"
23   "Said he come to take the sea BATHS--that's what I said."
24   "Well, then, how's he going to take the sea baths if it ain't on the sea?"
25
26   The counts:
27                   Period:   6 times
28                    Comma:   6 times
29            Question Mark:   3 times
30         Exclamation Mark:   1 times
31                    Colon:   0 times
32                Semicolon:   0 times
33                   Others: 279 times
```

Here is another program that uses a switch statement. This time, the program uses a char data for directing the flow. This program receives four pieces of information about a person (name, age, gender, and phone number) from the user, and stores the information in four variables. The program then receives a text input from the user. The program examines the first character of the text input, obtained using charAt (0). If the character matches one of the four letters ('N', 'A', 'G', and 'P') representing the four pieces of information, the program prints the information; otherwise, the program prints an error message.

The program uses String variables, name, gender, and phone, to store information about the name, gender, and phone number (Line 6). The program uses a String variable, choice, to record the input the user enters as the choice of information to recall (Line 6). The program uses an int variable, age, to record the age (Line 7). The program uses interactions with the user to receive values for the four variables (Lines 11–18). To recall information, the program prints a prompt, and then receives input in the variable choice (Lines 20–22). Then, the program examines choice.charAt (0) in a switch statement to decide which variable to recall (Lines 26–33). Any invalid choice is directed to the default : in Line 34.

---

[1]Samuel Langhorne Clemens (November 30, 1835 to April 21, 1910), known by his pen name Mark Twain, was an American writer.

```
1    import java.util.*;
2    public class SelectionByChar
3    {
4      public static void main( String[] args )
5      {
6        String name, gender, phone, choice;
7        int age;
8
9        Scanner keyboard = new Scanner( System.in );
10
11       System.out.print( "Type name: " );
12       name = keyboard.next();
13       System.out.print( "Type age: " );
14       age = keyboard.nextInt();
15       System.out.print( "Type gender: " );
16       gender = keyboard.next();
17       System.out.print( "Type phone: " );
18       phone = keyboard.next();
19
20       System.out.println( "Enter information to recall." );
21       System.out.print( "  A(ge), G(ender), N(ame), P(hone): " );
22       choice = keyboard.next();
23
24       switch ( choice.charAt( 0 ) )
25       {
26         case 'A': System.out.println( "The age is " + age );
27           break;
28         case 'G': System.out.println( "The gender is " + gender );
29           break;
30         case 'N': System.out.println( "The name is " + name );
31           break;
32         case 'P': System.out.println( "The phone is " + phone );
33           break;
34         default:  System.out.println( "Unsupported selection!" );
35       }
36     }
37   }
```

Listing 10.10 A program that uses a switch statement for recalling memory

Here are some execution examples of the code. In the first example, the user asks to recall the age by entering "A":

```
1    Type name: Emily
2    Type age: 30
3    Type gender: Feale
4    Type phone (use dash): 333-333-3333
5      A(ge), G(ender), N(ame), P(hone): A
6    The age is 30
```

In the second example, the user asks to recall the name by entering the prefix "Nam" of "Name":

```
1    Type name: Dwight
2    Type age: 32
3    Type gender: Male
4    Type phone (use dash): 123-123-1122
5      A(ge), G(ender), N(ame), P(hone): Nam
6    The name is Dwight
```

In the third example, the user asks to recall the phone number by entering "Pine", whose first letter is 'P':

```
1   Type name: George
2   Type age: 40
3   Type gender: Male
4   Type phone (use dash): 343-343-3344
5     A(ge), G(ender), N(ame), P(hone): Pine
6   The phone is 343-343-3344
```

In the last example, the user enters "Q", but there is no matching choice, so the program prints the error message:

```
1   Type name: Caroline
2   Type age: 23
3   Type gender: Female
4   Type phone (use dash): 333-222-1111
5     A(ge), G(ender), N(ame), P(hone): Q
6   Unsupported selection!
```

10.3   Using a String Data in a Switch Statement

An alternate version of the memory recall program show next uses a switch statement that examines the value of a String data. In this version, to recall information, the user must type the exact name of the information to recall. The program handles the input that the user enters in a non-case-sensitive manner by converting it to all lowercase using the method toLowerCase() of String (Line 22).

```
1    import java.util.*;
2    public class SelectionByString
3    {
4      public static void main( String[] args )
5      {
6        String name, gender, phone, choice;
7        int age;
8
9        Scanner keyboard = new Scanner( System.in );
10
11       System.out.print( "Type name: " );
12       name = keyboard.next();
13       System.out.print( "Type age: " );
14       age = keyboard.nextInt();
15       System.out.print( "Type gender: " );
16       gender = keyboard.next();
17       System.out.print( "Type phone: " );
18       phone = keyboard.next();
19
```

Listing 10.11 A program for recalling memory (part 1). The part responsible for receiving data from the user

```
20      System.out.println( "Enter information to recall." );
21      System.out.print( "  age, gender, name, phone: " );
22      choice = keyboard.next().toLowerCase();
23
24      switch ( choice )
25      {
26        case "age": System.out.println( "The age is " + age );
27          break;
28        case "gender": System.out.println( "The gender is " + gender );
29          break;
30        case "name": System.out.println( "The name is " + name );
31          break;
32        case "phone": System.out.println( "The phone is " + phone );
33          break;
34        default:  System.out.println( "Unsupported selection!" );
35      }
36    }
37  }
```

Listing 10.12 A program for recalling memory (part 2). The part responsible for recalling information

Here are a couple execution examples of the code:

```
1  Type name: Darrell
2  Type age: 18
3  Type gender: Male
4  Type phone (use dash): 555-555-5555
5    Age, Gender, Name, Phone: age
6  The age is 18
```

```
1  Type name: Eden
2  Type age: 19
3  Type gender: Female
4  Type phone (use dash): 777-888-9999
5    Age, Gender, Name, Phone: name
6  The name is Eden
```

Summary

- A switch statement allows selecting an action to perform based on the value of a data. The possible data types that can be used in a switch statement are: `char`, `int`, `long`, `short`, and `String`.
- Each case value in a switch statement is specified using `case VALUE:` where `VALUE` is a literal matching the type of the variable examined in the switch statement.
- No two cases appearing in a switch statement have the same values.
- `default:` is a keyword that corresponds to "otherwise".
- If `break` is encountered during the execution of the body of a switch statement, the execution is immediately terminated.

Exercises

1. **Converting to and from a switch statement, 1**   Convert the following switch statement to an equivalent if-else statement:

```
1  switch ( a )
2  {
3    case 1: System.out.println( "A" ); break;
4    case 2: System.out.println( "B" ); break;
5    case 3: System.out.println( "C" ); break;
6    default:
7  }
```

2. **Converting to and from a switch statement, 2**   Convert the following switch statement to an equivalent if-else statement:

```
1  switch (a)
2  {
3    case 1: System.out.println( "X" );
4    case 2: System.out.println( "Y" ); break;
5    case 3: System.out.println( "Z" ); break;
6    default:
7  }
```

3. **Converting to and from a switch statement, 3**   Convert the following switch statement to an equivalent if-else statement:

```
1  switch ( a )
2  {
3    case 1: System.out.println( "i" );
4    case 2: System.out.println( "ii" );
5    case 3: System.out.println( "iii" ); break;
6    default:
7    case 4: System.out.println( "iv" ); break;
8  }
```

4. **Converting to and from a switch statement, 4**   Convert the following if-else statement to an equivalent switch statement:

```
1  if ( a == 0 )
2  {
3    System.out.println( "A" );
4  }
5  else if ( a == 1 )
6  {
7    System.out.println( "B" );
8  }
9  else
10 {
11   System.out.println( "C" );
12 }
```

5. **Converting to and from a switch statement, 5**   Convert the following if-else statement to an equivalent switch statement:

```
1  if ( a == 0 )
2  {
3    System.out.println( "F" );
4  }
5  else if ( a == 1 )
6  {
7    System.out.println( "T" );
8  }
```

6. **Converting to and from a switch statement, 6**   Convert the following switch statement to an equivalent if-else statement, where a is an int data:

```
1  switch ( a )
2  {
3    case 0: System.out.println( "X" ); break;
4    case 1: System.out.println( "Y" ); break;
5    case 3: System.out.println( "W" );
6    case 2: System.out.println( "Z" ); break;
7    default: System.out.println( "?" );
8  }
```

Programming Projects

7. **Processing a sequence of 2d movements**   Write a program named Movements2D that receives a sequence of characters composed solely of 'U', 'D', 'L', and 'R' from the user, and processes it as a sequence of moves in the two-dimensional grid, where the initial position is $(0, 0)$. The letters 'U', 'D', 'L', and 'R' correspond to increases the y-coordinate by 1, decreases the y-coordinate by 1, increases the x-coordinate by 1, and decreases the x-coordinate by 1. Use a switch statement to process an individual letter. Use a for-loop to go through the input, and for each move made, print the new location. For instance, if the input sequence is "ULDDRU", the output of the program must be:

```
1  (0,1)
2  (-1,1)
3  (-1,0)
4  (-1,-1)
5  (0,-1)
6  (0,0)
```

The characters other than 'U', 'D', 'L', and 'R' will be treated as "not moving".

8. **Processing a sequence of 3d movements**   Write a program named Movements3D that receives a sequence of characters composed solely of 'F', 'B', 'U', 'D', 'L', and 'R' from the user, and processes it as a sequence of moves in the three-dimensional grid, where the initial position is $(0, 0, 0)$. The letters 'F', 'B', 'U', 'D', 'L', and 'R' increases the x-coordinate by 1, decreases the x-coordinate by 1, increases the z-coordinate by 1, decreases the z-coordinate by 1, increases the y-coordinate by 1, and decreases the y-coordinate by 1. Use a switch-statement to process an individual letter. Use a for-loop to go through the input, and for each move made, print the new location. For example, if the input sequence is "UFLDDRUB", the output of the program must be:

1	(0,0,1)
2	(1,0,1)
3	(1,-1,1)
4	(1,-1,0)
5	(1,-1,-1)
6	(1,0,-1)
7	(1,0,0)
8	(0,0,0)

The characters other than the six letters will be treated as "not moving".

9. **Rotating vowels**   Write a program named RotateVowels that receives a String data from the user, and replaces each letter in the input corresponding to a vowel to another vowel. The replacing rule is as follows: 'a' become 'e', 'e' become 'i', 'i' become 'o', 'o' become 'u', 'u' become 'a', 'A' become 'E', 'E' become 'I', 'I' become 'O', 'O' become 'U', 'U' become 'A', and any other character stays the same. For example, the method returns "Luaos" when given "Louis" as input, and returns "Iest" when given "East" as input. Write the code so that the method builds its output using a StringBuilder object. The program reads the examines the input character by character, and then appends the character after conversion to the StringBuilder object. Use a switch statement in determining which character must be appended.

10. **Treasure hunting in 2D**   Write a program named TreasureHunting2D that plays the game of finding a treasure hidden at a location on the 2D grid, where the coordinates are integers between 1 and 10, where the player can make at most ten guesses and the program provides up to two pieces of advice depending on the players's guesses.

- The first piece of advice is based upon the Manhattan distance between the true location and the guess, where the distance value is the sum of the absolute difference in the x-coordinates and the absolute difference in the y-coordinates.

  (a) If the distance is 0, the program announces:
  "You have found the treasure!".
  (b) If the distance is between 1 and 3, the program announces:
  "The treasure is very close.".
  (c) If the distance is between 4 and 6, the program announces:
  "The treasure is somewhat close.".
  (d) If the distance is greater than 6, the program announces:
  "The treasure is not close.".

- The second piece of advice is given in the second round and onwards, and appears only when the guess is still incorrect. The advice informs if the present guess is closer than the previous guess with the statement, "You are closer.", "You are farther.", or "The same distance.".

Make sure that after the user has correctly found the location, the execution of the loop-body will skip even if there are more rounds remaining.

While-Loops and Do-While Loops

11

11.1 Using While-Loops

11.1.1 The Syntax of While-Loops

The while-loop is a loop that only requires a continuation condition. The structure of a while-loop is simple:

```
1  while ( CONDITION )
2  {
3     STATEMENTS;
4  }
```

The meaning of this while-loop is "as long as CONDITION has the value of true, execute STATEMENTS". The diagram in Fig. 11.1 shows how a while-loop works. The for-loop and while-loop can simulate each other. First,

```
1  while ( CONDITION )
2  {
3     STATEMENTS;
4  }
```

is equivalent to the for-loop without initialization and update, as shown next:

```
1  for ( ; CONDITION; )
2  {
3     STATEMENTS;
4  }
```

Second,

```
1  for ( INITIALIZATION ; CONDITION; UPDATE )
2  {
3     STATEMENTS;
4  }
```

© Springer Nature Switzerland AG 2018
M. Ogihara, *Fundamentals of Java Programming*,
https://doi.org/10.1007/978-3-319-89491-1_11

Fig. 11.1 A diagram that
represents the while-loop

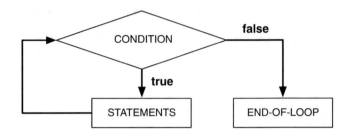

is equivalent to:

```
1  INITALIZATION;
2  while ( CONDITION )
3  {
4    STATEMENTS;
5    UPDATE;
6  }
```

We saw earlier that executing next on a Scanner object after obtaining its last token results
in a run-time error of NoSuchElementException. In our example (List 3.1), we attempted to
obtain five tokens from a String data with only four tokens, thereby intentionally produced the
run-time error. It is possible to prevent an attempt to read beyond the last token by using the method
hasNext() mentioned in Chap. 3. This method returns a boolean that represents whether or not
at least one token is remaining.

The next program demonstrates the use of hasNext for reading all the tokens from an input
String with an indefinite number of tokens. The method hasNext appears in the continuation
condition (Line 7):

```
1   import java.util.Scanner;
2   public class BeyondLimitNew
3   {
4     public static void main( String[] args )
5     {
6       Scanner tokens = new Scanner( "My age is 20" );
7       while ( tokens.hasNext() )
8       {
9         String aToken = tokens.next();
10        System.out.println( aToken );
11      }
12    }
13  }
```

Listing 11.1 A program that reads all tokens from a String using a Scanner object

Here is an interactive version of the program, where the tokens are obtained from a String that
the user enters:

The formal study of programming languages categorizes loops into two types, **definite loops** and
indefinite loops, depending on whether the number of repetition is determined at the start of the loop
or it is dynamically determined during the execution of the loop. The former type includes the for-loop
and the latter includes the while-loop. Although for-loops and while-loops are interchangeable, there
are situations where the use of one type appears more appropriate than the user of the other type.

```
1   import java.util.Scanner;
2   public class TokenReadingWithInput
3   {
4     public static void main( String[] args )
5     {
6       String aToken, tokens;
7       Scanner keyboard = new Scanner( System.in );
8       System.out.print( "Enter a String: " );
9       tokens = keyboard.nextLine();
10      while ( keyboard.hasNext() )
11      {
12        aToken = keyboard.next();
13        System.out.println( aToken );
14      }
15    }
16  }
```

Listing 11.2 A program that reads all tokens from a `String` obtained from the user

11.1.2 Summing Input Numbers Until the Total Reaches a Goal

Our next example is a program that receives a series of integers from the user, and presents its running total after receiving each number. The program keeps receiving numbers from the user until the total reaches a preset goal. The program uses three `int` variables (`input`, `total`, and `goal`) to record the input from the user, the total of the input values, and the goal. The program initializes `total` with the value of 0 and uses the value of 1000 for `goal`. The process of receiving one integer and then adding its value to `value` can be code as follows:

```
1         input = keyboard.nextInt();
2         total += input;
```

The program repeats this until the value of `total` exceeds `goal`. Using a while-loop, the repetition can be coded as follows:

```
1         while ( total <= goal )
2         {
3           input = keyboard.nextInt();
4           total += input;
5         }
```

Following is a source code of the program. The program uses a `Scanner` object `keyboard` instantiated with `System.in` (Line 6). The declarations of the `int` variables and their initializations appear in Line 7. In the while-loop, the program prints a prompt (Line 10), receives an input (Line 11), updates the total (Line 12), and reports the present values of `input` and `total` (Line 13) using `printf`. After exiting the loop, the program announces that the goal has been reached (Line 15).

Here is one execution example:

```
1   Enter input: 34
2   Input=34, Total=34
3   Enter input: 543
4   Input=543, Total=577
5   Enter input: 987
6   Input=987, Total=1564
7   The total has exceeded 1000.
```

```
1  | import java.util.*;
2  | public class UpToLimit
3  | {
4  |   public static void main( String[] args )
5  |   {
6  |     Scanner keyboard = new Scanner( System.in );
7  |     int input, total = 0, goal = 1000;
8  |     while ( total <= goal )
9  |     {
10 |       System.out.print( "Enter input: " );
11 |       input = keyboard.nextInt();
12 |       total += input;
13 |       System.out.printf( "Input=%d, Total=%d%n", input, total );
14 |     }
15 |     System.out.printf( "The total has exceeded %d.%n", goal );
16 |   }
17 | }
```

Listing 11.3 A program that receives input numbers until the total exceeds a preset bound

The loop can be quickly finished by entering a large number:

```
1  | Enter input: 355555
2  | Input=355555, Total=355555
3  | The total has exceeded 1000.
```

If the numbers entered, the loop lingers for a long time:

```
1  | Enter input: 1
2  | Input=1, Total=1
3  | Enter input: 2
4  | Input=2, Total=3
5  | Enter input: 4
6  | Input=4, Total=7
7  | Enter input: 8
8  | Input=8, Total=15
9  | Enter input: 16
10 | Input=16, Total=31
11 | Enter input: 32
12 | Input=32, Total=63
13 | Enter input: 64
14 | Input=64, Total=127
15 | Enter input: 128
16 | Input=128, Total=255
17 | Enter input: 256
18 | Input=256, Total=511
19 | Enter input: 512
20 | Input=512, Total=1023
21 | The total has exceeded 1000.
```

11.1.3 Integer Overflow

The next example is a program that receives a positive initial value from the user, and then keeps updating the value with the multiplication by 2. The program uses an `int` variable named `number` to store the input number as well as the value after each update. Since the number of bits allocated for int is finite, the repeated doubling will eventually produce a value greater than the largest value an int can represent. We call such a phenomenon an **overflow**. If doubling is the cause of overflow, the value of the int variable immediately after the overflow is negative. Therefore, the program uses the continuation condition while (number >= 0) in the while-loop (Line 10). Lines 6–8 are responsible for receiving the initial value from the user. To ensure that the initial value is strictly positive, the program substitutes a nonpositive input with 1. This conditional substitution is accomplished using the assignment number = Math.max(1, number) (Line 9). In the loop-body, the program reports the value of number (Line 12). An overflow will occur at Line 13, after reporting the value of number prior to doubling. Therefore, to report the negative value generated, the program has another statement to report the value of number (Line 15).

```
1   import java.util.*;
2   public class IntegerOverflow
3   {
4     public static void main( String[] args )
5     {
6       Scanner keyboard = new Scanner( System.in );
7       System.out.print( "Enter number number: " );
8       int number = keyboard.nextInt();
9       number = Math.max( 1, number );
10      while ( number > 0 )
11      {
12        System.out.println( "The number is " + number );
13        number *= 2;
14      }
15      System.out.println( "The number is " + number );
16    }
17  }
```

Listing 11.4 A program that demonstrates an overflow with multiplication by 2

Here is one execution of the code:

```
1   Enter number: 35
2   The number is 35
3   The number is 70
4   The number is 140
5   The number is 280
6   The number is 560
7   The number is 1120
8   The number is 2240
9   The number is 4480
10  The number is 8960
11  The number is 17920
12  The number is 35840
13  The number is 71680
14  The number is 143360
15  The number is 286720
16  The number is 573440
17  The number is 1146880
18  The number is 2293760
19  The number is 4587520
20  The number is 9175040
21  The number is 18350080
22  The number is 36700160
```

```
23  The number is 73400320
24  The number is 146800640
25  The number is 293601280
26  The number is 587202560
27  The number is 1174405120
28  The number is -1946157056
```

The last value -1946157056 is the result of multiplying 1174405120 by 2.

11.1.4 Vending Machines

Here is another example of the while-loop. In this example, we imitate the process of depositing coins into a vending machine for a purchase. Acceptable coins are the nickel (5 cents), the dime (10 cents), and the quarter (25 cents). While an actual vending machine takes one coin in one deposit, the program here takes multiple coins of the same kind in one deposit.

To receive multiple coins of a kind in one deposit, we design the program so that it asks the user to enter which coin she is depositing and how many. To specify the coin the user enters a String value. Depending on whether the String starts with 'N', 'D', or 'Q', the coin specification becomes the nickel, the dime, or the quarter. After receiving this input, the program sets the value of an int variable named inc to 5, 10, or 25, on the nickel, dime, and quarter. If the input is not one of the three, the program sets the amount of inc to 0. After this, if the value of inc is not 0, the program asks the user to enter how many coins of that kind she wants to deposit. The program increases the deposit by the product of this quantity and inc. The program repeats this two-step depositing process until the total deposit becomes greater than or equal to a target amount, target. target is an int constant with the value of 175 (that is, a dollar and 75 cents).

The program uses a while-loop to build the deposit:

$$\text{while (total < target)}$$

To determine the value of inc, the program uses a switch statement:

```
1       switch ( token.charAt ( 0 ) )
2       {
3         case 'N': inc = 5; break;
4         case 'D': inc = 10; break;
5         case 'Q': inc = 25; break;
6         default: inc = 0;
7       }
```

Here, token is the input that the user enters when given a prompt for the coin type, and so token.charAt (0) is the very first character of the input. The switch statement examines this character and takes an appropriate action. The user may enter more characters after the first one, but those extraneous characters are ignored. After exiting the loop, the program reports the total deposit (Line 28) and announces that the user can make a purchase (Line 29).

Here is an execution example of the program:

```
1   import java.util.*;
2   public class VendingDeposit
3   {
4     public static void main( String[] args )
5     {
6       Scanner keyboard = new Scanner( System.in );
7       int total = 0, inc, count, target = 175;
8       String token;
9       while ( total < target )
10      {
11        System.out.printf( "Deposit is %d cents%n", total );
12        System.out.println( "What coin do you deposit? " );
13        System.out.print( "N for Nickel, D for Dime, Q for Quarter: " );
14        token = keyboard.next();
15        switch ( token.charAt( 0 ) )
16        {
17          case 'N': inc = 5; break;
18          case 'D': inc = 10; break;
19          case 'Q': inc = 25; break;
20          default: inc = 0;
21        }
22        if ( inc > 0 ) {
23          System.out.print( "How many? " );
24          count = keyboard.nextInt();
25          total += inc * count;
26        }
27      }
28      System.out.printf( "Deposit is %d cents%n", total );
29      System.out.println( "Now you can make a selection." );
30    }
31  }
```

Listing 11.5 A program that mimics the process of depositing coins in a vending machine

```
1   Deposit is 0 cents
2   What coin do you deposit?
3   N for Nickel, D for Dime, Q for Quarter: N
4   How many? 5
5   Deposit is 25 cents
6   What coin do you deposit?
7   N for Nickel, D for Dime, Q for Quarter: D
8   How many? 3
9   Deposit is 55 cents
10  What coin do you deposit?
11  N for Nickel, D for Dime, Q for Quarter: N
12  How many? 2
13  Deposit is 65 cents
14  What coin do you deposit?
15  N for Nickel, D for Dime, Q for Quarter: Q
16  How many? 2
17  Deposit is 115 cents
18  What coin do you deposit?
19  N for Nickel, D for Dime, Q for Quarter: D
20  How many? 3
21  Deposit is 145 cents
22  What coin do you deposit?
23  N for Nickel, D for Dime, Q for Quarter: N
24  How many? 2
25  Deposit is 155 cents
26  What coin do you deposit?
27  N for Nickel, D for Dime, Q for Quarter: Q
28  How many? 2
29  Deposit is 205 cents
30  Now you can make a selection.
```

It is possible to determine the value of `inc` using a switch-statement with no `break` appearing in it, as follows:

```
1      inc = 0;
2      switch ( token.charAt( 0 )
3      {
4        case 'Q': inc += 15;
5        case 'D': inc += 5;
6        case 'N': inc += 5;
7      }
```

The amount 15 for `'Q'` is the difference between a quarter and a dime, and the amount 5 for `'D'` is the difference between a dime and a nickel.

11.1.5 The Collatz Conjecture

Our next example is the program for testing the **Collatz Conjecture**, also known as the $3x + 1$ Problem, due to Lothar Collatz.[1] The conjecture states that every positive integer can be transformed to 1 by successively applying the following transformation:

(*) if the number is an even number, divide it by 2; otherwise, multiply it by 3 and then add 1 to it.

For example, 7 turns into 1 by following the procedure as follows:

$$7 \to 22 \to 11 \to 34 \to 17 \to 52 \to 26 \to 13 \to 40 \to$$
$$20 \to 10 \to 5 \to 16 \to 8 \to 4 \to 2 \to 1$$

Portuguese scholar Tomás Oliveira e Silva has been conducting extensive research on this conjecture.[2] Through computer simulation, he has found that the conjecture is valid up to 5×2^{60}.

Consider receiving an input from the user and checking whether or not the conjecture holds for the input by repeatedly applying the transformation rule until the number becomes 1. We design the code using three methods, `update`, `method`, and `main`, as follows:

- The method `update` receives an integer as a formal parameter, applies the transformation rules *just once* to the number, and returns the number generated.
- The method `test` receives a positive integer as a formal parameter, and performs the test on the number. After each application of the rule, the method prints the number generated.
- The method `main` interacts with the user to receive input numbers, and then performs the test on them. The user can test the conjecture on an indefinite number of inputs. The program terminates when the user enters a non-positive number.

The source code of the program is shown next. After the program header, the method `update` appears. The formal parameter of the method is an `int` named `number`. The method returns an `int` value (Line 7). The actions to be performed by the method are as follows:

---

[1] Lothar Collatz (July 6, 1910 to September 26, 1990) was a German mathematician.
[2] The page of his work on this topic is: http://sweet.ua.pt/tos/3x_plus_1.html.

- The method checks whether or not the input number is a multiple of 2 with number % 2 == 0 (Line 9).
- If the input number is a multiple of 2, then the method returns number / 2 (Line 11).
- Otherwise, the method returns number * 3 + 1 (Line 13).

Note that a return statement immediately terminates the execution of a method, so we do not need else in Line 13.

```
1   // experimenting with Collatz Conjecture
2   import java.util.*;
3
4   public class Collatz
5   {
6      // execute update and return the value
7      public static int update( int number )
8      {
9         if ( number % 2 == 0 )
10        {
11           return number / 2;
12        }
13        return number * 3 + 1;
14     }
```

Listing 11.6 A program that tests the Collatz Conjecture (part 1). The method update

The method test has an int data named input as its formal parameter (Line 16). The method uses a variable named number and applies the transformation rule to the value stored in number. The initial value of number is equal to the value of input. The method uses a variable named round to record how many times the transformation rule has been applied to the input. The initial value of round is 0. The declarations and initializations of the two variables appear in Line 18. After reporting the value of input (Line 19), the method enters a while-loop with the continuation condition number > 1 (Line 20). The loop terminates when the value of number becomes less than or equal to 1. In the loop-body, the method applies the transformation rule using the method update, replaces the value of number with the value returned (Line 22), adds 1 to round (Line 23), and reports the values of round and number (Line 24). To report the value of round, the method allocates 4 character spaces.

```
15    // test the conjecture
16    public static void test( int input )
17    {
18       int round = 0, number = input;
19       System.out.println( "input = " + input );
20       while ( number > 1 )
21       {
22          number = update( number );
23          round ++;
24          System.out.printf( "%4d: %d%n", round, number );
25       }
26    }
27
```

Listing 11.7 A program that tests the Collatz Conjecture (part 2). A part that performs the test on one number

We can expect the following different outcomes depending on the value of `input`:

- if `input <= 1`, the loop terminates without executing;
- if `input >= 2` and the conjecture holds for `input`, the loop eventually terminates;
- if `input >= 2` and the conjecture does not hold for `input`, the loop never terminates.

The method `main` uses a variable, `input`, to store the input from the user. The initial value of `input` is 1 (Line 33). The while loop in the method continues so long as `input >= 1` (Line 34). Therefore, the initial value of the variable makes the loop run. In the loop-body, the method obtains a new value for `input` (Lines 36 and 37). If the number entered is greater than or equal to 1 (Line 38), the method calls `test` (Line 40). After quitting the loop, the method prints a message (Line 43).

```
28    public static void main( String[] args )
29    {
30       System.out.println( "Testing the Collatz Conjecture" );
31       Scanner keyboard = new Scanner( System.in );
32
33       int input = 1;
34       while ( input >= 1 )
35       {
36          System.out.print( "Enter a positive integer: " );
37          input = keyboard.nextInt();
38          if ( input >= 1 )
39          {
40             test( input );
41          }
42       }
43       System.out.println( "...quitting" );
44    }
45 }
```

Listing 11.8 A program that tests the Collatz Conjecture (part 3). The method `main`

Here are some execution examples of the program:

```
1    Testing the Collatz Conjecture
2    Enter a positive integer: 15
3    input = 15
4        1: 46
5        2: 23
6        3: 70
7        4: 35
8        5: 106
9        6: 53
10       7: 160
11       8: 80
12       9: 40
13      10: 20
14      11: 10
15      12: 5
16      13: 16
17      14: 8
18      15: 4
19      16: 2
20      17: 1
```

```
21   Enter a positive integer: 17
22   input = 17
23       1: 52
24       2: 26
25       3: 13
26       4: 40
27       5: 20
28       6: 10
29       7: 5
30       8: 16
31       9: 8
32      10: 4
33      11: 2
34      12: 1
35   Enter a positive integer: 0
36   ...quitting
```

11.1.6 Covnerting Decimal Numbers to Binary Numbers

The next program obtains the binary representation of a nonnegative decimal integer named `value`. The program uses the following logic:

- If `value` is equal to 0, then the representation is 0.
- Otherwise, initialize a `String` variable with an empty `String`, and then repeatedly divide `value` by 2, and insert the remainder of the division at the start of the `String` variable.

The next program incorporates this idea. The method `main` receives the input from the user (Line 14), stores it in an `int` variable named `number` (Line 15), and then calls the method `convert` (Line 16). `convert` is the method for executing the conversion. The method `main` stores the returned value in `result` (Line 16), and then prints the value of `result` (Line 17). This series of action is in a while-loop. The loop is repeated until the user enters a negative integer as the value to convert to binary.

The `convert` method receives an `int` value `number` as its formal parameter (Line 21). The method works as follows:

- If the value `number` is 0, the method returns `"0"` immediately (Lines 25).
- The method initializes a `String` variable named `binary` with the value of `""` (Line 27).
- The method repeats the following while `number > 0` (Line 28).
  - The method computes `number % 2` and stores it in a variable named `bit` (Line 30).
  - The method updates `binary` by inserting the value of `bit` (Line 31).
  - The method divides `number` by 2 (Line 32).
- After exiting the loop, the method returns `binary`.

The method modifies the value of the formal parameter `number`, but not the value of the actual parameter. If `number < 0`, the method returns an empty `String`.

```
1   import java.util.*;
2
3   public class ConvertToBinary
4   {
5     public static void main( String[] args )
6     {
7       Scanner keyboard = new Scanner( System.in );
8
9       int number = 0;
10      String result;
11
12      while ( number >= 0 )
13      {
14        System.out.print( "Enter an integer: " );
15        number = keyboard.nextInt();
16        result = convert( number );
17        System.out.printf( "%d --> %s%n", number, result );
18      }
19    }
20
21    public static String convert( int number )
22    {
23      if ( number == 0 )
24      {
25        return "0";
26      }
27      String binary = "";
28      while ( number > 0 )
29      {
30        int bit = number % 2;
31        binary = bit + binary;
32        number /= 2;
33      }
34      return  binary;
35    }
36  }
```

Listing 11.9 A program that obtains the binary representation of a nonnegative integer

Here is an execution example of the code:

```
1   Enter an integer: 0
2   0 --> 0
3   Enter an integer: 17
4   17 --> 10001
5   Enter an integer: 19
6   19 --> 10011
7   Enter an integer: 21
8   21 --> 10101
9   Enter an integer: 1027
10  1027 --> 10000000011
11  Enter an integer: 987654321
12  987654321 --> 111010110111100110100010110001
13  Enter an integer: -1
14  -1 -->
```

We can attach, to the conversion method, a line that shows the current value of number and the current value of binary during the course of the conversion while-loop.

```
1   import java.util.*;
2
3   public class ConvertToBinaryInAction
4   {
5     public static void main( String[] args )
6     {
7       Scanner keyboard = new Scanner( System.in );
8
9       long number = 0;
10      String result;
11
12      while ( number >= 0 )
13      {
14        System.out.print( "Enter an integer: " );
15        number = keyboard.nextLong();
16        result = convert( number );
17        System.out.printf( "%d --> %s%n", number, result );
18      }
19    }
20
21    public static String convert( long number )
22    {
23      if ( number == 0 )
24      {
25        return "0";
26      }
27      String binary = "";
28      while ( number > 0 )
29      {
30        int bit = (int)( number % 2 );
31        binary = bit + binary;
32        number /= 2;
33        System.out.printf( "%10d, %s%n", number, binary );
34      }
35      return  binary;
36    }
37  }
```

Listing 11.10 A program that obtains the binary representation of a nonnegative integer while showing the progress on the calculation

Here are some execution examples with additional output:

```
1   Enter an integer: 9
2       Digits, Binary
3            4, 1
4            2, 01
5            1, 001
6            0, 1001
7   9 --> 1001
```

```
8    Enter an integer: 1027
9         Digits, Binary
10            513, 1
11            256, 11
12            128, 011
13             64, 0011
14             32, 00011
15             16, 000011
16              8, 0000011
17              4, 00000011
18              2, 000000011
19              1, 0000000011
20              0, 10000000011
21   1027 --> 10000000011
22   Enter an integer: -1
23   -1 -->
```

11.1.7 Infinite Loops and Their Termination

An infinite loop is a loop that is designated to run forever. An infinite loop is constructed with true as the continuation condition. An infinite loop usually has a condition for termination inside the body. In Sect. 7.5.2, we saw the use of break to terminate a for-loop. break can be used to terminate a while-loop as well. Consider computing the number of times a pattern represented by a String variable named pattern appears in an input String variable named input. We can use an infinite loop for the task. We use a variable named pos to maintain the start position of the search in input. We also use a variable named count to record the number of occurrences of the pattern. The initial value is 0 for both pos and count. We use input.indexOf(pattern, pos) to check whether or not pattern appears in input at or after position pos. If the return value of indexOf is negative, we terminate the loop; otherwise, the return value is the position at which pattern appears, so we add one to count and update the value of pos with the returned value plus 1. The following code captures this idea:

```
1     int count = 0, pos = 0;
2     while ( true )
3     {
4        int res = input.indexOf( pattern, pos );
5        if ( res < 0 )
6        {
7           break;
8        }
9        count ++;
10       pos = res + 1;
11    }
```

11.2   Using Do-While Loops

11.2.1 The Syntax of Do-While Loops

The do-while loop is a variant of while-loops, where the execution of the loop-body precedes the termination condition evaluation.

The structure of a do-while loop is:

```
1  do
2  {
3     STATEMENTS
4  } while ( CONDITION );
```

The semicolon that appears is necessary.

We can rewrite a do-while loop using a while-loop. The following do-while loop

```
1  do
2  {
3     STATEMENTS;
4  } while ( CONDITION );
```

is equivalent to

```
1  STATEMENTS;
2  while ( CONDITION )
3  {
4     STATEMENTS;
5  }
```

Since a while-loop is an indefinite loop, we can write the program so that it will run forever using `true` as the termination condition.

```
1  while ( true )
2  {
3     STATEMENTS;
4     if ( CONDITION )
5     {
6        break;
7     }
8  }
```

11.2.2 "Waiting for Godot"

Here is a simple program that uses a do-while loop.

Consider receiving a series of tokens from the user until the user enters "Godot", when the execution terminates (where, of course, the "Godot" comes from a play by Samuel Beckett[3] titled *Waiting for Godot*). We store the user input to a `String` variable named `input`, and build a do-while loop using the condition `!input.equals( "Godot" )`. In other words, the program will run until the user enters `"Godot"`.

---

[3]Samuel Barclay Beckett (April 13, 1906 to December 22, 1989) was an Irish novelist and playwright. *Waiting for Godot* is an avant-garde play that features conversations between two men waiting for Godot, who never shows up.

If the code uses a while-loop, we need to assign some initial value other than the "Godot". Otherwise, the loop terminates immediately without asking the user to enter an input. If the code uses a do-while loop, the initialization is unnecessary.

Here is the version that uses a while-loop:

```
1  import java.util.*;
2  public class Godot
3  {
4    public static void main( String[] args )
5    {
6      Scanner keyboard = new Scanner( System.in );
7      String input = "";
8      while ( !input.equals( "Godot" ) )
9      {
10       System.out.println( "This program is called \"Godot\"." );
11       System.out.print( "Enter input: " );
12       input = keyboard.nextLine();
13     }
14     System.out.println( "Terminating the program." );
15   }
16 }
```

Here is the version that uses a do-while loop:

```
1  import java.util.*;
2  public class DoWhileGodot
3  {
4    public static void main( String[] args )
5    {
6      Scanner keyboard = new Scanner( System.in );
7      String input;
8      do
9      {
10       System.out.println( "This program is called \"Godot\"." );
11       System.out.print( "Enter input: " );
12       input = keyboard.nextLine();
13     } while ( !input.equals( "Godot" ) );
14     System.out.println( "Terminating the program." );
15   }
16 }
```

11.2.3 Converting Decimal Numbers to Binary Numbers (Reprise)

Let us look back at the decimal-to-binary conversion program. In that program, a while-loop is used to repeat the interaction with the user indefinitely, and the loop was terminated when the user entered a negative value as an input. To prevent the loop from terminating without executing its body, the program assigned a nonnegative initial value to the variable. As in the case of the "Godot" program, if we use a do-while loop, such initialization is unnecessary.

```
1   import java.util.*;
2
3   public class ConvertToBinaryDoWhile
4   {
5     public static void main( String[] args )
6     {
7       Scanner keyboard = new Scanner( System.in );
8
```

Listing 11.11 A program that obtains the binary representation of a nonnegative integer using a do-while loop (part 1)

```
9         int number;
10        String result;
11
12        do {
13          System.out.print( "Enter an integer: " );
14          number = keyboard.nextInt();
15          result = convert( number );
16          System.out.printf( "%d --> %s%n", number, result );
17        } while ( number >= 0 );
18      }
19
20      public static String convert( int number )
21      {
22        if ( number == 0 )
23        {
24          return "0";
25        }
26        String binary = "";
27        do
28        {
29          int bit = number % 2;
30          binary = bit + binary;
31          number /= 2;
32          System.out.printf( "%10d, %s%n", number, binary );
33        } while ( number > 0 );
34        return  binary;
35      }
36  }
```

Listing 11.12 A program that obtains the binary representation of a nonnegative integer using a do-while loop (part 2)

11.3 CTRL-D

Previously, to receive an indefinite number of input data from the user, we asked the user to enter a specific value to indicate the end of input. For example, in the decimal-to-binary conversion program, we asked the user to enter a negative integer to stop the program. Instead of using a special value, it is possible to use a special key to detect the end of input. The special key is called CTRL-D. The key can be entered by simultaneously pressing the "control" key and the 'D' key. When the method hasNext is called, if CTRL-D pressed before any other key, the method hasNext immediately returns true. Otherwise, hasNext waits until the return key is pressed, and then returns false.

Suppose keyboard is a Scanner object instantiated with System.in. We can write a while-loop of the following form:

```
1  while ( keyboard.hasNext() )
2  {
3    READ_TOKEN_AND_REACT;
4  }
```

The next code demonstrates the use of this code. The program receives an indefinite number of integers from the user, and computes their total. The program accepts input until the user enters CTRL-D. The program uses three int variables, input, total, and count, for recording the input, the total, and the number of inputs. The last two variables have the initial value of 0. The program does not produce a prompt for individual inputs. It only announces at the beginning:

"Enter inputs. End with a CTRL-D"

The while-loop appears in Lines 9–14. At the end, the program prints the number of inputs entered and their total.

```
1  import java.util.*;
2  public class HasNextNoPrompt
3  {
4    public static void main( String[] args )
5    {
6      Scanner keyboard = new Scanner( System.in );
7      int input, total = 0, count = 0;
8      System.out.println( "Enter inputs.  End with a CTRL-D" );
9      while ( keyboard.hasNext() )
10     {
11       input = keyboard.nextInt();
12       total += input;
13       count ++;
14     }
15     System.out.printf( "Count=%d, Total=%d%n", count, total );
16   }
17 }
```

Listing 11.13 A program for computing the total of integer input values

Here is one execution of the program. The inputs are: 10, 11, 12, 13, and 14. Each input line is followed by the return key. After entering 14 followed by the return key, the user presses CTRL-D. The CTRL-D does not echo.

```
1  Enter inputs.  End with a CTRL-D
2  10
3  11
4  12
5  13
6  14
7  Count=5, Total=60
```

Here is another execution. The user enters the same input numbers as before, but adds CTRL-D after some numbers. The CTRL-D entered after a number is ignored but echoes as ^D.

```
1   Enter inputs.   End with a CTRL-D
2   10
3   11^D
4   12 ^D
5   13 ^D
6   14
7   Count=5, Total=60
```

The effect of CTRL-D as the end of input is permanent, meaning that once a Scanner object encounters CTRL-D as the result of hasNext, the result of hasNext will always be false and an attempt to read another token will result in a run-time error, NoSuchElementException. To resume reading from the keyboard, a new Scanner object must be instantiated with System.in.

The next program is a variant of the previous program. This time, the program produces the prompt "Enter input: " for each input number. The program accomplishes this by executing System.out.print("Enter input: ") at two places (Lines 8 and 14). The one before entering the while-loop is necessary because the loop begins by waiting for an input.

```
1    import java.util.*;
2    public class HasNext
3    {
4      public static void main( String[] args )
5      {
6        Scanner keyboard = new Scanner( System.in );
7        int input, total = 0;
8        System.out.print( "Enter input: " );
9        while ( keyboard.hasNext() )
10       {
11         input = keyboard.nextInt();
12         total += input;
13         System.out.printf( "Input=%d, Total=%d%n", input, total );
14         System.out.print( "Enter input: " );
15       }
16       System.out.println( "\nEnd of the program." );
17     }
18   }
```

Here is an execution example of the code:

```
1    Enter input: 340
2    Input=340, Total=340
3    Enter input: 35
4    Input=35, Total=375
5    Enter input: 98
6    Input=98, Total=473
7    Enter input: -180
8    Input=-180, Total=293
9    Enter input: ^D
10   End of the program.
```

In Line 9, the user enters CTRL-D, and the CTRL-D echoes as ^D. Whenever CTRL-D is followed by the return key, it appear as ^D. In the program, the ensuing return key appears in the String literal in Line 16.

To see the difference between having and not having the return key immediately after CTRL-D, let us compare the following two new programs. The two programs are variants of the previous program with slightly different Line 16: HasNext01 prints "...End of the program" and HasNext02 prints "\n...End of the program".

```
1   import java.util.*;
2   public class HasNext01
3   {
4     public static void main( String[] args )
5     {
6       Scanner keyboard = new Scanner( System.in );
7       int input, total = 0;
8       System.out.print( "Enter input: " );
9       while ( keyboard.hasNext() )
10      {
11        input = keyboard.nextInt();
12        total += input;
13        System.out.printf( "Input=%d, Total=%d%n", input, total );
14        System.out.print( "Enter input: " );
15      }
16      System.out.println( "...End of the program." );
17    }
18  }
```

```
1   import java.util.*;
2   public class HasNext02
3   {
4     public static void main( String[] args )
5     {
6       Scanner keyboard = new Scanner( System.in );
7       int input, total = 0;
8       System.out.print( "Enter input: " );
9       while ( keyboard.hasNext() )
10      {
11        input = keyboard.nextInt();
12        total += input;
13        System.out.printf( "Input=%d, Total=%d%n", input, total );
14        System.out.print( "Enter input: " );
15      }
16      System.out.println( "\n...End of the program." );
17    }
18  }
```

Here are execution examples of the two programs. In both executions, the user enters: 10, 20, and CTRL-D.

```
1   Enter input: 10
2   Input=10, Total=10
3   Enter input: 20
4   Input=20, Total=30
5   Enter input: ...End of the program.
```

```
1  Enter input: 10
2  Input=10, Total=10
3  Enter input: 20
4  Input=20, Total=30
5  Enter input: ^D
6  ...End of the program.
```

11.4 Approximating the Square Root of a Real Number

Let's learn how to use a while-loop to approximate the square root of a number. Our goal is to write an application that receives a positive floating point number from the user, and then calculates an approximation of its square root. We will store the input in a variable named `original` and the approximated square root in a variable named `root`. To accomplish the goal, we use a simple strategy called **binary search**, that involves an indefinite loop. Later, we will see binary search in Sect. 13.5.2.

During the course of calculation, we manipulate two `double` variables, `high` and `low`. We ensure that the two variables have the following properties:

- The value of `high` is greater than or equal to the actual value of the square root.
- The value of `low` is smaller than or equal to the actual value of the square root.

In other words, the two properties are:

$$\texttt{high * high >= original and low * low <= original.}$$

We call a condition that is sustained throughout the execution of an indefinite loop a **loop invariant**. The conjunction of the above two properties is the loop invariant of the algorithm.

We initialize `high` with the value of `original + 0.5` and `low` with the value of 0. Since the square of (`original + 0.5`) is equal to `original * original + original + 0.25` and `original` is positive, the first condition is met. Furthermore, since `original` is positive, the second condition is met.

In the do-while loop, we execute the following:

Step 1 We obtain a candidate for the square root. This is the half-way point between `high` and `low`, i.e., (`high + low`) `/ 2`. We store the candidate in `root`.

Step 2 We store the square of `root` in a variable named `square`.

Step 3 We store the value of `original - square` in another variable, `diff`.

Step 4 If `diff` is equal to 0, the value of `root` is the square root we are looking for, so we terminate the loop.

Step 5 If `diff` is positive, we update `low` with the value of `root`.

Step 6 If `diff` is negative, we update `high` with the value of `root`.

Step 7 We terminate the loop if `diff` becomes smaller than the value of a predetermined positive constant, `SMALL`.

The loop invariant is sustained when the value of `low` or `high` is updated. Furthermore, if the value of `low` or `high` is updated, then the value of `high−low` decreases to its half. We thus can anticipate that the value of `root` gets close to the actual value of the square root very quickly.

Based upon these observations, we hope that the loop will terminate eventually by either finding the actual value of the square root or finding that the value of `diff` has become smaller than the value of `SMALL`. However, this is not always the case. This is because the floating point number representation has a finite number of bits. To prevent such a situation from happening, we store the value of 10^{-12} in `SMALL`.

Next is the code of `SquareRoot` that implements the above idea. The declaration of the constant `SMALL` appears in Line 4. The input from the user is received in Line 9. The variables `high` and `low` are declared and initialized as planned in Line 10. We use an `int` variable `round` to record the number of rounds that have been executed (Line 12). The initial value of `round` is 0.

```
1   import java.util.*;
2   public class SquareRoot
3   {
4     public static double SMALL = 0.0000000000001;
5     public static void main( String[] args )
6     {
7       Scanner keyboard = new Scanner( System.in );
8       System.out.print( "> " );
9       double original = keyboard.nextDouble();
10      double high = original + 0.5, low = 0;
11      double root, square, diff;
12      int round = 0;
```

Listing 11.14 A program for approximating the square root (part 1). The initialization of the variables

The continuation condition of the do-while loop is "the absolute value of `diff` is greater than or equal to `SMALL`". This is expressed as `diff >= SMALL || diff <= -SMALL` (Line 28). In the loop-body, the program adds 1 to the count (Line 15), stores the value of (`high + low`) / 2 in `root` (Line 16), and prints the values of `root` and `count`. The program then stores the square of `root` in `square` (Line 17) and stores the difference of the original from the square in `diff` (Line 18). Next, the program updates the values of `high` and `low` as follows: (Lines 20–27):

- If `diff > 0`, the program updates `low` with the value of `root`.
- If `diff < 0`, the program updates `high` with the value of `root`.

Finally, after exiting the loop, the program reports the values of the `root` and `square` (Line 29).

Here are execution examples of the program. First, we approximate the square root of 2.

```
1    > 2
2    Round=001,Value=1.250000000000000
3    Round=002,Value=1.875000000000000
4    Round=003,Value=1.562500000000000
5    Round=004,Value=1.406250000000000
6    Round=005,Value=1.484375000000000
7    Round=006,Value=1.445312500000000
8    Round=007,Value=1.425781250000000
9    Round=008,Value=1.416015625000000
10   Round=009,Value=1.411132812500000
11   Round=010,Value=1.413574218750000
12   Round=011,Value=1.414794921875000
13   Round=012,Value=1.414184570312500
14   Round=013,Value=1.414489746093750
15   Round=014,Value=1.414337158203125
```

```
13    do
14    {
15      round ++;
16      root = ( high + low ) / 2;
17      System.out.printf( "Round=%03d,Value=%.15f%n", round, root );
18      square = root * root;
19      diff = original - square;
20      if ( diff > 0 )
21      {
22        low = root;
23      }
24      else if ( diff < 0 )
25      {
26        high = root;
27      }
28    } while ( diff >= SMALL || diff <= -SMALL );
29    System.out.printf( "Root=%.15f, Square=%.15f%n", root, square );
30  }
31 }
```

Listing 11.15 A program for approximating the square root (part 2). The loop for approximation

```
16  Round=015,Value=1.414260864257813
17  Round=016,Value=1.414222717285156
18  Round=017,Value=1.414203643798828
19  Round=018,Value=1.414213180541992
20  Round=019,Value=1.414217948913574
21  Round=020,Value=1.414215564727783
22  Round=021,Value=1.414214372634888
23  Round=022,Value=1.414213776588440
24  Round=023,Value=1.414213478565216
25  Round=024,Value=1.414213627576828
26  Round=025,Value=1.414213553071022
27  Round=026,Value=1.414213590323925
28  Round=027,Value=1.414213571697474
29  Round=028,Value=1.414213562384248
30  Round=029,Value=1.414213557727635
31  Round=030,Value=1.414213560055941
32  Round=031,Value=1.41421356122095
33  Round=032,Value=1.414213561802171
34  Round=033,Value=1.414213562093210
35  Round=034,Value=1.414213562238729
36  Round=035,Value=1.414213562311488
37  Round=036,Value=1.414213562347868
38  Round=037,Value=1.414213562366058
39  Round=038,Value=1.414213562375153
40  Round=039,Value=1.414213562370605
41  Round=040,Value=1.414213562372879
42  Round=041,Value=1.414213562374016
43  Round=042,Value=1.414213562373448
44  Round=043,Value=1.414213562373163
45  Round=044,Value=1.414213562373021
46  Round=045,Value=1.414213562373092
47  Root=1.414213562373092, Square=1.999999999999992
```

Next, we approximate the square root of 3.

```
 1  > 3
 2  Round=001,Value=1.750000000000000
 3  Round=002,Value=0.875000000000000
 4  Round=003,Value=1.312500000000000
 5  Round=004,Value=1.531250000000000
 6  Round=005,Value=1.640625000000000
 7  Round=006,Value=1.695312500000000
 8  Round=007,Value=1.722656250000000
 9  Round=008,Value=1.736328125000000
10  Round=009,Value=1.729492187500000
11  Round=010,Value=1.732910156250000
12  Round=011,Value=1.731201171875000
13  Round=012,Value=1.732055664062500
14  Round=013,Value=1.731628417968750
15  Round=014,Value=1.731842041015625
16  Round=015,Value=1.731948852539063
17  Round=016,Value=1.732002258300781
18  Round=017,Value=1.732028961181641
19  Round=018,Value=1.732042312622070
20  Round=019,Value=1.732048988342285
21  Round=020,Value=1.732052326202393
22  Round=021,Value=1.732050657272339
23  Round=022,Value=1.732051491737366
24  Round=023,Value=1.732051074504852
25  Round=024,Value=1.732050865888596
26  Round=025,Value=1.732050761580467
27  Round=026,Value=1.732050813734531
28  Round=027,Value=1.732050787657499
29  Round=028,Value=1.732050800696015
30  Round=029,Value=1.732050807215273
31  Round=030,Value=1.732050810474902
32  Round=031,Value=1.732050808845088
33  Round=032,Value=1.732050808030181
34  Round=033,Value=1.732050807622727
35  Round=034,Value=1.732050807419000
36  Round=035,Value=1.732050807520864
37  Round=036,Value=1.732050807571795
38  Round=037,Value=1.732050807546330
39  Round=038,Value=1.732050807559062
40  Round=039,Value=1.732050807565429
41  Round=040,Value=1.732050807568612
42  Round=041,Value=1.732050807570204
43  Round=042,Value=1.732050807569408
44  Round=043,Value=1.732050807569010
45  Round=044,Value=1.732050807568811
46  Round=045,Value=1.732050807568911
47  Round=046,Value=1.732050807568861
48  Root=1.732050807568861, Square=2.999999999999943
```

Summary

- A while-loop is a loop whose control requires the continuation condition only.
- A do-while loop is a variant of the while-loop, where the evaluation of the continuation condition occurs at the end of loop-body.
- An infinite loop takes the form of `while ( true ) { ... }`.
- It is possible to use an infinite loop with a mechanism for terminating the loop.
- CTRL-D is a key combination that indicates the end of input.
- The method `hasNext` of `Scanner` shows whether or not the CTRL-D is at the start of the input sequence.

Exercises

1. **A while-loop for printing numbers with leading 0s** Write a while-loop that produces the following output:

```
1   002:
2   004:
3   006:
4   008:
5   010:
```

2. **A do-while loop for printing two numbers per line** Write a do-while loop that produces the following output:

```
1   001.0,002.0
2   003.0,004.0
3   005.0,006.0
4   007.0,008.0
5   009.0,010.0
```

3. **A while-loop that produces a bit complex number output** Write a while-loop with a single `printf` statement inside the loop-body, and produces the following output:

```
1    +1024?
2    +0512?
3    +0256?
4    +0128?
5    +0064?
6    +0032?
7    +0016?
8    +0008?
9    +0004?
10   +0002?
11   +0001?
```

4. **Converting a for-loop to a do-while loop** Convert the following for-loop to an equivalent do-while loop:

```
1   for ( int index = 1; index <= 15; index = index + 3 )
2   {
3       System.out.println( index );
4   }
```

5. **Converting a for-loop to a while-loop**   Convert the following for-loop to an equivalent while-loop:

```
for ( int index = 10; index >= 0; index = index - 2 )
{
  System.out.println( index );
}
```

6. **Converting a while-loop to a do-while loop**   Suppose that the following while-loop is part of a method that returns an `int`. Convert this loop to an equivalent do-while loop such that the `return` statement appears only after the do-while loop.

```
Scanner keyboard = new Scanner( System.in );
int a, count = 0;
while ( true )
{
  count ++;
  System.out.print( "Enter an int: " );
  a = keyboard.nextInt();
  if ( a == 0 )
  {
    return count;
  }
}
```

7. **Substrings with while-loop**   Suppose `word` is a `String` variable that is not `null`. Write a while-loop that produces all the nonempty suffixes of `word`, starting with the shortest one and ending with the longest one. Use an index variable that specifies the position where the suffix begins. For example, if `word` has the value `"sebastian-ibis"`, then the program must produce the following output:

```
s
is
bis
ibis
-ibis
n-ibis
an-ibis
ian-ibis
tian-ibis
stian-ibis
astian-ibis
bastian-ibis
ebastian-ibis
sebastian-ibis
```

8. **Random walk on a torus**   A torus is a three-dimensional structure resembling a doughnut. A torus has a two-dimensional geometry. The points on the torus can be referred to using x- and y-coordinates. We consider here the case where both coordinates are integers between 0 and `boundary - 1` for some integer `boundary` greater than or equal to 2. For both dimensions, each coordinate value v has two neighbors. If v is between 1 and `boundary - 2`, the two neighbors are v - 1 and v + 1. If v is equal to 0, the two neighbors are `boundary - 1` and 1. If v is equal to `boundary - 1`, the two neighbors are v - 1 and 0. In this manner, each point on the grid has exactly four direct neighbors.

Consider the step-wise process where a point p that is located on such a grid randomly changes its location by moving to one of the four direct neighbors at each step. For each neighbor, the probability of moving to the neighbor is 25%. The initial location of p is the origin (0,0). Write a program, RandomWalkTorus, that simulates this process. The program must receive the value for boundary from the user and repeat the process until the point returns to the origin. After each step, the program must report the location of the point along with the number of steps it has executed.

The program may work as follows:

```
1   Enter the value for the boundary: 4
2   Round=1, Position=(3,1)
3   Round=2, Position=(2,2)
4   Round=3, Position=(3,1)
5   Round=4, Position=(0,0)
```

9. **A simple number generation**   Using a do-while loop, write a program, WaitForZero, that repeats the following: randomly generate an integer between 0 and 9 and print the number generated, one per line. Use a do-while loop. Terminate the program when a 0 has been generated.

10. **A simple number generation plus**   Using a while-loop, write a program, WaitForThree Zeros, that repeats the following: randomly generate an integer between 0 and 9 and print the number generated. The loop must be terminated when three 0's have been generated consecutively.

11. **Waiting for a pattern, no.1**   Using a while-loop, write a program, WaitForZeroOne, that generates a random sequence of numbers between 0 and 9, and stops when a 1 is generated after a 0. The program must report each number generated in one character space. The numbers are printed in a single line, but after printing 60 characters, the program goes to the next line. Furthermore, after printing the required number of random digits, if the last line has few than 60 characters, the program goes to the next line before ending the program.

The output of the program may look like this one:

```
1   % WaitForZeroOne
2   77733064868796293377126313131127118073325787026191539790 4279
3   313954419098344974921682097061190863460556325728765420418607
4   475305949271044338127842098973290463257596466804635930484292
5   1715082201
6   %
```

12. **Waiting for a pattern, no.2**   Using a do-while loop, write a program WaitForZeroOneTwo that generates a random integer sequence of numbers between 0 and 9 and stops when the last three numbers generated become 0, 1, and 2 in this order. The program must report each number generated in one character space. The numbers are printed in a single line, but after printing 60 characters, the program goes to the next line. Furthermore, after printing the required number of random digits, if the last line has few than 60 characters, the program goes to the next line before ending the program.

13. **Guessing game**   Write a program named Guess that plays a guessing game with the user. The program randomly selects an integer from {1, ..., 9} using the code (int) (Math.floor(1 + Math.random() * 9)). The program then prompts the player to keep entering guesses. Each time the player enters a guess, the program must report the guess is correct or not. When the correct guess has been made, the program must terminate. Before terminating, the program must report how many guesses the player has made to arrive at the correct guess.

```
1    Enter your guess: 5
2    Your guess is not correct.
3    Enter your guess: 4
4    Your guess is not correct.
5    Enter your guess: 3
6    Your guess is not correct.
7    Enter your guess: 4
8    Your guess is not correct.
9    Enter your guess: 6
10   Your guess is correct.
11
12   You have found the answer with 5 guesses.
```

14. **Max and min simultaneously**   Write a program named MaxAndMin.java that receives an indefinite number of real numbers from the user (as double values) and computes the maximum and the minimum of those that have been received. The program must terminate when the user enters 0, ignoring the 0 in the calculation of max and min. The program must use a boolean variable that is initialized with the value of false. Each time a number is received, the program must store true to this variable. During the execution of the loop, if the value of this variable is false, the program records the number that the user has entered as the maximum and minimum; if the value of this variable is true and the number the user has entered is not 0, the program compares the number with the maximum and the minimum to perform updates. After the loop, if the value of the boolean variable is true, the program reports the maximum and the minimum.

15. **Decimal to binary conversion**   Write a program named DecimalToBinaryWithBuilder that receives a nonnegative long value from the user and produces its binary representation. Use a StringBuilder object in constructing the representation. The bit insertion must use the method insert of StringBuilder, and the return value must be the String that the builder represents. The program also must check whether the input from the user is nonnegative. If it is negative, the program must warn the user and halt immediately.

    Here is one execution example.

```
1    Enter a nonnegative integer: 3445844276438276431
2    The binary representation of 3445844276438276431 is
3    10111111010010000011001000111001101000001101010100110010100111
```

Programming Projects

16. **BMI with a while-loop**   Write a program named BMIWhile that repeats the following: receive the weight and the height from the user, compute the BMI value determined by the two input values, and print the result on the screen (weight, height, and the BMI) with exactly two digits after the decimal point for each quantity. Use a while-loop in the code. Terminate the program when the user enters a nonpositive value for either weight or height.

17. **The area of triangle with a while-loop**   Write a program named TriangularAreaWhile that repeats the following: receive three sides of a triangle, compute the area of the triangle specified by the sides, and print the result on the screen (the lengths, and the area). The program must use an infinite while-loop while (true) and exit the loop if either one of the values entered is nonpositive or if one of the values entered is strictly greater than the sum of the other two (since such a triangle is impossible). The condition for exiting the loop must be the disjunction of six comparisons. To compute the area, use Heron's formula:

$$\sqrt{s(s-a)(s-b)(s-c)}$$

where $s = (a + b + c)/2$.

18. **The area of triangle with a while-loop, alternative** In the previous problem, we used the disjunction of six conditions as the condition for breaking the loop. Rewrite the program by replacing this condition with the disjunction of just two conditions with some pre-computation. Let min and max be the minimum and the maximum of the three sides. Then we have the following properties:
    - One of the sides is nonpositive if and only if min is nonpositive.
    - One side is longer than the sum of the other two if and only if two times max is greater than the sum of the three.

19. **Three-digit Mastermind** Mastermind is a game of two players. Mastermind is played as follows: Each player initially selects a four-digit number consisting of numerals 1 through 9 in which no digits appearing more than once. The players keep these numbers to themselves. After the initialization, the two players take turns in guessing the number the other player has. The player who guesses the number correctly first wins the game.

    When the opponent of a player makes a guess, the player having the secret number must answer whether or not the number matches the selected number; if not, the player must report the number of "hits" and the number of "misses", where a "hit" is a digit of the secret number appearing at exactly the same position in the guess and a "miss" is a digit of the secret number appearing at a different position in the guess. For example, for a secret number 9478, a guess 3417 has one hit (the 4) and one miss (the 7).

    We consider here a simplified version as follows:
    - The number of digits is not four but three.
    - The play is one-sided, meaning that only the first player selects a secret number and the second player tries to guess it correctly.
    - The first player is played by a computer program.
    Since no two digits can be equal in a secret number, the smallest possible number is 123 and the largest possible number is 987.

    Write a program named MastermindSimple that plays the role of the first year (the player that selects a secret number) as follows:

    (a) The program has a method

    ```
    public static boolean isLegit( int n )
    ```

    that checks whether or not the number n is between 123 and 987, none of the three digits of n are 0, and the three digits of n are pairwise distinct.

    (b) The program has a method

    ```
    public static int generate()
    ```

    that generates a random integer between 123 and 987 that passes the test. The method uses an infinite while-loop. In the loop, the method generates a random integer between 123 and 987, and returns the number if it passes the isLegit test.

    (c) The program has a method

    ```
    public static int countHit( int number1, int number2 )
    ```

    that returns, assuming that number1 and number2 have already passed the isLegit test, the number of hits when number1 is a guess and number2 is a secret.

    (d) The program has a method

    ```
    public static int countMiss( int number1, int number2 )
    ```

    that returns, assuming that number1 and number2 have already passed the isLegit test, the number of hits when number1 is a guess and number2 is a secret.

(e) The program uses either a while-loop or a do-while loop. In the loop, the program receives an integer guess from the user, stores the guess in an `int` variable named `guess`, and does the following:

    i It checks if the guess is legitimate using the `isLegit` method. If it is not legitimate, the program informs that the guess is not legitimate.

    ii Otherwise, if the guess is equal to the secret, the program congratulates the user and terminates the loop.

    iii Otherwise, the program counts the hits and the misses and reports the counts.

The program may work as follows:

```
1    Enter your guess: 123
2    No.Hits=0, No.Misses=0
3    Enter your guess: 456
4    No.Hits=2, No.Misses=0
5    Enter your guess: 457
6    No.Hits=1, No.Misses=1
7    Enter your guess: 467
8    No.Hits=0, No.Misses=2
9    Enter your guess: 478
10   No.Hits=0, No.Misses=1
11   Enter your guess: 567
12   No.Hits=0, No.Misses=3
13   Enter your guess: 756
14   Congratulations! You've guessed it right!
```

20. **Count the number of occurrences of "the"** Write a program, `CountThe`, that receives a series of `String` data from the user by way of `nextLine` of the class `Scanner`, concatenates the input lines into a single `String` data, and then in the concatenated data, counts the occurrences of the three-letter pattern `"the"`. To allow the user to enter any number of lines, use a while-loop that terminates when the user enters CTRL-D. To identify all the occurrences of `"the"`, use a variable that represents the start position of the search. The initial value of this variable is 0. When the search finds an occurrence at a position, the program updates the value of this variable with the position value plus 3 (the length of the literal `"the"`). The loop continues until either no more occurrence is found or the value of the variable representing the start position of search becomes greater than or equal to the length of the input.

    The program may run as follows:

```
1    Enter text (CTRL-D to stop) > Here is the program you need to write.
2    Enter text (CTRL-D to stop) > Your program solves the problem of finding
3    Enter text (CTRL-D to stop) > all the occurrences of the String literal
       "the"
4    Enter text (CTRL-D to stop) >  in the input character sequence that the
       user
5    Enter text (CTRL-D to stop) >  enters.
6    Enter text (CTRL-D to stop) > ^D
7    The number of occurrences is 7.
```

21. **Count the number of occurrences of either "the" or "an"** Extend the solution to the previous problem and write a program `CountTheAn` that computes the number of occurrences of either "the" or "an".

Part III

Arrays and Objects

Arrays

12

12.1 Arrays

12.1.1 The Structure of an Array

An **array** is a finite sequence of elements of some common data type, where an element of an array can be accessed by combing the name given to the array and the position of the element in the sequence, called **index**. Arrays are reminiscent of number sequence. In mathematics, an element of a number sequence is specified by the name of the sequence and the subscript representing the position of the element in the sequence, e.g., n_0 and n_9. In Java, numbers surrounded by square brackets specify positions and the positions always start from 0.

To declare an array data type, a pair of matching square brackets is attached as a suffix, as shown next. The first is an array of `int` values, the second is an array of `String` values, and the last declaration is an array of `double` values.

```
1   int[] myIntegers;
2   String[] myWords;
3   double[] someNumbers;
```

Arrays are objects, so before accessing their individual elements, they must be instantiated. An array is instantiated with its number of elements. We call the number of elements in an array the **length** or **size** of the array. The length specification appears inside a pair of square brackets `[]` after the type specification of the individual elements. Examples of the length specification are shown next. Line 4 instantiates a 10-element array of `int` values, Line 5 instantiates a 17-element array of `String` values, and Line 6 instantiates a 40-element array of `double` values.

```
1   int[] myIntegers;
2   String[] myWords;
3   double[] someNumbers;
4   myIntegers = new int[ 10 ];
5   myWords = new String[ 17 ];
6   someNumbers = new double[ 40 ];
```

© Springer Nature Switzerland AG 2018
M. Ogihara, *Fundamentals of Java Programming*,
https://doi.org/10.1007/978-3-319-89491-1_12

Fig. 12.1 A view of an
array. The array has length
11 and the indexes are 0
through 10

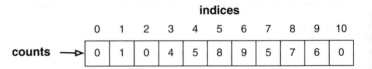

Given an array that has been instantiated, we can obtain the number of elements in the array by attaching `.length` to the name of the array. Unlike the method `length` of `String`, the `.length` attached to an array is something called an instance variable (we will learn in detail what instance variables are in Chap. 16) that is publicly accessible but cannot be modified.

An individual element (or a slot) in an array can be specified with its name followed by a pair of brackets that contains inside the index to the element, e.g., `a[ 7 ]` and `b[ 9 ]`. Since the indexes in arrays always start from 0, given an array of some N elements, the index of the last element is N - 1. This means that if `x` is the name of an array, its elements are thus `x[ 0 ], ..., x[ x.length - 1 ]`.

Using the same examples as before, the code:

```
1  int[] myIntegers;
2  String[] myWords;
3  double[] someNumbers;
4  myIntegers = new int[ 10 ];
5  myWords = new String[ 17 ];
6  someNumbers = new double[ 40 ];
7  System.out.println( myIntegers.length );
8  System.out.println( myWords.length );
9  System.out.println( someNumbers.length );
```

produces the output:

```
1  10
2  17
3  40
```

We often use a drawing like the one in Fig. 12.1 to visualize an array. Each square is an element of the array and `counts` is the name of the array. The numbers appearing above the elements are indices to the elements.

12.1.2 Computing the Number of Occurrences

12.1.2.1 Computing Distributions

Consider receiving an indefinite number of exam scores and computing the score distribution. The scores are integers between 0 and 100, so there are 101 possible scores. We group the scores into eleven bins: 0..9, 10..19, ..., 90..99, and 100, where the last bin is exclusively for 100, the highest possible score. The task is to count, for each bin, the scores that belong to it, and then report the counts and print a histogram.

We use an `int` array named `counts` for recording the counts.

```
int[] counts = new int[ 11 ];
```

The elements of counts are assigned indexes from 0 to 10. Given a score, score, the index of the bin that score belongs to can be obtained by the quotient by 10. We store this quotient in an int variable, position, and then increase counts[position] by 1. The statement counts is treated as an int variable.

```
1  int position = score / 10;
2  counts[ position ] ++;
```

At the time of instantiation, each element of the array is initialized with the default value of its data type. The array counts is an array of int data, so the initial value of its elements is 0. No scores have been entered yet at the time of instantiation, so the counts must be set to 0 for all the bins before starting to receive the scores. Thus, there is no need for explicit initialization.

Here is the first part of the source code, where the program receives the scores. The program declares an int array counts and instantiates it as an 11-element array (Line 8). The program asks the user to start entering numbers and enter CTRL-D to report the end of input (Lines 10 and 11). To receive input, the program uses a while-loop with keyboard.hasNext() as the continuation condition. As we saw in Chap. 11, keyboard.hasNext() returns false only when the user enters CTRL-D at the start of the input sequence. In the loop-body, the program receives a new score using keyboard.nextInt(), and then stores it in the variable score (Line 14). The program determines the index of the bin in the manner we have discussed, and then stores it in the variable position (Line 15). The program then increases counts[position] by 1 (Line 16).

```
1   import java.util.*;
2   public class ScoreDist
3   {
4     public static void main( String[] args )
5     {
6       Scanner keyboard = new Scanner( System.in );
7
8       int[] counts = new int[ 11 ];
9
10      System.out.println( "Enter scores in the range 0..100." );
11      System.out.println( "When you are done, enter CTRL-D." );
12      while ( keyboard.hasNext() )
13      {
14        int score = keyboard.nextInt();
15        int position = score / 10;
16        counts[ position ] ++;
17      }
18
```

Listing 12.1 A program for computing the distribution of scores in range 0..100 (part 1).

The program must produce two types of output from the counts thus obtained, a numerical output and a bar-histogram. In both outputs, the program uses the numbers 0, 10, ..., 90, 100 as the representatives of the bins. These representative numbers are equal to ten times the indexes to the bins. In the bar-histogram output, the program prints a horizontal line of hash marks for each bin. The lengths of the lines are equal to the counts. The histogram can be generated using a double for-loop.

```
19    System.out.println( "The histogram:" );
20    for ( int index = 0; index <= 10; index ++ )
21    {
22      System.out.printf( "%3d:%d%n", index * 10, counts[ index ] );
23    }
24
25    System.out.println( "The bar histogram:" );
26    for ( int index = 0; index <= 10; index ++ )
27    {
28      System.out.printf( "%3d:", index * 10 );
29      for ( int i = 1; i <= counts[ index ]; i ++ )
30      {
31        System.out.print( "#" );
32      }
33      System.out.println();
34    }
35  }
36 }
```

Listing 12.2 A program for computing the distribution of scores in range 0..100 (part 2).

An execution example of the code appears next:

```
1  Enter scores in the range 0..100.
2  When done, enter either CTRL-D.
3  0 11 22 33 44 55 66 77 88 99 89 97 96 95 100 79 77 75 56 51 51 68
4  The histogram:
5    0:1
6   10:1
7   20:1
8   30:1
9   40:1
10   50:4
11   60:2
12   70:4
13   80:2
14   90:4
15  100:1
16  The bar histogram:
17    0:#
18   10:#
19   20:#
20   30:#
21   40:#
22   50:####
23   60:##
24   70:####
25   80:##
26   90:####
27  100:#
```

We now change the histogram to a cumulative histogram, where the cumulative count at index i is the number of all scores satisfying `score / 10 <= i`. In other words, each score value, `score`, is counted in all the bins whose indexes are greater than or equal to `score / 10`.

We obtain the cumulative counts in an array named `cumulative` in two step. We obtain the noncumulative counts, `counts`, as before, and then, for each value of `index` between 0 and 10, calculate `cumulative[ index ]` as the total of `counts[ 0 ]`, ..., `counts[ index ]`. In this two-step calculation, we use the fact that for each value of `index` between 1 and 10, `cumulative[ index ]` is equal to `cumulative[ index - 1 ] + counts[ index ]`, and compute the cumulative counts using a series of additions as shown next. Since 0 is the smallest index value, `cumulative[ 0 ]` is equal to `counts[ 0 ]`.

```
20    cumulative[ 0 ] = counts[ 0 ];
21    for ( int index = 1; index <= 10; index ++ )
22    {
23       cumulative[ index ] = cumulative[ index - 1] + counts[ index ];
24    }
```

The next is the source code for producing a cumulative histogram. The program uses two arrays (Lines 8 and 9). The program prints the same instruction as before (Lines 11 and 12), and generates the counts in the same manner as before (Lines 13–18).

```
1   import java.util.*;
2   public class ScoreDistCumulative
3   {
4     public static void main( String[] args )
5     {
6       Scanner keyboard = new Scanner( System.in );
7
8       int[] counts = new int[ 11 ];
9       int[] cumulative = new int[ 11 ];
10
11      System.out.println( "Enter scores in the range 0..100." );
12      System.out.println( "When you are done, enter CTRL-D." );
13      while ( keyboard.hasNext() )
14      {
15        int score = keyboard.nextInt();
16        int position = score / 10;
17        counts[ position ] ++;
18      }
19
```

Listing 12.3 A program for computing a cumulative distribution (part 1).

After computing the cumulative counts, the program produces a cumulative bar-graph using the same algorithm as before (Lines 27–35).

```
20        cumulative[ 0 ] = counts[ 0 ];
21        for ( int index = 1; index <= 10; index ++ )
22        {
23           cumulative[ index ] = cumulative[ index - 1] + counts[ index ];
24        }
25
26        System.out.println( "The bar histogram:" );
27        for ( int index = 0; index <= 10; index ++ )
28        {
29          System.out.printf( "%3d:", index * 10 );
30          for ( int i = 1; i <= cumulative[ index ]; i ++ )
31          {
32             System.out.print( "#" );
33          }
34          System.out.println();
35        }
36     }
37 }
```

Listing 12.4 A program for computing a cumulative distribution (part 2).

With the same input sequence as before, the program produces the following output:

```
1  % java ScoreDistCumulative
2  Enter scores in the range 0..100.
3  When done, enter either CTRL-D.
4  34 5 6 7 88 99 100 98 80 78 67 88 98 99 87 77 61 76 38 48 95 85
5  The bar histogram:
6      0:###
7     10:###
8     20:###
9     30:#####
10    40:######
11    50:######
12    60:########
13    70:##########
14    80:###############
15    90:###################
16   100:####################
```

12.1.2.2 Simulating the Action of Throwing Two Dice

Our next example is a program for computing, by simulation, the probability distribution of the number that is "rolled" by "throwing" two fair dice. The number that is "rolled" ranges from 2 to 12. The program simulates the action of throwing two dice repeatedly, and computes the frequencies that these numbers are "rolled". At the end, the frequencies are converted to percentages. The program receives how many "rolls" must be made from the user.

The program uses a 13-element array of double data named rates to record the frequencies. For each number i between 2 and 12, the program uses rates[i] to record the number of times i is "rolled". The counts are converted to percentages using the same array, so the data type of the elements of the array are not int but double.

Here is the declaration of the array:

```
double[] rates = new double[ 13 ];
```

Previously, in Sect. 7.5, we used the formula `(int)( Math.random() * 6 ) + 1` to simulate the throw of one die. Since we use a pair of dice, we use the sum of two copies of this formula:

```
1    int pos = (int)( Math.random() * 6 ) + 1
2               + (int)( Math.random() * 6 ) + 1;
```

By combining the two occurrences of +1, we obtain:

```
1    int pos = (int)( Math.random() * 6 )
2               + (int)( Math.random() * 6 ) + 2;
```

We cannot simplify the formula further. In other words, neither

```
int pos = (int)( Math.random() * 6 + Math.random() * 6 ) + 2;
```

nor

```
int pos = (int)( Math.random() * 12 ) + 1;
```

are equivalent to the formula used in the program.

Here is a source code for the program. As mentioned earlier, the program uses a 13-element array of `double`, `rates` (Line 6). The program receives the number of times that the dice are "rolled" from the user, and stores it in the variable `rounds` (Lines 10 and 11). The program uses a for-loop to produce the required number of rolls (Line 13). At each round of the for-loop, the number generated is stored in an `int` variable, `pos` (Lines 15 and 16). The value of `pos` is between 2 and 12. The program increases `rates[ pos ]` by 1.

```
1    import java.util.*;
2    public class TwoDice
3    {
4      public static void main( String[] args )
5      {
6        double[] rates = new double[ 13 ];
7
8        Scanner keyboard = new Scanner( System.in );
9
10       System.out.print( "Enter the no. of trials: " );
11       int rounds = keyboard.nextInt();
12
13       for ( int i = 1; i <= rounds; i ++ )
14       {
15         int pos = (int)( Math.random() * 6 )
16                    + (int)( Math.random() * 6 ) + 2;
17         rates[ pos ] ++;
18       }
19
```

Listing 12.5 A program that simulated the action of throwing two dice (part 1).

After finishing the simulation, the program converts the counts to percentages. The program accomplishes this by multiplying each count by 100 and then dividing it by rounds (Lines 20–23). Since the data type of the elements of the array is double, the value of rates[pos] * 100 is already double, so although rounds is an int value, the division is correctly calculated. To print the percentage values (Lines 25–28), the program uses the printf format of %2d:%6.2f%%n, where the %% instructs to print the percent sign. Since the numbers that are "rolled" are between 2 and 12, the iterations in the for-loops (Lines 20 and 25) start from 2, ignoring the indexes 0 and 1. In fact, the first two elements rates[0] and rates[1] exist, but are not accessed at all.

```
20        for ( int pos = 2; pos <= 12; pos ++ )
21        {
22          rates[ pos ] = rates[ pos ] * 100 / rounds;
23        }
24
25        for ( int pos = 2; pos <= 12; pos ++ )
26        {
27          System.out.printf( "%2d:%6.2f%%%n", pos, rates[ pos ] );
28        }
29      }
30 }
```

Listing 12.6 A program that simulated the action of throwing two dice (part 2).

Here is the result of running the program with 10,000 throws:

```
1  Enter the no. of trials: 10000
2   2:   2.83%
3   3:   5.43%
4   4:   8.13%
5   5: 11.25%
6   6: 14.11%
7   7: 16.90%
8   8: 13.67%
9   9: 10.82%
10 10:   8.56%
11 11:   5.41%
12 12:   2.89%
```

Here is the result of running the program with one million throws:

```
1  Enter the no. of trials: 1000000
2   2:   2.77%
3   3:   5.54%
4   4:   8.36%
5   5: 11.07%
6   6: 13.88%
7   7: 16.63%
8   8: 13.90%
9   9: 11.17%
10 10:   8.33%
11 11:   5.56%
12 12:   2.78%
```

12.1.2.3 Initialization of an Array

As mentioned earlier, when an array of some type T is instantiated, the initial value of each element of the array is the default value for the type T. Specifically, the initial value is 0 for each number type, the character with index 0 for char (often denoted as \0), false for boolean, and null for all other types. The value null is printed as the String literal "null" when processed with System.out.print, printf, or println. null is not an object, so no instance method can be applied to it. For example, the code

```
1   String[] data = new String[ 10 ];
2   System.out.println( data[ 0 ].length() );
```

produces a run-time error NullPointerException at the second line.

12.1.3 ArrayIndexOutOfBoundsException

An attempt to access an element of an array using an invalid index leads to a run-time error ArrayIndexOutOfBoundsException.

Suppose we have a program that receives a series of String values from the user, stores the elements of the series in an array, and then interactively recalls an element of the data at the index the user specifies. The interaction with the user is repeated using a do-while loop that is terminated when the user enters a negative index for a query. The elements of the series may contain the white space character, so the program uses nextLine to read the elements of the series. While any negative value is interpreted as the signal for termination, the program treats any nonnegative value as a valid index. Given such a program, the user may enter a large index value to make ArrayIndexOutOfBoundsException occur.

A source code for this program is shown next. The programs asks for the number of elements in the series at the start (Line 8). To receive an integer input from the user, we have exclusively used nextInt in the past. However, now that the elements of the array are to be read using nextLine, it is a good idea to read every input with nextLine. Unfortunately, there is no Scanner method that reads an input line, coverts it to an integer, and returns the integer. Fortunately, we can use the method Integer.parseInt for converting a String data to an integer. Integer.parseInt is a static method of class Integer. If the String does not represent an integer, for example, "#$%", the method produces a run-time error and the execution halts at that point. The program uses Integer.parseInt to convert the input line to an integer, and stores the value in an int variable, dim (Line 9).

The program then runs as follows: The program instantiates data as an array of String data having length dim (Line 11). The program then uses a for-loop that iterates the sequence 0, ..., dim - 1 using a variable named index, and receives the elements of the array, where each element is read with nextLine (Lines 14–18). In the do-while loop (Lines 19–27), the program receives an index to an element to recall (Lines 21–22), and if the index is nonnegative (Line 23), prints the data stored at the index (Line 25). The continuation condition of the do-while loop is index >= 0, so the loop terminates when index < 0.

```
1   import java.util.*;
2
3   public class StringArrayPlain
4   {
5     public static void main( String[] args )
6     {
7       Scanner keyboard = new Scanner( System.in );
8       System.out.print( "Enter the no. of data: " );
9       int dim = Integer.parseInt( keyboard.nextLine() );
10
11      String[] data = new String[ dim ];
12
13      int index;
14      for ( index = 0; index < dim; index ++ )
15      {
16        System.out.printf( "Enter line at position %d: ", index );
17        data[ index ] = keyboard.nextLine();
18      }
19      do
20      {
21        System.out.print( "Enter position (negative to quit): " );
22        index = Integer.parseInt( keyboard.nextLine() );
23        if ( index >= 0 )
24        {
25          System.out.printf( "At %d we have %s%n", index, data[ index ] );
26        }
27      } while ( index >= 0 );
28    }
29  }
```

Listing 12.7 A program that builds an array of String data and then presents its contents.

In the following execution example, the user enters a non-existing index 9 for a 9-element array, thereby makes ArrayIndexOutOfBoundsException occur.

```
1   Enter the no. of data: 9
2   Enter line at position 0: Tomato
3   Enter line at position 1: Green Pepper
4   Enter line at position 2: Lettuce
5   Enter line at position 3: Pickle
6   Enter line at position 4: Black Olive
7   Enter line at position 5: Jalapeno Pepper
8   Enter line at position 6: Honey Mustard
9   Enter line at position 7: Mayonnaise
10  Enter line at position 8: Hot Sauce
11  Enter position (negative to quit): 0
12  The value at 0 is Tomato
13  Enter position (negative to quit): 2
14  The value at 2 is Lettuce
15  Enter position (negative to quit): 3
16  The value at 3 is Pickle
17  Enter position (negative to quit): 9
18  Exception in thread "main" java.lang.ArrayIndexOutOfBoundsException: 9
19     at StringArrayPlain.main(ArrayDataPlain.java:23)
```

The run-time error ArrayIndexOutOfBounds can be prevented from happening by changing the condition in Line 23 to if (index >= 0 && index < dim).

12.2 Relative Indexing

12.2.1 The Concept of Relative Indexing

The program that simulates the "rolls" of two dice, uses an array consisting of 13 slots, ignoring the first two slots. The code that appears next is an alternate one that uses an array of exactly 11 slots. In the program, we think of a slot index i as representing i + 2 as the number that is "rolled". The changes from the previous program are highlighted. They are:

- The length of the array has been changed to 11 (Line 6).
- The + 2 in the formula for determining the number that is "rolled" has been removed, since 2 was to be subtracted from the number generated by the formula (Lines 15 and 16).
- The range of index has been changed to 0, ..., 10 in the for-loops (Lines 20 and 25).
- The number represented by the index value pos has been changed to pos + 2 (Line 27).

```
1   import java.util.*;
2   public class TwoDiceExact
3   {
4     public static void main( String[] args )
5     {
6       double[] rates = new double[ 11 ];
7
8       Scanner keyboard = new Scanner( System.in );
9
10      System.out.print( "Enter the no. of trials: " );
11      int rounds = keyboard.nextInt();
12
13      for ( int i = 1; i <= rounds; i ++ )
14      {
15        int pos = (int)( Math.random() * 6 )
16                + (int)( Math.random() * 6 );
17        rates[ pos ] ++;
18      }
19
20      for ( int pos = 0; pos <= 10; pos ++ )
21      {
22        rates[ pos ] = rates[ pos ] * 100 / rounds;
23      }
24
25      for ( int pos = 0; pos <= 10; pos ++ )
26      {
27        System.out.printf( "%2d:%6.2f%%%n", pos + 2, rates[ pos ] );
28      }
29    }
30  }
```

Listing 12.8 A program for simulating the action of throwing two dice that uses an array of eleven elements.

The idea we used can be summarized as: *use the relative distance from a fixed number as an array index.* We call this idea **relative indexing**. To obtain a relative index from a given index, we subtract a fixed number, called the **base index**. In the above simulation, the base index is 2. Relative indexing allows programmers to avoid using slots that are not part of the computation.

12.2.2 Calculating the BMI for a Range of Weight Values

Consider computing the BMI value for a fixed height (in inches) and a range of integer weight values (in pounds), where the range is specified with its minimum and maximum. Suppose the minimum and the maximum are stored in `int` variables, `minWeight` and `maxWeight`. Since the weight values are integers, we can use an array of `double` data with `maxWeight + 1` elements, and use only the elements of array at indexes between `minWeight` and `maxWeight`. With the use of relative indexing, the array length can be reduced to `maxWeight - minWeight + 1`, where the element at an index i represents the BMI for the weight `minWeight + i`.

The following program uses this relative indexing. The program receives the minimum and maximum weights from the user, and stores them in variables, `minWeight` and `maxWeight` (Line 8 and 9). The program receives the height from the user and stores it in a variable, `height` (Line 10). The program uses `minWeight` as the base index. The size of the range of weights, `maxWeight - minWeight + 1`, is stored in an `int` variable, `size` (Line 11). The program instantiates an array of `double` data, `bmi` (Line 12). Then, for each index value i between 0 and `size - 1` (Line 13), the program stores the BMI value for the height equal to `height` and the weight equal to `minWeight + i` in `bmi[ i ]` (Line 15). At the end, the program prints the BMI values thus calculated along with their weights (Lines 17–20).

```
1   import java.util.*;
2   public class BMIFixedHeight
3   {
4     public static void main( String[] args )
5     {
6       Scanner keyboard = new Scanner( System.in );
7       System.out.print( "Minimum weight, maximum weight, height: " );
8       int minWeight = keyboard.nextInt();
9       int maxWeight = keyboard.nextInt();
10      double height = keyboard.nextDouble();
11      int size = maxWeight - minWeight + 1;
12      double[] bmi = new double[ size ];
13      for ( int i = 0; i < size; i ++ )
14      {
15        bmi[ i ] = 703.0 * ( minWeight + i ) / height / height;
16      }
17      for ( int i = 0; i < size; i ++ )
18      {
19        System.out.printf( "%3d:%5.2f%n", ( minWeight + i ), bmi[ i ] );
20      }
21    }
22  }
```

Listing 12.9 A program that computes the BMI value for a range of weights.

Here is an execution example of the code.

```
1   Minimum weight, maximum weight, height: 155 167 67
2   155:24.27
3   156:24.43
4   157:24.59
5   158:24.74
6   159:24.90
7   160:25.06
```

```
 8   161:25.21
 9   162:25.37
10   163:25.53
11   164:25.68
12   165:25.84
13   166:26.00
14   167:26.15
```

12.2.3 Counting the Occurrences of Characters

Next, consider computing the number of times each letter of the alphabet appears in an input line, after converting each uppercase letter to lowercase. The program receives an input line from the user, and then converts it to all lowercase with the method `toLowerCase()`. Since there are 26 letters in the lowercase alphabet, the program uses a 26-element `int` array, `count`, for counting the occurrences of the letters, where the elements $0, \dots, 25$ correspond to the letters `'a'`, ..., `'z'`. In the ASCII table, the 26 letters occupy consecutive positions starting from 97, so subtracting 97 from a lowercase letter produces its position in the array `count`, and adding 97 to an index value produces the position of the corresponding letter in the ASCII table. The number 97 can be substituted with the letter `'a'` wherever needed.

The program receives an input from the user, stores it in a variable named `line` (Line 8), and then generates its lowercase version, `lineLower` (Line 9).

```
 1   import java.util.*;
 2   public class LetterCount
 3   {
 4     public static void main( String[] args )
 5     {
 6       Scanner keyboard = new Scanner( System.in );
 7       System.out.print( "Enter: " );
 8       String line = keyboard.nextLine();
 9       String lineLower = line.toLowerCase();
10
```

Listing 12.10 A program that counts the occurrences of letters (part 1). The part responsible for receiving input.

The program then instantiates an array of 26 elements, `count` (Line 11). The program uses a for-loop to examine the characters of `lineLower` (Line 12). The program stores the character being examined in a `char` variable named `c` (Line 14). The program then obtains the relative index of `c` in a variable named `index` by subtracting `'a'` from `c` (Line 15). If `c` is a lowercase letter, then the value of `index` must be between 0 and 25. The program checks if the value of `index` is between 0 and 25 (Line 16) and if so, increases `count[ index ]` by 1 (Line 18).

```
11       int[] count = new int[ 26 ];
12       for ( int pos = 0; pos <= lineLower.length() - 1; pos ++ )
13       {
14         char c = lineLower.charAt( pos );
15         int index = c - 'a';
16         if ( index >= 0 && index <= 25 )
17         {
18           count[ index ] ++;
19         }
20       }
21
```

Listing 12.11 A program that counts the occurrences of letters (part 2). The part responsible for generating counts.

To present the result, the program prints the input line (Line 22), the lowercase version (Line 23), and a header line (Line 24). The program then uses a for-loop that iterates over the sequence $0, \ldots, 25$ with a variable named `index` (Line 25). The character represented by `index` is obtained by converting the relative index to its absolute index with the addition of a ', and then casting of `(char)` on the absolute index. In other words, `(char)( 'a' + index )` produces the letter (Line 28). The count corresponding to the letter is `count[ index ]` (Line 28). The program prints the letter and the count using `printf` with the format of `"%6c: %2d%n"` (Line 27). The format instructs to allocate six character spaces to the letter and two character spaces to the count.

```
22       System.out.printf( "Input: %s%n", line );
23       System.out.printf( "Lower: %s%n", lineLower );
24       System.out.println( "Letter:count" );
25       for ( int index = 0; index <= 25; index ++ )
26       {
27         System.out.printf( "%6c: %2d%n",
28             (char)( 'a' + index ), count[ index ] );
29       }
30     }
31 }
```

Listing 12.12 A program that counts the occurrences of letters (part 3). The part responsible for printing the result.

Next is an execution example of the code:

```
1 Enter: I can write programs in Java.  I want to learn more.
2 Input: I can write programs in Java.  I want to learn more.
3 Lower: i can write programs in java.  i want to learn more.
```

```
4   Letter:count
5          a:   6
6          b:   0
7          c:   1
8          d:   0
9          e:   3
10         f:   0
11         g:   1
12         h:   0
13         i:   4
14         j:   1
15         k:   0
16         l:   1
17         m:   2
18         n:   4
19         o:   3
20         p:   1
21         q:   0
22         r:   5
23         s:   1
24         t:   3
25         u:   0
26         v:   1
27         w:   2
28         x:   0
29         y:   0
30         z:   0
```

In this example, since the input line is short, several letters have 0 as their counts. Since each letter-count pair does not require more than 12 character spaces, we can expect to be able to reduce the number of output lines by skipping letters whose counts are 0 and by printing multiple letter-count pairs in each line of output.

The program LetterCountNeat prints the result using this idea. Both LetterCount and LetterCountNeat have the same code for receiving the input and generating counts (except for the class declaration), so only the remaining part of the program for LetterCountNeat is presented here.

LetterCountNeat prints up to four letter-count pairs in one line. The header for the letter-count output has been revised to:

"Letter:count Letter:count Letter:count Letter:count"

(Lines 24 and 25). To emphasize that a count is associated with the letter it is printed together, the format for the count has been changed to %-6d. This means that the number will be printed immediate after the colon.

To print multiple letter-count pairs while ignoring letters that did not appear, the program uses a new int variable named p. The variable p represents the number of letter-count pairs that have been printed so far. We scan the elements, as before, using the variable index. Each time a letter with a positive count is encountered, the program takes the following action: (a) it prints the letter-count pair, (b) it increases p by 1, and (c) if the value of p is a multiple of 4, it prints the newline. Furthermore, to ensure that the output of the program ends with a newline, if the value of p is not a multiple of 4 after exiting the loop, the program prints the newline.

The next code implements this idea. Line 29 is for checking if the count is positive, Lines 31 and 32 are for printing the letter-count pair, Line 33 is for increasing the value of p, and Lines 34–37 are for adding the newline after printing four pairs. Lines 40–43 handle the last newline.

```
22        System.out.printf( "Input: %s%n", line );
23        System.out.printf( "Lower: %s%n", lineLower );
24        System.out.println(
25            "Letter:count Letter:count Letter:count Letter:count" );
26        int p = 0;
27        for ( int index = 0; index <= 25; index ++ )
28        {
29          if ( count[ index ] > 0 )
30          {
31            System.out.printf( "%6c:%-6d",
32                (char)( 'a' + index ), count[ index ] );
33            p ++;
34            if ( p % 4 == 0 )
35            {
36              System.out.println();
37            }
38          }
39        }
40        if ( p % 4 != 0 )
41        {
42          System.out.println();
43        }
44      }
45 }
```

Listing 12.13 A new version of the program that counts the occurrences of letters.

The output of the new program with the same input as before is shown next:

```
1  Enter: I can write programs in Java.  I want to learn more.
2  Input: I can write programs in Java.  I want to learn more.
3  Lower: i can write programs in java.  i want to learn more.
4  Letter:count Letter:count Letter:count Letter:count
5      a:6         c:1         e:3         g:1
6      i:4         j:1         l:1         m:2
7      n:4         o:3         p:1         r:5
8      s:1         t:3         v:1         w:2
```

Here is the output with another input:

```
1  Enter: Old MacDonald Had a Farm
2  Input: Old MacDonald Had a Farm
3  Lower: old macdonald had a farm
4  Letter:count Letter:count Letter:count Letter:count
5      a:5         c:1         d:4         f:1
6      h:1         l:2         m:2         n:1
7      o:2         r:1
```

12.3   Arrays of `boolean` Data

We often use a `boolean` variable as a check mark and an array of `boolean` data as a series of check marks. Here, we study the use of an array of `boolean` data using a source code for a program that finds prime numbers.

A non-zero integer m is a **divisor** of another integer n if the remainder of n divided by m is 0. If m is a divisor of n, we say that n is **divisible** by m. A positive integer $n \geq 2$ is a **prime number** (or simply a **prime**) if 1 and n are the only positive divisors of n. In other words, n is prime if and only if for all m, $2 \leq m \leq n - 1$, the remainder of n divided by m is 0. An integer $n \geq 2$ that is not a prime number is called a **composite number**. The 16 smallest prime numbers are as follows:

$$2, 3, 5, 7, 11, 13, 17, 19, 23, 29, 31, 33, 37, 41, 43, 47$$

It is known that there are infinitely many prime numbers.

Every positive integer $n \geq 2$ can be expressed as the product of prime numbers, where the same prime number may appear multiple times. This decomposition is unique, if the order of appearance of the prime numbers is ignored. For example, 100 is the product of prime numbers 2, 2, 5, and 5. The primality of a number $n \geq 3$ thus can be tested by examining if any prime number less than n divides n. In other words,

($\star$) a positive number $n \geq 3$ is a prime number if and only if no prime number p between 2 and $n - 1$ divides n.

Consider discovering, given some maximum number, limit, all the prime numbers between 2 and limit. The property ($\star$) suggests the following algorithm: Repeat (a) and (b) for all values of n starting with 2 and ending with limit:

(a) Using a loop, test if n is divisible by any prime number less than n.
(b) If n is divisible by a prime number less than n, record n as composite; otherwise, record n as prime.

We implement this algorithm using an array of boolean values, flags. flags has limit + 1 elements. At the end of the calculation, we establish a condition: for each index i >= 2, flags[i] is true if and only if i is prime.

There are multiple ways to implement the determination of a primality of n by testing if any smaller prime number divides n (such a strategy is called **trial division**). Here is a simple one. We tentatively store true to flags[n]. We then execute trial divisions by the primes between 2 and n - 1. If one of the primes in that range is found to be a divisor of n, we change the value of flags[n] to false. The idea can be encoded as follows:

```
1        flags[ n ] = true;
2        for ( int m = 2; m <= n - 1; m ++ )
3        {
4            if ( flags[ m ] && n % m == 0 )
5            {
6                flags[ n ] = false;
7            }
8        }
```

Since the value of flags[n] does not change from false to true, the loop can be terminated as soon as the value changes to false:

```
1        flags [ n ] = true;
2        for ( int m = 2; m <= n - 1; m ++ )
3        {
4          if ( flags [ m ] && n % m == 0 )
5          {
6            flags [ n ] = false;
7            break;
8          }
9        }
```

If break is executed, the final value of m is strictly less than n; otherwise, the final value of m is equal to n. Thus, the value of flags [n] is equivalent to the condition m < n.

```
1        for ( int m = 2; m <= n - 1; m ++ )
2        {
3          if ( flags [ m ] && n % m == 0 )
4          {
5            break;
6          }
7        }
8        flags [ n ] = m == n;
```

Using a while-loop, this can be written as:

```
1        int m = 2;
2        while ( m <= n - 1 && !( flags [ m ] && n % m == 0 ) )
3        {
4          m ++;
5        }
6        flags [ n ] = m == n;
```

Because of the truncation rule in conditional evaluation (see Sect. 6.2.4), the second term ! (flags [m] && n % m == 0) is evaluated only if m < n. By using DeMorgan's laws, we obtain:

```
1        int m = 2;
2        while ( m <= n - 1 && ( !flags [ m ] || n % m != 0 ) )
3        {
4          m ++;
5        }
6        flags [ n ] = m == n;
```

This is the version that is used in the next program PrimeFinding.

The first part of the code executes the trial division algorithm as we have developed. The program receives the value of limit from the user (Lines 7 and 8), instantiates the array flags as boolean[limit + 1] (Line 10). Lines 11–19 are for determining the elements of flags. When the value of n is equal to 2, no trivial division is made. Since the initial value of the array elements is true and 2 is a prime number, the programs works when n is equal to 2.

To print the prime numbers that have been discovered, the program uses the idea from LetterCountNeat. This time, the program prints each prime number with its position (represented by p) (Line 30). The primes appear in increasing order.

```
1   import java.util.*;
2   public class PrimeFinding
3   {
4     public static void main( String[] args )
5     {
6       Scanner keyboard = new Scanner( System.in );
7       System.out.print( "Enter limit: " );
8       int limit = keyboard.nextInt();
9         //---- prime discovery
10      boolean[] flags = new boolean[ limit + 1 ];
11      for ( int n = 2; n <= limit; n ++ )
12      {
13        int m = 2;
14        while ( m < n && ( !flags[ m ] || n % m != 0 ) )
15        {
16          m ++;
17        }
18        flags[ n ] = m == n;
19      }
20        //---- inventory
21      int p = 0;
22      for ( int n = 2; n <= limit; n ++ )
23      {
24        if ( flags[ n ] )
25        {
26          p ++;
27          System.out.printf( "%5d:%-8d", p, n );
28          if ( p % 4 == 0 )
29          {
30            System.out.println();
31          }
32        }
33      }
34      if ( p % 4 != 0 )
35      {
36        System.out.println();
37      }
38    }
39  }
```

Listing 12.14 A program that finds all prime numbers less than or equal to a given bound.

Here is an execution example of the code:

```
Enter limit: 1000
    1:2          2:3          3:5          4:7
    5:11         6:13         7:17         8:19
    9:23        10:29        11:31        12:37
   13:41        14:43        15:47        16:53
   17:59        18:61        19:67        20:71
   21:73        22:79        23:83        24:89
   25:97        26:101       27:103       28:107
   29:109       30:113       31:127       32:131
   33:137       34:139       35:149       36:151
   37:157       38:163       39:167       40:173
   41:179       42:181       43:191       44:193
   45:197       46:199       47:211       48:223
   49:227       50:229       51:233       52:239
```

15	53:241	54:251	55:257	56:263
16	57:269	58:271	59:277	60:281
17	61:283	62:293	63:307	64:311
18	65:313	66:317	67:331	68:337
19	69:347	70:349	71:353	72:359
20	73:367	74:373	75:379	76:383
21	77:389	78:397	79:401	80:409
22	81:419	82:421	83:431	84:433
23	85:439	86:443	87:449	88:457
24	89:461	90:463	91:467	92:479
25	93:487	94:491	95:499	96:503
26	97:509	98:521	99:523	100:541
27	101:547	102:557	103:563	104:569
28	105:571	106:577	107:587	108:593
29	109:599	110:601	111:607	112:613
30	113:617	114:619	115:631	116:641
31	117:643	118:647	119:653	120:659
32	121:661	122:673	123:677	124:683
33	125:691	126:701	127:709	128:719
34	129:727	130:733	131:739	132:743
35	133:751	134:757	135:761	136:769
36	137:773	138:787	139:797	140:809
37	141:811	142:821	143:823	144:827
38	145:829	146:839	147:853	148:857
39	149:859	150:863	151:877	152:881
40	153:883	154:887	155:907	156:911
41	157:919	158:929	159:937	160:941
42	161:947	162:953	163:967	164:971
43	165:977	166:983	167:991	168:997

12.4   Using Multiple Arrays

We often use multiple arrays having the same lengths to manipulate a sequence of elements, where each element consists of multiple data.

Consider writing a program that receives names (as String data) and scores (as double data) for some number of people. The user specifies the number of people, and then, for each person, enters the name and the score. The program records the names and scores, and retrieves them upon user's request. For retrieval, the user specifies a range of scores with its lower and upper bounds. The program then finds all the scores that are in the range, and then prints the scores with their associated names.

The program NameScore accomplishes this task. The initial part declares some variables that are used throughout the program. num is the number of people to appear on the list (Line 10), names and scores are the arrays to record the names and the scores (Lines 7 and 8). flags represents which persons' scores are in the range specified by the user (Line 9). Each time the user specifies a range of scores, the elements of flags are recalculated as follows: for each index i, true is stored in flags [i] if the value of scores [i] is in the specified range, and false is stored otherwise.

```
1   import java.util.*;
2   public class NameScore
3   {
4     public static void main( String[] args )
5     {
6       Scanner keyboard = new Scanner( System.in );
7       String[] names;
8       double[] scores;
9       boolean[] flags;
10      int num;
11
```

Listing 12.15 A program that receives names and scores and performs search (part 1).

Next, the program receives the number of people to appear on the list, and then stores the number in num (Lines 12 and 13). num is then used to instantiate the length for each of the three array instantiations (Lines 14–16). Then, using a for-loop, the program receives the names and the scores from the user (Lines 18–23).

```
12      System.out.print( "Enter the number of people: " );
13      num = keyboard.nextInt();
14      names = new String[ num ];
15      scores = new double[ num ];
16      flags = new boolean[ num ];
17
18      for ( int i = 0; i < num; i ++ )
19      {
20        System.out.printf( "Enter name and score for person %d: ", i );
21        names[ i ] = keyboard.next();
22        scores[ i ] = keyboard.nextDouble();
23      }
24
```

Listing 12.16 A program that receives names and scores and performs search (part 2).

The interaction for retrieval uses a `String` variable named `answer` (Line 25). The interaction is repeated indefinitely using a do-while loop (Line 26). At the end of the loop-body, the user is asked to respond to the question of whether or not the program should continue (Line 50). The response is stored in a `String` variable named `answer` (Line 51). If the response does not start with `'y'`, the loop is terminated (Line 52).

To retrieve scores, the program receives two `double` values from the user, and stores them in `double` variables, `low` and `high` (Lines 27–29). The program uses a variable named `count` to record the number of scores that have passed the test (Line 31). The program uses a for-loop that iterates over the sequence of valid index values with a variable named `i` (Line 32). For each index value of `i`, the program stores the value of (`scores[ i ] >= low && scores[ i ] <= high`) in `flags[ i ]` (Line 34), and then, if the value obtained is `true` (Line 35), increases the value of `count` by 1 (Line 37). The program announces the value of `count` after completing the recalculation of the elements in `flags` (Line 40). To report which scores are in the range, the program uses a for-loop again with the iteration variable `i` (Line 42). If `flags[ i ]` has the value of `true` (Line 44), the program prints `i`, `names[ i ]`, and `scores[ i ]` in one line using the format `"%3d %10s %6.2f%n"`. This means that three character spaces are allocated for `i`, ten character spaces are allocated for names [i], and six character spaces with exactly two digits after the decimal point are allocated for scores [i].

```
25        String answer;
26        do {
27          System.out.print( "Enter the lower and upper limits: " );
28          double low = keyboard.nextDouble();
29          double high = keyboard.nextDouble();
30
31          int count = 0;
32          for ( int i = 0; i < num; i ++ )
33          {
34            flags[ i ] = ( scores[ i ] >= low && scores[ i ] <= high );
35            if ( flags[ i ] )
36            {
37              count ++;
38            }
39          }
40          System.out.println( "The count is " + count + "." );
41
42          for ( int i = 0; i < num; i ++ )
43          {
44            if ( flags[ i ] )
45            {
46              System.out.printf( "%3d %10s %6.2f%n",
47                  i, names[ i ], scores[ i ] );
48            }
49          }
50          System.out.print( "Continue (y/n)? " );
51          answer = keyboard.next();
52        } while ( answer.startsWith( "y" ) );
53      }
```

Listing 12.17 A program that receives names and scores and performs search (part 3).

Here is an example of how the program works:

```
1   Enter the number of people: 15
2   Enter name and score for person 0: Anna 80.0
3   Enter name and score for person 1: Bill 90.5
4   Enter name and score for person 2: Christy 97.5
5   Enter name and score for person 3: Dave 79.5
6   Enter name and score for person 4: Emily 81.0
7   Enter name and score for person 5: Fred 86.0
8   Enter name and score for person 6: Gail 95.0
9   Enter name and score for person 7: Harry 92.5
10  Enter name and score for person 8: Irene 98.0
11  Enter name and score for person 9: Jack 99.0
12  Enter name and score for person 10: Kim 93.5
13  Enter name and score for person 11: Luis 74.5
14  Enter name and score for person 12: Mimi 76.0
15  Enter name and score for person 13: Nick 77.0
16  Enter name and score for person 14: Olga 84.5
17  Enter the lower and upper limits: 0 100
18  The count is 15.
19     0       Anna  80.00
20     1       Bill  90.50
21     2    Christy  97.50
22     3       Dave  79.50
```

```
23  │    4         Emily   81.00
24  │    5          Fred   86.00
25  │    6          Gail   95.00
26  │    7         Harry   92.50
27  │    8         Irene   98.00
28  │    9          Jack   99.00
29  │   10           Kim   93.50
30  │   11          Luis   74.50
31  │   12          Mimi   76.00
32  │   13          Nick   77.00
33  │   14          Olga   84.50
34  │ Continue (y/n)? y
35  │ Enter the lower and upper limits: 0 50
36  │ The count is 0.
37  │ Continue (y/n)? y
38  │ Enter the lower and upper limits: 70 80
39  │ The count is 5.
40  │    0          Anna   80.00
41  │    3          Dave   79.50
42  │   11          Luis   74.50
43  │   12          Mimi   76.00
44  │   13          Nick   77.00
45  │ Continue (y/n)? n
```

12.5   String Methods That Return an Array

In Chap. 9, we mentioned two String methods that each return an array, toCharArray and split. For a String data w, the method call w.toCharArray() returns an array of char that is equal to the character-by-character representation of w. The method split receives a String parameter p. For a String data w and a String parameter p, the method call w.split(p) returns an array of String generated by splitting w by viewing p as the delimiter. For example, suppose w is equal to the String literal "-ab:cd::ef-". The return value of w.toCharArray() is an 11-element array:

```
{ '-', 'a', 'b', ':', 'c', 'd', ':', ':', 'e', 'f', '-' }
```

The return value of w.split("::") is a 2-element array:

```
{ "-ab:cd", "ef-" }
```

The return value of w.split(":") is a 4-element array:

```
{ "-ab", "cd", "", "ef-" }
```

and the return value of w.split("-") is a 3-element array:

```
{ "", "-ab:cd::ef-", "" }
```

We can use the method split when multiple data values appear in one line and the values are separated with some common delimiter. Suppose we need to convert a String data line into an int array, assuming that line consists of some integer values separated by tab-stops in between (for example, "10\t20\t30"). One approach to solving this problem is to read line twice using Scanner as follows:

```
1    Scanner sc = new Scanner( line );
2    int count = 0;
3    while ( sc.hasNext() )
4    {
5       count ++;
6       sc.next();
7    }
8    int[] data = new int[ count ];
9    Scanner sc = new Scanner( line );
10   for ( int i = 0; i < count; i ++ )
11   {
12      data[ i ] = sc.nextInt();
13   }
```

Since the tokens are separated by tab-stops, split can be used as follows:

```
1    String[] tokens = line.split( "\t" );
2    int[] data = new int[ tokens.length ];
3    for ( int i = 0; i < tokens.length; i ++ )
4    {
5       data[ i ] = Integer.parseInt( tokens[ i ] );
6    }
```

Summary

- An array is a series of data of some common data type.
- The declaration of an array type requires an empty pair of matching brackets at the end, such as int[] and String[].
- An array data type is an object data type, so requires an instantiation.
- The instantiation of an array requires the specification of the number of elements in the series that it represents. The number is provided in a pair of brackets after he type of the individual elements, such as new int[10].
- The value of the length specified in an instantiation must be nonnegative.
- For an array x, x.length returns the number of elements in x.
- An individual element in an array can be accessed by combining the name of the array and its index in the form: name[index].
- When a program tries to access an element of an array at an invalid index, an run-time error ArrayIndexOutOfBoundsException occurs.
- Relative indexing is a concept that represents the absolute index with the combination of the base index and the distance from the base index.

Exercises

1. **Simple questions about an array** Suppose an array dataValues has been constructed using the following code fragment:

```
1    int[] dataValues = new int[20];
2    for ( int index = 0; index < 20; index ++ )
3    {
4       dataValues[ index ] = index + 1;
5    }
```

State the value of each of the following after the execution of the code:

(a) dataValues.length

(b) dataValues[10]

(c) dataValues[15] - dataValues[5]

2. **An array of random numbers with no duplication** Write a program, RandomNumberArray, that generates a random array of int data whose length, size, is specified by the user. The elements in the array must satisfy the following conditions:

- The range of the array elements is 0 through 10 * size - 1.
- No two elements in the array are equal to each other.

The task can be accomplished by a series of, possibly repetitive, random number generation. To generate a random number at index i, the program generates a candidate according the first rule, and then checks whether the same number appears in any positions between 0 and i - 1. If the number already appears, the program generates a new random number. It repeats this process until a random number not appearing in positions 0 through i - 1 is generated.

Here is an execution example of the intended program:

```
1   Enter the size: 0:109
2   1:100
3   2:23
4   3:57
5   4:123
6   5:22
7   6:137
8   7:120
9   8:1
10  9:60
11  10:146
12  11:68
13  12:8
14  13:52
15  14:96
```

3. **The second maximum in an array** Write a program, SecondMaximum, that receives a positive integer from the user, generates an array of random real numbers between 0 and 10,000, whose length is equal to the integer that the user has entered, and then computes the second largest number appearing in the array. The program may fail to work properly if the number that the user enters is less than or equal to 0. If the number that the user enters is 1, the second largest number is undefined, but the program must report the only element of the array as the second largest number.

4. **Random string** Write a program, RandomString, that receives a positive integer from the user, and then generates a String of random characters whose length is equal to the integer that the user has specified. The program must use table look-up in the following manner. The program instantiates a 26-element array of char values whose elements are 'a' through 'z'. It then creates a random String data of the specified length by selecting, for each character position of the String, a random position between 0 and 25, and then appending the element in the table at that random position to the String being generated.

Here is an execution example of the program:

```
1   Enter the length: 20
2   ylufdstaeldwbyvotdph
```

5. **The standard deviation of elements in an array** The standard deviation of a series of numbers, $a_1, \cdots, a_n$, is given by the following formula:

$$\sqrt{\frac{\sum_{i=1}^{n}(a_i - \text{the average})^2}{n-1}}$$

Write a program, StdDev that generates an array of random real numbers greater than or equal to 0 and less than 10,000, and then computes the standard deviation of the elements in the array. The user specifies the length of the array. Since the formula has $n-1$ in the denominator, the length of the array must be greater than or equal to 2. To obtain an integer greater than or equal to 2, the program keeps asking the user to enter a value for the length until the value entered is greater than or equal to 2. After the calculation, the program must print the elements in the array, the average, and the standard deviation. Each real number, when printed, must be formatted by allocating four character spaces before the decimal point and ten digits after the decimal point.

The following is an execution example of the program:

```
1    Enter the length: 1
2    Enter the length: 0
3    Enter the length: 10
4       0: 8695.0374293399
5       1: 4425.0711045508
6       2:  187.4407268688
7       3: 6606.5239258968
8       4: 8713.3827987525
9       5: 1437.1711093935
10      6: 2549.7630539290
11      7: 7171.4009860844
12      8: 6077.1461415774
13      9: 7729.9647709803
14   average = 5359.2902047373
15   stddev = 3059.5779033118
```

6. **Counting decimals**   Write a program, CountDecimals, that receives an indefinite number of tokens from the user, and then, in the series of tokens, computes the number of occurrences of each decimal. The program must report the count of each decimal on the screen at the end.

The program may work as follows:

```
1    > CSC120
2    > CSC220
3    > BIL169H
4    > ECO101
5    > 0: 3
6    1: 4
7    2: 3
8    3: 0
9    4: 0
10   5: 0
11   6: 1
12   7: 0
13   8: 0
14   9: 1
```

The ' > ' appearing at the start of the first four lines is the prompt.

7. **Modification to the prime number finding problem**   The prime number discovery program we discussed in this chapter prints all the primes it has discovered. Write a new version, PrimeFindingNew, where the program produces an array of int data consisting of the prime numbers that have been discovered, and then prints the elements in the array.

One way to generate such an array is to collect all the indexes at which the elements of `flags` are `true`. To accomplish this, the program may scan the `flags` to obtain the number of times `true` appears as an element. This is the length of the array to be returned. After that, the program can instantiate an array of `int` data whose length is equal to the count that just has been obtained. Then, the program stores in the array the indexes at which the elements of `flags` are `true`.

8. **toCharArray** Write a program, `MyToCharArray`, that receives an input line from the user, converts it to an array of `char` values, and prints the elements in the array. The program must generate the output with six elements per line with three character spaces allocated to the indexes and one character space allocated for the element, as shown in the example below.

The program may work as follows:

```
1   Enter your input: This is a test of toCharArray.
2      0:T,    1:h,    2:i,    3:s,    4: ,    5:i
3      6:s,    7: ,    8:a,    9: ,   10:t,   11:e
4     12:s,   13:t,   14: ,   15:o,   16:f,   17:
5     18:t,   19:o,   20:C,   21:h,   22:a,   23:r
6     24:A,   25:r,   26:r,   27:a,   28:y,   29:.
```

Programming Projects

9. **The distribution of token lengths** Write a program, `TokenLengthDist`, that receives an indefinite number of tokens from the user, and then computes the distribution of the lengths of the tokens. Treat any token having length greater than 15 as having length exactly 16. The user specifies the end of input by entering CTRL-D. To count, the program uses an array of length 17 and ignores slot 0.

The program may work as follows:

```
1    Below enter any number of tokens. At the end enter CTRL-D.
2    I am writing a program by the name of TokenLengthDist. This is an
         interesting problem to solve.
3    1:2
4    2:6
5    3:1
6    4:2
7    5:0
8    6:1
9    7:3
10   8:0
11   9:0
12   10:0
13   11:1
14   12:0
15   13:0
16   14:0
17   15:0
18   16:1
```

10. **The Birthday Paradox** The "Birthday Paradox" states: the chances are 50–50 for a group of random 23 people to contain a pair of people having the same birthdays. Write a program, `BirthdayParadox`, that tests this paradox as follows: The program creates a 365-element array of `boolean` values (initially the elements are all `false`). The program also initializes an `int` variable that plays the role of a counter to 0. For an indefinite number of times, the program generates a random integer between 0 and 364. After generating each random integer, if the element of the array at the randomly generated index is `false`, then the program changes the

element of the array to `true`, and increases the value of the counter by 1; otherwise, the program exits the loop. After exiting the loop, the program reports the final value of the counter.

The program may work as follows (two runs):

```
% java BirthdayParadox
Found a collision at round 27
% java BirthdayParadox
Found a collision at round 48
```

11. **More on the Birthday Paradox** As a continuation of the previous problem, write a program `BirthdayParadoxStats` that receives a positive integer `r` from the user, executes the experiment as described in the previous question `r` times, stores the `r` counter values thus generated in an array of `int` data having `r` elements, and then reports the contents of this `r`-element array. The output of the result must produce 15 elements per line, as follows:

```
Enter the number of rounds: 200
 33  21  33  26  36  51  47  44  34  29   4  21  23  19  10
 21  33  13  48  59  37  12  11  31  30  54   8  28  19  29
 40   4   9  26  33  19  10  30  16  60   5  34  16  31  25
 38  30  19  44  31  48  43  30  20  25   4  16  50  15  32
 13  19  25  30  48  35  26  38  20  33   6  20  26  33  54
 25   6  37  27  35  11  10  28  29   6  21   7   7  30  43
 20  22  14  30  14  16  23  37  25  47  38  15  25  27   9
 19  15  27  31  29  25  10  33  15  13  15  30  44  34  39
 15  50  10  22   9  14  28  38  31  37   8  23  21  31  34
 30  30  28  18  17  36  12  14  32  22  40  18  44  35  10
 31  81  11  20  21  21  33  12  48  21  12  23  26  30  15
  7  20  41  14  12  27  27  10  36   6  32  38  35  34  22
 47  18   3  14   6  33  20  34  24  20  51  11  10  20  30
 24  21  21  21  31
```

12. **Random permutation of N things** Write a program, `RandomNThings`, that receives a positive integer `num` from the user, and then generates a random permutation of indexes `0, ..., N - 1`. The following algorithm can be used to accomplish this task:
   - Instantiate an array, `perm`, having length `num`.
   - For each index i between 0 and `N - 1`, store i in `perm[ i ]`.
   - Use a for-loop that iterates over the sequence `0, ..., num - 2` with a variable, `j`. At each round, generate a random integer between `j` and `num - 1`, store the integer in a variable, `k`, and then exchange the values between `perm[ j ]` and `perm[ k ]`.

13. **Generating a random rectangle in a range** Write a program, `RandomRectangle`, that receives a positive integer from the user, and then prints a rectangle. Let `size` be the variable in which the integer that the user enters is recorded. The coordinates of the rectangle should be integers between 0 and `size` (that is, the value `size` is included in the range). Each side of the rectangle should be either parallel to the horizontal axis or parallel to the vertical axis.

To represent the rectangle generated, use the coordinates of the lower left corner and the upper right corner. Since there are four values total in the representation, use a four-element array of `int` values for the representation, where the four elements in the array are the x-coordinate of the lower left corner, the y-coordinate of the lower left corner, the x-coordinate of the upper right corner, and the y-coordinate of the upper right corner in this order.

The following algorithm can be used for the task.

- Select four random integers between 0 and `size` and store them in a four-element array of `int` values, `coord`.
- If either `coord[ 0 ] == coord[ 2 ]` or `coord[ 1 ] == coord[ 3 ]`, go back to the first step.
- If either `coord[ 0 ] > coord[ 2 ]`, exchange the values between them.
- If either `coord[ 1 ] > coord[ 3 ]`, exchange the values between them.

The Class `Arrays` and Resizing Arrays

13

13.1 The Class `Arrays`

`Arrays` is a class that provides static methods for manipulating and examining arrays. The class `Arrays` belongs to the package `java.util`, so the class must be imported, using one of the following two:

```
import java.util.Arrays;
import java.util.*;
```

Here are some methods of `Arrays`. Let T be any data type.

- `boolean Arrays.equals( T[] x, T[] y )`
  This method returns a `boolean` value representing whether or not the two arrays x and y have the same lengths, and the elements are equal between x and y at all positions. If T is a primitive data type, the equality between elements is tested with `==`. If T is an object data type, the result depends on how the equality method, `equals`, is executed in the class T.
- `void Arrays.fill( T[] x, T v )`
  This method fills the array x with the value v.
- `void Arrays.fill( T[] x, int fromIndex, int toIndex, T v )`
  The method stores v in the elements x[fromIndex], ..., x[toIndex - 1].
- `T[] Arrays.copyOf( T[] x, int copyLength )`
  This method returns an array consisting of the first copyLength elements of the array x.
  If the copyLength is greater than x.length, the method stores the default value of the data type T in the remaining copyLength - x.length elements of the returned array.
- `void Arrays.sort( T[] x )`

© Springer Nature Switzerland AG 2018
M. Ogihara, *Fundamentals of Java Programming*,
https://doi.org/10.1007/978-3-319-89491-1_13

This method rearranges the elements of x in increasing order. If T is a primitive data type, < is used for comparison, but a tie can be broken arbitrarily. If T is an object data type, T must admit comparison with a method named compareTo (see Chap. 17 for comparable data types).

- void Arrays.sort(T[] x, int fromIndex, int toIndex)

  This is a variant of sort. Sorting is applied only on the elements having indexes between fromIndex and toIndex - 1.

The next program demonstrates the use of the methods through a series of actions.

Step 1:   The program instantiates a String array of ten elements.

Step 2:   The program fills the array with a String literal "abc" using Arrays.fill.

Step 3:   At each index of the array, the program generates a random four-letter String data and stores it at the index.

Step 4:   The program creates a copy of the array having the same length as the original using Arrays.copyOf.

Step 5:   The program compares the original and the copy using Arrays.equals.

Step 6:   The program sorts the elements of the copy using Arrays.sort.

Step 7:   The program compares the original and the copy using Arrays.copyOf.

After each action, the program announces the action that has been performed, and then prints the contents of the relevant arrays. To print the contents of an array, the program uses a method named print. The method receives an array as its formal parameter, and then prints all the elements in the array in just one line, with one white space attached in front of each element (Line 8).

```
1    import java.util.*;
2    public class ArraysMethods
3    {
4      public static void printArray( String[] data )
5      {
6        for ( int p = 0; p < data.length; p ++ )
7        {
8          System.out.print( " " + data[ p ] );
9        }
10       System.out.println();
11     }
12
```

Listing 13.1 A program that demonstrates the use of methods from class Arrays (part 1). The method for printing an array

To generate a random String in Step 3, the program uses a method named randomString. The method randomString receives an int value as its formal parameter, len, and returns a random String object having length len (Line 13). To accomplish this, the method generates len random lowercase letters and connects them into one String data. A for-loop is used to count from 1 to len (Line 16). To generate a single random letter, the method generates a random relative index between 0 and 25 with the formula appearing in Line 18:

```
int diff = (int)( Math.random() * 26 );
```

The method then converts the relative index value, diff, to the absolute index in the ASCII table by adding it to 'a', and then casting (char) to the sum, as appearing in the right-hand side of Line 19:

```
(char)( 'a' + diff )
```

The value of this char is appended directly to a String variable, value. The initial value of this variable is " " (Line 15). The method at the end returns this value (Line 21). If the value of len is negative, the method does not execute the loop-body, so the return value of the method is an empty String.

```
13    public static String randomString( int len )
14    {
15      String value = "";
16      for ( int j = 1; j <= len; j ++ )
17      {
18        int diff = (int)( Math.random() * 26 );
19        value += (char)( 'a' + diff );
20      }
21      return value;
22    }
23
```

Listing 13.2 A program that demonstrates the use of methods from class Arrays (part 2). The method for randomly generating a (gibberish) character sequence of length len

The remainder of the code is the method main. The method main performs the following seven-step action.

1. After creating the initial array named data (Line 26), the program announces that it has created an array (Line 27), and then prints the contents of data (Line 28).
2. The program fills data with "abc" (Line 30), announces that it has filled data (Line 31), and then prints the contents of data (Line 32).
3. The program fills data with random elements (Lines 34–37), announces that it has stored random elements (Line 38), and then prints the contents of data (Line 39).
4. The program creates a copy of data having the same length, stores it in copied (Line 41), announces that it has created a copy (Line 42), and then prints the contents of copied (Line 43).
5. The program prints the result of comparing between data and copied (Line 45).
6. The program sorts copied (Line 47), announces that it has sorted copied (Line 48), and then prints the contents of copied (Line 49).
7. The program prints the result of comparing between data and copied (Line 50).

The probability that an 10-element array of random String data is already sorted is $10!/10^{10}$. The probability that the value of the equality test is still true in (7) is thus approximately 0.000363. This means that we can anticipate that the result of the equality test is very likely to change from true to false.

The code for the method main is presented next, with the calls to Arrays methods highlighted:

```
24    public static void main( String[] args )
25    {
26       String[] data = new String[ 10 ];
27       System.out.println( "Before assignment" );
28       printArray( data );
29
30       Arrays.fill( data, "abc" );
31       System.out.println( "Filled with \"abc\"" );
32       printArray( data );
33
34       for ( int pos = 0; pos < 10; pos ++ )
35       {
36          data[ pos ] = randomString( 4 );
37       }
38       System.out.println( "Filled with random Strings" );
39       printArray( data );
40
41       String[] copied = Arrays.copyOf( data, data.length );
42       System.out.println( "A copy has been generated" );
43       printArray( copied );
44
45       System.out.printf( "Equality:%s%n", Arrays.equals( data, copied ) );
46
47       Arrays.sort( copied );
48       System.out.println( "The copy has been sorted" );
49       printArray( copied );
50       System.out.printf( "Equality:%s%n", Arrays.equals( data, copied ) );
51    }
52 }
```

Listing 13.3 A program that demonstrates the use of methods from class Arrays (part 3). The method main

Here is an execution example of the code:

```
1  Before assignment
2   null null null null null null null null null null
3  Filled with "abc"
4   abc abc abc abc abc abc abc abc abc abc
5  Filled with random Strings
6   sbbo zgqz qzwa wgjj kvii nyff tcot ided hugg ndgj
7  A copy has been generated
8   sbbo zgqz qzwa wgjj kvii nyff tcot ided hugg ndgj
9  Equality:true
10 The copy has been sorted
11  hugg ided kvii ndgj nyff qzwa sbbo tcot wgjj zgqz
12 Equality:false
```

13.2   Reordering Elements in an Array

Programmers often encounter a situation where the order of some elements in an array must be rearranged. Such a task can be accomplished by:

- instantiating a new array with the same length as the original,
- storing the elements of the original in the new array at their respective new positions, and then,
- replacing the original array with the new array.

In addition, if either the number of elements that are affected by the rearrangement is small or the rearrangement is highly regular, the task can be accomplished without using another array. We call rearranging the order without using another array **reordering elements in place**. A key idea in reordering elements in place is the **element swap**. The element swap is exchanging values between two elements.

Suppose x and y are variables of some type T. To swap the values between x and y, we can use a temporary storage, say temp of the same type T, and execute:

```
1  T temp = x;
2  x = y;
3  y = temp;
```

or in the reverse order:

```
1  T temp = y;
2  y = x;
3  x = temp;
```

We can use this technique for exchanging values between two elements of an array. Suppose myData is an array of type T. Suppose, also, p and q are valid indexes of this array. In other words, the values of p and q are between 0 and myData.length - 1. We can swap values between myData[p] and myData[q] using a temporary storage, temp, of type T as follows:

```
1  T temp = myData[ p ];
2  myData[ p ] = myData[ q ];
3  myData[ q ] = temp;
```

The following program demonstrates the use of this technique for element swapping.

The program uses an array literal. The syntax for creating an array literal of elements of type T is:

$$\text{new } T[]\{ \text{ ELEMENT\_1, } \ldots, \text{ ELEMENT\_K } \}$$

where ELEMENT_1, ..., ELEMENT_K are the elements of the array. For example, the code:

```
1  String[] a;
2  int[] b;
3  a = new String[]{ "ABC", "DEF", "GHI" };
4  b = new int[]{ 10, 9, 8, 7, 6 };
```

instantiates an array of String data having length three and stores it in a, and then instantiates an array of int data having length five and stores it in b.

In the program, we use a 16-element array of String data, words. Initially, the elements of the array are the words from the title of a Pink Floyd tune: *Several Species of Small Furry Animals Gathered Together in a Cave and Grooving With a Pict* from their album *Ummagumma*.[1] We then swap elements between indexes 3 and 5.

The code demonstrates the modification by printing the elements of the array each time a change takes place on it. To print the contents, it uses a method named printArray (Line 3). The formal parameter of the method is an array of String data named words. The method uses a for-loop that iterates over the sequence 0, ..., words.length - 1 with a variable named i (Line 5), and prints each element with one white space preceding it. As we have done previously, the format to be used for inserting the white space is " " + words[index]. Since the length of words can be possibly large, the program prints the newline after printing eight elements successively in one line as well as after printing all the elements. Since the value of i starts from 0, after printing eight elements successively in one line, the value of i has the remainder 7 when divided by 8. Since the last valid index is words.length - 1, the condition for testing if the newline character must be printed is

$$i \ \% \ 8 \ == \ 7 \ || \ i \ = \ words.length \ - \ 1$$

```
1   public class ArraySwap
2   {
3     public static void print( String[] words )
4     {
5       for ( int i = 0; i < words.length; i ++ )
6       {
7         System.out.print( " " + words[ i ] );
8         if ( i % 8 == 7 || i == words.length - 1 )
9         {
10          System.out.println();
11        }
12      }
13    }
```

Listing 13.4 A program that swaps elements between two positions in an array (part 1). The method print

The main part of the program goes as follows:

1. Create a String[] literal words that holds the words from the title of the song, using the syntax for creating an array literal (Lines 16–19), and then print the contents of the array (Line 20).
2. Copy the value at position 3 to a temporary variable named temp (Line 22).
3. Copy the value at position 5 to position 3 (Line 24), and then print the contents of the array (Line 24).
4. Finalize the swap by copying the value from temp to position 5 (Line 26), and then print the contents (Line 27).

---

[1]Pink Floyd is a British Rock band that was formed in 1968 and disbanded in 2012. It is one of the most successful rock bands in history. *Ummagumma* is their double vinyl album that was issued in 1969.

```
14    public static void main( String[] args )
15    {
16      String[] words = new String[]{
17        "Several", "Species", "of", "Small", "Furry", "Animals",
18        "Gathered", "Together", "in", "a", "Cave", "and",
19        "Grooving", "With", "a", "Pict" };
20      print( words );
21
22      String temp = words[ 3 ];
23      words[ 3 ] = words[ 5 ];
24      print( words );
25
26      words[ 5 ] = temp;
27      print( words );
28    }
29 }
```

Listing 13.5 A program that swaps elements between two positions in an array (part 2). The method `main`

Figure 13.1 illustrates the series of actions performed on the array elements.

Fig. 13.1 Swapping values between two array elements

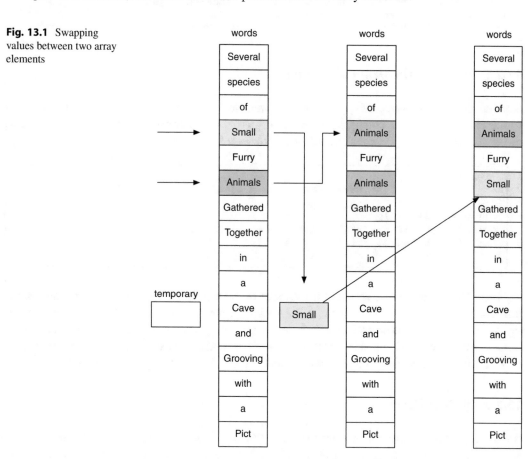

Fig. 13.2 Reversing the order of appearance of elements in an array

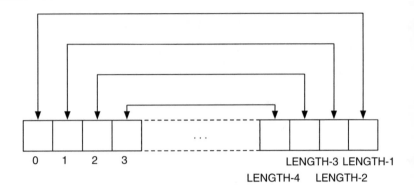

The result of executing the code is as follows:

```
1   Several Species of Small Furry Animals Gathered Together
2   in a Cave and Grooving With a Pict
3   Several Species of Animals Furry Animals Gathered Together
4   in a Cave and Grooving With a Pict
5   Several Species of Animals Furry Small Gathered Together
6   in a Cave and Grooving With a Pict
```

13.2.1 Reversing the Order of Elements

Suppose data is an array of type T and we want to reverse the order in which the elements appear in data. To accomplishing the task, we swap elements between indexes i and data.length - 1 - i for all values of i between 0 and data.length / 2 - 1.

```
1   T temp;
2   for ( int i= 0; i <= data.length / 2 - 1; i ++ )
3   {
4       temp = data[ i ];
5       data[ i ] = data[ data.length - 1 - i ];
6       data[ data.length - 1 - i ] = temp;
7   }
```

Figure 13.2 visualizes the action of the reversal by exchange. The choice of the maximum value data.length / 2 - 1 is important. In the case where data.length is an even number, say 2 * m, the innermost exchange is between the indexes m - 1 and m. In the case where data.length is an odd number, say 2 * m + 1, the innermost exchange is between the indexes m - 1 and m + 1, so the unique middle element, the one located at index m, is untouched.

13.2.2 Cyclic Shifting

Another application of element swapping is **cyclic shifting**. Cyclic shifting is to move all the elements in one direction and placing the displaced element at the other end. Depending on whether the elements move to lower indexes or higher indexes, we call the action the **left cyclic shift** and the **right cyclic shift**. Here is the more formal definition of cyclic shifting. Suppose we have an array named x having length n at hand.

Fig. 13.3 The results
obtained by executing
cyclic shifts

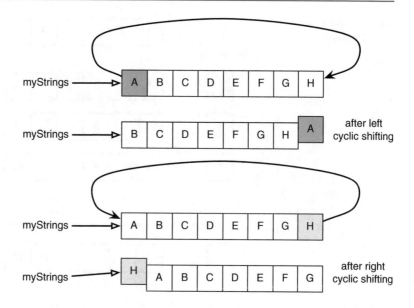

after left
cyclic shifting

after right
cyclic shifting

- By **left cyclic shifting** of x, we mean to move, concurrently, x[1], ..., x[n - 1] to x[0], ..., x[n - 2] and x[0] to x[n - 1].
- By **right cyclic shifting** of x, we mean to move, concurrently, x[0], ..., x[n - 2] to x[1], ..., x[n - 1] and x[n - 1] to x[0].

Figure 13.3 visualizes the two cyclic shifts.

An in-place cyclic shift can be accomplished as follows:

1. Save the element that needs to rotate around (that is, the element that needs to move from one end to the other) in a temporary storage. This creates an unoccupied slot in the array.
2. While the destination of the element in the temporary storage becomes unoccupied, find the element that needs to move into the slot that is presently unoccupied, and move the element to its destination.
3. Moving the displaced element to its destination.

The program `ArrayCyclicShifting` demonstrates both left and right cyclic shifting using the above algorithm of successive relocation (Fig. 13.4). The program creates an array of random integers between 0 and 99, and then performs a series of cyclic shifts while printing the contents of the array at the beginning and after each cyclic shift. The first part of the source code is the method `printArray`. This method prints the elements of an array of `int` data that is given as the parameter (Line 3). The method prints all the elements of the array in one line by using the `printf` format of `" %2d"`. Since the elements of the array are between 0 and 99, exactly three character spaces will be used for an element.

Fig. 13.4 An algorithm
for left cyclic shift

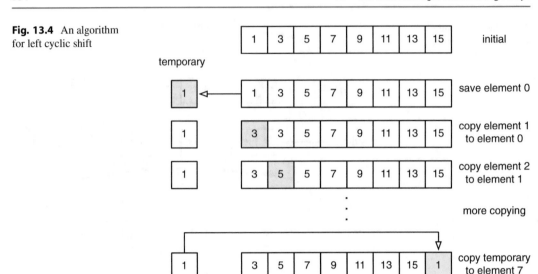

```
 1   public class ArrayCyclicShift
 2   {
 3     public static void printArray( int[] numbers )
 4     {
 5       for ( int index = 0; index < numbers.length; index ++ )
 6       {
 7         System.out.printf( " %2d", numbers[ index ] );
 8       }
 9       System.out.println();
10     }
11
```

Listing 13.6 A program that performs cyclic shifting (part 1). The method printArray

Next, we present the method for left cyclic shift, leftCyclicShift. The method has an array
of int data, numbers, as its formal parameter (Line 12). The algorithm that method executes is as
follows:

1. Store numbers[0] in an int variable named temporary (Line 15).
2. Using a for-loop that iterates over the sequence 1, ..., numbers.length - 1 with a
   variable named index, store the value of numbers[i] in numbers[i - 1] (Lines
   16–19).
3. Store the value in temporary in numbers[numbers.length - 1] (Line 20).

After completing the shift, the method prints the contents of the array using the method printArray
(Line 21).

```
12   public static void leftCyclicShift ( int [] numbers )
13   {
14      System.out.println( "Left Cyclic Shift" );
15      int temporary = numbers [ 0 ];
16      for ( int index = 1; index < numbers.length; index ++ )
17      {
18         numbers [ index - 1 ] = numbers [ index ];
19      }
20      numbers [ numbers.length - 1 ] = temporary;
21      printArray ( numbers );
22   }
23
```

Listing 13.7 A program that performs cyclic shifting (part 2). The method for left cyclic shifting

The method for right cyclic shifting, `rightCyclicShift`, moves the elements in the opposite direction (Line 24), by executing the following algorithm:

1. Store `numbers [ numbers.length - 1 ]` in an `int` variable named `temporary` (Line 27).
2. Using a for-loop that iterates over the sequence `numbers.length - 2`, ..., 0 with a variable named `index`, store the value of `numbers [ i ]` in `numbers [ i + 1 ]` (Lines 28–31).
3. Store the value saved in `temporary` in `numbers [ 0 ]` (Line 32).

```
24   public static void rightCyclicShift ( int [] numbers )
25   {
26      System.out.println( "Right Cyclic Shift" );
27      int temporary = numbers [ numbers.length - 1 ];
28      for ( int index = numbers.length - 1; index >= 1; index -- )
29      {
30         numbers [ index ] = numbers [ index - 1 ];
31      }
32      numbers [ 0 ] = temporary;
33      printArray ( numbers );
34   }
35
```

Listing 13.8 A program that performs cyclic shifting (part 3). The method for right cyclic shifting

The last part of the code is the method `main`. The method `main` does the following:

1. Instantiate an array of 20 elements (Line 38) with random integers in the range 0..99 (Lines 39–42).
2. Print the contents of the array (Line 44).
3. Execute the right cyclic shift method twice (Lines 46 and 47). (The right cyclic method prints the contents of the array before returning.)
4. Execute the left cyclic shift once (Line 48). (The left cyclic method prints the contents of the array before returning.)

```
36    public static void main( String[] args )
37    {
38      int[] numbers = new int[ 20 ];
39      for ( int index = 0; index < numbers.length; index ++ )
40      {
41        numbers[ index ] = (int)( Math.random() * 100 );
42      }
43      System.out.println( "Original" );
44      printArray( numbers );
45
46      rightCyclicShift( numbers );
47      rightCyclicShift( numbers );
48      leftCyclicShift( numbers );
49    }
```

Listing 13.9 A program that performs cyclic shifting (part 4). The method `main`

Here is the result of executing the program:

```
1  Original
2    1 49 24 90 46 58 56   2 58 27 34 64 73 20 33 48 15   0 12 10
3  Right Cyclic Shift
4   10   1 49 24 90 46 58 56   2 58 27 34 64 73 20 33 48 15   0 12
5  Right Cyclic Shift
6   12 10   1 49 24 90 46 58 56   2 58 27 34 64 73 20 33 48 15   0
7  Left Cyclic Shift
8   10   1 49 24 90 46 58 56   2 58 27 34 64 73 20 33 48 15   0 12
```

13.3   Modifications of an Array That Require Resizing

13.3.1 Insertion and Deletion

Once an array has been instantiated, its length cannot be changed. To add an element to an existing array or to remove an element from an array, one must create a new array where the elements appear in their designated places, and then replace the array is currently used with the new one. Suppose the array that is currently used has the name `oldArray`. Here are specific steps to follow to insert an element, say x, to this array at some index p.

1. Instantiate a new temporary array, say `newArray`.
2. For all indexes i that are strictly smaller than p, copy `oldArray[ i ]` to `newArray[ i ]`.
3. Place x in `newArray[ p ]`.
4. For all indexes i that are strictly greater than p, copy `oldArray[ i ]` to `newArray[ i + 1 ]`.
5. Assign `newArray` to `oldArray`.

Figure 13.5 visualizes this action. In the middle three steps, there is no overlap among the destinations of the elements, so the orders of the three steps can be permuted.

To remove the element at some index p, we execute the following algorithm:

1. Instantiate a new temporary array with a different name, say `newArray`.
2. For all indexes i that are strictly smaller than p, copy `oldArray[ i ]` to `newArray[ i ]`.

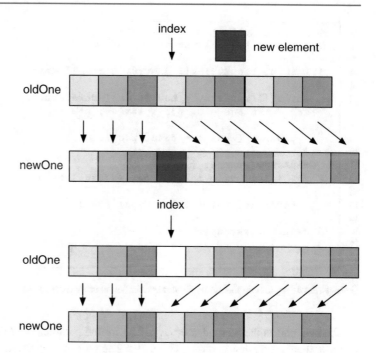

Fig. 13.5 Insertion of an element in an array

Fig. 13.6 Deleting an element from an array

3. For all indexes i that are strictly greater than p, copy oldArray[i] to newArray[i - 1].
4. Set newArray to oldArray.

We can visualize this action in a figure like Fig. 13.6. In the middle two steps, there is no overlap among the destinations of the elements, so the order of the two steps can be switched.

The following program, ResizeArray, demonstrates the methods for insertion and removal we have just discussed using arrays of String values. The program uses an array, data, for maintaining a list of String values. The program initializes the array by receiving its length and individual elements from the user. The program then repeats interactions with the user to (a) insert an element to the array, (b) remove an element from the array, or (c) present the elements of the array. This is repeated until the user instructs the program to terminate. The insertion and removal are carried out by methods, insert and remove. Both insert and remove return a new array constructed from the original by making the requested modifications. The method main calls these two methods, and replaces data with the array that the methods return.

The first part of the code is the method insert. The formal parameters of the method are a String array named data, an int value named target, and a String object w. As mentioned above, the return type of the method is an array of String data (Line 4). The task to be performed is to return an array created from data by inserting w at index target. The method executes the following algorithm to accomplish the task:

1. Create a new array named newArray whose length is data.length + 1 (Line 6).
2. Copy each element data[pos] whose index, pos, is smaller than target to newArray[pos] (Lines 7–10).
3. Store w in newArray[target] (Line 11).
4. Copy each element data[pos] whose index, pos, is greater than target to newArray[pos + 1] (Lines 12–15).
5. Return newArray (Line 16).

```
1   import java.util.*;
2   public class ResizeArray
3   {
4     public static String[] insert( String[] data, int target, String w )
5     {
6       String[] newArray = new String[ data.length + 1 ];
7       for ( int pos = 0; pos < target; pos ++ )
8       {
9         newArray[ pos ] = data[ pos ];
10      }
11      newArray[ target ] = w;
12      for ( int pos = target; pos < data.length; pos ++ )
13      {
14        newArray[ pos + 1 ] = data[ pos ];
15      }
16      return newArray;
17    }
18
```

Listing 13.10 A program that demonstrates resizing of an array (part 1). The class header and the method `insert`

The next part is the method, `remove`. The formal parameters of the method are a `String` array `data` and an `int` value `target` (Line 19). The task to be performed is to return an array created from `data` by removing the element at index `target`. To accomplish the required task, the method does the following:

1. Create a new array `newArray` whose length is `data.length - 1` (Line 21).
2. Copy each element `data[ pos ]` whose index, `pos`, is smaller than `target` to `newArray[ pos ]` (Lines 22–25).
3. Copy each element `data[ pos ]` whose index, `pos`, is greater than `target` to `newArray[ pos - 1 ]` (Lines 26–29).
4. Return `newArray` (Line 30).

```
19    public static String[] remove( String[] data, int target )
20    {
21      String[] newArray = new String[ data.length - 1 ];
22      for ( int pos = 0; pos < target; pos ++ )
23      {
24        newArray[ pos ] = data[ pos ];
25      }
26      for ( int pos = target + 1; pos < data.length; pos ++ )
27      {
28        newArray[ pos - 1 ] = data[ pos ];
29      }
30      return newArray;
31    }
32
```

Listing 13.11 A program that demonstrates resizing of an array (part 2). The method `remove`

In the method `main`, the program receives the initial length of the array from the user (Line 37), instantiates a new array with the number of elements specified by the user (Line 38), and then receives the initial elements that to be stored in the array from the user (Lines 40–44). The variable `pos` to specify a position in the array is declared outside the for-loop (Line 39). This variable is used in other places of the code.

```
33    public static void main( String[] args )
34    {
35       Scanner keyboard = new Scanner( System.in );
36       System.out.print( "Enter size: " );
37       int size = keyboard.nextInt();
38       String[] data = new String[ size ];
39       int pos;
40       for ( pos = 0; pos < data.length; pos ++ )
41       {
42          System.out.printf( "Enter element %d: ", pos );
43          data[ pos ] = keyboard.next();
44       }
45
```

Listing 13.12 A program that demonstrates resizing of an array (part 3). The part responsible creating the initial array

Two `String` variables, `value` and `answer`, are used for interaction (Line 46). The available actions are presented with the first letters of the names of the actions. The first letters of the action names are `'I'`, `'R'`, `'V'`, and `'Q'` (Lines 49). The user enters an action to be performed as a `String` value, and this is stored in `answer` (Line 50). To direct the execution, the program uses an if-else statement (Line 51)

In the case where the first character is `'I'` (Line 51), the action to be performed is insertion. The program receives the position of insertion, `pos`, and the element, `value`, to be inserted (Lines 53–56). The program then calls `insert( data, pos, value )`, and then substitutes `data` with the array that the method returns (Line 57).

In the case where the first character is `'R'` (Line 59), the action to be performed is removal. The program receives the position where the element to be removed is located, and stores it in the variable `pos` (Lines 61 and 62). The program then calls `remove( data, pos )`, and then substitutes `data` with the array that the method returns (Line 63).

In the case where the first character is `'V'` (Line 65), the action to be performed is showing the data. Using a for-loop, the program prints the elements, one element per line, with their indexes (Lines 67–70).

In all other cases, there will be no action to be performed, but in the case where the first character is `'Q'`, the program exits the loop and terminates (Line 72).

```
46        String value, answer;
47        do
48        {
49          System.out.print( "(I)nsert, (R)emove, (V)iew, (Q)uit? " );
50          answer = keyboard.next();
51          if ( answer.startsWith( "I" ) )
52          {
53            System.out.print( "Enter position: " );
54            pos = keyboard.nextInt();
55            System.out.print( "Enter value: " );
56            value = keyboard.next();
57            data = insert( data, pos, value );
58          }
59          else if ( answer.startsWith( "R" ) )
60          {
61            System.out.print( "Enter position: " );
62            pos = keyboard.nextInt();
63            data = remove( data, pos );
64          }
65          else if ( answer.startsWith( "V" ) )
66          {
67            for ( pos = 0; pos < data.length; pos ++ )
68            {
69              System.out.printf( "%3d:%s%n", pos, data[ pos ] );
70            }
71          }
72        } while ( !answer.startsWith( "Q" ) );
73      }
74    }
```

Listing 13.13 A program that demonstrates resizing of an array (part 4). The do-while-loop

In the following execution example, the user enters the last names of eight of his favorite operatic singers: George London, Dietrich Fischer-Dieskau, Astrid Varnay, Karita Mattila, Renee Fleming, Birgit Nilsson, Wolfgang Windgassen, and Ben Heppner. The user makes some changes by adding Christa Ludwig, removing Windgassen, and then adding Elisabeth Schwartzkopf.[2] Note that the array length is 8 at the start and the index position of the last element is 7, so to append the element at the end, the user enters 8.

---

[2]George London (May 30, 1920 to March 24, 1985) was a Canadian concert and operatic bass-baritone. Dietrich Fischer-Dieskau (May 28, 1925 to May 18, 2012) was a German concert and operatic baritone. Ibolyka Astrid Maria Varnay (April 25, 1918 to September 4, 2006) was a Swedish-born American operatic soprano. Karita Marjatta Mattila (born September 5, 1960) is a Finnish concert and operatic soprano. Renée Fleming (born February 14, 1959) is an American concert and operatic soprano. Birgit Nilsson (May 17, 1918 to December 25, 2005) was a Swedish concert and operatic soprano. Wolfgang Windgassen (June 26, 1914 to September 8, 1974) was a heldentenor. Thomas Bernard Heppner (born January 14, 1956) is a retired Canadian tenor. He is a Companion of the Orders of Canada. Christa Ludwig (March 16, 1928–) is a retired German concert and operatic mezzo-soprano. Dame Olga Maria Elisabeth Friederike Schwarzkopf (9 December 1915 to 3 August 2006) was a German soprano. She was a Dame Commander of the Most Excellent Order of the British Empire.

```
 1  Enter size: 8
 2  Enter element 0: London
 3  Enter element 1: Fischer-Dieskau
 4  Enter element 2: Varnay
 5  Enter element 3: Mattila
 6  Enter element 4: Fleming
 7  Enter element 5: Nilsson
 8  Enter element 6: Windgassen
 9  Enter element 7: Heppner
10  (I)nsert, (R)emove, (V)iew, (Q)uit? I
11  Enter position: 8
12  Enter value: Ludwig
13  (I)nsert, (R)emove, (V)iew, (Q)uit? V
14    0:London
15    1:Fischer-Dieskau
16    2:Varnay
17    3:Mattila
18    4:Fleming
19    5:Nilsson
20    6:Windgassen
21    7:Heppner
22    8:Ludwig
23  (I)nsert, (R)emove, (V)iew, (Q)uit? R
24  Enter position: 6
25  (I)nsert, (R)emove, (V)iew, (Q)uit? V
26    0:London
27    1:Fischer-Dieskau
28    2:Varnay
29    3:Mattila
30    4:Fleming
31    5:Nilsson
32    6:Heppner
33    7:Ludwig
34  (I)nsert, (R)emove, (V)iew, (Q)uit? I
35  Enter position: 2
36  Enter value: Schwartzkopf
37  (I)nsert, (R)emove, (V)iew, (Q)uit? V
38    0:London
39    1:Fischer-Dieskau
40    2:Schwartzkopf
41    3:Varnay
42    4:Mattila
43    5:Fleming
44    6:Nilsson
45    7:Heppner
46    8:Ludwig
47  (I)nsert, (R)emove, (V)iew, (Q)uit? Q
```

13.3.2 Adjoining Two Arrays

Next, we consider adjoining two arrays. Suppose we have at hand two arrays, list1 and list2, whose elements are of some data type T, and we want to create a new array list3 by appending the elements of list2 after the elements of list1. This task can be accomplished by instantiating list3 as an array of length list1.length + list2.length, copying the elements from list1 to the positions 0, ..., list1.length-1, and then copying the elements of list2 to the positions list1.length, ..., list1.length+list2.length-1.

```
1    T[] list3 = new T[ list1.length + list2.length ];
2    for ( int index = 0; index < list1.length; index ++ )
3    {
4      list3[ index ] = list1[ index ];
5    }
6    for ( int index = 0; index < list2.length; index ++ )
7    {
8      list3[ list1.length + index ] = list2[ index ];
9    }
```

This code can be shorten slightly with the use of the method `copyOf` of the class `Arrays`. The method call `Arrays.copyOf( list1, list1.length + list2.length )` returns an array of length `list1.length + list2.length`, whose first `list1.length` elements form an exact copy of `list1`. We obtain the array returned by the method call, and then copy the elements of `list2` to their respective positions.

```
1    // java.util.Arrays must be imported
2    T[] list3 = Arrays.copyOf( list1, list1.length +  list2.length );
3    for ( int index = 0; index < list2.length; index ++ )
4    {
5      list3[ list1.length + index ] = list2[ index ];
6    }
```

13.4   args

The formal parameter of the method `main`, `String[] args`, is an array that represents the tokens that appear after the command, when a Java program is executed from a command line interface. The array holds the tokens that follow the name of the Java program in the command line. For example, if `Foo` is a Java class name and `java Foo c1 c2` is typed as a command line, the array `args` of the method `main` of `Foo` has length two with elements, `"c1"` and `"c2"`. The character sequence that appears after the command are interpreted with the syntax of the command line interface. In the case of Unix-like environments, characters including ' | ', ' > ', ' < ', and ' ; ', serve as some type of punctuation. All the tokens appearing after any of these characters will be ignored when creating `args`.

Here is a program that simply prints the elements of the array one by one:

```
1   public class Args
2   {
3     public static void main( String[] args )
4     {
5       System.out.printf( "args has length %d.%n", args.length );
6       for ( int index = 0; index < args.length; index ++ )
7       {
8         System.out.printf( "args[%d] = %s%n", index, args[ index ] );
9       }
10    }
11  }
```

Listing 13.14 A program that prints the length and the elements of `args`

We present one execution example of the code. In the example, "% " is the prompt, "java Args" is the execution command, and "10.0 -k, -n abc" is the sequence that follows the command.

```
1  % java Args 10.0 -k, -n abc
2  args has length 4.
3  args[0] = 10.0
4  args[1] = -k,
5  args[2] = -n
6  args[3] = abc
```

If a semicolon appears, the part that follows is considered to be another command. In the following case, the semicolon splits the command into two separate commands, and so the program is executed twice.

```
1  % java Args 10.0 -k, -n abc; java Args -foobar -x
2  args has length 4.
3  args[0] = 10.0
4  args[1] = -k,
5  args[2] = -n
6  args[3] = abc
7  args has length 2.
8  args[0] = -foobar
9  args[1] = -x
```

13.5 Searching for an Element in an Array

13.5.1 Sequential Search

Searching in an array is the problem of checking, given some array a and a data key, if key is already an element of a. A simple solution to the problem is to examine the elements of the array in order. Such search is called the **sequential search**. Suppose that a is an array of String data and key is a String value. A sequential search can be executed as follows:

```
1   boolean found = false;
2   int i;
3   for ( i = 0; i < a.length; i ++ )
4   {
5     if ( a[ i ].equals( key ) )
6     {
7       found = true;
8       break;
9     }
10  }
```

The value of found represents whether or not a match has been found. The value of i at the end is the location of the first match. If there is no match, the value of i at the end is a.length. We can convert the code fragment to a method that reports the outcome with an int return value. The conversion needs two return statements. One substitutes the action inside the if-statement and the other substitutes the action after the for-loop. Typically, the internal one returns the index at which a match is found, the external one returns a special value, e.g., -1.

```
1    for ( int i = 0; i < a.length; i ++ )
2    {
3      if ( a[ i ].equals( key ) )
4      {
5        return i;
6      }
7    }
8    return -1;
```

13.5.2 Binary Search

In the case where the data type of the elements of the array permits comparison and the array elements are already sorted, **binary search** can be used to speed up the search.

A typical binary search executes a loop with two indexes, say `low` and `high`, and maintains the following loop invariant:

(*) `0 <= low, low <= high, high <= names.length`, and if a key appears in the array, its index is between `low` and `high - 1`.

The loop goes as follows:

(A) Initialize `low` with `0` and `high` with `names.length`. The condition (*) holds.

(B) If `low == high`, because of (*), it can be guaranteed that the key does not appear in the array, so report that `key` does not appear in the array.

(C) If `low < high`, compute `(low + high)/2` and store the value in an `int` variable, `mid`.
  (i) If `names[ mid ].equals( key )`, the key has been found, so report the discovery and terminate the search.
  (ii) If `names[ mid ].compareTo( key ) < 0`, it means that all the elements at indexes `<= mid` are smaller than `key`, so update `low` with the value of `mid + 1`. The condition (*) still holds.
  (iii) Similarly, if `names[ mid ].compareTo( key ) > 0`, it means that all the elements at indexes `>= mid` are greater than `key`, so update `high` with the value of `mid`. The condition (*) still holds.

The number of elements in the search range (between the indexes `low` and `high - 1`) is `high - low`. Because `mid` is chosen to be a half-way point between `low` and `hight`, when either `low` or `high` is updated in Steps C-ii or C-iii, the number of elements in the search range decreases at least by one half. This means that for an initial range size of N, the number of times the loop-body is executed is at most $\lceil \log_2 N \rceil$. Even if there are one million elements in the array, it will require at most 20 probes to complete the search.

Suppose the result of comparing between the search key and the array element is stored in an `int` variable named `result`. We can use the following code for binary search. The loop terminates when the value of `result` becomes 0 (meaning a match has been found) or the value of `low` becomes `high` (meaning the search range has size 0). After the loop, the outcome of the search can be determined based on the value of `result`. Furthermore, if it is 0, the value of `mid` is the location of the match that has been found.

```
1     int mid, low = 0, high = names.length, result = -1;
2     while ( result != 0 && low < high )
3     {
4       mid = ( low + high ) / 2;
5       result = names[ mid ].compareTo( key );
6       if ( result < 0 )
7       {
8         low = mid + 1;
9       }
10      else if ( result > 0 )
11      {
12        high = mid;
13      }
14    }
15    if ( result == 0 )
16    {
17      System.out.println ( key + " was found at " + mid );
18    }
19    else
20    {
21      System.out.println ( key + " was not found" );
22    }
```

13.6 Arrays with Capacity and Size

Instead of resizing an array each time an element is inserted or removed, a fixed array can be used by remembering how many slots of the array are currently occupied. We call it an **array with capacity and size**. An array with capacity and size employs the following principles:

- We call the length of the array the **capacity**. This is the maximum number of elements you can store in the array.
- The length of the array is greater than or equal to the largest possible number of elements that need to be present in the array at the same time.
- An `int` variable is used to record the number of data being stored. We call it the **size** of the storage.
- The elements being stored in the array appear consecutively, at indexes between 0 and `size - 1`.
- A more data can be stored in the array if and only if the size is strictly less than the capacity.
- The element order in the array need not be preserved.

Figure 13.7 shows a drawing of such an array.[3] Since the element order need not be preserved, the following strategies can be used for implementing addition and removal.

- If `size < capacity`, a new element can be added to the array. To accomplish this, store the new element at index `size`, and then increase the value of `size` by 1.
- If `0 <= p` and `p < size`, the element at p can be eliminated. To accomplish this, copy the element at `size - 1` (the last element) to p, and then decrease the value of `size` by 1.

Both operations require just one element change in the array. Figure 13.8 shows these ideas.

---

[3] Joanne Brackeen (born July 26, 1938) is an American jazz pianist and composer. Terri Lyne Carrington (born August 4, 1965) is an American jazz drummer, composer, and producer. Carmen Mercedes McRae (April 8, 1922 to November 10, 1994) was an American jazz singer. Linda May Oh (born 1984 in Malaysia) is a Jazz bassist and composer. Esperanza Emily Spalding (born October 18, 1984) is an American jazz bassist and singer. Blossom Dearie (April 28, 1924 to February 7, 2009) was an American jazz singer, composer, and pianist.

Fig. 13.7 The concept of an array with capacity 8 and size 5. The slots 0 through 4 are presently occupied

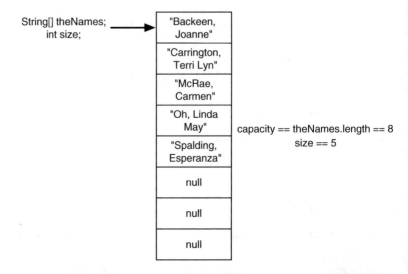

Fig. 13.8 The concept of an array with capacity and size. The figure shows the result of two consecutive actions: to insert `"Dearie, Blossom"` and then to remove `"McRae, Carmen"`. `"Dearie, Blossom"` appears in two position after the removal, but the one at position 5 will not be accessed because `size` is now equal to 5

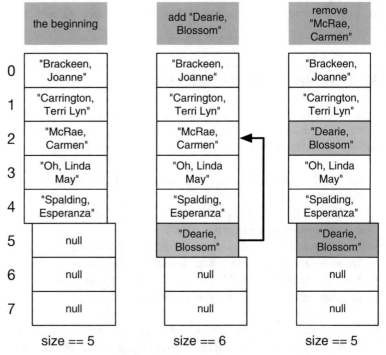

The program `FixedSizeUnsorted` is an example of arrays with capacity and size. The application receives an initial set of `String` data from the user, and then interacts with the user to make modifications and perform examinations on the data. The operations that are available on the data are adding elements in succession, removing one element, viewing the collection, and searching for all the elements matching a key specified by the user. The program uses four global variables, `String[] theNames`, `int capacity`, `int size`, and `Scanner keyboard` (Lines 6–10). The variables represent the array, the capacity of the array, the size of the array, and the keyboard with which to receive input from the user. The method `main` consists of two method calls: `setup` (Line 12), for setting up the initial array, and `action` (Line 13), for performing the interaction with the user.

```
1   import java.util.*;
2   // Using an array of fixed size
3   public class FixedSizeUnsorted
4   {
5     // global variables
6     public static int size, capacity;
7     public static String[] theNames;
8     public static Scanner  keyboard;
9     // main
10    public static void main( String[] args )
11    {
12      setup();
13      action();
14    }
```

Listing 13.15 A program that uses an array with capacity and size (part 1). The global variables and the method main

The method setUp instantiates the array after receiving the capacity from the user (Lines 19–21), and then sets size to 0 (Line 22). The method uses Integer.parseInt for converting a String data to an integer.

```
15    // initial set up
16    public static void setup()
17    {
18      keyboard = new Scanner( System.in );
19      System.out.print( "Enter capacity: " );
20      capacity = Integer.parseInt( keyboard.nextLine() );
21      theNames = new String[ capacity ];
22      size = 0;
23    }
```

Listing 13.16 A program that uses an array with capacity and size (part 2). The method for the initial set up

The method action is for interacting with the user. The user chooses one from five actions: 'A' for adding multiple elements, 'R' for removing an element, 'P' for printing all the elements, 'S' for searching for an element with a key, and 'Q' for quitting the program. The method uses a char variable, c, to record the choice of action (Line 27). This is the first letter of the user input (Lines 30–32). By choosing 'Q', the user can terminate the loop that starts in Line 28. The flow is controlled with a switch statement.

- For the action of adding elements, the program receives an indefinite number of lines from the user, and calls add for each line entered (Lines 36–46). The user can stop the addition by entering an empty line (Line 47). The empty line is not added to the array.
- For the action of removing and element, the program receives the index of the element to be removed, and then calls the method remove. The input line that the user enters for the index is converted to an integer using Integer.parseInt (Lines 50–51).
- For the action of searching for elements with a key, the program receives a search key from the user, and then calls search (Lines 54–55).
- For the action of printing the array, the program calls print (Line 58).

After quitting the loop, the method prints a message stating that it is terminating the program (Line 61).

```
24   // action
25   public static void action()
26   {
27     char c;
28     do
29     {
30       System.out.print(
31           "A(dd), R(emove), P(rint), S(earch), Q(uit): " );
32       c = ( keyboard.nextLine() ).charAt( 0 );
33       switch ( c )
34       {
35         case 'A':
36           System.out.println(
37               "Enter new names, empty line to finish: " );
38           String name;
39           do
40           {
41             System.out.print( "> " );
42             name = keyboard.nextLine();
43             if ( name.length() != 0 )
44             {
45               add( name );
46             }
47           } while ( name.length() != 0 );
48           break;
49         case 'R':
50           System.out.print( "Enter an index for removal: " );
51           remove( Integer.parseInt( keyboard.nextLine() ) );
52           break;
53         case 'S':
54           System.out.print( "Enter a search key: " );
55           search( keyboard.nextLine() );
56           break;
57         case 'P':
58           print();
59       }
60     } while ( c != 'Q' );
61     System.out.println( "Closing..." );
62   }
```

Listing 13.17 A program that uses an array with capacity and size (part 3). The method that interacts with the user for modifications and examinations

The method search (Line 63) executes sequential search for elements containing a given search key. Like the example in Sect. 13.5.1, the program uses an indicator variable, found, to record whether or not any match has been found. The initial value of the variable is false (Line 54). The program uses a for-loop that iterates over all the valid indexes with a variable named pos (Line 67). In the loop-body, a match is tested with theName[pos].indexOf(key) >= 0 (Line 69). If this condition is true, the program stores true in the variable found, and then prints the element theName[pos] with the value of pos (Lines 72 and 73). The value change of found is only from false to true. After the loop, if the indicator variable found remains false, it means that no match has been found, so the program reports that no match has been found (Line 76–78).

In the method `print`, the programs uses a for-loop that iterates over the sequence of valid indexes, `0, ..., size - 1`, to print the elements with their indexes (Lines 84–87).

```
63      // method for searching
64      public static void search( String aName )
65      {
66        boolean found = false;
67        for ( int pos = 0; pos < size; pos ++ )
68        {
69          if ( theNames[ pos ].indexOf( aName ) >= 0 )
70          {
71            found = true;
72            System.out.printf(
73                "Found at %04d in %s\n", pos, theNames[ pos ] );
74          }
75        }
76        if ( !found )
77        {
78          System.out.println( "Not found" );
79        }
80      }
81      // method for printing data
82      public static void print()
83      {
84        for ( int pos = 0; pos < size; pos ++ )
85        {
86          System.out.printf( "%04d:%s%n", pos, theNames[ pos ] );
87        }
88      }
```

Listing 13.18 A program that uses an array with capacity and size (part 4). The methods for searching and printing

The method `add` (Line 90) is for adding a single element. The program first checks if there is space left in the array with the condition `size < capacity` (Line 92). If there is space left, the program places the new element in the array at index `size`, and then increases the size by 1 (Line 94). The two actions can be compressed into a single line:

$$\texttt{theNames[size ++] = aName}$$

If there is no space left, the program prints an error message (Line 98).

```
89      // method for insertion
90      public static void add( String aName )
91      {
92        if ( size < capacity )
93        {
94          theNames[ size ++ ] = aName;
95        }
96        else
97        {
98          System.out.println( "The storage is full." );
99        }
100     }
```

Listing 13.19 A program that uses an array with capacity and size (part 5). The method for adding a single element

The method `remove` (Line 102) is for removing an element. The program checks if the value of `index` is valid with the condition `index >= 0 && index < size` (Line 103). If the value is valid, the program copies the last element to the suggested position, and then decreases `size` by 1. The two actions can be combined into a single statement (Line 105):

$$\text{theNames[index] = theNames[- size].}$$

Since the - appears before `size`, the decrement occurs before the assignment to `theName[index]`.

```
101     // method for removal
102     public static void remove( int index ) {
103       if ( index >= 0 && index < size )
104       {
105         theNames[ index ] = theNames[ -- size ];
106       }
107       else
108       {
109         System.out.println( "The specified position does not exist." );
110       }
111     }
```

Listing 13.20 A program that uses an array with capacity and size (part 6). The method for removing an element

Here is an execution example of the code, where the names of several notable female jazz musicians appear as data to be stored.[4]

```
 1   java FixedSizeUnsorted
 2   Enter capacity: 100
 3   A(dd), R(emove), P(rint), S(earch), Q(uit): A
 4   Enter new names, empty line to finish:
 5   > Joanne Brackeen
 6   > Terri Lyn Carrington
 7   > Blossom Dearie
 8   > Diana Krall
 9   > Carmen McRae
10   > Linda May Oh
11   > Sarah Vaughan
12   > Dianne Reeves
13   > Norma Winstone
14   > Nancy Wilson
15   >
16   A(dd), R(emove), P(rint), S(earch), Q(uit): P
17   0000:Joanne Brackeen
18   0001:Terri Lyn Carrington
19   0002:Blossom Dearie
20   0003:Diana Krall
21   0004:Carmen McRae
22   0005:Linda May Oh
```

[4]Diana Jean Krall (born November 16, 1964) is a Canadian jazz pianist and singer. She is an Officer of the Order of Canada and an officer of the Order of British Columbia, Canada. Dianne Reeves (born October 23, 1956) is an American jazz singer. Sarah Lois Vaughan (March 27, 1924 to April 3, 1990) was an American jazz singer. Cassandra Wilson (born December 4, 1955) is an American jazz musician, vocalist, songwriter, and producer. Nancy Wilson (born February 20, 1937) is an American singer, who has won three Grammy awards. Norma Ann Winstone (born 23 September 1941) is a British jazz singer and lyricist. She has the rank Most Excellent Order of the British Empire.

```
23   0006:Sarah Vaughan
24   0007:Dianne Reeves
25   0008:Norma Winstone
26   0009:Nancy Wilson
27   A(dd), R(emove), P(rint), S(earch), Q(uit): A
28   Enter new names, empty line to finish:
29   > Cassandra Wilson
30   > Norma Winstone
31   >
32   A(dd), R(emove), P(rint), S(earch), Q(uit): S
33   Enter a search key: Wilson
34   Found at 0009 in Nancy Wilson
35   Found at 0010 in Cassandra Wilson
36   A(dd), R(emove), P(rint), S(earch), Q(uit): R
37   Enter an index for removal: 0
38   A(dd), R(emove), P(rint), S(earch), Q(uit): P
39   0000:Norma Winstone
40   0001:Terri Lyn Carrington
41   0002:Blossom Dearie
42   0003:Diana Krall
43   0004:Carmen McRae
44   0005:Linda May Oh
45   0006:Sarah Vaughan
46   0007:Dianne Reeves
47   0008:Norma Winstone
48   0009:Nancy Wilson
49   0010:Cassandra Wilson
50   A(dd), R(emove), P(rint), S(earch), Q(uit): Q
51   Closing...
```

Summary

■ The class `Arrays` provides a number of useful methods.

■ Using a temporary variable, the values can be exchanged between two variables. Similarly, using a temporary variable, the values can be exchanged between two array elements.

■ Using the idea of temporary variables, the elements of an array can be circularly moved and the appearance order of elements in an array can be reversed.

■ Changing the length of an array requires an instantiation of a new array.

■ Sequential search is the standard search method of an element in an array.

■ If the elements are sorted, binary search can be used in place of sequential search.

■ An array with capacity and size can be used to store an indefinite number of elements in an array.

Exercises

1. **A method that checks some property of an array, 1**

```
1   public static int matched( int[] a )
2   {
3     int count = 0;
4     for ( int pos = 0; pos < ( a.length + 1 ) / 2; pos ++ )
5     {
6       if ( a[ pos ] == a[ a.length - pos - 1 ] )
7       {
8         count ++;
9       }
10    }
11    return count;
12  }
```

For each of the following int arrays, state the value returned by the method:
   (a) [0, 1, 2, 3, 3, 2, 1, 0]
   (b) [0, 1, 2, 3, 0, 1, 2]
   (c) [0, 1, 2, 3, 4, 3, 2, 1, 0]

2. **A method that checks some property of an array, 2**   For each of the following int arrays, state the value returned by the method:

```
1   public static int matched( int[] a )
2   {
3     int count = 0;
4     int offset = a.length/2;
5     for ( int position = 0; position < offset; position ++ )
6     {
7       if ( a[ position ] == a[ offset + position ] )
8       {
9         count ++;
10      }
11    }
12    return count;
13  }
```

   (a) {8, 7, 6, 8, 7, 6, 5}
   (b) {0, 1, 4, 7, 1, 4}
   (c) {0, 1, 2, 3, 4, 3, 2, 1, 0}

3. **Copying and then sorting**   Write a method named copyAndSort(double[] data) that returns the sorted version of data. Use methods from Arrays so that the source code does not have loops.

4. **Search for a key**   Write a public static method, searchForProbe, that returns if an array contains a search key, where the method receives an array of String data and a String data as the search key. If the array contains the key, method must return one of the indexes at which the key appears; otherwise, the method must return -1.

5. **Count matches in an array**   Write a public static method named countMatches that returns the number of elements in an array of String data that are equal to a given key. The method has two formal parameters. One is the array in which the key is searched for, and the other is the search key.

6. **Counting elements in an array whose values are in a range** Write a public static method named `searchInRange` that returns the number of elements in an array of `int` values that are strictly greater than a given `int` value and strictly less than another given `int` value. The formal parameters of the method are the array in which the numbers are sought, the lower bound, and the upper bound.

7. **Counting elements in an array whose values are outside a range** Write a public static method named `searchOutOfRange` that receives an array of `int` values and two additional `int` values as formal parameters, and returns the number of elements in the array that are either less than the first `int` value or greater than the second `int` value.

8. **Is a sequence increasing?** Write a public static method named `isIncreasing` that returns a `boolean` representing whether or not the elements in an array of `int` values are strictly increasing. The method receives the array as its formal parameter.

9. **Is a sequence decreasing?** Write a public static method named `isNondecreasing` that returns a `boolean` representing whether or not the elements of an array of `int` values are non-decreasing. The method receives the array as its formal parameter.

10. **Is a sequence pairwise distinct?** Write a public static method named `isDistinct` that returns a `boolean` representing whether or not two arrays of `int` values have no elements in common. The arrays are given as formal parameters. The elements in the array and their order of appearance must be preserved, so `Arrays.sort` cannot be performed on the parameters.

11. **Even number checking** Write a public static method named `evenParityCheck` that returns a `boolean` representing whether or not any even number appears in an array. The method receives the array as its formal parameter.

12. **lastIndexOf an element** Write a method named `lastIndexInArray` that computes the last position at which a given key appears in the array, where the type of the elements and the key is `char`. If the key does not appear in the array, the method should return `-1`. The method receives the array and the key as its formal parameters.

13. **secondToLastIndexOf an element** Write a method named `secondToLastIndexInArray` that computes the second to last position at which a given key appears, where the type of the elements and the key is `char`. If the key does not appear in the array more than once, the method should return `-1`. The method receives the array and the key as its formal parameters.

14. **Computing (max–min) of array elements** Write a method named `valueWidth` that returns the difference between the largest and the smallest numbers appearing in an array, where the array elements are `int` values. The method receives the array as its formal parameter.

15. **Characters occurring only once** Write a method named `singlyOccurringCharCount` that receives a `String` data, and then returns, of those characters appearing in the `String`, how many appear just once in it. Use the method `toCharArray` of `String` to obtain an array version of the class `String`, and then use the method `sort` of the class `Arrays` to obtain a sorted list of the characters in the array.

16. **Sorting** Write a program, `RandomArraySort`, that generates an array of random `int` data, and then sorts the array. The user specifies the length of the array as well as the value range of the elements in the array with its minimum and maximum. After generating the array randomly, the program prints the elements of the array, sorts the elements using `Arrays.sort`, and then prints the elements again. Design and use a method for printing the elements of an array of `int` values. The format is five elements per line, 12 character spaces per element, flush right, and without currency punctuation. Since the longest `int` without punctuation requires 11 character spaces, this should put at least once space between the elements in the same line.

The program may run as follows:

```
1   Enter size, the smallest, and the largest: 20 -1000000 1000000
2   ********Before sorting
3        817304      -680967      580358      698246     -552187
4        401077      -481882     -967384      664908      839001
5        185968      -462035      341899     -940863     -260153
6       -832638       225017      136135     -310982     -391535
7   ********Before sorting
8       -967384      -940863     -832638     -680967     -552187
9       -481882      -462035     -391535     -310982     -260153
10       136135       185968      225017      341899      401077
11       580358       664908      698246      817304      839001
```

17. **A simple merge of three arrays**   Write a program, SimpleThreeMerge, that generates three arrays of random integers with identical lengths, and then merges the three into one. The user specifies the length as well as the range of the values of the array elements. The array generated by merging should be three times as long as the individual arrays. The array should contain the elements of the first array in the first third in the order they appear, the elements of the second array in the second third in the order they appear, and the elements of the third array in the last third in the order they appear. The program must print the elements of the individual arrays as well as the elements of the array that contains all three. Design and use a method for printing the elements of an array of int values. The format is five elements per line, 12 character spaces per element, flush right, and without currency punctuation. Since the longest int without punctuation requires 11 character spaces, this should put at least once space between the elements in the same line. The program may run as follows:

```
1   Enter size, the smallest, and the largest: 10 -100000000 100000000
2   ********Data 1
3      -33384206    -28969551     47024306    -33694198     -6858007
4       84681217    -72689949    -60679845    -99988760     -1229077
5   ********Data 2
6      -21488327     66203194    -60898244     31539203    -45065541
7       71798105      3208921    -12009976    -91486999     86835731
8   ********Data 3
9      -22300371    -18684131     46783358      6312420    -20064955
10     -42988143     59528769     62786162    -43964318    -65677842
11  ********Merged
12     -33384206    -28969551     47024306    -33694198     -6858007
13      84681217    -72689949    -60679845    -99988760     -1229077
14     -21488327     66203194    -60898244     31539203    -45065541
15      71798105      3208921    -12009976    -91486999     86835731
16     -22300371    -18684131     46783358      6312420    -20064955
17     -42988143     59528769     62786162    -43964318    -65677842
```

Programming Projects

18. **Merging three sorted arrays so that there are no duplicates**   Write a method named threeMerge that receives three sorted arrays of int values, and then returns a new array, in which all the elements of the three arrays appear in nondecreasing order. Let a, b, and c be the three arrays and let merged be the array to be returned. Suppose we use three int variables p, q, and r as indexes to the elements of the three arrays. The initial value is 0 for each of the three index variables. We can write a source code for merging as follows:

```
1    for ( int i = 0; i < merged.length; i ++ )
2    {
3      if ( X ) { merged[ i ] = a[ p ++ ]; }
4      else if ( Y ) { merged[ i ] = b[ q ++ ]; }
5      else { merged[ i ] = c[ r ++ ]; }
6    }
```

Assuming a tie can be broken arbitrary, figure out what conditions can be used where indicated with X and Y.

19. **Write-in election**   Write a program, `Election`, that computes the tally in a write-in election, and announces the winner. Since the votes are write-in, there is no predetermined set of candidates. Whoever appears the most in the votes is the winner. The user enters the individual votes, one vote per line, and ends entering with either typing an empty line or pressing CTRL-D. To compute the tally, the program uses two arrays, a `String[]` variable, `names`, and an `int[]` variable, `counts`. Upon receiving a single vote, the program checks if the name on the vote appears in `names`, and if it does, the program adds 1 to the value of the element in `count` at the position corresponding to the name; if the name does not appear in `names`, the program extends both arrays by one element, stores the name in `names` at the last position and stores 1 in `counts` at the last position. In this manner, the two arrays will have the same lengths. The initial length is 0 for both arrays.

Here is an example of how the program may run:

```
1    ############################################
2    # Enter the votes, one vote per line.      #
3    # End with either CTRL-D or an empty line.#
4    ############################################
5    Frodo
6    Sam
7    Pippin
8    Frodo
9    Frodo
10   Pippin
11   Pippin
12   Pippin
13   Sam
14   Sam
15   Pippin
16
17   Frodo received 3 votes.
18   Sam received 3 votes.
19   Pippin received 5 votes.
20   --------
21   The winner is Pippin!
```

20. **Sorting two arrays and merging them into one sorted array**   Write a program, `TwoMerge`, that generates two arrays of an identical length that are filled with random integers, sorts them, and merges the sorted two arrays into one sorted array. The user specifies the length and the range of the numbers to be generated with its minimum and maximum. The program must print the elements of the individual and the merged arrays. Write a method for printing the elements of an array of `int` values. The format is five elements per line, 12 character spaces per element, flush right, and without currency punctuation. Also, write a method for merging two sorted arrays having the same lengths into one. Merging two sorted arrays can be accomplished using the

following idea: Concurrently examine the elements of the two arrays in the order they appear, one element at a time from each array, selecting whichever the smaller of the two as the next element in the merged array. The program may run as follows:

```
 1   Enter size, the smallest, and the largest: 20 -100 100
 2   ********Data 1
 3          -94           -84           -82           -81           -73
 4          -68           -62           -50           -49           -47
 5          -31           -24           -20            11            21
 6           23            51            53            59            66
 7   ********Data 2
 8          -86           -84           -79           -75           -71
 9          -64           -53           -45           -30           -28
10          -25           -24             3             6            42
11           48            50            65            69            87
12   ********Merged
13          -94           -86           -84           -84           -82
14          -81           -79           -75           -73           -71
15          -68           -64           -62           -53           -50
16          -49           -47           -45           -31           -30
17          -28           -25           -24           -24           -20
18            3             6            11            21            23
19           42            48            50            51            53
20           59            65            66            69            87
```

21. **Reading double tokens and quantifying changes**   Write a program, NumberTokens, that receives a sequence of floating point numbers of an indefinite length from the user, and reporting the results of comparing the numbers after the first one to their immediate predecessors. The comparison has three outcomes: 'U' to mean "significantly greater than the predecessor", 'D' to mean "significantly smaller than the predecessor", and "neither". The "significance" of difference is measured by the absolute difference compared to a fixed positive threshold. In other words, the present value is significantly greater than its predecessor if the present value is greater than the predecessor plus the threshold, and the present value is significantly smaller than its predecessor if the present value is smaller than the predecessor minus the threshold. The threshold is entered after the input number sequence is entered, so the input sequence must be stored in an array.

The program may run as follows:

```
 1   Enter numbers, empty line to stop
 2   > 3.4 5.3 9.0 -1.7 -24.5 -23 -22 -21 -19 0 18
 3   > 17 19 20 23.7 8.5 7.5 2.5
 4   >
 5   Enter threshold (a negative to stop): 5
 6   --DD----UU----D-D
 7   Enter threshold (a negative to stop): 10
 8   --DD----UU----D--
 9   Enter threshold (a negative to stop): 20
10   ---D-------------
11   Enter threshold (a negative to stop): -1
```

Multidimensional Arrays

14

14.1 Rectangular Arrays

14.1.1 Defining Multi-Dimensional Arrays

Arrays may have more than one dimension. We call arrays having more than one dimension **multi-dimensional arrays**. For an integer $N \geq 1$, an N-dimensional array as a type is declared with N pairs of brackets []. In the following code, mDouble is declared as a two-dimensional array of double and myFlags is declared as a three-dimensional array of boolean.

```
1  double[][] myDouble;
2  boolean[][][] myFlags;
```

In an instantiation of a multi-dimensional array, the length must be specified for at least one dimension, but not necessarily for all of them. In the following code, the first line instantiates a two-dimensional array whose first dimension has length 11 and whose second dimension has length 35, and the second line instantiates a three-dimensional array whose first dimension has length 3. In the second array, the three elements myFlags[0], myFlags[1], and myFlags[2] are expected to be two-dimensional arrays, but they are presently null and so their shapes are unknown yet.

```
3  myDouble = new double[ 11 ][ 35 ];
4  myFlags = new boolean[ 3 ][][];
```

In an instantiation of a multi-dimensional array, if one dimension is without length specification, so must be its subsequent dimensions. Therefore,

```
myDouble = new double[][ 7 ];
myFlags = new boolean[ 5 ][][ 4 ];
```

are both syntactically incorrect.

© Springer Nature Switzerland AG 2018
M. Ogihara, *Fundamentals of Java Programming*,
https://doi.org/10.1007/978-3-319-89491-1_14

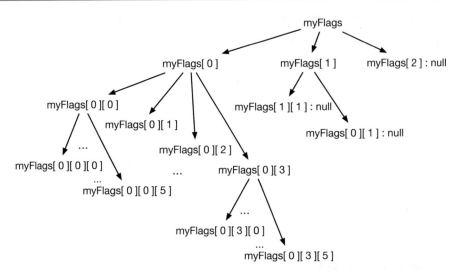

Fig. 14.1   The structure of a multi-dimensional array. The word "nulll" indicates subarrays that are `null`

After Line 4 of the above code example, possibly different two-dimensional arrays can be assigned to the three elements of `myFlags`. For example,

```
5   myFlags[ 0 ] = new boolean[ 4 ][ 6 ];
6   myFlags[ 1 ] = new boolean[ 2 ][];
```

assigns a 4-by-6 array to `myFlag[ 0 ]` and a two-dimensional array with first dimension having length 2 to `myFlag[ 1 ]`, but keeps `myFlags[ 2 ]` as `null`. A sub-array element of a multi-dimensional array can be accessed by specifying indexes to consecutive dimensions, where the values of the indexes start from 0 in every dimension that is already defined. Each sub-array element of a multi-dimensional array that is not equal to `null` can be inquired for the length of its first dimension using `.length`. In other words, after Line 6, `myFlags.length`, `myFlags[ 0 ].length`, and `myFlags[ 1 ].length` produce the values 3, 4, and 7 respectively, and for all i between 0 and 3, `myFlags[ 0 ][ i ].length` produces the value 6. For other index specification, such as `myFlags[ 1 ][ 0 ]`, whose subarray is `null` leads to `NullPointerException`. Figure 14.1 shows the structure of `myFlags`.

For a multi-dimensional array with length specifications for all of its possible dimensions, if its length specifications are uniform (for example, 3-by-5-by-6), we call it a **regularly shaped array**; otherwise, we call it an **irregularly shaped array** or a **jagged array**. We call a two-dimensional regularly shaped array a **rectangular array**, and a rectangular array whose dimensions have the same lengths a **square array**.

14.1.2 Summing the Elements in Subsequences

Consider computing the summation of elements for all subsequences of a number sequence $a_0, \ldots, a_{N-1}$. The task is to obtain

$$s(i, j) = \sum_{k=i}^{j} a_k = a_i + \ldots + a_j$$

for all i and j such that $0 \leq i \leq j \leq N - 1$. For all $0 \leq j < i \leq N - 1$, $s(i, j)$ is defined to be 0. Including the cases where the value is trivially 0, there are N possibilities for both i and j, so we can view the task as calculating the elements of a regularly-shaped two-dimensional array, both of whose dimensions have length N. Suppose the input sequence is represented by an array of int, a, whose length is n. The goal is to produce a two-dimensional array of int, sums [n] [n]. The declaration and the instantiation of the two-dimensional array can be as follows:

```
1  int [] [] sums;
2  sums = new int [ a.length ] [ a.length ];
```

We note the following three properties:

- For all i and j such that i > j, sum [i] [j] must become 0. Since the default value of int is 0, this property is already satisfied.
- For all i, sums [i] [i] must become a [i].
- For all i and j such that i < j, sum must satisfy the condition sum [i] [j] == a [j] + sums [i] [j - 1].

These properties suggest the following strategy for computing the table. For each row i, store a [i] in sums [i] [i], and then using a for-loop that iterates over the sequence i + 1, ..., a.length - 1 with another int variable named j, store a [j] + sums [i] [j - 1] in sums [i] [j].

The following source code is based upon these observations. The method readData is for obtaining an input number sequence from the user. The method has the return type of int [] (Line 9). The user first specifies the length of the sequence. This value is stored in an int variable named len (Line 11). After instantiating an array numbers with new int [len] (Line 12), the program receives the elements of the array from the user (Lines 13–17), and then returns the array (Line 18).

```
1   import java.io. * ;
2   import java.util. * ;
3   // computer all partials sums of an array
4   public class PartialSumsAll
5   {
6     // read an array from a given scanner
7     public static int [] readData ()
8     {
9       Scanner keyboard = new Scanner ( System.in );
10      System.out.print ( "Enter the length: " );
11      int len = keyboard.nextInt ();
12      int [] numbers = new int [ len ];
13      for ( int pos = 0; pos < len; pos ++ )
14      {
15        System.out.printf ( "Enter element at %d: ", pos );
16        numbers [ pos ] = keyboard.nextInt ();
17      }
18      return numbers;
19    }
20
```

Listing 14.1 A program that computing partial sums using a two-dimensional array (part 1). The method readData

The method partialsAll receives a one-dimensional int array, oneD, as its formal parameter, and returns a two-dimensional array whose elements are the values of the summations. The program instantiates a two-dimensional array as `oneD.length` by `oneD.length` (Line 24). The method then executes a double for-loop to fill this array. The external for-loop generates the row index with a variable named `rowPos` (Line 25). For each value of `rowPos`, the method stores `oneD[ rowPos ]` in `twoD[ rowPos ][ rowPos ]` (Line 27), and then using an internal for-loop, generates the column index values `rowPos + 1, ..., oneD.length - 1` with a variable named `colPos` (Line 28), and stores `twoD[ rowPos ][ colPos - 1 ] +oneD[ colPos ]` in `twoD[ rowPos ][ colPos ]` (Lines 30 and 31). After the double for-loop, the method returns `twoD` (Line 34).

```
21      // compute the partial sums of an input array
22      public static int[][] partialsAll( int[] oneD )
23      {
24        int[][] twoD = new int[ oneD.length ][ oneD.length ];
25        for ( int rowPos = 0; rowPos < oneD.length; rowPos ++ )
26        {
27          twoD[ rowPos ][ rowPos ] = oneD[ rowPos ];
28          for ( int colPos = rowPos + 1; colPos < oneD.length; colPos ++ )
29          {
30            twoD[ rowPos ][ colPos ]
31                = twoD[ rowPos ][ colPos - 1 ] + oneD[ colPos ];
32          }
33        }
34        return twoD;
35      }
36
```

Listing 14.2 A program that computing partial sums using a two-dimensional array (part 2). The method `partialsAll`

The method `print` is for printing the data of a two-dimensional array (Line 38). The program uses a double for-loop to generate row-column index pairs with variables `rowPos` and `colPos` (Lines 40 and 42), and then prints `twoD[ rowPos ][ colPos ]` using the format `%5d` (Line 44). At the end of each row, the method prints the newline (Line 46).

```
37      //-- print
38      public static void print( int[][] twoD )
39      {
40        for ( int rowPos = 0; rowPos < twoD.length; rowPos ++ )
41        {
42          for ( int colPos = 0; colPos < twoD.length; colPos ++ )
43          {
44            System.out.printf( "%5d", twoD[ rowPos ][ colPos ] );
45          }
46          System.out.println();
47        }
48      }
49
```

Listing 14.3 A program that computing partial sums using a two-dimensional array (part 3). The method `print`

The method `main` obtains a one-dimensional array from the user by calling `readData` (Line 53), computes the partial sums by calling `partialsAll` (Line 54), and then prints the contents of the partial sums by calling `print` (Line 55).

```
50    //-- main
51    public static void main( String[] args )
52    {
53      int[] a = readData();
54      int[][] sums = partialsAll( a );
55      print( sums );
56      // print( partialsAll( readData() ) );
57    }
58  }
```

Listing 14.4 A program that computing partial sums using a two-dimensional array (part 4). The main part

Alternatively, the three method calls appearing in the method `main` can be combined into one:

```
print( partialsAll( readData() ) );
```

Here is an execution example of the program:

```
1   Enter the length: 5
2   Enter element at 0: 10
3   Enter element at 1: 13
4   Enter element at 2: 17
5   Enter element at 3: -30
6   Enter element at 4: -5
7      10    23    40    10      5
8       0    13    30     0     -5
9       0     0    17   -13    -18
10      0     0     0   -30    -35
11      0     0     0     0     -5
```

14.2   Jagged Arrays

Consider receiving the names and scores for a number of people, and then computing the average score for each person, where the numbers of scores available can be different from person to person. We can use a two-dimensional jagged array for recording the scores, an array of `String` data to record names, and an array of `double` data to record the average scores.

The first part deals with the instantiation of the arrays. The user enters the number of people whose records are available. The program stores this number in a variable named `nPeople` (Lines 8 and 9), and then instantiates the three arrays (Lines 11–13).

```
1   import java.util. *;
2   public class Jagged
3   {
4     public static void main( String[] args )
5     {
6       Scanner keyboard = new Scanner( System.in );
7
8       System.out.print( "Enter # of people: " );
9       int nPeople = keyboard.nextInt();
10
11      double[][] data = new double[ nPeople ][];
12      String[] names = new String[ nPeople ];
13      double[] average = new double[ nPeople ];
14
```

Listing 14.5 A program that receives the names and scores for a number of students and reports the averages of the scores (part 1). The part responsible for receiving the number of people and creating array variables

The next is the part for receiving the names and scores. The program uses a for-loop that iterates over the sequence 0, ..., nPeople - 1 with a variable named index. At each round, the program receives the name of the person (Lines 17 and 18), receives the number of scores for that person, stores the number in a variable named size (Lines 19 and 20), instantiates data[index] with new double[size] (Line 21), and then uses an interior for-loop to generate column indexes 0, ..., size - 1 with a variable named col (Line 23) to receive the elements data[index][0], ..., data[index][size - 1] (Line 25).

```
15      for ( int index = 0; index < nPeople; index ++ )
16      {
17        System.out.printf( "Enter name for %d: ", index );
18        names[ index ] = keyboard.next();
19        System.out.printf( "Enter #entries %d: ", index );
20        int size = keyboard.nextInt();
21        data[ index ] = new double[ size ];
22        System.out.printf( "Enter %d data: ", size, index );
23        for ( int col = 0; col < size; col ++ )
24        {
25          data[ index ][ col ] = keyboard.nextDouble();
26        }
27      }
28
```

Listing 14.6 A program that receives the names and scores for a number of students and reports the averages of the scores (part 2). The part responsible for receiving the names and the scores

The calculation of the averages requires a double for-loop. The external for-loop iterates over the sequence 0, ..., nPeople - 1 with a variable named index (Line 29). The internal for-loop iterates over the sequence 0, ..., data[index].length - 1 with a variable named col (Line 31). The program stores the total of the scores appearing in that row in average[index] (Line 33). Then, with the division by data[index].length, the program scales the total stored in average[index] to the average.

```
29    for ( int index = 0; index < nPeople; index ++ )
30    {
31       for ( int col = 0; col < data[ index ].length; col ++ )
32       {
33          average[ index ] += data[ index ][ col ];
34       }
35       average[ index ] /= data[ index ].length;
36    }
37
```

Listing 14.7 A program that receives the names and scores for a number of students and reports the averages of the scores (part 3). The part responsible for computing the averages

The last part of the code handles the output. Again, the program uses a double for-loop (Lines 38 and 42) for accessing the individual scores. The program also prints the name (Line 40) and the average (Line 47) for each person.

```
38    for ( int index = 0; index < nPeople; index ++ )
39    {
40       System.out.printf( "Name at %d is %s%n", index, names[ index ] );
41       System.out.print( "The data are: " );
42       for ( int col = 0; col < data[ index ].length; col ++ )
43       {
44          System.out.printf( " %.3f", data[ index ][ col ] );
45       }
46       System.out.println();
47       System.out.printf( "Average is %.3f%n", average[ index ] );
48    }
49    }
50 }
```

Listing 14.8 A program that receives the names and scores for a number of students and reports the averages of the scores (part 4). The part responsible for reporting the results

Here is an execution example of the code.

```
 1  Enter # of people: 4
 2  Enter name for 0: Amelia
 3  Enter #entries 0: 5
 4  Enter 5 data: 90 91 92 93 84
 5  Enter name for 1: Brittany
 6  Enter #entries 1: 4
 7  Enter 4 data: 89 91 89 94
 8  Enter name for 2: Carolyn
 9  Enter #entries 2: 3
10  Enter 3 data: 75 76 77
11  Enter name for 3: Diane
12  Enter #entries 3: 4
13  Enter 4 data: 100 89 99 97
14  Name at 0 is Amelia
15  The data are:   90.000 91.000 92.000 93.000 84.000
16  Average is 90.000
17  Name at 1 is Brittany
18  The data are:   89.000 91.000 89.000 94.000
19  Average is 90.750
20  Name at 2 is Carolyn
21  The data are:   75.000 76.000 77.000
22  Average is 76.000
23  Name at 3 is Diane
24  The data are:   100.000 89.000 99.000 97.000
25  Average is 96.250
```

Summary

■ By attaching multiple bracket pairs, [], to a data type, multi-dimensional arrays can be declared.

■ An instantiation of a multi-dimensional array requires the length specification for the first dimension.

■ In an instantiation of a multi-dimensional array, if the length specification of one dimension is skipped, then the length specification must be skipped for all the dimensions that follow.

Exercises

1. **Creating and printing a jagged array** Write a program, CreatePrintJagged, that instantiates a two-dimensional jagged array of double values that has ten rows. The lengths of the ten rows should be 0, ..., 9 in this order. For each individual element of the array, the program generates a random real number between 100 and 200. After generating the array, the program prints the elements of the array, one row per line. For printing the numbers, the program must use %9.4f. In this manner, without additional spacing, one whitespace appears before each number.

2. **Converting a square array to a one-dimensional array, part1** Write a method, rectangularArrayToLinear, that converts a two-dimensional rectangular array of int values to a one-dimensional array of int values by concatenating the elements of the rows of the array.

3. **Converting a square array to a one-dimensional array, part2** Write a method, rectangularArrayToLearnAlt, that converts a two-dimensional rectangular array of

int values to a one-dimensional array of int values by concatenating the elements of the columns of the array.

4. **Converting a one-dimensional array to a square array, part 1** Write a method, breakIntoSquareArray, that converts a one-dimensional array of int values, to a two-dimensional square array of int, where the length of the one-dimensional array may not be a perfect square. The return type of the method is int[][]. Find the largest perfect square that is less than or equal to the length of the one-dimensional array. Use the square root of the largest square as the length of each dimension of the square array. Place the elements of the one-dimensional array should be placed in the two-dimensional array in the row major order. If the length of the one-dimensional array is not a perfect square, there will be elements that are not included in the square array.

5. **Converting a one-dimensional array to a square array, part 2** Write a method, breakIntoSquareArrayAlt, that converts a one-dimensional array of int to a two-dimensional square array of int, where the length of the one-dimensional array may not be a perfect square. The return type of the method is int[][]. Find the largest perfect square that is less than or equal to the length of the one-dimensional array. Use the square root of the largest square as the length of each dimension of the square array. Place the elements of the one-dimensional array should be placed in the two-dimensional array in the column major order.

6. **Square array** Write a method, isArraySquare, that receives a two-dimensional array of double values, and then returns a boolean value representing whether or not the array is a square array. The method must return true if the array has 0 rows.

7. **Rectangular array** Write a method, isArrayRectangle, that receives a two-dimensional array of double values, and then returns a boolean value representing whether or not the array is a rectangular array. The method must return true if the array has 0 rows.

8. **Diagonal array** A square matrix is said to be a diagonal matrix if its all 0 except where the row index is equal to the column index. Write a method, isDiagonal, that checks whether or not a two-dimensional array is a diagonal array. The formal parameter of a method is a two-dimensional array of double values. The method must return a boolean value representing whether or not the array is a diagonal array.

9. **Upper-triangular array** A two-dimensional array is an upper-triangular array if it is a square array and is all 0 except where the column index is greater than or equal to the row index. Write a method, isUpperTriangular, that checks if a two-dimensional array is a upper-triangular array. The formal parameter of a method is a two-dimensional array of double values. The method must return a boolean value representing whether or not the array is an upper-triangular array.

Programming Projects

10. **Sudoku checking** Sudoku is a number puzzle in which the goal is to complete a 9-by-9 table that is partially filled. When completed, the table must satisfy the following conditions:
    - In each row, 1 through 9 must appear exactly once each.
    - In each column, 1 through 9 must appear exactly once each.
    - The 9-by-9 table can be naturally divided into nine 3-by-3 subtables. The third requirement is that in each 3-by-3 subtable, 1 through 9 must appear exactly once each.

    Write a method, sudokuSolutionCheck, that receives a 9-by-9 two-dimensional array of int values as its formal parameter, and then returns whether or not the array represents a Sudoku solution. The method may halt with ArrayIndexOutOfBoundsExceptions if the row or column dimension of the array is smaller than 9 or the array contains an element smaller than 1 or greater than 9.

11. **Sudoku checking with holes**   Continuing on the previous problem, suppose that a partial solution to a Sudoku puzzle is represented by a 9-by-9 array of int values, where the elements are from 0 through 9 with 0 means that the value of the square is yet to be determined. Write a method, sudokuPartialSolutionCheck, that receives a 9-by-9 array of int values as its formal parameter, and then returns whether or not the partial solution represented by the array contains no violations of the three rules given in the statement of the previous question.

12. **Bingo card generation**   Bingo is a game played by any number of players and one master. Each player has a card on which a 5-by-5 table of numbers is printed, where the numbers are chosen from 1, ..., 99 with no duplication and the center of the table has no number written. No two players have the same tables. To play the game, the master generates a random permutation of the number sequence 1, ..., 99, and then announces the numbers as they appear in the permuted sequence. Each time the master announces a number, each player checks if the number that just has been announced appears on her card. If so, she crosses out the number on her card. The center is thought of as being crossed out. If one row, one column, or one diagonal has been completely crossed out on her card, a player receives a prize and leaves the game.

Suppose we use a 5 × 5 array of int values to encode a Bingo card, with −1 representing any number that has already been crossed out. Write a program, BingoCardGenerate, that generates a random Bingo card where the center is the only place that the number has been crossed out. A simple solution will be to conduct a random exchange on an array { 1, ..., 99 } 25 times, fill the array with the first 25 numbers on the permuted sequence, and then change the center to −1.

Here is a possible output of the program:

```
1    23   9 15 77 67
2    64 19 86  7 45
3    24 68 -1 74 22
4    78 34 63 59 40
5    39 25  8  1  2
```

13. **Bingo checking**   Continuing on the previous question, suppose we use a 5×5 array of boolean values to encode the places of a card that have been crossed out. In the encoding, true means "crossed out" and false means "has not been crossed out". Write a method, bingoCheck, that receives a 5-by-5 boolean table, and then determines whether or not the player can claim the completion to receive a prize.

Class `File` 15

15.1 Class `File`

15.1.1 The File Path and the Instantiation of a `File` Object

As mentioned in Chap. 3, data can be read from text files with methods applied to `Scanner` objects instantiated with objects of type `File`. `File` is a class that represents files (including non-text files and file folders). To use `File` in a program, `File` must be imported by one of the following two import statements:

```
import java.io.File;
import java.io.*;
```

The `*` appearing the second import statement is a wildcard.

A `File` object can be instantiated with a file path as a parameter. A file path is a character sequence that represents a series of relative movements from a folder to another, starting with the present working folder and ending with a folder or a non-folder file (called a **regular file**).

Each "relative" movement specifies moving to a specific child folder, staying in the present folder, or moving to the parent folder. The specification of the child folder in the first case is by its name. The present folder and the parent folder are represented by `.` and `..`, respectively. For example, the folder name sequence

```
[ .., Documents, programs, test ]
```

specifies: moving to the parent folder, moving to the `Documents` folder, and then moving to the `programs` folder. The last entry `test` refers to a file or a folder named `test` residing in the folder `programs`. A `String` representation of a path is the concatenation of the movements and the name at the end with a special delimiter appearing in between. The delimiter is the backslash, `\`, in the case of the Windows and the forward slash, `/`, in the case of the others. Thus, the `String` representation of the file path is

```
"..\Documents\programs\test"
```

for the Windows, and

```
"../Documents/programs/test"
```

© Springer International Publishing AG, part of Springer Nature 2018
M. Ogihara, *Fundamentals of Java Programming*,
https://doi.org/10.1007/978-3-319-89491-1_15

for the other systems. If the separator character appears consecutively (for instance, ///), it is treated as just one separator.

The **absolute file path** to a file is the path that starts from the root of the file system. In the case of Windows, the root is specified by a single letter corresponding to the drive name (quite often, the drive name is C) followed by :\. In the case of other operating systems, the root is specified by the forward slash, /. An absolute file path may depend on how the file system is built and how the path is created in the program, so it may contain ., .., or consecutive appearances of the folder separator character. An absolute file path with such occurrences is redundant, and can be simplified into one that contains no such occurrences. We call such an absolute path without redundancy a **canonical path**. If p is a file path ending with a folder and q is a relative path, the concatenation p and q with the separator character between them is also a file path.

File has three constructors that receive a String data as a parameter. They are File(String p), File(File f, String p), and File(String f, String p). In the last two, f and p are expected to represent a folder and a relative file path respectively. Let us take a look at an example. Suppose a file records.txt has the canonical path /Users/maria/docs/records.txt (in a non-Windows system), and this file is accessed from a Java program located in a folder whose canonical path is /Users/maria/javacode. Then, File objects representing records.txt can be instantiated using any one of the following f0, ..., f5:

```
File f0 = new File( "/Users/maria/docs/records.txt" );
File f1 = new File( "../docs/records.txt" );
File f2 = new File( new File( "../docs", "records.txt" ) );
File f3 = new File( "../docs", "records.txt" );
File f4 = new File( "../../maria", "docs/records.txt" );
File f5 = new File( "../../maria/docs", "records.txt" );
```

The absolute paths of the five File objects, in the order of appearance, are as follows:

```
f0: /Users/maria/docs/records.txt
f1: /Users/maria/javacode/../docs/records.txt
f2: /Users/maria/javacode/../docs/records.txt
f3: /Users/maria/javacode/../docs/records.txt
f4: /Users/maria/javacode/../../maria/docs/records.txt
f5: /Users/maria/javacode/../../maria/docs/records.txt
```

The instantiation of a File object does not guarantee the validity of the path, let alone the existence of the file specified by the path.

15.1.2 File Methods

Class File has many instance methods. Table 15.1 summarizes the instance methods that are covered in this chapter.

There are methods that inquire about the properties of the file represented by the File object. exists returns a boolean value representing whether or not the file indeed exists. canRead returns a boolean value representing if the file represented by the File object is readable. canWrite returns a boolean value representing if the file represented by the File object can be overwritten. canExecute returns a boolean value representing if the file represented by the File object can be executed. isDirectory returns a boolean value representing if the file represented by the File object is a folder. isFile returns a boolean value representing if the file represented by the File object is a regular file.

Table 15.1 A list of File methods

Name	Return type	Action
exists()	boolean	Returns whether or not f exists
canRead()	boolean	Returns whether or not f exists and can be read
canWrite()	boolean	Returns whether or not f exists and can be overwritten
canExecute()	boolean	Returns whether or not f exists and can be executed
isDirectory()	boolean	Returns whether or not f exists as a folder
isFile()	boolean	Returns whether or not f exists as a regular file
getName()	String	Returns the name of f
getAbsolutePath()	String	Returns the absolute path to f
getAbsoluteFile()	File	Returns a File object instantiated with the absolute path to f
getCanonicalPath()	String	Returns the canonical path to f
getCanonicalFile()	File	Returns a File object instantiated with the canonical path to f
getParentPath()	String	Return the paths to the parent of f, where the parent is determined based on the absolute path to f
getParentFile()	File	Returns the parent of f as a File object, where the parent is determined based on the absolute path to f
length()	long	Returns the byte size of f
createNewFile()	boolean	Attempts to create the file f; returns whether or not the attempt was successful
delete()	boolean	If f exists, attempts to remove f; returns whether or not the attempt was successful
mkdir()	boolean	Attempts to create f as a folder; returns whether or not the attempt was successful
renameTo(File g)	boolean	In the case where f exists, attempts to change the path to f to the path specified in g; returns whether or not the attempt was successful
listFiles()	File[]	If f exists and is a folder, return an array of File objects consisting of all the files in f; otherwise, return null

To simplify the description, we assume that the methods are applied to a File object f. All methods on this list take no parameters, except for renameTo

There is a group of File methods that provide information related to the file paths of the file represented by the File object. getName returns a String object that is equal to the name of the file. getAbsolutePath returns a String object representing the absolute path to the file represented by the file object. getAbsoluteFile returns a File object instantiated with the absolute path obtained by getAbsolutePath. getCanonicalPath returns a String object representing the canonical path to the file represented by the file object. getCanonicalFile returns a File object instantiated with the canonical path obtained by getCanonicalPath. getParent returns a String object representing the canonical path to the parent. getParentFile returns a File object instantiated with the path returned by getParent. Furthermore, if the File object represents a file folder, listFiles returns an array of File objects representing the files in the folder. If the File object does not represent a file folder, listFiles returns null.

Finally, there is a group of methods used for creating, removing, and renaming. createNewFile attempts to create the file represented by the File object as a regular file. mkdir attempts to create the file represented by the `File` object as a file folder. `delete()` attempts to remove the file represented by the `File` object. `renameTo( File g )` attempts to change the path to the file represented by the `File` object to that of g. These four methods return a `boolean` value representing whether or not the attempt was successful.

15.1.3 Exception Handling

15.1.3.1 Error Handling Imposed by the Compiler

A `throws` declaration is a declaration attached to the header of a method. It formally associates a run-time error type with the method. For an error type E, the declaration takes the form of `throws  E` and appears immediately after the closing parenthesis of the parameter declaration in the method header. If a method M calls another method N, and N has a `throws  E` declaration, then the Java compiler enforces that the code of M specifies how to handle a run-time error of type E originating from N. Thus, if a throws declaration in a method of an imported class, every method that calls the method must specify how to handle the error. One of the `File` methods introduced in Sect. 15.1.1, `createNewFile`, declares `throws  IOException`.

Suppose we have the following program that attempts to create a folder named `"testDir"`, and then in the folder, attempts to create a file named `"testFile.txt"`.

```
1   import java.io.*;
2   public class FileTest
3   {
4     public static void main( String[] args )
5     {
6       File dir = new File( "testDir" );
7       boolean success = dir.mkdir();
8       File testFile = new File( dir, "testFile.txt" );
9       success = testFile.createNewFile();
10    }
11  }
```

An attempt to compile the program results in the following error message:

```
1   FileTest.java:9: error: unreported exception IOException; must be caught
        or declared to be thrown
2           success = testFile.createNewFile();
3                                            ^
4   1 error
```

The message states that the method `createNewFile` has a `throws  IOException` declaration but the present source code does not specify how to handle the error.

15.1.3.2 "Throwing" a Run-Time Error

There are two ways to handle a formally declared error that may result from a method call. One is to attach a `throws` declaration of the same error type to the method declaration:

```
    public ... M( ... ) throws E
```

With this declaration, if an error of type E occurs during the execution of its code, M reports the error back to its direct superior. If the present execution of M is due to a method call to M appearing in another method Q, then the superior is Q. If there is no such Q, M must be the method `main` of some program, so the superior is JVM. In the latter case, JVM terminates the program after reporting the error on the screen.

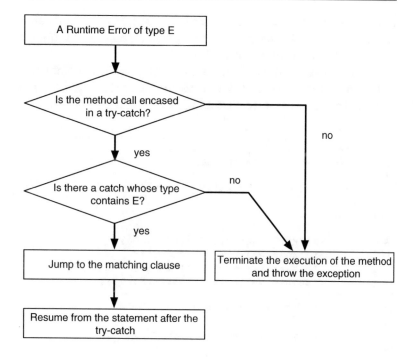

Fig. 15.1 The mechanism for handling run-time errors

A method cannot have more than one `throws` declaration. This limitation creates an issue when a method makes calls to multiple methods and they have different error types in their `throws` declarations. Fortunately, the Java run-time error types are organized as a tree, so any common ancestor of the different error types can be used as the error type in the `throws` declaration. `Exception` is the error type at the root of the tree, so in a situation where different run-time errors need to be handled, `Exception` can be used.

15.1.3.3 "Catching" a Run-Time Error

The other way to handle a formally declared run-time errors is to "catch" the error. The syntax for "catching" a run-time error of type E that originates from a method call to N is as follows: enclose a code block that includes the method call to N in a pair of curly brackets with a keyword `try` preceding the open bracket, and then immediately after the close bracket, add another pair of brackets preceded by a phrase `catch (E e)`. Some code can be placed inside the second pair of brackets. The lowercase letter e appearing in the parentheses represents an object representing the error that has occurred.

```
1    try
2    {
3        ... N( ... )
4    }
5    catch (E e)
6    {
7        ...
8    }
```

If an error of type E occurs during the execution of the `try` block, the execution of the block is immediately terminated, and then the execution of the `catch` block begins. After completing the code in the `catch` block, the execution jumps to the section immediately after the `catch` block. If an error of type E does not occur and no other run-time error occurs, the execution of the `try`-

block completes, and the execution reaches the section immediately after the catch block. Multiple catch clauses can be attached to one try block, if none of the error types appearing in the multiple catch clauses are ancestors of another.

Figure 15.1 summarizes the mechanism used to handle run-time errors.

Returning to the previous code example that failed to compile, any run-time error originating from createNewFile can be handled using a try-catch as follows:

```
1   import java.io.*;
2   public class FileTestCatch
3   {
4     public static void main( String[] args )
5     {
6       try
7       {
8         File dir = new File( "testDir" );
9         boolean success = dir.mkdir();
10        File testFile = new File( dir, "testFile.txt" );
11        success = testFile.createNewFile();
12      }
13      catch ( IOException e )
14      {
15        System.out.println( "Error!" );
16      }
17    }
18  }
```

Listing 15.1 A program that demonstrates the use of try and catch

The difference between throwing and catching is that the former immediately terminates the execution of the method while the latter does not. Regardless of which approach is used to handle IOException, the class IOException needs to be imported. IOException is in the java.io package.

15.1.3.4 A Demonstration of Try-Catch

The following program demonstrates the use of try-catch for handling run-time errors.

The program receives two file paths from the user. The program instantiates a File object f with the first path and another File object g with the second path, and then executes a series of actions using two methods. The first method is called showExistence (Line 5). The method receives two File objects, f and g, as its formal parameters. The method prints information about the existence of the two files using the format "Existence: %s=%s, %s=%s%n" (Lines 7 and 8). The first and the third %s placeholders are for the file names, and the second and the fourth %s placeholders are for the return values of exists.

The second method of the program is called creationPlay (Line 10). This method has a throws IOException declaration. The method receives two File objects, f and g, as its formal parameters, and executes a series of actions. After each action, the method calls showExistence(f, g) to print the existence status of the two files. Here is the series of actions creationPlay performs:

1. Print the canonical paths of f and g obtained by calling getCanonicalPath (Lines 13 and 14).
2. Try to create the files specified by f and g using createNewFile (Lines 19 and 21).
3. Try to move f to itself using renameTo (Line 25).

```
1   import java.util.*;
2   import java.io.*;
3   public class FileCreate
4   {
5     public static void showExistence( File f, File g )
6     {
7       System.out.printf( "Existence: %s=%s, %s=%s\n\n",
8           f.getName(), f.exists(), g.getName(), g.exists() );
9     }
```

Listing 15.2 A program that demonstrates the use of `File` methods for creating, deleting, and renaming files (part 1). The method `showExistence`

4. Try to move f to g using `renameTo` (Line 27).
5. Try to create the files specified by f and g as folders using `mkdir` (Lines 31–34).
6. Try to delete the files specified by f and g using `delete` (Lines 37–40).

In Steps 2 through 6, `creationPlay` announces the action it is about take. Since each method that is called returns a `boolean` value, the call is placed in `System.out.println`. This has the effect of printing the return value on the screen.

```
10    public static void creationPlay( File f, File g ) throws IOException
11    {
12      System.out.println( "The two input files" );
13      System.out.println( "File1 = " + f.getCanonicalPath() );
14      System.out.println( "File2 = " + g.getCanonicalPath() );
15      System.out.println( "----Their initial state" );
16      showExistence( f, g );
17
18      System.out.print( "----Create File1 -> " );
19      System.out.println( f.createNewFile() );
20      System.out.print( "----Create File2 -> " );
21      System.out.println( g.createNewFile() );
22      showExistence( f, g );
23
24      System.out.print( "----Rename File1 to File1 -> " );
25      System.out.println( f.renameTo( f ) );
26      System.out.print( "----Rename File1 to File2 -> " );
27      System.out.println( f.renameTo( g ) );
28      showExistence( f, g );
29
30      System.out.print( "----Create File1 as a folder -> " );
31      System.out.println( f.mkdir() );
32      System.out.print( "----Create File2 as a folder -> " );
33      System.out.println( g.mkdir() );
34      showExistence( f, g );
35
36      System.out.print( "----Delete File1 -> " );
37      System.out.println( f.delete() );
38      System.out.print( "----Delete File2 -> " );
39      System.out.println( g.delete() );
40      showExistence( f, g );
41    }
```

Listing 15.3 A program that demonstrates the use of `File` methods for creating, deleting, and renaming files (part 2). The method `creationPlay`

The method main (Line 42) receives two file paths from the user (Lines 46 and 47). The method instantiates a File object from each path, and then calls the method creationPlay with two File objects as actual parameters. Since the two File objects are not used anywhere else in the method main, this group of actions can be compressed into one line by placing the constructor calls inside the call to creationPlay (Line 50). A constructor does not have a return statement (see Chap. 16), but can be viewed as a method that returns an object of the type the constructor represents. The call appearing in Line 50 takes advantage of this fact. If the method call to creationPlay is successful, the method main prints a message (Line 51) and halts.

The program handles IOException that may originate from creationPlay (Line 53) using try-catch. If creationPlay produces a run-time error of IOException, the execution jumps to Line 53 without executing Line 51. There are two actions to be performed in the catch block. One is to print the information stored in e. This is accomplished by the method call e.printStackTrace() (Line 55). This method is available for all data types representing run-time errors. The method prints the series of method calls, starting from main, that have ultimately resulted in the run-time error at hand. The other action to be performed is to print a message to inform that a run-time error has occurred (Line 56). After producing the message on the screen, the program terminates because there is no statement after the catch block.

```
42    public static void main( String[] args )
43    {
44       Scanner keyboard = new Scanner( System.in );
45       System.out.print( "Enter two paths: " );
46       String p1 = keyboard.next();
47       String p2 = keyboard.next();
48       try
49       {
50          creationPlay( new File( p1 ), new File( p2 ) );
51          System.out.println( "Operations completed without errors" );
52       }
53       catch ( IOException e )
54       {
55          e.printStackTrace();
56          System.out.println( "---Program terminated---" );
57       }
58    }
59 }
```

Listing 15.4 A program that demonstrates the use of File methods for creating, deleting, and renaming files (part 3). The method main

Here are two examples of executing the program. The first example shows a case where the program executes the tasks without run-time errors.

```
 1  Enter two paths: tmp1 tmp2
 2  The two input files
 3  File1 = /Users/ogihara/file/tmp1
 4  File2 = /Users/ogihara/file/tmp2
 5  ----Their initial state
 6  Existence: tmp1=false, tmp2=false
 7
 8  ----Create File1 -> true
 9  ----Create File2 -> true
10  Existence: tmp1=true, tmp2=true
11
12  ----Rename File1 to File1 -> true
13  ----Rename File1 to File2 -> true
14  Existence: tmp1=false, tmp2=true
15
16  ----Create File1 as Directory -> true
17  ----Create File2 as Directory -> false
18  Existence: tmp1=true, tmp2=true
19
20  ----Delete File1 -> true
21  ----Delete File2 -> true
22  Existence: tmp1=false, tmp2=false
23
24  Operations completed without errors
```

Note that (i) immediately after moving the first file to the second file, the first file ceases to exist (Line 14), and (ii) the attempt to create the second file as a directory returns `false` (Line 17) because the second file already exists as a regular file.

The second example shows a case where the creation of the new file at the beginning of the series produces `IOException`. In this specific case, the error occurs because the directory `foo1` that appears in the first path does not exist.

```
 1  Enter two paths: foo1/foo2 foo3
 2  The two input files
 3  File1 = /Users/ogihara/file/foo1/foo2
 4  File2 = /Users/ogihara/file/foo3
 5  ----Their initial state
 6  Existence: foo2=false, foo3=false
 7  ----Create File1 -> java.io.IOException: No such file or directory
 8     at java.io.UnixFileSystem.createFileExclusively(Native Method)
 9     at java.io.File.createNewFile(File.java:1012)
10     at FileCreate.creationPlay(FileCreate.java:19)
11     at FileCreate.main(FileCreate.java:47)
12  ---Program terminated---
```

The printout generated by the call `e.printStackTrace()` starts in the middle of Line 7, after `"-> "` and ends in Line 11. Line 12 is the output produced by the print statement appearing in the `catch` block. Lines 8 through 10 present the chain of method calls that has led to the run-time error. The elements in the sequence appear one method call per line, starting from the most recent ones. By following the sequence from the end, we learn that the method `main` called the method `creationPlay` in Line 47 of the source code, the method `creationPlay` called the method `createNewFile` of `java.io.File` in Line 19 of the source code, the method `createNewFile` called the method `createFileExclusively` of `java.io.UnixFileSystem` in Line 1012 of the source code, and that method `createFileExclusively` generated the run-time error.

15.1.4 File Listing

The next program uses the method listFiles to take an inventory of the parent directory of the file specified in args [0]. After that, for each file appearing in the list, the program tests its properties using canExecute, canRead, canWrite, isDirectory, and isFile, and then reports the results. For each file, the program prints the results of the five tests. It also prints the name and the size of each file.

The first part of the source code is the method directoryPlay. The formal parameter of the method is a File object, home (Line 5). The method obtains the parent folder of home by using the method getParentFile, and stores the File object that is returned in a File variable named parent (Line 7). Next, the method obtains an array consisting of all the files residing in the folder parent using the method listFiles, and stores the returned array in an array of File objects named list (Line 8). The method then instantiates a rectangular array of boolean values named flags. In flags, the method stores the results of executing the five property tests for all files in the folder parent. The length of the first dimension of flags is the length of list and the length of the second dimension is 5, since the number of tests to be performed is 5 (Line 9). The method also instantiates an array of long values, size (Line 10), and an array of String values, name (Line 11). The method stores the file lengths in size and the file names in name for all files in the list. The length is thus list.length for both arrays.

After these array instantiations, the method examines the files appearing in the list. Using a for-loop, the method generates the index sequence 0, ..., list.length - 1 with a variable named i. At each round, the method executes the five tests, canExecute, canRead, canRead, isDirectory, and isFile, in this order, and stores the results in flags[i][0], ..., flags[i][4] (Lines 14–18). The program also obtains the file length and the file name using the methods length and getName, and stores the returned values in their respective arrays, size and name.

```
1   import java.io.*;
2   import java.util.*;
3   public class FileExplore
4   {
5     public static void directoryPlay( File home )
6     {
7       File parent = home.getParentFile();
8       File[] list = parent.listFiles();
9       boolean[][] flags = new boolean[ list.length ][ 5 ];
10      long[] size = new long[ list.length ];
11      String[] name = new String[ list.length ];
12      for ( int i = 0; i < list.length; i ++ )
13      {
14        flags[ i ][ 0 ] = list[ i ].canExecute();
15        flags[ i ][ 1 ] = list[ i ].canRead();
16        flags[ i ][ 2 ] = list[ i ].canWrite();
17        flags[ i ][ 3 ] = list[ i ].isDirectory();
18        flags[ i ][ 4 ] = list[ i ].isFile();
19        size[ i ] = list[ i ].length();
20        name[ i ] = list[ i ].getName();
21      }
```

Listing 15.5 A program that demonstrates the use of File methods for examining properties of files (part 1). The part responsible for taking the inventory

The method prints the inventory thus obtained, but before that, the method prints the name of home, the absolute path to home, the name of parent, and the absolute path to parent that are obtained using the methods getName and getAbsolutePath (Lines 22–25). The method prints the inventory one file per line. The information that it prints consists of the index to the file in the file list, the five boolean values stored in the array flags, the file length, and the file name. The format it uses is the following:

```
%05d:%6s%6s%6s%6s%6s%8d %s%n
```

The first placeholder, %05d, is for the index, the next five occurrences of %6s are for the five boolean values, the next one, %8d, is for the file length, and the very last one, %s, is for the file name. To beautify the table, the program prints header lines (Line 26–28).

```
22    System.out.printf( "Home: %s%n", home.getName() );
23    System.out.printf( "Absolute Path: %s%n", home.getAbsolutePath() );
24    System.out.printf( "Parent: %s%n", parent.getName() );
25    System.out.printf( "Absolute Path: %s%n", parent.getAbsolutePath() );
26    System.out.println( "Parent's File List\n------------------" );
27    System.out.println(
28        "Index: Exec? Read?Write?IsDir?IsFil?    Size Name" );
29    for ( int i = 0; i < list.length; i ++ )
30    {
31      System.out.printf( "%05d:%6s%6s%6s%6s%6s%8d %s%n",
32          i, flags[ i ][ 0 ], flags[ i ][ 1 ], flags[ i ][ 2 ],
33          flags[ i ][ 3 ], flags[ i ][ 4 ], size[ i ], name[ i ] );
34    }
35 }
```

Listing 15.6 A program that demonstrates the use of File methods for examining properties of files (part 2). The part responsible for printing the results

The last part of the code is the method main. The method has a throws IOException declaration (Line 37). The program needs one file path to start. The actions that the method main performs are as follows:

- Ask the user to enter a path (Line 38).
- Instantiate a Scanner object (Line 39).
- Receive a file path from the user and store it in a String variable named path (Line 40).
- Instantiate a File object f with the path (Line 41).
- Instantiate a File object g with the canonical path obtained from f (Line 42).
- Call the method directoryPlay with g as the actual parameter.

```
36  public static void main( String[] args ) throws IOException
37  {
38    System.out.print( "Enter path: " );
39    Scanner keyboard = new Scanner( System.in );
40    String path = keyboard.nextLine();
41    File f = new File( path );
42    File g = f.getCanonicalFile();
43    directoryPlay( g );
44  }
45 }
```

Listing 15.7 A program that demonstrates the use of File methods for examining properties of files (part 3). The method main

Here is one execution example:

```
 1  Enter path: ../..
 2  Home: CSC120
 3  Absolute Path: /Users/nancy/Documents/CSC120
 4  Parent: Documents
 5  Absolute Path: /Users/nancy/Documents
 6  Parent's File List
 7  ------------------
 8  Index: Exec? Read?Write?IsDir?IsFil?      Size Name
 9  00000: false  true   true false   true   18436 .DS_Store
10  00001: false  true   true false   true       0 .localized
11  00002:  true  true   true  true false      476 archives
12  00003:  true  true   true  true false      204 classical.txt
13  00004:  true  true   true  true false      136 cranium
14  00005:  true  true   true  true false      714 CSC120
15  00006:  true  true   true  true false      578 CSC527
16  00007:  true  true   true  true false      204 easy
17  00008: false  true   true false   true  132102 eceSeminarOct2017.docx
18  00009:  true  true   true  true false      272 fiances
19  00010:  true  true   true  true false      306 frank
20  00011:  true  true   true  true false      612 globaltheme
21  00012:  true  true   true  true false      204 india.txt
22  00013:  true  true   true  true false      102 letters
23  00014:  true  true   true  true false      204 Microsoft User Data
24  00015:  true  true   true  true false      204 MitsuCollection.txt
25  00016: false  true   true false   true17438298 Mult_Pattern_2_EdXX.docx
26  00017:  true  true   true  true false      204 MyCollection.txt
27  00018:  true  true   true  true false      170 papers
28  00019:  true  true   true  true false      782 pdfs
29  00020:  true  true   true  true false      340 Projects
30  00021:  true  true   true  true false     1020 Resume
31  00022:  true  true   true  true false      442 reviews
32  00023:  true  true   true  true false      578 temp
33  00024:  true  true   true  true false      374 temporary
```

15.2   Using Scanner Objects to Read from Files

Suppose theFile is a File object that refers to a text file. Then, the Scanner object instantiated with new Scanner(theFile) makes it possible to read the contents of theFile. Since the constructors of File do not check the validity of the file paths provided, the file represented by theFile may not exist. In such a case, the constructor throws a run-time error FileNotFoundException. FileNotFoundException belongs to java.io and is a descendant of IOException. To handle FileNotFoundException, java.io.FileNotFoundException must be imported by one of the following two import statements:

```
1  import java.io.*;
2  import java.io.FileNotFoundException;
```

The next program demonstrates how to read from a text file that contains scores for a group of students. The number of scores available differs from student to student. The file begins with an integer token that specifies the number of students whose scores appear in the file. This is followed by the information for individual students. The information for an individual student consists of the name of the student, the number of scores available for the students, and the individual scores for the student. The actual number of scores that appear must match the stated number of scores. Furthermore, the actual number of students whose records appear in the file must match the number of students stated in the first line of the file. The names are free of delimiters, so can be read with the method `next`.

Here is a sample score file:

```
1   8
2   Judy   5 80.5   82.0   85.0   92.0   95.0
3   King   6 89.0   87.5   77.5   100.0 95.5   98.0
4   Linda 3 94.5   95.5   96.5
5   Monty 4 75.5   80.0   90.0   65.0
6   Nancy 2 100.0 100.0
7   Oliver  1 99.0
8   Patty 3 97.5   95.0   92.5
9   Quincy  2 84.0   89.0
```

Listing 15.8 A sample data file for the score reading data program

Here is a program that reads a file whose contents are in this format. The program receives a path to the file from the user, and then stores it in a `String` variable named `path` (Lines 7–9). The program instantiates a `File` object with the file path, and then stores it in a variable named `theFile` (Line 10). The program instantiates a `Scanner` object `fileScanner` with `theFile` (Line 13). Since the instantiation of a `Scanner` object may result in `FileNotFoundException`, the instantiation is placed in a `try-catch`. The `try` block contains the instantiation of the `Scanner` object and all the remaining actions of the program. The corresponding `catch` appears much later (Line 37). The program reads the first token of the file using `nextInt`, and stores the number in an `int` variable named `lineNumber` (Line 14). The program instantiates an array of `String` data having length equal to `lineNumber`, and stores the array in a variable, `names` (Line 14). The program instantiates a jagged array having length `lineNumber`, and stores the array in a variable, `scores` (Line 15). Each row of `scores` is `null` immediately after the instantiation. The program then reads the data for individual students using a double for-loop. The exterior loop iterates over the indexes to the students, `0, ..., lineNumber - 1`, with a variable named `i` (Line 17). The internal loop iterates over the indexes to the scores (Line 22). The actions to be performed in the double for-loop are as follows:

- Read the name and store it in `names [ i ]` (Line 18).
- Read the number of scores, and store it in an `int` variable named `size` (Line 20).
- Instantiate the row `data [ i ]` with `new double[ size ]` (Line 21).
- Use a for-loop to read the individual scores and store them in `data [ i ][ 0 ], ..., data [ i ][ size - 1 ]` (Lines 22–25).

The number of students can be obtained with `names.length`. To obtain the number of scores available for the student at index `i`, `data [ i ].length` is used. To print the data, the program allocates ten character spaces for the name (Line 29), and ten character spaces with two digits after the decimal point (in other words, `%10.2f`) for each score (Line 32).

```
1    import java.util.*;
2    import java.io.*;
3    public class ReadTable
4    {
5      public static void main( String[] args )
6      {
7        Scanner keyboard = new Scanner( System.in );
8        System.out.print( "Enter file path: " );
9        String path = keyboard.nextLine();
10       File theFile = new File( path );
11       try
12       {
13         Scanner fileScanner = new Scanner( theFile );
14         int lineNumber = fileScanner.nextInt();
15         String[] names = new String[ lineNumber ];
16         double[][] data = new double[ lineNumber ][];
17         for ( int i = 0; i < lineNumber; i ++ )
18         {
19           names[ i ] = fileScanner.next();
20           int size = fileScanner.nextInt();
21           data[ i ] = new double[ size ];
22           for ( int col = 0; col < size; col ++ )
23           {
24             data[ i ][ col ] = fileScanner.nextDouble();
25           }
26         }
27         for ( int i = 0; i < names.length; i ++ )
28         {
29           System.out.printf( "%10s", names[ i ] );
30           for ( int col = 0; col < data[ i ].length; col ++ )
31           {
32             System.out.printf( "%10.2f", data[ i ][ col ] );
33           }
34           System.out.println();
35         }
36       }
37       catch ( FileNotFoundException e )
38       {
39         System.out.printf( "The file %s does not exist%n", path );
40       }
41     }
42   }
```

Listing 15.9 A program that reads the names and scores of students from a file

Here is the result of executing the code on the data file presented earlier.

```
1    Enter file path: dataTable.txt
2        Judy     80.50     82.00     85.00     92.00     95.00
3        King     89.00     87.50     77.50    100.00     95.50     98.00
4       Linda     94.50     95.50     96.50
5       Monty     75.50     80.00     90.00     65.00
6       Nancy    100.00    100.00
7      Oliver     99.00
8       Patty     97.50     95.00     92.50
9      Quincy     84.00     89.00
```

The try-catch of the program is designed to handle FileNotFoundException. It does not handle other types of run-time errors. For example, consider a file dataTableErroneous.txt that was created by changing the number appearing at the very start of the file to 9 and retaining the remaining contents of the file. Since the number of students that is stated is larger than the actual number of students, the program results in a run-time error of NoSuchElementException as follows:

```
1   Enter file path: dataTableErroneous.txt
2   Exception in thread "main" java.util.NoSuchElementException
3       at java.util.Scanner.throwFor(Scanner.java:862)
4       at java.util.Scanner.next(Scanner.java:1371)
5       at ReadTable.main(ReadTable.java:20)
```

However, if the user provides a file path to a non-existing file, the program prints the error message in the catch clause and halts as follows:

```
1   java ReadTable
2   Enter file path: fooBar.txt
3   The file fooBar.txt does not exist
4   % ...
```

People often use the "tab-delimited" format for data files. The following is a "tab-delimited" version of the data file we have just used, where the number of people or the numbers of scores does not appear. However, the information is presented one person per line and the entries in each line are separated by a tab-stop.

```
1   Judy    80.5    82.0    85.0    92.0    95.0
2   King    89.0    87.5    77.5    100.0   95.5    98.0
3   Linda   94.5    95.5    96.5
4   Monty   75.5    80.0    90.0    65.0
5   Nancy   100.0   100.0
6   Oliver  99.0
7   Patty   97.5    95.0    92.5
8   Quincy  84.0    89.0
```

Listing 15.10 A sample data file for the score reading data program. The file is without dimensional information

Suppose we must read from the tab-delimited version instead, and generate names and data, what should we do?

To decompose one line of data, we can choose from two strategies, as we discussed in Sect. 12.5. One strategy is to process the line twice with Scanner, the other is to use the method split of String. Regardless of which strategy is to be used, we must read the entire line using the method nextLine. Suppose we have just obtained one line of the file, and the student is at index i. Suppose that the line is stored in a String variable named w. With the first strategy, the performed actions will be as follows:

1. Instantiate a Scanner object with w as the parameter.
2. Run a while-loop with hasNext as the continuation condition, and obtain the number of tokens, say m, appearing in w.
3. Instantiate data[i] by new double[m - 1].
4. Instantiate the Scanner object again, and read the tokens from w. Store the very first token in names[i] and store the rest in data[i].

The second strategy takes advantage of the fact that the entries in each line are separated by a tab. With that strategy, the actions to be performed are as follows:

1. Split w into an array of String data using w.split("\t"), and store it in an array, say tokens.
2. Store tokens[0] in names[i].

3. Instantiate `data[ i ]` by `new double[ tokens.length - 1 ]`.
4. Using `Double.parseDouble`, convert `tokens[ 1 ]`, ..., `tokens[ tokens.length - 1 ]` to double values, and then store them in `data[ i ][ 0 ]`, ..., `data[ i ][ tokens.length - 2 ]`. `Double.parseDouble` is the `double` version of `Integer.parseInt`.

We use the latter strategy in our program.

The source code has the method `main` at the beginning. The method declares `throws IOException`. As before, the program obtains a file path from the user, and then instantiates a new `File` object (Lines 7–10). However, this time, the program verifies the existence and the readability of the specified file (Line 11). The program calls the method `theWork` only when the two tests return `true` (Line 13).

```
1   import java.util.*;
2   import java.io.*;
3   public class ReadTableGuess
4   {
5     public static void main( String[] args ) throws FileNotFoundException
6     {
7       Scanner keyboard = new Scanner( System.in );
8       System.out.print( "Enter file path: " );
9       String path = keyboard.nextLine();
10      File theFile = new File( path );
11      if ( theFile.exists() && theFile.canRead() )
12      {
13        theWork( theFile );
14      }
15    }
16
```

Listing 15.11 A program that reads the score data from a file without dimensional information (part 1). The method `main`

The next method, `getLineNumber`, is for obtaining the number of lines in a file. The method `getLineNumber` executes the following series of action:

- Instantiate a `Scanner` object (Line 19).
- Store the value of 0 to an `int` variable `lineNumber` (Line 20).
- While there is a line remaining in the file (Line 21), read one line without saving it (Line 23) and increase `lineNumber` by 1 (Line 24).

```
17    public static int getLineNumber( File f ) throws FileNotFoundException
18    {
19      Scanner fileScanner = new Scanner( f );
20      int lineNumber = 0;
21      while ( fileScanner.hasNextLine() )
22      {
23        fileScanner.nextLine();
24        lineNumber ++;
25      }
26      fileScanner.close();
27      return lineNumber;
28    }
29
```

Listing 15.12 A program that reads the score data from a file without dimensional information (part 2). The method `getLineNumber`

- Close the Scanner object (Line 26) and return the value of lineNumber (Line 27).

The formal parameter of the method theWork is a File object named theFile. The method obtains the number of lines in the file with a call to getLineNumber, and then stores the returned value in its a variable, lineNumber (Line 32). The method instantiates the arrays names and data as before (Lines 33 and 34). The method then reads the individual lines. The line numbers are generated in the variable line. At each line, the method executes the following:

- Read one full line and store it in oneLine (Line 40).
- Call oneLine.split("\t") to obtain an array of String data, and store it in tokens (Line 41).
- Store tokens[0] in names[line] (Line 42).
- Store tokens.length - 1 in size (Line 43).
- Instantiate (data[line]) with new double[size] (Line 44).
- Use a for-loop that iterates over the sequence 0, ..., size - 1 with a variable named col, store Double.parseDouble(tokens[col + 1]) in data[line][col] (Lines 45–48).

After this, a section for printing the data appears. The source code is exactly the same as before.

```
30    public static void theWork( File theFile ) throws FileNotFoundException
31    {
32        int lineNumber = getLineNumber( theFile );
33        String[] names = new String[ lineNumber ];
34        double[][] data = new double[ lineNumber ][];
35
36        Scanner fileScanner = new Scanner( theFile );
37
38        for ( int line = 0; line < lineNumber; line ++ )
39        {
40            String oneLine = fileScanner.nextLine();
41            String[] tokens = oneLine.split( "\t" );
42            names[ line ] = tokens[ 0 ];
43            int size = tokens.length - 1;
44            data[ line ] = new double[ size ];
45            for ( int col = 0; col < size; col ++ )
46            {
47                data[ line ][ col ] = Double.parseDouble( tokens[ col + 1 ] );
48            }
49        }
50        for ( int row = 0; row < names.length; row ++ )
51        {
52            System.out.printf( "%10s", names[ row ] );
53            for ( int col = 0; col < data[ row ].length; col ++ )
54            {
55                System.out.printf( "%10.2f", data[ row ][ col ] );
56            }
57            System.out.println();
58        }
59    }
60 }
```

Listing 15.13 A program that reads the score data from a file without dimensional information (part 3). The part responsible for data reading and printing

15.3   Using PrintStream to Write to Files

Java has a number of classes for writing data to files. PrintStream is one of them. The class belongs to java.io, so the class must be imported. A PrintStream object can be instantiated with a File object as the parameter. Like the constructors of Scanner, the PrintStream constructor that takes a File object as the parameter has a throws FileNotFoundException declaration. This error occurs when the file path to the File object has a non-existing file folder. We are already very much familiar with PrintStream, because System.out has type PrintStream. We can use methods print, printf, and println on any PrintStream object that is instantiated with a File object. The way the methods work is exactly the same as the way they work for System.out. The only difference is that the output is generated not on the screen, but in a file.

Here is a program that converts the contents of a text file to all uppercase and saves the result in another file. The method main has a throws FileNotFoundException declaration (Line 6). The program obtains two file paths from the user (Lines 10 and 12), instantiates two File objects with the paths (Lines 14 and 15), opens the first file as an input file (Line 16), and opens the second file as an output file (Line 17). Then, the program enters a loop for converting the texts line by line (Line 18). The single statement appearing in the loop-body combines three actions: reading one line, applying toUppercase to the line, and writing the line in the output file (Line 20).

```
1   import java.util.Scanner;
2   import java.io. * ;
3   // Convert a file contents to all upper case
4   public class ToUpper
5   {
6     public static void main( String[] args ) throws FileNotFoundException
7     {
8       Scanner keyboard = new Scanner( System.in );
9       System.out.print( "Enter input file path: " );
10      String fInName = keyboard.next();
11      System.out.print( "Enter output file path: " );
12      String fOutName = keyboard.next();
13      assert !fInName.equals( fOutName ) : "The file names are equal!";
14      File fIn = new File( fInName );
15      File fOut = new File( fOutName );
16      Scanner scanner = new Scanner( fIn );
17      PrintStream stream = new PrintStream( fOut );
18      while ( scanner.hasNext() )
19      {
20        stream.println( scanner.nextLine().toUpperCase() );
21      }
22    }
23  }
```

Listing 15.14 A program that turns file contents of a file to all upper case and saves it to a new file

The Assert Statement In Line 13 of the program, we see

    assert !fInName.equals(fOutName): "The file names are equal!"

This line must be interpreted as:

if the condition !fInName.equals(fOutName) is false (equivalently, fInName is equal to fOutName), produce an error message "The file names are equal!", and halt immediately after that.

This is almost identical to the IllegalArgumentException we have used before. The difference is that the assert statements are active only if the program is executed with a special option -ea of the command java. In other words, in the two executions

```
1  java -ea ToUpper
2  java ToUpper
```

the first one executes the assert statement and the second one ignores it. The type of a run-time error generated by assert is AssertionError. We show the result of executing the code on the following file. The file contains the lyrics to the original 1892 version of the song *America the Beautiful*:

```
1   O beautiful for halcyon skies,
2   For amber waves of grain,
3   For purple mountain majesties
4   Above the enameled plain!
5   America! America!
6   God shed His grace on thee,
7   Till souls wax fair as earth and air
8   And music-hearted sea!
9
10  O beautiful for pilgrim feet
11  Whose stern, impassioned stress
12  A thoroughfare for freedom beat
13  Across the wilderness!
14  America! America!
15  God shed His grace on thee
16  Till paths be wrought through wilds of thought
17  By pilgrim foot and knee!
18
19  O beautiful for glory-tale
20  Of liberating strife,
21  When once or twice, for man's avail,
22  Men lavished precious life!
23  America! America!
24  God shed His grace on thee
25  Till selfish gain no longer stain,
26  The banner of the free!
27
28  O beautiful for patriot dream
29  That sees beyond the years
30  Thine alabaster cities gleam
31  Undimmed by human tears!
32  America! America!
33  God shed His grace on thee
34  Till nobler men keep once again
35  Thy whiter jubilee!
```

Listing 15.15 The lyrics to *America the Beautiful*

Here is the result of executing the code:

```
1  O BEAUTIFUL FOR HALCYON SKIES,
2  FOR AMBER WAVES OF GRAIN,
3  FOR PURPLE MOUNTAIN MAJESTIES
4  ABOVE THE ENAMELED PLAIN!
5  AMERICA! AMERICA!
6  GOD SHED HIS GRACE ON THEE,
7  TILL SOULS WAX FAIR AS EARTH AND AIR
8  AND MUSIC-HEARTED SEA!
9
10 O BEAUTIFUL FOR PILGRIM FEET
11 WHOSE STERN, IMPASSIONED STRESS
12 A THOROUGHFARE FOR FREEDOM BEAT
13 ACROSS THE WILDERNESS!
14 AMERICA! AMERICA!
15 GOD SHED HIS GRACE ON THEE
16 TILL PATHS BE WROUGHT THROUGH WILDS OF THOUGHT
17 BY PILGRIM FOOT AND KNEE!
18
19 O BEAUTIFUL FOR GLORY-TALE
20 OF LIBERATING STRIFE,
21 WHEN ONCE OR TWICE, FOR MAN`''S AVAIL,
22 MEN LAVISHED PRECIOUS LIFE!
23 AMERICA! AMERICA!
24 GOD SHED HIS GRACE ON THEE
25 TILL SELFISH GAIN NO LONGER STAIN,
26 THE BANNER OF THE FREE!
27
28 O BEAUTIFUL FOR PATRIOT DREAM
29 THAT SEES BEYOND THE YEARS
30 THINE ALABASTER CITIES GLEAM
31 UNDIMMED BY HUMAN TEARS!
32 AMERICA! AMERICA!
33 GOD SHED HIS GRACE ON THEE
34 TILL NOBLER MEN KEEP ONCE AGAIN
35 THY WHITER JUBILEE!
```

When the program is run with the -ea option, if we provide identical file paths for the two files, the program halts with an error message as follows:

```
1  Enter input file path: foo
2  Enter output file path: foo
3  Exception in thread "main" java.lang.AssertionError: The file names are
       equal!
4    at ToUpper.main(ToUpper.java:13)
```

When the program is run without the option of -ea, if we provide identical files paths for the files, the programs halts with an error, but the error message is different:

```
1  Enter input file path: foo
2  Enter output file path: foo
3  Exception in thread "main" java.io.FileNotFoundException: foo (No such
       file or directory)
4    at java.io.FileInputStream.open(Native Method)
5    at java.io.FileInputStream.<init>(FileInputStream.java:131)
6    at java.util.Scanner.<init>(Scanner.java:611)
7    at ToUpper.main(ToUpper.java:16)
```

Summary

- File is a class for specifying files with file paths. The class offers many methods for obtaining the properties of the files as well as obtaining paths to the files. They include canRead, canWrite, isDirectory, isFile, length, listFiles, getName, getCanonicalPath, and getAbsolutePath. Furthermore, the class offers methods for creating and removing actual files specified in File objects. They include mkdir, delete, and createNewFile.
- A Scanner object can be used to read data from a file specified by a File object.
- Instantiation of a Scanner object with a File object has a throws FileNotFound Exception declaration.
- A PrintStream object can be used to write data to a file specified by a File object.
- System.out is a PrintStream object.
- The constructor of a PrintStream object with a File object as the parameter has a throws FileNotFoundException declaration.
- The declaration, throws ERROR_TYPE, attached to a method header officially announces that the method may throw a run-time error of the type. A method that calls such a method must handle a run-time error of the type generated as a result of the method call.
- Attachment of a throws declaration can be used to resolve the requirement to handle formally declared run-time errors.
- A try-catch clause can be used to handle run-time errors.
- Multiple catch clauses can be attached to a single try clause.
- An assert statement generates a run-time error if a condition does not hold.
- An assert is active only when the program that contains it is executed with the -ea option.
- The run-time errors in Java form a tree.

Exercises

1. **Questions about File methods**
   (a) Is the following statement true? If a File is instantiated with a file path and if the file specified the path does not exist, then FileNotFoundException is thrown.
   (b) Name the File method that returns whether or not a given file is a directory.
   (c) Name the File method that attempts to create a given file as a directory.
   (d) Name the File method that returns whether or not a given file exists.
   (e) Name the File method that returns whether or not a given file can be read.
   (f) Name the File method that returns whether or not a given file can be overwritten.
   (g) Name the File method that returns whether or not a given file can be executed.
   (h) Name the File method that, when the file specified by the File object is a folder, provides an array of File objects representing the files in the folder.

2. **Reading from a file** Suppose a file, FooBar.txt, consists of the following four lines:

```
1   a_____10.5_
2   _bb_____20.5_
3   __
4   _ccc____-30.5
```

where each _ represents the whitespace. Suppose a Scanner object reader has been instantiated with a constructor call new Scanner(new File("FooBat.txt")), and then the following has been executed:

```
1   while ( reader.hasNext() )
2   {
3     System.out.println(reader.next());
4   }
```

State how many lines of output are produced by this code.

3. **Reading a two-dimensional array**   Write a program, ReadMatrix, that reads the elements of a two-dimensional matrix of floating point values stored in a file into a two-dimensional array, and then prints the elements of the array on the screen. The file name should be supplied in args[0]. Assume that, in the data file, the first token is the number of rows, the second token is the number of columns, and after these two tokens, the elements of the matrix appear in the row-major order. In the output, print the dimensions of the matrix, and then print the elements of the matrix, one row per line, with the entries appearing in the line same, where the entries appear with exactly three digits after the decimal point and exactly one whitespace in between. For example, if the contents of the input file are:

```
1    3
2    4
3    0.1
4    0.4
5    0.7
6    1.0
7    3.5
8    3.4
9    3.3
10   3.2
11   -1.0
12   1.0
13   -2.0
14   2.0
```

the output must look like:

```
1    3
2    4
3    0.100 0.400 0.700 1.000
4    3.500 3.400 3.300 3.200
5    -1.000 1.000 -2.000 2.000
```

4. **Reading a two-dimensional array and computing the row- and column-wise averages**
   Write a program, MatrixAverage, that reads the elements of a two-dimensional matrix of floating point values stored in a file into two-dimensional array, and then computes the row- and column-wise averages of the matrix. The file name is given as args[0]. The format used in the input file is:
   • the number of rows,
   • the number of columns, and
   • the entries of the matrix in the row-major order.

5. **Reading and printing**   Write a program, Punctuate, that reads the tokens appearing in a text file, and prints the tokens on the screen as follows:
   • If the token ends with one of the following punctuation marks, print the newline after the token: the period, the exclamation mark, the question mark, the colon, the semicolon, and the comma.
   • Otherwise, print one whitespace after the token.

6. **Reading numbers while calculating their running total** Write a program, RunningTotal, that reads data from file, and computes and prints the running total of the numbers it encounters. All the tokens appearing in the file are integers. The program receives the file path from the user using Scanner.

7. **Searching for a key in a text file** Write a program named ReadAndSearch that receives a keyword and a file path from the user, and looks for all the occurrences of the key in the file. The program processes the contents of the file by reading them line by line. The program keeps track of the number of lines that have been read and uses it as the line number. Each time it finds that the line has an occurrence of the search key in it, the program prints the line number corresponding to the line.

Programming Projects

8. **Character counting** Write a program named ASCIICounting that receives a file path from the user, and then reads the contents of the file to produce the number of occurrences of each character in the region of characters with indexes 0–127 in the ASCII table. The ' \n' appearing at the end of each line will be ignored when counting the character occurrences. After reading the file, the program prints the characters and their counts for all the characters that have been found in the file. The character with a count of 0 will be ignored in the output. The format to be used in producing the character-count pair on the screen is '%c':%-6d. The code must use a try-catch to handle the case in which the file path that the user specifies is not valid.

Here is an execution example:

```
1   Enter file name: ASCIICounting.java
2   ' ':402    '!':1      '"':6      '%':4      '&':2      '’':2
3   '(':20     ')':20     '*':2      '+':10     ',':2      '-':1
4   '.':17     '/':4      '0':9      '1':3      '2':3      '6':2
5   '7':2      '8':2      ':':1      ';':19     '<':3      '=':14
6   '>':2      'A':2      'C':3      'E':2      'F':4      'I':3
7   'L':1      'N':2      'O':1      'S':9      '[':10     ']':10
8   'a':29     'b':2      'c':19     'd':11     'e':32     'f':7
9   'g':8      'h':10     'i':58     'j':2      'l':12     'm':7
10  'n':46     'o':35     'p':20     'r':33     's':23     't':56
11  'u':13     'v':4      'w':7      'x':5      'y':6      '{':11
12  '}':11
```

9. **Character distribution** As an extension of the previous question, write a program ASCIIDistComparison that compares the ASCII character distributions of two files. The user specifies the paths to the files. For each file, the program produces a 128-dimensional array of int values representing the frequencies of the 128 characters. The program computes the difference between the two 128-dimensional arrays, and reports the differences on the screen. Use the same printing format as in the previous problem.

Here is an execution example of such a program:

```
1   Enter file name 1: file1.txt
2   Enter file name 2: file2.txt
3   ' ':7      '!':5      '"':-30    '%':5      '&':2      '’':8
4   '(':-10    ')':-10    '*':-6     '+':4      ',':-14    '-':-1
5   '.':-27    '/':9      '0':-12    '1':5      '2':2      '3':-7
6   '4':-4     '5':-4     '6':2      '7':5      '8':4      '9':-7
7   ':':-1     ';':-21    '<':2      '=':-6     '>':1      'A':3
8   'B':-8     'C':17     'D':5      'E':-1     'F':13     'G':-1
9   'I':-2     'L':-1     'M':-5     'N':9      'O':-3     'P':-2
10  'R':-10    'S':-19    'T':-3     'W':-4     '[':4      '\':-230
11  ']':4      'a':-26    'b':-53    'c':2      'd':-18    'e':-63
```

12	'f':35	'g':-27	'h':-39	'i':8	'j':2	'k':-21
13	'l':-37	'm':-22	'n':-9	'o':13	'p':7	'q':-1
14	'r':-16	's':-31	't':-30	'u':-29	'v':-3	'w':-1
15	'x':3	'y':-27	'{':5	'|':-2	'}':5	

10. **Character distribution plus** Revise the previous program to write a new one named `ASCIIDistComparisonPlus`. This time, the program additionally reports the character for which the difference is the largest.

With the same input files, the output may be as follows:

```
1   Enter file name 1: file1.txt
2   Enter file name 2: file2.txt
3   ' ':7      '!':5      '"':-30    '%':5      '&':2      ''':8
4   '(':-10    ')':-10    '*':-6     '+':4      ',':-14    '-':-1
5   '.':-27    '/':9      '0':12     '1':5      '2':2      '3':-7
6   '4':-4     '5':-4     '6':2      '7':5      '8':4      '9':-7
7   ':':-1     ';':-21    '<':2      '=':-6     '>':1      'A':3
8   'B':-8     'C':17     'D':5      'E':-1     'F':13     'G':-1
9   'I':-2     'L':-1     'M':-5     'N':9      'O':-3     'P':-2
10  'R':-10    'S':-19    'T':-3     'W':-4     '[':4      '\':-230
11  ']':4      'a':-26    'b':-53    'c':2      'd':-18    'e':-63
12  'f':35     'g':-27    'h':-39    'i':8      'j':2      'k':-21
13  'l':-37    'm':-22    'n':-9     'o':13     'p':7      'q':-1
14  'r':-16    's':-31    't':-30    'u':-29    'v':-3     'w':-1
15  'x':3      'y':-27    '{':5      '|':-2     '}':5
16  Max. difference of -230 for '\'.
```

11. **Printing the text shape to a file** Write a program, `TextShape`, that reads a text file and prints the "shape" of the text line into another file. For a `String` data w, by "shape" of w, we mean a `String` data generated from w by converting each character occurring between the first non-space character and the last non-space character to '#'.

The user specifies the input file and the output file to execute this program.

For example, the "shape" of

```
1   A BCDEFG
2   HIJKLM
3     NOPQ RS T UV
4   W X Y Z
```

is

```
1   #######
2    ######
3     ############
4   #######
```

Make sure that the program works when the input file contains a nonempty line consisting solely of ' '.

12. **Converting each tab-stop to an equivalent series of ' '** Write a program named `TabConvert` that reads from a file and produces an output where each tab-stops appearing in the input file is substituted with a series of ' ', so that when printed the appearance of the input file and the appearance of the output are exactly the same. Assume that the tab-stop positions are multiples of 8. The program receives the paths to the input and output files from the user. In the program, write a method `convert` whose action is to receive a `String` value without the newline character as the formal parameter, and then return a tab-stop free `String` value that has the same appearance as the parameter when printed with no indentation.

Designing Object Classes

16

16.1 Packaging a Group of Data as an Object

16.1.1 The Position of a Game Piece

In Java, object classes are used to assemble a set of data as a unit.

The header of the source code for an object class is the same as the header of the source code for a non-object class. Specifically, the header takes the form of `public class CLASS_NAME`. Declarations about implementation and extension (see Chap. 17) may appear after the class name. The possible components of an object class are: **instance variables** (defined as if they were global variables), **instance methods**, **constructors**, constants, and static methods.

In this chapter, we explore how to write a source code for an object class. We start with a series of programs for manipulating the position of a game piece placed on a game board. We assume that the board has two-dimensional integral coordinates (that is, the position of a piece is represented as a pair of integers), for instance, as shown in Fig. 16.1.

The user specifies the initial position of the piece, and then interacts with the program to change its position. The new position of the piece is specified with the numbers of squares that the piece must move along the x- and y-axes. If the move is possible, the program updates the position. The program then asks whether or not the user wants to move the piece again. If the user answers "yes", the series of actions is repeated; otherwise, the program terminates.

The following program, `UsePositionZero`, is the initial version of the program. The program does not use a custom object class. It uses two `int` variables, `xPos` and `yPos`, for representing the position (Line 7). The program receives the initial values for the two variables in Lines 9–11. Then the program enters a do-while loop (Line 14). In the loop-body, the program first reports the present position of the piece. In reporting the position, the program uses the format `(%d,%d)` with `xPos` and `yPos` supplied to the two placeholders (Line 15). The program then asks the user to enter the amounts of move, and changes the coordinates with the amounts that the user enters (Lines 17–19). The program then reports the new position using the same format (Line 21). The program then asks the user whether or not the program should continue (Line 23). The response is stored in a `String` variable named `answer` (Line 24). The loop is terminated if the response does not start with `"y"` (Line 25).

© Springer Nature Switzerland AG 2018
M. Ogihara, *Fundamentals of Java Programming*,
https://doi.org/10.1007/978-3-319-89491-1_16

Fig. 16.1 An 8 × 8 game board. The X represents a position of a game piece

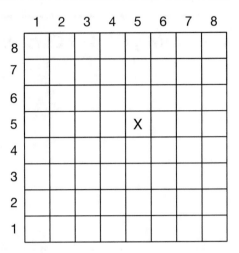

```
1   import java.util.*;
2   public class UsePositionZero
3   {
4     public static void main( String[] args )
5     {
6       Scanner keyboard = new Scanner( System.in );
7       int xPos, yPos;
8
9       System.out.print( "Enter the initial x y: " );
10      xPos = keyboard.nextInt();
11      yPos = keyboard.nextInt();
12
13      String answer = "";
14      do {
15        System.out.printf( "The current position: (%d,%d)%n", xPos, yPos );
16
17        System.out.print( "By how much do you want to shift x and y? " );
18        xPos += keyboard.nextInt();
19        yPos += keyboard.nextInt();
20
21        System.out.printf( "The new position: (%d,%d)%n", xPos, yPos );
22
23        System.out.print( "Continue (y/n)? " );
24        answer = keyboard.next();
25      } while ( answer.startsWith( "y" ) );
26    }
27  }
```

Listing 16.1 The initial version of the program that manipulates the position of a game piece

Here is an example of executing UsePositionZero:

```
1   Enter the initial x y: 1 3
2   The current position: (1,3)
3   By how much do you want to shift x and y? 2 7
4   The new position: (3,10)
5   Continue (y/n)? y
6   The current position: (3,10)
7   By how much do you want to shift x and y? 10 -8
8   The new position: (13,2)
9   Continue (y/n)? y
10  The current position: (13,2)
11  By how much do you want to shift x and y? -1 -1
12  The new position: (12,1)
13  Continue (y/n)? n
```

We want to write new versions of UsePositionZero, where the two coordinates are treated as one unit. To accomplish this, we define an object class PositionFirst. An object of PositionFirst has two data components, x and y, representing the x- and y-coordinates of the position. Both x and y are int variables. They are declared as instance variables. Figure 16.2 visualizes the way PositionFirst encompasses the two instance variables in it.

Fig. 16.2 The instance variables of a PositionFirst object

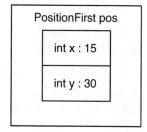

Here is the source code of PositionFirst. The declarations of x and y are given in Line 3 of the source

```
3       int x, y;
```

The lack of the static attribute signifies that they are instance variables.

The constructor for PositionFirst starts at Line 4.

```
4       public PositionFirst( int xValue, int yValue )
5       {
6           x = xValue;
7           y = yValue;
8       }
```

The constructor stores the values xValue and yValue given as the formal parameters in the instance variables x and y.

The general format of a constructor is

$$public\ CLASS\_NAME(\ PARAMETERS\ )$$

This format is different from the format of method declarations, since there is no return type.

There is only one instance method in `PositionFirst`. The method is named `shift` (Lines 9–12). The method `shift` has two formal parameters, `xDiff` and `yDiff`, and adds their values to the instance variables. The header of the method does not have the static attribute. The lack of the attribute signifies that the method is an instance method.

```
1   public class PositionFirst
2   {
3      int x, y;
4      public PositionFirst( int xValue, int yValue )
5      {
6         x = xValue;
7         y = yValue;
8      }
9      public void shift( int xDiff, int yDiff )
10     {
11        x += xDiff;
12        y += yDiff;
13     }
14  }
```

Listing 16.2 Class `PositionFirst`

Recall that the use of a constructor requires the special keyword of new. For a pair of `int` data `startX` and `startY`,

new PositionFirst(startX, startY)

produces a new `PositionFirst` object whose instance variables `x` and `y` have values `startX` and `startY`. For example,

PositionFirst myPos = new PositionFirst(1, 3);

constructs a `PositionFirst` object with coordinates (1,3) and assigns it to `myPos`.

The class `PositionFirst` does not have the method `main`. We write a separate class, `UsePositionFirst`, for handling the interactions with the user. To run `UsePositionFirst`, both `PositionFirst.java` and `UsePositionFirst.java` need to be compiled. The two files can be compiled individually:

```
1   % javac PositionFirst.java
2   % javac UsePositionFirst.java
```

or jointly:

```
% javac PositionFirst.java UsePositionFirst.java
```

The source code of `UsePositionFirst` is an adaptation of the source code of `UsePosition Zero`. The program uses a `PositionFirst` object, `pos`, to store coordinates (Line 7). To instantiate `pos`, the constructor of `PositionFirst` is called (Line 10). The actual parameters of the constructor are two calls of `keyboard.nextInt()` (Line 10). The return value of the first call `keyboard.nextInt()` becomes the first actual parameter, ad the return value of the second call `keyboard.nextInt()` becomes the second actual parameter. The x- and y- coordinates of `pos` are accessed with `pos.x` and `pos.y` (Lines 14 and 18). Moving the position is accomplished by calling the method `shift` (Line 16). The actual parameters of the method call are two calls to `keyboard.nextInt()` (Line 16).

```
1  import java.util.*;
2  public class UsePositionFirst
3  {
4    public static void main( String[] args )
5    {
6      Scanner keyboard = new Scanner( System.in );
7      PositionFirst pos;
8
9      System.out.print( "Enter the initial x y: " );
10     pos = new PositionFirst( keyboard.nextInt(), keyboard.nextInt() );
11     String answer = "";
12     do {
13       System.out.printf( "The current position: (%d,%d)%n",
14           pos.x, pos.y );
15       System.out.print( "By how much do you want to shift x and y? " );
16       pos.shift( keyboard.nextInt(), keyboard.nextInt() );
17
18       System.out.printf( "The new position: (%d,%d)%n", pos.x, pos.y );
19       System.out.print( "Continue (y/n)? " );
20       answer = keyboard.next();
21     } while ( answer.startsWith( "y" ) );
22   }
23 }
```

Listing 16.3 A program that plays with the position of a game piece using an object of type `PositionFirst`

Here is an execution example of the program:

```
1  Enter the initial x y: -100 -100
2  The current position: (-100,-100)
3  By how much do you want to shift x and y? 1000 1000
4  The new position: (900,900)
5  Continue (y/n)? y
6  The current position: (900,900)
7  By how much do you want to shift x and y? 345 9870
8  The new position: (1245,10770)
9  Continue (y/n)? y
10 The current position: (1245,10770)
11 By how much do you want to shift x and y? -1397 760
12 The new position: (-152,11530)
13 Continue (y/n)? n
```

16.1.2 Private Instance Variables and the `toString` Method

The class `PositionFirst` permits direct access to the instance variables via the attachment of their names, for instance, `pos.x`. This direct access is utilized in Lines 14 and 18 of the source code of `UsePositionFirst`, where the program reports the position of the piece. However, the direct accessibility of instance variables can be problematic for the following reasons:

- If the name and/or type of an instance variable changes, all the direct accesses to the variable appearing in other source codes must be updated accordingly. For instance, if the name x in PositionFirst changes to xxx, the two occurrences of pos.x in UsePositionFirst must be changed to pos.xxx.
- In the case where an instance variable is a number and is directly accessible, an attachment of a short-hand expression to a direct access to the variable may modify the value inadvertently. Such an error is often difficult to identify. For instance, suppose that a programmer intends to store the value of pos.x + 1 in r, but accidentally writes r = pos.x ++ instead of r = pos.x + 1. The execution of the assignments stores the value of pos.x in r and adds 1 to pos.x.

These problems can be avoided by making the instance variables inaccessible from any class other than PositionFirst, and providing alternatives for accessing and modifying their values. To make an instance variable inaccessible from other source codes, an attribute of private must be attached in its declaration as follows:

```
    private int x, y;
```

Suppose this modification has been applied to the instance variables, x and y, of PositionFirst. Then, PositionFirst compiles, but UsePositionFirst does not. Here is the compilation error message:

```
 1  UsePositionFirst.java:13: error: x has private access in PositionFirst
 2        System.out.printf( "The current position: (%d,%d)%n", pos.x, pos.y
          );
 3                                                                ^
 4  UsePositionFirst.java:13: error: y has private access in PositionFirst
 5        System.out.printf( "The current position: (%d,%d)%n", pos.x, pos.y
          );
 6                                                                       ^
 7  UsePositionFirst.java:18: error: x has private access in PositionFirst
 8        System.out.printf( "The new position: (%d,%d)%n", pos.x, pos.y );
 9                                                            ^
10  UsePositionFirst.java:18: error: y has private access in PositionFirst
11        System.out.printf( "The new position: (%d,%d)%n", pos.x, pos.y );
12                                                                   ^
13  4 errors
```

The message states that the instance variables of PositionFirst are private and so cannot be accessed.

By reading the error message, we learn that the errors originate from the places where the program attempts to access the values of x and y. To resolve the problem, we introduce instance methods, getX and getY, that return the values of x and y.

Here is the class PositionPrivate in which the above modifications have been incorporated. The methods getX and getY appear in Lines 14–17 and Lines 18–21. Both take no parameters and execute just one statement. The actions to be performed by the constructor are the same as before (Lines 6 and 7). The method shift is untouched (Lines 9–13).

```
1   public class PositionPrivate
2   {
3     private int x, y;
4     public PositionPrivate( int xValue, int yValue )
5     {
6       x = xValue;
7       y = yValue;
8     }
9     public void shift( int xDiff, int yDiff )
10    {
11      x += xDiff;
12      y += yDiff;
13    }
14    public int getX()
15    {
16      return x;
17    }
18    public int getY()
19    {
20      return y;
21    }
22  }
```

Listing 16.4 Class `PositionPrivate`

We call methods that offer access to the values of instance variables `getters` (or `accessors`), and methods that offer ways to change the values of instance variables `setters` (or `modifiers`). In `PositionPrivate`, `getX` and `getY` are getters and `shift` is a setter.

The program `UsePositionPrivate` is derived from `UsePositionFirst` by changing the type of `pos` to `PositionPrivate` (Lines 7 and 10) and changing the direct accesses `pos.x` and `pos.y` to their respective instance methods `pos.getX()` and `pos.getY()` (Lines 14 and 20).

```
1   import java.util.*;
2   public class UsePositionPrivate
3   {
4     public static void main( String[] args )
5     {
6       Scanner keyboard = new Scanner( System.in );
7       PositionPrivate pos;
8
9       System.out.print( "Enter the initial x y: " );
10      pos = new PositionPrivate ( keyboard.nextInt(), keyboard.nextInt() );
11      String answer = "";
```

Listing 16.5 Class `UsePositionPrivate` (part 1)

```
12       do
13       {
14         System.out.printf( "The current position: (%d,%d)%n",
15             pos.getX(), pos.getY() );
16         System.out.print( "By how much do you want to shift x and y? " );
17         pos.shift( keyboard.nextInt(), keyboard.nextInt() );
18
19         System.out.printf( "The new position: (%d,%d)%n",
20             pos.getX(), pos.getY() );
21         System.out.print( "Continue (y/n)? " );
22         answer = keyboard.next();
23       } while ( answer.startsWith( "y" ) );
24     }
25  }
```

Listing 16.6 Class UsePositionPrivate (part 2)

Again, from the user's point of view, the program works exactly the same way as before.

```
1   Enter the initial x y: -23 54
2   The current position: (-23,54)
3   By how much do you want to shift x and y? 23 -54
4   The new position: (0,0)
5   Continue (y/n)? y
6   The current position: (0,0)
7   By how much do you want to shift x and y? 0 4
8   The new position: (0,4)
9   Continue (y/n)? y
10  The current position: (0,4)
11  By how much do you want to shift x and y? 4 -100
12  The new position: (4,-96)
13  Continue (y/n)? n
```

16.1.3 Using Constants in an Object Class

The position programs we have seen so far allow an arbitrary value for each coordinate. However, in a real game, the area in which the game pieces are placed is finite. For instance, in Chess, the area is 8 by 8, and in the Japanese Chess, Shogi, the area is 9 by 9. Based on this observation, we modify PositionPrivate to create a new version, PositionConfined, where the coordinates have an upper bound and a lower bound. The constants that define the lower and upper bounds are MINIMUM and MAXIMUM. They are defined as follows:

```
1   public static final int MINIMUM = 1;
2   public static final int MAXIMUM = 8;
```

These constants are public, so their values can be accessed from outside by attaching their names to PositionConfined. For example, an external program can print the values of these constants by:

```
1   System.out.println( "The maximum is " + PositionConfined.MAXIMUM );
2   System.out.println( "The minimum is " + PositionConfined.MINIMUM );
```

The code produces the following output:

```
1   The maximum is 8
2   The minimum is 1
```

Having bounds on the coordinates means that we need to enforcing the bounds. There are two places for the user to suggest an invalid position, when the user specifies the initial position and when the user specifies the amounts of movement. We handle the two situations as follows:

- If the suggested initial position is outside the boundary, we use some default position.
- If the suggested movement will push the position outside the boundary, we do not move the piece.

The default coordinates are defined with two additional constants, DEFAULT_X and DEFAULT_Y. Both are int type and have the value of 1. In the program, they are defined as follows:

```
1   public static final int DEFAULT_X = 1;
2   public static final int DEFAULT_Y = 1;
```

We introduce a new method inRange (Line 10) for checking if a suggested value for a coordinate is in the range of valid coordinate values. inRange receives an int value z as its formal parameter, and returns a boolean value representing whether or not z is in the range. More precisely, the method returns z >= MINIMUM && z <= MAXIMUM (Line 12). The variable z can be for x or for y. We make inRange a public static method. This means that the method is available to other source codes without having to instantiate a PositionConfined object. The usage of the message from outside should be like: PositionConfined.inRange(10).

Using inRange, the constructor now works as follows:

- Tentatively assign the default values to the instance variables (Lines 17 and 18).
- If both parameters are valid (Line 19), assign the values of the parameters to the instance variables.

The new version of shift uses inRange to check whether or not the suggested coordinates, x + xDiff and y + xDiff, are valid (Line 28). If both are valid, the method updates the instance variables with the suggested coordinates, and returns true (Lines 30–32). Otherwise, the method retains the present values and returns false (Line 34). The return type of shift has been changed from void to boolean.

The methods getX and getY are the same as before (Lines 36–43). A new method has been introduced in PositionConfined. The name of the method is toString. The method toString returns the String that presents the two coordinate values in the format we have been using to print the positions (Lines 44–47). The formatted String is produced using String.format.

```
1   public class PositionConfined
2   {
3     public static final int MINIMUM = 1;
4     public static final int MAXIMUM = 8;
5     public static final int DEFAULT_X = 1;
6     public static final int DEFAULT_Y = 1;
7
8     private int x, y;
9
10    private static boolean inRange( int z )
11    {
12      return z >= MINIMUM && z <= MAXIMUM;
13    }
14
15    public PositionConfined( int xValue, int yValue )
16    {
17      x = DEFAULT_X;
18      y = DEFAULT_Y;
19      if ( inRange( xValue ) && inRange( yValue ) )
20      {
21        x = xValue;
22        y = yValue;
23      }
24    }
25
26    public boolean shift( int xDiff, int yDiff )
27    {
28      if ( inRange( x + xDiff ) && inRange( y + yDiff ) )
29      {
30        x += xDiff;
31        y += yDiff;
32        return true;
33      }
34      return false;
35    }
36    public int getX()
37    {
38      return x;
39    }
40    public int getY()
41    {
42      return y;
43    }
44    public String toString()
45    {
46      return String.format( "(%d,%d)", x, y );
47    }
48  }
```

Listing 16.7 Class PositionConfined

Now that we have revised PositionPrivate to PositionConfined, we revise UsePositionPrivate too. The new program is UsePositionConfined. The new version uses PositionConfined instead of PositionPrivate. The program captures the return value of the method shift, and stores it in a boolean variable, res (Line 18). If the value of res is true, the program prints the new position (Lines 19–22). Otherwise, it prints a special message "-----UNSUCCESSFUL-----" (Lines 23–26).

```
1   import java.util.*;
2   public class UsePositionConfined
3   {
4     public static void main( String[] args )
5     {
6       Scanner keyboard = new Scanner( System.in );
7       PositionConfined pos;
8
9       System.out.print( "Enter the initial x y: " );
10      pos = new PositionConfined(
11          keyboard.nextInt(), keyboard.nextInt() );
12      String answer = "";
13      do
14      {
15        System.out.println( "The current position: " + pos.toString() );
16        System.out.print( "By how much do you want to shift x and y? " );
17
18        boolean res = pos.shift( keyboard.nextInt(), keyboard.nextInt() );
19        if ( res )
20        {
21          System.out.println( "The new position: " + pos.toString() );
22        }
23        else
24        {
25          System.out.println( "--------UNSUCCESSFUL--------" );
26        }
27        System.out.print( "Continue (y/n)? " );
28        answer = keyboard.next();
29      } while ( answer.startsWith( "y" ) );
30    }
31  }
```

Listing 16.8 Class UsePositionConfined

Here is an execution example of the program. The error message is generated two times during the execution.

```
1   Enter the initial x y: 4 4
2   The current position: (4,4)
3   By how much do you want to shift x and y? 3 3
4   The new position: (7,7)
5   Continue (y/n)? y
6   The current position: (7,7)
7   By how much do you want to shift x and y? 10 20
8   --------UNSUCCESSFUL--------
9   Continue (y/n)? y
10  The current position: (7,7)
11  By how much do you want to shift x and y? -7 -7
12  --------UNSUCCESSFUL--------
13  Continue (y/n)? y
14  The current position: (7,7)
15  By how much do you want to shift x and y? 1 -2
16  The new position: (8,5)
17  Continue (y/n)? n
```

Fig. 16.3 A black box.
What is inside the box
cannot be seen from the
user

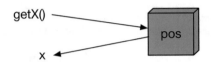

16.1.4 Information Hiding

An important concept in the design of object classes is **information hiding** (or **black box**). Information hiding refers to the idea that, by making its instance variables private, the users of an object class can be oblivious to how the information is represented in the object class and how the information is manipulated (see Fig. 16.3). For instance, a programmer of UsePositionConfined needs to know how to call the constructor and instance methods of PositionConfined, but does not need to know how the two coordinates are represented in the class. Using information hiding, the task of writing a source code for a program can be easily split among multiple programmers.

To demonstrate how information hiding works, we rewrite the class PositionConfined into PositionFancy. PositionFancy combines the two coordinate values, x and y, into a single int variable using the formula 16 * x + y. The first part of the code defines the same constants and the inRange method as PositionConfined:

```
 1   public class PositionFancy
 2   {
 3     public static final int MINIMUM = 1;
 4     public static final int MAXIMUM = 8;
 5     public static final int DEFAULT_X = 1;
 6     public static final int DEFAULT_Y = 1;
 7
 8     private static boolean inRange( int z )
 9     {
10       return z >= MINIMUM && z <= MAXIMUM;
11     }
12
```

Listing 16.9 Class PositionFancy (part 1). The constants and the method inRange

The second part of the source code presents how to go back and forth between two values and on value. The name of our only instance variable is w (Line 11). In representing the multiplicative factor of 16, the program uses a constant named SCALE (Line 13). Given x and y, the program combines the two using the formula x * SCALE + y. The method combine is a private instance method that combines two coordinate values, and stores the result in w (Lines 17–20). Because of the change in the encoding, both getX and getY need different codes. The method getX returns w / SCALE (Lines 19–22), and the method getY returns w % SCALE (Lines 23–26).

```
1     private int w;
2
3     private static final int SCALE = 16;
4
5     private void combine( int x, int y )
6     {
7       w = x * SCALE + y;
8     }
9     public int getX()
10    {
11      return w / SCALE;
12    }
13    public int getY()
14    {
15      return w % SCALE;
16    }
17
```

Listing 16.10 Class PositionFancy (part 2). The part responsible for combining the two coordinate values and splitting the combined number into two coordinate values

Next we see the constructor (Lines 30–37) and the method shift (Lines 39–47). The actions of the form x = VALUE1 and y = VALUE2 have been substituted with a method call, combine(VALUE1, VALUE2).

```
30    public PositionFancy( int xValue, int yValue )
31    {
32      combine( DEFAULT_X, DEFAULT_Y );
33      if ( inRange( xValue ) && inRange( yValue ) )
34      {
35        combine( xValue, yValue );
36      }
37    }
38
39    public boolean shift( int xDiff, int yDiff )
40    {
41      if ( inRange( getX() + xDiff ) && inRange( getY() + yDiff ) )
42      {
43        combine( getX() + xDiff, getY() + yDiff );
44        return true;
45      }
46      return false;
47    }
48
```

Listing 16.11 Class PositionFancy (part 3). The constructor and the method shift

Next we see the new version of the method toString. In building the String to be returned, toString uses the instance methods getX and getY.

```
49      public String toString()
50      {
51         return String.format( "(%d,%d)", getX(), getY() );
52      }
53
```

Listing 16.12 Class PositionFancy (part 4). The method toString

The last part of the code is a new method, toTable, that produces the position of the piece using eight lines of String, where the position appears as a '#' in an 8-by-8 square of '.'. The eight lines correspond to the y-coordinates of 8, 7, ..., 1 from top to bottom. For example, (7,2) is represented as:

```
. . . . . . . .
. . . . . . . .
. . . . . . . .
. . . . . . . .
. . . . . . . .
. . . . . . . .
. . . . . . #.
. . . . . . . .
```

and (3,8) is represented as:

```
. . #. . . . .
. . . . . . . .
. . . . . . . .
. . . . . . . .
. . . . . . . .
. . . . . . . .
. . . . . . . .
. . . . . . . .
```

To generate this visual encoding, PositionFancy uses two char constants, HERE and ELSEWHERE (Lines 54 and 55). HERE is the character that appears at the position represented by the PositionFancy object pos and ELSEWHERE is the character that appears at other places in the 8-by-8 diagram. Defining the two types of characters as constants makes it easy to make changes in the future.

To build the output, the program uses a StringBuilder object, builder. First, the program obtains the coordinate values using the getters and stores them in variables x and y (Lines 59 and 60). The program uses a double for-loop in building the contents of the StringBuilder object. The external loop iterates over the decreasing sequence MAXIMUM, ..., MINIMUM with a variable named i (Line 62). The internal loop iterates over the increasing sequence MINIMUM, ..., MAXIMUM with a variable named j (Line 64). In the body of the internal loop, if (i == y && j == x) (Line 66), the method appends HERE to builder (Line 68); otherwise, it appends ELSEWHERE (Line 72). Each time the internal loop concludes, the method appends '\n' (Line 75). At the conclusion of the external loop, the method returns the String represented by builder, obtained by calling the method toString (Line 77).

```
54      public static final char HERE = '#';
55      public static final char ELSEWHERE = '.';
56
57      public String toTable ()
58      {
59        int x = getX();
60        int y = getY();
61        StringBuilder builder = new StringBuilder();
62        for ( int i = MAXIMUM; i >= MINIMUM; i -- )
63        {
64          for ( int j = MINIMUM; j <= MAXIMUM; j ++ )
65          {
66            if ( i == y && j == x )
67            {
68              builder.append( HERE );
69            }
70            else
71            {
72              builder.append( ELSEWHERE );
73            }
74          }
75          builder.append( "\n" );
76        }
77        return builder.toString();
78      }
79    }
```

Listing 16.13 Class PositionFancy (part 5). The toTable method

The application written with PositionFancy is UsePositionFancy. In this application, the movement of the position is limited to one space, either only horizontally or only vertically. The four possible movements are thus left, up, down, and right, and they are represented with the letters 'h', 'j', 'k', and 'l'. In addition, the letter 'q' represents the termination of the program.

As before, the program asks the initial position from the user (Line 9), and then instantiates a PositionFancy object with the input from the user (Line 10). After this, the program enters a do-while loop (Line 13). To report the present position, the program uses the method toTable (Line 14). Since the String data that the method returns has the newline at the end, the program uses System.out.print instead of System.out.println. The program then prompts the user to enter the action to be performed (Lines 15 and 16), and receives input from the user (Line 17). The program uses a switch statement (Line 18) to perform the action. The method shift takes two parameters. The program calls shift(-1, 0) for 'h', shift(0, -1) for 'j', shift(0, +1) for 'k', and shift(+1, 0) for 'l' (Lines 20–23). Since the y-coordinate in the visual encoding decreases from MAXIMUM to MINIMUM, "down" (the letter 'j') must be represented with the decrease in the value of y, and "up" (the letter 'k') must be represented with the increase in the value of y. The return value of the method shift is ignored. Since the position is visually presented and the visual presentation takes up many lines, the reporting of the new position immediately after making a move has been eliminated. The program terminates if the command chosen is 'q' (Line 25).

```
1   import java.util.*;
2   public class UsePositionFancy
3   {
4     public static void main( String[] args )
5     {
6       Scanner keyboard = new Scanner( System.in );
7       PositionFancy pos;
8
9       System.out.print( "Enter the initial x y: " );
10      pos = new PositionFancy( keyboard.nextInt(), keyboard.nextInt() );
11
12      String answer = "";
13      do {
14        System.out.print( pos.toTable() );
15        System.out.print(
16            "Enter h,j,k,l to move left, down, up, right; q to quit: " );
17        answer = keyboard.next();
18        switch( answer.charAt( 0 ) )
19        {
20          case 'h': pos.shift( -1, 0 ); break;
21          case 'j': pos.shift( 0, -1 ); break;
22          case 'k': pos.shift( 0, +1 ); break;
23          case 'l': pos.shift( +1, 0 ); break;
24        }
25      } while ( !answer.startsWith( "q" ) );
26    }
27  }
```

Listing 16.14 Class UsePositionFancy

Here is an execution example of the code:

```
1   Enter the initial x y: 1 2
2   ........
3   ........
4   ........
5   ........
6   ........
7   ........
8   #.......
9   ........
10  Enter h,j,k,l to move left, down, up, right; q to quit: j
11  ........
12  ........
13  ........
14  ........
15  ........
16  ........
17  ........
18  #.......
```

```
19   Enter h,j,k,l to move left, down, up, right; q to quit: j
20   |........
21   |........
22   |........
23   |........
24   |........
25   |........
26   |........
27   |#.......
28   Enter h,j,k,l to move left, down, up, right; q to quit: k
29   |........
30   |........
31   |........
32   |........
33   |........
34   |........
35   |#.......
36   |........
37   Enter h,j,k,l to move left, down, up, right; q to quit: k
38   |........
39   |........
40   |........
41   |........
42   |........
43   |#.......
44   |........
45   |........
46   Enter h,j,k,l to move left, down, up, right; q to quit: l
47   |........
48   |........
49   |........
50   |........
51   |........
52   |.#......
53   |........
54   |........
55   Enter h,j,k,l to move left, down, up, right; q to quit: l
56   |........
57   |........
58   |........
59   |........
60   |........
61   |..#.....
62   |........
63   |........
64   Enter h,j,k,l to move left, down, up, right; q to quit: l
65   |........
66   |........
67   |........
68   |........
69   |........
70   |...#....
71   |........
72   |........
```

```
73    Enter h,j,k,l to move left, down, up, right; q to quit: l
74    ........
75    ........
76    ........
77    ........
78    ........
79    ....#...
80    ........
81    ........
82    Enter h,j,k,l to move left, down, up, right; q to quit: l
83    ........
84    ........
85    ........
86    ........
87    ........
88    .....#..
89    ........
90    ........
91    Enter h,j,k,l to move left, down, up, right; q to quit: l
92    ........
93    ........
94    ........
95    ........
96    ........
97    ......#.
98    ........
99    ........
100   Enter h,j,k,l to move left, down, up, right; q to quit: l
101   ........
102   ........
103   ........
104   ........
105   ........
106   .......#
107   ........
108   ........
109   Enter h,j,k,l to move left, down, up, right; q to quit: l
110   ........
111   ........
112   ........
113   ........
114   ........
115   .......#
116   ........
117   ........
118   Enter h,j,k,l to move left, down, up, right; q to quit: q
```

16.2   An Object Class Representing a Bank Account

Here, we write an application for keeping track of the balances of bank accounts. The application allows the user to create a list of bank accounts, and then execute transactions on individual accounts or between two accounts on the list. An account is represented by the account name and the balance. We select String as the data type for the former and int as the data type for the latter. We assume that the balance is represented in cents. The largest balance that an int can represent is greater than 2 billion cents, or 20 million dollars. The amount is sufficient for our application.

The class BankAccount has two instance variables. They are a String variable, name, and an int variable, balance. The class has the following five instance methods:

- getName() returns a String data representing the account name.
- getBalance() returns an int data representing the balance.
- getBalanceString() returns a String data representing the balance in dollars, with the dollar sign and the currency punctuation.
- deposit(int amount) attempts to deposit the amount represented in the parameter and returns a boolean value representing whether or not the deposit was successfully made. The method does not change the balance if the amount is not positive.
- withdraw(int amount) attempts to withdraw the amount represented in the parameter and returns a boolean value representing whether or not the withdrawal was successfully made. The method does not change the balance if the amount is either nonpositive or greater than the balance.

A source code for the class BankAccount appears next. All the instance variables are private. The constructor receives two formal parameters, a String value, name, and an int value, startBalance. The latter represents the initial balance of the account. The constructor stores these values in their respective instance variables. However, the value provided for balance may be nonpositive. If that happens, the constructor uses 1 cent as the initial balance. This choice is expressed as the assignment balance = Math.max(1, startBalance) appearing in Line 9. As for the account name, since the instance variable and the parameter have the same names, they have to be distinguished. This is accomplished by attaching the prefix this. to the instance variable. This appears in Line 8:

```
this.name = name;
```

The assignment without this., i.e.,

```
name = name;
```

stores the value of the formal parameter name to itself (this is legitimate, since formal parameters can be treated as variables). This means that the instance variable name retains its default value null. The prefix this. means "the instance method or the instance variable of this class". In the source code of an object class, the prefix this. can be attached to any reference to its instance variable and any reference its instance methods.

The five instance methods are written as follows: The method getName returns the value of name (Lines 12–15) and the method getBalance returns the value of balance (Line 18). For getBalanceString, the program splits the amount into the dollar amount and the residual dollar amount by dividing balance by 100. The quotient is used as the former, and the remainder is used as the latter. These two quantities are given to String.format with the format of $%,d.%02d, and the String generated is returned (Line 22). In deposit (Line 25), if the value of amount at most 0 (Line 27), false is immediately returned (Line 28). Otherwise, the method adds the amount to balance (Line 30) and returns true (Line 31). In withdraw, if the amount is strictly negative or the amount exceeds the balance (Line 36), the method returns false (Line 38). Otherwise, the method subtracts the amount from the balance, and then returns true (Lines 39 and 40).

```
1   public class BankAccount
2   {
3     private String name;
4     private int balance; // in cents
5
6     BankAccount( String name, int startBalance )
7     {
8       this.name = name;
9       balance = Math.max( 1, startBalance );
10      // since the balance have to be positive
11    }
12    public String getName()
13    {
14      return name;
15    }
16    public int getBalance()
17    {
18      return balance;
19    }
20    public String getBalanceString()
21    {
22      return String.format( "$%,d.%02d", balance / 100, balance % 100 );
23    }
24
25    public boolean deposit( int amount )
26    {
27      if ( amount <= 0 ) {
28        return false;
29      }
30      balance += amount;
31      return true;
32    }
33
34    public boolean withdraw( int amount )
35    {
36      if ( amount <= 0 || amount > balance ) {
37        return false;
38      }
39      balance -= amount;
40      return true;
41    }
42  }
```

Listing 16.15 Class BankAccount

SomeBankAccounts is our application program. SomeBankAccounts receives information for some bank accounts from the user, and then interacts with the user to make transactions on the accounts. At the start of the program, the user specifies how many bank accounts are to be handled. The user then provides the names and the initial balances of the accounts. The program enters a loop in which it interacts with the user to perform transactions. The available actions in each round are: (a) making a deposit to one account, (b) making a withdrawal from one account, and (c) transferring money from one account to another. If the requested action fails, the program reports the failure. Here are the methods that perform the three actions.

The method `deposit` attempts to make a deposit of an amount given in the second parameter to the account given in the first parameter (Line 4). To accomplish this, the method calls the instance method `deposit` on the specified account, and then checks its return value (Line 6). If the return value is `false`, the method prints an error message (Line 8).

The method `withdraw` works in a similar manner. The method attempts to make a withdrawal of the amount given in the second parameter from the account given in the first parameter (Line 12). To accomplish this, the method calls the instance method `deposit` on the specified account, and then checks its return value (Line 14). If the return value is `false`, the method prints an error message (Line 16).

The method `transfer` attempts to withdraw the amount given in the third parameter from the account given in the first parameter, and then deposits it to the account given in the second parameter (Line 20). To accomplish the task, the method first attempts the withdrawal (Line 23). If this attempt is successful, the deposit can be made without checking, so the method makes the deposit (Line 25). Otherwise, the method prints an error message (Line 29).

```
1   import java.util.*;
2   public class SomeBankAccounts
3   {
4     public static void deposit( BankAccount acc, int amount )
5     {
6       if ( !acc.deposit( amount ) )
7       {
8         System.out.println( "Deposit unsuccessful" );
9       }
10    }
11
12    public static void withdraw( BankAccount acc, int amount )
13    {
14      if ( !acc.withdraw( amount ) )
15      {
16        System.out.println( "Withdrawal unsuccessful" );
17      }
18    }
19
20    public static void transfer( BankAccount from, BankAccount to,
21        int amount )
22    {
23      if ( from.withdraw( amount ) )
24      {
25        to.deposit( amount );
26      }
27      else
28      {
29        System.out.println( "Transfer unsuccessful" );
30      }
31    }
32
```

Listing 16.16 A program that manipulates with a list of bank accounts (part 1). The methods `deposit`, `withdraw`, and `transfer`

The method `initial` handles the initialization of the individual accounts on the list. The method returns a `BankAccount` object (Line 33). The parameter of the method `index` is an `int` value presumably representing the index to the bank account that is to be generated. The value `index` is used just for presenting a prompt (Line 37). The method receives the name using `nextLine` (Line 38), and the initial balance (Lines 39 and 40). The method uses `nextLine` to receive an input line, and then converts the input line to an `int` value using `Integer.parseInt`. The method then combines the values to instantiate a `BankAccount` object, and then returns this object.

The method `actionPrompt` prints the prompt. The method receives an array of `BankAccount` objects as its formal parameter (Line 44). The method prints the name and the balance of all the accounts (Lines 46–52). To obtain the name and the balance, the method uses `getName` and `getBalanceString` of `BankAccount`. After printing the account information, the method presents the available actions (Lines 53–57). The actions have numbers from 1 to 4, where 4 is for terminating the program.

```
33    public static BankAccount initial( int index )
34    {
35       Scanner keyboard = new Scanner( System.in );
36
37       System.out.printf( "Enter name for account #%d: ", index );
38       String name = keyboard.nextLine();
39       System.out.printf( "Enter amount for account #%d: ", index );
40       int amount = Integer.parseInt( keyboard.nextLine() );
41       return new BankAccount( name, amount );
42    }
43
44    public static void actionPrompt( BankAccount[] allAccounts )
45    {
46       System.out.println( "------" );
47       for ( int i = 0; i < allAccounts.length; i ++ )
48       {
49          System.out.printf( "%2d: %s has the balance of %s%n", i,
50             allAccounts[ i ].getName(),
51             allAccounts[ i ].getBalanceString() );
52       }
53       System.out.println( "-----Select action" );
54       System.out.println( "1. Deposit to an Account" );
55       System.out.println( "2. Withdrawal from an Account" );
56       System.out.println( "3. Transfer Between Accounts" );
57       System.out.println( "4. Quit" );
58    }
59
```

Listing 16.17 A program that manipulates with a list of bank accounts (part 2). The methods `initial` and `actionPrompt`

The final part of the program is the method `main` (Line 60). The method receives the number of accounts, `size`, from the user (Lines 64 and 65), and instantiates an array of `BankAccount` objects, `theAccounts`, having `size` elements (Line 66). The method uses a for-loop that iterates over the sequence 0, ..., size - 1 with a variable named i. For each value of i, the method calls initial(i), and stores the returned BankAccount object in theAccounts[i] (Lines 67–70).

```
60    public static void main( String[] args )
61    {
62        Scanner keyboard = new Scanner( System.in );
63        int choice, amount, size, index, index2;
64        System.out.print( "Enter the Number of Accounts: " );
65        size = Integer.parseInt( keyboard.nextLine() );
66        BankAccount[] theAccounts = new BankAccount[ size ];
67        for ( int i = 0; i < size; i ++ )
68        {
69            theAccounts[ i ] = initial( i );
70        }
```

Listing 16.18 A program that manipulates with a list of bank accounts (part 3). The preparation in the method main

The method then commences a do-while loop (Line 72). The action to be performed in the do-while loop is as follows:

Step 1: The method prints the prompt using actionPrompt (Line 73).

Step 2: The method prompts the user to enter the choice (Line 75) and obtains the choice of the user. The choice is converted to an int using Integer.parseInt (Line 75).

Step 3: If the choice is 1, the action to be performed is a deposit (Line 76). The method receives the index to the account (Lines 78 and 79), receives the amount to deposit (Lines 80 and 81), and performs the task by calling the method deposit with the element of the BankAccount array at the index and the amount specified (Line 82).

Step 4: If the choice is 2, the action to be performed is a withdrawal (Line 84). The method receives the index to the account (Lines 86 and 87), receives the amount to deposit (Lines 88 and 89), and performs the task by calling the method withdraw with the element of the BankAccount array at the index and the amount specified (Line 90).

Step 5: If the choice is 3, the action to be performed is a transfer (Line 92). The method obtains the index to the destination account of the transfer and the index to the source account of the transfer (Lines 94–97), and then obtains the amount of transfer (Lines 98 and 99). The transaction is performed by calling the method transfer with the elements of the BankAccount array at the two indexes and the amount specified as the actual parameters (Line 100). The two indexes can be equal to each other. If the two indexes are equal to each other, the money is withdrawn (if the amount specified is valid) from the account specified by the two identical indexes and deposited back to it.

Step 6: The program terminates if the choice is 4 (Line 102).

```
71      do
72      {
73        actionPrompt( theAccounts );
74        System.out.print( "Enter your choice: " );
75        choice = Integer.parseInt( keyboard.nextLine() );
76        if ( choice == 1 )
77        {
78          System.out.print( "Enter account index: " );
79          index = Integer.parseInt( keyboard.nextLine() );
80          System.out.print( "Enter amount: " );
81          amount = Integer.parseInt( keyboard.nextLine() );
82          deposit( theAccounts[ index ], amount );
83        }
84        else if ( choice == 2 )
85        {
86          System.out.print( "Enter account index: " );
87          index = Integer.parseInt( keyboard.nextLine() );
88          System.out.print( "Enter amount: " );
89          amount = Integer.parseInt( keyboard.nextLine() );
90          withdraw( theAccounts[ index ], amount );
91        }
92        else if ( choice == 3 )
93        {
94          System.out.print( "Enter account origination index: " );
95          index = Integer.parseInt( keyboard.nextLine() );
96          System.out.print( "Enter account destination index: " );
97          index2 = Integer.parseInt( keyboard.nextLine() );
98          System.out.print( "Enter amount: " );
99          amount = Integer.parseInt( keyboard.nextLine() );
100         transfer( theAccounts[ index ], theAccounts[ index2 ], amount );
101       }
102     } while ( choice != 4 );
103   }
104 }
```

Listing 16.19 A program that manipulates with a list of bank accounts (part 4). The loop in the method `main`

Here is an execution example of the program, presented in two parts:

```
1   Enter the Number of Accounts: 3
2   Enter name for account #0: My Saving
3   Enter amount for account #0: 10000000
4   Enter name for account #1: My Checking
5   Enter amount for account #1: 100000
6   Enter name for account #2: Her Saving
7   Enter amount for account #2: 20000000
8   ------
9    0: My Saving has the balance of $100,000.00
10   1: My Checking has the balance of $1,000.00
11   2: Her Saving has the balance of $200,000.00
12  -----Select action
13  1. Deposit to an Account
14  2. Withdrawal from an Account
15  3. Transfer Between Accounts
16  4. Quit
```

```
17  Enter your choice: 1
18  Enter account index: 0
19  Enter amount: 5000000
20  ------
21   0: My Saving has the balance of $150,000.00
22   1: My Checking has the balance of $1,000.00
23   2: Her Saving has the balance of $200,000.00
24  -----Select action
25  1. Deposit to an Account
26  2. Withdrawal from an Account
27  3. Transfer Between Accounts
28  4. Quit
29  Enter your choice: 3
30  Enter account origination index: 2
31  Enter account destination index: 1
32  Enter amount: 5000000
33  ------
34   0: My Saving has the balance of $150,000.00
35   1: My Checking has the balance of $51,000.00
36   2: Her Saving has the balance of $150,000.00
37  -----Select action
38  1. Deposit to an Account
39  2. Withdrawal from an Account
40  3. Transfer Between Accounts
41  4. Quit
42  Enter your choice: 2
43  Enter account index: 2
44  Enter amount: 999900
45  ------
46   0: My Saving has the balance of $150,000.00
47   1: My Checking has the balance of $51,000.00
48   2: Her Saving has the balance of $140,001.00
49  -----Select action
50  1. Deposit to an Account
51  2. Withdrawal from an Account
52  3. Transfer Between Accounts
53  4. Quit
54  Enter your choice: 4
```

16.3 Array with Capacity and Size (Reprise)

In Sect. 13.6, we studied arrays with capacity and size. We wrote an application using an array with capacity and size to manipulate a list of names `String`, where we enabled the user to add an element, remove an element, search for an element, and see all the elements. In this section, we study how to convert the class to a general purpose object class for maintaining an indefinite number of `String` objects.

To develop the general purpose class, we do the following:

- We will turn the global variables into instance variables.
- We will remove `main` and `action` methods, since they are irrelevant.
- We will convert the method `setup` to a constructor, where the constructor takes `int` data, `capacity`, as its formal parameter, instead of asking for input from the user.
- We will convert the method `add` to an instance method that adds just one element.
- We will convert the remaining methods (`search`, `remove`, and `print`) to instance methods. We will remove the `static` attribute from the header of the methods.

- We will add new methods, getCapacity and getSize, as getters.

Here is a code for ArrayWithCapacity. The global variables are now private instance variables (Lines 4 and 5). They are int variables, size and capacity, and a String[] variable, theNames. The constructor takes an int value, capacity, as the formal parameter (Line 7). The constructor saves the value of the parameter to the instance variable, capacity. Here we use this. for distinction (Line 9). The constructor then instantiates the array using the capacity value as the length (Line 10) and assigns 0 to size (Line 11). The getters getCapacity (Lines 14–17) and getSize (Lines 19–22) return the values of capacity and size.

```
1   // Using an array of fixed size
2   public class ArrayWithCapacity
3   {
4     private int size, capacity;
5     private String[] theNames;
6
7     public ArrayWithCapacity( int capacity )
8     {
9       this.capacity = capacity;
10      theNames = new String[ capacity ];
11      size = 0;
12    }
13    public int getCapacity()
14    {
15      return capacity;
16    }
17    public int getSize()
18    {
19      return size;
20    }
```

Listing 16.20 The first part of class ArrayWithCapacity

The method search (Lines 21–36) is the same as before, except that it is now an instance method. Since the previous version used the variables as global variables, just removing the attribute of static is enough to make this adjustment.

```
21    public void search( String aName )
22    {
23      boolean found = false;
24      for ( int pos = 0; pos < size; pos ++ )
25      {
26        if ( theNames[ pos ].indexOf( aName ) >= 0 )
27        {
28          found = true;
29          System.out.printf( "Found %s at %d%n", theNames[ pos ], pos );
30        }
31      }
32      if ( !found )
33      {
34        System.out.println( "Not found" );
35      }
36    }
```

Listing 16.21 The search method of the class ArrayWithCapacity

The way the method `print` works (Lines 37–43) is the same as before:

```
37   public void print ()
38   {
39     for ( int pos = 0; pos < size; pos ++ )
40     {
41       System.out.printf ( "%4d:%s%n", pos, theNames[ pos ] );
42     }
43   }
```

Listing 16.22 The method for printing the data in class `ArrayWithCapacity`

The method `add` (Lines 44–54) is now designed to take only one element to add:

```
44   public void add( String aName )
45   {
46     if ( size < capacity )
47     {
48       theNames[ size ++ ] = aName;
49     }
50     else
51     {
52       System.out.println ( "The storage is full." );
53     }
54   }
```

Listing 16.23 The method for adding an element in `ArrayWithCapacity`

The method `remove` (Lines 55–65) is the same as before, except that the instance variables appear in place of the global variables:

```
55   public void remove( int index )
56   {
57     if ( index >= 0 && index < size )
58     {
59       theNames[ index ] = theNames[ -- size ];
60     }
61     else
62     {
63       System.out.println ( "The specified position does not exist." );
64     }
65   }
```

Listing 16.24 The method for removing an element in class `ArrayWithCapacity`

Now we can use this new class to rewrite the application. Important points to note are:

- This time, we use an `ArrayWithCapacity` object, since we have packed all the relevant components in it (Line 9). We use

  ```
  ArrayWithCapacity array = new ArrayWithCapacity( capacity );
  ```

  for instantiation.

- We use method calls `array.add( name )` (Line 19), `array.remove( index )` (Line 23), `array.search( key )` (Line 27), and `array.print ()` (Line 29) for actions.

```
1   import java.util.*;
2   // Using an array of fixed size
3   public class UseArrayWithCapacity {
4     // main
5     public static void main( String[] args ) {
6       Scanner keyboard = new Scanner( System.in );
7       System.out.print( "Enter capacity: " );
8       int capacity = Integer.parseInt( keyboard.nextLine() );
9       ArrayWithCapacity array = new ArrayWithCapacity( capacity );
10      char c;
11      do {
12        System.out.print( "What do you want to do?\n"
13          + "A(dd), R(remove), P(rint), S(earch), Q(uit): " );
14        c = keyboard.nextLine().charAt( 0 );
```

Listing 16.25 A new version of the program that uses an array with capacity and size (part 1)

```
15          switch ( c )
16          {
17            case 'A':
18              System.out.println(
19                  "Enter new names, empty line to finish: " );
20              String name;
21              do
22              {
23                System.out.print( "> " );
24                name = keyboard.nextLine();
25                if ( name.length() != 0 )
26                {
27                  array.add( name );
28                }
29              } while ( name.length() != 0 );
30              break;
31            case 'R':
32              System.out.print( "Enter index: " );
33              array.remove( Integer.parseInt( keyboard.nextLine() ) );
34              break;
35            case 'S':
36              System.out.print( "Enter a key: " );
37              array.search( keyboard.nextLine() );
38              break;
39            case 'P':
40              array.print();
41              break;
42          }
43        } while ( c != 'Q' );
44        System.out.println( "Closing..." );
45      }
46   }
```

Listing 16.26 A new version of the program that uses an array with capacity and size (part 2)

By appropriately modifying the key matching criterion, indexOf (key) >= 0, it is possible to design a class for maintaining a list of objects of a type other than String.

Summary

- If the instance variables of an object class are public, the program of the object class may access the variable by attaching the names of the instance variables to the object name with a comma in between.
- To prohibit access to instance variables from any outside class, the attribute of private can be attached.
- To distinguish between an instance variable and a formal parameter having the same name, the attribute of this. can be attached to it.
- Information hiding refers to the idea that an object class can be written so that the user of the object class does not need to know what the instance variables of the object class are.
- Methods for accessing values of instance variables (not necessarily as they are) are called getters (or accessors).
- Methods for changing values of instance variables (not necessarily as they are) are called setters (or modifiers).
- It is possible to convert an existing program to a container class that has a certain functionality by changing the global variables to instance variables.

Exercises

1. **Terminology question** State the differences between "private" instance variables and "public" instance variables.

2. **Class Car** Write a class named Car for recording information about a car. The class has three getters:
   - getMake () returns the make of the car as a String value,
   - getModel () returns the model of the car as a String value, and
   - getYear () that returns the year the car was made as an int value.

   The class has four setters:
   - setMake (String make),
   - setModel (Sting model),
   - setYear (String year), and
   - setYear (int year) (by way of method overloading).

   Write two constructors for the class,
   - Car (String make, String model, String year) and
   - Car (String make, String model, int year).

   Choose appropriate instance variables.

3. **An object class DoDo** Suppose DoDo is an object class that provides access to two instance variables, a String value, word, and an int value, quantity. Write a constructor public DoDo (String word, int quantity) that instantiates an object of the class by storing the first value in the instance variable word and the second value in the instance variable quantity. Also, write getters for word and quantity.

4. **Using instance methods**   Let `Stats` be a class designed for maintaining the statistics of some collection of real numbers. The class does not necessary have to maintain the numbers in the collection, but has to satisfy the following properties:

- There is one constructor. The constructor has no formal parameters. The constructor initializes the collection of as the empty set.
- The class has a void method `add( double x )` that incorporates the value `x` into the collection.
- The class has an `int` method `size()` that returns the number of values that have been incorporated.
- The class has a `double` method `average()` that returns the average of the numbers that have been incorporated.
- The class has a `double` method `variance()` that returns the variance of the numbers that have been incorporated, where the variance is the mean of the square of the difference between the individual values from the average. Note that the variance is given as:

$$\text{(the sum of the square of the values)} - \text{(the square of the average)}$$

In this exercise, write a Java program `CalcStats` that

- opens a data file whose name is given as `args[ 0 ]`,
- uses a `Stats` object to incorporate all the numbers appearing in the file, and then
- prints the three pieces of information that can be obtained from the object using the accessor methods.

For example, if the contents of the file `numbers.txt` are:

```
1   3
2   4
3   5
4   6
5   7
6   8
7   9
8   10
```

the program runs as follows

```
1   % java CalcStats numbers.txt
2   The count is 8
3   The average is 6.500000
4   The variance is 5.250000
```

5. **Writing class `Stats`**   Write the class `Stats` whose function was defined in the previous question.

6. **A class for a point in the three-dimensional space**   Write a class named `ThreeDPoint` for recording a point in a three-dimensional real space, where the instance variables are in `double`. There should be methods for individually accessing the three coordinates and methods for individually modifying them.

Programming Projects

7. **A class for a linear equation over three unknowns**   Write a class named `ThreeDLinear` for recording a linear equation $ax + by + cz = d$, where x, y, z are unknowns and a, b, c, d are coefficients. The class has only one constructor that takes values for a, b, c, and d and stores the values in their respective instance variables. The class has four accessors to obtain the values of the coefficients. The class has three other instance methods:

- `public ThreeDLinear scale( double s )`: This method returns a new `ThreeDLinear` object in which all the coefficients are scaled by `s`.
- `public ThreeDLinear plus( ThreeDLinear o )`: This method returns a new `ThreeDLinear` object that corresponds to the equation whose coefficients are generated by adding the coefficients of `this` and those of `o`.
- `public ThreeDLinear minus( ThreeDLinear o )`: This method returns a new `ThreeDLinear` object that corresponds to the equation whose coefficients are generated by subtracting the coefficients of `o` from the coefficients of `this`.

8. **Class for a complex numbers** Write a class named `ComplexNum` for recording a complex number. The class must have two `double` instance variables, `real` and `imaginary`. An object of this class represents the complex number `real + imaginary * i` (where i is the root of $\sqrt{-1}$). Write the instance method `size` that returns, in `double`, the value of $real^2 - imaginary^2$.

9. **Class `MilitaryTime`** Write a class named `MilitaryTime` for representing the time of a day in 24 h. The class must have two accessors, `getHours()` and `getMinutes()`. Both of them must return an integer. The class has two additional instance methods, `advance(MilitaryTime o)` and `rewind(MilitaryTime o)`. The former advances the time by the amount of time represented by `o`. The latter rewinds the time by the amount of time represented by `o`.

10. **Class `TicTacToe`** Write a class named `TicTacToe` for representing a configuration of Tic-Tac-Toe. Tic-Tac-Toe is a game played by two people on a 3×3 grid. The two players take turns and mark one square of the grid with letters assigned to them (O and X). The player who has produced a row, a column, or a diagonal of the same letters wins the game. We view a configuration of the game as a 3×3 two-dimensional array of `char`. We use two characters, `'O'` and `'X'`, for the markings and the whitespace for available squares. The constructor of `TicTacToe` creates the blank configuration (that is, the configuration in which no square has been marked). We use a pair of integers between 0 and 2 to specify a square. The class has the following methods:

- `boolean isAvailable( int x, int y )`: returns whether or not the row x column y square of the grid is blank.
- `boolean isO( int x, int y )`: returns whether or not the row x column y square of the grid is an `'O'`.
- `boolean isX( int x, int y )`: returns whether or not the row x column y square of the grid is an `'X'`.
- `void setO( int x, int y )`: sets the row x column y square of the grid to `'O'`.
- `void setX( int x, int y )`: sets the row x column y square of the grid to `'X'`.

11. **The 15 puzzle** The 15 Puzzle is a puzzle played with 15 pieces placed on a 4×4 grid. The sizes of the pieces are equal to the size of any square of the grid. The pieces are numbered 1 through 15. At the start of the game the pieces are placed on one of the 16 squares of the grid with no overlap, so there is only one open square. During the course of the puzzle, the player can move a piece from any one of the neighboring squares (from left, right, above, or below) to the open square. The goal of the puzzle is to reorder the pieces so that 1..4 appear in the top row from left to right, 5..8 appear in the next row from left to right, 9..12 appear in the next row, and 13..15 in the bottom row, with the rightmost square open, as shown in the following diagram:

$$
\begin{array}{cccc}
1 & 2 & 3 & 4 \\
5 & 6 & 7 & 8 \\
9 & 10 & 11 & 12 \\
13 & 14 & 15 &
\end{array}
$$

To play the puzzle, the player herself scrambles the order of the pieces, by randomly moving the pieces according to the rule. Every 15 puzzle configuration generated from the goal configuration in this manner is solvable.

Write a class named `Config15` whose object represents a configuration of the 15 puzzle. The class must have three instance variables. The first is a 4×4 array of `int` values, where the numbers $0, \ldots, 15$ appear exactly once. In this array, 0 represents the open square. The second and the third instance variables are the row and the column indexes of the open square. The constructor takes an array in this format and copies the contents of the array to the instance variable, and then search for an open square to assign values to the row and column instance variables.

There should be the following instance methods.

- `boolean isSolved()`: This method returns whether or not the configuration represented by the object is the final configuration.
- `boolean pullDown()`: This method pulls the piece above the open square into the open square. The move is not possible if the open square is in the first row. The method returns as a `boolean` value indicating whether or not the move was successful.
- `boolean pullUp()`: This method moves the piece in the square immediately above the open square. The move is not possible if the open square is in the last row. The method returns whether or not the move has been successful.
- `boolean pullLeft()`: This method moves the piece in the square immediately to the left of the open square. The move is not possible if the open square is in the first column. The method returns whether or not the move has been successful.
- `boolean pullRight()`: The method moves the piece in the square immediately to the right of the open square. The move is not possible if the open square is in the last column. The method returns whether or not the move has been successful.
- `int get( int i, int j )`: The method returns the value of the array at row `i` and column `j`.
- `int getOpenRow()`: The method returns the value of the row index of the open space.
- `int getOpenCol()`: The method returns the value of the column index of the open space.

12. **File exploration using an array with capacity**   Modify the code for `ArrayWithCapacity` to write a code `FileArrayWC` for maintaining a list of `File` objects. The class has the following instance methods:

- `int getCapacity()`: returns the capacity.
- `int getSize()`: returns the size.
- `File get( int index )`: returns the object at position `index`.
- `void add( File f )`: adds f.
- `void remove( int index )`: removes the file at `index`.
- `int[] search( String key )`: returns an array of indexes at which the canonical path to the `File` object has `key` appearing in it.

Using this class, write an application `UseFileArrayWC` that allows the user to do the following:

(a) Adding one file by specifying its file path.

(b) Adding all files in a folder by specifying a path to the folder.

(c) Removing a file at a specific index.

(d) Searching for files with a key.

(e) Viewing all files.

(f) Writing the data to a file.

For searching and viewing, write a method named `present` that receives a `FileArrayWC` object named `data` and an `int []` object named `indexes` as parameters, and then prints all the files in `data` whose positions appear in `indexes`. To print an item, present the index, readability, writability, executability, whether it is a folder or not, along with the canonical path. The four `boolean` properties are represented by the letters `'r'`, `'w'`, `'x'`, and `'d'`. For each of the four properties, if the file does not possess the property, we print `' '`. Here is an example of the output, where the array has only three elements, 0, 1, and 2.

```
1    0 rwxd /Users/ogihara/Documents/CSC120/codeVer1
2    1 rwxd /Users/ogihara/Documents/CSC120/bookDraft
3    2 rw   /Users/ogihara/Documents/CSC120/code/UseFileArrayWC.classVer1
```

To view the data, define a one-parameter version of the method `present` that takes a `FileArrayWC` object `data` and calls the two-parameter version, where the second parameter is an array whose elements are `0, ..., data.getSize() - 1`. That way, all the elements will be printed. Each time the program writes the data into a file, it receives a name of the data file from the user. The very first line of the output is the size. After the first line, the canonical paths of the elements appear, one file per line. A `throws IOException` declaration can be added to each method that makes a call to some `File` method that has the declaration of `throws IOException`.

Interfaces, Inheritance, and Polymorphism

17

17.1 Interface

17.1.1 The Structure of an Interface

An **interface** is a template for building a Java class. The components of an interface are static methods, constants, and **abstract methods**. An abstract method is a method header followed by a semicolon and is without a body. All abstract methods have public visibility. An abstract method specifies only its syntax, but not its semantics.

A class written based upon an interface must turn each abstract method into one with a body having the same visibility, the same return type, the same name, the same parameter type signature, and the same `throws` declaration (if any) as the abstract one. We call this action **overriding**. A class C **implements** an interface I if its header formally states so, in the following manner:

```
public class C implements I
```

If the source code of C has this declaration, the constants and the methods (both static and abstract) appearing in I are automatically included in the source code of C, so they can be used without specifying the name of the interface. We call this mechanism **inheritance**. It is not possible to instantiate an object of I, but it is possible to declare the data type of an object to be I. We call this mechanism **polymorphism**.

An object class may implement multiple interfaces. If a class C implements interfaces I1, ..., Ik, the declaration uses the keyword `implements` only once and places the interfaces with commas in between in the following manner:

```
public class C implements I1, ..., Ik
```

The names of the interfaces may appear in any order.

17.1.2 A Simple Pizza Application

17.1.2.1 A Simple Pizza Class

Let us learn how to write and use interfaces by working on an application for building a menu at a pizza shop. The application will consist of (a) a class for an individual pizza, (b) a class for a

© Springer Nature Switzerland AG 2018
M. Ogihara, *Fundamentals of Java Programming*,
https://doi.org/10.1007/978-3-319-89491-1_17

menu, and (c) a main application class. The information available for a pizza is its name and price. To simplify the problem, we assume that pizzas can be added to the menu, or removed from the menu, but cannot be edited, meaning that it is not possible to change the names or prices of pizzas. In such a setting, changing the name or price of a pizza on the menu must be accomplished by removing the pizza from the menu, and then adding a revised version to the menu. Since the names or prices of pizza objects cannot be changed, we need only two functions in our pizza objects. The two functions are obtaining their names and obtaining their prices. We encode these requirements in our interface, `PizzaSimpleint`, that is shown next. The required functions, `getName` and `getPrice`, are stated in Lines 3 and 4 as abstract methods.

```
1   public interface PizzaSimpleInt
2   {
3     public String getName();
4     public double getPrice();
5   }
```

Listing 17.1 The code for `PizzaSimpleInt`

We write an implementation, `PizzaSimple`, of the interface. The coding idea for `PizzaSimpleInt` is straightforward. We use a `String` instance variable, `name`, for the name and a `double` instance variable, `price`, for the price. We assume that the value of `price` represents the price in dollars.

The class has a declaration, `implements PizzaSimpleInt` (Line 1). The instance variables are declared in Lines 3 and 4 as private variables. The constructor receives the name and price as parameters, and stores their values in the instance variables. Since the parameters and the instance variables have the same names, the prefix `this.` is attached to the instance variables to distinguish between the two (Line 8 and 9). The getters are overridden in Lines 11–18.

```
1   public class PizzaSimple implements PizzaSimpleInt
2   {
3     private String name;
4     private double price;
5
6     public PizzaSimple( String name, double price )
7     {
8       this.name = name;
9       this.price = price;
10    }
11    public String getName()
12    {
13      return name;
14    }
15    public double getPrice()
16    {
17      return price;
18    }
19  }
```

Listing 17.2 The code for `PizzaSimple`

17.1.2.2 Using an Interface as a Data Type

PizzaSimpleCollection is an object class representing a collection of pizzas, and PizzaSimpleMain is the main application program. Before halting, PizzaSimpleMain records the menu in a text data file. A path to the data file can be specified at the start of the program as args[0]. If the program starts with no such argument, PizzaSimpleMain asks for a file path from the user. Before starting interactions for building the menu, PizzaSimpleMain checks if the file specified by the file path exists, and if so, reads the data from the file. If the file does not exist, the program starts with no pizzas on the menu, and uses the file only for recording data. Since the file may be used at the start and at the end, we memorize the file path as an instance variable of PizzaSimpleCollection.

PizzaSimpleInt is an interface, so has no constructor. However, PizzaSimpleInt can be used as a data type. For instance, we can declare a PizzaSimpleInt variable, and then assign a PizzaSimple object to the variable, as shown next:

```
1  PizzaSimpleInt pizzaX;
2  pizzaX = new PizzaSimple( Hawaiian, 15.50 );
```

PizzaSimpleCollection uses an array of PizzaSimpleInt as the list of pizzas on the menu:

```
private PizzaSimpleInt[] list;
```

To get started, the constructor instantiates list as a 0-element array of PizzaSimpleInt:

```
list = new PizzaSimpleInt[ 0 ];
```

The format of the data files is as follows:

- The first line of the data file is the number of pizzas recorded in the file.
- Following the first line, the information appears for the individual pizzas on the menu. Each pizza is recorded in two lines. The first line for the name and the second line for the price. The number of pizzas recorded appear in this manner must match the number of pizzas stated in the first line.

Here is a sample data file:

```
1   5
2   Four Cheese
3   12.5
4   Nettuno
5   11.0
6   Capriccioso
7   14.0
8   Alfredo
9   14.5
10  Meat Lover's
11  13.5
```

In addition to reading from the data file (at the start of the program) and saving the information to the data file (at the end of the program), PizzaSimpleCollection has three functions, adding a pizza, deleting a pizza, and viewing the entire collection.

17.1.2.3 Instance Variables and Constructors

The class `PizzaSimpleCollection` involves file access, so needs imports. They are stated in Lines 1 and 2. In addition to the instance variable `list` of type `PizzaSimpleInt []`, the class has a `File` instance variable named `theFile` (Lines 5 and 6). The file path to the data file is recorded using this `File` object. During the execution of the program, `list.length` will be equal to the number of pizzas on the menu.

The class `PizzaSimpleCollection` has two constructors. The first constructor (Line 8) receives a `File` data, `f`, as its formal parameter. The constructor stores the value of `f` to the instance variable `theFile` (Line 10), instantiates `list` as a 0-element array of `PizzaSimpleInt`, and then calls the method `read` to add from the data stored in the data file `f`.

The method `read` has a `throws FileNotFoundException` declaration, so the constructor has the same declaration.

```
1   import java.util.*;
2   import java.io.*;
3   public class PizzaSimpleCollection
4   {
5      private PizzaSimpleInt [] list;
6      private File theFile;
7
8      PizzaSimpleCollection( File f ) throws FileNotFoundException
9      {
10        theFile = f;
11        list = new PizzaSimpleInt[ 0 ];
12        read();
13     }
14     PizzaSimpleCollection( String name ) throws FileNotFoundException
15     {
16        this( new File( name ) );
17     }
18
```

Listing 17.3 The code for `PizzaSimpleCollection` (part 1). The instance variables and the constructors

The second constructor (Line 14) receives a `String` data `name` as its formal parameter. The required action of the constructor is to execute the code for the first constructor with `new File( name )` in place of `f`:

```
1      theFile = new File( name );
2      list = new PizzaSimpleInt[ 0 ];
3      read();
```

In writing this code, we can recycle the code for the first constructor by calling it, as shown in Line 16:

```
      this( new File( name ) );
```

If a constructor calls another constructor of the same class, the keyword of `this` is used as the name of the constructor. The call of another constructor from the same class has to appear in the first line of the code. The code like:

```
1     File g = new File( name );
2     this( g );
```

makes sense, but is syntactically incorrect.

17.1.2.4 Reading Data

The method `read` checks if the file specified by `theFile` exists, and if so, reads the data from the file. Despite this check, there still remains the possibility that the constructor of a `Scanner` throws `FileNotFoundException`. Therefore, the method `read` has the `throws FileNotFoundException` declaration (Line 19). If `theFile` passes this existence check (Line 21), the program instantiates a `Scanner` object to read data from the file (Line 23). The method reads the number of pizzas recorded in the file using `nextLine` and `Integer.parseInt` (Line 24). The method then instantiates an array of `PizzaSimpleInt` data whose length is equal to the number of elements specified in the first line (Line 25).

After the initialization, the method `read` uses a for-loop to read the remainder of the file contents in pairs of lines. The first line of a pair is the name of the pizza (Line 28) and the second line is the price (Line 29). The method uses `Double.parseDouble` to convert the second line to a `double` value, instantiates a `PizzaSimple` object with the name and price, and stores it in its designated position in the array (Line 30). After completing the process of reading information, the method closes the `Scanner` object (Line 32).

```
19    public void read() throws FileNotFoundException
20    {
21       if ( theFile.exists() )
22       {
23          Scanner scanner = new Scanner( theFile );
24          int size = Integer.parseInt( scanner.nextLine() );
25          list = new PizzaSimpleInt[ size ];
26          for ( int index = 0; index < size; index ++ )
27          {
28             String name = scanner.nextLine();
29             double price = Double.parseDouble( scanner.nextLine() );
30             list[ index ] = new PizzaSimple( name, price );
31          }
32          scanner.close();
33       }
34    }
35
```

Fig. 17.4 The code for `PizzaSimpleCollection` (part 2). The method `read`

17.1.2.5 Writing Data

The method `write` records the data in the file specified by `theFile`. The method has a `throws FileNotFoundException` declaration (Line 36). The method instantiates a `PrintStream` object with `theFile` (Line 38). The method writes the length of the array `list` in one line, and then uses a for-loop to write the information of the individual pizzas in two lines. To accomplish this, the method uses the getters of `PizzaSimpleInt`. After completing the process of writing the data into the data file, the method closes the `PrintStream` object by calling the method `close` (Line 33).

```
36     public void write() throws FileNotFoundException
37     {
38       PrintStream stream = new PrintStream( theFile );
39       stream.println( list.length );
40       for ( int index = 0; index < list.length; index ++ )
41       {
42         stream.println( list[ index ].getName() );
43         stream.println( list[ index ].getPrice() );
44       }
45       stream.close();
46     }
47
```

Listing 17.5 The code for `PizzaSimpleCollection` (part 3). The method `write`

17.1.2.6 Adding a Pizza to the List

The method `add` receives a `String` data, name, and a `double` data, `price`, as formal parameters (Line 48). These parameters represent the name and price of a new pizza to be added to the menu. Since `list.length` must be equal to the number of pizzas on the menu, the array must be extended. The method generates a new array of `PizzaSimpleInt` to increase its capacity by one. This is accomplished by calling `Arrays.copyOf`. The copy length is `list.length + 1` (Line 50). The array returned by `copyOf` is stored in `listNew`. The designated position of the new pizza is `list.length`. The method stores a new `PizzaSimple` object instantiated with the two parameters in the designated position (Line 51). After that, the method stores the array in `list` (Line 52).

```
48     public void add( String name, double price )
49     {
50       PizzaSimpleInt[] listNew = Arrays.copyOf( list, list.length + 1 );
51       listNew[ list.length ] = new PizzaSimple( name, price );
52       list = listNew;
53     }
54
```

Listing 17.6 The code for `PizzaSimpleCollection` (part 4). The method `add`

17.1.2.7 Removing a Pizza from the List

The method `delete` receives an `int` data, `index`. This is the index to the element to be removed (Line 55). The removal necessitates resizing of the array. Like `add`, the method uses `Arrays.copyOf`. This time, the copy length is `list.length - 1` (Line 57). The array `copyOf` returns has the elements correctly at their designated positions for all indexes before `index`. Therefore, the elements located after `index` are copied manually (Line 58-61).

```
55   public void delete( int index )
56   {
57     PizzaSimpleInt[] listNew = Arrays.copyOf( list, list.length - 1 );
58     for ( int pos = index + 1; pos < list.length; pos ++ )
59     {
60       listNew[ pos - 1 ] = list[ pos ];
61     }
62     list = listNew;
63   }
64
```

Listing 17.7 The code for `PizzaSimpleCollection` (part 5). The method `delte`

17.1.2.8 Viewing the Elements of the List

The method `view` (Line 65) is for printing the menu. For each pizza, the method prints its position in the collection, its name, and its price using the format `%3d:%s:$%.2f%n` (Lines 69 and 70).

```
65   public void view()
66   {
67     for ( int index = 0; index < list.length; index ++ )
68     {
69       System.out.printf( "%3d:%s:$%.2f%n", index,
70         list[ index ].getName(), list[ index ].getPrice() );
71     }
72   }
73 }
```

Listing 17.8 The code for `PizzaSimpleCollection` (part 6). The method `view`

The source code of `PizzaSimpleCollection`, has only two occurrences of `PizzaSimple` (Lines 30 and 51). If there is an alternate implementation of `PizzaSimpleInt`, using the alternate in place of `PizzaSample` is easy. We only have to rewrite the two places where `PizzaSimple` appears.

17.1.2.9 The Pizza Collection Main Class

`PizzaSimpleMain` is the main class that handles interactions with the user. The method `main` has a `throws FileNotFoundException` declaration, because it uses `PizzaSimpleCollect-ion`. At the start, if the length of `args` is positive (Line 8), the program instantiates `PizzaSimple Collection` object named `data` with `args[ 0 ]` (Line 10); otherwise, the program asks the user to enter a file path, and then uses the input for instantiation (Lines 14 and 15). In both cases, the constructor of `PizzaSimpleCollection` attempts to read the data from the specified file only if the file exists, so if the user provides an invalid file path, no data will be read at the start. The program uses a `String` variable named `input` to record the input from the user. The initial value of `input` is an empty `String` (Line 17).

The interactions with the user are repeated using a do-while loop until the user enters an input starting with `"Q"` as her choice of action (Lines 18 and 38). In the loop-body, the program prompts the user to enter the choice of action to be performed (Lines 20 and 21), receives an input, and stores it in `input` (Line 22). The execution is then directed using a `switch` statement based upon the first character of the input from the user (Line 24). If the character is `'V'`, the method executes `data.view()` (Line 26). If the character is `'A'`, the method receives the name (Lines 28 and 29) and the price (Lines 30 and 31) from the user, stores them in variables, `name` and `price`, and calls `data.add( name, price )` (Line 32). If the character is `'D'`, the method receives an input line from the user, converts it to an integer on the fly using `Integer.parseInt`, and calls `data.delete` with this integer as the actual parameter (Lines 35 and 36). If the character is `'Q'`, nothing happens inside the switch statement, and the loop is terminated (Line 38). Before halting the program, the program calls `data.write()` to save the data. `Double.parseInt` and `Integer.parseInt` are used to read the price of the new pizza and the index to the element to be removed.

```
1   import java.util.*;
2   import java.io.*;
3   public class PizzaSimpleMain
4   {
5     public static void main( String[] args ) throws FileNotFoundException {
6       Scanner keyboard = new Scanner( System.in );
7       PizzaSimpleCollection data;
8       if ( args.length > 0 )
9       {
10        data = new PizzaSimpleCollection( args[ 0 ] );
11      }
12      else
13      {
14        System.out.print( "Enter data file name: " );
15        data = new PizzaSimpleCollection( keyboard.nextLine() );
16      }
17      String input = "";
18      do
19      {
20        System.out.println( "Enter your choice by first letter" );
21        System.out.print( "View, Add, Delete, Quit: " );
22        input = keyboard.nextLine();
23
24        switch ( input.charAt( 0 ) )
25        {
26          case 'V': data.view(); break;
27          case 'A':
28            System.out.print( "Enter name: " );
29            String name = keyboard.nextLine();
30            System.out.print( "Enter price: " );
31            double price = Double.parseDouble( keyboard.nextLine() );
32            data.add( name, price );
33            break;
34          case 'D':
35            System.out.printf( "Enter index: " );
36            data.delete( Integer.parseInt( keyboard.nextLine() ) );
37        }
38      } while ( !input.startsWith( "Q" ) );
39      data.write();
40    }
41  }
```

Listing 17.9 The code for `PizzaSimpleMain`

Suppose that the name of the previous sample data file is `pizzaSimpleData.txt`. The program can be initiated with the file path to the file as `args [ 0 ]` as follows:

```
% java PizzaSimpleMain pizzaSimpleData.txt
Enter your choice by first letter
View, Add, Delete, Read, Quit: V
   0:Peperoni:$10.50
   1:Four Cheese:$12.50
   2:Nettuno:$11.00
   3:Meat Lovers:$13.00
Enter your choice by first letter
View, Add, Delete, Quit: A
Enter name: Capricciosa
Enter price: 14
Enter your choice by first letter
View, Add, Delete, Quit: D
Enter index: 0
Enter your choice by first letter
View, Add, Delete, Quit: V
   0:Four Cheese:$12.50
   1:Nettuno:$11.00
   2:Meat Lovers:$13.00
   3:Capricciosa:$14.00
Enter your choice by first letter
View, Add, Delete, Quit: Q
```

The data file has been updated. If we execute the `cat` command on the file, we see that there are now five pizzas.

```
% cat pizzaSimpleData.txt
5
Four Cheese
12.5
Nettuno
11.0
Capriccioso
14.0
Alfredo
14.5
Meat Lover's
13.5
```

17.2   Subclasses and Superclasses

17.2.1 Extending Existing Classes and Interfaces

The pizza menu building program that we have just seen has only the name and the price as information for a pizza. We will extend the program by adding information about the ingredients. We also add a search function that allows the user to look for pizzas having an ingredient. In developing this program, we will recycle `PizzaSimpleInt` and `PizzaSimple` and develop a new interface `PizzaComplexInt` an its implementation `PizzaComplex`. We will then slightly modify `PizzaSimpleCollection` and `PizzaSimpleMain` to obtain `PizzaComplexCollection` and `PizzaComplexMain`. To recycle the source code for `PizzaSimpleInt` and the source code for `PizzaSimple`, we use the keyword of `extends` as follows:

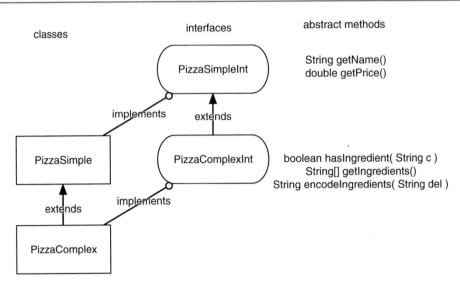

Fig. 17.1 The two interfaces and the two classes. The pointy arrows represent extensions and the circle-head arrows represent implementations

```
public interface PizzaComplexInt extends PizzaSimpleInt
```

and

```
public class PizzaComplex extends PizzaSimple implements PizzaComplexInt
```

When X extends Y, the unit type must agree between X and Y, meaning that X is a class if and only if Y is a class, and that X is an interface if and only if Y is an interface. If the type of the two units is class, we say that X is a **subclass** of Y and Y is a **superclass** of X. If the type is interface, we say that X is a **sub-interface** of Y and Y is a **super-interface** of X. As for the source codes we have at hand, PizzaComplex is a subclass of PizzaSimple, PizzaSimple is a superclass of PizzaComplex, PizzaComplexInt is a sub-interface of PizzaSimpleInt, and PizzaSimpleInt is a super-interface of PizzaComplexInt.

By declaring X extends Y, all non-private components that appear in Y are automatically included in X. This means that the two abstract methods of PizzaSimpleInt are already declared (as abstract methods) in PizzaComplexInt, and all the public parts of PizzaSimple (the constructor and the two getters) are available in PizzaComplex. This phenomenon is called **inheritance** too.

If a class X extends a class Y, the constructor of Y can be referenced using the keyword of super. The class X may override public methods in Y. If X does that, the pre-override version of the method can be referred to by attaching the prefix of super.

Figure 17.1 presents the relations among the two interfaces and the two classes.

Here is the code for PizzaComplexInt. Three new abstract methods are introduced.

```
1   public interface PizzaComplexInt extends PizzaSimpleInt
2   {
3       public boolean hasIngredient( String in );
4       public String[] getIngredients();
5       public String encodeIngredients( String del );
6   }
```

Listing 17.10 The code for `PizzaComplexInt`

We expect these abstract methods, when implemented, to operate as follows:

1. `hasIngredient( String c )` returns a `boolean` value representing whether or not the pizza has an ingredient whose name matches the keyword `c`.
2. `getIngredients()` returns the list of ingredients as an array of `String` data.
3. `encodeIngredients( String del )` returns a one-line encoding of the ingredients of the pizza, with the `String` represented by `del` appearing in between.

   The reason that the method `encodeIngredients` receives a delimiter as a parameter is that one-line encodings of ingredients are generated in two different situations. One is when presenting the information of a pizza on the screen. The other is when recording the information of a pizza in a data file. For the former, we may want to use a very short delimiter so that there will be wraparounds. For the latter, we may want to use a delimiter (such as the tab-stop) that does not appear in the names of pizzas. By parameterizing the delimiter, it is possible to handle the two different situations using just one method.

17.2.2 Writing Extensions

17.2.2.1 Writing a Subclass

Including the two abstract methods declared in `PizzaSimpleInt`, `PizzaComplexInt` has a total of five abstract methods. Since `PizzaComplex` has the `extends PizzaSimple` declaration, `PizzaComplex` only has to implement the three abstract methods that are introduced in `PizzaComplexInt`. We will use a private `String[]` instance variable named `ingredients` to represent the ingredients, where each element of the array is the name of one ingredient (Line 3). The constructor of `PizzaSimple` requires two parameters, `name` and `price`. The constructor of `PizzaComplex` has one more parameter. This parameter is an array of `String` data, `ingredients` (Line 5). Because `PizzaComplex` is a subclass of `PizzaSimple`, a `PizzaSimple` object is automatically included in a `PizzaComplex` object (as shown in Fig. 17.2). If the constructor of `PizzaComplex` does not call the `PizzaSimple`, the instance variables declared in `PizzaSimple` will have their default values (that is, `null` for `name` and 0 for `price`). Since `PizzaSimple` does not have setters for `name` or `price`, it is thus necessary to call the constructor of `PizzaSimple` to assign values to `name` and `price`. The way to call for the `PizzaSimple` constructor is:

```
super( name, price )
```

This is reminiscent of `this(...)` that is used to refer to another constructor of the same object class. The remaining action of the constructor `PizzaComplex` is to copy the value of the parameter

Fig. 17.2 A
`PizzaComplex` object

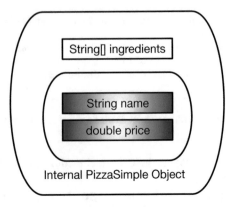

String[] ingredients

String name

double price

Internal PizzaSimple Object

PizzaComplex Object

`ingredients` to the instance variable `ingredients`. Because the parameter and the instance variable have the same names, the code attaches the prefix `this.` to the instance variable to distinguish it from the parameter. As in the case of the constructor call `this(...)`, the constructor of the superclass `super(...)` must be called at the start of the constructor.

```
1   public class PizzaComplex extends PizzaSimple implements PizzaComplexInt
2   {
3      private String[] ingredients;
4
5      public PizzaComplex( String name, double price, String[] ingredients )
6      {
7         super( name, price );
8         this.ingredients = ingredients;
9      }
10
```

Listing 17.11 The code for `PizzaComplex` (part 1). The header, the instance variable, and the constructor

The three abstract methods appearing in `PizzaComplexInt` are overridden in `PizzaComplex` as follows: The method `getIngredients` returns the array `ingredients` (Lines 11–14). A program that receives an ingredient list through the method `getIngredients` from a `PizzaComplex` object cannot shrink or extend the array, but can change the individual ingredients of the array. This is because the method provides a reference to the instance variable `ingredients`. To ensure that such modifications will never occur, the method can return a copy of the array instead of the array itself. Such a copy can be generated by `Arrays.copyOf( ingredients, ingredients.length )`.

```
11   public String[] getIngredients()
12   {
13     return ingredients;
14   }
15
```

Listing 17.12 The code for `PizzaComplex` (part 2). The implementation of the method `getIngredients`

To implement `hasIngredient`, the program uses a for-loop called a **"for-each" loop**. Given an array a whose elements are of type `T`,

$$\text{for (T x : a) \{ ... \}}$$

means to iterate over the elements of a with the iteration variable x. A for-each loop is available for all arrays and all classes that implement an interface `Iterable`. We will discuss the interface `Iterable` in the next chapter. In the case of arrays, the elements appear in the increasing order of their indexes.

In the source code of `PizzaComplex`, we use a for-each loop with the following expression (Line 18): `for ( String in : ingredients )` This loop retrieves the elements of the array `ingredients` one after another and stores them in the variable `in`. The method checks whether or not the keyword c appears somewhere in the name `in`. However, since the user may switch between the lowercase and the uppercase on some letter when typing the search key, the method uses the uppercase version of c and the uppercase version of `in` instead (Line 20). This means that the search is not case-sensitive. If there is a match, the method returns `true` immediately (Line 22). Completing the loop without returning means that there was no match. For this reason, the method returns `false` (Line 24).

```
16   public boolean hasIngredient( String c )
17   {
18     for ( String in : ingredients )
19     {
20       if ( in.toUpperCase().indexOf( c.toUpperCase() ) >= 0 )
21       {
22         return true;
23       }
24     }
25     return false;
26   }
27
```

Listing 17.13 The code for `PizzaComplex` (part 3). The implementation of the method `hasIngredientsPizzaComplexInt`

The implementation of `encodeIngredients` (Line 28) uses a `StringBuilder` (Line 30). The method uses a for-loop to iterate over the sequence `0, ..., ingredients.length - 1` with a variable named j (Line 31). The method appends the `String ingredients[ j ]` (Line 33), and then if j is not the last one (Line 34), appends the delimiter `del` (Line 36). This has the effect of concatenating all the ingredients with `del` in between. After completing the loop, the method returns the `String` represented by the `StringBuilder` object (Line 39).

Interfaces, Inheritance, and Polymorphism

```
28   public String encodeIngredients( String del )
29   {
30     StringBuilder builder = new StringBuilder();
31     for ( int j = 0; j <= ingredients.length - 1; j ++ )
32     {
33       builder.append( ingredients[ j ] );
34       if ( j < ingredients.length - 1 )
35       {
36         builder.append( del );
37       }
38     }
39     return builder.toString();
40   }
41 }
```

Listing 17.14 The code for `PizzaComplex` (part 4). The implementation of the method `encodeIngredients`

17.2.2.2 A Class for a Collection of `PizzaComplex` Data

In `PizzaComplexCollection`, the type of the pizza array is `PizzaComplexIt[]` (Line 5). The class defines two delimiters to be used as a parameter for the method `encodeIngredients` of `PizzaComplexInt`. The delimiters are called `SEPARATOR` and `COMMA`. `SEPARATOR` is used when recording the data in a file and its value is `"\t"` (Line 8). `COMMA` is used when printing the ingredients on the screen, and its value is `",  "` (Line 9). As before, there are two constructors, one that receives a file path (Line 11) and the other that takes a `File` object (Line 15). The order between the two is deliberately switched in this version, to emphasize that the order of appearance of the two constructors can be arbitrary.

```
1    import java.util.*;
2    import java.io.*;
3    public class PizzaComplexCollection
4    {
5      private PizzaComplexInt[] list;
6      private File theFile;
7
8      private static final String SEPARATOR = "\t";
9      private static final String COMMA = ", ";
10
11     PizzaComplexCollection( String name ) throws FileNotFoundException
12     {
13       this( new File( name ) );
14     }
15     PizzaComplexCollection( File f ) throws FileNotFoundException
16     {
17       theFile = f;
18       list = new PizzaComplexInt[ 0 ];
19       read();
20     }
21
```

Listing 17.15 The code for `PizzaComplexCollection` (part 1). The header, the constants, the instance variables, and the constructor

The data file now has three lines for each pizza. The third line is an encoding of the ingredients generated by calling encodeIngredients(SEPARATOR). The data file looks like this one:

```
1   6
2   Four Cheese
3   14.0
4   Mozzarella      Parmesan        Ricotta Gorgonzola
5   Pepperoni
6   10.0
7   Pepperoni
8   Nettuno
9   14.0
10  Tuna     Pasta Sauce       Onion    Green Pepper
11  Capricciosa
12  14.5
13  Olive    Ham      Mozzarella       Artichoke
14  Meat Lovers
15  15.0
16  Pepperoni        Ham      Sausage Bacon    Mozzarella
17  Veggie
18  12.5
19  Onion    Green Pepper      Tomato  Mozzarella       Olive
```

The method read is similar to the previous one. To split the ingredient line to an array, read calls the method split for String with SEPARATOR as the delimiter (Line 33). The name, price, and ingredients that are read from the file are then given to the constructor of PizzaComplex, and the PizzaComplex object generated by the constructor is stored in the list (Line 34).

```
22     public void read() throws FileNotFoundException
23     {
24       if ( theFile.exists() )
25       {
26         Scanner scanner = new Scanner( theFile );
27         int size = Integer.parseInt( scanner.nextLine() );
28         list = new PizzaComplexInt[ size ];
29         for ( int index = 0; index < size; index ++ )
30         {
31           String name = scanner.nextLine();
32           double price = Double.parseDouble( scanner.nextLine() );
33           String[] ingredients = scanner.nextLine().split( SEPARATOR );
34           list[ index ] = new PizzaComplex( name, price, ingredients );
35         }
36         scanner.close();
37       }
38     }
39
```

Listing 17.16 The code for PizzaComplexCollection (part 2). Reading from file

The method write works similarly to the method write of PizzaSimple. It records
the data in the file specified by theFile (Line 40). The difference from the previous
version is that there is the third line for each a pizza. The method uses the method call
encodeIngredients(SEPARATOR) to generate the encoding for the third line (Line 48).

```
40    public void write() throws IOException
41    {
42      PrintStream stream = new PrintStream( theFile );
43      stream.println( list.length );
44      for ( int index = 0; index < list.length; index ++ )
45      {
46        stream.println( list[ index ].getName() );
47        stream.println( list[ index ].getPrice() );
48        stream.println( list[ index ].encodeIngredients( SEPARATOR ) );
49      }
50      stream.close();
51    }
52
```

Listing 17.17 The code for PizzaComplexCollection (part 3). The method write

The method add (Line 53) works similarly to the method add that is defined in PizzaSimple.
It receives the name, price, and ingredients for a new pizza and adds the PizzaComplex object
instantiated with the three values at the end of the list (Lines 56–57). It uses Arrays.copyOf to
generate a copy of the present list with one additional slot (Line 55). The method delete (Line 61)
works in the same manner as before.

```
53    public void add( String name, double price, String[] ingredients )
54    {
55      PizzaComplexInt[] listNew = Arrays.copyOf( list, list.length + 1 );
56      listNew[ list.length ]
57          = new PizzaComplex( name, price, ingredients );
58      list = listNew;
59    }
60
61    public void delete( int index )
62    {
63      PizzaComplexInt[] listNew = Arrays.copyOf( list, list.length - 1 );
64      for ( int pos = index + 1; pos < list.length; pos ++ )
65      {
66        listNew[ pos - 1 ] = list[ pos ];
67      }
68      list = listNew;
69    }
70
```

Listing 17.18 The code for PizzaComplexCollection (part 4). The methods add and delete

The method `view` works in a very similar manner to the method `view` in `PizzaSimple` (Line 71). This time, there is an ingredient list to be attached after the price. The list is generated using `encodeIngredients` with `COMMA` as the delimiter (Line 77). The method `search` takes `String` data `c` as the search key (Line 81). For each element in the list, `search` calls the method `hasIngredient` with `c` as the search key (Line 85), and if `hasIngredient` returns `true`, prints the pizza contents using the same format as the format `view` uses (Lines 87–89).

```
71   public void view()
72   {
73     for ( int index = 0;  index < list.length;  index ++ )
74     {
75       System.out.printf( "%3d:%s:$%.2f:%s\n", index,
76           list[ index ].getName(), list[ index ].getPrice(),
77           list[ index ].encodeIngredients( COMMA ) );
78     }
79   }
80
81   public void search( String c )
82   {
83     for ( int index = 0;  index < list.length;  index ++ )
84     {
85       if ( list[ index ].hasIngredient( c ) )
86       {
87         System.out.printf( "%3d:%s:$%.2f:%s\n", index,
88             list[ index ].getName(), list[ index ].getPrice(),
89             list[ index ].encodeIngredients( COMMA ) );
90       }
91     }
92   }
93 }
```

Listing 17.19 The code for `PizzaComplexCollection` (part 5). The methods `view` and `search`

The main class `PizzaComplexMain` works in a very similar manner to `PizzaSimpleMain`. The major differences are as follows:

- The pizza menu is now represented by a `PizzaComplexCollection` object (Line 6).
- The menu for actions that is presented to the user now includes an option for searching (Line 21).
- To add a new pizza, the user is asked to enter the name, the price, and then the ingredients with commas in between (Line 32). The input is then split using the comma as the delimiter (Line 33). The array becomes the third parameter of the method call to `add`.
- The switch statement has one additional anchor with the literal `'S'` (Line 40). This anchor is for directing the action to search. The program receives a search key from the user (Line 41), and calls the method `search` (Line 42).

```
1    import java.util.*;
2    import java.io.*;
3    public class PizzaComplexMain
4    {
5      public static void main( String[] args ) throws IOException {
6        PizzaComplexCollection data;
7        Scanner keyboard = new Scanner( System.in );
8        String input = "";
9        if ( args.length > 0 )
10       {
11         data = new PizzaComplexCollection( args[ 0 ] );
12       }
13       else
14       {
15         System.out.print( "Enter data file name: " );
16         data = new PizzaComplexCollection( keyboard.nextLine() );
17       }
18
19       do {
20         System.out.println( "Enter your choice by first letter" );
21         System.out.print( "View, Add, Delete, Search, Quit: ");
22         input = keyboard.nextLine();
23
24         switch ( input.charAt( 0 ) )
25         {
26           case 'V': data.view(); break;
27           case 'A':
28             System.out.print( "Enter name: " );
29             String name = keyboard.nextLine();
30             System.out.print( "Enter price: " );
31             double price = Double.parseDouble( keyboard.nextLine() );
32             System.out.print( "Enter ingredients separated by comma: " );
33             String[] ing = keyboard.nextLine().split( "," );
34             data.add( name, price, ing );
35             break;
36           case 'D':
37             System.out.printf( "Enter index: " );
38             data.delete( Integer.parseInt( keyboard.nextLine() ) );
39             break;
40           case 'S':
41             System.out.printf( "Enter key: " );
42             data.search( keyboard.nextLine() );
43         }
44       } while ( !input.startsWith( "Q" ) );
45       data.write();
46     }
47   }
```

Listing 17.20 The code for `PizzaComplexMain`

Suppose the name of the `PizzaComplex` menu data file is `pizzaComplexData.txt`. Here is an execution example that starts with this file as the data file:

```
1   % java PizzaComplexMain
2   Enter data file name: pizzaComplexData.txt
3   Enter your choice by first letter
4   View, Add, Delete, Search, Quit: V
5      0:Four Cheese:$14.00:Mozzarella, Parmesan, Ricotta, Gorgonzola
6      1:Pepperoni:$10.00:Pepperoni
7      2:Nettuno:$14.00:Tuna, Pasta Sauce, Onion, Green Pepper
8      3:Capricciosa:$14.50:Olive, Ham, Mozzarella, Artichoke
9      4:Meat Lovers:$15.00:Pepperoni, Ham, Sausage, Bacon, Mozzarella
10     5:Veggie:$12.50:Onion, Green Pepper, Tomato, Mozzarella, Olive
11  Enter your choice by first letter
12  View, Add, Delete, Search, Quit: A
13  Enter name: Hawaiian
14  Enter price: 13.00
15  Enter ingredients separated by comma: Ham,Pineapple
16  Enter your choice by first letter
17  View, Add, Delete, Search, Quit: V
18     0:Four Cheese:$14.00:Mozzarella, Parmesan, Ricotta, Gorgonzola
19     1:Pepperoni:$10.00:Pepperoni
20     2:Nettuno:$14.00:Tuna, Pasta Sauce, Onion, Green Pepper
21     3:Capricciosa:$14.50:Olive, Ham, Mozzarella, Artichoke
22     4:Meat Lovers:$15.00:Pepperoni, Ham, Sausage, Bacon, Mozzarella
23     5:Veggie:$12.50:Onion, Green Pepper, Tomato, Mozzarella, Olive
24     6:Hawaiian:$13.00:Ham, Pineapple
25  Enter your choice by first letter
26  View, Add, Delete, Search, Quit: S
27  Enter key: ham
28     3:Capricciosa:$14.50:Olive, Ham, Mozzarella, Artichoke
29     4:Meat Lovers:$15.00:Pepperoni, Ham, Sausage, Bacon, Mozzarella
30     6:Hawaiian:$13.00:Ham, Pineapple
31  Enter your choice by first letter
32  View, Add, Delete, Search, Quit: Q
```

17.3   Polymorphism

An object of class `PizzaComplex` can be treated as a data of type `PizzaComplex`, type `PizzaComplexInt`, type `PizzaSimple`, and of `PizzaSimpleInt`. To treat it as a different (but legitimate) type, we use casting. Casting is accomplished by placing, in front of the data, the alternate data type in parentheses. For example, to treat a `PizzaComplex` object p as a `PizzaSimple` object, we write: `(PizzaSimple)p` When a data is treated as a super-type, we call it **up-casting**. When a data is treated as a subtype, we call it **down-casting**. Up-casting is always possible, but down-casting may not be possible. To treat a `PizzaSimple` object as a `PizzaComplex` object, we need to ensure that the object is indeed a `PizzaComplex` object. Suppose we have an array of `PizzaSimpleInt` type, some of whose elements may be `PizzaComplex` objects. To see if an element can be treated as a `PizzaComplex` object, we can use a special operation `instanceof`:

$$(x \; instanceof \; T)$$

The operation examines the type of x, and returns `true` if the actual type of x can be treated as type T.

We can write, for instance, the following code to utilize the casting and `instanceof`:

```
1    public void pizzaTest( PizzaSimpleInt p )
2    {
3      System.out.println( p.getName() );
4      System.out.println( p.getPrice() );
5      if ( p instanceof PizzaComplex )
6      {
7        String[] in = ( (PizzaComplex)p ).getIngredients();
8      }
9    }
```

We call the idea that an object can be treated as more than one type **polymorphism**. In Java, every object is a subclass of class Object. This organizational structure comes in handy when one wants to create an array of objects with mixed types.

As mentioned earlier, the run-time errors are in a tree. For instance, FileNotFoundException is a subclass of IOException, IOException is a subclass of Exception, Exception is a subclass of Throwable, and Throwable is a subclass of Object.

17.4   Boxed Data Types

The primitive data types are not object types, so they are not subclasses of Object. The Java Development Kit contains many useful classes and interfaces that take data types parameters (see the next chapter). Those parameters cannot be primitive data types. To make such classes and interfaces available for primitive data types, Java offers eight object data types that correspond to the eight primitive data types. We call these data types the **boxed data types**. The eight boxed data types are: Boolean, Byte, Character, Double, Float, Integer, Long, and Short. They correspond to: boolean, byte, char, double, float, int, long, and short. Java provides automatic conversions from each primitive data type to its boxed type, and vice versa. For example, if a data of type int is supplied where a data of type Integer is demanded, Java automatically converts the int data to an equivalent Integer data, and if a data of type Integers is supplied where a data of type int is demanded, Java automatically converts the Integer data to an equivalent int data. We call the automatic conversion from a primitive data type to its boxed type **auto-boxing**, and the automatic conversion from a boxed data type to its un-boxed data type **auto-unboxing**. The automatic conversion fails to work in the case where the value of null needs to be unboxed. This results in NullPointerException.

We can write programs using the boxed type of integers with null being interpreted as "undefined". For example, consider computing, with a Scanner object named sc, the maximum of the numbers appearing in an indefinitely long sequence of int values. Suppose we use a variable named max to record the maximum of the numbers we have received so far. For each number received, the program will compare it with max to update max. When the first number arrives, there is no previous number. Therefore, the first number must be used as the initial value of max. By using a boolean variable named noNumbersYet that records whether or not at least one number has been received, we can distinguish the case between the first number and the rest as follows:

```
 1  boolean noNumbersYet = true;
 2  int max;
 3  while ( sc.hasNext() )
 4  {
 5     int nextNumber = sc.nextInt();
 6     if ( noNumbersYet || max < nextNumber )
 7     {
 8        max = nextNumber;
 9     }
10     noNumbersYet = false;
11  }
12  if ( noNumbersYet )
13  {
14     System.out.println( "max is undefined" );
15  }
16  else
17  {
18     System.out.println( "max is " + max );
19  }
```

We use the disjunction || in the first condition inside the while-loop to truncate the conditional evaluation. At the end of the loop-body, we set the value of noNumbersYet to false, so the second time around, the second condition, max < number, is tested.

By using Integer instead, we can make max assume the role of the boolean variable.

```
 1  Integer max = null;
 2  while ( sc.hasNext() )
 3  {
 4     int nextNumber = sc.nextInt();
 5     if ( max == null || max < nextNumber )
 6     {
 7        max = nextNumber;
 8     }
 9  }
10  if ( max == null )
11  {
12     System.out.println( "max is undefined" );
13  }
14  else
15  {
16     System.out.println( "max is " + max );
17  }
```

17.5 Interface Comparable

Comparable is a frequently used interface. Objects of a class implementing this interface can be compared with each other using the method compareTo. If a class T implements this interface, an array of elements of T can be sorted using Arrays.sort. Since the compareTo method takes as its parameter another object to compare to, the specification of Comparable in the declaration of a class is a bit complicated. Instead of simply stating:

```
public class T implements Comparable
```

the declaration must state:

```
public class T implements Comparable <T>
```

The `<T>` part is called the **generic type parameter**. We study generic parameters in Chap. 18. We extend `PizzaComplex` so that its objects are comparable with each other by adding an implementation of `Comparable`. The new class is called `PizzaUltra`.

Since `PizzaUltra` does not have an additional instance variable, the constructor of `PizzaUltra` calls the constructor of the superclass `PizzaComplex` (Line 5) with `super`. All the instance methods in `PizzaComplex` are available in `PizzaUltra`.

The header of the new class is:

```
1   public class PizzaUltra extends PizzaComplex implements
2       Comparable<PizzaUltra>
3   {
4     public PizzaUltra( String name, double price, String[] ingredients )
5     {
6       super( name, price, ingredients );
7     }
8   }
```

The code does not compile in the above form, because the class has not yet overridden the method `compareTo`. The error message shown next is generated when an attempt is made to compile the code.

```
1   PizzaUltra.java:1: error: PizzaUltra is not abstract and does not override
        abstract method compareTo(PizzaUltra) in Comparable
2   public class PizzaUltra extends PizzaComplex implements
        Comparable<PizzaUltra>
3               ^
```

To resolve the problem, we must write a public `int` method `compareTo` that takes another `PizzaUltra` object as a parameter. The header of the method must look like this one:

```
public int compareTo( PizzaUltra o )
```

There are three instance variables in `PizzaComplex`. They are a `String` variable, name, a `double` variable, `price`, and a `String[]` variable, `ingredients`. Assuming that no two pizzas on the menu have the same names, we naturally choose to compare pizzas by their names. Because the instance variables are declared to be private variables, `PizzaUltra` does not have direct access to the names. For this reason, the following code for `compareTo` fails:

```
1     . . .
2     public int compareTo( PizzaUltra o )
3     {
4       return this.name.compareTo( o.name );
5     }
6     . . .
```

with the following error message:

```
1   PizzaUltra.java:11: error: name has private access in PizzaSimple
2       return this.name.compareTo( o.name );
3                                      ^
4   PizzaUltra.java:11: error: name has private access in PizzaSimple
5       return this.name.compareTo( o.name );
6                   ^
7   2 errors
```

To resolve the problem, we use the getter, getName, as follows:

```
1   public class PizzaUltra extends PizzaComplex implements
2       Comparable<PizzaUltra>
3   {
4     public PizzaUltra( String name, double price, String[] ingredients )
5     {
6       super( name, price, ingredients );
7     }
8
9     public int compareTo( PizzaUltra o )
10    {
11      return getName().compareTo( o.getName() );
12    }
13  }
```

Listing 17.21 The code for PizzaUltra

Now that we have implemented Comparable, we can sort any pizza list. We specifically use the capability at two occasions. One is after reading the data from the data file. The other is after adding a new pizza. The code for the collection class is essentially the same as before, with the use of PizzaUltra. Since the elements of the array are now PizzaUltra, at the end of the methods add and read, the array is sorted using Arrays.sort. The source code for PizzaUltraCollection is presented next with the differences from PizzaComplexCollection highlighted:

```
1   import java.util.*;
2   import java.io.*;
3   public class PizzaUltraCollection
4   {
5     private PizzaUltra[] list;
6     private File theFile;
7
8     private static final String SEPARATOR = "\t";
9     private static final String COMMA = ", ";
10
11    PizzaUltraCollection( String name ) throws IOException
12    {
13      this( new File( name ) );
14    }
```

Listing 17.22 The code for PizzaUltraCollection (part 1)

```
15    PizzaUltraCollection( File f ) throws IOException
16    {
17       theFile = f;
18       list = new PizzaUltra[ 0 ];
19       read();
20    }
21
22    public void read() throws FileNotFoundException
23    {
24       Scanner scanner = new Scanner( theFile );
25       int size = Integer.parseInt( scanner.nextLine() );
26       list = new PizzaUltra[ size ];
27       for ( int index = 0; index < size; index ++ )
28       {
29          String name = scanner.nextLine();
30          double price = Double.parseDouble( scanner.nextLine() );
31          String[] ingredients = scanner.nextLine().split( SEPARATOR );
32          list[ index ] = new PizzaUltra( name, price, ingredients );
33       }
34       Arrays.sort( list );
35       scanner.close();
36    }
37
38    public void write() throws IOException
39    {
40       PrintStream stream = new PrintStream( theFile );
41       stream.println( list.length );
42       for ( int index = 0; index < list.length; index ++ )
43       {
44          stream.println( list[ index ].getName() );
45          stream.println( list[ index ].getPrice() );
46          stream.println( list[ index ].encodeIngredients( SEPARATOR ) );
47       }
48       stream.close();
49    }
50
51    public void add( String name, double price, String[] ingredients )
52    {
53       PizzaUltra addition = new PizzaUltra( name, price, ingredients );
54       PizzaUltra[] listNew = Arrays.copyOf( list, list.length + 1 );
55       listNew[ list.length ] = addition;
56       Arrays.sort( listNew );
57       list = listNew;
58    }
59
60    public void delete( int pos )
61    {
62       PizzaUltra[] listNew = new PizzaUltra[ list.length - 1 ];
63       for ( int i = 0; i < pos; i ++ )
64       {
65          listNew[ i ] = list[ i ];
66       }
```

Listing 17.23 The code for PizzaUltraCollection (part 2)

```
67      for ( int i = pos + 1; i < list.length; i ++ )
68      {
69         listNew[ i - 1 ] = list[ i ];
70      }
71      list = listNew;
72   }
73
74   public void view()
75   {
76      for ( int index = 0; index < list.length; index ++ )
77      {
78         System.out.printf( "%3d:%s:$%.2f:%s%n", index,
79             list[ index ].getName(), list[ index ].getPrice(),
80             list[ index ].encodeIngredients( COMMA ) );
81      }
82   }
83
84   public void search( String c )
85   {
86      for ( int index = 0; index < list.length; index ++ )
87      {
88         if ( list[ index ].hasIngredient( c ) )
89         {
90            System.out.printf( "%3d:%s:$%.2f:%s%n", index,
91                list[ index ].getName(), list[ index ].getPrice(),
92                list[ index ].encodeIngredients( COMMA ) );
93         }
94      }
95   }
96 }
```

Listing 17.24 The code for `PizzaUltraCollection` (part 3)

The main class, `PizzaUltraMain`, has the same code as `PizzaComplexMain`, except that it now uses `PizzaUltraCollection` instead of `PizzaComplexCollection`.

```
1  import java.util.*;
2  import java.io.*;
3  public class PizzaUltraMain
4  {
5     public static void main( String[] args ) throws IOException {
6        PizzaUltraCollection data;
7        Scanner keyboard = new Scanner( System.in );
8        String input = "";
9        if ( args.length > 0 )
10       {
11          data = new PizzaUltraCollection( args[ 0 ] );
12       }
13       else
14       {
15          System.out.println( "Enter data file name: " );
16          data = new PizzaUltraCollection( keyboard.nextLine() );
17       }
18
```

Listing 17.25 The code for `PizzaUltraMain` (part 1)

```
19      do {
20        System.out.println( "Enter your choice by first letter" );
21        System.out.print( "View, Add, Delete, Search, Quit: " );
22        input = keyboard.nextLine();
23
24        switch ( input.charAt( 0 ) )
25        {
26          case 'V': data.view(); break;
27          case 'A':
28            System.out.print( "Enter name: " );
29            String name = keyboard.nextLine();
30            System.out.print( "Enter price: " );
31            double price = Double.parseDouble( keyboard.nextLine() );
32            System.out.print( "Enter ingredients separated by comma: " );
33            String[] ing = keyboard.nextLine().split( "," );
34            data.add( name, price, ing );
35            break;
36          case 'D':
37            System.out.printf( "Enter index: " );
38            data.delete( Integer.parseInt( keyboard.nextLine() ) );
39            break;
40          case 'S':
41            System.out.printf( "Enter key: " );
42            data.search( keyboard.nextLine() );
43        }
44      } while ( !input.startsWith( "Q" ) );
45      data.write();
46    }
47 }
```

Listing 17.26 The code for `PizzaUltraMain` (part 2)

Summary

- An interface is a template for a class.
- An interface may declare static methods and constants.
- Each instance method declared in an interface is abstract.
- Each component appearing an interface must have the public visibility.
- An interface cannot declare instance variables.
- An interface cannot be instantiated, but can be used as a data type.
- To declare formally that a class is built upon an interface, the keyword `implements` must be used.
- The keyword `implements` appears after the class name in the class declaration.
- A class that implements an interface must override all the abstract methods appearing in the interface.
- All the components of an interface are available to each class that implements it.
- An interface can be extended to another interface.
- A class can be extended to another class.
- The keyword to use in declaring an extension is `extends`.
- The prefixes of "super-" and "sub-" are used to refer to the original unit that is extended and the unit that extends the original respectively.

- The public components of a superclass are available to its subclasses. They can be accessed as if they are part of the subclasses.
- The private components of a superclass are not available to its subclasses.
- Inheritance refers to a concept that an implementation has all the public components of an interface it implements and that a subclass can use all the public components of a subclass.
- When a class has multiple constructors and one constructor uses another, the other constructor is referenced to by this(...).
- For a class to initialize the instance variables defined in its superclass, super(...) is used to call the constructor of the superclass.
- this(...) and super(...) must appear at the start of the constructor.
- An instance method of a superclass can be called with the prefix of super.
- It one class/interface X extends another, Y, a data of type X can be treated as type of Y. We call this phenomenon polymorphism.
- To check whether or not an object x can be treated as a data of type T, the operator instanceof can be used as: x instanceof T.
- A boxed data type is an object-class version of a primitive data type. There are eight boxed data types corresponding to the eight primitive data types.
- Java automatic converts between a primitive data type and its boxed type. The automatic conversion from a primitive data type to its boxed type is called auto-boxing and the conversion in the reverse direction is called auto-unboxing.
- Comparable is an interface that defines an abstract method compareTo. If a class implements this interface, the objects from the class can be compared.
- Declaring an implementation of Comparable requires a type parameter.

Exercises

1. **Implementing an Interface MyCarInt**   Let MyCarInt be an interface defined as follows:

```
1  public interface MyCarInt
2  {
3    public int getYear();
4    public String getMake();
5    public String getModel();
6  }
```

Write a class named MyCar that implements this interface.

2. **Implementing an Interface DogInt**   Let DogInt be an interface defined as follows:

```
1  public interface DogInt
2  {
3    public int getAge();
4    public String[] getBreed();
5    public boolean hasBlood( String key );
6  }
```

We assume that the age of a dog is represented in months. The first method returns the age of the dog as an `int` representing the number of months. The method returns an array of `String` data representing the names of the breeds in the mix, for instance, { `"Yorkshire Terrier",` } { `"Dachshund"`, `"Maltese"` }. The method `hasBlood` checks if a breed name given as the parameter matches one of the elements in the breed list. Write a class named `Dog` that implements this interface.

3. **Writing an interface for `BankAccount`**   We previously studied a class `BankAccount` for recording the name and the balance of a bank account. Suppose that the class is one that implements an interface `BankAccountInt` in which all the instance methods appear as abstract methods. Write this interface.

4. **Writing an interface `DateInt`**   Consider the following interface, which is for recording the year, the month, and the day value of a date on or after January 1, 1900.

```
1   public interface DateInt
2   {
3      public int getYear();
4      public int getMonth();
5      public int getDay();
6      public static boolean isLeapYear( int year )
7      {
8         ...
9      }
10  }
```

The static method `isLeapYear` returns a `boolean` representing whether or not the year that the formal parameter specifies is a leap year. After the introduction of the Gregorian calendar in the year 1582, the determination of a leap year is made using the following rule: a year Y is a leap year if and only if Y is either a multiple of 400 or a multiple of 4 and not a multiple of 100. For example, the year 2000 is a leap year but 2100 is not one. Assuming the year to be tested for a leap year is greater than 1582, write the static method `isLeapYear`.

5. **Implementing an interface `DateInt`**   Write a class named `DataZero` that implements the interface `DateInt` from the previous question. The class has one constructor. The constructor receives three `int` values as parameters. The three values represent the year, the month, and the day. Write the constructor so that if the combination of year, month, and day is invalid, it throws an `IllegalArgumentException`.

6. **Implementing an interface `DateInt`**   Continuing on the previous question, write a new class `DateNew` that extends `Date` and implements `Comparable<DateNew>`.

Programming Projects

7. **Comparable class `StudentBasicInt`**   Write an interface named `StudentBasicInt` for recording information of a single student. The interface has three abstract methods that are expected to be implemented as getters, `String getFamilyName()`, `String getOtherNames()`, and `int getRank()`. The expected actions of these methods are to return the family name, the other names, and an integer representing the academic rank (1 for freshman, 2 for sophomore, 3 for junior, and 4 for senior). The interface should define `int` constants, `FRESHMAN`, `SOPHOMORE`, `JUNIOR`, and `SENIOR` representing these four ranks. The interface must define setters

void setFamilyName(String o), void setOtherNames(String o), and void setRank(int o), which store the names and the rank.

8. **Implementing the interface StudentBaseInt**   Write a class named StudentBase that implements the interface StudentBaseInt from the previous question. Furthermore, write a class StudentBaseMaster with just one static method public static StudentBaseInt create(String a, String b, int c)   that   returns   a StudentBaseInt object instantiated with the three parameters a, b, and c, that represent the family name, the other names, and the rank.

9. **Writing an application for reading and presenting StudentBaseInt data**   Write an application class named StudentBaseApp that reads StudentBaseInt data from a file, and stores it in the same file after modifications. Possible modifications are adding a new student and changing information of a student. The file path must be received from the user. The data file must contain the number of students in the first line. After stating the number of students in the data file, the information for each student appears in three lines. The three lines representing the family name, the other names, and the rank. The program should store the student record in an array of StudentBaseInt and use StudentBaseMaster to instantiate each element of the array.

Generic Class Parameters and the Java Collection Framework

18

18.1 `ArrayList`

18.1.1 Maintaining a Collection of Merchandise Items

Consider writing an application that interacts with the user to build a list of merchandise items. Each item is represented by its name and price (in dollars). Like the pizza applications from the previous chapter, the application must allow the user to read data from a file, write the data to a file, add an item, remove an item, and view the data. In addition, the program must allow the user to revise the name as well as the price of an item. Furthermore, the program must allow the user to rearrange the items on the list in the increasing order of the names or in the increasing order of the prices.

In building the application, we write the following classes:

- an object class named `Merchandise` whose objects represent a merchandise item,
- an object class named `PriceComparison` whose objects perform price comparison between `Merchandise` objects,
- an object class named `MerchandiseCollection` whose objects are collections of `Merchandise` objects, and
- an application class named `MerchandiseMain` that provides the method `main`.

18.1.2 The Class for Merchandise Item

`Merchandise` objects are compared with respect to their names using the `compareTo` method of `Merchandise`. Here is the initial part of the code for `Merchandise`. The class header (Line 1) has the `implements Comparable<Merchandise>` declaration. We plan to use a private `String` variable, `name`, and a private `int` variable, `price`, as the instance variables. The two variables represent the name and the price of a merchandise item. The constructor receives the values for these two variables, and then stores them in the instance variables. Since the parameters have the same names as the instance variables, `this.` is used for distinguishing between the instance variables and the parameters (Lines 8 and 9).

© Springer Nature Switzerland AG 2018
M. Ogihara, *Fundamentals of Java Programming*,
https://doi.org/10.1007/978-3-319-89491-1_18

```
 1   public class Merchandise implements Comparable< Merchandise >
 2   {
 3         // instance variables
 4      private String name;
 5      private int price;
 6         // constructor
 7      public Merchandise( String name , int price)
 8      {
 9         this.name = name;
10         this.price = price;
11      }
```

Listing 18.1   The class Merchandise (part 1). The class header, the instance variables, and the constructor

Next we show the getters, the setters, and the method compareTo. The method compareTo relies on the method compareTo of the class String.

```
12         // getters
13      public String getName ()
14      {
15         return name;
16      }
17      public int getPrice ()
18      {
19         return price;
20      }
21         // setters
22      public void setName( String name )
23      {
24         this.name = name;
25      }
26      public void setPrice( int price )
27      {
28         this.price = price;
29      }
30         // for implementing Comaparable
31      public int compareTo( Merchandise o )
32      {
33         return name.compareTo( o.name );
34      }
35   }
```

Listing 18.2   The class Merchandise (part 2). The getters, the setters, and the comparator

18.1.3 The Comparator Class

PriceComparator is an object class that implements an interface Comparator. Comparator is similar to Comparable, and is defined with a generic type parameter, say <T>. However, unlike Comparable, Comparator must be imported, and it is in the java.util package.

Comparator has only one abstract method, compare. The method compare receives two data of type T and returns an int value. This is not from the actual source code for Comparator, but after removing the comments, we can imagine that the source code is like this one:

```
1  public interface Comparator <T>
2  {
3    public int compare( T o1, T o2 );
4  }
```

The generic type parameter is highly complex topic. We only see a small fraction of coding with generic type parameters in this book. We mention the following general rules about generic type parameters:

- Any single capital letter can be used as a generic type parameter, so there are only 26 possibilities for a type parameter.
- Classes and interfaces that require multiple type parameters can be defined.
- To declare a class or an interface with multiple generic type parameters, assign distinct letters to the generic types, use a single pair of <> where the parameters appear together with commas in between (for instance, <T, K, E>).

Here is a source code for PriceComparator. The first line of the code is the required import statement. In Line 2, the generic type parameter appearing in Comparator is substituted with the actual data type, Merchandise. The method compare receives two Merchandise objects, and compares their prices by simply subtracting one price value from the other. Like the method compareTo of Comparable, the method compare is expected to report the result of comparison by the sign of the return value. In other words, the return value is strictly positive if o1 is greater than o2, strictly negative if o1 is smaller than o2, and 0 if o1 is equal to o2.

```
1  import java.util.Comparator;
2  public class PriceComparator implements Comparator< Merchandise >
3  {
4    public int compare( Merchandise o1, Merchandise o2 )
5    {
6      return o1.getPrice() - o2.getPrice();
7    }
8  }
```

Listing 18.3 The class PriceComparator

The code for PriceComparator does not have an instance variable. There is no need to define a constructor, but still a constructor can be called with new PriceComparator().

18.1.4 The Collection of Merchandise Items That Uses ArrayList

18.1.4.1 ArrayList
To write the class MerchandiseCollection, we use the class ArrayList, from the java.util package. ArrayList is a class for maintaining a list of objects. ArrayList improves upon the arrays with capacity and size from Sect. 13.6. Following are some features of ArrayList:

- The elements in the list are given unique indexes starting from 0, and can be retrieved or changed with their indexes.
- It is possible to insert an element at a specific position, while preserving the order of appearance of other elements.
- For removing an element at a specific index, `ArrayList` shifts all the elements appearing after the index. The order of appearance of the remaining elements is thus preserved.
- There is no explicit limit on the number of elements to store the list.
- The class implements an interface `List`. `List` is in the package `java.util`. Because `ArrayList` implements `List`, for-each loops can be used to iterate over the elements in an `ArrayList`.
- An `ArrayList` object takes a generic type parameter with it. An instantiation of an `ArrayList` requires the specification of the type of the elements stored in the list.

If T is an object type, the declaration of an `ArrayList` data type, `list`, for storing elements of type T, and its instantiation will be as follows:

```
1    ArrayList<T> list;
2    list = new ArrayList<T>();
```

`ArrayList` offers many instance methods, here is a short list:

- `int size()`: The method returns the number of elements currently stored in the list.
- `boolean add( T e )`: The method attempts to add the element e at the end of the list, and then returns whether or not the operation was successful.
- `boolean add( int index, T e )`: The method attempts to inserts the element e at the position index in the list, and then returns whether or not the operation was successful.
- `void clear()`: The method removes all the elements from the list.
- `T get( int index )`: The method returns the element at position index.
- `T remove( int index )`: The method attempts to remove the element at position index, and then returns the element removed.
- `T set( int index, T e )`: The method replaces the element at position index with e, and then returns the element that was stored at index prior to the replacement.

18.1.4.2 The Instance Variables, the "Getters", and the "Setters"

Here is a source code for `MerchandiseCollection`. The class has two imports, `java.util.*` and `java.io.*`. There is only one instance variable, `theList`. The type of the instance variable is `ArrayList<Merchandise>`. The variable is instantiated with `new ArrayList<Merchandise>()`. The instantiation produces an object of `ArrayList<Merchandise>` with no elements being stored in the list.

```
1    import java.io.*;
2    import java.util.*;
3    public class MerchandiseCollection
4    {
5          //---- instance variable
6       private ArrayList<Merchandise> theList;
7          //---- constructor
8       public MerchandiseCollection()
9       {
10         theList = new ArrayList<Merchandise>();
11      }
```

Listing 18.4 The class `MerchandiseCollection` (part 1). The class header, the instance variable, and the constructor

The "getters" and "setters" appear next. The method `size()` (Lines 13) returns `theList.size()` (Line 15). The returned value is the number of merchandise items stored in the list. The method `getName( int i )` (Lines 17) obtains the element at index `i` and returns its names. This is accomplished by `theList.get( i ).getName()` (Line 19). The method `getPrice( int i )` (Lines 21) obtains the element at index `i` and returns its price. This is accomplished by `theList.get( i ).getPrice()` (Line 23).

```
12         //---- getters
13      public int size()
14      {
15         return theList.size();
16      }
17      public String getName( int i )
18      {
19         return theList.get( i ).getName();
20      }
21      public int getPrice( int i )
22      {
23         return theList.get( i ).getPrice();
24      }
```

Listing 18.5 The class `MerchandiseCollection` (part 2). The "getters"

The method `add( String name, int price )` (Line 26) adds a merchandise item composed of `name` and `price` at the end of the list (Line 28). The method `remove( int i )` (Line 30) removes the element at `i` (Line 32). The method `set( int i, String name, int price )` (Line 34) replaces the name and price of the element at `i` with the values given as parameters (Lines 36 and 37).

```
25          //---- setters
26     public void add( String name, int price )
27     {
28        theList.add( new Merchandise( name, price ) );
29     }
30     public void remove( int i )
31     {
32        theList.remove( i );
33     }
34     public void set( int i, String name, int price )
35     {
36        theList.get( i ).setName( name );
37        theList.get( i ).setPrice( price );
38     }
```

Listing 18.6   The class `MerchandiseCollection` (part 3). The "setters"

18.1.4.3 The File Read/Write

The data format for a merchandise collection requires two lines per item, with the first line representing the name and the second line representing the price. The name may contain the white space character. Since the length of an `ArrayList` is not fixed, the data file does not need to provide information about how many elements are in the list.

Reading the data from a file is accomplished using the method `read`. The method `read` receives a file path as its formal parameter (Line 40). The method opens a `Scanner` to read from the `File` object instantiated with the file path (Line 42). So long as there is a token remaining in the file (Line 43), the method reads one line as the name, and then another line as the price. The second line is converted to an `int` value using `Integer.parseInt`. These two values are passed to the method `add`. This sequence of actions is compressed into a single statement appearing in Line 45. The method has a `throws FileNotFoundException` declaration because the constructor of a `Scanner` may throw an exception of the type. After reading is completed, the `Scanner` is closed using method `close` (Line 47).

Writing the data to a file is accomplished using the method `write`. The method receives a file path as its parameter (Line 49). The method opens a `PrintStream` with the file specified in the formal parameter (Line 51). Then, the method uses a for-each loop to iterate over the elements in the list. The loop header `for ( Merchandise m : theList )` (Line 52) implies that the elements are retrieved in sequence from the list `theList`, the type of the elements is `Merchandise`, and the element can be referred to by the variable `m`. For each element retrieved, the method writes two lines into the file. The first line is the name and the second is the price. The `printf` in Line 54 accomplishes both using the format `%s\n%d\n`, where the first placeholder is for the name and the second is for the price. After finishing to write the information of the elements, the method closes the stream using the method `close`. This method also has a `throws FileNotFoundException` declaration.

18.1.4.4 The Sorting Methods

The last part of `MerchandiseCollection` has two methods for rearranging the elements in the list. In the case of arrays, sorting is accomplished using the method `sort` in the class `Arrays`. In the case of `ArrayList`, the class that provides the functions for sorting is `Collections`. The method `sortByName` (Lines 59–62) sorts the elements using the method `compareTo` that is natively available in the class `Merchandise`.

```
39        //---- read & write
40        public void read( String fileName ) throws FileNotFoundException
41        {
42          Scanner sc = new Scanner( new File( fileName ) );
43          while ( sc.hasNext() )
44          {
45            add( sc.nextLine(), Integer.parseInt( sc.nextLine() ) );
46          }
47          sc.close();
48        }
49        public void write( String fileName ) throws FileNotFoundException
50        {
51          PrintStream st = new PrintStream( new File( fileName ) );
52          for ( Merchandise m : theList )
53          {
54            st.printf( "%s\n%d\n", m.getName(), m.getPrice() );
55          }
56          st.close();
57        }
```

Listing 18.7 The class MerchandiseCollection (part 4). The methods read and write

The method sortByPrice (Lines 63–66) sorts the elements using the method compare defined in the class PriceComparator. The method sort of Collections has a version that receives the comparison method as an additional parameter. The accepted type for the parameter is a Comparator<T> where T is the type of the elements in list. Since we have written a class PriceComparator that implements Comparator<Merchandise>, an object of PriceComparator can be used as the method for comparison. Line 65 has new PriceComparator() as the second parameter, and the object returned by the constructor is passed to the method sort.

```
58        //--- sorting
59        public void sortByName()
60        {
61          Collections.sort( theList );
62        }
63        public void sortByPrice()
64        {
65          Collections.sort( theList, new PriceComparator() );
66        }
67     }
```

Listing 18.8 The class MerchandiseCollection (part 5). The methods sortByName and sortByPrice

18.1.5 The Main Class

18.1.5.1 The Method for Printing Prompt

In MerchandiseMain, the user is presented with as many as 11 choices for an action to be performed, including one to terminate the program. The class has a method, printPrompt, to print these choices neatly. The choices are presented in a table-like manner with three choices appearing in one line, as shown next:

```
1   ----Choose action to be performed----
2      1. add an item      2. remove an item   3. view list
3      4. sort by name     5. sort by price    6. change item
4      7. change name      8. change price     9. read from a file
5      10. write to a file 0. quit
```

The source code of print Prompt appears next.

```
1   import java.util.*;
2   import java.io.*;
3   public class MerchandiseMain
4   {
5     public static void printPrompt()
6     {
7       System.out.println( "----Choose action to be performed----" );
8       System.out.printf(
9             "  %-20s%-20s%-20s\n  %-20s%-20s%-20s\n"
10          + "  %-20s%-20s%-20s\n  %-20s%-20s\n",
11            "1. add an item", "2. remove an item", "3. view list        ",
12            "4. sort by name", "5. sort by price", "6. change item",
13            "7. change name", "8. change price", "9. read from a file",
14            "10. write to a file", "0. quit" );
15    }
16
```

Listing 18.9 The class MerchandiseMain (part 1). The method print Prompt

18.1.5.2 The Method main

The method main of MerchandiseMain uses a MerchandiseCollection variable, data, to record the collection (Line 19), a Scanner variable, keyboard, to receive input from the keyboard (Line 20), a String variable, name, to store the name information (Line 21), and three int variables, choice, price, and pos, for storing the index to the action to be performed, the price value, and the position of a merchandise item in the list (Line 22). The method is a large while-loop whose continuation condition is choice != 0 (Line 23). The initial value of choice is 1, so the loop-body is executed at least once.

The loop-body is placed in a try-catch. The try-part conducts all the necessary action. The catch-part is for recovering from some anticipated run-time errors. The choice of action is received after presenting the prompt (Lines 26–28).

18.1.5.3 Adding and Removing

After receiving the number indicating the action to be performed, the program uses a switch-statement to direct the flow to the required method. The choice 1 is for adding an item (Line 31). The program receives the name (Lines 32 and 33) and the price (Lines 34 and 35), and then calls the method add of the MerchandiseCollection variable data with the name and price received (Line 36). The program uses nextLine exclusively to receive input from the user. To interpret the input from the user as an integer, the program uses Integer.parseInt. If the user enters a String data that

```
17    public static void main( String[] args )
18    {
19      MerchandiseCollection data = new MerchandiseCollection();
20      Scanner keyboard = new Scanner( System.in );
21      String name;
22      int choice = 1, price, pos;
23      while ( choice != 0 )
24      {
25        try {
26          printPrompt();
27          System.out.print( "Enter your choice: " );
28          choice = Integer.parseInt( keyboard.nextLine() );
```

Listing 18.10 The class MerchandiseMain (part 2). The start of the method main, including the variable declarations, the start of the loop, and the try-clause

cannot be converted to an integer, a run-time error of NumberFormatException occurs. This error is handled by a catch-clause appearing in Lines 91 and 92. NumberFormatException may occur in other places of the code, and all of them are handled by this catch-clause. For removing an item (Line 38), the program receives the position of the item to be removed (Lines 39 and 40), and then calls the method remove (Line 41).

```
29        switch ( choice )
30        {
31        case 1: // add
32          System.out.print( "Enter the name: " );
33          name = keyboard.nextLine();
34          System.out.print( "Enter the price: " );
35          price = Integer.parseInt( keyboard.nextLine() );
36          data.add( name, price );
37          break;
38        case 2: // remove
39          System.out.print( "Enter the position: " );
40          pos = Integer.parseInt( keyboard.nextLine() );
41          data.remove( pos );
42          break;
```

Listing 18.11 The class MerchandiseMain (part 3). The part that handles adding and removing an item

18.1.5.4 Viewing and Sorting

Choices 3, 4, and 5 are for viewing and sorting the elements. The program presents the data on the screen after sorting, so the choice 3 can be thought of as a special case where sorting is not performed at all. The three cases have the same entry points (Lines 43–45) and the following series of actions is performed:

- If the action is sorting by the name (i.e., the choice is 4), call sortByName (Lines 46–49).
- If the action is sorting by the price (i.e., the choice is 5), call sortByPrice (Lines 50–53).
- If the action is viewing the data (i.e., the choice is 3), call neither.

After sorting the elements, the program prints the items on the list using a for-loop, where the number of items in the list is obtained using the method `size` (Line 54). For each item, the program prints the index, the name, and the price (Lines 56–58).

```
43            case 3: // view
44            case 4: // sort by name
45            case 5: // sort by price
46              if ( choice == 4 )
47              {
48                 data.sortByName();
49              }
50              else if ( choice == 5 )
51              {
52                 data.sortByPrice();
53              }
54              for ( pos = 0; pos < data.size(); pos ++ )
55              {
56                 System.out.printf( "%3d: %s : $%,d\n", pos,
57                       data.getName( pos ), data.getPrice( pos ) );
58              }
59              break;
```

Listing 18.12 The class `MerchandiseMain` (part 4). The part that handles sorting and viewing the data

18.1.5.5 Making Changes

The choices 6, 7, and 8 are for making changes on an element in the list. The three cases have the same entry points (Lines 60–62). If the choice is 6, the change is for both the name and the price. If the choice is 7, the change is for the name only. If the choice is 8, the change is for the price only. The program first obtains the index to the item to be updated, and stores it in the variable `pos` (Lines 63 and 64). To handle the three possibilities in one place, the program obtains the present values of the name and price of the item at `pos`, and stores them in `name` and `price` (Lines 65 and 66). The idea is that the item at `pos` will be updated with the values of `name` and `price`, but prior to the update, the user will be asked to provide new values for the two variables. Which of the two variables the user can update depends on the choice of the action.

- If the choice is not 8 (i.e., the choice is either 6 or 7), the new name is obtained and stored in `name` (Lines 68–72).
- If the choice is not 7 (i.e., the choice is either 6 or 8), the new price is obtained and stored in `price` (Lines 73–77).

Finally, the program stores the values of `name` and `price` by calling the method `set` (Line 78).

```
60        case 6: // change
61        case 7: // change name
62        case 8: // change price
63          System.out.print( "Enter the position: " );
64          pos = Integer.parseInt( keyboard.nextLine() );
65          name = data.getName( pos );
66          price = data.getPrice( pos );
67          System.out.printf( "The item is: %s : $%,d\n", name, price );
68          if ( choice != 8 )
69          {
70             System.out.print( "Enter the new name: " );
71             name = keyboard.nextLine();
72          }
73          if ( choice != 7 )
74          {
75             System.out.print( "Enter the new price: " );
76             price = Integer.parseInt( keyboard.nextLine() );
77          }
78          data.set( pos, name, price );
79          break;
```

Listing 18.13 The class MerchandiseMain (part 5). The part that is responsible for changing the name and the price

18.1.5.6 File Read/Write

If the choice is 9, the program receives a file path from the user, and then calls the method read (Lines 80–83). If the choice is 10, the program receives a file path from the user and calls the method write (Lines 84–87). In the case where the choice is 0, the program prints a message to inform that the program will terminate (Lines 88 and 89).

```
80        case 9: // read from a file
81          System.out.print( "Enter an input file path: " );
82          data.read( keyboard.nextLine() );
83          break;
84        case 10: // write to a file
85          System.out.print( "Enter an output file path: " );
86          data.write( keyboard.nextLine() );
87          break;
88        case 0: // quit
89          System.out.println( "...Terminating" );
90        }
```

Listing 18.14 The class MerchandiseMain (part 6). The part responsible for reading from a data file and writing to a data file

There are two catch-clauses. One is for catching a run-time error that occurs when the user enters a line that cannot be interpreted as an integer, and the other is for catching FileNotFoundException (Lines 93 and 94). The program prints an error message stating the error, and then returns to the loop.

Here is an example of using the program. Consider maintaining a list of real estate properties, with the address and the price. Suppose a text file, propertyData.txt, has seven properties in the format readable by the program, as follows:

```
91        } catch ( NumberFormatException e ) {
92            System.out.println( "Incorrect input!!!" );
93        } catch ( FileNotFoundException e ) {
94            System.out.println( "No such file found|!!" );
95        }
96      }
97    }
98  }
```

Listing 18.15 The class `MerchandiseMain` (part 7). The `catch` clauses

```
1   10 Wilkinson Road
2   343450
3   11 Wilkinson Drive
4   766000
5   34 Coral Way
6   807500
7   7900 Plainview Drive
8   195500
9   7000 Flamingo Drive
10  790000
11  1 Presidential Place
12  1535000
13  2 Marigold Terrace
14  615000
```

Starting with this file, we can manipulate the data as follows:

```
1   ----Choose action to be performed----
2     1. add an item       2. remove an item   3. view list
3     4. sort by name      5. sort by price    6. change item
4     7. change name       8. change price     9. read from a file
5     10. write to a file 0. quit
6   Enter your choice: 9
7   Enter an input file path: propertyData.txt
8   ----Choose action to be performed----
9     1. add an item       2. remove an item   3. view list
10    4. sort by name      5. sort by price    6. change item
11    7. change name       8. change price     9. read from a file
12    10. write to a file 0. quit
13  Enter your choice: 5
14    0: 7900 Plainview Drive : $195,500
15    1: 10 Wilkinson Road : $343,450
16    2: 2 Marigold Terrace : $615,000
17    3: 11 Wilkinson Drive : $766,000
18    4: 7000 Flamingo Drive : $790,000
19    5: 34 Coral Way : $807,500
20    6: 1 Presidential Place : $1,535,000
21  ----Choose action to be performed----
22    1. add an item       2. remove an item   3. view list
23    4. sort by name      5. sort by price    6. change item
24    7. change name       8. change price     9. read from a file
25    10. write to a file 0. quit
26  Enter your choice: 1
27  Enter the name: 71 Canary Drive
28  Enter the price: 199700
```

```
29   ----Choose action to be performed----
30      1. add an item        2. remove an item    3. view list
31      4. sort by name       5. sort by price     6. change item
32      7. change name        8. change price      9. read from a file
33      10. write to a file 0. quit
34   Enter your choice: 1
35   Enter the name: 2 Atkins Road
36   Enter the price: 280000
37   ----Choose action to be performed----
38      1. add an item        2. remove an item    3. view list
39      4. sort by name       5. sort by price     6. change item
40      7. change name        8. change price      9. read from a file
41      10. write to a file 0. quit
42   Enter your choice: 4
43      0: 1 Presidential Place : $1,535,000
44      1: 10 Wilkinson Road : $343,450
45      2: 11 Wilkinson Drive : $766,000
46      3: 2 Atkins Road : $280,000
47      4: 2 Marigold Terrace : $615,000
48      5: 34 Coral Way : $807,500
49      6: 7000 Flamingo Drive : $790,000
50      7: 71 Canary Drive : $199,700
51      8: 7900 Plainview Drive : $195,500
52   ----Choose action to be performed----
53      1. add an item        2. remove an item    3. view list
54      4. sort by name       5. sort by price     6. change item
55      7. change name        8. change price      9. read from a file
56      10. write to a file 0. quit
57   Enter your choice: 2
58   Enter the position: 2
59   ----Choose action to be performed----
60      1. add an item        2. remove an item    3. view list
61      4. sort by name       5. sort by price     6. change item
62      7. change name        8. change price      9. read from a file
63      10. write to a file 0. quit
64   Enter your choice: 3
65      0: 1 Presidential Place : $1,535,000
66      1: 10 Wilkinson Road : $343,450
67      2: 2 Atkins Road : $280,000
68      3: 2 Marigold Terrace : $615,000
69      4: 34 Coral Way : $807,500
70      5: 7000 Flamingo Drive : $790,000
71      6: 71 Canary Drive : $199,700
72      7: 7900 Plainview Drive : $195,500
73   ----Choose action to be performed----
74      1. add an item        2. remove an item    3. view list
75      4. sort by name       5. sort by price     6. change item
76      7. change name        8. change price      9. read from a file
77      10. write to a file 0. quit
```

```
78   Enter your choice: 8
79   Enter the position: 7
80   The item is: 7900 Plainview Drive : $195,500
81   Enter the new price: 205000
82   ----Choose action to be performed----
83      1. add an item        2. remove an item    3. view list
84      4. sort by name       5. sort by price     6. change item
85      7. change name        8. change price      9. read from a file
86      10. write to a file 0. quit
87   Enter your choice: 5
88      0: 71 Canary Drive : $199,700
89      1: 7900 Plainview Drive : $205,000
90      2: 2 Atkins Road : $280,000
91      3: 10 Wilkinson Road : $343,450
92      4: 2 Marigold Terrace : $615,000
93      5: 7000 Flamingo Drive : $790,000
94      6: 34 Coral Way : $807,500
95      7: 1 Presidential Place : $1,535,000
96   ----Choose action to be performed----
97      1. add an item        2. remove an item    3. view list
98      4. sort by name       5. sort by price     6. change item
99      7. change name        8. change price      9. read from a file
100     10. write to a file 0. quit
101  Enter your choice: 10
102  Enter an output file path: propertyData2.txt
103  ----Choose action to be performed----
104     1. add an item        2. remove an item    3. view list
105     4. sort by name       5. sort by price     6. change item
106     7. change name        8. change price      9. read from a file
107     10. write to a file 0. quit
108  Enter your choice: 0
109  ...Terminating
```

The execution example has resulted in the following revised data file, `propertyData2.txt`:

```
1    71 Canary Drive
2    199700
3    7900 Plainview Drive
4    205000
5    2 Atkins Road
6    280000
7    10 Wilkinson Road
8    343450
9    2 Marigold Terrace
10   615000
11   7000 Flamingo Drive
12   790000
13   34 Coral Way
14   807500
15   1 Presidential Place
16   1535000
```

18.2 The Dynamic Maintenance of the Largest K Values

We often encounter a problem of writing a code for selecting, from an indefinite number of elements, a fixed number of, say k, best ones. A straightforward solution to this problem is to store all the elements in a list, sort the list, and then select the k best ones. However, if the total number of elements considered is much larger than k, this approach may be slightly wasteful of memory. An alternative to this approach is to use a shorter list, whose length will be no more than k + 1. At the start the list has 0 elements. Each element is added to the list, and the elements in the list are sorted. After that, if the list has k + 1 elements, the "worst" of the k + 1 elements is removed, thereby bringing the length of the list back to k. When all the elements have been processed, the list consists of the k best ones.

Using ArrayList, this idea can be easily implemented. Let E be a generic data type that represents the data type of the elements to be processed, such that E is comparable. We use an ArrayList<E> variable, theList, to maintain the best elements that have seen so far. We initialize theList with new ArrayList<E>(). To process a new element, say o, we add o to theList, use Collections.sort to sort the list, and if theList.size() is equal to k + 1, remove the candidate at position 0, because sort sorts the element in increasing order. After all the candidates have been processed, we may need to access the best ones. The access is provided by the method get(int i) that returns the element at rank i in the list.

Here is the class TopK written based upon the above discussion. The syntax for stating that E has compareTo is <E extends Comparable<E>>. Since E is the parameter associated with TopK, the overall class declaration becomes the one in Line 2:

```
public class TopK<E extends Comparable<E>>
```

The class has two instance variables (Lines 4 and 5). One is an ArrayList<E> named theList and the other is an int variable, k. The variable k specifies the number of elements to keep. The constructor receives the value for k, stores it in this.k (Line 9), and instantiates the list (Line 10).

```
1   import java.util.*;
2   public class TopK< E extends Comparable< E > >
3   {
4      private ArrayList<E> theList;
5      private int k;
6
7      public TopK( int k )
8      {
9         this.k = k;
10        theList = new ArrayList<E>();
11     }
```

Listing 18.16 The class TopK (part 1)

The method get receives an int value named i as the parameter (Line 12), and returns the element at rank i. This is accomplished by returning the element obtained through get(k - i) of the list because the elements appear in the decreasing order of their ranks (Line 14). The method add receives an element o of type E (Line 16), adds it to theList using the method add of ArrayList, sorts the list using Collections.sort, and then, if the length of theList is equal to k + 1 (Line 20), removes the element at index 0 using the method remove of ArrayList (Line 22).

```
12    public E get( int i )
13    {
14      return theList.get( k - i );
15    }
16    public void add( E o )
17    {
18      theList.add( o );
19      Collections.sort( theList );
20      if ( theList.size() == k + 1 )
21      {
22        theList.remove( 0 );
23      }
24    }
25  }
```

Listing 18.17 The class TopK (part 2)

Here is a source code for testing the class TopK. The program instantiates a TopK<Integer> object top with the value of k set to 10 (Line 6). The program then adds integers 1, ..., 10,000 one after another in top (Lines 7–10), and then retrieves the recorded top ten elements (Line 11–14). Since the elements appear in increasing order. The program generates ranks from 1 to 10 with a variable named i (Line 11), and prints the element located at rank i (Line 13).

```
1  public class TopKTest
2  {
3    public static void main( String[] arg )
4    {
5      System.out.println( "Test using integers 1..10000" );
6      TopK<Integer> top = new TopK<Integer>( 10 );
7      for ( int i = 1; i <= 10000; i ++ )
8      {
9        top.add( i );
10     }
11     for ( int i = 1; i <= 10; i ++ )
12     {
13       System.out.printf( "%2d: %d\n", i, top.get( i ) );
14     }
```

Listing 18.18 The class TopKTest (part 1). Top 10 of 1, ..., 10,000

The program then repeats the same action, this time with a 10,000 random real number with values 0 and 1,000,000 (Lines 17–20). The instantiation (Line 16) uses new TopK<Double>(10).

```
15      System.out.println( "Test using random double" );
16      TopK<Double> newtop = new TopK<Double>( 10 );
17      for ( int i = 1; i <= 10000; i ++ )
18      {
19         newtop.add( Math.random() * 1000000 );
20      }
21      for ( int i = 1; i <= 10; i ++ )
22      {
23         System.out.printf( "%2d: %f\n", i, newtop.get( i ) );
24      }
25   }
26 }
```

Listing 18.19 The class `TopKTest` (part 2). Testing with random real numbers

Here is an execution example of the code. In the first test, the top ten numbers are 10,000, ..., 9991 and the program correctly identifies them. In the second test, the top ten numbers are expected to be close to the upper bound, 1,000,000. In the example, the top ten numbers are indeed greater than 999,000.

```
1  Test using integers 1..10000
2   1: 10000
3   2: 9999
4   3: 9998
5   4: 9997
6   5: 9996
7   6: 9995
8   7: 9994
9   8: 9993
10  9: 9992
11 10: 9991
12 Test using random double
13  1: 999990.863047
14  2: 999867.865257
15  3: 999831.136887
16  4: 999685.778237
17  5: 999663.635342
18  6: 999629.397141
19  7: 999591.778661
20  8: 999538.840688
21  9: 999424.382109
22 10: 999248.272207
```

18.3 The Java Collection Framework

18.3.1 The Framework

The `List` and its implementation `ArrayList` belong to a large group of interfaces, abstract classes, and concrete classes, called the **Java Collection Framework**. The Java Collection Framework provides various tools for dynamically maintaining a collection of data through such actions as adding, removing, and searching. Some interfaces and classes in the framework are shown in Fig. 18.1. Like `ArrayList`, all interfaces and classes in the framework take a generic type parameter. In the following description, we use E to refer to the generic type parameter.

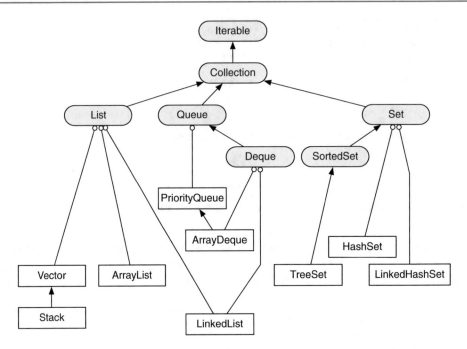

Fig. 18.1 The Java Collection Framework. The squashed rectangles represent interfaces and the rectangles represent classes. The arrows represent extensions and the round-head arrows represent implementations

An interface Iterable<E> is at the top of the hierarchy in the diagram. Iterable<E> defines only one method, iterator. The method iterator returns an object of type Iterator<E>. Iterator<E> is an interface that defines two abstract methods that enable iterative access to the elements in some collection of data of type E. The two methods are hasNext and next. The method hasNext returns a boolean value. The return value of hasNext is interpreted as the indication of whether or not there is any element remaining in the iteration. The method next returns an object of type <E> and is interpreted as the next element in the iteration. If a class implements Iterable<E>, for-each loops are available. The two methods are reminiscent of the methods having the same names in Scanner. Although the methods have the same names, Scanner does not implement Iterable<String>.

In the diagram, an interface Collection<E> appears immediately under Iterable<E>. Collection<E> is a collection of data of type E. The elements in the collection may not appear sequentially. Here are some methods of Collection<E>.

- add(E o): This method attempts to add the data o of type E to the collection, and then returns a boolean indicating whether or not the attempt was successful.
- clear(): This method empties the collection. The return type is void.
- contains(Object o): This method returns a boolean value representing whether or not the collection contains an element matching o.
- isEmpty(): This method returns a boolean representing whether or not the collection is empty.

- `remove( Object o )`: This method removes one occurrence of an object matching `o`. The method returns a `boolean` representing whether or not such an element has been removed.
- `size()`: This method returns an `int` representing the number of elements in the collection.

The interfaces `List<E>`, `Queue<E>` (pronounced "cue" as in the "billiard cue"), `Deque<E>` (pronounced "deck" as in the "deck of cards"), `Set<E>`, and `SortedSet<E>` extend `Collection<E>`, and represent certain organizations of the elements in the collections.

- `List<E>` is a sequential list of data. Like arrays, `List<E>` assigns sequential indexes starting from 0 are assigned to its elements. The elements are accessible with their indexes.
- `Queue<E>` is a sequential list of data, but only the element at one end can be examined or removed, elements can be added only at the other end.
- `Deque<E>` is a sub-interface of `Queue<E>` and is a "double-ended" version of `Queue<E>`. Addition, examination, and removal can be made at each end, but nowhere else in the collection.
- `Set<E>` is a set of data without duplication.
- `SortedSet<E>` is a sub-interface of `Set<E>`, where the elements are in order.

18.3.2 Some Classes from the Framework

`ArrayList<E>` we studied earlier in the chapter is a class that implements `List<E>`.

Here we explore two additional classes, `LinkedList<E>` and `HashSet<E>`, from the diagram. The former implements `List<E>`, `Queue<E>`, and `Deque<E>`. The latter implements `Set<E>` and `SortedSet<E>`. `LinkedList<E>` uses a chain of objects. Each object in the chain holds a value of type E, a reference to its next object, and a reference to its previous object. The chain has two ends, the "head" and the "tail". The "previous" object of the "head" is `null` and the "next" object of the "tail" is `null`. As in the case of `ArrayList<E>`, `LinkedList<E>` provides the methods `add( E o )`, `get( int i )`, `set( int i, E o )`, and `remove( int i )`. In addition, the class offers access to the "head" and the "tail" (see Fig. 18.2). Here are some methods available in `LinkedList<E>` beyond those defined in `List<E>`.

- `addFirst( E o )` inserts `o` to the chain as its "head" element (the present "head", if it exists, will become the "next" element of the new "head"). The return type of this method is `void`.
- `addLast( E o )` inserts `o` to the chain as its "tail" element (the present "tail", if it exists, will become the 'previous" element of the new "tail"). The return type of this method is `void`.
- `getFirst()` returns the "head" element of the chain, if it exists.
- `getLast( E o )` returns the "tail" element of the chain, if it exists.
- `removeFirst()` removes the "head" element of the chain, if it exists, and returns it.
- `removeLast( E o )` removes the "tail" element of the chain, it if exists, and returns it.

Because `LinkedList<E>` offers access to each end of the list, the function to be performed in `Deque<E>` are already available in `LinkedList<E>`. The abstract methods of `Queue<E>` and of `Deque<E>` are overridden in `LinkedList<E>` through adaptations of the above methods. Here are some of such methods. For `Queue<E>`, we have the following:

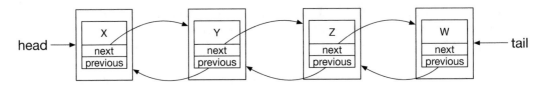

Fig. 18.2 A LinkedList. X, Y, Z,and W are the data elements in the collection. next and previous present the references to the "next" and "previous" elements

- offer(E o) adds the element o at the "head" of the queue, and returns a boolean representing whether or not the attempt was successful.
- peek() returns, without removing, the element at the "head" of the queue. If the queue is empty, the method returns null.
- poll() removes the element at the "head" of the queue and returns it. If the queue is empty, the method returns null.

The methods for Deque<E> that are overridden in LinkedList<E> include the following:

- offerFirst(E o) adds the element o at the "head" of the queue, and returns a boolean representing whether or not the element has been added.
- offerLast(E o) adds the element o at the "tail" of the queue and returns a boolean representing whether or not the element has been added.
- peekFirst(E o) returns, without removing it, the "head" element of the queue.
- peekLast(E o) returns, without removing it, the "tail" element the queue.
- pollFirst(E o) removes and returns the "head" element of the queue.
- pollLast(E o) removes and returns the "tail" element of the queue.

HashSet<E> uses a structure called a **hash table** to record the elements in the collection. A hash table is an array. Each element has an assigned index in the array. The assigned index is calculated from a value given by a so-called **hash function**. The index of an element is the remainder of the value of the hash function of the element when divided by the length of the array. Adding an element, removing an element, and search for an element are carried out by examining the array at the assigned index of the element. Since the assigned indexes are based upon the hash function, it may happen that two elements to be stored in the hash-table have the same indexes. We call such a phenomenon a **collision**. Collisions are usually resolved by allocating a list of E to each slot of the array, rather than making each slot available for one element exclusively (see Fig. 18.3). Adding an element, removing an element, and searching for an element are executed on the list at the index assigned to the element. The order in which the elements appear in the HashSet<E> depends on the length of the hash table, the hash function, and the mechanisms used for adding an element and removing an element on the lists representing the slots of the hash table. HashSet<E> implements add(E o), clear(), contains(Object o), remove(Object o), isEmpty(), and size().

Fig. 18.3 A hash table

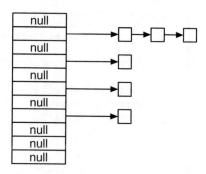

18.3.3 A Demonstration

We present a program that demonstrates how the interfaces List, Queue, and Set operate. List and Queue are implemented with LinkedList and Set is implemented with HashSet. For the type parameter, String is chosen.

The method main of the class calls three methods, listExperiment, queueExperiment, and setExperiment (Lines 6–8). They demonstrate the use of List<String>, Queue <String>, and Set<String>. The three methods have common tasks: (i) add the elements from a String array constant SEQUENCE (appearing in Lines 11–13), (ii) remove some elements, and then (iii) print the contents of the collection.

The task (iii) is accomplished by the method printInfo. The method printInfo receives a Collection<String> data named c as its parameter (Line 15). The methods executes the following:

- The method reports the size of c obtained by the method size of Collection<String> (Line 18).
- The method reports the contents of c using the for-each loop (Lines 19–24).
- The method prints, for each element from SEQUENCE, whether or not the element appears in the collection c. The method contains of Collection<String> is used for this purpose (Lines 25–29).

The method listExperiment (Line 32) instantiates a LinkedList<String> object, and then assigns the object to a List<String> variable named myList (Line 35). The method then adds each element of SEQUENCE successively twice using the method add of List<String> (Lines 36–40). Next, the method removes the element at position 3 (the position indexes start from 0) three times successively (Lines 41–47). To remove an element, the method uses the method remove of List<String> (Line 43). Since the method remove of List<String> returns the element that has been removed, listExperiment reports the element returned after each removal (Line 44). Furthermore, immediately after each removal, using the method get of List<String>, the method prints the element at index 3 (Lines 45 and 46). Next, listExperiment replaces the element at position 3 with a new String literal, "jackie", using the method set of List<String>, and reports the element at index 3 after the modification (Lines 48–51). Finally, the method calls printInfo to print the information about myList (Line 52).

```
1    import java.util.*;
2    public class CollectionExperiment
3    {
4      public static void main( String[] args )
5      {
6        listExperiment();
7        queueExperiment();
8        setExperiment();
9      }
10
11     public static final String[] SEQUENCE = new String[]{
12         "suzie", "grace", "carol", "deborah", "janis"
13     };
14
15     public static void printInfo( Collection<String> c )
16     {
17       System.out.println();
18       System.out.printf( "The collection has %d elements\n", c.size() );
19       System.out.print( "The elements are:" );
20       for ( String w : c )
21       {
22         System.out.print( " " + w );
23       }
24       System.out.println();
25       System.out.println( "The results of membership tests are:" );
26       for ( String w : SEQUENCE )
27       {
28         System.out.printf( "%20s:%s\n", w, c.contains( w ) );
29       }
30     }
31
```

Listing 18.20 The class `CollectionExperiment` (part 1). The method `main`, the array constant `SEQUENCE`, and the method `printfInfo`

After the initial insertion of the elements, the contents of `myList` are expected to be:

```
"suzie", "suzie", "grace", "grace", "carol", "carol", "deborah",
                 "deborah","janis", "janis"
```

with the second occurrence of `"grace"` at position 3. Removing the element at position 3 three times successively must turns this to:

```
"suzie", "suzie", "grace", "deborah", "deborah", "janis", "janis"
```

and changing the element at position 3 to `"jackie"` must change the contents to:

```
"suzie", "suzie", "grace", "jackie", "deborah", "janis", "janis"
```

The method `queueExperiment` (Line 54) instantiates a `LinkedList<String>` object, and then assigns the object to a `Queue<String>` variable named `myQueue` (Line 58). The method then adds each element of `SEQUENCE` successively twice using the method `offer` of `Queue<String>` (Lines 59–63). Next, the method examines the head element using the method `peek` of `Queue<String>` (Lines 66 and 67) and then removes the head element of `myQueue` using the method `poll` of `Queue<String>` (Lines 68 and 69). The method repeats this action three times. Finally, the method calls `printInfo` to print the information about `myQueue` (Line 71).

```
32   public static void listExperiment()
33   {
34     System.out.println( "-----Linked List Demo-----" );
35     List<String> myList = new LinkedList<String>();
36     for ( String w : SEQUENCE )
37     {
38       myList.add( w );
39       myList.add( w );
40     }
41     for ( int i = 1; i <= 3; i ++ )
42     {
43       String y = myList.remove( 3 );
44       System.out.printf( "Removed the element at 3 %s\n", y );
45       y = myList.get( 3 );
46       System.out.printf( "The new element at 3 is %s\n", y );
47     }
48     myList.set( 3, "jackie" );
49     String z = myList.get( 3 );
50     System.out.println( "Changed the element at 3 to \"jackie\"" );
51     System.out.printf( "The new element at 3 is %s\n", z );
52     printInfo( myList );
53   }
54
```

Listing 18.21 The class CollectionExperiment (part 2). The experiment with a List<String> data

```
55   public static void queueExperiment()
56   {
57     System.out.println( "-----Queue Demo-----" );
58     Queue<String> myQueue = new LinkedList<String>();
59     for ( String w : SEQUENCE )
60     {
61       myQueue.offer( w );
62       myQueue.offer( w );
63     }
64     for ( int i = 1; i <= 3; i ++ )
65     {
66       String y = myQueue.peek();
67       System.out.printf( "The head is %s\n", y );
68       y = myQueue.poll();
69       System.out.printf( "The head %s has been removed\n", y );
70     }
71     printInfo( myQueue );
72   }
73
```

Listing 18.22 The class CollectionExperiment (part 3). The experiment with a Queue<String> data

After the initial insertion of the elements, the contents of myQueue are expected to be:
"suzie", "suzie", "grace", "grace", "carol", "carol", "deborah",

Removing the head element three times in a row must turn this set to:

"grace", "carol", "carol", "deborah", "deborah", "janis", "janis"

The method `setExperiment` (Line 74) instantiates a `HashSet<String>` object, and then assigns the object to a `Set<String>` variable named `myQueue` (Line 77). The method then adds each element of `SEQUENCE` successively twice using the method `add` of `Set<String>` (Lines 78–82). Next, the method removes `"suzie"` using the method `remove` and `Set<String>` (Lines 83 and 84). Finally, the method calls `printInfo` to generate a report about `mySet` (Line 85).

```
74    public static void setExperiment()
75    {
76       System.out.println( "-----Set Demo-----" );
77       Set<String> mySet = new HashSet<String>();
78       for ( String w : SEQUENCE )
79       {
80          mySet.add( w );
81          mySet.add( w );
82       }
83       mySet.remove( "suzie" );
84       System.out.printf( "Removed %s\n", "suzie" );
85       printInfo( mySet );
86    }
87 }
```

Listing 18.23 The class `CollectionExperiment` (part 4). The experiment with a `Set<String>` data

After the initial insertion of the elements, the contents of the list are expected to be the set consisting of:

"suzie", "grace", "carol", "deborah", "janis"

Removing `"suzie"` must turn this set to:

"grace", "carol", "deborah", "janis"

Here is the result of executing the program.

```
1    -----Linked List Demo-----
2    Removed the element at 3 grace
3    The new element at 3 is carol
4    Removed the element at 3 carol
5    The new element at 3 is carol
6    Removed the element at 3 carol
7    The new element at 3 is deborah
8    Changed the element at 3 to "jackie"
9    The new element at 3 is jackie
10
11   The collection has 7 elements
12   The elements are: suzie suzie grace jackie deborah janis janis
13   The results of membership tests are:
14               suzie:true
15               grace:true
16               carol:false
17             deborah:true
18               janis:true
```

```
19   -----Queue Demo-----
20   The head is suzie
21   The head suzie has been removed
22   The head is suzie
23   The head suzie has been removed
24   The head is grace
25   The head grace has been removed
26
27   The collection has 7 elements
28   The elements are: grace carol carol deborah deborah janis janis
29   The results of membership tests are:
30                   suzie:false
31                   grace:true
32                   carol:true
33                deborah:true
34                   janis:true
35                   -----Set Demo-----
36   Removed suzie
37
38   The collection has 4 elements
39   The elements are: carol janis grace deborah
40   The results of membership tests are:
41                   suzie:false
42                   grace:true
43                   carol:true
44                deborah:true
45                   janis:true
```

Note that the order in which the elements are retrieved from the set is different from the order in which the elements are added to the set.

Summary

- A generic type parameter is a parameter for an object type.
- A generic type parameter is represented with an upper case letter inside a pair of "greater than" and "less than" symbols, < >.
- Comparable<E> is an interface with one abstract method compareTo.
- Comparator<E> is an interface that defines an abstract method compare that compares two items of type E.
- Iterable<E> is an interface with one abstract method iterator that returns a data of type Iterator<E>.
- Iterator<E> is an interface with two abstract methods hasNext and next.
- For-each loops can be applied to an object of a class implementing Iterable<E>.
- ArrayList<E> is a class that builds a list of an indefinite length.
- The Java Collection Framework is a large body of interfaces and classes. The framework provides ways to maintain dynamic collections of data. Major units in the framework include interfaces Iterable<E>, Iterator<E>, Collection<E>, List<E>, Queue<E>, Dequeue<E>, Set<E>, and SortedSet<E> and classes ArrayList<E>, LinkedList<E>, and HashSet<E>.

Exercises

1. **A class for a bottom K list**   The class TopK was designed to maintain the largest k elements in a sequence of an indefinite number of elements of some type E, where E is a class parameter, where E extends Comparable<E>. Write a class, BottomK, for maintaining the smallest k elements instead.

2. **A class for a pair of values**   Write a class, Pair, that takes two class parameters, K and E, where K extends Comparable<K>. An object of the class has a pair of instance variables, one being of type K and the other being of type E. A constructor for Pair<K, E> receives values for the two variables and stores them in the instance variables. The class has a "getter" for each of the two variables, getOne and getTwo. The class is also expected to be comparable with respect to the first instance variable. The header for the class is:

```
1    public class Pair< E extends Comparable<E>, K> implements
2        Comparable< Pair< E,K > >
```

3. **A Collatz Conjecture competition**   Recall that Collatz Conjecture states that every positive integer can be converted to 1 with successive applications of the following transformation rule: if the number is even, divide it by 2; otherwise, multiply it by 3 and then add 1. Write a program, CollatzCompetition, that receives three input integers, say num, max, and k, from the user, generates num random integers between 1 and max, and among the random numbers generated, finds which k numbers require the most transformation steps before becoming 1. The minimum possible value for k is 3. If the user enters a number less than 3, the number must be adjusted to 3.
   Here is a possible output of the program:

```
1    Testing the Collatz Conjecture
2    Enter  #Trials, Max, K: 10000 1000000 10
3    rank=10   length=436     number=775035
4    rank=9    length=369     number=900093
5    rank=8    length=361     number=772009
6    rank=7    length=361     number=781862
7    rank=6    length=357     number=293199
8    rank=5    length=356     number=815273
9    rank=4    length=348     number=747070
10   rank=3    length=344     number=270847
11   rank=2    length=344     number=270222
12   rank=1    length=343     number=789302
```

In keeping the top 10, use the class Pair<Integer, Integer> written in the previous question, where the first element of the pair is the number of steps that the first number had to undergo before becoming 1.

4. **The set of unique tokens**   Write a program, UniqueTokens, that produces an ordered list of tokens that appear in a file, where the path to the file is given by args [0]. The program must use a Set<String> variable instantiated with HashSet<String> to record the tokens. After opening the file, the program scans all the tokens in the file, and adds the tokens to the set using the method set of the class Set<String>. After finishing collecting the tokens, the program generates an ArrayList<String> consisting of all the tokens appearing in the set. To accomplish this, the program retrieves all the tokens in the set using a for-each loop, and adds it to the list. After building the list, the program sorts it using Collections.sort. Finally, the program prints the tokens, say three tokens per line, to produce the output.

Here is the output generated by supplying the source code of TopK.java that was presented in this textbook:

1	(	)	);
2	+	0	1
3	=	==	>
4	ArrayList<E>	ArrayList<E>();	Collections.sort(
5	Comparable<	E	TopK(
6	TopK<	add(	class
7	extends	get(	i
8	if	import	int
9	java.util.*;	k	k;
10	new	o	private
11	public	return	theList
12	theList.add(	theList.get(	theList.remove(
13	theList.size()	theList;	this.k
14	void	{	}

To produce this output, the program uses printf with 22 character spaces allocated for each token.

5. **The set of unique tokens, keeping only the alphabet, the apostrophe, and the dash** As a variation of the previous question, write a program, UniqueTokensAlt, that generates a sorted list of the tokens appearing in a given file, where all the characters other than the letters of the alphabet, the apostrophe, and the dash are converted to the whitespace during the process of reading tokens, and each uppercase letter is converted to lowercase.

To accomplish the task, the program reads the input file line by line, transforms the line to a new String that contains only the letters, the apostrophe, the dash, and the whitespace, and then reads the tokens from the newline using a Scanner. The transformation should be done as follows: convert the line to all lowercase, instantiate a StringBuilder object, append the characters of the lowercase version after replacing each character that is not a lowercase letter, an apostrophe, or a dash to a whitespace. For example,

$$\texttt{System.out.printf("\textbackslash\%s\textbackslash n", "abc");}$$

must be converted to:

$$\texttt{system out printf s n abc}$$

The tokens obtained from this String are "system", "out", "printf", "s", "n", and "abc". Here is the output of the program with the source code of TopK.java as the input.

1	add	arraylist	class
2	collections	comparable	e
3	extends	get	i
4	if	import	int
5	java	k	new
6	o	private	public
7	remove	return	size
8	sort	thelist	this
9	topk	util	void

6. **A comparator for File** Write a class, CompareFile, that implements Comparator <File>. The comparison should be based upon the names of the File objects accessed with getName.

Programming Projects

7. **Name and count**   Write a class named NameAndCount for recording a String data named name and an int data named count. A constructor for the class takes two values, one for the name and the other for the count, and stores the two values in the instance variables. The class must be comparable, with the declaration of implements Comparable<NameAndCount>. The class has a "getter" for the name, named getName, and a "getter" for the count, named count. For "setters", there is a method named increment that increases the value of count by 1. There is another instance method equals, which receives a String data as its parameter, and returns a boolean value indicating whether or not the contents of the String data is equal to the contents of name. Additionally, the class must implement the compareTo method, which returns the result of comparing the values of count.

8. **A comparator for the NameAndCount**   Write a class named CompareNameAndCount that implements Comparator<NameAndCount>. The comparison should be based upon the names.

9. **Taking an inventory**   Using the NameAndCount class from the previous question, write a program NameInventory that takes an inventory of the tokens appearing in a file, where the file path is given by args[0]. The program instantiates a LinkedList of NameAndString objects and retrieves all the tokens from the file. For each token it retrieves, the program scans the list for a match with the token using the equals method. If there is a match, the program increases the count by calling the method increment of the NameAndCount object that matches the token. If there is no match found, the program adds a new NameAndCount object with the token and the initial count of 1. After incorporating all the tokens, the program sorts the collection, and prints the names with their counts.

   The program can be used to count votes in a write-in election. Here is the result of processing the file containing one million random tokens that are chosen from a set of five names:

```
1              Ron:19799              Dudley:19883         Hermione:20058
2              Draco:20125            Harry:20135
```

Online and Recursive Algorithms

19

19.1 Online Algorithms

19.1.1 The Definition of Online Algorithms

Online algorithms are those that process an indefinite amount of data using a fixed number of variables. Sections 7.6 and 8.5 presented programs for computing the Fibonacci sequence $\{F_i\}_{i \geq 0}$ defined by: $F_0 = 1$, $F_1 = 1$, and for all $i \geq 2$, $F_i = F_{i-1} + F_{i-2}$. In generating the values of $F_2, F_3, \ldots$, the programs used three `long` variables, `f`, `fp`, and `fpp`, where they represented the values of F_i, F_{i-1}, and F_{i-2}. Prior to computing the value of F_i, the programs copied the value of `fp` to `fpp` and then the value of `f` to `fp`. In this manner, regardless of how many elements of the sequence needed to be generated, the program needed just three variables (and an index variable representing `i`). The two programs represent the concept of online algorithms.

An **online algorithm** uses a set of variables that is initialized and updated during the execution of the algorithm. Their initialization is very important. For the computation of Fibonacci numbers, the initialization consists of storing the value of 1 to both `fp` and `fpp`. Here we recall the program from Chap. 7 that we used to compute the Fibonacci numbers.

```
1   long f, fp = 1, fpp = 1;
2   Scanner keyboard = new Scanner( System.in );
3   System.out.print( "Enter n: " );
4   int n = keyboard.nextInt();
5   for ( int i = 2; i <= n; i ++ )
6   {
7     f = fp + fpp;
8     System.out.println(
9         i + "\tf=" + f + "\tfp=" + fp + "\tfpp=" + fpp );
10    fpp = fp;
11    fp = f;
12  }
```

Listing 19.1 The initialization and the update in the computation of the Fibonacci numbers

© Springer Nature Switzerland AG 2018
M. Ogihara, *Fundamentals of Java Programming*,
https://doi.org/10.1007/978-3-319-89491-1_19

Another example of online algorithms is the computation of the maximum and the minimum in the series of numbers. This example was presented in Sect. 7.4. The program initialized the variables that represent the maximum and the minimum with the first number entered. After that, the program updated the two variables each time a new number arrived.

```
1     System.out.print( "Enter Data No. 1: " );
2     input = keyboard.nextInt();
3     max = input;
4     min = input;
5     for ( int round = 2; round <= nData; round ++ )
6     {
7       System.out.print( "Enter Data No. " + round + ": " );
8       input = keyboard.nextInt();
9       if ( max < input )
10      {
11        max = input;
12      }
13      if ( min > input )
14      {
15        min = input;
16      }
17    }
```

Listing 19.2 A program that computes the maximum and the minimum in a series of numbers. This part of the code is from Chap. 7

19.1.2 Computing Recurrences

We generalize the online computation for the Fibonacci numbers and write programs for computing the elements of sequences generated by linear recurrences. We first consider first-order recurrences. Suppose a sequence $s_0, s_1, s_2, \ldots$ is defined by the linear recurrence:

$$s_n = as_{n-1} + b \text{ for all } n \geq 1$$

where a, b, and s_0 are integers. Consider computing $s_1, \ldots, s_n$, given a, b, s_0, and n as input. This problem can be solved using an online algorithm. In addition to a, b, and s_0, our program receives n, and then generates the sequence $s_1, \ldots, s_n$ and reports their values. Since s_i may quickly grow, we use long for storing the value of s_i.

Here is a source code for our solution. We use a long variable, previous, to record s_{i-1} and a long variable, sValue, to record s_i (Line 8). The value of sValue is updated using the assignment sValue = a * previous + b (Line 21). The update occurs immediately before the assignment to sValue (Line 20). The coefficients, a and b, are stored in variables named a and b. Their values are received in Lines 12 and 13. The initial value, s_0, is received as the value for sValue in Line 11. After receiving the value for n in Line 15, the program enters a while-loop (Line 17).

```
 1   import java.util.*;
 2   public class RecurrenceFirst
 3   {
 4     public static void main( String[] args )
 5     {
 6       Scanner keyboard = new Scanner( System.in );
 7       int a, b, i, n;
 8       long sValue, previous;
 9
10       System.out.print( "Enter s_0, a, b for s_n = a * s_{n-1} + b: " );
11       sValue = keyboard.nextInt();
12       a = keyboard.nextInt();
13       b = keyboard.nextInt();
14       System.out.print( "Enter n: " );
15       n = keyboard.nextInt();
16       i = 0;
17       while ( i < n )
18       {
19         i ++;
20         previous = sValue;
21         sValue = a * previous + b;
22         System.out.printf( "%3d: %d%n", i, sValue );
23       }
24     }
25   }
```

Listing 19.3 A program for computing a first-order linear recurrence

Here is an execution example of the code:

```
 1   Enter s_0, a, b for s_n = a * s_{n-1} + b: 1 3 2
 2   Enter n: 20
 3     1: 5
 4     2: 17
 5     3: 53
 6     4: 161
 7     5: 485
 8     6: 1457
 9     7: 4373
10     8: 13121
11     9: 39365
12    10: 118097
13    11: 354293
14    12: 1062881
15    13: 3188645
16    14: 9565937
17    15: 28697813
18    16: 86093441
19    17: 258280325
20    18: 774840977
21    19: 2324522933
22    20: 6973568801
```

We extend the program to handle second-order recurrences of the form:

$$s_n = as_{n-1} + bs_{n-2} + c, \text{ for all } n \geq 2$$

where s_0 and s_1 are integers, and a, b, and c are integer coefficients.

Like the programs for computing the Fibonacci sequence, the computation is dependent on two previous numbers in the sequence. We use two long variables, previous for s_{n-1}, and previousPrevious for s_{n-2}.

```
1   import java.util.*;
2   public class RecurrenceSecond
3   {
4     public static void main( String[] args )
5     {
6       Scanner keyboard = new Scanner( System.in );
7       int a, b, c, i, n;
8       long previousPrevious, previous, sValue;
9
10      System.out.print( "Enter s_0, s_1, "
11          + "a, b, c for s_n = a * s_{n-1} + b * s_{n-2} + c: " );
12      previous = keyboard.nextInt();
13      sValue = keyboard.nextInt();
14      a = keyboard.nextInt();
15      b = keyboard.nextInt();
16      c = keyboard.nextInt();
17      System.out.print( "Enter n: " );
18      n = keyboard.nextInt();
19      i = 1;
20      while ( i < n )
21      {
22        i ++;
23        previousPrevious = previous;
24        previous = sValue;
25        sValue = a * previous + b * previousPrevious + c;
26        System.out.printf( "%3d: %d%n", i, sValue );
27      }
28    }
29  }
```

Listing 19.4 A program for computing a second-order linear recurrence

Here is one execution example:

```
1   Enter s_0, s_1, a, b, c for s_n = a * s_{n-1} + b * s_{n-2} + c: 1 2 1 1
        0
2   Enter n: 20
3     2: 3
4     3: 5
5     4: 8
6     5: 13
7     6: 21
8     7: 34
```

```
 9        8: 55
10        9: 89
11       10: 144
12       11: 233
13       12: 377
14       13: 610
15       14: 987
16       15: 1597
17       16: 2584
18       17: 4181
19       18: 6765
20       19: 10946
21       20: 17711
```

If the program receives 1 for each of s_0, s_1, a, and b, and receives 0 for c, the sequence generated is equal to the Fibonacci sequence.

19.1.3 Computing the Factorial Function

For a positive integer n, the factorial of n, denoted by $n!$, is the product of all integers between 1 and n. For integers n less than or equal to 0, the factorial of n is defined to be 1. Here are some first few values of the factorial:

$$0! = 1$$

$$1! = 1$$

$$2! = 2$$

$$3! = 6$$

$$4! = 24$$

$$5! = 120$$

Consider computing the factorial of a given positive integer n.

It is easy to see that to compute $n!$ for $n \geq 1$, we only have to multiply the value of $(n - 1)!$ by n. The next code implements this idea. The value of factorial increases very quickly. There is a formula called **formula!Stirling's** that provides an approximate real value for the factorial as follows:

$$n! \approx \sqrt{2\pi n}\left(\frac{n}{e}\right)^n$$

Therefore, we use a long to store the value of the factorial.

Here is the source code of our program. The program receives the value for n from the user (Line 8). If the value of n is positive, the program enters the process of computing the factorial (Line 9). To compute the factorial, the program initializes a long variable, factorial, with the value of 1 (Line 11), and then enters a for-loop that iterates over the sequence 1, ..., n with a variable named i (Line 12). At each round, the program updates the value of factorial with factorial * i, and then prints the value of i and factorial using the format %2d:%d (Line 15).

```
1   import java.util.*;
2   public class Factorial
3   {
4     public static void main( String[] args )
5     {
6       Scanner keyboard = new Scanner( System.in );
7       System.out.print( "Enter a positive integer: " );
8       int n = keyboard.nextInt();
9       if ( n > 0 )
10      {
11        long factorial = 1;
12        for ( int i = 1; i <= n; i ++ )
13        {
14          factorial *= i;
15          System.out.printf( "%2d:%d%n", i, factorial );
16        }
17      }
18    }
19  }
```

Listing 19.5 A program that computes the factorial function using an online algorithm

Here is an execution example of the program:

```
1   Enter a positive integer: 20
2    1:1
3    2:2
4    3:6
5    4:24
6    5:120
7    6:720
8    7:5040
9    8:40320
10   9:362880
11  10:3628800
12  11:39916800
13  12:479001600
14  13:6227020800
15  14:87178291200
16  15:1307674368000
17  16:20922789888000
18  17:355687428096000
19  18:6402373705728000
20  19:121645100408832000
21  20:2432902008176640000
```

The program computes the value of n! correctly for the values of *n* up to 20. As shown next, the value that the program produces for 21 is negative:

```
1   Enter a positive integer: 22
2    1:1
3    2:2
4    3:6
5    4:24
6    5:120
7    6:720
8    7:5040
```

```
 9 | 8:40320
10 | 9:362880
11 |10:3628800
12 |11:39916800
13 |12:479001600
14 |13:6227020800
15 |14:87178291200
16 |15:1307674368000
17 |16:20922789888000
18 |17:355687428096000
19 |18:6402373705728000
20 |19:121645100408832000
21 |20:2432902008176640000
22 |21:-4249290049419214848
23 |22:-1250660718674968576
```

If computing approximate values of factorials (instead of their exact values) is acceptable, we can use `double` instead of `long` to obtain factorials for much larger values of n. To generate an output that is easy to read, we use the `printf` format of `%e`. This is a format for the exponential representation, where a floating point number is presented as AeB, where A is a real number with precisely one digit before the decimal point and B is an integer. A and B collective mean "A × 10 raised to the power of B". For instance, $1.346201e+241$ means 1.346201×10^{241}. The format for the number i is changed from `%2d` to `%3d`.

```
 1 |import java.util.*;
 2 |public class FactorialDouble
 3 |{
 4 |  public static void main( String[] args )
 5 |  {
 6 |    Scanner keyboard = new Scanner( System.in );
 7 |    System.out.print( "Enter a positive integer: " );
 8 |    int n = keyboard.nextInt();
 9 |    if ( n > 0 )
10 |    {
11 |      double factorial = 1;
12 |      for ( int i = 1; i <= n; i ++ ) {
13 |        factorial *= i;
14 |        System.out.printf( "%3d:%e%n", i, factorial );
15 |      }
16 |    }
17 |  }
18 |}
```

Listing 19.6 A program that approximates the factorial function using `double` in place of `long`

Here is how the program computes the factorial, with the middle 130 lines of output omitted:

```
1 |Enter a positive integer: 150
2 |  1:1.000000e+00
3 |  2:2.000000e+00
4 |  3:6.000000e+00
5 |  4:2.400000e+01
6 |  5:1.200000e+02
7 |  6:7.200000e+02
8 |  7:5.040000e+03
9 |  8:4.032000e+04
```

```
10      9:3.628800e+05
11     10:3.628800e+06
12    ...
13    140:1.346201e+241
14    141:1.898144e+243
15    142:2.695364e+245
16    143:3.854371e+247
17    144:5.550294e+249
18    145:8.047926e+251
19    146:1.174997e+254
20    147:1.727246e+256
21    148:2.556324e+258
22    149:3.808923e+260
23    150:5.713384e+262
```

The program can compute the approximate factorial if n as large as 170, which is the limit.

```
1     % java FactorialDouble
2     Enter a positive integer: 173
3     ...
4     151:8.627210e+264
5     152:1.311336e+267
6     153:2.006344e+269
7     154:3.089770e+271
8     155:4.789143e+273
9     156:7.471063e+275
10    157:1.172957e+278
11    158:1.853272e+280
12    159:2.946702e+282
13    160:4.714724e+284
14    161:7.590705e+286
15    162:1.229694e+289
16    163:2.004402e+291
17    164:3.287219e+293
18    165:5.423911e+295
19    166:9.003692e+297
20    167:1.503617e+300
21    168:2.526076e+302
22    169:4.269068e+304
23    170:7.257416e+306
24    171:Infinity
25    172:Infinity
26    173:Infinity
27    %
```

Infinity is a special value of the boxed class Double that represents the positive infinity.

19.2   Recursive Algorithms

19.2.1 Computing the Factorial Function Recursively

We say that a problem has a "recursive solution" if it has the following properties:

1. The "size" of each input to the problem can be measured as a nonnegative integer.

2. It is easier to solve the problem for an input having a smaller size than to solve the problem for an input having a larger size.
3. The problem for inputs having the smallest sizes is trivial.
4. For solving the problem for a non-trivial input, the following strategy can be used: generate inputs having smaller sizes, solve the problem for the smaller inputs, and then integrate the solutions to generate a solution for the input at hand.

If the above action of solving the problem is coded as a method whose parameter represents the input, the code for the method contain calls to itself. We such calls **recursive calls**. Java permits programs to have recursive calls.

Consider, again, computing the factorial of a positive integer n. Since the factorial of n is the factorial of $n - 1$ times n for all $n \geq 2$, a recursive algorithm for computing the factorial can be stated as follows:

- If n <= 1, return 1. This is the trivial case.
- If n >= 2, compute the factorial of n-1 using a recursive call, compute the product of the value returned by the recursive call and n, and then return the product.

Next appears a program that computes the factorial using recursive methods.

In the method main (Line 16), the program receives an input number from the user, and then stores it in an int variable named number (Lines 18–20). If the value of number is between 0 and 20 (Line 19), the program calls the method compute with number as the actual parameter.

The method compute (Line 4) performs the following actions:

1. Print the value of the formal parameter n (Line 6).
2. Declare a long variable, returnValue, and store 1 in it (Line 7).
3. If n > 1, replace the value of returnValue with the product of compute (n - 1) and n (Lines 8–11). A recursive call appears in Line 10.
4. Print the values of n and returnValue using the format n=%-4dn!=%30d.

```
1   import java.util.*;
2   public class FactorialRecursive
3   {
4     public static long compute( int n )
5     {
6       System.out.printf( "input=%d%n", n );
7       long returnValue = 1;
8       if ( n >= 2 )
9       {
10        returnValue = compute( n - 1 ) * n;
11      }
12      System.out.printf( "n=%-4dn!=%30d\n", n, returnValue );
13      return returnValue;
14    }
15
16    public static void main( String[] args )
17    {
18      Scanner keyboard = new Scanner( System.in );
19      System.out.print( "Enter value between 0 and 20: " );
20      int number = keyboard.nextInt();
21      if ( number >= 0 && number <= 20 )
22      {
23        compute( number );
24      }
25    }
26  }
```

Listing 19.7 A program that computes the factorial function recursively double in place of long

Here is one execution of the program:

```
1   Enter value between 0 and 20: 10
2   input=10
3   input=9
4   input=8
5   input=7
6   input=6
7   input=5
8   input=4
9   input=3
10  input=2
11  input=1
12  n=1    n!=                              1
13  n=2    n!=                              2
14  n=3    n!=                              6
15  n=4    n!=                             24
16  n=5    n!=                            120
17  n=6    n!=                            720
18  n=7    n!=                           5040
19  n=8    n!=                          40320
20  n=9    n!=                         362880
21  n=10   n!=                        3628800
```

Line 12 where the program prints the values n and returnValue does not occur until the recursive call is completed. The following series of figures illustrates how the recursive calls are handled (Figures 19.1, 19.2, 19.3, 19.4, 19.5, 19.6, 19.7, 19.8, 19.9, 19.10, and 19.11).

Fig. 19.1 The value passing that occurs during the computation of the factorial (part 1)

Fig. 19.2 The value passing that occurs during the computation of the factorial (part 2)

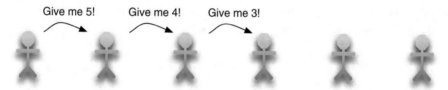

Fig. 19.3 The value passing that occurs during the computation of the factorial (part 3)

Fig. 19.4 The value passing that occurs during the computation of the factorial (part 4)

Fig. 19.5 The value passing that occurs during the computation of the factorial (part 5)

Fig. 19.6 The value passing that occurs during the computation of the factorial (part 6)

Fig. 19.7 The value passing that occurs during the computation of the factorial (part 7)

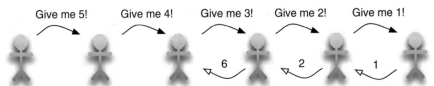

Fig. 19.8 The value passing that occurs during the computation of the factorial (part 8)

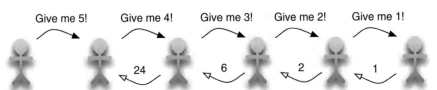

Fig. 19.9 The value passing that occurs during the computation of the factorial (part 9)

Fig. 19.10 The value passing that occurs during the computation of the factorial (part 10)

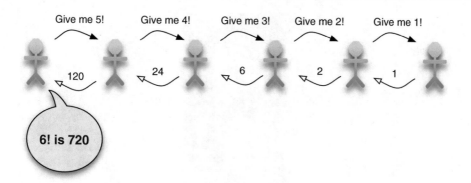

Fig. 19.11 The value passing that occurs during the computation of the factorial (part 11)

19.2.2 The Greatest Common Divisor of Two Integers

The **greatest common divisor (GCD)** of two integers is the largest positive integer that divides both numbers. For example:

- GCD(20, 35) = 5,
- GCD(14, 5) = 1,
- GCD(−121, −143) = 11, and
- GCD(0, 191) = 191.

There is an algorithm for computing the GCD efficiently, called **Euclid's Algorithm.**[1] Given two nonnegative integers, m and n, Euclid's algorithm performs the following updates until n becomes 0:

1. Store the value of $m\%n$ to r.
2. Replace m with n.
3. Replace n with r.

When the repetition terminates (which is when n becomes 0), the value of m is the GCD of m and n.
   For instance, using the algorithm, the GCD of 14 and 35 is obtained as follows:

m	n	$r = m\%n$
14	35	14
35	14	7
14	7	0
7	0	N/A

The GCD is 7. Here is the GCD between 10,458 and 2505 is calculated using Euclid's algorithm.

---

[1] Euclid is a mathematician who was born in the mid-fourth century, BCE.

m	n	$r = m\%n$
10,458	2505	438
2503	438	315
438	315	123
315	123	69
123	69	54
69	54	15
54	15	9
15	9	6
9	6	3
6	3	0
3	0	N/A

This means that the GCD of the two numbers is 3.

Euclid's algorithm can be implemented as follows, using a while-loop whose continuation condition is m >= 1 && n >= 1.

```
1  import java.util.Scanner;
2  public class GCD
3  {
4    public static void main( String[] args )
5    {
6      Scanner keyboard = new Scanner( System.in );
7      int m, n, r;
8      System.out.print( "Enter two numbers: " );
9      m = keyboard.nextInt();
10     n = keyboard.nextInt();
11     if ( m >= 1 && n >= 1 )
12     {
13       System.out.printf( "The GCD of %d and %d is ", m, n );
14       while ( n > 0 )
15       {
16         r = m % n;  // obtain residual
17         m = n;  // m is the divisor
18         n = r;  // r is the residual
19       }
20       System.out.println( m );
21     }
22   }
23  }
```

Listing 19.8 A program that computes the GCD using a while-loop

We can encode Euclid's algorithm as a recursive algorithm. In this recursive algorithm, the input consists of two numbers. Our implementation uses two parameters, a and b, whose values are nonnegative. The input size is the value of the second parameter. If the input size is 0, the method returns the first number as the GCD. Otherwise, the method makes a recursive call with the first and second parameters simultaneously substituted with b and a % b.

Here is a program GCDRecursive that computes the GCD of two positive input numbers using recursive calls. The recursive version has a method named GCD for computing the GCD. The method returns the value of the GCD of its two parameters, a and b. At the start of the method, it prints the parameters (Line 6). Then, if the value of b is 0, the method returns 0 (Lines 7–10); otherwise, it makes a recursive call (Line 11).

```
1   import java.util.Scanner;
2   public class GCDRecursive
3   {
4     public static int GCD( int a, int b )
5     {
6       System.out.println( "a = " + a + ", b = " + b );
7       if ( b == 0 )
8       {
9         return a;
10      }
11      return GCD( b, a % b );
12    }
13    public static void main( String[] args )
14    {
15      Scanner keyboard = new Scanner( System.in );
16      System.out.print( "Enter two numbers: " );
17      int m = keyboard.nextInt();
18      int n = keyboard.nextInt();
19      if ( m >= 1 && n >= 1 )
20      {
21        int r = GCD( m, n );
22        System.out.printf( "The GCD of %d and %d is %d%n", m, n, r );
23      }
24    }
25  }
```

Listing 19.9 A program that computes the GCD using recursive calls

Here are some execution examples of the program.

```
1   Enter two numbers: 2435 98643
2   a = 2435, b = 98643
3   a = 98643, b = 2435
4   a = 2435, b = 1243
5   a = 1243, b = 1192
6   a = 1192, b = 51
7   a = 51, b = 19
8   a = 19, b = 13
9   a = 13, b = 6
10  a = 6, b = 1
11  a = 1, b = 0
12  The GCD of 2435 and 98643 is 1
```

```
1   Enter two numbers: 108 81
2   a = 108, b = 81
3   a = 81, b = 27
4   a = 27, b = 0
5   The GCD of 108 and 81 is 27
```

Fig. 19.12 An example of
the tower of Hanoi

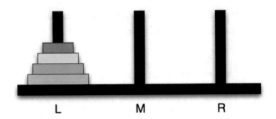

L   M   R

```
 1   Enter two numbers: 35986 56789
 2   a = 35986, b = 56789
 3   a = 56789, b = 35986
 4   a = 35986, b = 20803
 5   a = 20803, b = 15183
 6   a = 15183, b = 5620
 7   a = 5620, b = 3943
 8   a = 3943, b = 1677
 9   a = 1677, b = 589
10   a = 589, b = 499
11   a = 499, b = 90
12   a = 90, b = 49
13   a = 49, b = 41
14   a = 41, b = 8
15   a = 8, b = 1
16   a = 1, b = 0
17   The GCD of 35986 and 56789 is 1
```

19.2.3 The Tower of Hanoi

19.2.3.1 The Problem Statement

Legend says that there is a temple in a remote place in Hanoi, where the monks are counting the time by moving 64 disks (Fig. 19.12). The monks can move one disk at a time on the tick of a clock. The disks have a hole in the middle, and they are placed on a pole through their holes. There are three poles at the site. The 64 disks were originally placed on the first pole, in the decreasing order of their diameters, with the smallest disk at the top. The monks have been given the task of moving all 64 disks to the second pole. In moving the disks, the monks have to abide by the following rule: no disk can be placed on a disk with a smaller diameter. In other words, during the execution of the task, on each of the three poles, the disks are placed in the decreasing order of their diameters.

Legend has it that the world ends when the monks have completed the task.

The monks have been working on the task, generation after generation, but they have not finished yet.

When will the world end?

19.2.3.2 Our Solution

Let's see if we can determine the actions of the monks by computation.

We formalize the problem as follows: We assign the position numbers 0, 1, and 2 to the three poles. We assign the names L, M, and R to them. We use the phrase "move 2 to L and R" to mean the action of moving the 2nd smallest disk from Pole L to Pole R. We envision that M is the final destination of the disks.

The solution for moving two disks is as follows:

```
1   Move 1 from L to R
2   Move 2 from L to M
3   Move 1 from R to M
```

The solution for moving four disks is as follows:

```
1    Move 1 from L to R
2    Move 2 from L to M
3    Move 1 from R to M
4    Move 3 from L to R
5    Move 1 from M to L
6    Move 2 from M to R
7    Move 1 from L to R
8    Move 4 from L to M
9    Move 1 from R to M
10   Move 2 from R to L
11   Move 1 from M to L
12   Move 3 from R to M
13   Move 1 from L to R
14   Move 2 from L to M
15   Move 1 from R to M
```

Figure 19.13 shows the process.

We can generalize these solutions to the following general solution:

- The smallest disk can be moved freely.
- To move $N \geq 2$ disks to a designated location, all of the top $N - 1$ disks must be moved to a pole that is neither the present pole nor the designated pole. The N-th disk then must be moved to the designated location. After that, the top $N - 1$ disks that were previously moved to the temporary pole must be moved to the designated location.

We encode this idea into our program. Our program receives the input (the number of disks to move) as args[0] and produces the solution.

We use a static String array constant NAMES that contains the names "L", "M", and "R" (Line 4). We use a void method named solve for producing a solution on the screen (Line 5). The method solve receives three int parameters. The first one, number, is the number of disks to be moved. The second parameter, fromPole, is the current location (0, 1, or 2) of the disks to be moved. The third parameter, toPole, is the target location (0, 1, or 2) of the disks to move. We anticipate that the value of fromPole to be different form the value of toPole. Since the poles are numbered 0, 1, and 2, the sum of the three possible pole indexes is 3. Thus, given the two indexes, fromPole and toPole, we can identify the index to the remaining pole using the formula:

$$3 - \text{fromPole} - \text{toPole}$$

The actions to be performed in solve are as follows:

Fig. 19.13 The solution
to a small Tower of Hanoi
problem. The top two
drawings of disks and
poles represent the first
four moves. The bottom
two drawings of disks and
poles represent the next
three moves. The numbers
appearing on the arrows
represent the step numbers

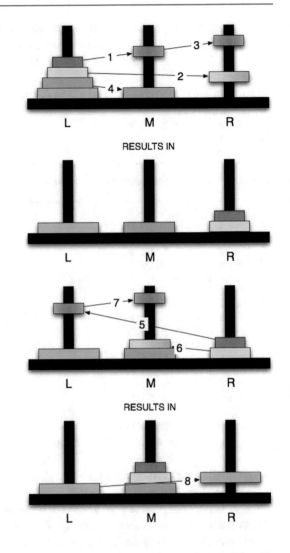

- If the number of disks to be moved (stored in the parameter number) is equal to 1 (Line 7), print the solution: move number from NAMES[fromPole] to NAMES[toPole] (Lines 9 and 10).
- If the number of disks to be moved is greater than 1 (Line 12), execute the following:
  - Obtain the index to the remaining pole and store it in a variable named remainder (Line 14).
  - Print the solution for moving number - 1 disks from NAMES[fromPole] to NAMES[remainder] using a recursive call solve(number - 1, fromPole, remainder) (Line 15).
  - Print the action for moving the disk number from NAMES[fromPole] to NAMES[toPole]. (Lines 16 and 17).
  - Print the solution for moving number - 1 disks from NAMES[remainder] to NAMES[toPole] using a recursive call solve(number - 1, remainder, toPole) (Line 18).

```
 1   import java.util.*;
 2   public class Hanoi
 3   {
 4     static final String[] NAMES = { "L", "M", "R" };
 5     static void solve( int number, int fromPole, int toPole )
 6     {
 7       if ( number == 1 )
 8       {
 9         System.out.printf( "Move %d from %s to %s%n", number,
10             NAMES[ fromPole ], NAMES[ toPole ] );
11       }
12       else
13       {
14         int remainder = 3 - fromPole - toPole;
15         solve( number - 1, fromPole, remainder );
16         System.out.printf( "Move %d from %s to %s%n", number,
17             NAMES[ fromPole ], NAMES[ toPole ] );
18         solve( number - 1, remainder, toPole );
19       }
20     }
21     public static void main( String[] args )
22     {
23       solve( Integer.parseInt( args[ 0 ] ), 0, 1 );
24     }
25   }
```

Listing 19.10 A program that solves the Tower of Hanoi problem

19.2.3.3 Will the World End Soon?

Let's return to the legend and figure out when the world ends according to the legend. Suppose the number of disks is n. How many moves must the monks make to complete the task? The number of moves is 1 for $n = 1$ and 3 for $n = 2$. In general, for $n \geq 2$, the required number of moves is:

$$\text{the required number of moves for } n - 1 \text{ disks} +$$
$$1 (\text{for the } n\text{-th disk}) +$$
$$\text{the required number of moves for } n - 1 \text{ disks.}$$

If we use T_n to represent the required number of moves for n disks, the above observation gives:

$$T_1 = 1 \text{ and for } n \geq 2, T_n = 2T_{n-1} + 1.$$

By adding the value of 1 to both sides of the recurrence, we obtain

$$T_n + 1 = 2(T_{n-1} + 1).$$

Since $T_1 + 1 = 2$, we have

$$T_n + 1 = 2^n,$$

and thus,

$$T_n = 2^n - 1.$$

For $n = 64$, this is

$$18,446,744,073,709,551,615$$

Even if the monks are able to move one disk per second, it will take 585 billion years to complete the task. Luckily, we will not live to see the end of the world.

Summary

- An online algorithm is an algorithm that computes some values on an indefinite series of data using a fixed number of variables.
- A recursive algorithm is one that uses a call to itself to reduce a bigger input to a smaller input.

Exercises

1. **Computing the parity of a number sequence**   Write a program named `CumulativeParity` that receives an indefinite number of integers from the user, and computes the parity (odd or even) of the total of the numbers. It is possible to express the parity of a single integer num by `Math.abs( num ) % 2`. Write the code so that it computes the total and, at the end, prints the parity of the number.

2. **Computing the parity of number sequence, using boolean**   Write a program named `CumulativeParityAlt` that receives an indefinite number of integers from the user, and computes the "even parity" (whether or not the total is even). This time, the solution should be different from the one for the previous problem.

   The parity can be expressed as a `boolean` value using the condition `num % 2 == 0`. With this conversion, `true` represents the even parity, and `false` represents the odd parity. For two parity values, `p1` and `p2`, of two numbers in `boolean`, the parity of the sum of the two numbers can be computed by the condition `p1 == p2`. Assume that the parity before the user starts entering input is `true`. For example, if the user enters 10, −4, 5, 8, 9, and 1 in this order, the parity changes as follows: `true`, `true`, `false`, `false`, `true`, `false`.

3. **Computing the total of the number tokens in a file**   Write a program named `TotalNumberToken` that reads the tokens appearing in a file, and computes the total of all the tokens that can be treated as integers. The user will specify a file path as `args[ 0 ]`. The program must read each token as a `String`, and then convert it to an integer using `Integer.parseInt`. An attempt to convert a token that does not represent an integer results in a run-time error of `NumberFormatException`. The run-time error can be processed using a `try-catch` so the program execution will continue.

4. **Top two numbers**   Write a program named `ComputeTopTwo` that receives a series of integers from the user, and computes the largest two of the numbers. Use `Integer` variables to record the largest two of the numbers that have been entered so far.

5. **Testing if an input is a palindrome**   A word is a *palindrome* if the word reads the same forwards and backwards. Write a method named `recursivePalindrome` that receives a `String` object `word` as the formal parameter. The method must return a `boolean` value representing whether or not the word is a palindrome. We can use the following rules in making the decision:
   - If `word` has length 0 or 1, then it is a palindrome.
   - If `word` has length 2 or higher, then it is a palindrome if and only if (a) the first character of `word` is equal to the last character of `word` and (b) `word` without the first and the last characters is a palindrome.

   To incorporate the second rule in the recursive calculation, test (a) first and if that test fails, return `false` immediately.

6. **GCD of many integers**   We can extend the idea of computing the GCD recursively to compute the GCD of two or more integers. The GCD of $(n_1, \ldots, n_k)$, $k \geq 2$, is the largest positive integer that is a divisor of all of them. Design a recursive method `multiGCD` that takes an `int` array `series` as its formal parameter, and returns the GCD of the numbers in the sequence. We assume that all the numbers in the series, except for the last one, are strictly positive.

Programming Projects

7. **Computing a list of all primes recursively**   Consider computing a list of all primes less than or equal to a given number using a recursive method. Suppose we use a method `allPrimes( int n )` to accomplish this task. The return type of the method is `List<Integer>`. The `List<Integer>` object contains all the primes less than or equal to `n`. The list that the method returns is empty if `n <= 1` and is a list containing only 2 if `n == 2`. If `n > 2`, the method first calls `allPrimes( n - 1 )` to obtain a list of all the primes less than or equal to `n - 1`. The method then determines whether or not `n` is a prime by examining the remainder of `n` by each member in the list. If none of the divisions produce 0 as the remainder, the method adds `n` at the end of the list, since `n` is found to be a prime. Otherwise, the method keeps the list as it is. Finally, the method returns the list. Write a program named `RecursiveFindPrimes` that receives the value for `n` from the user, calls `allPrimes( n )` to obtain the list of primes, and then prints the members of the list thus obtained. Use either `LinkedList<Integer>` or `ArrayList<Integer>` as an implementation of `List<Integer>`.

8. **Top-3 numbers**   Write a program named `TopThreeIntegers` that receives an indefinitely long series of integers from the user, and computes the largest three numbers appearing in the series. After some initial prompting, the user starts entering the elements in the sequence, terminating the sequence with CTRL-D. There will be no prompting during the input of the sequence. The program expects that the user will enter at least three numbers before entering CTRL-D. To compute the largest three, the program may use the following online algorithm:

   - Use three variables, `first`, `second`, and `third`, to store the largest, the second largest, and the third largest numbers among the numbers that the user has entered so far.
   - Store the very first input in `first`.
   - Receive the second number. Compare it with the value of `first` to determine the larger and the smaller of the first two numbers, and update the values of `first` and `second` accordingly.
   - Receive the third number. Compare it with the values of `first` and `second` to determine the ranking of the first three numbers to determine the values of the three variables. Update the values of the three variables accordingly.
   - Receive the remaining numbers one after another using a while-loop. After receiving a new number, compare the new number with `first`, `second`, and `third` to perform updates.

Index

© Springer Nature Switzerland AG 2018
M. Ogihara, *Fundamentals of Java Programming*,
https://doi.org/10.1007/978-3-319-89491-1

Printed in the United States
By Bookmasters